GENERAL SIR ARTHUR COTTON

HIS LIFE AND WORK

GENERAL SIR ARTHUR COTTON

HIS LIFE AND WORK

BY HIS DAUGHTER

LADY HOPE

WITH SOME

FAMINE PREVENTION STUDIES

BY

WILLIAM DIGBY

His "were imperial works and worthy kings" - MILTON

GYAN

Published by

GYAN

Gyan Publishing House
5, Ansari Road
Daryaganj, New Delhi-110002
Phone: 011-47034999, 9811692060
E-mail: books@gyanbooks.com

Distribution Network
gyanbooks.com
India, USA, Canada, UK, Australia, France

ISBN : 978-81-212-3429-0 (PB)
First Published, London, 1900

2nd Impression 2020

Printed at: Gyan Press, Delhi.

General Sir Arthur Cotton His LIfe and Work
Author: Lady Hope

GENERAL SIR ARTHUR COTTON

R.E. K.C.S.I

HIS LIFE AND WORK

BY HIS DAUGHTER

LADY HOPE

WITH SOME

FAMINE PREVENTION STUDIES

BY

WILLIAM DIGBY C.I.E

PORTRAITS MAPS AND ILLUSTRATIONS

His "were imperial works and worthy kings"—MILTON

LONDON

HODDER AND STOUGHTON

27 PATERNOSTER ROW

MCM

Elliott & Fry, photo

Walker & Cockerell, ph. sc.

TO

MY BELOVED MOTHER

WHOSE INTEREST AND SYMPATHY

THROUGH A LONG LIFE

CHEERED AND SUPPORTED

MY FATHER

IN HIS ARDUOUS TASKS

FOR THE BENEFIT OF

HUMANITY

THIS RECORD OF HIS

LIFE AND WORK

IS

DEDICATED

Preface

IN placing before my readers the Memoir of my Father, and his life work for the benefit of India, in its deliverance from the disastrous effects of Famine, as well as its increased prosperity, I have felt that I am only undertaking a task which it was my bounden duty to accomplish to the best of my ability.

So near his heart lay this ever burning question, so fervent were his desires that his schemes for a far more general irrigation of the country should be carried out to the full, and so heart-breaking was the grief to him, as time rolled on, that the absolute fulfilment of his dearest wishes was either postponed, or neglected, that when his long and earnest life had closed, I felt it incumbent upon me to obey the request he had so often made, in his own touching and pathetic way, that I would gather together the various papers and documents which he had left, and make use of them for the benefit of India, and the supplying of its vast needs.

A duty thus inculcated by one so beloved, whose slightest wish had always been a law to me, could only be undertaken in the spirit of loyal obedience, and a true desire to further his highest ideals.

My father was truly an empire maker, as he was an empire lover; no one ever more zealously longed for the spread of England's civilisation, her privileges and her blessings over distant lands where, hidden too often behind the curtain of natural beauty, or surface intellectuality, there lies a hidden depth of misery and darkness, such as we, in our favoured country, can scarcely know.

With regard to India's temporal interests, he always felt that vast quantities of water might be saved from rushing wastefully into the ocean by tank storage and canal distribution, thus both irrigating and navigating the country as a preliminary to all questions of railway locomotion. "First," he would say, "enrich the country, and then lay down railway lines as advisable."

All these points are fully entered into in the book which I have ventured to place before the British public. Careful calculations are given as regards the increase of revenue by these simple means; and when we compare the statements of profit and loss we have to throw into the famine balance the gigantic consideration of the loss of human life, which, after all, is infinitely more precious than any monetary revenue, or the value of funds spent on irrigation works.

So serious is this subject, so vast in its various phases, that it commands from us a definite and diligent enquiry as to the possibility of lessening these dire evils, and effecting a universal improvement throughout our Indian possessions. My father used sometimes to say,—"I am a man of one idea"; but though it was true that the question of Indian irrigation was the leading feature of his public life, he had a vast number of other interests, every one of them tending towards the benefit of mankind, and the increased prosperity of our own nation, with its multitude of dependencies, and its ever-widening interests throughout the world. He carried on his own shoulders, as few men do, the weight of the needs of others,—other men's sorrows affecting him as though they were his own; in fact, through sheer sympathy and a strong sense of responsibility, he *felt* them to be his own.

In his ceaseless study of these great considerations he discovered remedies, and his practical nature seemed to show him at once how these remedies were to be applied.

Now that his lips are silenced, and his pen is laid down, I fervently ask that my readers may themselves look into these great questions, and study them from his point of view, in the light of information now freshly placed before them.

With regard to the writing of the book, I have to acknowledge very gratefully the help given to me by Mr. William Digby, C.I.E., the devoted ardour he has shown in the arrangement of some of its chapters, and the information he has collected in support of this great question of irrigation in India, and its consequent prevention of famine.

I also thank Mr. Walch for his kindness in permitting me to use quotations from some of the pages of his book, on *The Engineering Works of the Godavari Delta*, with photographs of both its scenery and irrigation systems, and I am indebted to the India Office for latest particulars regarding irrigation canals which have been incorporated in the irrigation and navigation map.

To other friends who have shown their sympathy with me, and have helped in various ways to forward my labours in connection with this volume, I here tender my grateful and lasting thanks.

E. R. HOPE.

Table of Contents

PAGE

Preface vii

An Appreciation of Sir Arthur Cotton 3

CHAPTER I

Family History—A Notable Band of Brothers—Early Days and Characteristics 7

CHAPTER II

Young Manhood—The Beginnings of Great Issues 14

CHAPTER III

Arthur Cotton as a Traveller 26

Appendix: Water in Australia 46

CHAPTER IV

The Beginnings of Great Duties 50

CHAPTER V

Preparing for the Great Work—The Redemption of the Godavari District 70

CHAPTER VI

The District of Godavari—Before and After its Transformation . 77

Appendix: The Testimony of a Native Indian Official 89

PAGE

CHAPTER VII

Part 1.—The "most Beneficent and Profitable" Irrigation Work in the World: its Inception, its Construction, its Success . . . 93

Appendices:

Prosperous Households in Godavari 144
The River and the Delta 145
The Approval of Government 146
A Friendly Civilian 147
A Big Gale and a Hard Test 148
A Civilian Estimate of the Work 148
The Benefits, Too Many for Enumeration 149
What was Done in Twelve Months 149
The Chief Civilian Officials' Testimony 149

Part 2.—Lady Cotton's Reminiscences 151

CHAPTER VIII

Indian Family Life—Furlough—Home Life—The Star of India—Retirement 163

CHAPTER IX

Earnest Endeavours and Energetic Labours on Behalf of India's Prosperity 184

CHAPTER X

Examination in a House of Commons Committee Room—The Parliamentary Committee of 1872 209

A Commons' Debate—Severe Attack—Speeches by Lord George Hamilton 214

[Memorandum in Reply by Sir Arthur Cotton, with Appendices A to F] 224

Mr. Henry Fawcett 257

Rt. Hon. John Bright 258

Sir George Campbell 261

General Sir George Balfour 262

PAGE

The Select Committee of 1878: its Constitution, its Methods, its Result 264

Appendices:

Report of the Select Committee 306

Memorandum by Sir A. Cotton on the Report of the Committee . . 309

CHAPTER XI

Railways *versus* Irrigation and Navigation Canals 328

Appendices:

The Governor-General of India on Irrigation Extension 382

Sir R. Temple on Irrigation Done and To Be Done 384

How Water was Wasted in 1877 386

Obiter Dicta by Sir Geo. Campbell 388

Colonel Fischer on the Grand Central Reservoir, and other matters . 393

CHAPTER XII

The Cost of a Famine in Lives and Money. 400

Appendix: What the 1900 Famine is Costing People and Country . 416

CHAPTER XIII

Is Famine in India due to an Insufficiency of Rain? 418

Appendix: Through the Famine Districts, by Vaughan Nash . . 427

CHAPTER XIV

The Money, Moral, and Material, Value to India of Sir Arthur Cotton's Work 433

CHAPTER XV

Work for All India 437

The Ganges Canal: Controversy with Sir Proby Cautley, K.C.B. 469

CHAPTER XVI

Work in England for India 475

CONTENTS

PAGE

CHAPTER XVII

Life in England—Letters from Florence Nightingale, Sir Bartle Frere, Sir Colin Scott-Moncrieff, R.E., and others . . 492

CHAPTER XVIII

Many Interests at Home and Abroad 513

Appendix: A Modern Seer and a New Hope for British Agriculture . 541

CHAPTER XIX

The Mainspring and Secret of Arthur Cotton's Life, Character, and Characteristics 548

CHAPTER XX

The Eventide of Life and Peace 560

Illustrations and Maps

TO FACE PAGE

General Sir Arthur Cotton, R.E., K.C.S.I. (*Frontispiece*)

Combermere Abbey 7

Sir Arthur Cotton and his Brothers 9

Mother and Father of Sir Arthur Cotton. 12

Lieutenant Arthur Cotton, R.E. 16

Gorge of the Godavari—Looking up Stream 77

Dowlaisweram Anicut—from near the Under Sluices . . 80

Maddur Branch of Anicut 105

Irrigated Lands, after Harvest 109

Sketch Map of the Godavari Delta, showing Irrigation and Navigation Works 122

Head of Main Canal, Eastern Delta. 129

Mukkamala Lock 131

A Houseboat for Canal Travel—Eastern India . . . 135

The Gunnaram Aqueduct crossing the Godavari River . . 141

Pennumantra Bridge, Gostanadi and Velpur Canal . . . 157

Alamur Lock Weir, from below, Coringa Canal . . . 163

Woodcot, Dorking 497

Sir Arthur Cotton (aged 94) standing in front of 6ft. high English Wheat 513

Sir Arthur Cotton (aged 94) standing in front of Maize grown by him in 1896 537

IRRIGATION AND NAVIGATION MAP OF INDIA, prepared by Sir A. Cotton, and brought up to date from statistics at the India Office . . . . *in pocket at end of book*

"If we have done our duty at least to this part of India, and have founded a system which will be a source of strength and wealth and credit to us as a nation, it is due to

ONE MASTER MIND,

which, with admirable industry and perseverance, in spite of every discouragement, has worked out this great result. Other able and devoted officers have caught Colonel Cotton's spirit and have rendered invaluable aid under his advice and direction, but for this first creation of genius we are indebted to him alone.

"Colonel Cotton's name will be venerated by millions yet unborn, when many, who now occupy a much larger place in the public view, will be forgotten; but, although it concerns not him, it would be, for our own sake, a matter of regret if Colonel Cotton were not to receive due acknowledgment during his lifetime."—*Minute by the Government of Madras*, SIR CHARLES TREVELYAN, *Governor*.

An Appreciation of Sir Arthur Cotton

THE biographies of eminent Anglo-Indians constitute a large library in themselves. Probably there is not one of the biographies of which its subject was not worthy of the honour of permanent record. India has afforded unequalled opportunities for the display of the highest altruistic qualities of which our race is capable. "Englishmen and Englishwomen will work, and have worked, for India until they drop."[1] In the foremost rank of such Englishmen, Arthur Thomas Cotton stands second to none. It is no biographer's enthusiasm which declares that he is, without doubt, the greatest benefactor of British birth the Indian people have ever known. More people have had enough to eat day by day, have worn sufficient and comfortable clothing, have lived in good houses, have had something to spare for the conveniences of life, because Sir Arthur Cotton laboured for India, than can be placed to the credit of any other man of whom I have read or heard. Again, I say this is no biassed eulogium. In chapter XIV. of this work will be found, in statistical form, so far as that is possible, what Arthur Cotton's work

[1] Mr. Vaughan Nash, Special Famine Correspondent of the *Manchester Guardian*, in letter dated April, 1900.

represents to the Indian Government and to the people themselves. To that chapter I ask attention if any reader should consider my words overstrained.

Sir Arthur Cotton's influence is ineffaceably stamped on three portions of the eastern coast of the Madras Presidency. What is true of this region might have been true, in a modified measure, of many other parts of India, especially of some of those provinces which now (July, 1900) are the scenes of awful suffering, had Sir Arthur Cotton's ripe experience not been overborne by administrative jealousy and by official unacquaintance with what really could be done by means of irrigation in almost every part of India.

In the homes of many thousands of families in India, living in comfort, "Cōtōn,"[1] with what he did, is an honoured, almost worshipped, entity; in Britain, it is probable that, owing to his manifold activities by voice and pen throughout many years, no other Anglo-Indian has ever been so widely known. A discussion recently took place in a London assemblage on the causes of famines in India. Incidentally, Sir Arthur Cotton's name was mentioned. Subsequently, one of the leading public men of the metropolis remarked: "Sir Arthur Cotton's name has been mentioned. We, here, know Sir Arthur Cotton; we believe in Sir Arthur Cotton and in what he did for India. He came to us here, and he told us what India needs; we want to see his policy prevail."

What Arthur Cotton did in India was sorely needed. What he would have done is still more sorely needed.

[1] In one of his letters, quoted later, Sir Arthur Cotton asks his correspondent whether the people, to whom reference was made, could really pronounce the short "o," adding that in Northern Madras his name was pronounced as though the "o" were long.

Because his counsel was not followed, again and again have destitution and hideous suffering overtaken vast multitudes, while the progress of one-sixth of the population of the whole world has been arrested. What has been will again be. A few years hence, an even more disastrous famine than that of to-day will afflict our Indian fellow-subjects, a continuing decadence of country and people will prevail, *unless* the readers of this biography, and the English people generally, determine that Sir Arthur Cotton's works shall follow him.

Therefore

is it that this biography is offered to Arthur Cotton's countrymen and countrywomen, with the hope that its narrative of his work and teaching will carry conviction to many minds and produce such beneficent consequences that the present sorrowful condition of India's population shall, so far as widespread irrigation can ensure this, become a matter of regretful historical interest only.

COMBERMERE ABBEY.

p. 7.

CHAPTER I

Family History—A Notable Band of Brothers —Early Days and Characteristics

GENERAL SIR ARTHUR COTTON, R.E., K.C.S.I., was born on May 15, 1803. He was the tenth son of Mr. Henry Calveley Cotton, who was himself the tenth son of Sir Lynch Cotton, the fourth holder of a baronetcy created, in 1677, in the person of Sir Robert Cotton, K.B., M.P. for Cheshire. The family is of considerable antiquity. As early as the twelfth century, the Abbey of Combermere, with its "surrounding demesne, lands, woods, and timbers," is described by an early historian. In the year 1153, its first abbot was "still surviving." He was followed by other abbots, several of whom were granted fresh privileges and additional lands. In the year 1535, "the site of the monastery, with its church, bell tower, the lake of Combermere, and cemetery, was granted to George Cotton, and Mary his wife, by the King's letters patent," the king being Henry VIII.

Through the handsome Catherine of Beragne the descent of the Cottons may be traced from the Plantagenets. They appear to have served their king and country through several centuries. Sir George Cotton, the second son of John Cotton, of Cotton, in Shropshire, was an esquire of the body to Henry VIII. His younger brother, Sir Richard Cotton, Knight Comptroller of the Household, was a Privy Councillor in the reign of Edward VI. Henry Cotton, younger son of Sir Richard Cotton, was appointed by Queen Elizabeth to the see of Salisbury.

Sir Robert Cotton, grandson of Sir Richard, added

largely to the wealth and importance of the family by his marriage with Hester, daughter of Sir Robert Salisbury, of Llewenny, county Denbigh.

Sir Robert Salisbury Cotton, his grandson, is described as "a most frank and hospitable gentleman, and as having dispensed a daily hospitality even more than proverbially Cheshire." His descendant, Sir Stapleton Cotton, distinguished himself in military service in 1817, and received the title of Baron Combermere. Like his kinsman, the subject of this memoir, Sir Stapleton gained his distinction in India. He was the hero of Bhurtpore. He displayed great personal bravery, even wished to lead the storming-party when a breach had been made. The would-be stormer of the breach was Commander-in-Chief in India at the time! He was afterwards Field-Marshal, Constable of the Tower, and Colonel of the 1st Life Guards. This is the testimony which is given to his courage: "Lord Combermere, commonly so careful of the life of the humblest soldier, too imprudent with his own, could with difficulty be restrained from leading the foremost of the stormers of the breach his sappers and miners had made in the walls."

Arthur Cotton was not the only distinguished member of his family. Six of his brothers made their mark in their day, and did useful service for mankind. A portrait of each of them, with Arthur in the centre, faces this page. Of his brothers Sir Arthur has left some record.

Sir Sydney Cotton was a very able officer. He commanded at Peshawur during the Mutiny, and had, as prisoners, five thousand of the mutineers, whom he had disarmed. Among his other services was the raising of the 21st Lancers. When he had been some months in command at Peshawur, a friend of mine sent one of the senior officers of the Adjutant-General's Department at Calcutta, and asked: "How is Sydney Cotton getting on in Peshawur?" The reply was: "This is the way he is getting on. Before he went there we never had an hour's

SIR ARTHUR COTTON AND HIS BROTHERS.

p. 9

freedom from anxiety, night or day, about the place Since he went there we have never had one hour s anxiety." Happily he had to work with two of the finest men in India at the time: Sir Herbert Edwardes, the Commissioner, and General Lushington. Peshawur was at that time the station on which more depended than upon any other. It was one of the principal providential facts in the Mutiny that the defence was in the hands of three such officers as those I have named.

In the second volume of Bosworth-Smith's *Life of Lord Lawrence*, the references to General Cotton are many. John Lawrence found in the intrepid commander at Peshawur one who seconded all the stern measures which the civil ruler felt necessary. The manner in which incipient mutiny was checked by some of the disaffected regiments being sent to outpost duty "against an imaginary invasion of the Mohmunds," or nearly marched off their legs "in their amazing race for Delhi," was masterly. Lord Lawrence's biographer remarks that it was fortunate for Lawrence himself that he had such trustworthy coadjutors. ". . . in Edwardes, in Nicholson, in Cotton, at Peshawur, he had admirable lieutenants, men with whom to think was to act, to see a danger was to overcome it, men who worked behind his back as hard as, perhaps harder than, they would have worked under his eye."[1] Again: "No officer could have managed better than Brigadier S. Cotton, and if he is superseded, I do not know what will happen."[2]

One most important matter provided occasion for a difference of opinion between Lawrence on the one hand, and Cotton, Edwardes, and others, on the other. The peril which existed while Delhi remained untaken led Lawrence to look ahead, and to seek permission from Lord Canning to abandon Peshawur if he thought well. While he was in correspondence with the Viceroy, he wrote to Edwardes: "Pray think of what I have said, and consult Brigadiers

[1] *Life of Lord Lawrence*. By R. Bosworth-Smith, M.A., vol. ii. p. 45.

[2] *Ibid*., p. 69.

S. Cotton and Nicholson, but nobody else. No man will retrace his steps more unwillingly than myself. But there is a point when to hold on savours more of obstinacy than of wisdom." General Cotton was not convinced, nor were the other officers consulted. They could not conceive that, under any circumstances, it was wise to abandon Peshawur. They resisted the civil head of affairs by argument and persuasion. Lord Canning took a like view with those who were for holding on, and, on August 7, telegraphed to Lawrence, "Hold on to Peshawur to the last." By this time, however, the tide had turned against the mutineers, and Lawrence no longer urged even the possibility of retirement. It may be interesting to add that the Prince Consort, at Windsor, said to Sir John Lawrence, "I have read your paper on the abandonment of Peshawur, and entirely agree with you."

Richard Lynch Cotton was educated at the Charterhouse, and became an undergraduate at Worcester College in Oxford. In 1815 he was elected to a Fellowship at Oriel, and in 1823 became Vicar of Denchworth. He resigned this living on being appointed Provost of the college by the Duke of Wellington, who was then Chancellor of the University.

Charles Conyers Cotton was, for many years, in the Civil Service of India, retiring when he married Miss Egerton, of Oulton Hall. He lived at Knolton Hall, in Cheshire.

Hugh Calveley Cotton worked with his brother Arthur in the Indian Irrigation Works, and eventually had the sole charge of the Kurnool Anicut.

Admiral Francis Vere Cotton retired early from his naval command, and lived during the latter years of his life in Shropshire.

General Frederick Cotton, C.S.I., was the youngest of the brothers, and is the only one now surviving of that large family. He was in the Royal Engineers in India, and assisted his brother in the Tanjore, Godavari, and other works. He was born in 1807, is a retired Major-General, H.E.I.C.S., and received the Companionship of the Star of India in 1868 for his meritorious service in the Public Works Department. He is ninety-two years of age, and, though suffering from impaired sight, is still mentally alert, proof of which may be seen in an article from his pen in *Blackwood's Magazine* for May, 1900. It is entitled, "Value of the Water of the Great Rivers of India." The good sense with which he deals with this question, and with the prospects of future extension of irrigation, is most marked.[1]

It was an interesting sight to see these brothers together when they happened to meet, as they did occasionally, at some family gathering. They were a noble body of men, handsome, clever, brilliant in conversation; their callings were useful and without a blemish; not one of them had

[1] Much will be found in later chapters concerning the great use to which Indian rivers may be put. On this point the veteran Engineer remarks: "We have an example, set us by some engineer of former ages, which is so to the point of what is wanted at the present day that I must quote it. Quite in the south of the Peninsula there is a river —the Viga, if I remember right—the water of which was so admirably utilized that only in exceptional years did a drop of it reach the sea. The river was dammed here and there, and the channels, leading the water off for irrigation, had tanks to store water for the perfecting of the crop after the freshes ended, which is exactly the principle on which the great rivers should be treated as far as possible. There has been an idea of late that if water is to be stored it will be necessary to find sites for enormous lakes in which to collect it. It is true that the larger the reservoirs are the cheaper the cost of storing water will be. But, if the value of the water is what I hope I have proved it to be, that is not the first consideration. To explain how sites may be formed everywhere, I would ask my readers to look at the Trigonometrical survey map of the Peninsula of India, where they will find that almost any shallow valley is made, by an embankment across it, into a retaining reservoir. These tanks, so called, being dependent upon the local rains, are valueless in seasons of drought, and, in consequence, do nothing to secure the Peninsula from famine. This would not be the case if a stream, led from a never-failing river, ran through the country to supply them. Indeed, our great hydraulic engineer, Sir Arthur Cotton, had a scheme for making such an artificial river to secure the supply of these tanks. But I only call attention to the possibility to show that, as every part of India has its valleys, there is no good reason why water should not be stored on the old native river Viga system in all parts of the country."

a personal enemy, so honourable had been their lives through all the vicissitudes of their different careers. Some of them, however, because of the strength and honesty of their convictions, had very determined opponents, Arthur in particular. But his most inveterate opponent, who, perhaps, was the late Sir George Campbell, K.C.S.I., testified to his great ability and the nobleness of his aims.

Arthur's early life, as well as his future career, owed much to the careful training and admirable judgment of his mother. Mrs. Calveley Cotton was a very remarkable woman, strong both mentally and physically.

Arthur's bent of mind was curiously shadowed forth in his earliest days in certain traits of character and conduct which were observed by one of his sisters. She and her mother were one day walking in a town with young Arthur by their side, when they remarked on the strange look of the water running in the gutter, wondering what could have given it the colour of blood. Suddenly Arthur disappeared. Hours after the little fellow returned home, having traced to its source the cause of the discoloured stream,—dye works, some distance away. She remembered, too, that often in the nursery he would play with his bread and milk, instead of eating it. When asked the cause of his delay, he replied, "I am making canals."

His brothers, also, remembered that when they were out walking on a rainy day, Arthur would be continually lagging behind, busily tracing small channels in the road with the point of his stick; he would divert the rain-water through the channels, making systems of communication between them.

As an instance of his fearlessness, we are told that, when a boy at school, he had a younger brother (George, one of those who died early) with him, who, unfortunately, incurred the dislike of the head-master, and was bullied and ill-treated in such a way that he was losing both health and spirits, much to Arthur's distress. Finding no means of relief, and having to submit to the rule of the school,

MRS. HENRY CALVELEY COTTON
(Mother of Arthur Cotton).

MR. HENRY CALVELEY COTTON
(Father of Arthur Cotton).

p. 12.

which was that every boy should place his home letters upon the master's desk before despatching them, the elder brother wrote a full account of the grievances to which the younger one was subjected by the cruelty of a master, and described the effect they were having upon him ; this done, he placed the open letter upon the master's desk for inspection. The master read apparently every word of its contents and allowed the letter to be sent, evidently cowed by the boy's decision and firmness of resolution.

At the age of fifteen he obtained a cadetship for India, and joined the military seminary at Addiscombe, near Croydon, where the cadets intended for the Artillery and Engineer service of the East India Company then received their education.

CHAPTER II

Young Manhood—The Beginnings of Great Issues

ARTHUR COTTON was a boy of only sixteen and a half when, towards the end of 1819, he left Addiscombe, after a career marked by much diligence in study and uniform good conduct. Nowadays few careers are begun so early as was his. More than that, when begun, they are not often pursued with assiduity. Life is taken much more easily by the young at the end of the century than it was at the beginning. This is becoming matter of common complaint and is engaging literary attention simultaneously in London and New York at the time these pages are being revised for the printer. "There is no doubt," says one distinguished writer, "that a very large number of young persons are not willing to work hard. They are anxious to do, in return for their pay, just as little as they can." These pages will show that Arthur Cotton's strenuous nature had no sympathy with any disposition of that kind. So well had he worked at Addiscombe, that he obtained an appointment in the Royal Engineers without having to undergo any examination. To him an examination would have been as naught. But the honour of admission without paying a toll was his, and he deserved it. I believe this is the only instance on record of admission into the scientific corps of Royal Engineers being obtained without an examination.

Second-Lieutenant Cotton was stationed at Chatham, but he was not allowed to remain long at the Depôt. In a short time (on the 31st of January, 1820) he was posted to the Ordnance Survey in Wales. Not unnaturally his early experience was subsequently often in his mind. He was at the most impressionable of ages. His duties took him on foot from place to place, through what was at that time a very wild and lonely country, sparsely populated, and difficult of access on account of the fewness of roads. His surveying tour was successful. He presented an admirable report, covering all the phases of the work entrusted to him, and received high praise for what he had done.

For a year and a half he remained at Chatham, and, in May, 1821, when he was just eighteen, having been appointed to service in India, he embarked for Madras, at which city he arrived in September, after what, for those days, was not a long voyage, extending, as it did, over only four months;—now, the globe may be circled in a little more than half that time. He was attached to the office of the Chief Engineer for the Presidency, and spent nearly a year acquainting himself with the character of the public works he was likely to be called upon to undertake.

In May, 1822, office work came to an end; Lieut. Cotton received the appointment of Assistant to Captain Fullerton, Superintending Engineer of the Tank Department, Southern Division. A most responsible duty was assigned to him, nothing less than the survey of the Paumben Pass, a narrow channel in the causeway of rocks, which forms what is known as Adam's Bridge, between the mainland of India and the island of Ceylon—a bridge of religious and historic importance to Hindus, inasmuch as across it Hanumān, the Monkey-god,[1] led his forces for the conflict with Rāvana and the Rākshasas, which occurred in Ceylon. This was the beginning of a work upon which, at a later date, the young Engineer found useful occupation; the passage now allows of vessels of a few hundred tons

[1] Hanumān himself jumped from India to Ceylon at one bound; his followers found the rocks, which a young Englishman, in after ages, was to remove, useful in following their chief.

passing through. Fifty years after, Sir James Elphinstone, Bart., M.P., made a strenuous effort in the House of Commons to secure imperial funds for the enlarging of the passage to such an extent that ocean-going steamers for Madras and Calcutta and the East Coast ports could reach their destination without passing around Ceylon. Again and again, during the course of the agitation, it seemed as if the work might be taken in hand, but, eventually, the effort was in vain; nothing was accomplished. One notable engineering work still awaits its engineer. Little beyond survey work was done by the young Lieutenant in 1822, as he was recalled to the supervision of tank repairs in the districts of Coimbatore, Madura, Tinnevelly, Trichinopoly, and Tanjore, where was laid the foundation of that complete knowledge of water—its storage and distribution—which was to bear such wonderful fruit there and in other parts of the Presidency.

Lieutenant Cotton soon after proceeded to headquarters, where he remained until 1824. During this time his outdoor work was chiefly in connection with the erection of military buildings at St. Thomas' Mount, a military station a few miles south of Madras.

The first Burmese war was pending, and troops were being drafted from India to the Land of Pagodas. Among those who expressed a desire to join the expedition was Lieutenant Cotton, who, then only twenty, proceeded to the front. He was associated for some time with the gunboats, reconnoitring, fighting, and eventually with the storming of the fortresses of Mergui and Tavoy. He was engaged in defending Rangoon, and afterwards took part in the assault on the stockades of Kakien. Here he distinguished himself by taking the lead, as the only engineer officer with one of the columns of the main army. He led the storming party against seven forts and stockades; he served also in the trenches, and was engaged in all the most notable actions of that time.

One of these exploits is thus described in his own words:—

LIEUTENANT ARTHUR COTTON, R.E. p. 16.

"The place taken was Mergui, the southern fort of the coast of Tenasserim, in Burma, not far from the north of Penang. The force was detached from Rangoon about August 24, and sailed direct to Tavoy, in the centre of the coast of Tenasserim, which surrendered, and we then sailed to Mergui, which is beautifully situated on rising ground some miles up the river, where there is good anchorage for ships. One face of the fort is on the river bank, with batteries which were silenced by the men-of-war, while the transports were at anchor half a mile below. The west face of the fort was built, on a line perpendicular to the river, of solid teak timber twelve or fifteen feet high, and had a gate about a quarter of a mile from the river. The force was landed near the shipping, and, according to the utter want of anything like military order usual at that time, the men—soldiers, sepoys, and pioneers—all rushed up to the gate without any arrangement.

"When we reached the gate, exposed to the fire from some flankers, I found there was only one ladder at the spot, which I planted beside the gate, and looked round for others, when a young officer of the 60th called to two or three officers and men by name to follow him, and leading them in—all four—he dropped down on the inside, cut off from all possible help. I looked for more ladders, and was planting a second against the gate, when it was opened by our fine fellow inside, and we rushed in, and carried the whole place in half an hour, capturing the Governor.

"All this without a single order from the officer in command, and if we had not had the most contemptible enemy in the world, we should at least have suffered terrible loss. As it was, our loss was only thirty or forty men.

"The splendid young officer who led, and who would now, of course, have been a V.C., was never mentioned; nor do I believe the staff officer, who wrote the report, knew what had happened, for he was not at the gate, I think. This is a specimen of the whole war. Nobody could now believe the way in which things were then done. Every loss we suffered was solely from the want of any

2

sort of preparation or military arrangement. The Burmese are the greatest cowards in the world, and had not an idea of stratagem. They never thought of fighting us in the open. When the Governor of Tavoy, who was on board one of our vessels, saw the men rush up to the fort, as if it were play, he threw down the telescope, saying, 'If that's the way you fight, who can stand before you?' Then he went and hid himself in his cabin."

It will be readily realized that if in actual fighting such loose arrangements prevailed, in commissariat and general control of supplies the defects would be very bad. They were bad indeed. Great hardships were suffered by all the force. Not only were the provisions scant in quantity, but they were exceedingly bad in quality. The sick in hospital died by hundreds owing to the want of suitable food.

My father, even after a lapse of so many years, retained detailed memories of those days of peril. He used to tell us that once he was with a small party of men every one of whom was shot down except himself. Several officers, who were his contemporaries, have told us how one day, when the fight was at its hottest, he was seen alone leading a troop of men into the thick of the battle, cheering them on, and cutting his way through the enemy's flank as he went.

It was whilst stationed in Burma that he acquired a dislike to card-playing, a dislike which lasted all his life. He was invited by one of the principal officers to dine with him. This officer was a man of high standing in the army, and much looked up to by the younger men. After dinner Lieutenant Cotton was asked to play. Although he had been well accustomed to the card table in his parent's home in Cheshire, he had never played for money, but being a very youthful subaltern he accepted this invitation as a command, and thought it his duty to play. The more he played, the more deeply he lost, and when he rose from the table he was a poorer man by twenty pounds. His pay was very small, but he had in his possession bank-notes of that exact value, sent to him by his father in a recent letter, that he might purchase some necessaries which otherwise he would have wanted—and wanted in vain. For the moment he could hardly realize the fact that every penny of his money had now to be handed over to his superior officer; however, so it was. Needing the money very badly, he greatly regretted this loss. But he had lost. He might have refused to play, but having consented to take a hand, he had no resource save to part with the much cherished bank-notes, and, of course, he paid. However, he had learned his lesson, and vowed that, so long as he lived, he would never play cards again. This resolution was a lasting one; he could never bear the sight of cards in the house, and never allowed his children to play with them.

Lieutenant Cotton returned to Madras after the Burmese campaign was ended. During the voyage, while sitting on the deck of the ship one evening, admiring the sea and the sky illuminated with stars, the thought struck him forcibly: "Who made these worlds? Upon whose handiwork am I gazing now? It is the work of God, the great Creator." He had never been what is called a religious man, and had never specially studied his Bible. This thought so impressed him that it brought naturally with it the practical enquiry: "If there be a great Creator, if He made the world, the sun, the moon, and the stars, what do I know of Him? Has He ever spoken? If so, what are His words? The Bible is the Word of God. I ought to read it; I should like to know what He says."

There and then, on the impulse of the moment, he went into the saloon where the ship's officers and some of the passengers were playing cards. As he entered, he asked the question: "Is there a Bible on board the ship?"

A loud shout of laughter greeted this question; he was asked if he were going to turn religious. However, on again making his request, it was suggested that some one present possessed a Bible, which was packed in the bottom of his box. It was brought and handed over to him. It may be said, from that hour until the last day of his life, his chief delight was in the study of the Scriptures. He pored over the Bible that was lent him; the rest of the voyage was full of the deepest interest, as he drank in its new life-giving truth, new and precious to him.

The result of this experience, and the change that now took place in his life and thoughts, were in no sense transient. His future career was in every way influenced by it; his hours, both of toil and pleasure, were marked by a sense of the presence of the Unseen Saviour. His whole nature was characterized by devotion to his Bible, which he always spoke of as "The Word of God," to the teachings of which everything must be subordinated. His motives, pursuits, and interests were all coloured by his prevailing study.

On reporting himself, after arrival in Madras, Lieutenant Cotton was appointed to act as Superintendent Engineer, Central Division, Tank Department. Early in the following year he was confirmed in the appointment. His duties were of the same character as those he performed before he proceeded to Burma, the inspection and repair of Irrigation Works, but now with more of personal responsibility than before. The arduous nature of the work, towards the end of 1827, led to a breakdown of health in the shape of an attack of jungle fever and inflammation of the lungs; short leave to the Neilgherries, the chief mountain range in Southern India, was granted. Leave over and health restored, the young Engineer was ordered to the Paumben Pass to make a thorough survey of it, and to commence trifling improvements. Work was really begun, but only in a tentative way. A mere pittance of £300 to £400 was granted, but with this small sum the worst obstacles in the channel were removed and the Pass deepened two or three feet.

After eight years' service, he was promoted to the rank of Captain. Then opportunity offered for the beginning of one of the great works which will, through all time, be associated with the name of Arthur Cotton. He was appointed to the separate charge of the Cauveri Irrigation, which formed part of the Southern Division, with oversight and responsibility in regard to the Paumben works. Special study was given to the needs of the Tanjore district, and the moods of the Coleroon River were regarded in almost every possible light, with the view of making that great stream of the utmost possible service. The need for wide-reaching works was exceptionally great. Absolute ruin stared Tanjore and the adjoining districts in the face. "Since the completion of the scheme they are reckoned the richest parts of the Presidency, and Tanjore returns the largest revenue [of any district] in the Empire. Land under the silt-charged waters of the Kistna yields at the most Rs. 8 per acre, while in Tanjore the State often receives twice as much."[1]

Plans for the earlier works were evolved and received sanction. They were the product of 1828 and 1829, and on the first of January, 1830, the great work was begun by Lieutenant Fred. Cotton, younger brother of the Superintending Engineer, cutting through the Grand Anicut to construct the sluices. Having got the work started Captain Cotton had perforce to surrender to repeated attacks of jungle fever, and obtained sick leave to Europe, delivering over charge during January, 1830. He was away from his sphere of labour for two and a half years, twelve months of which were spent on the return journey.[2]

When he returned to England life had a new aspect for him; he saw everything in a fresh light. Hunting, card-playing, dancing, and other amusements and recreations, which formed a great portion of the interests of those among whom he spent his leisure time, were distasteful to him. He used often to describe what he felt when asked to join in these amusements, the hollowness of such a life, the way in which it pained him to see reasonable men and women thus employing their time; and I have heard some of his relatives describe him as

[1] *Irrigated India*, p. 158, by the Hon. A. Deakin.
[2] See Chapter iii.: "Sir Arthur Cotton as a Traveller."

sitting thoughtfully and quietly in one corner of the room while the others were engaged in various ways. The fact was, that he was seeking the Higher Life; he longed to know more of the true foundations of belief; he wanted to consecrate his energies to the Lord Who had so manifested Himself to his heart; his sole enquiry was: "How shall I live my life for Him? What shall I do for His glory and for the benefit of men?"

These questions he felt could not be answered amidst the county society in which he was then living. So, making his own choice, as usual, he went to a village in Oxfordshire, where one of his brothers, an earnest and devoted Christian, was a clergyman of the Church of England and a devoted student of Scripture. There my father remained for a time, helping him in his parish work.

So strongly had Captain Cotton impressed himself and his views in regard to the Cauveri upon the authorities that, despite his prolonged leave, his position was kept open for him, and he resumed charge in the autumn of 1832. The energy with which he threw himself into his duties may be judged from the fact that he had his completed project for the two Coleroon anicuts before the Government and sanction obtained in time for the preliminary works to be finished before the monsoon freshes in June occurred. What the work of the next half-dozen years really meant—alike to the district in which the Superintendent Engineer served and to his own reputation—requires separate treatment. It may suffice to state that prolonged and devoted toil brought about another breakdown in health. Complete change was again necessary, and, mindful of all the pleasure and strength he derived from a southern clime, Captain Cotton turned his steps towards Tasmania.[1] His visit on this occasion was destined to have important consequences upon the whole of his after life; there he was to find the partner of his

[1] The Service Rules at that time prevented his going again to England, and his choice lay between South Africa and Australia.

remaining days, the true, the loving, the cherished, companion in every scene through which he subsequently passed.

Captain Cotton was again in Hobart Town. One day as he was walking with his host, Captain Beecher, they saw a young lady coming towards them. Captain Beecher said to him: "Now I am going to introduce you to a girl whom I should really like you to know." He then told him of the self-denying, earnest, Christian life of his young friend, what a blessing she was in her own home, and how devoted and kind to the sick and poor living in the outskirts of the town. At this moment she came up to them: Captain Cotton was introduced, and he there and then made up his mind "if God would give him so great a gift, he would marry that girl." The young lady was Miss Elizabeth Learmonth, the daughter of Thomas Learmonth, Esq., a gentleman who had become a large landed proprietor in Australia, but who was at that time living with his family in Tasmania.

Her gentle smile and attractive manner won his heart at once; they met day after day. She found in him just what her heart needed—a wise, Christian, sympathising friend, who could help her in every way she desired.

After this, the accident described on pp. 38–39 made additional sick leave necessary, as Captain Cotton's health had been much impaired; he had to spend another year in the colony. Before the end of that time he and Miss Learmonth were engaged. The state of his health was the only objection in the mind of her parents to their union; of this they said, quite gravely: "To all appearance he won't live two years." Over these fears they often laughed in after life, especially when the day for keeping their golden wedding drew near.

So he returned to Madras alone, but only for a short time, the doctors saying that a longer rest and stay in the fine climate of Tasmania was necessary for him. October, 1841, saw him again in the island, and the marriage took place on the 29th of that month.

After another year and a half, spent in Tasmania, Captain and Mrs. Cotton returned to India, their voyaging made happier by the presence of a little daughter, two months old.

Two extracts from letters, written by him at this time, may be made. One gives Captain Cotton's ideas about books suitable for a Christian's reading.

"I wish," writes Captain Cotton, "to remind you of one thing, that it would be well, so far as you can judge or ascertain, for you to read none but first-rate books: I mention this, as it may not perhaps occur to you. If we were led into a treasury, and told to help ourselves, why should we fill our pockets with silver, when there was a heap of gold by its side? 'Take unto you the whole armour' (Eph. vi. 13). Naturally we seek for all sorts of things to arm ourselves with: the favour of great men, health, shutting our eyes to the light—anything but the armour of God—things which, so far from being armour themselves, are so vain that no armour can preserve them; nothing but the armour of God—that to which we are directed in His Word—can stand in the evil day. Let us hear what it is—'Having your loins girt about with truth.' The first thing that is done in hot climates, to prepare for great fatigues, is to wind something round the body to support it; for strength is the first thing required."

Again, to the same correspondent:—

"We arrived here (in Tasmania) without trouble; and found a home ready provided for us, with everything we could want. We can remain in this house for some time, and have almost arranged to take a little farm of Mr. D——'s, adjoining the Parsonage. It has a small cottage on it, is capable of irrigation, and has nearly every qualification that I wanted. I believe we shall be able to take possession of it at once, and as I have one engine already complete and put together, I can at once begin to irrigate. There is a garden in full cultivation with fruit trees."

There the first year of the married life of my parents

was spent in great happiness. My narrative will now go back to incidents, some of which happened prior to my father's marriage,—his various voyages and journeys, all of which I have gathered into one chapter.

CHAPTER III

Arthur Cotton as a Traveller

SEVENTY years ago it was possible to take things more leisurely than is now conceivable. Those were unhurried days; such days are never likely to return. My father's health was re-established by the rest and recreation he found in England; he was eager once more to be at work. Yet he could calmly contemplate an overland journey to India, which differed vastly from the two days' rapid run from London to Brindisi, and water journeying all the rest of the way. Our traveller zig-zagged through France and Switzerland, visited the Holy Land, crossed the Syrian desert with an Arab caravan, sojourned in Persia and at Bagdad, and made some of the most lasting and valued friendships of his life. He has left on record, in a number of letters to his relatives, entertaining glimpses of his travel-experiences. In the altered circumstances of travelling to-day they are of special interest.

Arthur's first letter was from Namur, reached by way of Ostend. He had proceeded thence to Bruges by the broad canal, handsomely bordered with trees and kept in beautiful order, in a boat extremely well fitted up. This is a mode of travel now unknown. Yet it had many charms. But for such an easy and quiet manner of journeying it is probable that Robert Browning could not have taken his ailing bride to sunny Italy and a new lease of life. From Bruges, my father travelled to

Ghent and Brussels, crossing and inspecting the field of Waterloo, on which he remarks with characteristic acumen :—

" With the help of a book we had with us we made out the site of the battle perfectly. It appeared to me the finest piece of ground for a general action that could be imagined; there was sufficient variety of level to show clearly the state of the field throughout, and at the same time not so much broken as to prevent any army from being used with full effect."

From Geneva to Lyons and other regions, and so by way of Avignon to Marseilles, he leisurely proceeded. Much of the country was of a dreary character, rocky and barren, and reminded him vividly of the worst parts of India.

"A very stony, bare, country with many low, rocky, hills quite destitute of vegetation, and several of them with old fortifications on them, like the very small Polygar forts in the Carnatic. If it had had the advantage of a few clumps of trees near the villages it would have been exactly like the worst parts of Coimbatore and Mysore." The advantage apparently was with the Indian scenery.

When at Marseilles he was told of the quarantine harbour formed by a breakwater uniting two islands five miles from the coast. He was not able to visit this work, though anxious to do so; ever on the watch for that which would help him in India, he wanted to see the breakwater so as to obtain a "hint with respect to the Madras Roads." His mind, it will be seen, was already anticipating the project, which he afterwards initiated, of a breakwater at Madras.

Society at Alexandria he found to be "an odd mixture of English, French, Italians, and various compounds of these people, with Greeks, Syrians, and others, some sitting on their heels, some on the ground, and some on their proper points of support; all the males had pipes or cigars in their mouths, and some had large beards, and wore the Arab dress." "It makes me quite sick," he adds, "to see Englishmen and Christians ashamed of their own dress and customs." The town, miserable place as it was then, had, however, "many beauties in his eyes, for everything looked like India."

From Alexandria he proceeded, again by canal, to the Nile; thence to Cairo, after a voyage of one hundred and twenty-five miles in six days. The Nile, he says, was "nearly full, and level with the surface of the country, which has a fine effect, but, in point of size, the river is nothing, not more than from three hundred to seven hundred yards broad, and the other branch is much smaller." Still comparing everything with the standard of India, he remarks: "Englishmen here are nearly in the same circumstances as in India; the Pasha treats them as well as possible, and, in general, all in authority do the same."

Of the Pyramids he expresses the disappointment so frequently felt as to their apparent diminutiveness. There is nothing with which to compare them. "There is," he remarks, "no high ground in their neighbourhood, so that they stand 'quite independent,' as C—— would observe. I could not, except once or twice for a moment, perceive that they were above thirty or forty feet high. The illusion is so complete and so extraordinary that, though I had heard of it, both respecting the Pyramids and also other stupendous objects of a similar kind, I could not have imagined it possible unless I had experienced it myself."

I was travelling in Egypt, in 1894, when my mother wrote: "Your letter of March 8 came this morning—such a treat to us both. Your father has such lovely, delightful, recollections of desert air and desert life, although his travels were not made under such comfortable circumstances as yours. He had no opportunity either of seeing the wonders you are seeing, having to keep with his caravan."

Arthur Cotton returned through the Nile delta to Alexandria. He carefully examined the system of irrigation there employed, and found it far inferior to irrigation in India.

After a long detention at Alexandria he embarked for Beyrout in an Italian brig, arriving there on January 4, 1833. A party was formed to proceed to Jerusalem, consisting of a young Pole on his way to Bagdad, a Danish missionary thoroughly acquainted with Syria, an Irishman born at Malta, a Dutchman, and Michael Trad, a young Syrian; "and it was of this hodge-podge," my father observes, "that an Arab who came to see us at an inn on the road asked if we were not all brothers—we were so much alike." He continues: "We had no want of languages among us, and found occasion at different times for Arabic, English, Spanish, Italian, Latin, Greek, Hebrew, French, and Hindustani; such is the variety of visitors to this place."

The party voyaged along the coast to Jaffa, and so by a roundabout route to Jerusalem. Afterwards he passed through Samaria, making a *détour* to take in Mount Carmel, and so to Damascus. He says: "I was glad to enter upon lands where I knew our Lord Himself had passed before me; almost every place was remarkable for some transaction in which the hand of God had especially appeared." In the vicinity of Mount Carmel the travellers experienced a tremendous storm, from which they found refuge in a convent on the mountain, and stayed there in wretched weather for two days. He commented on the so-called Holy Places at and near Jerusalem, saying: "Lies and absurdities and idolatry meet you at every step." "However," he adds, "forgetting these abominations" (alluding especially to the pretended issue of fire from the Sepulchre), "and remembering that here, indeed, our Saviour paid the price of my forgiveness, that this is the place where alone God has dwelt in a visible shape, and where our Saviour will again appear, as was positively declared at the time of His Ascension, it is full of interest. I went to the top of the Mount of Olives; on one side I saw the Dead Sea, the most decided mark that God is not unconcerned in what we are doing, and, on the other, Jerusalem, showing, in its degraded state, the consequence of rejecting the Saviour."

It has already been stated that one of the travellers was a young Syrian gentleman, in whom the missionaries in Syria were much interested, as he had decided tendencies towards the adoption of Christianity. He had a great friend, Assad Shidiak, like himself a member of one of the old families of the Lebanon, who held an appointment in a Maronite monastery, but had received the truth of the gospel in its simplicity, and had written a book on the subject. His influence and the teaching of the missionaries had told on Michael, who was of a very amiable disposition and much attached to some of the missionaries.

It was thought that the journey to Jerusalem and Damascus, which Captain Cotton was taking in company with the missionary, Mr. Nicolayson, might be helpful to Michael, who joined them as interpreter. Somewhere on the way to Jerusalem, a Major Skinner joined the party, and they travelled together, Michael making himself of the greatest use to them by his pleasant, ready, tact and kindly way of ingratiating himself with the Arabs and in smoothing over difficulties. Probably this Major Skinner was the English officer who, as a roadmaker, has left his mark on Ceylon only less emphatically than my father has left his on Indian deltas.

Some weeks had been spent in Jerusalem, and the party went to Damascus. Captain Cotton and Major Skinner were the first Europeans to ride into the city in Frankish clothes. The country had been in a very lawless state, and there were fears of an outbreak, but Ibrahim Pasha's strong rule was beginning to be felt, and no disturbance occurred. The head of the fanatical party was executed by Ibrahim's orders during Captain Cotton's visit.

While they were at Damascus, Michael heard that his friend, Assad Shidiak, had suffered much persecution in the monastery for his faith, and had actually been put to death there. A young English merchant in the city, named Todd, was much moved by Michael's distress, and laid the matter before Ibrahim Pasha, who at once offered him an escort of cavalry. He went direct to the monastery, and demanded admittance. Mr. Todd and the soldiers searched the place, the monks putting them off in vain with excuses, saying Shidiak had died of fever and had been buried. At last one old monk came to Mr. Todd and told him that Shidiak had been his loved friend, and he would show the niche in which he had been walled up, and for some time kept alive. He took Mr. Todd to the place, and pointed out where the wall had been broken down to take out the body, the stones still being about as when the workmen had finished their work. The monks were most subservient, offering refreshments to the escort as well as to Mr. Todd. The latter's reply was: "We will neither eat nor drink in this house on which the curse of God rests. He has seen your murder of His faithful servant." There had been a hope that they might have been in time to deliver the captive, but he had been some time dead.

From Damascus the party had planned to proceed to Bagdad, and were arranging for camels and horses, when Sherif Bey, the governor under Ibrahim Pasha, begged to be allowed to provide an escort and make all arrangements for them, the journey being a most dangerous one. This courtesy they gladly accepted. The Bey put them in charge of a sheikh, who had recently brought a large caravan from Bagdad, and was returning. He was a remarkable man, both in appearance and manners, who had frequently travelled to India with horses, remaining there until they were sold; so that he knew Europeans, and took great interest in the party thus placed under his charge.

They reached Bagdad in safety. The sheikh took them to sleep at his own house the first night. The next morning Captain Cotton went to the Mission House, where Mr. Groves, Mr. Parnell (afterwards Lord Congleton), and Mr. Cronin had been for two or three years.

The details of the desert journey are to be found in a letter to his mother, which my father sent from Bagdad on May 11, 1833. It more than justifies quotation in full, and was as follows:—

MY DEAR MOTHER,—

My last was dated Damascus, so you see I am making progress towards India, though not so rapidly as might be. After many delays and contradictory pieces of advice, we at length left that place, on the 3rd April, in company with a small caravan, and, after twenty-four days' hard marching, we arrived here in excellent health on the 26th. We have since discovered that the real cause of our difficulty in getting away from Damascus was the unwillingness of the sheik of the caravan to let us accompany it, for the Arab tribes are so sensible of the comparative riches of the Franks in general that, if they had discovered us in a caravan, it was to be expected that they would demand an enormous sum as tribute, and make the head of the caravan responsible. However, the sheik at last consented to our accompanying him, on condition that we were dressed like Arabs, and we had to pay a much larger sum than native travellers for our camels. The Pasha of Syria and the principal Bagdad merchants of Damascus committed us to the care of a sheik on whom they placed great dependence, and so we started as well cared for by men we never saw before as if we had been their sons and brothers. And the sheik did not fail in the smallest point of what he had been charged with, so that, excepting the unavoidable tedium of sitting twelve or fourteen hours a day on camels in a warm sun, I never made a journey in my life with less annoyance.

The caravan contained about six or seven hundred camels, divided into twelve or fourteen parties, each under its own sheik, and there were perhaps one hundred and twenty men with them, twenty or thirty of whom were mounted on dromedaries, armed with swords and matchlocks, and rode two or three miles in front, or on the flanks, according to where they expected the Arabs of the desert to attack them. When no danger was apprehended, the camels were spread over a great space, sometimes more than a mile in breadth, but when Arabs were in sight the whole body kept together. At night the whole party slept in a very small space, the camels packing quite as close as bales of goods, and we all amongst them ; from which we learnt that a stable is a garden of pinks and roses compared with the desert bedchamber of our nags.

However, you may suppose that after being on their backs for twelve hours, we had little time to consider whether we were near to or far from them at night. We usually started before sunrise, and continued without halt till near sunset, and sometimes till after that. The camels feed a great part of the day, as they go, wherever they find pasture, and there was no day on which they did not meet with abundance of such things as they like (which were chiefly strong aromatic plants), excepting on the banks of the Euphrates, where there was literally nothing.

At the time we crossed, the desert was in its greatest beauty, and you would be surprised at the variety of flowers ; I think I must have seen fifty, half of which would be prized in any flower garden in England. The camels require no water when there is green food for them, and ours did not taste it for twenty days. We passed only two wells, which were in the beds of streams, for as the camels did not need water, the caravan came as straight as possible, considering that the sheik had no compass, and so steered their feet as well as he could by the sun. The camels may well be called Ships of the Desert, in one respect, for when we were on a perfect plain and saw any of them approaching us, and while they were still beyond the horizon, they looked so like vessels at a distance at sea that I could perceive no difference, and when the mirage was spread over the horizon, the illusion was complete. If they are to be called ships, however, we must consider them as belonging to the navy of Lilliput, for our whole caravan only carried as much as a single one-masted vessel of one hundred tons would convey by sea, little more than a "flat." The desert at first consisted chiefly of a succession of very gentle undulations of ground, of gravelly soil covered, though very thinly, with aromatic plants, excepting in some spots where there was so much vegetation as to appear quite rich to eyes that had got a little accustomed to the desert.

Towards the Euphrates we passed plains of very great extent, without the smallest unevenness, not a plant or knoll rising one foot above the general level. The highest vegetable of any kind that we saw was the flower of a plant like rhubarb, which grew to the height of a foot and a half in some places.

After leaving Damascus two or three days, we did not see a single standing camp of Arabs, which you may suppose was not a very bitter disappointment to a peaceable man like me. We met two parties on the march. One of them took us for Ibrahim Pasha's army, and retreated without their property in great precipitation ; neither party offered to molest us.

The leaders of our caravan were of a very peaceful tribe, a great part of whom are at present living within the walls of Bagdad, and they pay a fixed tribute per camel to the strange tribes through which they pass. We came to the Euphrates in flood, and crossed it in boats ; it was quite full, and about one hundred and fifty yards broad. Between the Euphrates and Tigris we passed a real desert, for, though it was in the spring, not a blade of vegetation was to be seen in many parts. On arriving late at Bagdad, our sheik took us to his house, where we slept, and the next morning crossed the Tigris by a bridge of boats, and found a hearty welcome in the house of the missionaries.

Though we had so little trouble on our journey, I cannot tell you the delight with which we found ourselves among our countrymen again, and sheltered from the sun. On the last day we were seventeen and a half hours on our camels, and we rode about sixty miles, from which you may judge that I was not much the worse for wear. This, however, must be qualified in some degree, for I was not in a condition to be refreshed by the sight of a wooden-seat chair. The motion of the heavy camels is exceedingly fatiguing, but our sheik had provided us with a very delicate nag, that could walk as prettily as any young lady, so I suffered little comparatively; still, I found that it was not pleasant to make from forty thousand to fifty thousand low bows involuntarily in a day.

You may have heard that the year before last, out of sixty thousand inhabitants of Bagdad, fifty thousand died of the plague, and at the same time the whole city was laid several feet under water by a flood while an army was waiting to besiege it, which took up its ground before the wall as soon as the water retired. The present appearance of the city corresponds with these occurrences. In one night, when the flood first broke down the walls and entered the city, about one-fourth of the houses fell, and buried many persons in their ruins. Much of the space within the walls is now covered with heaps of ruins, and in the other parts there are whole streets without an inhabitant. There is scarcely a vestige remaining of the city's former magnificence; it once contained three millions.

We have received the greatest kindness from the missionaries and the Company's Resident here. They are the only English in the place. There is an easy way of getting to Bussorah by the Tigris, and we hope to start in a large boat on Tuesday, that is, in three days, and to reach Bussorah in four or five days; whence we have a good prospect of a vessel to Bombay. The climate of this place is at present delicious. My companion, Major Skinner, is one of the very few persons who can bear uncomfortable circumstances without annoying himself or anybody else. We hope to go on together.

Mr. Newman, of Oriel, an acquaintance of Richard's, was attached to this Mission, and I had a letter to him, but he left the place some months ago; the others, however, required no introduction to give us a hearty reception. Colonel Taylor, the Resident, also would have quartered us, if we had not been provided for. Christians and Mussulmans appear to have agreed to shew us kindness every step we have taken from England here, excepting, indeed, our friends in the plains of Esdraelon, and then we received instantaneous redress.

I begin to fear now that the Post Office people at Bombay will have given me up, and sent away my letters, which would be a very grievous disappointment; but I hope not. How little did I think that I should be so long without hearing of you!

An application has been made to the Director from this Pashalik for some of their officers to superintend public works and organize troops, and the Directors of the East India Company have consented to the arrangement; so that there is some hope of a strong and settled government being again established in these miserable countries where every man's hand is against his neighbour.

Among other works in contemplation is the establishment of a regular line of steam boats on the Euphrates, and the cutting of a canal to connect that river with Bagdad, at the expense of the Pasha, thereby completely establishing this as the most easy and expeditious line of communication from England to India. I hope and trust you are all in health and prosperity, as when I left you, but I wish I could know it.

A large packet of letters has lately arrived from Constantinople, but they have been rather a long time on the road. They bring wretched accounts of Ireland. There has been a very serious mutiny discovered in the Madras Army among the native officers and privates, but the end of it is not known here. Our Resident here is in a most extraordinary position with respect to the government, as none of the Arab tribes in the open country, or of the different parties in the cities, can trust one another's word in the least; whenever any disturbances break out, nothing can be settled without getting the Resident to be a party to the agreement, and they have the most entire confidence in the bare word of a Frank.

Some months ago the people in Bagdad rebelled, and attacked the Palace, and would certainly have put the Pasha to death had he not called upon the Resident, who interfered for him with the conspirators, and he was enabled to settle the business without further bloodshed. The same thing has taken place repeatedly in all parts of the Pashalik, so that what little peace is enjoyed here is by means of a man without any outward power whatever, solely his personal character, and that of his nation, being firmly established. I never saw so striking an instance of the effect of a single upright mind in the midst of a nation of faithless men.

My next letter, I hope, will be from Bombay. May God bless you, and all the members of the family. I send my kindest love to every one.

Ever your most affectionate Son,

ARTHUR.

One of the missionaries who welcomed my father to their homes at Bagdad, as mentioned in the letter, was Mr. Anthony N. Groves. His son, Henry, in an account of the mission, notices Captain Cotton's arrival; and, in another letter written quite recently, my father, referring to Henry Groves's death, says he remembers sleeping with him at this time on the roof of the Mission House. Mr. Groves afterwards accompanied him to Bombay.

They started from Bagdad on May 21, 1833, but were detained by my father's very dangerous illness at Bushire, on the Persian Gulf. The late Lord Congleton wrote to Mrs. Groves:—

"But for your kind husband, Captain Cotton would not, humanly speaking, have got through his illness at Bushire, so ill was he, and so near death. I doubt if he can remember anything about the matter."

He was, however (as he afterwards informed his friends), of the opinion that his grave was dug. "Michael," Mrs.

Groves says, "though most faithful in his attendance, was at times quite overpowered by the circumstances of his beloved master and friend, and almost broken-hearted at the thought of his death."

About the year 1863, Sir Arthur Cotton was recognised at a public meeting by a gentleman, whose name he could not remember, but who informed him that thirty years previously he was in command of the escort of the British Resident at Bushire, and had had charge of his funeral arrangements. My father often used to remark that "he supposed he was himself the only man who had ever visited his own grave."

After about twelve months from the time of his setting out from England Captain Cotton arrived at Bombay, and returned to Tanjore.

This, perhaps, may be the place in which to refer to other journeys made by my father. He visited Australia thrice and Mauritius once. The far-away days during which these journeys were taken, and the practical manner in which the traveller endeavoured to turn his observations and knowledge to the benefit of the country he visited, render a reference to them desirable.

He, who afterwards declaimed so strongly against the construction of railways in India because canals would so much more cheaply carry goods and provide means for cultivation, himself had charge of the construction of a small railway, which will be noticed in due course. At the conclusion of his work on the Red Hills Railway, near Madras, his health broke down, and he went to Tasmania on sick leave, a long, tedious, voyage in those days.

On his arrival in Tasmania he temporarily settled down at Hobart Town. Here he immediately occupied himself with experiments on a centrifugal steam engine, probably the precursor of the steam turbine, which at present is attracting such widespread attention. But the real rotary engine has even yet to establish itself. The idea of a rotary engine, I believe, was entirely his own. This engine he certainly made himself. Whilst studying its working when it was in motion, unhappily with a boiler of poor quality—the only one he could obtain—the boiler burst, and there was an explosion, which injured him most severely.

In describing this misfortune he took his usual optimistic view of the event by saying: "Yes, the boiler burst and injured both my legs, taking off the flesh of one of them, but I succeeded in getting one hundred and fifty revolutions a minute." This result compensated him for all his sufferings! For many months he could not walk, and all his life he suffered more or less from the result of this accident, especially after work which fatigued him, or in cold weather. It is an interesting fact, however, that he was always a great walker; even after he was seventy years of age he could go long distances on foot. His light, active, figure and wiry frame stood him in good stead, and his energetic habit of mind caused him to greatly enjoy long hours of climbing, or the exploring of new country.

For many weeks after the accident he lay dangerously ill in an hotel in Hobart Town. When he was able to be moved, he was invited to the house of a gentleman, who lived a few miles from Hobart Town on the bank of the Derwent, and there rest and the beautiful scenery did much to help his recovery He was able to be driven about the neighbourhood, which is, perhaps, amongst the most lovely in the world.

The river Derwent brings vessels of considerable size to Hobart Town, which lies at the foot of Mount Wellington. For eight months in the year the mountain is tipped with snow, while at its foot and for about two miles along its base the sides are covered with the most luxurious growth of plants of many kinds—blue, and red, and yellow—quite unknown in England or India. The charm to the invalid was great, and he improved much in that first change.

Then he became the guest of a family in the centre of

the island, where the scenery was less beautiful, but novel and peculiar, full of different interests, while the Christian society he enjoyed was always helpful and cheering. A farther move took him towards the north, to Norfolk plains, about sixteen miles from Launceston, where again he found Christian residents, whose hospitality and kindness he never forgot. He gradually recovered the power of riding and walking, and after some months returned to Hobart Town and India.

At the time of his first visit to Tasmania Sir John Franklin was governor of the island — a kind-hearted, genial, man, much beloved by those who knew him intimately. My father was a great favourite with him and Lady Franklin, and was often at Government House. He was warmly attached to the fine old explorer.

Before he left for India, the expedition of 1839 to the South Pole arrived in Tasmanian waters. The ships, *Erebus* and *Terror*, were anchored close together in the Derwent, and stayed there some months, Sir John greatly enjoying the society of his old fellow-midshipmen and friends, Sir James Ross and Captain Crozier, the latter of whom commanded the expedition. The society of so many scientific and Christian men was much valued by the community at large, especially by those who had the opportunity of meeting them constantly at Government House. Not many years later Sir John, with Captain Crozier and the same two ships, sailed for the North Pole, where both commanders perished, to the sorrow of many friends and to the grief of the nation.

A few years of strenuous toil in the Godavari Delta, and once more there was a breakdown in my father's health, so serious that the devoted Engineer was obliged to leave his work. Once more a voyage to Australia was determined upon. This time he was not alone. Wife and children were with him.

It so happened that at this time there was no vessel going direct from Madras to Melbourne, so he decided to break the journey at Mauritius, and we sailed for that island, the ship being under the command of a captain who had on board a half-caste family, a queer conglomeration of relatives, who occupied the stern cabin next to our own.

We arrived in the harbour of Port Louis, the beautiful capital of a beautiful island, on a lovely moonlight night. The sight was most impressive; many ships were anchored under the shadow of Peter Botte, a high mountain whose summit is crowned with a round rock which is poised on the point of another rock—a remarkable feature standing, as the mountain does, quite alone. A British man-of-war was among the ships at anchor; its band was playing some lively strains as we drew to our anchorage, then there was a pause, and, to our loyal and devoted ears came the welcome strains of "God Save the Queen."

We remained at Mauritius for two months. First we stayed for a few days at Port Louis; then, finding this place very hot—the climate being most oppressive—we went to the village of Cure Pipe, where we occupied a lovely cottage surrounded by fields, with a running brook close to the house, in which we—the younger ones at least—delighted to wade, and on the banks of which we could gather lovely wild flowers.

When we arrived at Mauritius my father was quite prostrated with weakness as the result of his severe illness, but from the day that we entered our cottage he began to revive, and his strength soon returned to him, so that we had the joy of seeing him restored to health before we were obliged to leave the island for Australia.

At the house of one of our friends near Port Louis there was an enormous tortoise, so large that three or four of us used to amuse ourselves by riding on its back together. It would carry us long distances. Now and then it would disappear and be away for days together. My father called us one Sunday morning to look through a telescope across the lake which adjoined our friend's property, and there we saw the tortoise's head bobbing up and down as it returned from one of its solitary rambles, swimming to us across this piece of water. I have sometimes heard doubts thrown on the enormous size of this creature as described by those who tell this story, but, in reading Admiral Keppel's life the other day, I found the same tortoise not only spoken of, but exhibited in a drawing as it walked along carrying on its back six men. Thus unexpectedly our description was corroborated.

From Mauritius we went to Australia to stay with my mother's relatives. During this time we had many interesting and curious experiences, but our great interest and pleasure was our father's companionship. He was at leisure and was constantly with us. He would take the greatest pains to teach us and give us information on every subject we could understand. When out for a day's ramble with him, we spent the heated hours of mid-day at an inn, where incidents revealing his exceeding kindliness occurred which are as fresh in my memory to-day as when they happened.

The inn was rather a notorious place in that lonely district, lonely then, but now densely populated, being in the neighbourhood of Geelong. There was no other inn near it for many miles. It went by the name of "The Squeakers," and was frequented by a very rough and desperate class of men. On one occasion a relative of ours, who had been riding a great distance, arrived at this inn so exhausted that he threw himself on the bed in a small room, divided only by a wooden partition from the drinking saloon, where a crowd of ruffians were seated. As he lay quite prostrate, too tired to move hand or foot, he heard them saying that they thought it would be a good plan to rob the gentleman, drag him out of his bed, and put him out of sight where no one would ever find him again. During the conversation he heard one voice clear and distinct, marked by a strong Scotch accent, say: "You'll nae touch him ; he's a guid man, he works hard. He has ridden fifty miles to-day, and I'll stand by him." This friendly word probably saved his life.

We used to go out early in the mornings to search for

manna. It is a strange thing that the manna described in the book of Exodus seems to be exactly reproduced in that colony. Every morning and evening we found it lying on the ground in large quantities on the sticks, on logs of trees, on blades of grass. It was white and sweet, and deliciously fresh and pleasant to the taste, but it would not keep. We used to collect it in bags, and enjoy it for our breakfast and tea; but if it was kept for a few hours it turned black and could not be eaten. It is generally thought that the manna of Australia is a kind of gum produced by an insect; it is snow white and very sweet. But I do not know that this explanation has ever been verified.

Whilst we stayed here, my father became friendly with the clergyman, the Rev. Mr. Hastie, a Scotchman, and used to go with him from place to place reading to the people. So great was the bond of sympathy between himself and this excellent man, that they corresponded afterwards, Mr. Hastie often saying how greatly he missed him when he was compelled to return to India.

My father was interested in the cattle farms belonging to his brothers-in-law, and also in their immense tallow works, which they had brought to great perfection. But he was even more interested in the plans, which he worked out with the most elaborate care, for the irrigation of the farms, for though, as a rule, rain was plentiful, it was uncertain in its fall, and he would often prophesy the serious results of one year without an ample water supply. He wanted to arrange for water storage on a very large scale, with simple canal systems from point to point, which would have made the owners quite independent, for a long time at least, of the fall of rain. Sad it is to remember that during the last week of his life he was reading a letter, which described the terrible drought then prevailing in that very part of the country. For a long period no rain had fallen, and this letter described the dying of the cattle and sheep from sheer inanition, dried-up stream-beds and the utter absence of grass everywhere. He looked up at me with that intense look which he would assume when conversing on subjects very near his heart, and said: "If they had only taken my advice, given so many years ago, they would have saved fortunes, and gained others over and over again."

This leads me to allude to the one vein of sadness that ran through his whole life. It was neither more nor less than the burden, which always weighed upon him, of the vast needs of India, coupled with the knowledge that, had he the power to apply the remedies, he could have met these needs, and thus have saved the country from much of its famine and poverty. The plans which he recommended were his own, but he never desired to keep his knowledge to himself. He was always ready to impart it, down to the smallest detail, to any one who would listen to him or take his advice. But here was the difficulty. His schemes were considered Utopian; yet he could always answer such a suggestion by pointing to his magnificent works carried out on the Coleroon and Godavari rivers, which have abundantly repaid the expenditure incurred, and have formed an oasis in India during the long years that have followed their completion.

As an appendix to this chapter I give a paper on "Water in Australia," written probably in 1850. Although half a century has passed, and enterprise in Australia is not wanting, there is still much in this paper of value.

It was soon after we left the hospitable home of our relations there that gold was discovered in the neighbourhood. I have heard my father tell the story. He said that a gentleman, who was riding across the country, had stopped at a house near and asked for luncheon. After he had finished his repast he rode away. As he was crossing a plain not far distant his horse threw him. Before he could reach it, it had galloped away. In pursuing the horse, he found himself in marshy ground, and, as he seized the reins, the horse kicked up some soil from the marsh. In this soil the gentleman noticed a glittering and a sparkling of some material, that looked to him very much like gold. He took up some of the earth in his hand, and the more closely he examined it the more he thought it could be nothing but fine grains of gold. There was no mistake. He rode straight back to the town and showed it to an expert, who told him that he had conjectured rightly—he had discovered a gold-field. In an incredibly short time the whole of that district was covered with small huts and tents; thousands of men arrived to try their luck in searching for the newly-found treasure. Of course, farming had to be abandoned there, and the owner moved to another part of the country.

St. Helena was a place we visited on our voyage to England some years later. A weird, desolate-looking, rock looming in the distance was our first sight of Napoleon Buonaparte's sea-girt prison. As the ship sailed into the harbour this tremendous mass of steep rock towered over us and looked an impregnable fortress. How was this summit ever to be reached? A small boat took us from the ship and scaling ladders were drawn down to the side of the rock, and we climbed up to the greener slopes above where the little town was.

After breakfast at the hotel, we rode on mules and ponies to the site of Napoleon's house and tomb. Our pathway lay through beautiful woods and the most luxuriant foliage. It was altogether a day to be remembered. The brilliant blue sky and the precipices that we passed as we explored the heart of the island were all most charming. The tomb, surrounded by an iron railing, was covered by a weeping willow—a beautiful spot, but an intense sadness seemed to rest over it, for it teemed with the interests of a great but broken life, and world-wide ambitions that had fallen like a crumbled ruin on this very spot. We afterwards went into the house where the valiant conqueror had lived during those long, sad, years of his history.

The weather at St. Helena was very changeable. Though the early morning had been brilliant, such heavy showers fell during our ride that our clothes were soaked through and through, and the result was, to myself, a serious illness, which began that day and lasted for many weeks. However great the penalty we had to pay for our sight-seeing on that day in June, we always felt that we had gained something in visiting this most interesting spot.

Appendix

WATER IN AUSTRALIA

The first thing beyond all others in Australia is this question of water and its storage. This great fundamental point, on which the whole future of the country hangs, is now publicly acknowledged. How could there be ever any doubt about this in a land subject at moderate intervals to droughts of twenty months or more. Of late there has been an additional hindrance in the matter, from the subject of Irrigation being taken up, which, in itself a very important one, has been, in the circumstances, a terribly mischievous one by greatly drawing off attention from the vital point, which is, of course, in the case of long droughts, the storage of water.

In this way the Committee sent to America was most mischievous, because there the sole question was distribution. They have the water in abundance.

But, having at last fixed attention on the real point, the next thing that should be kept in view is that there is abundant proof that the storage of water is a matter of extremely small cost. This ought to have been the very first subject of the inquiries of the Committee, because the whole tone of further proceedings must be essentially affected by the probable task.

A Committee ought to have been sent to India and to France, where large reservoirs have been constructed, to obtain rough estimates of the probable cost of storing in Australia by similar works. Not, of course, with the idea of forming anything approaching net estimates, but merely to form a judgment, such as whether one thousand or one million cubic yards could be stored for one pound sterling, that is, to ascertain whether the cost of storage would be a real hindrance or not. My conclusion, from experience in India, is that the cost will be found so insignificant that there cannot be a question about the immediate commencement of a complete system of storage for the whole country.

In India we certainly have, in the nature of the face of the country, extraordinary facilities for storing, and tens of thousands of tanks, containing from two hundred million cubic yards downwards, have been constructed, while there are many sites that would contain more than a thousand millions yet not occupied. One, on a main river which would require a bund one hundred feet high, and half a mile long, costing perhaps £200,000, would be converted into a lake ninety miles long by an average of about three miles wide, having a surface of eight hundred million square yards, and mean depth of ten yards, or a content of eight thousand million cubic yards, which would be forty thousand cubic yards per pound of capital expended, and a million cubic yards per pound of interest; or, if one thousand cubic yards would carry an acre of grass to completion, the charge would be a farthing per acre per annum.

And if in Australia it cost one hundred times as much, it would then be only two shillings per acre, a sum quite insignificant, even in respect of ordinary years, but what in respect of years of drought, when the lives of millions of sheep are in suspense! And it must be ever kept in view that when the country is filled up, it will not be a question of lives of sheep, but of men, as it is now in India, where five millions died in the last famine in spite of all the vast arrangements that were made to provide food, and even in Ireland, a little patch of land lying beside England, with the sea within easy reach of every part of it, some hundreds of thousands perished.

I am not acquainted with the nature of the surface of much of the country in Australia, and, therefore, can only attempt to give some material for calculating the cost of storage in one tract, for instance, the plains of the Darling. It must be, of course, in my hands, a mere rough sketch of what it might cost, but something like correct figures may be applied to this estimate by those who know the country.

Suppose the Darling has a fall of a foot per mile, and that a weir were built across it, throwing the water into a canal with a fall of nine inches per mile, into a tank twenty-four feet deep, formed by a circular embankment of earth ten yards high and ten miles in diameter.

Such a tank would cover two hundred and fifty million square yards of ground, and with a depth of eight yards contain two thousand million cubic yards of water. And if we allow five feet per annum for evaporation, or for a drought of two years, ten feet, it would leave fourteen feet for one, or seven feet for two, in case of an extreme drought, giving six hundred million cubic yards, or sufficient, I suppose, for six hundred thousand acres of corn or grass; that is, one thousand cubic yards per annum, or five waterings of one and a half inches each. The extreme evaporation recorded in India with half a gale of wind at 110° is half an inch per day, and the whole annual evaporation in the tropical part of the country is believed to be about six yards, or one-fifth of an inch per day. We may allow five feet in Australia near the tropics.

Now the earthwork in such tanks and canals would be about twenty-five million cubic yards, which, at one shilling per cubic yard, would be £1,250,000. To this amount must be added lining the upper part of the interior slope with loose stones to bear the work of the waves. The cost of this is, of course, quite uncertain. We may allow £250,000 for it with the weir and sluices, or £1,500,000 in all, the interest of which at six per cent. with management would be £90,000 a year for six hundred thousand acres, or three shillings per acre; or, if the value of the crop be £10, equal to one and a half per cent. upon it.

But this is only for an ordinary year, and supposing that twelve feet of water is always kept in the tank, at the end of the first year, what would be the value of this water in a great drought? Allowing a crop of grass to keep five sheep alive for the year per acre and no other benefit, at ten shillings per sheep, it would save the whole cost of the works in the one year.

But this also supposes that no advantage is taken of the formation of the ground. The works might cost one-tenth of this where the ground was favourable.

I only give this as a rude sketch of what I suppose might be done in the great plains of alluvium. What favourable valleys in the hilly country might be closed by short embankments is another great question. All the upper basins of the Darling, the Lachlan, the Murrumbudgee, and Murray, as well as other rivers, should be examined by men who have the peculiar talent for projecting such works, and who have obtained some knowledge of the subject from visiting the great works in France and India.

But it is, of course, of the utmost importance that an engineer should be found who has such a peculiar talent; besides which a statesman will be required who can take in a view of the vast question in all other respects.

We have a terrible instance of a great work undertaken by an engineer who was unequal to the project in the harbour at Madras, where half a million has been expended, and in the late hurricane all the ships ran out of it, judging the hurricane safer than the harbour.

But the great point I wish to urge is that I am fully assured from my experience that the cost of storing water will be found in Australia perfectly insignificant in comparison with the results which would be secured.

I should add two or three remarks :—

First. The effect of such a tank is not confined to the thousand square miles irrigated by it. A vast extent of country round would be refreshed by dew and rain from the evaporation of four hundred million cubic yards of water per annum from the surface of the tank; besides that, the state of the air would be greatly improved by the moisture, for in those lands the air is altogether too dry. And the temperature would be considerably moderated.

Secondly. The moment such water is available patches of plantation would be made over the whole neighbourhood, as has been done in whole kingdoms in India, greatly modifying the climate and increasing the rainfall and dew. If the vast plains of the Darling were thus sprinkled over with tracts and plantations, the whole country would be so improved for human occupation that it would be entirely and essentially changed.

Some day all this will be done. When it is, and when many thousands of families are finding prosperity and comfort on areas now almost worthless, it is to be hoped my father's wise prescience may not be altogether forgotten.

CHAPTER IV

The Beginnings of Great Duties

"The nature of the irrigation works in the Madras Presidency and their historic development are best illustrated in the great Cauveri[1] scheme, which supplies a delta stretching from above the town of Trichinopoly to the sea. The chief systems of Southern India are all on the east coast, all deltaic, all modern adaptations of ancient designs, and all make river waters available by the same class of works. Any one of them will serve as a key to the rest, and this particular scheme, as the largest and most profitable, is naturally selected to indicate the type."—Hon. A. DEAKIN, M.L.A.

CAPTAIN COTTON'S beginnings in Southern India as a semi-independent officer with scope to exercise his growing faculties synchronized with that period, in Great Britain and elsewhere, of eager hope as to what the application of science would do towards increasing the productivity of the earth and the happiness of the various races of mankind. In England this period was, in a measure, inaugurated by the publication of the famous Bridgewater Treatises. The effort of the human mind, which they represented, finds expression in the phrase then so widely current: "He who makes two blades of grass to grow where one grew before is a benefactor of his race." There is a passionate desire in men to see some tangible result of their labour, especially if that labour be of a strenuous character. The test is always applied to an

[1] The new spelling in Indian words gives Kaveri for Cauveri. It has been thought advisable to retain, so far as may be, the old spelling throughout: but no hard-and-fast rule has been adopted by me.

enterprise, material or moral: Does it pay? And, if not carried too far, the test is not an unworthy one.

My father, in 1836, stands at the threshold of the most distinguished part of a great career. Looking, as we are able to do, from the end to the beginning, it is possible to say of his notable achievements, that they have been altogether good. Their effects were and are beneficial only. A builder of empire, of that particular Empire of Britain of which he was one of the most admiring of sons, and which he regarded as guarded by and blessed of God, there is no record of human suffering in all he accomplished; the stones which go to make his niche of fame are nowhere cemented by human anguish or the shedding of blood. All he did has been of a character to make life more prosperous to many millions, and to satisfy abundantly the most elementary needs of human life. This done, all else was possible. Continually hungry and poverty-stricken people can make no progress. Such a tribute as this, when Arthur Cotton's most important achievements are first taken in hand by him, is due to him; it was in a spirit which was ever mindful of the gain which would result to humanity that he undertook and carried, with so strenuous a determination, his great projects to success. Not a little of his success was due to his intense zeal and powers of hard work. Only such a noble ambition as he cherished could have carried him through what he did, not simply in travelling through the districts in all seasons, but also in the preparation of elaborate reports for the consideration of the Government. No detail was too unimportant for his personal consideration, no toil too severe for him to endure.

What did Arthur Cotton do in Tanjore?

He devised a great scheme for controlling the river Cauveri, and saving its almost priceless water from running to waste.

To grapple with the Cauveri's current was no mean achievement. Colonel Caldwell, the first British Engineer to examine the river with care, which he did in 1804, was forcibly struck with the unusual character of the Cauveri; he predicted its total annihilation as a useful stream at no distant future, unless the river could be restored to what he believed to have been its original condition. My father's comment on this statement was as follows:—"But the evil, though progressive, is much slower than might at first be expected. The sand and heavier ingredients are deposited in the bed of the river, but a considerable portion of the firm soil, from its less specific gravity, remains longer in suspension, and is ultimately carried into the smaller channels, and from them into the rice fields, which it greatly enriches." It is clear *this* Engineer was not afraid of the vagaries of the stream.

"The original merit of conceiving the plan of so grappling with a great river like the Cauveri as to compel it to become an easily controlled agent cannot be impaired, and I may be permitted to express my admiration of the skill and courage they display, both in their design and execution." Thus said Colonel Baird Smith seventeen years after Captain Cotton's work had been begun. He further remarked: "The permanent prosperity of Tanjore is, without doubt, to be attributed in large measure to that first bold step taken by Colonel Cotton in the construction of the Upper Coleroon dam, under circumstances of great difficulty, with restricted means, against much opposition, and with heavy personal responsibilities."

There was no prosperity when Captain Cotton conceived his plan. On the contrary, the district was in a state of decay, the people, spiritless and suffering.

This testimony was the common opinion of every one capable of judging as to what was done. The official in charge of the district at the time (Mr. W. N. Kindersley, who is described by Sir Alexander Arbuthnot as "one of the ablest civil servants in the Madras Presidency") declared that there was "not an individual in the province who did not consider the upper anicut the greatest blessing that had ever been conferred upon it." Mr. Kindersley also expressed his conviction that "the name of its projector would, in Tanjore, survive those of all the Europeans who had ever been connected with it."

That was civilian testimony. What would a brother Engineer say of the project? Brother Engineers were not wanting in the expression of their opinions. They shared the view of Captain Cotton's superior, the Chief Engineer of the Presidency, Colonel Duncan Sim (afterwards Commanding Engineer throughout the siege of Delhi), who was deputed to report upon the conception and progress of the work. Colonel Sim's praise was unstinted. "Simple and natural," he wrote, "as this course [the project of the anicuts] may now appear, no one previously to Captain Cotton thought of recommending it, and it was attended by a degree of responsibility and risk which few would voluntarily have undertaken. For the talent and judgment displayed by Captain Cotton in his patient investigation of the causes which were affecting the rivers in Tanjore, and for the boldness with which he proposed, and carried into effect, what appeared to be the only remedy, I conceive that officer is entitled to the highest praise." The same fine characteristic was exhibited by my father in the Godavari works, and received like commendation. Colonel Sim, contemplating the unfinished work near Dowlaisweram, and understanding all that was involved in it, turning to Major Fred. Cotton, exclaimed: "I am astounded at your brother's professional daring." More than forty years later, similar credit from similar authority was given to the Engineer. Forty years are a long period in a man's life; time enough to be forgotten twice over. But Arthur Cotton was not forgotten, and, in 1882, the high tribute of 1839 was virtually repeated in the report of the Chief Engineer for Irrigation in that year, when he remarked that, "to Captain (now Sir Arthur) Cotton is due the entire credit of the series of works which have fulfilled the purposes for which they were designed with such remarkable success."

Colonel Duncan Sim's reading of Captain Cotton's

characteristics bears a moment's consideration. With unerring discernment he brings to light what really were the guiding principles of the daring Engineer's character. Originality of thought: " . . . no one previously to Captain Cotton thought of recommending" the simple and natural course he adopted; courage in the carrying out of his convictions: "attended by a degree of responsibility and risk which few would voluntarily have undertaken." Originality and courage, added to these was loyalty and conviction. If my father lived for any one thing more than another it was that he might press forward the use of water for navigation and irrigation. At a discussion in 1877, following a paper read by him at the East India Association, one of the speakers said: "If Sir Arthur Cotton would open his mind to the great value of railways at the same time that he urges the real importance of canals, his views would undoubtedly commend themselves more cogently to many people acquainted with India and the points at issue, and the aim, for which he so laboriously and conscientiously worked for many years, would be more speedily advanced." The response to this was instantaneous and in high indignation. "That is," retorted the righteously annoyed Engineer, "if I would either be a party to what I know is false or would help to conceal the truth as to the very essential and fundamental point of the whole matter, it would be the way to promote the truth." Sir Arthur's friends will not need that any emphasis should be given to the haughty pride with which this assertion of fidelity to principle was made.

It will be seen that, unlike many men, Arthur Cotton had not to wait for many years until the joy of seeing difficulties overcome had become mitigated by a want of recognition. Though he never sought for praise it is clear the recognition which his work extorted was gratifying to him. It could not well be otherwise. But praise never spoiled him, never developed conceit, never led to self-assertion; on the contrary, he modestly accepted what was said of that which he had done, and found in it an incentive to do something, immediately after, even more worthy of regard, even more useful in increasing the comfort and happiness of his fellows. From his earliest to his latest day this was a marked characteristic of his every act.

What, then, really was the work so highly praised for its conception and execution, and the financial results of which, as an investment of public money, were so marvellous and so gratifying? It was one which, as has already been stated, was destined to stamp Captain Cotton as an Engineer of pre-eminent gifts in hydraulic works, which, of all engineering works, are the most difficult to plan and to execute with complete success. The stability of bridges, for example, can be determined with mathematical accuracy, and they may be so designed as to be nearly independent of the action of water. But a system of dams and channels is no sooner established than the most watchful care[1] is needed to preserve it in efficiency; and any mistakes or oversight in the original design are

[1] Writing of the Sirhind canal, Mr. Deakin (*Irrigated India*, p. 214 and p. 224) says:—

"Every mile of the canal proves full of instruction as well as entertainment. Like a living organism, the great stream of water continually alters its environment, and is altered by it in time, so that the engineer's task is never over; he constantly meets new contingencies, and by the lessons of experience on his own or upon other canals learns to vary his expedients."

"Out of those far-off mountains and by this thirsty spectre land come the thin streams of water which are now filtered into the canal, to carry its boon of harvests for scores of miles into country almost as unprofitable as this. But in a few months there will be no longer this empty valley, and this quietness of air through which the voices of the Changras on the weir make a faint murmur. That great reef will then be hid in foam when the flood tide, spreading from bank to bank, and hoarsely roaring, will sweep down twelve feet to sixteen feet deep, half a mile wide, shifting its quicksands and shingle beds from side to side as a porter shifts his load, tossing its tangle of trees, grinding its ranks of boulders against the stubborn mass of stone and iron that will bar its way. . . . In the heat and in the storm the engineers will stand to their posts, and flinch from no contest with flood, fever, or famine, or with the river which they master (as their Government masters this people), to prevent the ruin which must certainly follow if its great subject forces should ever master them."

sure to make themselves manifest, and to require unforeseen and often very difficult remedies. Hence, discernment and foresight of a high order are essential in such designs. Captain Cotton's ascendancy in the possession of such qualifications was such as seemed unquestionable to those who were best acquainted with its engineering feats.

Before answering the question with which the preceding paragraph is opened, let this example of how the test: "Will it pay?" borne by Sir Alexander Arbuthnot, be recorded. Sir Alexander says:—

"The financial returns of these works have been such as have seldom resulted from any public undertaking. From the report above quoted, it appears that for six years after the construction of the anicuts, the annual profit on the capital expended was, in the case of the upper anicut, sixty-nine per cent., and in that of the lower anicut nearly one hundred per cent. The increased value of private property, due to the works, has been equally large, while in seasons of scarcity not only have these districts been preserved from the horrors of famine, but they have been enabled to pour large supplies of food into the adjoining districts."

My father shall be his own exponent as to what he wished exactly to do with what he had seen. "In considering how this noble river may be improved to the utmost," he wrote, "it immediately occurs that our grand object must be, not to let its waters run to waste into the sea. In high freshes an immense quantity is lost because it comes down faster than it can be applied to use; in low freshes a smaller, but still very large, quantity is lost at the very time that it is most required, because it is on too low a level for the lands to be irrigated by it. In the first case our object is to gain time, in the second to gain height.

"But, it is to the second point, namely the saving of water in low freshes, that I wish particularly to call the attention of Government, for the reasons already stated.

"The two plans usually adopted for raising the water from the bed of the river to a sufficient level to answer the purposes of irrigation are, first, by carrying a portion of the stream through a channel, having a less fall than the surface of the country till it has attained a level above that of the adjoining land ; and, second, by damming up the river.

"The first of these is preferable under certain circumstances, but it is very rarely indeed that the cost of diverting the water in a river can be secured in this way, for, generally, the cutting at the head of the channel must be so deep, and the channel must be of such great length to gain the required elevation, that it would be too expensive."

Of the scheme he recommended for approval he remarks :—

"The present cultivation of Tanjore would be entirely secured, except in extraordinarily bad years; not only would crops be saved that are now lost entirely, but by far the greater part of the whole district would be made to produce larger crops ; in extraordinarily deficient years the amount saved by the dam would be far greater than in ordinary years."

When lecturing at the School of Military Engineering at Chatham, many years after, he said the history of this work would give an idea of the state of things under the Company's government. "In '27," he observes, "I was sent to inspect it, as the people were stated to be nearly in a state of rebellion from its neglect. I found the works in utter disrepair; the Coleroon canal had six feet of silt in its bed, so that when it ought to have had eight feet of water flowing down it, it had two. Thus this work, which had a population of perhaps one hundred thousand and a revenue of £40,000 dependent upon it, had not been allowed £500 to keep it in repair. The Government could not afford it. Is it surprising the natives thought us savages? I made a small estimate of £3,500 for some immediate repairs, but knowing what its fate would be, I proceeded to Madras, and arrived just in time to hear, as I expected, that the Government could not squander such sums as this upon the wild demands of an Engineer. We had, however, a Governor at that time who was accessible, and I asked the Chief Engineer to go to him and speak to him about it. He said the papers had never been laid before him, and ordered the expenditure. In my ignorance at that time I thought the point was gained, as orders were sent to the Collector of the district, who had first called for my report on the case, and whose business it was, according to the absurd arrangement of that time, to execute the work. Soon after, I left the district, and did not return till '33, when to my astonishment I found that the Collector had not taken the trouble to spend the money, or the Government to enforce it; a small sum only had been spent, and the people were in such a state of rebellion that it had been feared troops would have to be sent into the district. Such was the inconceivable state of things under that admirable middle-class government."

The Cauveri is a large river rising in the range of mountains] known as the Western ghats, which, catching the strength of the south-west monsoon, fill all the rivers draining their slopes with very large volumes of water. It is the biggest of the rivers in the south of the Peninsula, and runs for some hundreds of miles before reaching the head of the delta, at which point it throws off its first effluent, called the Coleroon.

Here it should be remarked, what Arthur Cotton himself frequently stated, he was not dealing with a virgin river or with virgin soil. Indian rivers were turned to irrigating purposes centuries before the British obtained a footing on the continent. Indian rulers of ancient times vied with each other in the execution of works which in a great degree proved of exceeding benefit to the country.[1]

[1] "The practice of irrigation in India and in China antedates the historical epoch by an indeterminate period. The Greek Megasthenes, ambassador of Seleukos Nikator at the court of Sandrokothos, near Patna, who wrote an account of India three hundred years before Christ, says that then 'the whole country was under irrigation,' and very prosperous because of the double harvests, which by its means the people were enabled to reap each year. There are reservoirs in Ceylon and in Southern India more than two thousand years old."—*Irrigated India*, p. 141.

But even the most notable of these enterprises was marked by a paucity of idea and inadequacy of conception. In Tanjore and the adjoining district of Trichinopoly the indigenous works had proved comparatively successful. They, however, only made use of the river during the rains, when the water was least wanted. Our Engineer's conception and intention was to preserve the flood waters for the dry season. He did it. The doing of it removed the rice crops from the danger of utter destruction; rice being the staple article of food, what he did meant nothing less than rescue from starvation and misery for the whole population.

There was a singular appropriateness in the time at which the Coleroon was taken in hand. Within six months from the date of sanction of the plans, enough had been done before the monsoon burst, in what proved to be a dry season, to make the works most potent. So much water was stored, even at this early date from commencement, that much distress was prevented and the treasury instead of being depleted received additional revenue.

Arthur Cotton had great expectations as to what his anicuts would do. He thus expresses those ideas :—

"1st. An increased supply of water in Tanjore on one hundred days (counting those only on which the supply was deficient) would be ensured, the quantity varying from nothing to fifteen hundred thousand cubic yards per hour, or averaging five hundred thousand cubic yards per hour, and amounting in all to twelve hundred millions, or one-fifth of the total quantity that Tanjore received at present, which is on an average six thousand millions.

"2nd. It would entirely put an end to all disputes about the extension of the head of Seringam, etc.

"3rd. It would free the Trichinopoly ryots of Laulgoody entirely, and those of Seringam and part of Coanud in some measure, from the trouble and expense of making corumboes (temporary dams), and render the supply of water in their lands almost certain.

"4th. It would enable the people to use the early and

partial freshes to a much greater extent than at present, make the crop more rapid in its growth, and by both the harvest would be earlier, and consequently a more abundant supply would be left for the late lands.

"5th. It would greatly increase the effect of the under sluices, both by enabling us to open them oftener and also by giving a greater head of water. Hence there will be a most complete control over the level of the bed of the Cauveri, which is very important."

Again, he always considered, and reminded those who consulted him on this subject, that the value of irrigation works must be regarded as having two aspects :—

1st. *The additional revenue* brought to the Government by this method of employment of its public funds;

2nd. The consequent *increase in the value of the land itself* to the native community, and the *increase of their own incomes*; for which reason the land had a better saleable value. He added: "The price of land will greatly increase."[1]

Once more: "The increase in the value of property to individuals is at least proportionately great." He reckoned that, "the value of the dependent crop would be augmented from its actual amount of £200,000 to £258,125; and the annual revenue from £75,000 to £103,125."

With such results already assured, no wonder that Arthur Cotton's life-long efforts were put forth to prove and to emphasize the fact that, "if a hundredth part of the time, labour, and money that had been lost by droughts, or expended in trying to obviate the effects of scarcities, had been expended in providing against them, very much might have been effected."

Captain Cotton likewise explained that "it was undoubted that, in the worst year of drought that ever occurred, enough water had been allowed to flow into the sea which, if used, would have irrigated ten times as much grain as would

[1] The italics in these paragraphs are Sir Arthur Cotton's.

have supplied the whole population." He added: "The Carnatic, I acknowledge (like England and every other country), is not able to support a large population if nothing is done to provide water, when naturally it would be deficient, and to carry it off, when naturally it would be in excess; but I am fully assured that there is no reason whatever why it should not be one of the most populous and fertile countries in the world, if the energies of its Government were exerted, as they must be, to bring out the capabilities of the country." In this, he was at one with Burke, who, in a great speech on the Nawab of Arcot, spoke of the water resources of Southern India as the national bank of the country.[1]

Again, he argued most strongly that "the soil of these fertilized districts was by no means of especially good quality; its prosperous condition was owing entirely to its regulated supplies of river-water."

His next project was a similar work with regard to the

[1] "The Carnatic is not by the bounty of Nature a fertile soil. It is refreshed by few or no living brooks or running streams, and it has rain only at a season; but its product of rice exacts the use of water subject to perpetual command. This is the National Bank of the Carnatic, on which it must have a perpetual credit, or it perishes irretrievably. For that reason, in the happier times of India, a number, almost incredible, of reservoirs have been made in chosen places throughout the country. They are formed for the greater part of mounds of earth and stones, with sluices of solid masonry; the whole constructed with admirable skill and labour, and maintained at a mighty charge. In the territory contained in that map alone, I have been at the trouble of reckoning the reservoirs, and they mount to upwards of eleven hundred from the extent of two or three acres to five miles in circuit. From these reservoirs currents are occasionally drawn over the fields, and these watercourses again call for a considerable expense to keep them properly scoured and duly levelled. Taking the district in that map as a measure, there cannot be in the Carnatic and Tanjore fewer than ten thousand of these reservoirs of the larger and middling dimensions, to say nothing of those for domestic services, and the uses of religious purification. These are not the enterprises of your power, nor in a style of magnificence suited to the taste of your minister. These are the monuments of real kings, who were the fathers of their people,—testators to a posterity which they embraced as their own."—EDMUND BURKE.

Pallaur River, with its necessary provision of channels and reservoirs.

Indeed, from this time his active brain and earnest mind were ever at work, planning and scheming new enterprises, and always on a scale which was in accord with the size and volume of the rivers in question and the tracts of country which surrounded them. To these districts these huge forces of water must necessarily, in flood times, be an engine of destruction ; or, in drought, if not used—a loss, which could only cause famine, poverty, disease, and death ; on the other hand, they could be made productive of unlimited blessing and prosperity.

It was among the essential principles, always insisted upon by him, that the value of the irrigation works was not to be measured simply by the additional revenue yielded to the Government treasury, but that a much truer criterion is found in the enhancement of their income to the people and in the consequent saleable value of the land itself. Hence the importance of the observations which follow.

As to the profits of the people, he remarked, in a letter to the Board of Revenue, dated December 13, 1837, the year after the completion of the weirs, when noticing the increase of the revenue : "I believe the increase in the value of property to individuals is also at least proportionately great ; in Trichinopoly I have ascertained that the value of the lands in Seringam has actually doubled, and I am informed that the same is the case in the two South Arcot taluks. In Tanjore, also, I am assured that the price of land has greatly increased ; so, when it is considered that as much as five hundred and sixty thousand cawnies [1] of land are affected by the anicuts, the saleable price of which is, perhaps, £8,000,000, it does not seem too much to suppose that they have been the means of causing an increase of private property to the extent of no less a sum than £500,000."

To requote the remark on an earlier page of this

[1] A South-Indian term of land measurement.

chapter, "He who makes two blades of grass to grow where one grew before is a benefactor of his species," an extract from a letter from the Board of Revenue, written ten years after the construction of the anicuts, stating what was then officially known of their general results, may help to a reply :—

"Among the years succeeding 1836, some have been very bad and others equally good; but it is remarkable how uniform the rate of increase of production has continued, proving very clearly that the anicut has laid a new foundation of prosperity, so far as that may be measured by the productive power of the land. No other instrument could be employed to obtain the same results, because no other would tend in anything like the same degree to equalise the effects of favourable and unfavourable seasons, which are in themselves beyond any control."

The official figures showing the progress recorded fifteen and fourteen years respectively after commencement are :—

UPPER COLEROON ANICUT.

First cost	£8,340[1]
Subsequent repairs	£27,238
Number of years	15
Aggregate net increase of revenue	£208,291
Average annual profit	£12,702
Aggregate profit	£172,713
Annual percentage of profit on first cost	144 11/16

LOWER COLEROON ANICUT.

First cost	£74,231
Subsequent repairs	£3,997
Number of years	14
Aggregate net increase of revenue	£14,230
Average annual profit	£9,879
Aggregate profit	£130,876
Annual percentage of profit on first cost	133 1/16

[1] The late General Bell, R.E., states that the cost was greatly diminished owing to a singular circumstance. "The stone for the upper anicut was quarried near the site of the works, but no such resource being available within a long distance from the lower anicut, all the required stone (with, of course, the consent of the Brahmins) was procured from the boundary wall of an ancient temple, standing in the jungle not far off, and long since disused."

The profits were reckoned on the original outlay on the anicuts, which were the basis of the whole system of irrigation, reforming it in one year with, as has been shown, almost magical effect. All the outlay for fifteen years under the head of subsequent repairs, but including many new subsidiary works, was compared with the former outlay for the same number of years for repairs, and found to be considerably less, proving that the anicut had not only provided water for irrigation, but, with its subsidiary works, had rendered the management of the river less expensive. The saving in this respect was, therefore, added legitimately to the profit on the works. On this point an extract from a minute by the Hon. John Sullivan, Member of Council, dated Sept. 5, 1840, is explicit and valuable :—

"It is satisfactory to know that after some of the heaviest freshes that have ever been known in the Cauveri, no damage whatever has been done to the banks of either river. On the contrary, the civil engineer reports that Tanjore was never so free from breaches as it has been this year."[1]

The almost phenomenal activity of my father's mind,—to be noted again and again in this biography,—was, probably, never more strikingly manifested than at this time. To turn the flowing current of a large tropical river, with little of experience to guide one, might have been

[1] The Principal Collector of Tanjore wrote to the Board of Revenue, on August 11, 1838, as follows: "I trust the Board will be satisfied, from what has been said, that the season of fasli 1246, A.D. 1836, was beyond all comparison worse than that of fasli 1241, both as regards the freshes and the rains. But as long as there was water for it to act upon, the effects of the anicut were most satisfactory, and the inference was not only fair but obvious ; and that when, as was the case after the 25th September, the failure of the supply in the Agunda Cauveri was so great as to never afford a full river for a single day even with the assistance of the anicut ; without it the failure of the crops must have been incalculably greater than it was.

"I cannot conclude without observing that, whilst so much doubt appears to be entertained of the advantages of the anicut elsewhere, there is not an individual in the province who does not consider it the greatest blessing that has ever been conferred upon it."

supposed to be enough to occupy the mind of a young man still considerably under thirty. Not so, thought Arthur Cotton. A suggestion was made that the roadstead of Madras should be formed into an enclosed harbour, or, at least, a breakwater or breakwaters should be provided. Merchants and others interested in the sea-borne trade of the Presidency, hearing of his Paumben Passage work, and of his interest in everything which made water subservient to the purposes of man, invited his opinions. He complied with their request, and briefly urged :—

1st. That the work best calculated to counteract the surf should be unconnected with the shore;

2nd. That its shape should be a straight line parallel with the coast;

3rd. That it should be of rough stone;

4th. That it should not be within, nor much beyond, the outer line of the surf.

Colonel de Haviland, the Commandant of Engineers at Madras, approved of Captain Cotton's project and praised it highly, but the idea of such a breakwater was eventually relinquished, although at the time, so greatly did it commend itself to the gentlemen who had taken up the scheme, that at one meeting a very large sum of money was subscribed, with the intention of carrying out the plans.

On December 13, 1837, Captain Cotton addressed to the Board of Revenue an elaborate report on the duties of the Irrigation Department as a whole, but especially in relation to the numerous tanks referred to by Burke in the passage quoted on a preceding page. In this he treated, first, of the value of the works belonging to the Tank Department, not merely their capital value, as enterprises, but their annual value to the country if kept in good order; and then of the sum of money absolutely necessary year by year for this purpose. As to the then annual value, he shewed that it had greatly fallen off through want of attention. In conclusion, he remarked that, were these works all efficient, the annual value of the dependent crop would be augmented from its then value (£3,200,000) to £4,130,000, and the annual revenue from £1,180,000 to £1,650,000.

There is, in almost every district in the Madras Presidency, an immense number of tanks constructed to catch the rainfall and conserve it for irrigational purposes. Most, if not all of these, are of Indian origin. A vast proportion has been allowed to fall into disrepair, their beds being used, in parts, for the growing of crops instead of their whole area utilised for the storage of water. An example of this will at once occur to every one who knows the city of Madras,—in the magnificent (but unused) area of the Mylapur Tank, which runs by the side of the splendid road to St. Thomas's Mount, and is a boundary to the many-mansioned townlet of Nungumbaukum. These, says the Hon. A. Deakin, M.L.A. (one of the Delegates to England in 1900 in connection with the Commonwealth Bill), in his valuable work on *Irrigated India*,[1] are all sizes, according to the catchment, and serve for the watering of an immense area. Nowhere else in India is there such a multiplication of minor storages. Mr. Deakin further remarks :—"A calculation has been in circulation for some years, in which it is estimated that, if the embankments constructed with this end, within the Presidency, were added together, they would make a wall of earth six feet high, one and a half times round the globe."

Arthur Cotton's next work was the superintendence of the construction of a short railway from Madras to the Red Hills, a few miles distant, intended for the transport of road material to the city. At this spot is now situated the reservoir which supplies the city of Madras with water. Circumstances arose which prevented the com-

[1] P. 262, *Irrigated India: An Australian View of India and Ceylon, their Irrigation and Agriculture*, by the Hon. Alfred Deakin, M.L.A., formerly Chief Secretary and Minister of Water Supply of Victoria. London: W. Thacker & Co., 1893.

pletion of the line, but it afforded practical experience, which was of considerable use to him in the execution of the Godavari works years after, where railway lines played an important part in facilitating the prompt construction of the great dams.

In a report, which he prepared about this time, he discussed the question of railways relatively to improved common roads, and makes mention of the short line between Madras and the Red Hills in illustration of his views. He had evidently no full conception then of the noble scheme of waterways for irrigation and transport, which, a few years afterwards, he brought before the Government and the public, and of which he never ceased to be a zealous advocate. In the light of the knowledge he then possessed, he set himself to prove the advantage of railways over the best roads, as he afterwards proved the superiority of steamboat canals to railways. There was thus no inconsistency in his ideas and writings. The one problem always before him was the cheapest and most serviceable transport for India, and to his subsequent solution of the same he, for more than forty years, adhered with inviolable fidelity.

Major-General Fred C. Cotton, the sole surviving brother of my father, has favoured me with some notes on the subjects last-mentioned.

"The Red Hills railway," he says, "was the first railway made in India, and the idea, that my brother was opposed to a railway system being begun in India, was incorrect. Later he came to feel that, when once large capital was expended on railways, there would be no chance of the country having the cheaper water carriage, which was, and ever would be, less costly for the transport of its products over the great distance they would require to be moved In this he was quite right, and no one can doubt the value to India of a means of transport that would enable the producer, for instance, to undersell his competitors in the markets of other countries. Sir Arthur's expectations as to the fitness of canal-carriage seem never to have been rightly understood in England, perhaps because the canal system in this country is on so small a scale. The canals and river navigation of India, as he would have had it, would have admitted of steam being used as the locomotive power in impelling vessels of great tonnage, which the size of the rivers and the cheapness of land for canalization promised in every way. And, as has been found, the very limited amount of tonnage even a costly railway can deal with, makes them quite insufficient in power for the object he had in view and the real requirements of the country. I only write this note, because it appears to me that some explanation is advisable of Sir Arthur's opposition to the costly railway system being adopted, to the exclusion of the infinitely more economical and more suitable carriage by water.

"And I would add to these that, when it was determined,—contrary to the advice of the late Lord Derby (at that time Lord Stanley), somewhile Secretary of State for India,—to establish railways on the British system in India, every requisite for the purpose was immediately supplied: unlimited capital, qualified engineers in any number; rails, coaches, wagons, and locomotives needed only to be asked for to be forthwith supplied; the land, instead of being obtained through the expensive process of a Parliamentary committee, was provided directly by a decree of the Government; and, lastly, the necessary surveys were conducted with scarcely any difficulty through vast tracts of mostly level country. The broad rivers were entirely novel features; but these had, in many instances, been bridged by the Indian engineers, whose methods of construction were patterns of value to all future builders.

"On the other hand, a system of canal navigation would have required long and patient investigation and elaborate surveys by engineers accustomed to the construction and management of hydraulic works, and of such engineers very few then existed. It was no wonder, then, that, if such a system were thought of at all, it was rejected in favour of one perfectly easy of conception and execution, and needing only a guarantee to establish it all over the country."

CHAPTER V

Preparing for the Great Work—The Redemption of the Godavari District

THE bursting at Hobart Town of the boiler attached to the rotatory engine invented by Captain Cotton, with the resulting injury to himself, left alike its mark and influence upon him. When he reached Madras, he found himself in so unsatisfactory a state of health as to shrink from the heavy toil of an Engineer in charge of a Division. To him this was a serious disappointment. The long leave in Australia had afforded time for a consolidation of personal character and a great growth of mental force and professional zeal and acumen. India had taken hold of him. Not the India of Romance, but the India in Need. Consequently, it was with sorrow he felt himself unable to undertake what he wished to do. Arthur Cotton could afford to accept events with equanimity: he knew he was in God's hands, and was satisfied that, in His good time, the way would be made clear.

Weakened health necessitated light work, and light work was ready for him. It was, therefore, of signal benefit to himself, as well as to that part of the Madras Presidency in which his next service was to be performed, that he was appointed to superintend the building of a church at Vizagapatam, and also the construction of groynes on the beach at that place. Vizag, as it is familiarly called, was one of the most pleasant and salubrious stations in the northern districts.

Here he had a veritable rest, which well prepared him

for the engineering labours, which were to surpass all that he had, as yet, performed.

On their way from Madras to Vizagapatam the party had a direful experience. A cyclone burst in the Bay of Bengal, having (as is the wont of these circular storms) worked its way from that birthplace of the winds, in the neighbourhood of the Andaman Islands, whence have come so many destructive storms to devastate the Bay and to work havoc on the shores of Northern Madras and Orissa. Of this voyage my mother writes:—

"We left Madras for Vizagapatam, the sky all overclouded with the tokens of a hurricane coming on, and, before we had been on board many hours, the hurricane burst in all its fury. It was a remarkable voyage on account of the captain's wonderful presence of mind during the whole time the storm was raging. He behaved in a most Christian manner; no angry word was heard throughout the storm, nothing but his voice shouting, through a speaking trumpet, his orders to the officers; everything else was as quiet as possible.

"When the hurricane ceased we found that a ship, which had sailed from Madras at the same time as we had, had disappeared; the next morning the sea was strewn with wreckage, and a dismasted vessel was a striking object close by. The captain assembled all the crew and passengers, and thanked God for their deliverance. But the strain had been too great; his mind gave way immediately afterwards, and it was some time before he brought us into Vizagapatam."

Nowadays the warning cone on Madras beach would have told of the coming peril, and the beginning of the voyage would no doubt have been delayed. Few who have not witnessed a "Bay cyclone" can conceive the widespread destruction often caused. In 1872 one such storm burst upon the (then) unprotected roadstead of Madras.[1] The violence of the wind increased

[1] This storm was marked by the loss of the *Hotspur* (1,045 tons), the *Arbeg* (925), the *Armenian* (901), the *Invershine* (717), the *Misser*

as night came on, and blew with terrific fury throughout the hours of darkness, causing much devastation. When day broke such a scene of wreckage was revealed, as had never before been known. Several vessels—some English, some Indian coasting ships—were strewn along three miles of coast, while the iron pier, stretching a long distance through the surf to deep water, had been cut in two by an Indian ship, which had been driven clean through the structure and wrecked on the opposite side. A "Bay cyclone" exhibits Nature in one of her most fearsome moods.

The party arrived safely at Vizagapatam, and were not long in finding a rough dwelling on the top of an isolated hill called the Dolphin's Nose. Some disused artillery barracks were found of use.

Two years were spent in the pleasingly diversified duties of building a church at Waltair and protecting the beach with groynes and other consolidating works. My father describes his early work there as the construction of a series of groynes at certain distances. These were built of large stone blocks, unhewn, and piled above the highest water-mark for some fifty yards out to sea.

Often, in later years, when he was visiting English harbours, he would talk over this simple, and yet most efficient, method of resisting the force of the waves, and even proving an effective barrier against a heavy surf, such as that which ever breaks upon the Indian coast. He has told us how, in those early days, he was ridiculed by older men, who were more learned Engineers. To suppose for a moment that piles of rough, loose stones thrown together could possibly resist the encroachments of such a sea! It was ridiculous. However, his groynes proved a grand success; they did their work, which was all that was wanted of them. Nay, they did more than was ex-

(700), the *Burlington* (676), the *John Scott* (655), the *Kingdom of Belgium* (592), and seventeen native craft. Thirteen Europeans and six Indians were drowned. A breach was made in the pier, and traffic was not restored for fifteen months.—C. A. L.

pected, for they made a splendid beach and added to the available soil by the silting of the sand above them. "A first-rate beach," he would say, with one of his earnest, impressive, gestures, when talking it over in later years.

My mother says of the experiences of that time :—

"The view from the Dolphin's Nose was very fine. The hill rose abruptly from the sea, and the great depth, looked down upon from the top, was sometimes awe-inspiring. Hawks and other large birds of prey above wheeled ceaselessly in circles, uttering their wild, weird cry. One house only beside the barrack was on the hill. The Chaplain of Vizagapatam had built it, and lived there—an agreeable companion and friend, who often spent the evenings in our society, frequently in studying prophecy together."

As bearing in some degree on what Sir Henry Sumner Maine, distinguished among the eminent jurists who have served India as Legal Members of the Governor-General's Council, has discussed in his address, "The Influence of India upon English Thought," this may not be an inconvenient place in which to make a remark on the effect of the solitary, or semi-solitary, existence in which so many Anglo-Indian officials perforce spend most of their time, upon those who pass through this experience. India has produced a special kind of British Christian. The Lawrences, the Edwardeses, whose biographies have delighted and profited many thousands of God-fearing folk, are representative of a very large proportion of Anglo-Indian residents. A convinced British Christian in India and Ceylon becomes a man (or woman) of intense conviction, of close study of the Bible, of more than average earnestness of life. Arthur Cotton was one of the most conspicuous of these unostentatious but deeply faithful and conscientious followers of the Saviour. To the very religious mind and mood of the Hindu, the character of such an one appeals with great force. General Rundall, R.E., an old colleague of my father, brings this out with great force when he remarks :—

"His [Sir Arthur Cotton's] character, as known to a

large circle of friends, was that of a truly humble and consistent Christian, with deep and earnest religious convictions, which dominated his whole life, and which led him always to commit all his undertakings to God, in whom he believed and trusted. Utterly unselfish, and brimful of kindness to others, especially to the many young men who had the privilege of serving under him, ever considerate to the natives of India, who almost worshipped him for his self-denying labour in their behalf, and amongst whom he was known as 'The Sanyassee,' or devotee, he gained an influence over those brought in contact with him, which, with many, remained throughout their after life."

One stormy afternoon, when my father was returning from the beachworks—the wind was so boisterous he could hardly keep his feet—he saw a small native vessel being driven in against the rocks. The men on board were evidently helpless, and already a troop of wreckers had collected, and were watching for their prey. He hurried to the spot, and rushed on board the boat, with his stick driving back the greedy crowd, and defending the master and sailors. The vessel was loaded with cocoanuts, and many of these were stolen, but he managed to stand his ground till his sergeant came up, and the two men cleared the deck and delivered the overpowered crew from their foes. They also saved the little hoard of money, about two hundred rupees, which the wreckers would soon have found. He provided a shelter for them that night, and the next morning they all came up to the house, prostrated themselves and poured out evident thanks in a language which none of us understood.

Of Vizagapatam my father, in later years, at a time when he was planning a large project, nothing less than the making of that port one of the principal entrances to India, wrote thus:—

1st. Vizagapatam is the only place on the eastern coast of India, where there is no severe heat.

2nd. It has the best climate in India.

3rd. It is the natural point of outlet for all Northern India, by a direct railway to Allahabad, making it the cheapest and safest line from England to the North of India.

4th. It has *the* point of the eastern coast where, incomparably, the best harbour can be made by a single breakwater run out from the bold promontory of the Dolphin's Nose, south of the town.

5th. The adjoining territory provides an exceptional site for a first-class city.

6th. The whole tract from Vizagapatam to Ruripoor, three hundred miles, is the most fertile part of India. It rises to two thousand feet, and is suited to every kind of European enterprise—the planting of coffee, sugar, culture of the vine and fruit trees generally.

7th. There is hill country with a temperate climate, south of Ruripoor, and also the Central Provinces of India, rising to three thousand feet—a beautiful country, with a temperature down to frost in winter.

8th Water communication can be completed with the Punjab, by the valley of the Ganges and the coast, to Vizagapatam; the same to the great navigations of the delta of the Godavari and Kistna; also to Madras; by the Godavari to Berar, uniting the Punjab, the Upper Brahmaputra, Nagpore, and Madras in a first-class navigation of at least ten thousand miles, providing all North and East India with transit at one-tenth the cost of railways. Three or four thousand miles of these canals are already in operation.

9th. The line between Ruripoor and Allahabad passes through a field containing the best coal in India.

10th. Inland of the town site is an extensive piece of

> alluvial land, level with the sea, which can be cheaply made into an immense inner harbour.
>
> The outer harbour can be formed by blocks of granite of any size, from the Dolphin's Nose, costing nothing but the powder, loading, carriage by boats a few hundred yards, and discharging.

This was a noble scheme. What would have been the result had my father been given a free hand and been backed up at headquarters, especially in the India Office! Arthur Cotton, had he had his own way, would have more than half-regenerated India.

It was while engaged in this reclamatory work at Vizagapatam that he first became acquainted with the great Godavari river, which afterwards was to be the scene ot his most toilsome labours, his keenest anxieties, and his grandest success.

GORGE OF THE GODAVARI, LOOKING UP STREAM.

p. 77.

CHAPTER VI

The District of Godavari: Before and After Arthur Cotton worked his Magical Change

Before

WHEN Arthur Cotton was sent north to build a church and conserve a shore the Rajahmundry district was in distressful condition. He afterwards made wise use of the river, which ran through it, and, in recognition of what he had done, the district was no longer named after the town of Rajahmundry, but became a river-named region—the Godavari district. This district, whatever its name, contains some of the most beautiful scenery in India. Mr. Henry Morris, of the Madras Civil Service, at one time chief official in the district, writes:—[1]

"The gorge through which the Godavari enters the plains forms one of the most beautiful pieces of scenery in Southern India. . . .

"I have seen the gorge at both seasons; I have looked down on the river from the mountains which overhang it; and I have passed through the winding stream as the early morning sun gradually lighted up hill after hill, leaving the water in shade, and as the setting sun gradually left the valley in gloom; and I can confidently assert that I have never witnessed more exquisite scenery even on the Neilgherries or the Shevaroys. As the steamer glides into the gorge, the low, broken hills, which had previously adorned

[1] *A Descriptive and Historical Account of the Godavari District in the Presidency of Madras*, p. 4. London: Trubner & Co., 1878.

the bank of the river, disappear, and the mountains close up to the water's edge, in one place the two sides approaching each other as near as two hundred yards, and the precipitous banks appearing near enough even to be touched. They then open out, and again approach each other, forming successively beautiful little lakes, resembling Highland lochs, from which there is apparently no outlet. Sir Charles Trevelyan compares the scenery to that of the Rhine between Coblentz and Bingen, but it lacks the signs of human life which adorn, and the historical antiquities which beautify, the European stream."

Mr. Walch, in his most interesting book on *Engineering Works on the Godavari Delta* (p. 1), says :—

"The Godavari takes rank amongst the great rivers of India after the Ganges and the Indus. Rising some seventy miles north-east of Bombay, and only fifty miles from the Arabian Sea, it runs in a generally south-eastern direction across the peninsula, till, after a course of nearly ninety-nine miles, it falls into the Bay of Bengal about two hundred and fifty miles north of Madras. It receives the drainage from one hundred and fifteen thousand square miles, an area greater than that of England and Scotland combined, and its maximum discharge is calculated to be one and a half millions of cubic feet per second, more than two hundred times that of the Thames at Staines, and about three times that of the Nile at Cairo.

"Shortly after, the Godavari begins to wind amongst the spurs of the Eastern Ghats, which gradually close in on it, till it has to force its way through a gorge, which for two miles is so narrow that along the greater part of the distance a stone may be thrown from either bank to the middle of the stream. The hills here rise to a height of between two thousand and three thousand feet with steep, though not precipitous, sides, and are clothed from water's edge to summit with luxuriant tropical vegetation.

"Through this beautiful gorge, the river in its low stages glides with but little disturbance, and is easily navigated even by small boats, but during the floods it foams past its obstructions with a velocity and turbulence, which no craft that ever floated, could stem. So great is the action of the stream at such times, that the rocky bed has been scoured out to depths, popularly supposed to be unfathomable, but which, as the writer has himself ascertained, do really vary from one hundred to nearly two hundred feet. High floods rise quite fifty feet at the place, so that in the defile there is then a torrent from one hundred and fifty to two hundred and fifty feet in depth. For twenty miles beyond the gorge, the river winds in a succession of lake-like reaches amongst the eastern spurs of the hills, till near the village of Palaveram it emerges into the plains of the Eastern or Coromandel Coast. Small outlying hills, however, occur along its left bank for some twenty-five miles further; the last of these, which lies close to the river, is at Dowlaisweram, where the Godavery has attained a width of nearly four miles. It then divides into two branches and its delta begins.

"In its moderate freshes, the river brings down but little drift; when, however, it swells into a really high flood, its broad surface is plentifully strewn with floating *debris* of all kinds; giants of the forest, which have toppled into the water, whose roots and branches rise and fall with weird effect as they are rolled over and over in the stream; bamboos interlaced in wild confusion; jungle grasses and river rushes in tangled masses like floating islands, which the flood has deeply submerged or entirely washed away."

Of all the rivers in India, even the Ganges is hardly more sacred to the devout Hindu than is the Godavari. It is believed to flow from the same source as the Ganges, but underground, and it is frequently called by the same name. The eastern branch, after its division into several streams at Dowlaisweram, is called the Gautami, and, if possible, is looked on as more holy than the rest of the river. Once every twelve years a feast called Pushkaram is held on the banks of the river in turn with eleven other sacred streams of India, and pilgrims come from all parts of the land to bathe in its waters. At its source near Trimbak, in every part of its downward course, especially at the pagoda a little north of Rajahmundry, and at Kotaphali on the left bank of the eastern stream, it is considered to be peculiarly sacred at these times, and every sin is washed away in those who bathe in it. Crowds gather on the river bank morning, noon, and night, and convert the most favoured resort into huge standing camps for the twelve days during which the festival lasts."

But, while Nature was thus so lavish of her beauties and the stream was so sacred, there was much suffering in the land.

Factories for the manufacture of a special kind of cotton cloth, much in favour with the people, were, at a very early period, established by the East India Company. These, however, were discontinued as the Arkwright and other spinning and weaving inventions made use of by British manufacturers greatly cheapened the production of such fabrics and made the Indian cloth unprofitable. No other industry took their place, and there was much suffering among the people. Deterioration set in. There was nothing but the soil for the erstwhile spinners and weavers to turn to. Irregularities of rainfall—not uncustomary, but specially felt and noted because of the prevailing industrial distress—occurred, and, in 1833, famine followed. It is still referred to as The Great Famine.

"I have frequently asked a man his age," says Mr. Morris, "and he has been unable to state it. But he was quite ready to answer the question, 'How old were you at the time of the Great Famine?'"[1]

It was the old, too-familiar, story—not, necessarily, no rain, maybe too much of it falling at the wrong time, but —the life-sustaining water was not preserved against the day of need. In 1831 there was too much rain, in 1832 a cyclone caused serious damage to crops, in 1833 the supply was deficient.

The distress was terrible all over those northern districts. In the adjoining district of Guntoor, two out of five of all

[1] Morris's *Godavari*, p. 288.

DOWLAISWERAM ANICUT, FROM NEAR THE UNDER SLUICES.

p. 85.

the people died. Guntoor had five hundred thousand inhabitants when the famine began: there were but three hundred thousand when it had passed away. In Godavari itself one out of four perished.

"The crushing misery which gradually came upon the people and slowly destroyed them was appalling.

"As it increased from day to day, thousands emigrated to Madras and to other more fortunate districts.

"A stream of pilgrims flowed night and day towards the south.

"Madras being the seat of government, thousands repaired thither with the remnants of their household possessions, and with the children and dependents who had not died upon the road.

"In many cases the famishing parents sold their little perishing daughters to men, who carried them off to Hyderabad.

"The great northern road became one long graveyard.

"It was often most difficult to distinguish between the dying and the dead.

"It was directed that no one should be relieved at the public expense without undergoing the ordeal of working for this relief.

"Many of the better castes considered this worse than death, and refused to undergo the indignity of digging tanks, the work which was usually selected.

"Others accepted with shame the relief which was accompanied by such terms; and tenderly-nurtured women and high-born men were seen working at this manual labour under the direction of native overseers, while some decided to starve rather than submit to such degradation.

"The pressure of hunger made men lose all regard for others and thought for the rights of property.

"It became impossible to transport grain without the protection of armed escorts.

"When they heard of the approach of grain merchants with a convoy of food, the villagers would turn out *en masse* and strive to obtain possession of the grain by force.

"The usual routine of village life was most melancholy.

"During the day men could be seen prowling about the streets picking up anything edible, even from the most defiled sources, and at night women would go to the village well, and watch the water drop slowly into their brazen vessels, every drop being carefully prized and cherished."

"'Deeds of violence,' writes one who was evidently an eye-witness of these sad scenes, 'could not be altogether suppressed; and yet on the whole it was marvellous with what patience and submission this long period of calamity was endured—such pining want, such personal anguish, cattle dying from thirst in the fields, the little heirlooms of jewels and silver and gold ornaments parted with, the wail of famishing children, and yet no jacquerie, no fanatical outbursts against their rulers, in whose truth they still trusted.'"[1]

The two following seasons were fairly favourable but the region seemed cursed, for, in 1839, another cyclone burst. "which was more destructive than any that had occurred for nearly sixty years." The cyclone was accompanied by a tidal wave, which broke upon the shore, and caused an inundation at Cocanada and Coringa. "Ships were driven on land, some of the wrecked vessels were carried, it is said, four miles inland. The loss of life was very great. Very many of the native houses at Samulcotta were blown down; all the European houses except two were unroofed, and even in Rajahmundry some of the houses were nearly dismantled by the violence of the storm. The destruction of property was very great. The merchants' storehouses at Coringa and Ingaram were ruined, cattle and crops were destroyed, large tracts of land were rendered unfit for cultivation by the overflow of salt water, the tanks were filled and spoiled by the same cause, and the wells were filled with brackish and undrinkable water for some miles around."[2]

[1] From a letter to *The Times*, by E.L.K., in January, 1874, quoted in Morris's *Godavari*, pp. 289, 290.

[2] *Letters from Madras by a Lady*, p. 144. London: Murray.

Then defective rainfall and unfavourable seasons followed one another until terrible impoverishment resulted. But these things, rightly regarded, were no "curse." With all the variations of the seasons the means were there to ensure great prosperity. It seemed, of the officials, that "their eyes were holden so that they could not see."

In Madras an uneasy feeling had been aroused in the minds of the Governor and his Council, and Sir Henry Montgomery, Bart.,[1] then of the Madras Civil Service, was deputed "to make minute enquiries on the spot into the causes of the decline of the revenue and into the general condition of the people." A curious incident occurred. The Collector of the day, not unnaturally, in the uncriticised and unchecked manner in which Indian district administration was then carried on, imagined his work was to be called in question, and deeply resented Sir Henry's visit. He "did all that lay in his power to place obstacles in the way of the Commissioner obtaining information and prosecuting his inquiries."[2] The Collector was, of course, removed from the district and the Enquirer became Administrator as well.

What did Sir Henry Montgomery find? He found this distressing series of facts:—

1. The population at the end of twenty-one years, from 1821, was one-fourth less:—

1821–23	738,308
1842–43	561,041
Decrease	177,267

But, under normal circumstances, there should have been an increase of one per cent. per annum. So regarded, the loss was, really, not 177,267 but 332,310. How the population increased when Arthur Cotton had done his work will appear.

[1] Afterwards Member of the Council of the Secretary of State or India.

[2] Morris's *Godavari*, p. 291.

2. Neglect of works of irrigation.

3. Inefficiency and corruption of the village revenue authorities.

4. Extravagance by the zemindars and their mismanagement of their estates.

This was the Godavari to which Arthur Cotton devoted his thought and some of the most fruitful years of his life in India.

After

"*Taking all things into consideration, it may be questioned if there is a more beneficent or more profitable public work in the world.*" This is the deliberately-expressed verdict of the Hon. Alfred Deakin, M.L.A., of Victoria, Australia, after a most exhaustive enquiry in India into irrigation and its results.

1.—Population.

Naturally, with prosperity everywhere in the district, the population largely increased, more and more land was taken up, until, according to the latest reports, the people number over two millions.[1]

When the work was begun there were	In 1891, the Census recorded
561,041 inhabitants.	2,078,782 inhabitants.

Increase : 1,517,741, or, nearly 300 per cent.

With growth of population there has been growth of wealth, as, in every well-governed country, there always is. So far as the irrigated districts of India are concerned there is no such thing as over-population.

2.—Increase of Revenue.

From all sources in 1843–44.	Land Revenue only in 1898.
Rs. 17,25,841.	Rs. 60,19,224.
Increase .	Rs. 42,93,383.

Nearly two and a half times greater. Two hundred and

[1] *Statistical Abstract of British India*, No. 33, p. 14.

fifty per cent. increase. The revenue from all sources is reckoned in the earlier period figures, while only land revenue is reckoned in the above comparison. Take in all the figures for 1894–95 (the latest available to me), and the increase is Rs. 70,95,481,[1] a fourfold increase.

In the former period terrible suffering and widespread poverty; now, and for more than fifty years, general prosperity, a contented people. The district, as a whole, from a revenual point of view, has leaped from the thirteenth place among the twenty-two districts of the Madras Presidency to the second place. The first place, nevertheless, is Arthur Cotton's: it is the Tanjore district. His districts are, respectively, first and second, unchallenged, unchallengeable.

3.—Imports and Exports.

The year before the Anicut was commenced may, in this respect, be contrasted with the return for 1893–94, the latest available to me:—

1845–46.		1893–94.	
Imports.	Exports.	Imports.	Exports.
Rs. 3,88,749.	Rs. 9,07,774.	Rs. 37,06,953.	Rs. 1,54,59,084.

Combined Totals.

1893–94	Rs. 1,91,66,037
1845–46	12,96,523
Increase	Rs. 1,78,69,514

An increase of nearly fourteen hundred per cent.

4.—Additional Prosperity.

The statistics available whereby to estimate with reasonable care the additional wealth accruing to the district from its irrigational advantages relate only to the produce of the land. Even thus narrowly regarded, what is the result? The authorities reckon that the land revenue throughout India bears the proportion of one-twelfth [2] of

[1] Walch's *Godavari*, vol. i. p. 154.

[2] *Report of the Indian Famine Commissioners*, 1880, Part II., p. 112. This proportion is contested by Mr. Romesh Chunder Dutt, C.I.E.,

the gross value of the produce. On this assumption the land demand of the Godavari district being Rs. 6,019,224 p.a., this amount multiplied by twelve would represent total produce value of Rs. 72,230,688. Deduct from that sum one-twelfth to represent the land tax, there is left, in round figures, Rs. 66,000,000, say Rs. 60,000,000. In the same manner the dry crops (denied all irrigational facilities and subject to all fluctuations of the seasons) could not annually have been of more than Rs. 10,000,000 in value. There has, therefore, accrued as additional value ensured, with reasonable certainty, to the people, Rs. 50,000,000, or Rs. 25 per head per annum. No allowance is here made for receipts beyond those from the land, and Rs. 25 might, therefore, well be taken as representing the absolute additional benefit enjoyed by the people. But, for the purpose in view, under-statement rather than a full statement may be wisest. Consequently, I take Rs. 10 from the average amount and thus arrive at Rs. 15—a gold mohur, a coin employed in Indian currency for the past three centuries, though not now often seen in circulation. That is to say, during every year, on the average, each man, woman, and child in the Godavari district receives a gold mohur which would not have been theirs, but for Sir Arthur's work for the region in which they reside. This is one instance of admirable results following from British rule, and should make every one concerned in the government of India—that is, every British citizen—determine that other districts shall, so far as may be, share in the benefits which the Godavari district enjoys. Such great good could not occur in every instance, but everywhere some gain would be recorded.

5.—The Improved Condition of the People.

"The inhabitants of the district in general, and especially the agricultural classes, are most prosperous.

and other authorities, but, as I am dealing with official figures throughout, I must perforce take this official calculation. A deduction has, however, been made, as will be seen later on in this section.

"The condition of the ryots has decidedly improved since the great extension of irrigation consequent on the construction of the anicut and the canals dependent upon it.

"The prosperity of the ryots is evident to the most casual observer.

"The gradual substitution of tiled houses for thatched,

"the better dress which is being worn by the ryots,

"the more universal adoption of rice as an article of diet rather than Indian corn and other dry grains formerly in almost universal use,

"are all silent but certain indications of the improvement of the agricultural and even of the labouring classes."[1]

6.—General Benefit as noticed by a Stranger.

Mr. Deakin, whose exhaustive work on Indian Irrigation is frequently referred to by me in these pages, says of the anicut:—

"Before it was constructed there were but nineteen thousand acres imperfectly and irregularly watered from the river, and altogether sixty-nine thousand acres wetted from all sources; while now three hundred and sixty-four thousand acres have been added. There are three hundred and seventy miles of main canal, of which three hundred and thirty-nine are navigable, and eight hundred and forty-eight miles of distributaries. The accumulated surplus is over one million pounds, and the gross return sixteen per cent. on capital. The net revenue for 1888–89, after deducting interest and all charges, is £82,269, and the net profit 8·66 per cent. upon the investment. Need there be any further demonstration of the profitableness of irrigation in Madras?"

Again, Mr. Deakin remarks:—

"The maintenance occupies no less than two hundred and sixteen boats, including four steamers and eight steam dredges, the value of the floating part being £55,000, and

[1] Morris's *Godavari*, p. 87.

its annual cost £2,258. The reports every year note the construction of new works, whether as improvements, additions, or alterations. Very little Indian experience is required to show that a great irrigation scheme is essentially a living as well as reproductive work. It is never created at a blow, but invariably develops, and implies constant care, control, and amendment, as well as constant expenditure. Nevertheless it may not only pay such expenses, but leave a superb profit as well."[1]

7.—Succour to Distressed Regions.

"The grand system of canals in the Godavari district is approaching completion, but that of the Kistna is still backward. As the two deltas are, however, linked together by an admirable chain of navigable canals, not only are they thoroughly protected from a recurrence of such a famine as that by which they were decimated[2] in 1833, but they are able to contribute out of their abundance to the rest of India."[3]

[1] *Irrigated India*, pp. 255, 256.

[2] So far as Godavari is concerned this is an inadequate statement. The population was more than doubly "decimated" on that occasion—twenty-five per cent. of the population perishing.

[3] *Review of the Progress of Irrigation Schemes in relation to Famine Aspects.* By Col. (now General) F. H. Rundall, R.E., Inspector-General of Irrigation Works.

Appendix

THE TESTIMONY OF A NATIVE INDIAN OFFICIAL.[1]

CHANGES IN GODÁVARI DISTRICT SINCE THE CONSTRUCTION OF ANICUT.—*Noted by S. Nathamunni Mudaliar, Esq., Pensioned Tahsildar, Godávari.*

The construction of the anicut across the Godávari is a great boon to this part of the country. . . . In years of drought, famine was the inevitable lot of the people, and both men and cattle suffered. Since its construction, the district is intersected with canals, useful not only for purposes of agriculture, but also for navigation. There are two main canals in the Western delta —the Ellore and Narsápur canals. In the Central delta, there is one—the Amalapore canal. In the Eastern there are five—the Samalcottah, Cocanada, Coringa, Mandapeta and Bank canals. There is also a Bank canal in each of the other deltas. All these are navigable, and from these proceed a number of irrigation channels, and paddy transplantation has immensely increased. Sugar plantation, which was rare in this district, is now to be seen almost everywhere. The extent of cultivation is 794,829 acres as given in the jamabandi (revenue) report for 1887-88.

2. . . . The introduction of coasting steamers in addition to navigable canals afforded easy passage for transhipment of goods. The wealthier classes were much benefited and the condition of the ryots was so much improved by the general high prices that, instead of being in the hands of the sowcars, they were sowcars themselves. Even now, the majority of them are not in their hands. They have enough to pay for Government

[1] "Progress in the Madras Presidency during the past Forty Years," by S. Srinavasa Raghava Iyengar, C.I.E., now Dewan to H.H. the Maharaj-Gaikwa of Baroda, G.C.S.I., pp. ccxi., ccxii.

dues. The rich ryots lend money largely on inam [1] lands, taking them on long leases. The inamdars in general, being poor Brahmins, are not capable of cultivating the lands themselves, while the ryots have means enough of cattle, ploughs, and labourers. The famine of 1876 and 1877 brought in a considerable number of poor people from the neighbouring districts of Vizagapatam and Ganjam, who found employment here in various ways. They engaged themselves as field labourers, coolies, palanquin bearers and domestic servants. This rendered labour cheap. Most of them have remained here permanently, and some are so far improved in their condition as to become farmers themselves.

3. The vast increase in agriculture by irrigation has very materially improved the condition of ryots. They have learnt to build substantial and fashionable houses, and upstair buildings unlike their former thatched and slovenly ones. There has been considerable improvement in the manufacture of jaggery. Iron mills for extracting juice from sugar-cane are in general use now in the place of wooden ones, which are not so effective in getting out all the juice. There have not been any improvements in the implements of tilling. The ploughs of old are still in use, which do not furrow the land deep. Some years back, the Swedish plough was brought into this district and several experiments were made, but this was found too heavy for the ordinary bullocks here and the attempt to introduce it failed. Even the richer ryots found no use for it, for the land here requires no great tilling; it is flooded with canal water for some time before tilling and the land is easily turned up and transplanted. A second crop is also raised, but it is of inferior quality. It is only of three months' growth from February to April, and is chiefly used by the labouring classes. The land has become very valuable. An acre of lands sells from £10 to £30.

4. Prior to the anicut, the joint-rent system was in use. Each village was rented out jointly to the ryots of the village, and the leading men and men of substance were held responsible for the payment of Government dues. On account of paucity of product owing to failure of rain, the amarakam, as the leasing out was called, was a matter of very great difficulty. Nobody used to

[1] "Inam": a gift, especially a grant of land.

come forward to take up the village or a portion of it, and the tahsildars used to force it on some men of substance. It was really a painful sight. Now, the land has acquired so much value by irrigation that almost every inch of land is taken up and the Government dues easily paid. There is great competition among ryots to secure a right to the land. They come forward with darkhasts,[1] even at the end of the fasli, offering to pay assessment for the whole year, though they could derive no benefit in that year. The renting system has entirely disappeared except in the hill tracts, and the ryotwari has taken its place. By this system, each ryot deals directly with the Government and reaps all the benefit of his labour. He commands more respect now, enjoys more comforts, wears better clothes, and lives in a more comfortable way.

5. The Local Funds Acts have greatly added to the convenience of the people everywhere. Roads have multiplied; the indigenous schools considerably improved and their number increased; sanitation attended to; tanks and wells dug even in remote places. The number of village schools has so considerably increased that there are now four deputy-inspectors (sub-assistants) and one assistant-inspector for the whole district, in the place of one deputy-inspector some seven or eight years ago. There is besides an inspecting schoolmaster for each taluk. The sub-assistant inspectors are stationed, one at Narsápur, another at Ellore, a third at Rajamundry, and a fourth at Cocanada. The district is considerably in advance in this respect also.

6. The improvements in all directions, which have been the source of happiness to the people, have also been the source of great litigation. Much of the people's money goes to swell the revenue of civil courts and to fill the pleader's purse. People are more reckless in their proceedings and squander away their money, caring only to win their cause, good or bad. The country is in every way in a prosperous condition and it is quite unlike what it was prior to the construction of the anicut. Sir Arthur Cotton, to whose genius this gigantic work owes its existence, seems to have estimated the land revenue of the district at £220,000, and expected to realize £500,000 or £600,000 when the whole project was complete. Now, from the report for 1887-88, the land revenue appears to be £380,000 and odd. Other cesses,

[1] "Darkhast": an application to take up land for cultivation.

peishcush[1] from zemindari estates, quit-rent on inam and inam villages, come up to £140,000 and odd. Salt, abkári, opium, ferry fund and income-tax amount to upwards of £60,000. The grand total of the revenue of the district from all sources reaches nearly that amount which the great benefactor, Sir Arthur Cotton, roughly estimated some forty years ago.

[1] "Peishcush": the quit-rent taken for lands which for any reason are exempt from full assessment.

CHAPTER VII

PART I

The most "Beneficent and Profitable Irrigation"[1] Work in the World: its Inception, its Construction, its Success

"The Godavari anicut is, perhaps, the noblest feat of engineering skill which has yet been accomplished in British India. It is a gigantic barrier thrown across the river from island to island, in order to arrest the unprofitable progress of its waters to the sea, and to spread them over the surface of the country on either side, thus irrigating copiously land which has hitherto been dependent on tanks or on the fitful supply of water from the river. Large tracts of land, which had hitherto been left arid and desolate and waste, were thus reached and fertilized by innumerable streams and channels."—*Morris's Godavari*, p. 109.

THE Godavari district and its inhabitants had good reason, more than sixty years ago, for congratulation in the gentleman selected as Commissioner to inquire into the causes of the most serious retrogression. Sir Henry Montgomery, the Commissioner selected, had been Collector of Tanjore. He had seen the blessings bestowed on that district by the intelligent use of the river Cauveri, and the astonishing improvement which had followed the building of the Coleroon anicuts in 1835. He, therefore, when dealing with the remedial measures required for the "Rajahmundry" district, as the region was then called, strongly urged the thorough examination of the Godavari

[1] *Irrigated India*, by the Hon. A. Deakin, p. 255.

delta by an experienced engineer with a view to the development of its irrigation resources.

In the meantime my father had not himself been idle. Church erection and groyne-building were all very well in themselves, but they could not engross all his time. He, too, had had his thoughts directed to the distressful condition of the once prosperous district a little to the south of the scene of his labours.

As early as May, 1844, he addressed to the Board of Revenue a report on the Irrigation of the Delta of the Godavari, in connection with Sugar Cultivation in the Northern Circars.[1] He alludes to the loss of the export trade in cotton cloths, and the consequent impoverishment of a large part of the population; he then suggests the cultivation of sugar for export, believing this would be a promising substitute.

"An export trade," he wrote, "to other and richer countries has the most powerful tendency in every way to keep a population in a state of activity and industry. The effect of the failure of the export trade is already severely felt in these districts, and it must inevitably continue to decline, if some substitute for the cloth trade is not discovered. Happily sugar cultivation is calculated not only to fill this void, but to offer the fairest prospect of much more than compensation for the former trade. I have lately obtained what information I could on this subject, especially from Mr. Mackenzie, who has both cultivated the cane, and has also had a vacuum pan for manufacturing sugar."

Proceeding with his argument as to the fostering of an export trade being necessary, Captain Cotton continues—in observations which show how acutely he had studied the deeper aspects of matters which came before him—to say:—

"There are two ways in which diminution of price may

[1] This term, and that of the Ceded Districts, not infrequently occur. They refer to certain districts ceded to the British Government soon after the overthrow of the Mahrattas and in connection with the consolidation of the dominions of the Nizam of Hyderabad.

be produced, either by an increased produce of the article purchased, or by a diminished supply of the bullion with which it is purchased ; now, which of these two causes it has arisen from makes the whole difference. It is quite evident that while the revenue is collected in bullion, if a country is without the means of obtaining a constant supply from abroad, the quantity must rapidly diminish and its value increase, or, in other words, prices must fall ; and the diminution of the produce would be a poor remedy for this state of things ; it would only deprive the people of a part of their food, but in no degree improve the revenue, though it would certainly raise the price of grain. The only effectual remedy is to find an article of produce which can be exported to foreign countries, whence bullion can be obtained."

"The cultivation of sugar," he further remarks, "affects irrigation essentially, inasmuch as the same extent of land will not require, certainly, one-fourth of the quantity of water that paddy does, so that every acre of paddy land converted into land for the culture of sugar, will tend to relieve the other nunjah lands ; further, the water flowing down the river in the months of April and May, which is at present made no use of whatever, will be most valuable when applied to the sugar cane.

"The value of this cultivation may be shown in another way besides those mentioned. The produce of an acre is estimated to be worth about £15, while that of an acre of paddy is only £1 2*s.* So small an extent of cultivation as ten thousand acres would produce an export trade of £150,000 a year, taken at its cost of production ; and, as the small pan at Bimlipatam is capable of manufacturing one thousand five hundred tons a year, or about £30,000 in value, a single sugar factory containing five large pans would be sufficient for the manufacture of the above quantity. The general introduction of this new source of wealth is, therefore, calculated to make these districts the richest, as they are now the poorest,[1] in the Presidency,

[1] A prophecy fully verified by facts. Truly my father brought

and the revenue at present paid, would then be scarcely felt by the people.

"I trust the Board will excuse my thus attempting to bring this subject before them, distinctly with reference to the irrigation question. I have been, as it were, compelled to it from finding that the whole plan of my proceeding in the management of it must be fundamentally affected by the prospects of the foreign trade of the district; with a rapidly increasing produce of an article of foreign consumption, a much more bold system of improvement should be followed than would be advisable if the district was likely to remain in its present state."

In response to this report, and to the recommendation of Sir Henry Montgomery, the Board of Revenue, on August 5, 1844, requested Captain Cotton to "furnish a general report on the actual state of the irrigation of the first division, and its capabilities of improvement, more especially as connected with the Godavari and other rivers, which flow through it."

He, accordingly, submitted an elaborate report on the Delta of the Godavari, and added that "as respects soil, climate, and capabilities of irrigation, it can scarcely be surpassed by any part of the world." The requirements for an effective system of irrigation he stated to be :—

1st. The embankment of the rivers, to secure the crops from destruction by the river floods.

2nd. Dams, with channels of irrigation leading from the river, to bring its water from the level of its bed to that of the surface of the land.

3rd. Surplus channels, to lead off the floods caused by the local rains from the flat lands to the sea.

4th. Raised roads and bridges, to allow of the conveyance of produce to the markets, and to the coast, through a country which is otherwise, from its nature, impassable during the rains.

In describing the area to be affected, he says :—

the Godavari district from being the poorest to nearly the richest in the Presidency.

"After deducting sandy tracts, and sites of villages, besides channels of rivers, there remain one million acres of land fit for the cultivation of paddy, or sugar," which he shows could be utilized by a system of irrigation. He continues: "We have in this case all that the most timid could desire to encourage us to prosecute this undertaking."

His chief problem was how to deal with the river and bring it under control. In one sentence his determination may be given. He decided to build a masonry dam or anicut, twelve feet high, upwards of two and a quarter miles long, across the river bed, with embankments on the islands, of a total length of 7,365 feet.

This gigantic work needed not only the skill of a master mind, but the courage of one who was absolutely confident of the correctness of his plans; both for its commencement and for its final completion it had the absolute devotion of its originator. My father always felt, and acknowledged gratefully, that he owed in great measure the success of his schemes to the sympathy and powerful support given to them by the Marquis of Tweeddale, who was then Governor of Madras, and who ever remained one of his warmest friends. It was to the Governor's good offices that he owed the supplies, liberally granted though often very long in coming, for his Godavari projects.

He strongly recommended raised roads and bridges, so as to allow of the conveyance of produce to the markets and to the coast; many of these communications he was permitted to carry out. No detail was omitted in these deeply thought-out schemes.

Of the district itself, he writes: "I have no doubt that a complete system of irrigation here would increase the produce of lands now cultivated, by one-half, and that, with greatly diminished labour, so that food could be produced at one-half the cost that it now is."

It is interesting, too, to note, that the new roads and bridges were immediately utilised. In Tanjore, on one of the raised roads, the number of male travellers was found to be no less than twelve hundred in one day, and about one hundred tons of goods.

It cannot be wondered that, in his burning enthusiasm and his ceaseless desire for progress, he should write :—

"Would it not be unworthy of the Government of a civilized nation, after having had possession of a district for a long series of years, merely to put in repair old, partial, and radically defective, works, executed by the native governments under immense disadvantages, and suffered by us to go to ruin, when we have it in our power to construct a complete and general system of works, which will bring the last drop of water in the river to the surface of the lands, and put it all under complete control? One of the most striking facts in the whole of the proceedings of Europeans in India is the proneness, which there has been in past times, to lower ourselves to the level of the natives, and their modes of proceeding, when they had not the knowledge and science of the Western nations, instead of diligently applying the means which God has placed in our hands for the benefit of the countries He has given us charge of.

"In nothing has this been more shown than in irrigation, with this aggravation, however, that we have been far behind the native governments in keeping the works, such as they were, in order."

The real inwardness of the situation at this fateful time can be rightly explained only by him in whose mind the work, from start to finish, was already clear. Such an exposition is to be found in a letter that my father wrote to his brother, which, fortunately, is available for quotation.

RAJAHMUNDRY,
January 18, 1845.

MY DEAR FRED,—

We were greatly delighted to get your letter, and to hear such good accounts of your health. Sim writes that you are making yourself very useful. I was also pleased to hear you complain of not having heard of what I am doing, as all my acquaintances in these parts are tired of hearing about my plans, and I sadly want somebody to listen to me.

On taking charge of the Division, I made a run through Rajahmundry, and could not help seeing what it wanted, which was simply everything. So magnificent a country in such a state of ruin was the greatest disgrace to a civilized Government.

I immediately wrote a report recommending an anicut, channels, embankments, and roads, which I estimated roughly at £165,000. I then compared the results of forty years' gross neglect in this Delta, with those of forty years' attention in Tanjore. A few days after I had despatched this, I got a letter from the Board, calling upon me for projects for the improvement of all my districts, and especially the Godavari Delta (the latter would satisfy a moderate man for ten years), and relieving me from the ordinary duties of the Director. This looked well. I asked them for six officers, six or eight sappers, and others, telling them that I was done up, and could do nothing myself but look on. In answer to this I got one young hand to teach and two apprentice surveyors! With scarcely strength to ride ten miles, I started on this expedition to turn the Godavari out of its bed, and make it do something for its livelihood, a river only seven times the breadth of the Mississippi at a spot where I am now pitched! However, there were many helpful symptoms, too: the Court had expressly ordered something to be done for these unhappy Districts. Montgomery had been up here, was very well appreciated by the Marquis, and had strongly urged that I should be sent to try and do something with the river; a new Collector had just been appointed, who seemed both able and willing. As soon as ever I could get clear of my works at Vizagapatam, I put a sergeant in charge of them, and pitched on the bank of the Godavari. The more I worked the stronger I became, which was well, for I had to take, or help in, every line of level that was made, not having got one single level from my surveyors that wasn't altogether false.

One day I travelled ten miles, that is, one evening and morning, from which you may judge how I have recovered my strength.

I have now examined the river from the hills to the sea, and ascertained the levels all the way down, and also all others that are essential, and have satisfied myself as to the site of an anicut, and all the points necessary for preparing an estimate for it, and for the locks, sluices, etc., connected with it; and I am now preparing the papers as fast as I can, hoping to send them in, or take them myself, in a few weeks. Nothing can turn out better than this investigation. I find a site where an anicut twelve feet high will more than command the whole delta, and the land is level with the top of it within four miles on one side and two on the other, though the river is now twenty-eight feet deep in the floods, the country having a slope directly away from the river bank of from four to eight feet in a mile.

The banks of the river have a slope towards the sea of from one foot and a half near the hills to one foot (per mile) near the mouth. The bed has a very irregular fall, varying from four inches to three feet per mile, and averaging eight inches, the rise and fall being thirty-eight feet at the hills, and the banks there eighty feet above the sea. The site I have fixed upon is at the head of the delta, four miles below Rajahmundry. It commands two thousand square miles of the richest alluvial land, certainly about nine hundred thousand acres net, capable of yielding as paddy land £5,000,000 very easily; when the river is full, thirty-one feet deep on a standard at Rajahmundry, it contains ninety times as much water as could be used in the Delta, and enough for the whole of the lands when there is five and a half feet on the standard.

The river is here six thousand yards wide, including islands. The anicut would be five thousand yards; there is the finest hill of stone easily worked, and yet hard enough, on the spot, and first-rate hydraulic lime close at hand. My estimate for the anicut and its dependencies is £35,000, entirely of stone, the upper part all built of cut stone. I expect the anicut will abundantly pay by throwing water into the present petty channels, and that the return will be immediate. I do not propose sending estimates for any extent of new channels this year.

I also propose sending in an estimate to complete the embankment on the south side of the river, from the hills to the sea, this year.

B—— wrote me a note which made me sick, from which I gather the pains which the Board of Revenue have taken to throw cold water, not on the district, but on the plans. He says I ought not to write in my report what I, or even he, thinks would be best, but what I think the Government would consider advisable, which is certainly a good way of confirming them in a system which has ruined the district. However, I hear that the Marquis is more inclined to do something. I do not, however, really expect to be called to Madras.

Believe me,
Ever yours most affectionately,
ARTHUR.

Throughout this laborious period of his life one of his strongest characteristics was conspicuously exhibited. It ran through his whole career. That was his determination to minimise difficulties when obstacles arose to the fulfilment of any great purpose he had in view. He always tried to make little of them, and then never rested till they were overcome.

His praises of the Godavari district where he was working, showing his shrewd, prophetic instincts, may profitably be recorded here :—

"What this district may become if this matter be taken in hand, with only a small part of the energy it deserves, it is not easy to conceive. The unfailing river, an immense expanse of the richest soil, a safe and accessible port, a complete internal water communication, with teak forests, a climate and soil perfectly suited for sugar, and abundance of labour at only three-halfpence a day, form such a combination of advantages as, I suppose, cannot be found in the world, and certainly not under such a Government as ours. The climate being quite healthy, and free from excessive heat all along the sea-board, also opens it fully to the establishment of sugar works under European superintendence. Its situation, too, between the two great ports of Madras and Calcutta, makes it very convenient for commercial undertakings."

With an earnestly devoted mind, and strong common sense, he put these theories into practice; and his brother notices truly "the courage" with which he carried out these bold schemes, for they were unique in both conception and construction.

The four anicuts he built across the Godavari are not solid masses of masonry, but surface coatings of stone over the sand of the river bed. The idea was taken evidently from the so-called "Grand Anicut," which carried the surplus water of the Cauveri river into the Coleroon. This low weir—which is of unknown age—from its importance to Tanjore has always been carefully watched. Every year some small sum has been expended in restoring any breakage of its plastered surface; and it was well this attention was paid to it, for on its being cut into where sluices were opened, it was found that this "Grand Anicut" work was hardly more than a mass of rubbish, mud, stones, and logs of wood, the safety of which depended solely on its thin plastered surface.

The general reader is asked to pardon the somewhat long extracts which follow, and on no account to pass them by as of little moment. The distressful state of many parts of India during past and present years imposes upon the English public a deep responsibility. Keenest individual suffering, utter household ruin, distress almost inconceivable in this favoured land of ours, where now famine never comes (but once it was experienced here, as in India), all these are now ever present in India, and must all be remedied. Our Christian faith, our common humanity, our title to even ordinary respect among contemporary nations, to say nothing of the responsibility we owe to God, and our duty to those almost myriad millions committed to our care, impose upon us obligations which we may not, which we dare not, avoid. In saying that there is nothing—truly and literally nothing—within the wide scope of Indian statesmanship which, for remedial purposes, can even approach judiciously conceived and ably carried out irrigation works, I must not be considered as being unduly influenced by the deep affection I cherish for my father's views. I have been assured by men of ripe experience in, and prolonged study of, Indian questions, before whom the teachings of Sir Arthur Cotton have come, and by whom they have been considered, that while, before prosperity can be fully restored to India, many great enterprises will need to be undertaken, first and foremost comes—

THE WIDE EXTENSION OF IRRIGATION,

the carrying out of many, if not of all of my father's great projects.

Extension of irrigation must, in the near future, become a matter of searching discussion, maybe of keen controversy; they, I venture to submit, will be the most competent to deal with this question, who study it most closely. What my father wrote concerning the Godavari works will be helpful to this end. Therefore, I crave such patience on the part of the reader as may be necessary, though, for my own part, I am inclined to think the particulars will be entertaining enough in themselves to enchain interest.

As already stated, Major Cotton (in due course he had received a step in rank) finally decided to build the anicut at the head of the Delta, just below the village, at Dowlaisweram. The breadth of the Godavari at this place is, from bank to bank, rather over three and four-fifths miles, but of this more than a third is occupied by three islands and the head of the Central Delta, which separates the river into four channels.

The river bed was of pure sand, and the islands merely thin alluvial deposits over it, whilst floods, upwards of twenty-five feet in depth, swept one and a half millions of cubic feet of water per second past the spot. The problem, therefore, which the Engineer had before him, of how at such a site to deal with the river, and so bring it under control that even in its low stages it would be made to command almost all the deltaic lands, was no easy one. He decided to solve it by building a masonry dam, of dimensions which have already been described.

The execution of the proposed work would, he saw, be facilitated by the great regularity of the Indian seasons, which assured with almost absolute certainty a "working season" of some six months in each year, during which the discharge of the river would be no greater than could be diverted to any one or two of the branches, so that, in the others, work could go on untroubled by surface water. But the project was a bold one. The proposed work was without a prototype, except the anicut on a much smaller scale, which he himself had built in the Tanjore district, and it was to be carried out, where no engineering works of any size had ever been constructed, by means of rude Indian labour, and with apparatus, which was generally of quite a primitive character. The greatness of the task, and the difficulties which surrounded its execution, in no way daunted him. He never, for a moment, entertained the slightest misgiving as to the success of his scheme.

A COURAGEOUS NEW DEPARTURE: ECONOMY IN DAM CONSTRUCTION.

Owing to the difficulty of starting such a work in a region where neither appliances nor skilled workmen existed, Major Cotton, in a remark which indicated his readiness of resource in presence of a difficulty, applied for sanction to a change in mode of construction.

MADDUR BRANCH OF ANICUT.
Water about 7 ft. 6 in. over crest.

p. 105.

"I find," he wrote, "that the great quantity of cut-stone proposed will require so many more masons than the district can supply, so as to complete the work within a moderate time, that it would be very desirable, if possible, to give the work a form that will require less of this material. The facility of construction, involving the question of time is, next to security, the most important point. The delay of a year would, no doubt, cause a loss of ten or twenty thousand pounds, and much more some years hence. I find, from my late trials in the quarry, that it would probably take about one thousand stone-hewers and stone-cutters two years to prepare the requisite quantity of cut-stone; and from what I have yet been able to learn, I am afraid that nothing like this number could be procured. The section I now forward, therefore, is such as, by avoiding an overfall, excepting where the under-sluices occur, will admit of the principal part of the surface of the work being made of rubble work, pointed with concrete and finished with a surface of smoothed chunam, such as the sluices and other works are finished with in Tanjore, when not lined or covered with cut-stone. The principal part of the work will thus consist of loose stone, of which there is an unbounded supply, the greater part ready broken, and which can be brought to the work very rapidly by railroads.

"This is the mode of construction originally used at the ancient native work called the grand anicut, which has stood for so many centuries. Part of it has, indeed, been raised and covered with cut-stone, but a few years ago part of it was still without that protection. On cutting through the work to make the under sluices, the mass was found to consist of nothing but loose stone in mud, with the upper course only laid in chunam, and plastered with concrete. It has never required anything more than occasional renewals of the concrete, and has never been in any danger, or given cause for alarm.

"Here, where material is abundant on the spot, and skilled labour scanty, it is worth considering whether such a rude mode of construction may not be adopted with advantage. In my first report I proposed this kind of work, but I afterwards thought the employment of so vast a mass of materials would involve more delay than a more scientific construction.

"Since I sent in that report I have had much more opportunity of investigating the subject, and my main objection to the use of rude materials has been removed. I find that round timber, straight, hard, and durable, and perfectly suited for rails without sawing, can be obtained in great quantities at a most trifling cost. Such timber, from six to seven inches diameter, and twenty feet long, is procurable at from £2 to £2 10*s.* per hundred logs; so that sufficient for a mile of single railway, including cross pieces, that is, twenty thousand feet lineal, will cost from £20 to £25. Such rails added to a level on the surface, with flat two-inch iron screwed down upon it, makes an excellent temporary railroad at so moderate a cost that any length of it may be laid without an excessive expenditure; and by thus having several lines of railway a great mass of materials may be conveyed in a short time without confusion.

THE ANICUT MADE TO SERVE AS A BRIDGE.

"The section shows, however, another material alteration that I propose; and this is, to give the whole work a breadth of eighteen feet in the clear at the top, so as to provide both an ample roadway during the time that the river is low, that is during eight months in the year, and also to allow of a bridge being carried along it without altering the original work. It seems to me that, if this can be accomplished without exceeding the estimate, a very important point will be gained. To make the anicut fully answer the purpose of a bridge, while the river is low, I propose also to make the broad surface of the anicut two feet lower than the crown of the work; building a wall two feet high on the upper side, to keep the roadway dry and prevent accidents. It is to be observed that, as the under sluices will be of great capacity, they will discharge a large body of water, so that none will go over the work excepting while the freshes are high; and as during that time there is but little traffic in the country, the anicut will thus almost answer the whole purpose of a bridge."

From the report which convinced the Madras authorities, and afterwards the East India Directors in Leadenhall Street, that the work might well be taken in hand on Major Cotton's recommendation, the following paragraphs are taken:—

ESTIMATE FOR THE RIVER WORKS.

"The estimate for the works now proposed, viz. an anicut, the head sluices for two main irrigating channels, viz., one on the west side of the river and one at the head of the central tract (the upper part of which is called the Rallee estate), locks at each end for passing boats round the anicut, and those for carrying them past the head sluices into the irrigating channels, and the partial clearing of the present channels (which is all that is included in the present estimate), amounts to:—

	£	*s.*	*d.*
Anicut with six sets of forty under sluices	38,800	8	3
Five locks	1,841	19	3
Two head sluices	1,314	16	0
Excavations	1,400	0	0
Superintendence	1,200	0	0
Contingencies, etc.	3,000	0	0
Total . .	£47,557	3	6

"This sum is very small, whether the magnitude of the work or that of the expected results is considered. The length of the anicut will be four thousand two hundred yards; and it will be seen by the plans, that I propose to build it on a substantial and permanent plan, so as to be nearly independent of periodical repairs.

"The extraordinary advantages of the site will enable us to execute the work at a moderate cost. There is a hill of coarse, strong sandstone close to the spot. This stone is of a degree of hardness exactly suited to the case, neither too hard to be expensive in working, nor yet soft enough to be unfit for the purpose. There are also several hundred thousand tons of broken stone, the accumulation of ages from former quarryings, which will exactly suit for rubble work. All this latter material, therefore, will cost nothing but the carriage, and it is within eight hundred yards of the end of the anicut. As if everything should concur to facilitate the work, we have further in the immediate neighbourhood abundance of first-rate hydraulic limestone. There is also teak to be had in any quantity and of excellent quality, at about 1*s.* 3*d.* per cubic foot, including carpentering, for the lock and sluice gates. The cost of the masonry work, omitting the carriage, I have estimated at the rate at which it can be executed at present; but there is every reason to believe that, on a large scale and under European superintendence, the cost of every part of the operations may be considerably reduced. This part of the country is nearly without masonry works of any description, so that the natives are far behind those of the southern districts in all their modes of executing them. For instance, they burn their lime in heaps on the open ground, not even using a kiln of any kind. In such a state of things, it is not to be supposed that under European superintendence the cost cannot be diminished. For the carriage of materials I propose to use rails, as I have done with such good results in the execution of the bulwark at Vizagapatam, even though nothing but wood was used, with wooden wheels to the waggons.

THE PROBABLE LARGE PROFITS.

"Taking the cost at £47,500, we ought to consider that if there be a fair prospect of a return of thirty per cent., or £14,250 in direct revenue, besides the benefits to be derived by the inhabitants, there is more than ample ground to justify the construction of the works. One-third of this would be considered most abundant in England, and if it yielded only five per cent., or £2,375, it would

SIR ARTHUR COTTON AND HIS BROTHERS.

p. 9.

pay the Indian interest of the cost, and the benefits obtained by the ryots would be a clear advantage.

"The results of the anicut may be properly divided into two heads, viz., first, the ultimate results, when by means of additional channels of irrigation, drainage, etc., etc., the water is led to the whole of the lands commanded by the anicut; and second, the immediate results of the works now estimated for throwing water into the present channels, which will probably be realised to a great extent in the first year.

"First. We are to examine into the probable ultimate effects of the anicut.

"It is evident that, as the crown of that work will command the whole delta, there can be no possible reason why every acre of it should not be perfectly irrigated for one crop, that is, during the four months the freshes continue, and that all the best lands, to the extent that the Godavari can supply water, may be irrigated all the year round. The water from the anicut may, of course, be conveyed all the way to the Kistna, and it must necessarily affect all the country below the Colair lake, but it does not seem necessary here for me to go beyond the part of the delta lying in Rajahmundry.

"The following is a statement of the extent, revenue, etc., of these lands :—

DELTA.

	Sq. miles.		Acres.
Total extent of land in Rajahmundry	1,700	or	1,088,000
Deduct on account of sandy tracts, channels, roads, sites of villages, etc., one quarter			272,000
Remaining cultivable land . .			816,000
Or pooties at eight acres to the pooty			102,000
Or pooties at ten acres to the pooty			81,600

"The real measurement of the pooty is eight acres, but from the inquiries I have made it seems certain that, on an average the pooty, as entered in the village accounts, really contains about one pooty and a quarter or ten acres. I gather that the quantity of uncultivable land cannot exceed one-fourth of the whole, from the following returns of the contents of a large portion of the delta, taken from the village accounts :—

	Pooties.
Gross extent of land	12,583
Cultivable land in the same village . . .	9,878
Uncultivable land, being about one-fifth of the whole	2,705

"As no portion of the bed of the Godavari is included in these returns, the average of the whole of the delta to be deducted for waste must rather exceed the proportion of one-fifth, but can scarcely be so much as one-fourth.

"The total permanent assessment on these lands is as follows :—

	£	£
Peshcush of the villages now in the hands of Zemindars and Proprietors		13,000
Peshcush of villages under Government management . . .	43,700	
Permanent assessment of Government villages	72,300	
		116,000
Total .		£129,000

"We have thus, in a most palpable shape, a fair opening for an increase of revenue to the extent of £20,000, and of produce to the extent of £1,200,000, in the lands only that are in the hands of Government. If it be asked how is this great sum of money to be obtained, the answer is, Simply by converting the water of the Godavari into money instead of letting it run into the sea. At this moment, water is paid for by the sugar growers at about two shillings for eight hundred cubic yards, the cost of raising it by picottahs.[1] There are now about four hundred and twenty thousand cubic yards of water per hour flowing into the sea, worth, at the rate at which it is now actually and profitably purchased, £50 per hour or £1,200 per day, which for two hundred and forty days (the proportion

[1] Picottah : a kind of pump used for raising water for irrigation.

of the year in which the district is not supplied at all) gives £288,000. This water, if applied to the land, would be worth to the cultivators full £500,000. The whole of this is at present lost. Through the remainder of the year, that is, during the cultivation of the great crop, about four times this quantity, or one and three-quarter million cubic yards per hour, are allowed to flow into the sea, that might be profitably applied to the land, and in this way it may be understood by anybody how easily £1,000,000 a year may be lost. That some such amount is actually lost, just for a want of proper care of the district, is shown in such a way that the conclusion is inevitable, by the actual state of Tanjore. The only question is, what expenditure is required to give us the full benefit of our natural advantages? I have before estimated it roughly at £165,000, and the further examination of the district that I have since made has given me a more favourable view of the case than I had before. It has several facilities that I had not calculated upon, especially in respect to the site of the anicut, which I thought would be twenty miles further up the river. The site now proposed, being at the head of the delta, will save the conveyance of the water for twenty miles, and the construction of an aqueduct to carry the water to the central tract.

"My rough estimate for the whole of the works required to put the delta in good order is now as follows:—

	£
Present estimate for the Anicut with its locks, sluices, etc.	50,000
Embankments to the river	10,000
Irrigation channels	20,000
Drainage works	10,000
Sluices, locks, and other small works of masonry	10,000
Roads and bridges	20,000
Total	£ 120,000

"This expenditure may appear as absurdly small, as the estimate of the capabilities of the district appear large; but it is also very well supported by the case of Tanjore, if the circumstances of the two districts are considered. In my former report I calculated the total expenditure on improvements in Tanjore at £160,000 in forty years, during which time the revenue had risen £160,000; but here we have, in the first place, the prodigious advantages of the experience gained from all that has been done in Tanjore; and, secondly, what has been done there has been done piecemeal, while here we can make the improvements on one complete plan, which will make a very great difference. The cost of labour is also lower here, and materials are much cheaper."

THE APPROVAL OF "YOUR LOVING FRIENDS" OF LEADENHALL STREET.

Of course, absolutely final sanction had to come from the Honourable Company in London. This sanction seemed quite certain, and it was. So admirably is the whole position summarised by the précis writer that, although there may be some repetition, the whole communication may be quoted. In the quaint phraseology of "John Company's" communications with his subordinates in India, it was signed "We are, your loving friends," J. W. Hogg, and twelve other directors.

"Upon the whole, therefore, we may consider the anicut as:—

"First. Laying the foundation for the complete irrigation, for a rice crop, of the whole delta of the Godavari and part of that of the Kistna, in all three thousand square miles, or nearly two millions of acres.

"Second. Providing for leading out on the land of every drop of water of the Godavari, in the low freshes, and thus making use of what is now totally lost.

"Third. Opening the way for the conversion of the delta from a mere grain district to a sugar plantation.

"Fourth. Thus the produce of this tract, which at present probably does not exceed £300,000, would, when full advantage is taken of the water thus distributed over it, be increased to at least £2,000,000.

"Fifth. This tract, which now pays with great difficulty about £220,000, would then, with great ease, pay £500,000 or £600,000.

"Sixth. A complete system of internal navigation, intersecting the whole delta, would be established throughout the year.

"Seventh. Every village would be furnished with a stream of pure water for the people and cattle at all seasons.

"Eighth. The present estimate provides for the full irrigation of all the tracts at present partially irrigated by the principal channels of the Godavari.

"Ninth. It will give us at once the use of a large portion (about one-third) of the water of the low freshes during the whole summer, thus providing for sugar cultivation to the extent of about thirty thousand acres.

"Tenth. It will give a constant supply of water to those tracts which, like Tanuku taluk, are situated near the present channels, but which receive no benefit from them at all.

"Eleventh. It will put a famine in this or the neighbouring districts out of the range of probability.

"Twelfth. It will provide immediately two or three most important lines of water communications from Rajahmundry through the heart of the delta to the sea, available at all seasons.

"Thirteenth. It will have the important effect of showing to the people what can be done for them. At present they have no idea of the water being thrown into the channels during the summer; and, from the first moment that water is seen passing through any villages in the low freshes, the whole people of the delta will be awakened to its great capabilities, and will be prepared to welcome the opening of channels throughout the whole tract, and to extend the cultivation of sugar and other things which are at present limited by the want of water.

"Fourteenth. It may be estimated to yield £10,000, or twenty per cent. on the outlay in the first year, and at least £50,000, or cent. per cent. within ten years. This is much less than the new works in Tanjore yielded under circumstances which did not offer anything like the advantages that the state and capabilities of this district hold out.

"Fifteenth. But it seems to us that the most important point of all, in the present state of this district, is its capabilities as a sugar plantation; and the anicut will immediately provide for the most unlimited extension of that culture. When this work is executed there will not remain a single obstacle to this most valuable plant becoming the main produce of this district. Water would be provided for at least three thousand pooties, producing, with the Indian cane, sugar of the value of £130 per pooty, and with Mauritius cane, if we are rightly informed, double that sum, while grain produce is worth only £12 per pooty.

"The investigations of Major Cotton, the Civil Engineer of the Division, as detailed in his able and interesting Report of the 17th April, 1845, have shown the practicability of turning the waters of that river to the most profitable account by the construction of an anicut of such a height as to command the whole of the delta of the Godavari, and to supply to the rich alluvial soil of which that tract is composed, the means of constant irrigation.

"The work, which would be of a similar character to those already constructed in Tanjore, although considerably more extensive, appears to present fewer natural difficulties, and, in the immediate neighbourhood of the spot, abundance of stone fitted for building and for the manufacture of lime is to be found. The cost is estimated by Major Cotton at £47,575, although he is at the same time of opinion that the actual outlay will fall somewhat below this sum.

"Major Cotton's experience in the construction and results of similar works in Tanjore adds great weight to his opinion on this subject. We are, therefore, willing to rely on his representations, which, so far as regards the feasibility of the undertaking, have received the unqualified approval of the professional member of the Board of Public Works, Lieutenant-Colonel Lawe, the Chief Engineer, who has recorded a separate minute on the plan; and with respect to the high importance of the work, the Board of Revenue and the Collector entirely concur in opinion.

"We accordingly comply with your strong recommendation in favour of the project and sanction the proposed expenditure of £47,575 for carrying it into execution."

Busy scenes followed on the shores of the noble river. At one time over five thousand workmen were employed. But the great Engineer was seriously delayed and hindered for want of competent artisans. In one report he states:— "We have been much delayed from want of artificers in metals which has kept us back in the preparation of wagons and other apparatus."

As an indication of the considerable and varied establishment he had to call into being, the following paragraphs are of interest:—

"The quarry has been greatly extended, and railways carried through most part of it, though the length of the rock laid open is still rather too confined for the number of stone-cutters employed. But, having now four cranes and about sixteen wagons at work, the further opening of the quarry will proceed rapidly. One double railway is completed from the quarry to the river, and has been in use for some time. The wagons run the whole way of themselves, the road having a good slope. At present they are discharged on the side of the road, and the stones carried into the boats, which come up close to the end of the rails, but a wharf will soon be completed to enable all the small stones to be discharged into the boats at once. The other double railway is now within a short distance of the river, and materials for it are carried from the quarries by the wagons. Eighteen boats have been launched, and they answer very well. They are chiefly employed in carrying stone across the river, and it is at present deposited near the sites of the head sluices and locks, for which it will be first wanted. About one hundred and fifty tons a day are carried by water at present. On both lines of railway about four hundred tons a day of stones and gravel are conveyed, and this quantity will rapidly increase. At least fifty thousand tons of rough stone have been quarried and thrown in heaps near the railways in the quarry, and about eight thousand tons have been conveyed to the line of the anicut. Cut stone to the extent of twenty-five thousand cubic yards has been prepared. Two kilns have been kept burning for about two months, yielding now about two hundred parahs [1] of chunam a day each, and about four hundred garce [1] are now in store. The cutting and embanking for the railway from the limestone quarry to the river has been nearly completed, and a considerable part of the rails laid. It is two miles in length."

He continues:—

"At one time, when the first fresh was rising, some alarm was caused by the current cutting away the narrow point of land that divides the head of the channel on the Dowlaisweram side from the river, but it was protected by some stones and no harm was done.

"The new embankments between the wing-walls of the anicut, across Rallee and Muddoor islands, have stood excellently, having suffered neither from the rains nor the freshes. The water during the freshes flowed down the new cutting made on the Vijaisweram side for the head of the main channel, and this has thus been of considerable use this year. The cutting in Rallee head has not been carried far enough to communicate with any of the old channels.

"We are thus in a very fair position for commencing the operations of the season as early as the rains and freshes have permitted, and I hope very soon to be depositing one thousand tons of rough stone a day in the line of the work. We shall also shortly commence upon

[1] Indian measures.

the head sluices and locks. We have had from two thousand five hundred to three thousand five hundred people at work during the monsoon, and they have already begun to come in again in considerable numbers. I have every reason to believe they will come in greater numbers than we can employ, unless we undertake a large quantity of earthwork this year; for we shall not require above five thousand people at the anicut, now that we have got the principal railways in operation, and all the preparatory works executed.

"With respect to the progress of the work, I have great reason to be satisfied."

The strain upon a constitution by no means robust was too severe, how severe will be seen in the concluding portion of this chapter where Lady Cotton gives her reminiscences of that period. A breakdown in health occurred and sick leave to Australia was granted.

He himself refers to his ailing health, and expresses his sorrow at not being able to devote the time and attention he wished to what was going on. "It has been some additional hindrance to the progress of the works," he remarks, "that for the last six weeks, in the very height of the working season, I have been so completely broken in health as to be wholly unable to attend to the works personally, and to be only occasionally, even within doors, able to attend to business; and this must needs be the case in a measure, notwithstanding that the other officers are so remarkably effective. The loss of even an inexperienced officer would have been seriously felt."

To his brother Fred, he poured out his troubles thus:—

"I dare not think of the arrears of writing I am in to you, to the Board, and to everybody. I was overwhelmed with the outdoor work of the anicut, when I got a slight stroke of the sun, which, strange to say, I did not at first suppose it was, and applied no local remedy, but that of a little more sun, till I found myself quite floored, with a total inability to take food.

"The first attack was nothing, and had I poured a little cold water on the spot affected, it would have prevented any ill effect. As it was, local applications removed all the symptoms of headache and giddiness in a fortnight; but the mischief having in the meantime extended to the stomach, I was reduced as low as I almost ever was, and have been so completely shaken that I cannot walk a few hundred yards without feeling symptoms of illness of all sorts and kinds. I dare not visit any part of the works, *where I am wanted*, and it is only at times that I can attend to business indoors. There is every symptom of a complete break up, such as nothing but a continual residence in a temperate climate offers any hope of repairing in any degree. This is the very height of our operations, with the works in a most critical state, the freshes close at hand, and the monsoon already set in unusually early; so I am placed in very trying circumstances. I do not know how to leave the works to the responsibility of another man, in such a difficulty, and yet I am utterly unable to do the duties required of a chief engineer.

"We have had innumerable difficulties, and our expenditure this season has been serious, for I was obliged to push on the works, through thick and thin, to get them, if possible, into a state in which the monsoon would do them no serious harm; but, after all, they are far from being in a satisfactory condition.

"We have got one division of the anicut, across the widest channel (nearly a mile), finished off at a level three feet below that intended, and its lock, head sluices and under sluice very nearly ready for the freshes, all such giants compared with the southern works, having to provide for a depth of water of thirty feet, the head sluice with a waterway of twenty-six yards breadth, and the lock, one hundred feet by fifteen.

"A second channel has a similar anicut, well advanced, but the chunam will be so soft when the water goes over it, that it is very doubtful whether it will not be breached. The other sluices and one lock and all the wing walls are in such a state that I hope they will take no harm.

"But the two remaining channels across which I hope to have established good, strong, rough-stone dams, will, I fear, now be left entirely open, for there is hardly a possibility of our completing the dams sufficiently to prevent their breaching. Owing to the peculiar circumstances of the site, there does not seem reason to fear much mischief if these two channels are left open.

"I have been obliged to send in an additional estimate of £10,000 to complete the work, but, besides all the apparatus and buildings, railroads, boats, steamers, etc., that we have need of, there is about £5,000 worth of material and apparatus that has not yet arrived, or not been sent.

"You have no idea of the work of having to deal with a river of four miles broad on a straight line, and seven miles going round the heads of the lunkas (islands) that divide the channels, and this reduced from seventeen by a channel we cut for half a mile, where, if the water does not admit of a boat bringing the stone, etc., to the very spot, the probability is that there are one or two miles of heavy sand between the work and the material. Our people are not to be named with Malabarians, in any respect whatever; they are in general the poorest creatures possible, both as respects energy and skill, and the veriest slaves in the world.

"On the other hand, I have the most excellent set of officers—four of them—the hardest working fellows I ever saw. Young Haig, I think, is the most promising young engineer I have known. We have also some very good non-commissioned officers.

"I began this several days ago—I have been rather gaining strength since then; our monsoon has set in fully, but not violently, yet it has lowered the thermometer, which I think has had a good effect upon me. But I must soon make way for somebody who has life enough left in him to do the work. Orr is most competent to take up my engineering duties when I leave them.

"The matter is God's—not mine; and if He has a purpose of blessing the district, He will find instruments for His purpose. What the district seems to want above all is a Collector who would give himself up to promote its welfare, and who knows how to do it."

During his absence in Australia, Captain Orr, a trusted and valued Assistant, took Major Cotton's place at Dowlaisweram. A Committee was also appointed to investigate the works that had been carried out, and others that were still in progress. Those who had not before inspected the scene of his labours were struck with astonishment at the extraordinary progress of the works since their commencement about June, 1847, when some wells were sunk; after which nothing further could be done till after the subsidence of the freshes in October. In March, 1848 only four hundred yards of the rubble masonry forming the body of the anicut had been completed, and in the middle of June the work was again stopped by a very early rise of the river. Yet, when the Committee assembled about November, 1848, they found the first division of the anicut, one thousand four hundred yards in length, completed to the height of nine feet, and the third division, five hundred and twenty yards in length, also to a great extent finished.

Captain Orr, who had imbibed his chief's ardour and interest in the task, laboured most devotedly in carrying out the plans laid down. The construction of the anicut was as fruitful an occasion for anxiety as all such enterprises are. On one occasion Captain Orr had an example of the way in which, in engineering projects as in most else, it is the unexpected which happens. He had just reported he could "make all safe before the freshes set in," when he had to supplement his optimistic remark with the following story of disaster:—

"I have the painful duty to report the occurrence, yesterday afternoon, of very serious damage to that portion of the anicut which I have reported as all but completed across the Vijaisweram branch of the river.

"The front retaining wall was built quite across; only a small opening at one point, one foot square, being left near its base for the purpose of draining off the water, which oozed through the main temporary dam, and through a semi-circular embankment thrown round the opening, as an additional protection. The latter embankment was made practically of clay, was rivetted on both sides with grass rollers, and being so strong, and the same height as the anicut, was considered by me quite sufficient protection, even in the event of the main dam giving way. Things were in this perfectly satisfactory state, and the final closing of the opening was only delayed, that the adjoining masonry, being new, should have a few days to set before being subjected to the action of water. The river some days ago rose, in forty-eight hours, five inches, in addition to a similar rise which took place about a week before, but since Monday evening it seemed so steady that I was in hopes that the threatened danger of a fresh had passed. Yesterday afternoon, however, the river rose again suddenly, and at about 4 p.m. a very severe squall of wind broke over the works, blowing right down the river, which, piling up the pent up waters against the dams, caused them to breach. Being prepared for such an occasion, I still expected no injury to follow, but, unfortunately, we had not guarded against the unlooked-for, and at this season the unprecedented, contingency of a fresh accompanied by a gale causing such a rise of the river as eighteen inches in an hour, and that, too, while the river was passing freely over the whole length of the Rallee dam, and flowing two and a half feet deep through the Dowlaisweram under sluices. The consequence, I regret to say, was that the small semi-circular dam being topped by the waves, and soon breaching, brought such a pressure of water against the new and unbacked retaining wall that it gave way, and before the extension of the damage could be arrested, about twenty-two yards of the anicut on each side of the opening were washed away, and a breach some forty-four yards in width formed in the centre of the work. This untimely fresh, however, soon subsided, and before the regular season for floods the damage done was repaired."

To Captain Orr, in one of his reports, Major Cotton paid the following tribute:—

"I cannot conclude without noticing the invaluable aid derived from having an officer of Captain Orr's standing and ability to consult with in operations of this kind. The attention he has paid to railway works in England has also rendered him peculiarly useful here; but there is not a question connected with the whole management of the delta in which I do not find it of incalculable advantage to have him to consult with upon it. All the officers take the greatest interest in the work, and give me great satisfaction."

Imagine the forces which, in India, hydraulic engineers have to contend with! Here is a river four miles wide in which the water rises eighteen inches in an hour! The marvel is that, in presence of such difficulties, the accidents were not many and serious. So thorough, however, were his preparations for the enterprises he undertook that the casualties were very few indeed. But—

> "Be the day short, or be the day long,
> At length it cometh to evensong."

And, with Arthur Cotton's conceptions, despite difficulties, the end, the triumphant end, came without any excessive delay, nay, on the contrary, with unlooked-for expedition. Here is his gratifying statement as to the completion of the anicut and the beginning of channels of watering and navigation which his genius gave to the erstwhile distressed district. The map facing this page will show how the hand of Arthur Cotton is heavily scored on the soil of the district in ineffaceable lines, every line a source of salvation to past, present, and future generations of Indian cultivators.

In April, 1852, he had the happiness to be in the position to send the following report to the Board of Revenue at Madras:—

"I have the honour to report for the information of the Board the following results of an examination of the anicut lately made by Captains Orr and Hutchinson and myself:—

"Commencing from the Dowlaisweram side—

"First. The lock is in perfect order; no expense has been incurred on this work from the first (five years). I cannot help here mentioning the excellent workmanship of the lock gates, as I think they reflect much credit on Captain Hutchinson.

"Second. Head sluice also in good order, and without repairs from the first.

"Third. Under sluices, the same, with the exception that we have had to throw in a prodigious quantity of rough stone for the apron. It has repeatedly sunk one or two yards, and must now contain an enormous quantity of stone. It seems, however, now to be nearly settled, as it has sunk very little of late.

"Throughout the whole work not a rupee is required to repair damage sustained by the work last year. Only a quantity of stone had to be thrown into the apron of the Vijaisweram under sluice during the monsoon. This state of things is to me highly satisfactory. It seems to give a fair prospect of the actual cost of keeping the work itself in order being very insignificant. The alterations and additions proposed this year are all such as would not occur again; and they only amount to three and a half per cent. upon the total cost of the work. There is certainly every prospect that, including every alteration and improvement that can be thought of hereafter, the permanent annual expenditure on it will not be two per cent. upon the cost. One part of the work has now stood four monsoons, and, in one of them, an unprecedented flood. I think we may thus consider the anicut as fairly established. It is also to be considered, that a work like this is not like a bridge or a building, which is liable to be utterly destroyed. Almost the worst that could happen to it would be a breach of fifty or hundred yards, which could be repaired for £1,000 or £2,000, a trifle in comparison with the first cost. It is also observable that no alteration has been made in the original section of the work, excepting that the rough stone apron has been enlarged. The Dowlaisweram branch is just as originally planned, and no alteration of any consequence has been made in the others. I must, however, say, that here, as in the Coleroon, I would now prefer building a work with a vertical fall, as safer in a sandy river; and so I would in any place excepting one similar to the Kistna, where there is an unlimited supply of stone at very low rates, and where, consequently, twenty cubic yards of rough-stone could be obtained at the same cost as one of cut-stone. When I planned the Coleroon anicut, I considered that the great point in these rivers was to break the force of the water effectually, and prevent it scouring the lower channel; and what I have here seen makes me think still more of the importance of that principle. But I believe, where stone can be obtained very cheaply, a large mass of rough-stone, with a very long slope on the lower side, will be the cheapest and safest work in a sandy river.

"Can we see this large and important work, calculated so substantially to promote the real comfort of a million of people, thus brought to completion through so many difficulties and contingencies, without heartily acknowledging the goodness of God in thus prospering us and bringing the project so far to a successful issue, notwithstanding the opposition it has experienced from quarters from which I had every right and every reason to hope for, and from which I did confidently expect, most cordial and energetic support in carrying out a work of such unequalled magnitude in India (excepting that now on hand in the North-West), a work approved and ordered by the Home authorities, and calculated to be in every way so vast a public benefit? May we not hope that its accomplishment, with the abundant effects which have already resulted from it to the district, will lead to the adoption of such extensive works for the improvement of the country, and the promotion of the welfare of the people entrusted to our care, as will lead to an increasing appreciation of a Christian Government? There is nothing that the people more thoroughly appreciate, after peace, than public works, and especially those that furnish them with water. And I cannot but trust that this is only the beginning of a series of works worthy of our nation, our knowledge, our religion, and the extraordinary power God has been pleased to put into our hands. I say our religion, because I am sure it ought to lead us to do our utmost in every way to care for those who are thus committed to us.

"It remains for me to speak of the state of the bed of the river about the anicut, which will require to be carefully watched. . . .

"The rough-stone apron of the anicut throughout seems to be well established; there is no appearance of any sinking or disturbance of any consequence this year in any part. It is generally from fifteen to twenty yards broad. I am now, however, throwing in additional stone, according to this year's ordinary estimate, strengthening each branch according to the proportionate force of the water over it. To the Muddoor branch, as it is now higher than it has been hitherto, I propose adding considerably, and also to the Vijaisweram branch, which ought to have an abundantly large apron. The apron laid by Captain Orr last year stood most perfectly; but we can hardly take too much precaution on this point, especially as the cost of rough-stone is so moderate.

"I have now the honour to request that the establishment which I have recommended for the conservation of this important work may, if approved, be appointed without loss of time. A body of thoroughly trained men, under efficient superintendence, permanently resident on each portion of the work is essential, and should be immediately appointed, and housed, that they may be fully prepared for their duties before the freshes. No water works of any kind can ever be trusted to take care of themselves; but especially those in a delta require the most vigilant care; and both the cost of this work, and the vast amount of property dependent upon it, demand that no risk should be run about it. I trust that, whatever is decided as to precise arrangement of the superintendence of this system of works, authority may be granted for entertaining at once those that are required for the anicut and other works already executed, as a temporary arrangement."

The order of the Government on receipt ot the above was in cordial and appreciative terms:—

"The Right Honorable the Governor in Council has received with much satisfaction the report of Colonel Cotton on the state of the Godavari anicut, which may now be said to have arrived at completion, through the unceasing exertion and energy of Colonel Cotton and the officers associated with him in this great undertaking.

"It must be a highly gratifying termination of Colonel Cotton's immediate connection with the First Division, that he should have been enabled to notify to Government the complete stability of the anicut, and the success which has up to this period attended his plans; and in congratulating that officer on these happy results, the Governor in Council has much pleasure in recording his obligations to Colonel Cotton, Captain Orr, and the officers of the department under their orders, for their services on this occasion; and it will be his agreeable duty to bring the same to the notice of the Honourable the Court of Directors."

Later, the Court of Directors joined in this chorus of well-deserved praise. They declared they were constrained to record their very high opinion of the science, practical ability, and indefatigable labours of Major Cotton. "It is scarcely possible," they added, "to place that officer's qualifications as an Engineer of hydraulic works higher than they stood before, but the Godavari anicut is a new and splendid illustration of his powers of mind and self-devotion, from the exercise of which the country has already so largely benefited."

This must have been highly gratifying to the officer praised. But, it is certain that he received as much gratification in the recommendation which followed that the works be prosecuted with all possible diligence, and that the opening of the Rallee and other irrigating channels, required to extend to all parts of the district the benefit of the anicut, would receive early sanction.

ENTHUSIASTIC PRAISE FROM BENEFICIARIES OF IRRIGATION.

How greatly and gratefully what has been done is appreciated by those who have benefited therefrom, may be best stated in the words of the President and Members of the Local Reception Committee, Bezwada, a town on the Kistna, addressed to Sir M. E. Grant Duff, K.C.S.I., when, as Governor of Madras, he visited the northern districts. In their address the people say:—

"We, the President and Members of the Local Reception Committee, in the name of the people of Bezwada, desire to give your Excellency a right hearty welcome to this flourishing town. Perhaps no place in India more exemplifies the benefits of British rule than the picturesque spot you are now honouring with a visit. Before the beneficent scheme for irrigating this thirsty land came into operation, Bezwada was only a small village, and partly in ruins, from the people having died in the terrible Nandana famine, *i.e.* the Guntoor famine of the Nandana year, 1832. Now it is a town, and increasing year by year with such rapidity as to be a source of wonder to all who knew its former condition. Indeed, it seems likely to become again, as in ancient days it is said to have been, the largest town in these parts. In past times no part of India suffered more than this from the horrors of famine; and your Excellency's father pointed out the territory between the Godavari and Kistna as liable to these visitations in their severest form, and put on record a very terrible one. It often happened that whole villages were depopulated, and myriads of people perished for want of the water that flowed in abundance at their feet, and only just below the level of their dying crops, to be swallowed by the greedy ocean. As the huge volumes of water flowed grandly on, laden with rich, fertilising, yellow silt, gathered by the river in its course through the Deccan,

THE ENTHUSIASTIC GENERAL SIR ARTHUR COTTON CALLED IT 'LIQUID GOLD.'

The anicut, with its ramified system of canals, has certainly turned it into solid gold. At one stroke the mouths of a hungry and dying people have been filled with bread, and the coffers of the Government with money. In place of dashing madly on to be lost in the sea, the Kistna now spreads fertility and beauty on all sides, and had your Excellency come at a later period of the year, the extensive tracts of flat country between this and the coast would present you with a sight worth seeing. No longer struggling for a bare existence, or held in the grasp of sowcars—money-lenders—the people rejoice among their smiling crops, and the money-lenders have become almost extinct. Even in famine years the Kistna never fails to do its duty, and the dire poverty that existed during the childhood of middle-aged men is almost forgotten in the general prosperity; and it is meet that we should express gratitude to the good Government that has done these great things for us."

Like many others who have been privileged to work with Indians, Arthur Cotton found not a few upon whom he could rely, and whom he could trust implicitly. Pre-eminently amongst these was a Hindu Overseer named Veenem Veranah,[1] who seems to have been gifted with

[1] Such another one comes under my notice whilst I am revising these pages. Writing from Jaipur, Central India, on May 1, Mr. Nash, special correspondent of the *Manchester Guardian*, whose testimony to the value of irrigation canals will be quoted later, speaks: first, of Colonel Jacob [a man after Sir Arthur Cotton's own heart], and next, of his Indian assistant. "I am told that when Colonel Jacob goes about the country, the people of the irrigated districts surround him as if he were the god of water, and beseech him to give them canals. . . . The genius of the nullah is a famous organiser of transport, Dhaupat Rai, whose name will be familiar to officers who have been on service on the frontier and in the Soudan. Dhaupat is now in charge of the Imperial Service Transport Corps of Jaipur State, which he has turned to good use for famine purposes, and he is cultivating the nullah and organ-

HEAD OF MAIN CANAL, EASTERN DELTA.

p. 129.

exceptional qualifications for conducting engineering operations as well as for directing and managing large bodies of native labour. Of him Colonel Cotton thus wrote: "I cannot say less than that if we had not found an Indian of his remarkable qualifications, considering the state of the district when the works were commenced, I do not see how they could have been executed, for no European could have supplied his place, and no Indian at all equal to him has appeared." He was made a sub-engineer with the title of Rai Bahadur, and continued for many years to render excellent service in connection with the enterprises to the successful accomplishment of which he had so largely contributed.

On one of the walls of the anicut there is a tablet bearing the following inscription:—

V. VERANAH GARU,
RAI BAHADUR,
Sub-Engineer, D.P.W.,
Obiit, Oct., 1867.

Soon after the completion of the anicut, Arthur Cotton became Chief Engineer of the Presidency, and the charge of the Godavari works was assumed by his brother, Major (now General) F. C. Cotton; Captain Orr, who had been the chief executive officer in their construction, was placed in charge of the Kistna anicut, which is only second to the Dowlaisweram anicut in the grand results following from its construction.

Among those to whom tributes were paid was the sub-Collector, Mr. Henry Forbes. Of him, in warm language

ising the 7,000 workers employed in it as a sort of amusement. The little finger of this entirely competent person is worth a whole famine code and a league of red tape to the Jaipur durbar. His huts are dug out and solidly thatched; his gangs of workers know exactly what is the daily task, and do it; his orphans, clad in surprising jackets of yellow, are governed by five orphan corporals; his ambulance wagons are well horsed; and his depôts for the collection of the sick and starving are run with military precision."

of grateful eulogy, Sir Arthur wrote: "That we have made the progress that we have is entirely owing, under God, to Mr. Henry Forbes, whose vigorous and active measures have already raised the District to a degree that could not have been expected ; it may be said indeed that, as respects the getting public and private improvements effected, this District is ten years in advance of what it was a few months ago."

A STEAM TUG, AND HOW IT WAS OBTAINED.

Included in the many difficulties which sprang up, and which had to be removed, was the provision of a steam vessel. The plant or apparatus for carrying on the works was found to need a steam-tug, to be obtained from Calcutta. Sir Arthur, having heard of such a vessel, applied to the Board of Revenue to sanction its purchase by him. They did not see fit to comply with his request, telling him that it was not neceessary; he, knowing of what value it would prove in oversight and direction and, if need arose, for towing purposes, went to Calcutta and purchased one on his own responsibility. He considered it absolutely essential to the progress of the works at that time. When he had paid for it, he was met by what appeared to be an insurmountable difficulty; the Bay of Bengal was held to be too stormy a sea for the transit of so small a boat. Just as he was wondering what could be done in the matter, a man came to him and informed him that if he were only trusted, he, with one or two others, would take the boat safely down the bay and place it in the mouth of the Godavari, and that they were ready to do this at once. He accepted the offer, and in a very short time the steamer was plying up and down the river, and proved to be of very great use. So much was its value proved, that a small flotilla of similar steamers was built, and the authorities at Madras eventually generously acknowledged that they were not only a useful adjunct but were essential to the progress and completion of the enterprise.

MUKKAMALA LOCK.

p. 131.

Year by year Arthur Cotton's conception came nearer and nearer to fulfilment. Canal after canal, channel after channel, were made and opened, and ever more and more acreage was brought under the influence of the vivifying waters. In 1853 he expressed his satisfaction at seeing considerable progress made in cutting the great channels for draining the country near the Colair Lake. About a quarter of a million of cubic yards of earth had already been excavated, and about four thousand people were at work upon them. They were to complete a million cubic yards that year, and thus open the two main lines to a considerable breadth. "This alone will have so powerful an effect as to relieve this tract effectually when the rains are moderate; and," he adds, "I have no doubt that it will give a new character to the cultivation of this tract this year, by enabling the people to begin their cultivation much earlier."

It must have been with mingled gratification and sad reminiscence that he found himself able to write: "From about this time the success of the works became so apparent that money was more readily granted for their development."

So far, in these pages, the Godavari canals have been regarded in their aspect as irrigating media. Nothing has been said of their usefulness as respects navigation. But, though these pages have been temporarily silent on that point, Arthur Cotton's mind was not, for one hour, unmindful of the great service which his water-ways might render to the country in this respect. Indeed, he designed them almost as much for boat-traffic as for field-inundation. By this time, so strongly had he become convinced of the utility of, and even necessity for, the provision of cheap transit, that it is doubtful if he would have designed works which could not be made to serve the double purpose. There were arguments in plenty in favour of his views, not the least of which was that cultivators were frequently reluctant to take an irrigation supply unless they were assured of water carriage to take away the surplus crops which, without such opportunity, would be a drug to them, and would not repay the cost of cultivation.

IRRIGATION CANALS AS NAVIGATION ROUTES.

In the year to which we have now come—1853—he wrote :—

"The necessity for channels does not depend upon a great increase of exports, though that would render them much more valuable and important, nor even upon an export trade at all. The District must have communications for its internal traffic, whether it exports or not. A million of people cannot exist without interchange of commodities. And it is very much cheaper to make the irrigation channels navigable than to make roads ; besides that, the former will convey goods at a twentieth part of the rates by the latter.

"Again. The question seems to me rather to be what data are there to conclude that the export trade, which has increased in ten years from £30,000 to £140,000, should on a sudden become stationary, and that, too, when the quantity of produce is increasing, and the cost of obtaining that produce decreasing every year in consequence of the new works. The market for rice, tobacco, sugar, and oil-seeds is, in fact, in comparison with the extent of this delta, almost unlimited, and the quantity that will be taken from it depends upon one main thing, the cost of its production. If Rajahmundry can grow these things cheaper than it did, it may export a hundred times what it does now. The new works will certainly reduce the cost of produce, on an average, one-half and (of course always excepting extraordinary contingencies) nothing can stop the present increase of the export trade, unless we absolutely prevent the produce being conveyed to the coast by want of communications. I am informed that there is again a great increase of the export trade this year.

"The grounds on which I insist upon the necessity of making the channels navigable are these:—

"First. The actual present traffic on those that have been opened is abundantly sufficient to prove the necessity for them.

"Second. There is now a large and rapidly increasing foreign trade, the materials of which must be carried from the interior to the coast.

"Third. Among a population of close on a million of people there must be a large interchange of goods, if there are communications.

"Fourth. The delta is wholly without roads.

"Fifth. It is much cheaper to make the irrigation channels navigable than to make roads, and they are incomparably better means of transit.

"Sixth. To supply the people with means of raising a five-fold amount of produce, and give them no means of conveying the surplus to the towns and ports where it may be converted into money, seems to me the most palpable mistake.

"Seventh. If only one hundred thousand tons are moved by the channels annually (the exports alone are from forty thousand to fifty thousand tons already), and they are only conveyed on an average thirty miles, the cost of that traffic by land would be £40,000 a year; whereas by water it will not exceed £4,000, so that it would be equivalent to relieving the district from a charge of £36,000 a year, even if there were roads.

"Eighth. The cost of the navigation will be quite insignificant, perhaps on an average £20 a mile, the interest of which, divided among a traffic of only ten thousand a year, would be only one twenty-fourth of a penny per ton per mile; and for this the cost of transit would be reduced one penny farthing, even as compared with common roads, which would cost three or four times what the navigation will.

"Ninth. I must always insist upon the fundamental principle that where there is a considerable population it is the communications that make the traffic; and if there is little or no traffic the sole reason must be that there are no communications."

Quoting the above, Mr. Walch, in his book on the Godavari delta, proceeds to remark:—

"And so he went on with steady insistence, loyally backed up by the officers who followed him on the Delta Works; and there are now in the Godavari system alone nearly five hundred miles of canals which, besides carrying water for irrigation, are excellent lines of communication. Nor is this all. From the Godavari system navigation can, at three places, pass into the Kistna system with its three hundred miles of navigable canals, and from it again into the Buckingham Canal, which runs along the coast for one hundred and ninety-six miles from the end of the Kistna system to Madras, and for sixty-five miles further south. From Cocanada to the south end of the Buckingham Canal the length of canal navigation is four hundred and fifty miles.

"There cannot be the slightest doubt that the provision for cheap carriage, not only in and about the district itself, but also to the neighbouring districts and to an excellent seaport, contributed largely to the rapidity with which the Godavari irrigation developed, and the district sprang into prosperity. In this way the cost of the works especially required for navigation has been repaid over and over again, quite irrespective of the direct returns from boat licenses, and so on."

Thirty years later (1883) General Mullins, R.E., Chief Engineer for Irrigation, wrote:—

"The Irrigation and Navigation Works of the Godavari delta may well be a subject of congratulation, and I fully join in the opinion expressed by the Government of Madras, that the usefulness of this most successfully executed project, the development of which has been steadily going on during the last thirty-five years, is by no means to be measured by the direct pecuniary returns only, large as they have been. The present flourishing

A HOUSE-BOAT FOR CANAL TRAVEL IN EASTERN INDIA.

p. 135.

condition of the Godavari district, and the vast improvement it has undergone since the construction of the works, which provide for the irrigation of nearly six hundred thousand acres, afford the best possible evidence of the great benefits conferred on the people."

Still later, in January, 1890, further most interesting testimony is forthcoming concerning the navigation aspects of the district. The Hon. J. D. Rees, C.I.E., Member of the Viceregal Council, writes :—[1]

"After a brief halt at this historic site (Masulipatam), we travelled on along the coast of the district, which, in size, is about equal to the principality of Wales, and next morning arrived at Cocanada, in the Bay of Coringa, ten miles north of the Gautami mouth of the river Godavari. To the north and north-east of the anchorage low hills come down near the water's edge, relieving the coast from the barren and desolate appearance that it presents near Masulipatam. The harbour was alive with boats bearing on their sails huge red crosses, anchors, moons, and such-like devices, whereby their owners may recognise them from the distant shore. The collector, Mr. Power, met us on board, and another voyage ot six miles in a steam launch landed us between the groynes, which form, at once, an entrance to the town of Cocannada, and to the canals which extend thence to the great anicut of the Godavari, since the construction of which the trade of the town has advanced by 'leaps and bounds,' the value of its exports and imports having risen from £300,000 in 1862, to £740,000 in 1872, and £1,500,000 in 1888.

"Next morning, the 23rd, we rose early and left by canal for Rajamundry, a distance of forty-four miles, more or less. We were towed along, in a little convoy of house-boats, by the steam launch *Arthur Cotton*, named after the celebrated engineer who constructed the great Godavari Irrigation Works. In the river, from the head of the delta, there is a continual fall, consequently we had a continual rise, and passed three locks, one a double one, with a rise of eighteen feet. The canal banks were green,

[1] *Narrative of the Eleventh Tour of His Excellency the Right Honourable Lord Connemara*, G.C.I.E., *Governor of Madras, by J. D. Rees, Private Secretary.* I am indebted to Mr. Rees for his kind permission to make these quotations.

and banyans shaded the road, which ran alongside. All around us were fields of stubble, and innumerable straw-ricks. The character of the country, but for the palmyras, much resembles that of the Fens. When you get within a few miles of the great dam which stems the stream at Dowlaisweram, first one canal and then another takes off in different directions. After the separation of each canal the artificial waterway grows broader and broader, till, near Dowlaisweram, it becomes as wide as the Thames at Maidenhead, but probably contains a great deal more water. At last it ends in a lock; and, when we leave the boats and mount the banks, an expanse of water stretches some four miles before the eye. Immediately in front extends the first portion of the great anicut, which, with the help of three islands at the head of the delta, holds up the river, and diverts its waters on either side, so as to irrigate upwards of 612,000 acres of fertile rice-bearing lands, and to water with gold a delta of two thousand square miles. Every river in India is a Pactolus, but this great stream has been made more subservient to the wants of man than, perhaps, any other of its size in the world. Practically, at the present moment, it ends at this great anicut above which you see nothing but miles of water, and below which spread miles of yellow sand.

"It is the nature of such works that they are never finished. In 1852, the dam and some of the distribution works were completed for the exceedingly low figure of £150,000. Labour was then cheap, and material abounds on every side. Many times since have these titanic works been considered complete. In 1870, eighteen years later, they were completed, at a cost of £868,000, and now, in 1890, it is believed they are pretty well completed, at a cost of £1,180,000. Whatever they cost, however, so long ago as 1877, the returns directly due to the water distributed amounted to upwards of £2,000,000, and in 1879 it was calculated that goods of the value of upwards of £3,500,000 passed over the canals, while the value of the exports and imports of the district, which, in 1847, before the construction of the anicut, amounted to £170,000, had risen, in 1887, to upwards of £1,500,000. The great dam itself rises some fourteen feet above the level of the stream, and consists of three long portions and one short one, amounting, in the aggregate, to 3,982 yards in length. The navigable channels, which distribute the water, are

528 miles long, and the total lengths of distributive channels is not less than 1,600 miles.

"These steamers belong to the Irrigation Department, but fleets of private boats ply on river and canal, and carry passengers at ridiculously low rates. Competition has reached such a pitch that rival carriers are said to take passengers occasionally not only for nothing, but also to give them bananas to eat on the way. Nothing like this has yet been exhibited in England; though, occasionally, you can go from San Francisco to New York for the price of a journey from London to Edinburgh, from causes similar to those which operate here."

THE EXTRAORDINARY CHEAPNESS OF CONSTRUCTION.

It is sometimes urged that high prices must needs be paid for construction which is to last for many years. There are, doubtless, occasions when this is true. But there is no special virtue in high prices as such. That work is most deserving of praise which is most enduring and has cost least. Tested by this standard, Arthur Cotton's work everywhere, but especially in the Godavari delta, stands second to none. A Committee appointed to make an investigation into what had been done at Dowlaisweram anicut bore this striking testimony:—

"The rates are singularly low and, were each of them increased fifty per cent., the anicut might then be pronounced one of the cheapest works ever constructed, if its immense length, and its situation, with the endless difficulties arising therefrom, were duly considered.

"FOUNDER OF CHEAPEST SCHOOL OF ENGINEERING IN THE WORLD."

"And, it must be added, that this extraordinary cheapness was owing to the peculiar section of the anicut. It may, indeed, be safely affirmed that, had the works been projected by any other living engineer, their original cost would have been prohibitory. The comparatively small work of the Barrage in Egypt was built with the same object (as was this anicut) and cost £1,800,000, and was after all wanting in the security of the Godavari works.

This economical method of construction, originating with Colonel Cotton, has influenced the design of other similar hydraulic works in the Madras Presidency, and was the result of Colonel Cotton's appreciation of the old native engineers in India. So that there was no rashness in the design of the Godavari anicut section. It was simply confidence gained by Colonel Cotton's study of the ancient works, the stability of which had been proved during the lapse of ages. And thus he became the founder of the cheapest school of engineering in the world, as the Madras Engineering School undoubtedly was. Nor is it too much to say that if that school were fully understood, it would save millions of the money now being spent in all parts of the world, in retaining water for the supply of its great cities."

To the general reader the interest in the work lies mainly in the incidents of the hot official warfare which raged round this gigantic enterprise from beginning to end, and which seems to have been in no way relaxed even when the victory had been assured. The records teem, it is stated, with remonstrances from Colonel Cotton, and with replies, "now wrathful, now penned more in sorrow than in anger," on account of surprises sprung on the authorities in ever-increasing demands for funds. Well worth reading, as a commentary on Indian administration, is Colonel Cotton's despatch of November, 1852 (sent direct to Government in violation of all ordinary routine), with its pent-up indignation, restrained only by the soldier's sense of discipline; its withering complaints of the want of support; its entreaty for inquiry and inspection, for his "disappointment is that too little, not too much, interest has been shown respecting the works."

"An angry reply from the Governor seemed likely to bring things to an *impasse*, but the tide had happily turned, and the next report was so highly encouraging, that henceforth money was more readily granted; so that on one page we find a list of sums sanctioned on these works, at thought of which a few years earlier the revenue authorities would have stood aghast." Eventually there was recognition, "and in 1882 we have a notable despatch from the Secretary of State in which the total expenditure of £1,300,000 is reviewed, and which contains a cordial and gratifying acknowledgment from the Home Government of the success of the Works." [1]

To these remarks I add some notes, which have been given me by my uncle, General Fred. Cotton, on the valuable lesson of building dams in sandy beds.

"I think I am right in saying," says General Cotton, "and it may be of interest to those who are following Sir Arthur in his work in Hydraulic Engineering, that the most important step in his education was the lesson he learnt from the builder of the so-called grand anicut, which carried the surplus water of the Cauveri river into the Coleroon. This low weir is of unknown age, and, from its importance to Tanjore, always has been carefully watched. Every year some small sum has been expended in restoring any breakage of its plastered surface, and it was well this attention was paid to it. For on its being cut into for sluices being opened in it, which had for their object the removal, by the water discharged, of the accumulation of land in the Cauveri, it was found that this 'Grand' anicut work was hardly more than a mass of rubbish, mud, stones, and logs of wood, the safety of which depended solely on its then plastered surface. This was a fact not lost upon Sir Arthur, and it gave him, even with the slender means extended to the engineers of that period, the power to master and control the greatest river of the country. The fact was learned from an engineer of old times, but the courage with which Sir Arthur put the idea into practice in his great works was all his own. And, as been said by more than one of his profession, no English Engineer would have risked his reputation on the works he carried out so triumphantly. The four anicuts he built across the Godavari are not solid masses of

[1] "An Indian Romance." *Blackwood*, June, 1897.

masonry, but surface coatings of stone over the sand of the river bed, for which he substituted cut-stone for the plaster of the early engineers, but the principle was the same. The erections of these great works are not sufficiently studied in the present day. Indeed, the cheap School of Engineering, which he did much to introduce is, it appears, set aside for the extravagant system of England. And, after all, what is good engineering but economy! Any engineer can do anything with money; the question is how to do great things at little cost. In the sections above referred to, the use of well foundations is exemplified. The upper and lower retaining walls have wells for their foundation in sand of unknown depths. These wells are only six feet deep, and their sufficiency has been proved often; yet one hears still that in other parts of India, where they have been sunk in foundation, it has been thought necessary to sink them thirty or forty feet, till they come upon some solid ground stratum. It may be noted that a lighthouse, which had to be built on the sandy beach, on the coast of Madras, is founded upon wells eight feet deep, and never showed the slightest settlement."

Agreeably to a suggestion from the Board of Revenue, Major Cotton modified his section of the anicut [1] in the manner described in the following letter:—

"In reply to your letter respecting the mode of executing the curved surface of the anicut, I have the honour to reply, that I was afraid that the forming of the surface of the anicut with large stones, rudely fitted, would cause great delay, as every stone must be fitted on the work; however, upon considering the matter, though the stone is entirely without any regular shape, as in the localities mentioned, I thought it might be done sufficiently quickly; and I determined at all events to make a fair experiment, and I am happy to say that the result has far exceeded my expectations; about twenty-five square yards of half

[1] The character and extent of the modification will be found in the Irrigation Map of Godavari, which faces page 122.

THE GUNNARAM AQUEDUCT CROSSING THE GODAVARI RIVER.

p. 141.

a yard thick, composed of large stones, were prepared by crowbar men and stone-cutters at a cost of about fourteen annas a cubic yard, which would give under four shillings a cubic yard, including chunam (mortar), bricklayers, etc., the estimated rate for cut-stone being ten shillings. This was so well fitted that, with a good cement, it would do for an apron with an overfall, if the blocks were of a large size. I therefore consider the suggestion contained in the Board's letter a most important and valuable one. It seems entirely to remove the main difficulty in the execution of the work, as probably we shall be able to procure sufficient stone-cutters to complete the work in two years, if this kind of masonry is substituted for cut-stone everywhere, except in the lining of the sluices.

"The curved surface of the work according to the second section, if covered in this way, will be exceedingly strong, and much better than if covered with concrete, and the work will be considerably cheaper altogether than if it were executed according to the section first proposed."

Besides the anicut, which crossed the Godavari itself, an aqueduct of forty-nine arches, each of forty feet span, was built across an arm of the river. This was built entirely in one short season, and then overwhelmed with a flood, which subsided without having injured the work.

At no time did he claim that his work was perfection, though there are few men responsible for large undertakings, who came so near that ideal as did he. His own simple confession is contained in these words:—

"I cannot say that we have obtained all our experience without mistakes and accidents. There have been many of both; but we have found that they have helped to give us our present knowledge of Hydraulic Engineering in India, and a confidence which we never could have had, if we had attempted nothing. By God's blessing, all the great works were in the main successful, and are now in profitable operation."

"I have not the least doubt," he adds, "that both communications and irrigation will everywhere produce property to the value of much more than twenty times the outlay. The fact is that India, in its present unimproved state, is a mine of wealth far beyond that of any gold mine in the world. The richest mines in Australia only produce three and a half times the value of the labour bestowed on them, a man whose labour was worth £35 a year earning on an average £120 a year in mining."

Amongst the schemes now suggested, and for which estimates were sent in, there was one for works required in the central delta, between the two main branches of the Godavari. The chief of these was a great aqueduct already alluded to, remarkable in construction both in regard to boldness of design and execution.

Another was for providing irrigation to the lands on the left bank of the North-eastern Godavari: it included, among minor works, a channel twenty-four miles long to water forty-five thousand acres, and to become one of the great lines of navigation connecting the town and port of Coringa with the Godavari above the anicut, and so with the large towns of Ellore, Masulipatam, and all parts of the delta.

In reference to this matter he wrote: "How enormous is the loss sustained by the want of communications! No wonder the country yields so little revenue when the people are put to so great an expense merely for the conveyance of produce. If, as I feel confident is the case, a loss of much more than £7,500 would be sustained in the carriage of produce by this one line of thirty miles, if there were no canal—a line very far indeed inferior in extent of traffic to hundreds of miles of road in this Presidency—how large a proportion of the value of the labour of the population must be thus wasted! The money expended upon this channel, which, when completed, will be thirty-one miles in length, is about £5,000; probably £6,500 in all, will be the cost of it, or about £200 a mile. But this includes the making it a very capacious irrigation channel; and one half of the cost, at least, may be charged to the irrigation, leaving only £100 a mile for its cost as a navigable channel, a sum which, on *the calculation given above of fifty thousand tons a year, at two annas a mile, the cost of land carriage, would be repaid in two months.*

"The goods conveyed along it in the last three and a half months, that is, during the dullest time of the year, would have cost £1,500 to convey them by land, more than they have cost conveyed by water while the channel is yet in a very imperfect state.

"When people are relieved from this burthen, how can there be a doubt that a land revenue, which otherwise would be sufficiently heavy to paralyse the ryots, would leave them a surplus sufficient to enable them to be continually improving their lands?

"What becomes of the extraordinary idea that the country may be ruined by growing food too cheaply? The fact is undeniable that the districts that yield the largest revenue, in which the people are most comfortable, are those in which, by means of public works, the food is raised at the least expense and in the largest quantities. Tanjore, which for a long series of years has raised the greatest abundance of food, is that district in which land is most valuable; nor can a single instance be found of a district falling off in any way from the increased cheapness of production.

"It is easy to see that in the long run, a district which has to pay ten lakhs of bullion every year, to be sent to a distance, can much more easily do so when its food is grown so cheaply that it can afford to produce things cheaply for markets from which it can obtain bullion, than when the dearness and scarcity of food prevent it from selling things in other markets at a price which renders them marketable.

"But, whatever the theory is, the fact is undeniable that where grain is grown cheaply, a district flourishes, and the cheaper it is grown the more the district flourishes.

"It is not money, it is action which is wanted. If a small

portion of the money which is idle in every treasury were judiciously expended on public works it would not cause the smallest, even temporary difficulty, but would immediately improve the revenue collections, even those of the year in which the expenditure is made."

This chapter, perhaps, cannot be more fittingly concluded than by one more passage from his facile pen. Often speaking of the people's new resources, and consequent ability to trade with other places, and to purchase goods, from the want of which they had previously suffered severely, my father writes with regard to the increased traffic of the districts: "I am convinced that this prodigious change may be taken as a specimen of what may be effected in every branch of the social condition of the people of India. Hope, and consequently life, has been thrown into this population. They now begin to find that it is better really to work, and thus to live in comfort, than to pass their lives in sloth and abject poverty."

APPENDICES.

Taken from Mr. J. H. Morris's "History of Godavari."

I.—PROSPEROUS HOUSEHOLDS IN GODAVARI.

The ordinary dress of a ryot is very simple. Its cost varies according to the quality of the material, but the average value of a man's costume is from two to five rupees. It generally consists of a lower garment (dhóoati), of an upper garment (uttariyam), and of a turban or head-cloth (pága).

The house usually occupied by an ordinary ryot is as simple as his costume. It consists of one or two rooms built with mud, and thatched with palmyra leaves. The ploughing oxen, or the cows, frequently occupy part of the same building as the family. A few earthenware pots and brass utensils comprise the whole of the furniture, with the exception, perhaps, of a low cot or "charpoy," with the bottom made of tape. The increase of the family prosperity is chiefly seen in the better quality of the clothes worn, in the superior kind of food eaten, and especially in the greater number of jewels worn both by the men and by the women, particularly on the occasion of the usual Hindu feasts. A prosperous townsman generally inhabits a rather larger house than the peasant does. His house consists, perhaps, of three or four rooms, with a courtyard in the centre. A raised chunam seat—called in the south a "pial," and in the Telegu country *arugu*—is to be seen on each side of the entrance door, where the owner sits in the cool of the evening to hear the gossip of the day, and to chat with his friends. The utensils are very similar to those in an ordinary ryot's house, only of a better quality, and more numerous. There are more brass pots and dishes, and other vessels, all being kept scrupulously bright and clean. Some of the cups may be of silver. Of what we call furniture there is none, except a few chairs in the houses of the most wealthy, who may desire to imitate European manners. Generally there are a few lacquered wooden boxes to contain the family jewels, cooking utensils and palmyra leaf books, or perhaps a mat or two, or a rug to sit on. The general articles of food are rice, dhall, curds, and buttermilk, tamarinds and ghee—that is, clarified butter—and vegetables. Some of the lower castes eat meat and fish. The lowest orders live on raggi, or on Indian corn. The average monthly expense of the household of the middle class is about thirty shillings, and that of an ordinary ryot is eight shillings (pp. 87, 88).

[The average income throughout India is only two shillings and tenpence.]

THE RIVER AND THE DELTA.

The magnificent river to be utilised, after a course of several hundred miles across the Peninsula, enters at about sixty miles from the sea the alluvial country, which it has itself formed. "This alluvial land does not immediately expand to a great width from the point at which the river leaves the main range of the hills, there being still rising ground and detached patches of hills at a distance of from half a mile to five miles from the river, for a distance of twenty-three miles further; at the end of which distance two or three detached hills come close to it, the river divides into two streams, the alluvial country spreads out on both sides, and the delta may be properly said to commence, extending on the west side till it meets that of the Kistna at the Colair Lake, about forty miles, and on the east side about thirty-two miles to the shore of Coringa Bay." This was the delta which was to benefit by the projected irrigation. . . .

The country which was to be irrigated by means of the proposed anicut consisted, with the exception of a strip of sandy land bordering on the sea, of a noble expanse of rich alluvial land fit for almost any cultivation, if well supplied with water. It was estimated to contain about 1,300,000 acres, out of which, deducting one-fourth for sandy tracts near the sea, sites of villages, and channels of rivers, there would remain 1,000,000 acres fit for cultivation with paddy or sugar-cane (pp. 110, 111).

THE APPROVAL OF GOVERNMENT OF THE GREAT WORK.

The sanction and approval of the Madras Government were cordially given. "This great undertaking," they said, "appears to have been projected with the utmost care and circumspection. In 1844, the Government had under examination the general state of the Rajahmundry District, and entered upon a review ot the causes, which led to the deterioration of the revenues and the depressed state of the ryots; and it appeared that the total neglect of the works of irrigation under the Zemindari system, the apathy displayed by the Zemindars towards the improvement of their estates, and the evils attending the temporary and partial management of the local revenue officers, were amongst the chief causes of the impoverishment of a province on which Nature has bestowed so many advantages in soil and situation. The time has arrived for the introduction of such measures of improvement as will tend to promote the prosperity of this rich but hitherto neglected province, and his Lordship in Council feels satisfied that no measure is more calculated to produce an extensive beneficial effect than the project now under consideration.

"There seems no reason to doubt that an anicut across the Godavari will be as advantageous to the Rajahmundry district, as the Coleroon anicuts have been to the Tanjore and Trichinopoly districts; and it may be confidently expected, not only that a large annual amount of revenue, now difficult to collect, will be secured to Government without pressure on the ryots, but that a vast extent of the richest land will be made available for the cultivation of sugar and other valuable products.

"The difference between the calculations of the Collector and the Civil Engineer as to the probable increase of revenue that may be anticipated from the anicut is considerable; but if it had no other effect than that of securing to Government the sum of

£9,000 now annually lost, the object of its construction would be sufficiently gained. But, when it is considered that, exclusive of the extent to which Major Cotton is of the opinion the District of Rajahmundry will be benefited, the anicut will enable nearly 820,000 acres of land to be brought under perfect irrigation in the district of Masulipatam, it seems impossible to estimate, or to limit, the prospective advantages to the people and to the Government, that the completion of such a work is calculated to produce.

"One other point affords the strongest argument in favour of Major Cotton's project, that is, the frequent visitations of famine with which the Rajahmundry district has been afflicted, and from which the inhabitants have so dreadfully suffered; and if, as there is reason to believe, the proposed anicut will preserve the population of that province from the frightful scourge, there cannot be a question but that its construction should be advocated. His Lordship in Council resolves, therefore, to bring the correspondence on the subject of the projected undertaking to the notice of the Honourable Court of Directors, with the strong recommendation of this Government, that sanction be granted for the disbursement of the estimated amount, namely, £47,557, and that their orders be communicated in time for the commencement of the work at the beginning of the ensuing year.[1]

A FRIENDLY CIVILIAN.

That we have made the progress which we have is entirely owing to Mr. Henry Forbes, the Sub-Collector, whose vigorous and active measures have already roused the district to a degree that could not have been expected, and it may be said, indeed, that as respects the getting public and private improvements effected, the district is ten years in advance of what it was a few months ago. The people have come freely from all parts of the district, and both they and the native public servants now fully understand that the great improvements can be effected. The actual use of the Godavari water from the new channel as far as Samulcotta, over an entirely new tract, has also, no doubt, helped to enable the people to realise the practicability of improving the state of the district.

With respect to the estimate, as we have not yet trenched on the largest items, I cannot speak confidently, but so far as we

[1] *Minutes of Consultation o) the Madras Government, Revenue Department*, under date September 1, 1846.

have gone, I think there has been a fair result for the money expended. About £15,000 will be laid out in railways, boats, buildings, and machinery, all which will be of use in the execution of the remaining works included in the estimate of £120,000 (p. 128).

A BIG GALE AND A HARD TEST.

On September 16, 1849, an unprecedented rise in the Godavari occurred, accompanied by a very severe gale of wind, but the nearly completed anicut firmly stood the unwonted strain. The highest mark on the standard register at Rajahmundry was 31 feet, but this year the fresh rose to 33 feet 5 inches there, and to the height of 25 feet 4 inches at Dowlaisweram. The works came out of this very severe trial comparatively uninjured, although a good deal of damage was inflicted on the buildings of the establishment connected with them (pp. 125, 126).

A CIVILIAN ESTIMATE OF THE WORK.

Mr. Henry Forbes, the sub-Collector, wrote: "I cannot leave without regret a work which has been my daily occupation, and a source of constant interest to me, for four successive years; but I have seen it advance to such a point that my regret is unmingled with anxiety. Difficulties are now at an end; the Godavari is dammed from bank to bank; and to complete whatever may be left of the cut-stone work at Vijeswaram and to cover with cut stone the Ráli and Maddúru anicuts, alone remains to be done.

"From March 1, 1847, to April 30, 1850, there has been expended among the labourers for daily hire £23,913; and the total number of daily labourers employed having been 3,054,413, or the total population of the province five times told. In addition to this, there has at all times been a large number, particularly in the quarry, on regular monthly wages; and in this present year, when the building operations have been most extensive, there have been in constant employ 641 bricklayers and 365 stone-masons, of whom 308 bricklayers and 231 masons have been supplied from this district. Of the coolies working on daily hire, and taking the average at 6,500, about 1,200 have been furnished from Masulipatam and 5,300 from Rajahmundry. In this district each taluk has been called upon to supply a fixed number with reference to its size and population. The village officers have among themselves arranged the details of the quota from each village, and also for the regular relief of the parties at intervals of one month" (pp. 128, 129).

THE BENEFITS TOO MANY FOR ENUMERATION.

An endeavour has thus been made to give a brief, and, it is hoped, clear description of this invaluable work, as an appropriate close to the history of its construction. It would be difficult to enumerate all the benefits it has been the means of conferring on the people of the district, who still cherish the recollection of its founder in their household converse, and in their popular songs. "Peace hath her victories no less renowned than war," and few of her victories have such an enduring monument as the Godavari anicut (p. 180).

WHAT WAS DONE IN TWELVE MONTHS.

In the central delta the aqueduct has been completed, with the exception of the towing path. The channel above it, which had been almost destroyed by the river breaking in upon it in the flood, has been put in complete order, the main channel leading from it has been continued to tide water within four miles of the sea, and several miles of branch channels have been cut. It was highly interesting to pass over this aqueduct in a boat and see an ample stream of water thus thrown into the richest part of the district, in the height of the dry season, when a year before not a brick had been burnt towards the erection of this large work (p. 159).

THE CHIEF CIVILIAN OFFICIAL'S TESTIMONY.

I have thus endeavoured to describe both the anicut itself and the system of irrigation dependent on it, and to give an historical account of their construction. Little need be added in conclusion. It is impossible to overrate the value of these beneficent works. No one who has witnessed the very great advantage which they have proved to the people will consider that they have been the result of wasted or misspent money. The noble river, which formerly ran in comparative uselessness to the sea, has been restrained and bridled and sent abroad in a thousand channels to fertilize the land. The fluid, which is so precious in the arid climate of the East that it has been felicitously likened to "liquid gold," has been converted into capital, that has been repaid in what has proved better than the most enormous rate of interest, and has carried the blessings of fertility and contentment and peace to a region which, as in the great famine of 1833, was formerly desolated by the most terrible scarcity and drought (p. 164).

THE EARLY HISTORY OF THE PROJECT.

The final portion of the following brief narrative will serve to show how, in 1854, after the anicut had been in existence for several years, there was, in high quarters, scepticism as to the work, while the bit of early history calls for record:—

The whole story is so instructive that I cannot refrain from giving it a little more at large.

In 1779, Mr. John Sullivan, in his letter of February 3, fully explained to the Court of Directors the necessity for storing the waters of the Kistna and the Godavari.

In 1788, Lieutenant Lennon represented to the then Governor of Madras, that he had, in 1786, at his own expense, made a survey of the Godavari as far as where the Shevaroy falls into it.

In 1792, the Court of Directors, in their letter to Fort St. George, recognised the expediency of surveying the Kistna and Godavari, both with a view to irrigation and navigation. About thirty years after, the enterprising firm of Messrs. Palmer, at Hyderabad, attempted to navigate the Godavari as a private speculation, but were compelled to relinquish it, principally on account of the exactions of the various petty chieftains on the banks. It is only, in 1847, that an anicut is commenced across the Godavari. The paltry sum of £1,000 has only just been sanctioned by the Supreme Government for the survey of the Godavari, after a former refusal; and the last issue of the *Athenæum*[1] contains an account of the progress of the expedition of discovery as high as Chinnoor, two hundred and fifty miles from the port of Coringa. In spite of this, our present Governor, in his Minute on the Public Works Report, still continues to doubt whether the river will prove navigable, or the anicut stand. What an illustration of Horace does the Government afford! standing on the Godavari banks, with hands in pocket, and staring at the passing stream in stupid apathy since 1779:—

> "Rusticus expectat dum defluit amnis; at ille
> Labitur et labitur in omne volubilis annum."[2]

---

[1] A Madras newspaper.

[2] Pp. 299, 300, "A Letter to the Secretary of the Board of Control."

PART II

Lady Cotton's Reminiscences

The following interesting reminiscences by my mother (Lady Cotton) of her life in the Godavari district—to the breakdown of my father's health, owing to the enormous strain on his physical powers, which incapacitated him from further active work at the time—give indications of the great anxiety which weighed upon him at so critical a period in the progress of the works and which necessitated immediate and entire rest for both body and mind.

My dear husband, having sent in his plans for the improvement of the delta of the Godavari, was appointed to the charge of that district, and took up his position, with myself and baby, in a tope (or grove) on the bank of the river, about four miles from Rajahmundry.

There tents were pitched, and a rough building erected made with palmyra posts and thatched with palmyra leaves, which formed a happy home, full of large, wide, interests, as well as the interests private to myself as wife and mother.

Except for periodical attacks of jungle fever, God was very gracious to us in respect of health,—another dear little daughter was born to us in our rough house,—a sweet babe, who was her father's delight, and whose loving looks and ways, when he came in tired from his work, were always a refreshment to him. It pleased God to take her from us after about twelvemonths, and we buried her at Rajahmundry in a little graveyard looking down upon the river.

I have said our home was on the banks of the Godavari, but I ought rather to have said beside the river bed, for during nine months of the year, there lay before the encampment miles of dry and dazzling sand, in the centre of which ran what, in such circumstances, seemed a mere thread of water, and yet was of considerable width.

A village was near us, and the poor women coming from it were pitiful to see, as they toiled across the burning sand with naked feet—often carrying a child on one side, and a chatty, or earthen vessel, which might hold a couple of quarts, poised on their heads, it being their only supply of water for (it might be) a numerous household for the day.

It need not be said that the village and villagers were dirty in the extreme, and sickly too. The ground was dry and barren, no crops, no grass for the wretched-looking cattle during far the greater part of the year.

The thought comes now, how little begging there was, when the poverty was so great. The poor people could not at first seem to understand what the strangers had come among them to do, but they were always kindly and respectful, glad to see us and grateful for a gift, but never troublesome in any way.

When the floods came, after the rains had filled the springs and rivulets in the distant hills, there was a plentiful supply of water, a grand and noble river covered the sandy bed ; and looked beautiful indeed, but all too soon it disappeared, rushing on to the sea—of little use in any way to the land or people.

In 1847-48, the projected works were begun in earnest, and the tope became an active, busy scene ; about twelve officers and non-commissioned officers had been sent by Government to assist in brick-making, timber-cutting, stone-quarrying, working in iron and brass ; large workshops and busy, able workers gave promise of great improvements.

Soon thirteen hundred Indian workmen were employed. At first they were afraid to engage in the new occupations, and part of the labour had to be forced, but soon the work became popular among them, and when they found kindness was shown them, no oppression allowed, and regular daily pay given, they crowded to the spot and worked willingly and well. On Saturday, two days' pay was given, that they might have Sunday's rest, as on that day no work was allowed or done.

Every week evening, half-an-hour before closing time, the man in charge of each body of workers called the men separately by name, and gave them their day's wage in their hand, and at the hour for closing a gun was fired as the signal for every man to leave work and be free. This prevented their having to wait and lose their own time—away from their food and families, as is often the case, when so many coolies are employed together.

Men and women of different castes and from many different places being gathered together, the thought could not but occur to our missionary friends, "What an opportunity for preaching the gospel!" From several different missions workers came. The Rev. Henry Fox, C.M.S., then at Masulipatam, was one of these, and was greatly interested in the Telugu-speaking people.

Then there had been a mission conducted in the delta for several years; and Mr. Bowden, of that mission, used very frequently to visit the people.

There is little to say of fruit: one incident showed that the Word had not been spoken all in vain, and gave us hope. One of the missionaries was walking in the quarry, then a busy scene, and heard some of the workmen scoffing and taunting one of their number with belonging to Jesus Christ. Mr. Bowden asked the meaning of this, and while the man accused said nothing, the others persisted that it was true, that he was always thinking of Jesus Christ and His Word.

Mr. Bowden left the place, intending to take another opportunity of finding out more, and for that purpose went again to the quarry a day or two later. On entering it he met the man of whom he had heard these things, leaving his work, stricken with cholera, his companions still following him with taunts: "You need not be afraid to die, you'll go to Jesus Christ." He died that night, declaring himself a believer, and charging his wife to allow no heathen ceremonies when he was gone. Who can tell how many who heard the blessed news at that time believed, and entered into life!

So the time passed on in busy, interesting work. At last we were obliged to leave our home, as the neighbourhood had become too busy and noisy to be a pleasant place of residence, and another house, rather less rough and more commodious, was built for us, on the top of a low hill, a little farther from the river. It had several advantages and one disadvantage. Our hill had been found to contain a most convenient supply of stone, and a small railway had been made to convey it to the anicut. Sometimes the blasting in the quarry sent pieces of stone rattling upon our roof or falling round us. At a certain hour a messenger from the quarry would appear, requesting, with a salaam, that "Missis" would call in the children for safety, from, it might be, a score of blastings within a hundred yards of us! Our house was cracked in many places, the light appearing through the walls.

The snakes, too, were sadly disturbed by the blasting, and found the house a piece of comparatively undisturbed ground—a place of refuge! One evening an ayah, who had been left to watch the nursery, rushed into the sitting-room to tell us she had seen a large cobra glide into the room. We all went to see, and the children were taken elsewhere, but the snake was nowhere to be found. Still, the woman persisted that she knew it was there, so we bid her watch again. Very soon after we heard her scream; my husband got his gun, called a servant with a light, and went in. My sister and I listened eagerly; for some minutes there was no sound, then one barrel of the gun was fired, and I went to see what had happened. As I entered the nursery my husband fired again, with the muzzle of the gun under a chest of drawers, behind which the serpent had hidden itself. I can never forget the sight I saw—the cobra had raised itself to its full height, its hood was spread to its widest extent, its tongue protruded, and it was hissing in its rage and pain. It was powerless to do more, its back being broken ; it was soon despatched. We seldom went to bed without a provision of boots or brushes to throw at snakes.

On one occasion I went with the children to see a large blast, and we had been placed, as it was supposed, in a safe position, but the stones flew in an unexpected direction, and we had a narrow escape from very serious injury.

All this time the stones were being poured into the river bed, the anicut was progressing ; consequently the interest and excitement were great. The work was carried on with increased activity, and all the workers were labouring to the utmost of their strength, as the river might be expected to come down in flood on (or very near) the 20th June. All thoughts were fixed on the newly-completed anicut for many weeks before that time. Would it be ready, and would the masonry be dry and firm enough to stand when the great body of water reached it?

We had watched the swollen torrent in previous years, bearing down large logs of timber, and living trees up-rooted, roofs of houses, and dead animals (one year a large black bear). We could not but hope *that* year "the flood" might be delayed as long as possible. At this critical time the dear "Chief," worn out by the strain of labour, responsibility, and anxiety, became seriously ill ; a sunstroke, added to his labours, completely prostrated him, affecting him with severe nausea, so that, while support was specially needed, the name or smell of food even was loathsome to him. In this state he had been lying for some days and nights, and I had ceased thinking much of the anicut, because my heart was full of fears on his account.

After an anxious night, when the light was just beginning to dawn, I went out upon the hill a few steps to refresh myself with the sweet morning air. As I stood and looked towards the river, I was surprised to see one of the young officers making his way up the hill toward me at that very early hour. He soon arrived where I stood, and said he had brought bad news. There had been a perceptible rise in the river during the night. He had just been again to examine it, and there could be no doubt of a continued rise; the flood had begun. He ended his story with, "I have no hope that any part of the masonry will stand. The flood is coming nearly three weeks before its time!" I felt I dared not tell my husband. His life seemed hanging by a thread, and such news might cause his death.

I begged my informant to go away, and for a little longer at least to leave him in ignorance. But he wisely replied that would be of no use. As soon as the day had advanced he said the people would be sure to come with the news, and that I had much better go and break it as well as I could myself; he would remain to see whether I brought any orders for him. How I told the dreadful tidings I do not know. I am sure divine help was given to us both at that awful moment. I remember saying to him as he lay silent, knowing that nothing could be done to save the work, or hardly anything, "What would you do if you had no God to look to?" and he quietly answered, "I should destroy myself." But God *was* with him, "a very present help in trouble," and he was kept in wonderful peace.

The river rose and rose, until no vestige of the work could be seen, and we could only wait. Before the water had subsided, a steamer was sent from Madras to take him away for change, friends there being very anxious about his state; the Governor especially showed kind concern. One of the married officers most kindly offered to come into our house, and take charge of our children. So we left together, and went to Bangalore.

Before we left, or very soon after, I do not quite remember which, we heard that by God's most gracious care very little damage had been done to the anicut; the works stood beyond all expectation.

Thus far my mother writes. I resume my narrative:

The water came down on the occasion of these floods in

PENNUMANTRA BRIDGE, GOSTANADI AND VELPUR CANAL.

p. 157.

such tremendous power, that it took possession of the lowland on either side of the river, and during that time would wash away whatever obstacles might be within its reach. On one occasion we were absent from home; a friend told us of a strange sight that was witnessed. The water had taken possession of our house, which was on the lowland at that time, and had swept away furniture, boxes, baskets, and all sorts of articles from our dwelling rooms; amongst other treasures that floated down the stream were my father's cocked hat, in its tin box, and a very favourite book, which he and my mother had often read and studied together, marking with their pencils the passages they liked best. It was none other than *Madam Guyon's Autobiography*—a very rare book then, and written in old-fashioned English. So great a treasure could not possibly be lost, and the cocked hat must also, if possible, be saved. So a boat was sent out to the rescue; and, to this day, we have on our shelves the precious book, its leaves stained by that memorable flood.

It is interesting to me to look back to the Indian days, when the mingling of work and pleasure, which have been my lot all through life, first began. My father, as we have seen, was a man of earnest purpose. His devotion to his work, and the ardour with which he pursued it in all its details, even incurring severe hardships himself amidst his daily toil, left the mark of his own personality upon all those who were associated with him. It is not surprising, therefore, that on my own mind these early memories are clear and strong. The latter years of constant association with him, and knowledge of his life's interests, have helped to sustain and sharpen these memories; it is, therefore, with real pleasure that I am able to provide some reminiscences of those days.

To go back to my earliest recollections. I think I see him now when I was a tiny child in India. We were all living then in a rough temporary house on the banks of the Godavari. The house stood on a rocky hill, the further side of which was being quarried, for the erection of the great anicut. His lithe figure and rapid step are impressed upon my memory as he walked from the house or entered it in his holland blouse with a leathern belt round his waist and pith hat on his head, to keep off the rays of the morning sun. The heat was very great in this part of Southern India, but he never allowed it to interfere with his daily task. He often laughed over the care that many Englishmen took of themselves in that climate, saying that he never stayed at home for the heat, but worked just as he would have done in England, being out amongst his men, giving his orders, and carefully investigating every part of the operations throughout the district. For days together on his long expeditions he would live on milk and bananas, which he would purchase for a few pice from the people in the villages through which he passed.

Even in that great heat he would walk for hours, and never seemed to feel the effect at the time, though I remember that on one particular occasion, when he returned from a three days' absence which he had spent in travelling some distance by stages on foot, he walked straight into the house, without even greeting my mother, and threw himself down on the bed, where he instantly fell asleep and thus remained many hours. He then woke up quite refreshed, and was ready for his work. He was untiringly active, and too anxious, perhaps, to make every officer who worked with him carry out his long programme of unwearying effort, but not a hard chief to get on with, and all his coädjutors loved him.

He had the greatest love for Christian mission work ; he oved the missionaries too. He hardly asked or knew the section of the Church of Christ to which they belonged ; they were God's servants ; they were labouring for the souls of men ; they were carrying the personal message of the gospel, with its present blessedness and its future joys, to those around us who knew not the gospel. That was quite sufficient for him. The missionaries always had a ready access to the house, and a hospitable welcome when they came. Many and many a one could tell of his loving gifts and his self-denying kindness to them in their difficulties.

On Sunday a service was held for the English people; my father would often conduct the service himself—reading the prayers, giving out the hymns, and finally reading a sermon from the works of one of his favourite divines. Those happy days and Sunday services I well remember. We often went to church at six o'clock in the morning, as later on the heat would have been very trying.

His kindness to the people of the country was extraordinary and to all who worked under him; he was greatly beloved, and we have been told that his name is still well remembered, and that he is always looked upon by those who have benefited by his labours as their benefactor and friend. They could see the practical results of his daily toil in the free profusion of water, which passed from the channels which he cut, to their very doors, irrigating their fields and supplying their villages with the much-needed streams, which saved them from famine, and also delivered them from the consequences of flood.

Our servants were divided into different classes—one servant would not touch another's work; each must perform his or her duties according to his or her caste. The lowest caste of all are the sweepers, and they may not eat their food with any of the other servants, nor may they mix with them in any way. One of these poor women came one day to my mother, and said to her, "Please, Missis, advance one half rupee."

"What do you want it for, Letchee? You know I do not like to pay your wages in advance." (Letchee's wages were only six shillings a month, and she had to get her own food and everything else out of that.)

She would not say what was her reason for asking for the half rupee in advance, but only repeated her request, making very low salaams, bending her head nearly to the floor, "Please, Missis, advance one half rupee."

At last my mother said: "There it is then; I will give it you."

She next asked if she might go to the market at Rajahmundry, about ten miles from our house. She returned the same evening carrying a little child. The tiny creature had, as is usual, no clothes on; its head was shaved, all except a little black pigtail at the back. The wee baby was brought into my mother's room, and exhibited with great delight by its new mother. "Please, Missis," she said, "I very lonely. So buy baby . . . for one half rupee—in market."

From this eventful day, Letchee was seen performing her daily work with the baby sitting cross-legged in one corner of the room. She loved this little child very much, and would sing and talk to it all the time she was sweeping. When it died, after a year, she was quite broken-hearted.

Many a little present from humble givers was brought to us (the children) at the Godavari, as an expression of gratitude for my father's kindness. He and my mother did everything in their power to lessen the troubles and help to comfort the people in times of sickness and distress. Trays would be brought in to us often, laden with toys and animals made of sugar; and little articles of wood exquisitely carpentered by some of the men in the place were given to me.

I well remember many of the young officers who worked under my father: they were all more or less inspired with the spirit and energy which so continually moved him; but, more than that, his influence spiritually was beneficial to all those around him.

I never remember a dull moment in those early days of ours, when all hours of the day were alike filled with useful, pleasant recreation; they passed only too quickly. I think that when children live in an atmosphere of busy, useful work, they learn to realise the importance of time and its value; we were always taught to do something, and that there was no happiness in being idle. "If you want rest," my father used to say, "vary your employments. Nothing relieves the mind and body from fatigue like this."

His life, while in India, was indeed one of toil and exposure; still, he was always bright, genial, full of fun, and ready to devote his leisure hours to those around him, if only he could do anything calculated to give them happiness and amusement.

The wildness and solitude of some of these places in which we lived in South India could hardly be believed now. The jackals howled round the house through the nights and long twilight evenings. The rafters of the house were generally open; there were no ceilings to the rooms; more than once snakes have dropped down on to the floor in front of us, and once even, one fell on my mother's lap. On another occasion, she had lifted her baby from its cradle into her arms, for no apparent reason, but just that she wanted to rock the child more soundly to sleep on her own knee. As she did so, she saw something move in the little bed; she raised the pillow and a snake crawled out from under it.

Very often we travelled in tents from point to point, to the different places to which my father's engagements led him. I remember now, seeing him constantly surrounded by maps, which he used to study, making notes of the delta of the rivers, and planning out his canals. Life seemed too short for him, his active and mental work were carried out on so large a scale. Little as we understood of it while we were children, we always realised the importance of the weight of care, that rested on our father's shoulders.

There was an occasion of great danger to us all (already alluded to by my mother) when a huge rock in the quarry was being blasted, and we were allowed to stand in one particular spot, which was supposed to be at a very safe distance from the explosion, to see the rock shattered, and hear the noise that it would make. However, by some accident, the rock was burst in another direction from that intended, so that the splinters fell on all sides of us. My brother, who was a small child, and carried in a bearer's arms at the time, had an exceedingly narrow escape of being killed on the spot ; and I, a little child oı about eight years old, had my bonnet torn with the sharp stones that passed through it. Mercifully none of us were hurt.

ALAMUR LOCK WEIR, FROM BELOW, CORINGA CANAL.

p. 163.

CHAPTER VIII

Indian Family Life—Furlough—Home Life—The Star of India—Retirement

AS to our family life, while my father was engaged on his Godavari work, the days passed very pleasantly at Dowlaisweram. There was an early morning ride at five o'clock and breakfast on our return. Then two or three hours of lessons, and in the evening walks and rides or stories read aloud under the shade of the trees at the back of the house. About this time, my health not being good, I was sent to Madras to visit some relatives. We sailed from Coringa in a small Indian vessel, the captain of which was the kindest and most courteous of men. Our voyage proved an adventurous one, for, after we had been at sea two days, a terrific hurricane came on, and the ship was in great danger. Our experiences were not pleasant. My aunt and I were in one of the stern cabins, and in the middle of the night so rough were the waves that the ship lurched and rolled, the wind howled and the rain dashed against our port-hole, until at length the sea broke into the cabin, and the mattress on which I was laid on the floor was soaked with water; our alarm was very great, for there were now several inches of water in the cabin, and the movements of the ship having loosened the cords which bound our furniture to the walls of the cabin, it fell piece after piece on the floor, and finally "brought up" against the door, where it was piled in a large mass, threatening to fall on us at any moment. But when the morning came we could not make any one hear our cries of distress. The door was blocked, we could not hear if any one knocked, nor could they hear our voices from outside; the gale was still raging fiercely. I think it was eleven o'clock before help reached us.

When the captain went into his cabin which was adjoining ours, he shouted to us to ask how we were; we were then able to make him understand that we were in a difficulty, and could not reach our own door. He immediately sent for the ship's carpenter, who cut an opening between the two cabins. I was taken out from our surroundings, and put into the captain's berth; he spent the next few nights on deck whilst we occupied his cabin. It was indeed a relief when the storm died down, and the beautiful calm set in. The ship was not materially injured, and we were enabled to reach land in safety after a fortnight's tossing on the rough seas. This journey would ordinarily have taken about four days. Travel in India has vastly improved since those days. One of Sir William MacKinnon's British India steamers would now cover the distance in less than two days in any weather.

Leaving Madras, I went with my relatives to the hills, where my mother joined me in a short time. She told me that my father was coming and, to my great joy, took a cottage in these lovely surroundings: it was like so many of the hill cottages in India, bowered in roses, surrounded by strawberry beds, with many other English delights. Even in this charming place, we were exposed to the inroads of visitors not usually expected in a similar cottage in England—rats, centipedes, snakes, scorpions, and shiny green frogs, used to traverse our house as if it were their own. It is astonishing how speedily one gets used to this sort of thing, looking calmly on what seems, when described, very unpleasant.

We did not know exactly the day on which my father would be able to reach us, so our excitement was great when we were told, early one morning, that he had just arrived, after climbing the hills on foot and taking short cuts to reach us quickly. I forget for how many hours he had been walking, but I know that he had no sooner gone to rest after his morning meal, than a messenger came running to the house, asking if Colonel Cotton had arrived. Though my mother explained that he was resting after a long journey, the messenger would brook no delay. He kept on repeating that the lake at Ootacamund had disappeared.

"The lake all gone, all gone! Colonel Cotton come tell us what to do."

It was discovered that during the night the dam across the bottom of the lake had been swept away, and the waters, having burst their barriers, were flowing in torrents down the sides of the hills. No one could tell what the results might be. My father's presence was greatly needed and here, as elsewhere, he found work ready for him.

On leaving the hills he went to Madras, having been appointed chief engineer for the whole Presidency, a very important position. It necessitated our leaving the old home on the Godavari to take up our residence in the neighbourhood of Palaveram, six miles from Madras.

My mother and I made our journey from the Neilgherries to Madras alone. We travelled either by bullock-cart or palanquin, according to the state of the roads. Our palanquin bearers sang weird, monotonous songs all the way, in order, probably, to help them to keep step, and perhaps to make the journey seem shorter. Travel of this kind is now almost unknown, certainly to the ordinary visitor to India, and though our experiences were not specially exciting, they may perhaps bear record.

Late one evening the palanquin in which I was travelling, at a short distance from my mother's, was suddenly dropped and dark faces peered into it, curious to see the little white child. That child's terror may well be imagined, but her tears soon brought gentle and loving words from the onlookers, and the bearers took up their burden once more. Further on, when we were travelling in a rough cart drawn by bullocks, we came to a rest-house —practically an empty house, as travellers in India then generally needed only the shelter of a roof, for they carried bedding and other necessaries with them. There were but two rooms; the furniture consisted of one bed and a few chairs, all in a most dilapidated condition. Exhausted with the long journey and the heat, we were compelled to shelter and rest for a time, but, unfortunately, we found that our provisions were not fit to eat, having become stale and mildewed. We were dreadfully hungry and though the rest-house keeper could give us nothing whatever, my mother did not lose heart. The burning heat and solitude of that place we can never forget. Suddenly, to our intense surprise, we saw, through an open window, a native servant coming towards us. He was neatly dressed, as though in attendance on an English gentleman. Having attracted my mother's attention, he handed to her a note from a gentleman, who had pitched his tent close by, an Englishman, who had heard that a lady and her child had come to the lonely rest-house. The note merely contained a few lines, offering, in the kindest possible manner, whatever supplies my mother might desire, adding that his servants were at her disposal, and he hoped she would allow him to send round luncheon. Overcome with gratitude, my mother gladly accepted this offer, and before long, a tray of appetising provisions was brought. It was indeed, in the circumstances, a luxurious meal. Nor did the kindness of the giver end here. At sunset, when we started again on our journey, we found that our unknown benefactor's servants had brought us a bountiful supply of provisions for the rest of our journey to Bangalore, where we stayed with friends. The Maharajah of Mysore, who had heard of my father's achievements, gave a reception in our honour. To us that reception was a strange, but agreeable, experience. A goodly number were in attendance and not a little magnificence was displayed. The Maharaja treated us with great kindness, and offered us every hospitality. His gardens, formed of stiff little flower beds and white glistening fountains, out of which the water rose in columns, were picturesquely arranged.

His crowd of tame animals, and his innumerable servants occupied my attention, while my mother and our friends talked with the Maharajah himself.

At Madras we found my father waiting for us and we all went together to our new home. It was as airy and cool as any place could be in that southern land, a few hundred feet above the sea. From its terraces we looked down on one side to the plains stretching far away until lost in a haze of heat, on the other side over the Bay of Bengal towards the sunrising. We were only a few miles from Madras, and though busily engaged in office work during the day, my father found time in the early mornings and evenings to help in mission work, while my mother visited the soldiers' wives in the cantonment, arranged for mothers' meetings, and clothing clubs, besides caring for the sick. My father generally took the service on Sunday in our little church, as there was no resident chaplain; sometimes a clergyman from a distance came over to take duty.

About this time my father felt how unfit he was for life in the tropics. In a letter written to a relative he says: "My health has greatly improved by my tour, and physically I am well, but mentally very weary. There seems no probability of my being able to remain at my post. I fully expect that I must give up my duties, and my dear wife's health is so uncertain that she must, if possible, leave India. Every way seems closed to me, but He who has provided for us hitherto will not fail now to help and direct."

Medical advice made it clear that it was absolutely necessary for my father to have a prolonged rest; consequently we sailed for England on March 8, and arrived on July 2. The voyage occupied four months, during which time small-pox broke out on board, to the terror and agitation of the passengers. The first child affected died, the disease spread, and thirteen others found their last resting-place in the deep.

My father occupied himself during the voyage in reading, in making calculations and notes in connection with the many projects he was ever pondering, in talking them over with the passengers, and in winning all hearts, old and young, by his cheery and genial manner.

The captain of the ship in which we sailed, Mr. R. D. Crawford, one of Sir Arthur's early friends, writes of this voyage:—

"I had some misgivings as to how so active-minded a man would feel, with no direct occupation, on a voyage of three or four months; but he always appeared to be perfectly happy, and contributed greatly to the general cheerfulness. Soon after starting, he asked me to let him have the 'cuddy'[1] after breakfast each day for prayer and Bible reading; but I said as it was the only public room I feared interruptions, which, though I should regret them, I should not feel that I could use my authority to prevent. A day or so after he told me he had found in the steerage what he thought a suitable place. He kept up the reading and prayer there all the voyage, and most kindly told me that he felt I was right as to the 'cuddy.' I often attended myself, and realised what truly Christian feeling he showed in the matter. I remember I requested him to sit opposite to me at the table for the sake of general conversation. He consented at once, and we all benefited greatly by his talk. But his power of abstraction was so perfect that, on many days, I have said to those near me, 'We shall not get a word to-day from the Colonel,' and I was sure that he was too fully occupied to hear me.

"We had a good many children on board, and he felt much for one of them who, having been left completely to ayahs, could not talk with the rest, or understand them. Finding near the end of the voyage this child chatting merrily with the others, he was greatly pleased at the proof thus afforded of the superiority, over books, of learning orally first.

[1] East Indiaman equivalent for saloon in the big ocean steamers of to-day.

"Subsequently, he wrote a pamphlet instancing this, and got two men going to India to promise not to look at a book till, with a munshi, they had got words and accent, with the result that in two years the natives said they spoke just as one of themselves."

When we reached London, though it was the hottest July weather, my father felt the change intensely. His health was in so delicate a state that it was considered advisable that he should leave Town as soon as possible. He went for a short visit to Penge, near Beckenham, to renew his friendship with the Rev. Frederick Chalmers, who at the age of seventeen had fought side by side with him in the first Burmese war, and for whom he always cherished the deepest affection. Mr. Chalmers lived at the delightful house which, in after years, we learned to know and love so well—Beckenham Rectory. It was a large house and always full, for Mr. Chalmers and his wife as well as her beloved sister, Miss Marsh, and aged father, the Rev. William Marsh, D.D. (author of many once popular works, such as *English Hearts and English Hands*), dispensed an almost ideal hospitality. The hall door was always open; friends came and went in the pleasantest way, and every day, at noon, the family met in the drawing-room, or in the garden, or in Mr. Chalmers' study, for a short Bible reading.

In the *Memoir of the Rev. F. Chalmers* is an allusion to his first meeting with my father at Beckenham, after so long an absence:—

"Many were the pleasant meetings at Beckenham Rectory with friends of former days; but none more pleasant than the unexpected arrival of Sir Arthur Cotton. It was on a summer morning, and the doors were wide open to the sunny air; family prayer was just ending, when a stranger entered, unheard and unobserved, and knelt just behind Mr. Chalmers. As all the voices joined in the Lord's Prayer, the stranger's voice was heard amongst them, and scarcely had the last 'Amen' been said, before the friends and comrades—parted for thirty-six years—were clasped in each other's arms."

From Penge we went to Tunbridge Wells for a short time; but he longed for more quiet than is to be found in that somewhat lively resort, and was anxious to find a warm climate in which to spend the winter. Eventually he took a house at Weston-super-Mare, where we spent six months; from there we moved to a lovely place in Gloucestershire, on the Cotswold Hills. The luxury and delight of that old-fashioned house, and well-filled flower and fruit gardens, we shall never forget. To an Indian family the pleasures of English country life are indescribable, and certainly we enjoyed them to the full. My father very willingly helped the clergy of the neighbourhood in their work and enjoyed intercourse with some of the manufacturers, who had mills and cloth works beside the river, that flowed through our grounds, whose waters were stained with a deep indigo blue from the dyes that were used. It was in one of those villages that he gave an address at a Church Missionary Meeting, the notes of which we still have in his own handwriting. He said:—

"I have been more than thirty years in India, and having been generally throughout that time travelling about the country, I have had much opportunity of observing the progress of things among the native community; and nothing can be more certain in my mind than that, through missionary operations and other means which have operated in God's gracious providence, there has been a wonderful preparation for the spreading of the knowledge of our Lord and Saviour, Jesus Christ, throughout India.

"When He visited Samaria, He said to His disciples, 'Behold the fields are white already to harvest.' He clearly foresaw, not by Divine power, but by the signs that He had witnessed, the reception of the Truth at the preaching of Philip, which is afterwards recorded in the Acts. The signs He had seen were the simplicity of faith shown by the woman, who said, 'We know that Messiah cometh, who is called Christ; when He cometh, He will tell us all things.' The eagerness with which she ran to tell her fellow-townsmen that she had found the Messiah, and their ready reception of her testimony, and anxiety to keep Him among them, were all proof of ready faith.

"Here, I think, we may draw two inferences from what occurred on that occasion, which will bear directly on the matter about which we are met.

"First. Jesus says to His disciples, 'Say ye not, there are yet four months, and then cometh harvest?' as though He had said, 'How clear is your perception, and how strong your faith about the things which are seen and are proved!' Four months before harvest; that is when the blade has but just appeared, where there is nothing to be seen but what can scarcely be distinguished from grass or weed, you speak with the utmost assurance of a coming harvest, as if you already saw the reapers filling their hands with the golden corn. Why did He say this but to call His disciples to observe how well, were they equally observant about such things, they might discern the joyful symptoms of a coming spiritual harvest—of the time when a glorious crop should be gathering in.

"And, secondly, He says, 'Other men laboured, and ye are entered into their labours.'

"I think from this we must conclude that this poor woman had not obtained her faith, as it were, by accident, but that, at Samaria also, there had been humble, patient, persevering preachers of the coming Messiah, labouring diligently, hoping against hope, among these outcast Samaritans, according to almost universal experience, in spiritual things, as in material things, that when there is a harvest, there has been a seed time long before—this is of the greatest importance at this time, and worthy of our earnest consideration with reference, indeed, to the whole vast field of operations of this blessed society, but I would observe more expressly with reference to India, because I wish to speak of that which I have seen, and about which I am myself conversant.

"Would not our Lord say of India, 'Other men have laboured.' For how many years have simple, faithful, self-denying, practical and persevering men lived and died in that country!

"These men truly hoped against hope—they were indeed children of Abraham; they were opposed to the utmost by a so-called Christian Government, they encountered in all its strength, the madness, the stupidity, the love of sin, the system of idolatry, which Satan had been for so many ages training his dupes to raise against their own salvation; they laboured some ten, some twenty, some thirty years, often the case appearing more and more hopeless, with nothing to support them but the plain commands and promises of God, except that now and then God was pleased to remind them that when He would work, none would let, by giving them the soul of some poor perishing one for their hire, and these too often so weak that they were a constant trial to those who were trying to lead them in the way of Truth.

"At this time, how continually have they had to bear, in addition to so many trials, the blaspheming taunts of their ungodly countrymen, exulting over their small success. Perhaps many of them have died, without being favoured with even a few proofs that the Word they proclaimed was the power of God unto salvation, but, almost all, till of late years, without anything that would be called a harvest. It may be safely said of them—'They died in faith, not having reaped indeed, but having seen the fulfilment of the promises afar off.'

"But, now, what is the state of things? I am sure we have more than once to say, 'The fields are white already to harvest.'

"First. Government have, in a great measure, withdrawn their opposition.

"Second. Several of the local Governors are most heartily supporting the Missions, subscribing liberally to them, and presiding at the meetings."

From Gloucestershire we returned to London, where we spent the winter. A very sad winter it was, for whooping cough found its way into the nursery and the whole family became infected by it. My father was very ill, and my little sister, to our great grief, succumbed to it, leaving a blank that has never been filled.

We settled next at Barnet, within easy reach of London, where we remained for some years, and appreciated fully the ministry and work of the vicar, the Rev. W. Pennefather. My father, however, was not with us long. He was obliged to return to India. This was our first separation, and we all felt it keenly. It was followed by another trial, the death of my youngest brother at the age of six years.

Amongst the friends we saw at Barnet from time to time were Sir Herbert Edwardes, who had returned from India soon after the Mutiny, also Reginald Ratcliffe, who had bravely ventured on the race-course, and in other ways supported the open-air missions that were just then coming into vogue. The battle of life was as serious to him as the military engagements had been to Sir H. Edwardes and others whom we saw at that time.

I cannot pass over without further mention the name of Sir Herbert Edwardes—that most distinguished soldier and noble Christian, whose career was so much spoken of, and greatly noted at the time. I can call to mind his tall figure and handsome face, and his cordial, kindly manner. He had had many seasons of suffering and suspense, with regard not only to his military duties and the dangers to which he was exposed, but also on his wife's behalf, at that most terrible time, when she refused to leave his side, though in the utmost peril of her life, and it was not until he had sternly insisted on her removal to a safe place, that she at last, with many tears, quitted his side, and left him for a time, going with friends to a hill station in India, and thence to England. His bravery and indomitable determination to overcome difficulties are matters of history, and are beautifully told in the *Memoir* which records his life of usefulness, devotion, and courage. It is only to our personal knowledge of him that I refer here.

Amongst other interesting reminiscences of his life in India, and especially during the time of the Mutiny, Sir Herbert told us that one night, just after his wife had left, he was alone and looking forward with great anxiety to the coming day. He had noticed, when the troops had been paraded, the scowling expressions of the men and other threatening signs of probable insubordination. He had thrown himself on to the bed, hoping to get an hour's rest before what he feared would be a night of great responsibility and possibly of disaster. His orders were that he was to be called at once, should anything occur which demanded his presence. At midnight he heard the cry, "Sahib! Sahib!" He sprang up and, hastily pulling aside the curtain of the doorway, heard a loud hiss. He called for a light and there, above his head, was a large cobra with its hood spread. The servants soon despatched it, and the peril was past. "I returned to my room," he said, "with such a sense of God's care. I had been riding about the lines expecting my death every moment from muskets of angry men, and God has now shown me how death might have come in my quiet room but for His loving care and protection."

Not a few references have been made to the danger experienced from snakes. Every one who has lived in India knows of hair-breadth escapes. But, I believe, there is no record of any European—man, woman, or child—having died from snake-bite in India, at least for many years. I am told that a few years ago a discussion was raised in a Calcutta newspaper on this subject, when authentic instances of deaths of Europeans from snake-bite were sought, but none were forthcoming. Yet the latest returns show that in 1897 nearly twenty-one thousand Indian people perished from snake-bite. The habit of the native population of sleeping on the ground with the feet uncovered largely accounts for this great mortality. Deaths from this cause are hardly ever less, in any year, than the number given above.

Dr. Livingstone also was one of our heroes, having just returned from Africa. He took a small house near the Parsonage, where he and his family were gathered together after a long parting. He enjoyed the private life and domestic pleasures, which he had so nearly forgotten during his long residence in Africa, nor would he consent to be lionised, even in the smallest degree. The very power of English speech had almost forsaken him, and he had to hesitate for several seconds before he could give expression to his thoughts. On one memorable occasion he was asked to speak at a missionary meeting to be held in the schoolroom, and with many misgivings he undertook the task, but the result was nothing more nor less than a breakdown in the middle of his speech, for, as he expressed it, "the words would not come." In private intercourse he was delightful and would entertain and instruct us for hours together with reminiscences of his travels and adventures.

Amongst other friends resident in the neighbourhood, whose intercourse was a constant cheer to my mother, were Captain and Mrs. Trotter and their family, Mr. and Mrs. R. C. L. Bevan, Mr. and Mrs. Wilbraham Taylor, of Hadley Hurst, the Honble. Arthur (afterwards Lord) Kinnaird and his wife, and many others whom I might name.

General Colin Mackenzie was another of the friends whom we knew at this time. He also passed through the perils of the Mutiny, and not without personal danger. He was attacked at a defenceless moment by sepoys, and, as my father used to express it, was "almost cut to pieces by their sabres." It was said that he had thirty-seven sabre cuts on his body, but, owing to his vigorous constitution, and his wife's nursing, his life was spared. He was, indeed, a magnificent specimen of British manhood—tall, strong, and typically fair, with very handsome features. He visited the Godavari on one occasion, and it is recorded that "one of his first adventures was on the march from Madras, when, in endeavouring to cross the Godavari river at Rajahmundry, the strength of the current carried his horse off his feet. He disengaged himself, and swam, accoutred as he was, to the opposite bank, landing with his whip in his hand. His horse found his way to shore lower down."

His wife afterwards wrote of a visit from my father, as follows: "We had a delightful visit from Colonel Arthur Cotton, who did wonders for the Madras Presidency by his Irrigation Works. In ten years the revenue rose twenty-five per cent. and the exports were doubled. He told us of whole districts being depopulated by famine, and not a shadow of inquiry made, nor any remedy being thought of. Lord Dalhousie reported him to the Home Government as perfectly insufferable,' because he said the state of Cuttack was 'a disgrace to any Government.' He got out of the scrape by stating that it was 'formerly a disgrace, even to a Native Government, and that now *it was worse*,' neither of which facts could be denied.

"The Bhagavati, one of the rivers in Bengal, and, like all the rivers in that province, requires control, as otherwise it shapes its course yearly, cutting away banks and destroying property to an immense amount. There is not a stone in all Bengal, so there is nothing to oppose the progress of the water. A great part of the city of Murshidabad was threatened with destruction, and Major Mackenzie, being much concerned, took his friend to judge of the impending danger. Colonel Cotton sent in a plan for diverting the course of the current by 'groynes,' the whole expense of which would have been £2,000. Major Mackenzie backed the recommendation as strongly as possible. The Lieutenant-Governor supported it, but he and the President of Council were on such bad terms that whatever the one proposed the other opposed; the latter, as the acting representative of the Supreme Government, returned for answer that he 'did not see the Government was called upon to protect the city of Murshidabad!' And, of course, nothing was done."

Colonel Cotton had returned to Madras, but did not again occupy the post of Chief Engineer, to which he would have been entitled by seniority, had not the organisation of the Department of Public Works been altered, and the Chief Engineership allotted by selection and no longer by seniority. Colonel Cotton consequently became Commandant of Engineers without any special functions, and an informal adviser to the Government on engineering subjects.

During most of the troublous time of the Mutiny, he was in attendance on General Sir Patrick Grant. He went about with him from place to place, inspecting different stations, where it was thought danger might arise, but the Mutiny did not develop in the Madras Presidency, and he never once found himself in a disturbed district. He was at this time a guest of the Governor of Madras, for whom he had the greatest affection.

Although now Commandant of Engineers, and greatly occupied with military duties, Colonel Cotton was admitted to be the chief authority on all matters connected with irrigation ; not only in his own Presidency of Madras, but, generally, throughout India his counsel was found necessary, for in regard to irrigation he was without a peer. That this was emphatically so, will be apparent by an extract from Minutes of Consultation in the Public Works Department, dated May 15, 1858, when Sir Charles Trevelyan, Bart., was Governor of Madras. The final paragraphs of the Minutes were :—

"It is finally resolved that when pointing out to the Honourable Court of Directors the several difficulties which have been reviewed in these proceedings, the Government express their unanimous, strong, and earnest advocacy that all irrigation works which, on a comprehensive view of the wants of the country, may be deemed necessary to develop its undoubtedly great resources, be commenced at once boldly and on a large scale, be pressed forward throughout all times, and under all circumstances, and be looked on, and practically treated, as in fact they really are, as the most economical, because the most profitable, undertakings in which the Government could possibly engage. It is needless now again to bring forward the innumerable instances in which money has in this Presidency been most advantageously invested in irrigation works. The proceedings of Government have in this respect been only too desultory, too vacillating, and it is confidently asserted that India could be placed in a position to pay all her expenses and gradually discharge her debt far more readily and speedily by a judicious expenditure than by any scheme of retrenchment or reduction.

"It is right to add one remark to a paper otherwise too long. If we have done our duty at least to this part of India and have founded a system which will be a source of strength and wealth and credit to us as a nation, it is due to one master mind, which, with admirable industry and perseverance, in spite of every discouragement, has worked out this great result. Other able and devoted officers have caught Colonel Cotton's spirit and have rendered invaluable aid under his advice and direction, but for this great creation of genius we are indebted to him alone. COLONEL COTTON'S NAME WILL BE VENERATED BY MILLIONS YET UNBORN, WHEN MANY, WHO NOW OCCUPY A MUCH LARGER PLACE IN THE PUBLIC VIEW, WILL BE FORGOTTEN; but although it concerns not him, it would be, for our own sake, a matter of regret if Colonel Cotton were not to receive due acknowledgment during his own life-time."

At this time he reported to the Supreme Government on the project of irrigation in the Province of Orissa, which had been suggested by himself and entrusted to the Madras Irrigation and Canal Company. He also visited Calcutta, and gave a lecture on the subject of a dam across the Ganges at Rajmahal, and a canal therefrom for irrigation, navigation, and the supply of water to Calcutta, and subsequently reported on the same subject to Government.

Later on he reported, at the request of the Irrigation and Canal Company, on the Ganges Canal, with a view to a new project to be connected with it. His report, one of the ablest of his numerous writings, was printed without his knowledge, and fell into the hands of Sir Proby Cautley, who planned and executed the works of the canal, and who felt himself obliged to answer the criticisms of his work. Eventually it was fully acknowledged that Colonel Cotton's main objection to the site of the canal head on the hill, instead of in the plain country, was well founded.

In 1860 he left India,[1] and, on his arrival in England, received the honour of knighthood, and was entertained at a public banquet in London. No report of what passed at the banquet is on record; from all such manifestations

[1] The order passed by the Government of Madras is most cordial

Sir Arthur Cotton shrank with deep modesty which could not be shaken. Lord Halifax (then Sir Charles Wood, Secretary of State for India) conveyed the intimation of the offer of knighthood in the following letter :—

INDIA OFFICE,
Sept. 20, 1860.

DEAR COLONEL COTTON,—

I availed myself of the opportunity of my being in attendance on Her Majesty, at Balmoral, to bring before her your long continued and good services in the public

in its acknowledgment of his services. I reproduce it exactly as it appeared in the *Fort St. George Gazette*, Madras :—

MILITARY DEPARTMENT.

PROCEEDINGS OF THE MADRAS GOVERNMENT.

Read the following letter :—

From the officiating Secretary to the Government of India, Military Department, Fort William, 22nd December, 1859, No. 904, to the Secretary to Government, Military Department, Fort Saint George.

With reference to your letter, No. 3734, of the 21st October last, I am desired to acquaint you, for the information of the Government of Fort Saint George, that the proceedings of that Government in relation to the office of the Commandant of Engineers, are approved by the Government of India.

No. 3733, dated 21st October, 1859.

I am desired to observe, that when recently reducing the number of brigade commands in this Presidency, the reductions were carried out at once without reference to present incumbents ; but in the present case, the honourable the President in Council is disposed to approve of a different course, with a view, in some measure, to mark the valuable and signal services performed by Colonel Arthur Cotton, as especially noted in the minute of the honourable the Governor of Fort Saint George, dated the 17th October, 1859.

Order No. 121, 10th January, 1860.

[Communicated to the Commander-in-Chief, Commandant of the Engineers, and Pay Department.]

(*True Extract.*)

Acting Secretary to Government.

To the Adjutant-General.
" Commandant of Engineers.
" Military Auditor-General.
" Accountant-General.

works of Madras, and I have great pleasure in acquainting you that Her Majesty was pleased to signify her intention of conferring upon you the honour of knighthood in recognition of your services.

I remain, yours truly,

C. WOOD.

Col. Arthur Cotton.

Expression must be given to the view, strongly cherished by many of his friends, that Sir Arthur Cotton's remarkable services to India were never adequately recognised. This, one need hardly say, is no complaint of his; it is the complaint of his friends. He was a life-saver, not a life-destroyer. Had he killed in battle but a tithe, or a hundredth, of those he saved from suffering and premature death, he would have received the thanks of both Houses of Parliament, been made a peer, and have received a large grant from the public funds. That the opposite to this is the way we treat the heroes of peace shows how far our Christian nation is from the ideal which Christianity has set up. Mr. Deakin, speaking as one having no personal concern in Indian administration, is constrained to say:—

"It cannot be said that even upon the spot the services of the Engineers have been duly recognised by those entrusted with the control of the administration. Far-sighted viceroys have adopted a bold policy of expenditure upon irrigation works, and thoughtful members of other branches of the service have at times expressed their admiration for the ability which has made them a success; but the men themselves have rarely been rewarded as they deserved, either in view of the importance of their charge or its arduous conditions, even when measured against the always exhausting work of other officials in the same outlying districts."[1]

Again, he remarks: "Seeing their high character and great ability, recognising their physical trials when, in the

[1] *Irrigated India*, p. 230.

weary, wasting, feverish, autumn heats, the demands upon them culminate—the safety of the summer crops requiring them to be abroad daily, at a time of year when all the heads of the service have fled for relief to the coolness of the hills—it is not too much to say that, after all, the finest product of irrigation in India has been, and is, the gallant company of its Engineers. Enormous responsibilities are theirs, and they have discharged them with as much courage, and as much success as their brethren who have stormed the hill forts, or faced the tremendous odds of battle, planting the standard upon a territory which, even then, was but half won, seeing that it had next to be maintained by an endless struggle, no less severe, for fertility and against drought."

My father retired from his arduous labours in India, his health sadly broken, and his spirit worn and jaded by the constant struggle he passed through in his earnest, but often unsuccessful efforts to obtain the sympathy and interest that he desired from those in power, in order to continue and maintain the progress of the works which he had so much at heart. He was essentially a man who lived before his time. His ambitions were so great, and his sympathy so bound up with the interests of the people of that great country, to which, he considered, England owed such a debt of provision and protection, that he could not rest content with things remaining as they were, but always sought by every means in his power to alleviate the miseries which he witnessed in India, and to increase her prosperity. This burden weighed ceaselessly on his mind, and, much as he had been able to accomplish, he was always considering what more might be and ought to be done. He felt it his imperative duty to make India's wants known and to suggest remedies. He was never content to rest in the contemplation of the things that were past, but pressed ever forward to those which were to come. He had every confidence in his own plans, not only from his practical view of how these great and necessary works ought to be carried out, but also from the experience which the past had taught him. His schemes had proved far more beneficial than even he had estimated in his most sanguine moments. He had good reason to urge forward his crusade in season and out of season. Not irridescent anticipations, but sun-bathed successful projects, were the foundation of all that he urged. To carry out these great schemes he laboured incessantly both with his pen and by interviews with those in power. Yet so unwilling (or so unheeding) were those in authority to recognise the full significance of what Arthur Cotton had done, that at every turn he was met by the insuperable barrier, "No supplies." The furore of railways as the one means of communication in India had seized all in power, with disastrous consequences to that country.

When he returned to England at this time, he was, as I have said, broken down in health, and was advised to try a year's rest in some warm, sheltered place. He decided to go into the neighbourhood of the Gulf Stream, in the north-west corner of Devonshire. He was constantly liable to attacks of fever, and was so ill that when we reached Barnstaple, in search of a suitable house, he had to admit that he was quite unable to undertake even this simple task.

We had only been a few days in the town when a friend called and told us of a delightful place which was to be let. My mother drove over to inspect it, and found it replete with every comfort: fires burning in the rooms, lovely grounds, in fact everything that could be desired for our emergency. We were able to take possession at once, to the delight of us all. I shall never forget my father's gratitude for the provision of just such a home as he needed.

There was a very pretty drawing-room in this house, an oval-shaped room, with mirrors and china artistically disposed, besides Chippendale tables and other light articles of furniture. My father's first act on entering the house was to remove all the ornaments, and cover the tables with maps, papers, compasses, and measuring rules, as well as sundry other implements of his own particular craft. There was a good study, which was at his disposal, but his answer was: "Oh! I daresay I shall use that too. I like to see every room in the house fit for sensible employment, and I like to be reminded of India wherever I go." So nothing would induce him to allow the maps and papers to be removed.

He was very fond of colouring charts and maps, which he would spread on the floor, while he marked the course of the rivers, and the way in which canals for irrigation and navigation could be constructed. A map will be found, in pocket at end of book, showing India irrigated according to his ideas, and with the large storage centres which are necessary to maintain water in the channels in all conceivable circumstances.

CHAPTER IX

Earnest Endeavours to make India Prosperous rendered Futile by Official Inertness in India and in England

"I have heard the state of agriculture attributed to apathy of the natives, their want of enterprise, their dislike of change, but I cannot say that this view of the case is confirmed by my experience of the native character. I have generally found them open to the adoption of improvements, and to the introduction of any change, when satisfied that the same will prove personally beneficial; but, being poor, they are naturally very cautious in employing their labour in channels of which they have no experience. That the natives are not enterprising is true, but it is their poverty which is the cause. If they had the means and the education necessary, I believe you would not find them one whit behind ourselves in any enterprise which might be open to them."—JAMES THOMSON, *Merchant, President of the Madras Chamber of Commerce.*

THE closing years of Col. Cotton's official career, spent as they were at headquarters in Madras, afforded opportunity to him for taking a comprehensive view of the needs alike of the Madras Presidency and of India as a whole. He made full use of this opportunity. He propounded policies and put forward schemes, which, had the policies been accepted, and the schemes adopted, would have changed the whole history of the past half-century in India, and have given the future a hopeful, instead of the present almost hopeless, outlook. And, at this moment, when heart-rending accounts of the most awful human suffering is reaching this country from India, it is hard to restrain one's indignation at the indifference with which the later proposals of Sir Arthur were received at a time when, if they had been adopted, these troubles need not have occurred. The fight between him and his opponents, as will be shown again and again in these pages, was between railways and canals, or rather, between a few trunk lines of railway, and widespread navigation and irrigation canals. Because, in England, we are very familiar with the former, and know but little of the latter (to be almost more charitable in assigning a reason than the facts permit), railways were pushed more and more to the front, while water navigation and irrigation were relegated to the third place. Railways were an easy first, buildings and roads came second, with nearly twice as much money expended upon them as was spent upon the watering and improvement of the soil, though it was from this last the money had to come to enable the railways and the buildings and the roads to be constructed. An exact reversal of this policy, navigation and irrigation first, and railways third, would have worked such wonders in India, that the Empire would have been in the first rank of British dominions for prosperity, instead of being (the remark is deliberately made because it is founded upon Indian official publications), as it is now, perhaps the poorest and most distressful country in all the earth.

Colonel Cotton, in those last days of his in India, saw the existence of distress which would grow more acute in the future. In him,—

> "Old experience did attain
> To something of prophetic strain."

It was in earnest, even agonizing, terms, that he besought the rulers of India to apply to India the remedies which that country needed, and which were easily to hand, while he implored them not to introduce means foreign to the country's necessities;—not entirely in vain, for something irrigationally, although practically nothing navigationally, has been done. But the evils, against which Sir Arthur's remedies would have saved our Eastern Empire, have advanced in seven-leagued giant strides, while his remedies have been shuffled forward as with a slippered tread.

From Sir Arthur's writings during his last ten years in India I make some copious citations. Some of his remarks are fifty years old. They are as pertinent to the existing situation in India as though they were written this year. No one, who wishes to understand what may be done to lift India out of its present distressful and resourceless condition, can afford to leave these remarks unread. I commend them to my countrymen and countrywomen, in the prayerful confidence that some good will surely come to our unhappy Indian fellow-subjects from their republication at this particular time. Of the book then published, *The Times* remarked: "It is the solution of what has always been a most difficult and intricate problem, it sheds a flood of light over the dark future of our Indian possessions, and, while scarcely yielding in cogency of argument to mathematical demonstration, arrives at results at once practical and scientific—at once of general truth and immediate usefulness. Such as it is, we not only commend it to the study of India, of Presidents and Directors, but of every English gentleman who wishes to understand how the resources of modern science may be brought to bear on the happiness of individuals and communities, and how those principles, which every one is anxious to apply to his own estate, may be used for the regeneration of a mighty empire."[1]

Great would be the gain to India, if, once more, *The Times* would commend Sir Arthur Cotton's teachings, and so bring about "the regeneration of a mighty empire." These are among the observations which called forth the commendation of *The Times*:—

WHAT MAKES INDIA A POOR, AND ENGLAND A RICH, COUNTRY?

Why are the people poor? Because, being entirely without any means (excepting bullocks), which can be sub-

[1] *The Times*, Dec. 28, 1853.

stituted for human labour, it is as much as they can do to feed, clothe, and shelter themselves ; or rather, I should say, more than they can do, at least while they have to keep their rulers in luxury. This is the plain, indisputable answer to the question : Why are the Indian people poor? Now, as to the converse question : Why is England rich? That is, why has it the means of supplying itself with a thousand things beyond the mere necessaries of life? Because, though it contains only twenty-five millions of people, there is as much done by the aid of steam, water, roads, canals, railways, ports, docks, etc., as could be effected by the labour of perhaps two hundred millions of people without those aids ; and, having, therefore, the work of that number, while the necessaries of life are required for only one-eighth, there is, of course, an enormous surplus for other things. This is not peculiar to one country, for, if besides the labour of one hundred and forty millions in India, we had the work of another five hundred millions performed by roads, canals, railways, water, steam, etc., there would be in India also abundance of labour available for other things beyond producing the necessaries of life.

WHERE THE EVIL REALLY LIES? THE RULERS ARE MERE REVENUE COLLECTORS, THEY ARE NOT STATESMEN.

Now, where is the difficulty? Thousands want to lend money at four per cent. ; thousands of Europeans and Indians want employment as superintendents of works, etc. ; thousands of iron manufacturers and others in England want a sale for their goods ; tens of thousands of people in India want employment as labourers and artificers ; millions of ryots want water for millions of acres ; tens of thousands of miles of communication and means of carrying produce need to be constructed, and thus millions might be expended so as to yield ten, twenty, or fifty times the interest paid for them. Everything is ready except one thing. But there is, indeed, a difficulty, the difficulty which has kept India immersed in ignorance and poverty from the time we commenced our rule up to this day. It is this, that Englishmen, instead of coming to India to teach the natives the things which have made us what we are, sit down to learn of the natives the things that make them what they are. How wonderful it is, that the man who, if he were in England, would be certainly engaged in furthering everything in which England glories, should, in India, occupy himself from morning to night with this notable subject: the settlement of the land revenue of his district. He sees, for instance, that his district is paying £100,000 or £200,000 a year for the transit of goods, and that it cannot find a sale for what it produces for want of the means of sending it to places where it is saleable; and yet he is completely at a loss as to what can be done to relieve and improve it. He turns again to the "settlement," and tries once more what he knows has been tried a thousand times before in vain, how to make a district, steeped in poverty, pay additional revenue without increasing its resources. He sees and hears of capital, employed in almost every kind of public works, yielding fifty or one hundred per cent.; he sees that his own district, in producing certain articles of food, clothing, etc., pays double or treble what they could be procured for from another part of the country, if there were but cheap transit; whilst other districts are wanting, and paying double or treble for, things which could be got far more cheaply from his district; and yet he cannot think of anything to enrich his district except giving a little more time to the "settlement," or reading a few more thousand sheets of paper on that everlasting subject. Here is the real and sole difficulty. To remove it, one word from our rulers is all that is required; everything else is ready, and has long been ready. Let them only open a loan for twenty millions to begin with, order the expenditure of £30,000 a year in every district, purchase a million tons of rails and such other things as can be got at once for money, and will help towards the improvements of the resources of the country, and the whole difficulty is got over. This might be done to-morrow; nothing is required but that which has been so well done by the Governor-General, about the telegraph, be applied to everything else of this kind; that is, to say, "Let it be done." But, like everything else that has ever been done to promote the real welfare of India, it must come from without; it will never come from within, neither from the Court[1] nor the Civil Service. Every step in advance has been made not only without emanating from within, but in direct opposition to the utmost efforts of the Court as formerly constituted. The freedom of the press, the abolition of suttee, the admission of European merchants, missionaries, etc., steam communication, and now the electric telegraph, etc., etc., every one, without exception, has been hitherto, in some way or other, really forced upon the Indian House.

WHAT A SUFFICIENCY OF WATER WOULD ENABLE INDIA TO DO.

Now, if a community can purchase water at a certain price, and sell it again in the shape of sugar, rice, indigo, tobacco, pulse, cotton, etc., in unlimited quantities for fifty times as much as it cost, one would suppose that the question, as to how to make both ends meet, was settled. Such is, undoubtedly, the actual state of things in India. The prices of all exportable articles, whether rice or cotton for instance, are equally made of the cost of food and clothing. And if water be applied to diminish labour in raising articles of food, the proportion of the population set free thereby, will, of course, employ themselves in raising whatever their country is best suited to produce for foreign countries; and any quantity of cotton and other things can be sold to Europe, China, etc.

Port Philip, in Australia, has been loaded with wealth by discovering a thing which can be obtained at one-fourth its value, while India continues poor with a thing which can be obtained at one-fortieth of its value.

[1] The Court of Directors of the Honble. the East India Company.

THE USING, NOT THE HAVING MERELY, OF VALUE MAKETH RICH.

Nothing, therefore, can be more evident than that it is not the having a treasure in the country which makes it rich, but the taking every advantage of it. It is not the gold underground that made Port Philip rich, for it was not a bit the better for it for many years, but the digging it up and giving it in exchange for consumable things, etc. In the same way India will continue poor, even if water were ten times its present value, as long as it is not made the best use of, but still allowed to flow into the sea by millions of tons per second. The water that flows off in this way in an hour by the Godavari, is sometimes as much as four thousand million cubic yards, and is worth £800,000, or three times the whole revenue of Rajahmundry for a year. But, till it is made use of, the country continues just the same as if it had no such treasure.

How strange it seems that whilst the dullest labourer can perfectly understand the value of gold, the wisest statesman cannot perceive the value of that which is exchangeable for gold; so that though a hundred pounds worth of gold in the form of water can be obtained in India for £2 10*s*., no Indian statesman has yet been found wise enough to set a thousandth part of the population to work to obtain it; whereas, in Port Philip, when it was discovered that a hundred pounds worth of gold could be obtained for twenty-five pounds worth of labour, more than half the population were immediately employed in digging it up. Whenever the subject is stated, the defence is, "But, see what we are doing now! Look at the Ganges canal and the Godavari and Kistna works!" Suppose the Port Philippians had continued as poor as they were, and, upon somebody taunting them with neglecting their great treasure, they were to say in defence, "What shameful misrepresentations! Out of our sixty thousand people, we have got twelve people digging at Ballarat, and twelve at Mount Alexander," what should we think of their sense and activity? Yet twenty-four diggers bear the same proportion to the population of Port Philip as the sixty thousand employed in hydraulic works in India bear to the whole population of that country.

THE NEGLECT TO KEEP ANCIENT WORKS IN GOOD ORDER.

There is not a district in the Madras Presidency, except Tanjore, in which the old works are all in good repair.

It is not the ruinous wars that have kept us poor, but the most unaccountable neglect—a neglect the more extraordinary because it is not endured for a moment in other things. Let any man propose to provide money for wars by leaving buildings to go to ruin, and he would be thought mad; and yet this is only what is systematically done with works upon which the food of the people and the revenue depend.

India is like the field after an Indian battle; there is but one cry: "Water, Water." All that is wanted is water, and this want supplied, everything else will almost follow of course. Water for irrigation, and water for transit, will provide for everything else. Water is the universal solvent, and can solve that which has puzzled all the Indian wise men from Lord Cornwallis down to the present day, namely—the revenue settlement question. It has solved that question in Tanjore, the only district where it has been tried. When a man has to pay only twelve shillings a year for an acre of saleable land at four pounds ten shillings, the question is substantially solved. There may be, of course, a thousand questions of trifling importance about it, as there are about everything else; but the essential difficulty is gone. The real difficulty all along has been this—how to get twelve shillings of revenue out of a land on which the total profit was only ten shillings—and nothing but water can solve this; and it will assuredly do the same in every district of India where it is applied, by the simple process of making the profit on the land one pound or thirty shillings per acre.

COL. COTTON'S SINGULARLY ACCURATE PREDICTION.

Colonel Cotton, in his first report on the Godavari, made the following prediction :—

In examining the question of the propriety of such an outlay as this, there is one point which I consider deserving of particular attention; we are apt, generally, to think of a Government expenditure as if it were precisely similar to one made by a private individual; but, in countries circumstanced as these are, there is a vast difference, and especially in this particular case of Rajahmundry [afterwards Godavari] district. Ten thousand pounds cannot be spent in any district without a large portion of it immediately finding its way back to the Treasury, but, in this district, which is now suffering such difficulties from the immense diminution of specie, probably the greater part will be paid back in the course of the year. This additional circulation will enable many to pay their kists [taxes], who would otherwise not have done so; and perhaps there would be little more difference made by its disbursements, in respect of the state of the Treasury, than that such portion of the population as would otherwise have been not at all employed, or employed to little effect, would thus be usefully occupied. During three or four months the great bulk of the population are employed to very little purpose, where there is literally almost no capital to enable the landowners to make improvements. But an expenditure of £30,000 to £40,000 a year would put life and activity into the whole district. That part of the population which is just now, from the impoverished state of the district, a dead weight upon the rest from want of employment, would be provided for, and the supply of specie would give a great stimulus to the remainder. Indeed, I would state it as my opinion that, independently of the ultimate returns, the Treasury would not be at all the poorer at the end of the year; for such a disbursement, in the present state of the district, such an outlay seems to me more nearly allied to a loan from a landlord to his tenant, to be expended in improving his farm, than to simple expenditure.

"The revenue accounts of recent years," say the Public Works Commissioners, in a most elaborate and able report, "show how singularly accurate this prediction was."

The Commissioners themselves observe (section 269):—

"Even while the works are in progress and far from being complete, and while a large part of their effect is of necessity still undeveloped, the direct returns in revenue have amounted, taking each year's increase of revenue in comparison with the whole expenditure up to that time, to above sixty-two per cent. per annum on the capital laid out; and there is no doubt whatever that the future returns will be enormously larger, while to the people the change may be described as one from death to life: at so low a point were they before in poverty and indifference, so great is the contrast now in activity and energy. And all this has been obtained, it should be remembered, literally without any outlay, without any sacrifice of income whatever, for in every year of the progress of the work the increase of revenue has been materially in excess of the expenditure. It would be unsafe to reckon upon an equal measure of success in every instance, for the circumstances of Rajahmundry were peculiarly favourable, but we are bold to declare our firm conviction that there is no district in the country in which a similar expenditure would not be largely remunerative to the Government and a blessing to the people, though not in all to the same degree."

HAVE WE KEPT PACE WITH OUR INDIAN PREDECESSORS IN IRRIGATION?

In a work published in Madras in 1854, the question is asked: Is irrigation, on the whole, better or worse since the commencement of our rule? The writer answers his own question thus: "It is clear that the old works of irrigation are not kept in a sufficient state of repair. Their original cost is estimated at £15,000,000; their repairs cost annually £70,000; less than one-half of one per cent. on the prime cost. The estimated return to Government in the shape of assessment is £1,350,000 annually; the whole returns between Government and cultivators are £3,750,000, so that under two per cent. of their yearly return, and but four and two-thirds per cent. of the revenue derived from them by Government are expended in keeping them in order.

"This is evidently insufficient,[1] and the result is that the works not being in proper repair, so large a space of land is not now cultivated as formerly; and it is reckoned that in the twelve chief irrigation districts there are 1,262,906 acres of land, with an assessment of £475,480, once irrigated and cultivated, now lying waste, but capable of being again brought into cultivation, if the tanks and channels were put into proper repair; and many works are classed as in proper repair, though in fact they are not supplied with the full amount of water which they are capable of containing."

Mr. Dykes, in his *Salem*, informs us (p. 391) that there are in that district alone at the present time 8,864 wells, 218 dams, 164 small channels, and 1,017 small tanks, of which no use whatever is made.

Lieutenant Tyrrell writes as follows:—

"Regarding the present state of the country, it is deplorable to one who compares this old country with England or any country on the Continent; particularly when he comes to examine it attentively, and finds that there are tracts of ground, formerly cultivated, lying waste and overgrown with dense jungles; that broken tanks are met with constantly; and villages once large and flourishing are now perfectly deserted. The country here (Salem) is generally very fertile, and a good deal of grain is sown, but not one-half the quantity that might be raised. There are at least eight or ten broken or disused tanks that I have passed in a distance of thirty miles. One must have been of considerable size, the bund being about eighteen feet high. Towards the ghauts, particularly, are large tracts of land now deserted; the soil

[1] Colonel Sim, Chief Irrigation Engineer, is of this opinion. See his evidence before the Lords' Committee, 1853—Q. 8736–7.

is particularly fertile. They say that fever is the cause, but I am disposed to think that it is not so, as there are still some good villages who do not complain. Tengericottah is the most lamentable place; formerly a flourishing village, every requisite for extensive cultivation, now a perfect wilderness. A little engineering might supply an immense amount of water for irrigation."

This is declared to be no isolated picture applicable only to a peculiarly unfavourable district. "Lieut. Tyrrell is speaking of Salem, one of the finest collectorates in the Presidency; and there is no doubt that in whatever direction men push their enquiries away from the high roads into the less frequented tracts of the mofussil [country districts], similar reports will be the necessary result."

And the Commissioners come to the following general conclusion (sec. 240):—

"In short, all the works in the country, with a few exceptions, are in a state that may be called 'below par,' that is, they are below their state of full efficiency, and incapable of effecting their proper amount of irrigation. The tanks are in want of sluices, or such as they have are out of order, or they have no calingalahs, or such as they have are too small or too high, and so the stability of the tank is in danger; or the bank is low or weak, and the ryots are afraid to store a full tank; or their channels of supply have become choked up, and no longer bring a full supply of water. And as to the irrigating channels, many of them are in the condition described by Lieutenant Rundall, from the want of regulating works at their head; or they have become filled up by deposit, or the river has thrown up a bank in front of them, and they get no water; or they have too few outlets for irrigation, and the ryots cut through the bank; or the outlets are too large, and a vast quantity of water is wasted. Such is, unfortunately, the description which now applies to a very large proportion of all the irrigation works throughout the country, with the partial exception of the favoured districts of Tanjore and a part of Trichinopoly."

Nothing can be more satisfactorily proved by experience than the advantage of a liberal expenditure in repairing ancient works. For instance, in Tinnevelly, where operations have been confined to increasing the efficiency of existing works, and no attempt has been made to extend irrigation by new works. There (see *P.W.R.*, section 243) an outlay of £32,341 in fifteen years produced a direct return in revenue of £197,480, or about six for one, besides an addition of £3,000,000 to the income of the people.[1]

RESULTS ON BOTH SIDES OF THE RIVER.

Again, in South Arcot, in fourteen years, we have the following results :—

"Adding together the results on both sides of the river, the following are the facts :—The total cost of the anicut and all the connected works, inclusive of all repairs, to the end of 1850, is £45,667. The total aggregate excess of collections subsequently, over what they would have been in the same period at the average obtained before the improvements, is £180,029. Thus within a short period of fourteen years there has been a return of £37 10*s.* for every £10 expended, while the anicut and channels remain permanently valuable works. And taking their total original cost at £35,000, and assuming that annual repairs to the amount of even as much as two per cent. on that will be required to keep them in good order, we have the cost of these annual repairs £700 and £1,750, being interest at the rate of five per cent. on the original outlay, total £2,450, to set off against an annual gain of £12,875, being a net annual gain of above £10,000, clear of all expenses, obtained by an outlay of £35,000. And to this large gain to the Government must be added the share of the ryot to the amount yearly of £19,300 more; being an aggregate yearly net return of nearly £30,000 for an outlay of £35,000."[2]

THE ADVANTAGE GAINED IN EVERY DIRECTION FROM IRRIGATION WORKS.

". . . And this triumphant success, this magnificent addition to the revenue, is not to be gained by exaction, by trenching on the fair rights of property and industry; on the contrary, the noblest feature of all is that this vast gain to the Government is to be obtained by adding in a far higher degree to the wealth, comfort, and happiness of the people. The value of the crop on

[1] J. Bruce Norton, "Letter to the Secretary of the Board of Control," p. 33. [2] *Public Works Report*, sec. 247.

an acre of dry land does not exceed twelve shillings, but that of an acre of rice is forty shillings, and of an acre of sugar cane it is £23, being a gain of £1 8*s*. in the former case and £22 8*s*. in the latter. The gain to the producer, therefore, by the improvements in question, may be stated as follows, at a low estimate :—

	£
100,000 acres of sugar cane and other valuable products, at £20	2,000,000
11,000,000 acres of rice at Rs. 12 . .	1,320,000
Total	£3,320,000

"Reckoning the value of the crops at these moderate rates, and taking no notice of the fact that much of this will be land now altogether waste and unproductive, or of the certainty of the crops under river irrigation, compared with their precariousness at present, we find that the gain to the ryot is £3,320,000, and if he pays £300,000 in revenue, he will still be a clear gainer of £3,000,000 a year. It is no wonder that the greatest anxiety is displayed to get a share of the irrigation, or the greatest alacrity to use the water when so obtained; nor is there anything surprising in the striking change which Colonel Cotton so prominently remarks on in his later reports, as exhibiting itself in the character of the people, activity, enterprise, and life having taken the place of their former apathy and despondence."—(*P. W. R.*, secs. 264-5).

Other instances, the Samulcottah channel and the Wundy taluk, not less surprising, are given in detail; and in the Appendix Z to the *Public Works Report* will be found a tabular statement of all the undertakings within the last fourteen years, which shows a clear return to Government of sixty-nine and a half per cent. per annum on the cost of outlay; and a table of thirteen of such works is given in section 273 of the *Report*. The aggregate cost of those thirteen improvements was Rs. 2,34,901, and the total net annual gain in revenue, after deducting the annual charges, was Rs. 3,17,357, being at the rate of one hundred and thirty-four per cent. per annum on the capital expended.

WHAT THE NATIVE PRINCES DID.[1]

"The native princes, who constructed the tanks and channels of irrigation, knew quite well that from their very nature they must stand in need of constant repair. They therefore made a special provision for this necessity by subjecting every acre of land irrigated to a special cess for this particular purpose, which was in some instances contributed by the ryots, and in others, in equal parts from the ryots' share and the Government share of the produce, the revenue being in those times received in kind. We have not the means of determining whether this constitution of things was universal in all the provinces now forming this Presidency; but it certainly prevailed generally throughout those in which irrigation is most common, and it was probably universal all over the Carnatic at least.

"After the assumption of the government by the English it was determined to consolidate all the items, making up the land revenue into a single demand, and for the most part, this was a fixed sum in money for each acre or each cawny, the revenue in kind being commuted. In that operation the tank cess was included in the settlement, and was merged in the revenue; and the correlative duty of maintaining the works of irrigation in efficiency was fully recognised on the part of the Government. The only exception to this arrangement, we believe, was Tinnevelly, where, though the tank cess was commuted into money, and the proceeds included in the general revenue, a separate account of its amount has always been kept"—(sec. 454).

THE RESPONSIBILITY OF THE GOVERNMENT.

"These facts place the Government in a new position as to the works of irrigation. It now appears that these works are not by any means generally maintained out of the State revenue. As

[1] "It is no matter of surprise that the kings who devoted their treasures and their personal energies to the formation of tanks and canals have entitled their memory to traditional veneration as benefactors of their race and country. In striking contrast is the pithy remark of the author of the *Rajavalu* mourning over the extinction of the 'Great Dynasty,' and the decline of the country, that, 'because the fertility of the land was decreased, the kings who followed were no longer of such consequence as those who went before.'"—SIR EMERSON TENNENT, in his great work on *Ceylon*.

regards a large portion of them, the Government are in the position of trustees of a special fund, contributed wholly or in part by the holders of irrigated land, over and above, and independently of, the Government rent of the land, which latter was at first actually, and still is theoretically, a certain proportion of the year's produce for the maintenance of those works, originally constructed at the cost of the Government, by which the additional value was given to their property. Or, even granting that Government may be regarded as having contracted to maintain the works in consideration of these fees, and so are not responsible for the unexpended amount, even then the condition of their title to the money is that they shall keep the works in good repair. It thus appears that it is not simply a question of policy whether the Government shall keep the works in repair, nor even that there is a merely implied engagement to do so, but that it is a positive and express obligation to be fulfilled in return for an equivalent received. It must be admitted that this duty has not been performed, and private property has suffered great damage in consequence; and it now remains, therefore, to retrieve the past neglect, and bring up the works into a state of full efficiency as rapidly as possible—(sec. 465).

"But the last, and not the least consideration is behind, THE CERTAINTY OF PREVENTING THE AWFUL RECURRENCE OF FAMINE."[1]

AN IRRIGATED *versus* AN UNIRRIGATED DISTRICT. A COMPARISON BY SIR ARTHUR COTTON.

TANJORE: *Irrigated.*	GUNTOOR: *Unirrigated.*
In one district, Tanjore, a system of moderate, but actual, progress had been steadily pursued for fifty years, with the most extraordinary and unvarying success, by which the revenue has been increased from	In the district of Guntoor all such works are utterly neglected, and in one year a famine occurs which sweeps away two hundred and fifty thousand people out of five hundred thousand, and causes a loss of revenue in

[1] J. Bruce Norton, "Letter to the Secretary of Board of Control, 1854, p. 41."

£320,000 to £500,000 a year, while the saleable value of the land had equally advanced, till it is now (allowing for the difference in the value of money) equal to the value of land in England; and that this had been accomplished without any sudden extensive outlay of capital, producing a temporary difficulty, but by an average annual expenditure of about £4,000 a year, besides the current expenses for the repair of existing works. The total sum so expended is about £200,000, and the increase of revenue per annum is the same. The increase of private property in the value of the land is also about £3,000,000 or £3,500,000, indicating an addition of private income of £180,000 or £200,000 a a year. The money expended was employed in embanking the rivers, cutting channels for the distribution of water, and for drainage, constructing weirs, sluices, aqueducts, and other masonry works connected with the irrigation and drainage; in building many hundreds of bridges, and in the next ten or twelve years of £800,000, while not an acre of land is saleable. The sole cause which, has made this difference between these two districts, is the different degree of attention given to public works.

Let us suppose a district under a zemindary and village settlement from which almost every farthing that is collected (besides what is expended on the collection) is sent out of the district; the old and partial means of securing it a supply of food left to go to ruin, and not a mile of road made in it; not a reservoir of water constructed, not an embankment thrown up to prevent the water drowning any extent of crop; not a stream bridged, so that almost all its produce, except what can be consumed in the village where it grew, is utterly valueless. Besides this ordinary state of things, let us suppose a failure of local rain to occur, which, in consequence of its being unmitigated by a single tank of water, which borders the district for eighty miles, or a single channel leading water from an unfailing making one thousand miles of common road for facilitating transit.

All the districts around it have remained almost or quite stationary, excepting in so far as they have, though in a minor degree, had similar advantages granted to them. And still the expenditure in Tanjore has been so inadequate that the whole of its immense traffic is carried by common roads. Had a system of canals been added to the other works, it would probably have benefited to the extent of another £200,000 a year.

The district of Tanjore is taken care of, irrigated, and provided with common roads (though not with better communications), and the revenue steadily rises till from £200,000 it becomes £500,000 a year. The population increases from seven hundred thousand to eight hundred thousand, and the land reaches a saleable value of at least £4,000,000, equal to £24,000,000 in England.

river, it produces the utmost horrors of famine, sweeping off fully half of the population, and reducing the revenue at once by £140,000 a year, which is not fully recovered for twelve years.

Now this is a correct statement of the "progress" of Guntoor.

But, said one of the leading citizens of Madras,[1] writing

[1] Mr. John Bruce Norton, in a letter to the Secretary of the Board of Control, Robert Lowe. Mr. Norton's memory is still held in high

in 1854, let this matter be carried farther. Great as are the advantages which Tanjore possesses over the other districts of Southern India, let us suppose that, instead of a comparatively scanty expenditure upon her public works, a really liberal outlay had been made upon a well-considered, systematic plan, with a view still further to reduce the cost of transit. What would *then* have been her position? It is highly important to ascertain this, because in the pictures above drawn, much of her prosperity must undoubtedly be attributed to the improvement of works of irrigation. What follows from Col. Cotton's pen applies mainly to means of communication:—

"Now let us suppose," he says, "in the case of Tanjore that, instead of the petty trifling way in which it has been improved, a really intelligent and vigorous system had been pursued. Suppose, for instance, that instead of £4,000 a year even £10,000 only had been spent in the irrigation improvement, so that the district had been brought into tolerable order in that respect in twenty years instead of fifty, and that, by continuing the expenditure, water had been stored so as to supply it through the dry season, instead of having it, as now, without water for four months, so that it might have grown sugar and other valuable products, instead of rice only. And thus, long before this, the district might have been exporting one hundred thousand tons of sugar a year, worth £2,000,000, besides various other things. Let us suppose further, that, instead of merely during the last thirty years of the fifty, constructing very imperfect unmetalled roads, worked at fourpence-halfpenny per ton per mile, they had from the first commenced a system of steam canals, by which the transit could have been carried on at one-sixteenth of a penny per mile! At present there are just one thousand miles of road in the district; if the

esteem because of his public-spiritedness while in Madras. He may be remembered in England as one of the proprietors of *The Hour* newspaper, a daily journal which excited much interest during its too brief existence thirty years ago.

average traffic is equal to fifty tons of goods a day, the daily cost must be £300, or £320,000 a year. The steam canals, providing for the great bulk of this, would have relieved the district from an expenditure of £250,000 a year on the goods and passengers now moved, besides, probably, an equal sum gained in the additional value given to goods which are not moved at all at the present high rates. With these additional helps, an additional income in more valueable products of at least £1,000,000, and advantages in the transit worth £500,000 a year, the revenue might now be £1,000,000, instead of £500,000, and the net income of the people also one million more than it is at present. And all this might have been done without a rupee being paid out of the general treasury. The district would itself have paid for all these improvements from year to year out of the additional revenue it would have been yielding, just as of late in the Rajahmundy [now Godavari] district where, while £200,000 have been spent in eight years, £300,000 of additional revenue have been received. No reason whatever can be assigned why this should not have been done, and thus this one district, instead of paying £200,000 a year in mere revenue towards the late annual deficit of one million, might have paid £700,000 or seven-tenths of the whole deficit; and two districts so improved would have made a difference of our having, for the last thirty years, a surplus revenue upon all India, of half a million, instead of a deficit of one million. And, I think we may venture to say this would have been the case under that revenue system, which is the worst in India, according to Mr. [afterwards Sir George] Campbell, that is, even if every landowner had been allowed to manage his own land in his own way, and without the interference of his neighbours."

Sir Arthur was not without a sense of humour, as those who knew him best often found. He could be satirical, too, on occasion. It is true his satire was like summer evening lightning, illuminating rather than dangerous, but there it was. I give two instances, to be found in his writings of this period, of his humorous treatment of the great red-tapeism which then (and now almost as largely) prevailed in Indian administration.

THE GREAT PUTTY CASE.

A range of barracks is built by an Engineer at a cost of £30,000 or £40,000; there is a large saving on the estimate sanctioned, for which he officially receives the thanks of the Court of Directors. Some time afterwards a storm occurs, which breaks a few panes of glass valued at £7. The whole Presidency is at once in a state of excitement. The heads of that division of the army are directed to assemble a committee of officers to investigate this matter. Their report is referred to the Military Board, who, after patiently examining all the papers, and referring to all their records, forward all the documents to the Governor-in-Council, with a deliberate and elaborate report, in which they assure the Government that they have not hastily come to a decision, but have given their best energies to the investigation. They conclude that the cause of the windows being broken was the inferior quality of the putty used, and that, therefore, the Engineer ought to pay for them. All the papers connected with this intricate and vital matter are now examined by the Secretary to Government, who sends them in circulation to the Governor and the three members of Council. After a sufficient time has been given them to consider this weighty subject, and to record their individual sentiments in writing, the important day at length arrives when the whole is to be reviewed and discussed in Council. The flag is hoisted, his Excellency's carriage, with two troopers with drawn swords, in front, and three behind, enters the fort, and is drawn up at the gate of the Government Offices. It is followed by the Commander-in-Chief, and the two Councillors with their silver sticks. The Secretaries are summoned, and this solemn investigation is proceeded with, upon which the fate of £7 depends. It is, however, discovered that the decision of such an important question, by an assembly drawing among them salaries amounting to £40,000 or £50,000 a year, and the cost of whose weekly meetings in council may be calculated at about £1,000, would be too presumptuous. After much discussion, therefore, and probably, a second or third set of minutes, it is decided that the Secretary shall draw up a report embodying the opinions of the Council, to be submitted, with all the important documents connected therewith, to the honourable Court of Directors, and the Board of Control.

The thoughtless mail agent little thinks what he has got under his charge, when he receives the box containing this despatch, in the cabin on board the steamer. After many months, during which these papers have been the frequent subject of communication and discussion among the secretaries, directors, etc., etc., in London, another steamer proceeds with the freight of these papers, greatly increased in bulk and value by the opinions and decision of the august Board at home. They reach Madras, the Council is again assembled, the despatch is considered, a copy, with resolutions, etc., is sent to the Military Board, and, after having been circulated, considered, discussed, etc., by them, instructions are issued announcing that the honourable Court, of course with the concurrence of the Board of Control, have decided, for reasons duly stated, that the windows shall be mended at the expense of the Engineer. If a wing of the barracks had fallen down, of course, as a subaltern could not pay ten thousand pounds, there would be no alternative but to rebuild it at the public expense; but, as he can pay seven pounds, justice to the public service requires that he should be made an example of. In the meantime, as the officer is not in India, the matter lies over for a year or two. On his return, being surprised at the receipt of these orders, after having been officially thanked by the Court for having acquitted himself so well in the construction of this large building, he addresses the Chief Engineer, giving him, in a few words, reasons why he ought not to be held responsible for the loss of the £7, and, as he has not previously had an opportunity of speaking in his own behalf, the Chief Engineer draws up a minute on the subject, which is laid before the Military Board, who again considers the question, and once more report to Government. Nothing can exceed the condescending and unwearied patience of all the authorities. The Governor once more records a minute, the second member of Council minutes, the third member minutes, the Governor winds up by a fourth minute; by which time the subject is ripe for discussion. Again the Council assemble, consider, decide, and issue instructions to the

Military Board; and finally, the officer is told that he may keep his £7. And so ends the affair, till the report of the Governor-in-Council reaches the Court, when they will possibly order the matter to be taken up *de novo*, and thoroughly investigated. It should be mentioned that it was discovered at last that some brads had been omitted in fixing the glass, which was not likely to be discovered either by the President of the Board of Control, the twenty-four Directors and their Secretary, the Governor and Council of Madras and their Secretaries, the Military Board, the Chief Engineer, the General of the division, the Committee of Officers, or the Engineer himself, as none of them had ever served an apprenticeship to a glazier.

This is the literal history of an Indian question, which has recently been agitated.

ROAD-MAKING PECULIARITIES.

The history of communications in the Madras Presidency is one of the most curious of all the odd things that have occurred in the management of India. A sketch of this may be of great use as a warning to us in our future proceedings. The first roads made probably were those in Tanjore. When it was proposed to open one or two lines in that impassable sheet of irrigation it was immediately objected :—

"Well, this is a fine proposition, to make fine roads where there is not a horse or a cart to be found." There was not a mile in the whole delta over which a horse or a cart could have moved. After some struggling, however, a first attempt was made, and it was discovered that when there were cart roads, carts were used. But what was done in Tanjore was done without the least reference to any other part of the country. The questions were never asked: "But if roads are to be made, where are they most wanted? where will capital so expended produce the greatest results? which ought to be made first, etc., etc.?" Tanjore possessing the most active Government officers got roads, and the rest of the country generally remained without, as it is to this day. The next roads were probably those made by the Pioneers. The arrangements for these works were as follows: some lady at Madras having a favourite brother or cousin in one of the native regiments, took an opportunity at a pleasure ball given by the Quarter-Master-General, to ask him if he could not do something for her relation. Upon this he is put into the Pioneers, and in a few years he gets the command of a battalion. In the course of time some great public functionary being detained for weeks on an impassable line of country in his palanquin, becomes very sensible of the sufferings of the people in that neighbourhood from want of roads, and persuades the Government to send a battalion of Pioneers to make one. The whole management of the work, of course, falls to the officer so carefully selected to command them. He has never seen a road made ; he left England before he was old enough to entertain a thought about the roads he travelled over there. He has not an idea on the whole subject, nor a book to refer to. Of the principles on which the lines should be selected, as well as those on which the roads should be constructed, he is as utterly ignorant as the lady who recommended him for his appointment. He soon finds that a thousand men are lost upon a hundred miles of road, and obtains permission to employ a few thousand coolies, and thus, besides the cost of the Pioneers, a few lakhs of rupees are spent by a man who has not the slightest knowledge of, or even natural turn for, the work he is employed upon, and who possesses perhaps a low degree of general ability or zeal.

There is not the slightest exaggeration in this; it is a literal statement of the *usual* course of proceedings, in times past. No check of the remotest kind was exercised over these works, not a single professional officer had anything whatever to do with them. The Quarter-Master-General under whom they were carried on, was as perfectly ignorant of the matter and probably at least as indifferent about it, as the Executive Officers. Of the state of things a very distinct idea may be formed by the following anecdote. One of the officers commanding the Pioneers employed as above described, drew up a memo on the best construction for a road on cotton soil (black alluvial mud without sand or gravel mixed with it), and highly pleased with the knowledge he had attained, he sent it to the Quarter-Master-General. Struck by the remarkable talent displayed in the paper, the Quarter-Master-General sent a copy of it to all officers employed in that department; and that the utmost possible use might be made of it, he also sent a copy to the Chief Engineer, that he might circulate it through the corps. The plan was this, first a complete layer of large stones about a foot or a foot and a half thick were to be laid over the whole surface to be occupied by the road, and over these were then to be laid three feet of black cotton soil to raise the road to a sufficient height and prevent its being flooded. By this admirable arrangement almost any amount of money might be spent, as in such a situation the stones would have to be brought several miles, and, at the same time, the surface of the road being formed of the natural soil, but thoroughly loosened by being dug and thrown up, would be ten times worse than the original surface of the country. Such was the state of knowledge of road-making among those who conducted and who were entrusted, without check or supervision, with the expenditure of many tens of thousands of pounds.

The road from Masulipatam on the coast, three hundred miles north of Madras, to Hyderabad, a distance of two hundred and twenty miles, was one of those executed in this manner. When about £80,000 had been spent upon it, besides the pay of the Pioneers, the Court of Directors put a stop to it; and, as no metal of any kind was put on most of it, the road had never yet been practicable in the wet season, and even in the dry season, the communication was very little better, if at all. Then only about one hundred and twenty miles of the whole distance was meddled with; the money spent was, therefore, nearly £700 a mile before the work was began, or twice as much as would make an excellent road, and quite as much as would have made a good horse railroad (for there was not a single difficulty on the line), which would have reduced the cost of transit to one-twelfth of what it was and still is. The road from Madras to Poonamallee, eleven miles, was a similar case, and, as in this instance, the Pioneer officer was able to communicate constantly with the authorities in person, he was not so restricted about expenditure as in the other case; accordingly £44,000 was spent here, or £4,000 a mile. The Court of Directors now saw it was necessary to apply a remedy: and it was, to order that no more roads should be made. This was simple and effectual.

CHAPTER X

The Struggle in a House of Commons Committee Room,—with an Anticipatory Debate and Interludes

"God has said, From water all things are made. I consequently ordain that this jungle [Hissar district in the Punjab], in which subsistence is obtained with thirst, be converted into a place of comfort."
—AKBAR, 1568.

THE nearly forty years of arduous toil in India were matched by an almost equal period of so-called retirement to England, and the enjoyment of well-earned leisure. Sir Arthur Cotton's notions of retirement and leisure accord with some men's ideas of a busy career. He was always occupied in furthering some beneficial project or other. And, though it may appear that oftentimes he was but "beating the air," that he could not exhibit equal success in enterprises carried to completion such as marked his "active" forty years, it may yet be proved that, in the result, even more good will accrue from these later years than is apparent for the former period. For, if these pages convince a sympathising and responsible public that grave injustice has been done to India in the denial of widespread irrigation, Sir Arthur's projects will yet find completion. He has left behind him a rich record of material which, rightly understood and enthusiastically employed, will surely bring under safe cultivation not merely the miserably inadequate four millions of acres which Lord Curzon of Kedleston declared, in the Viceregal Council in April, 1900, was all that remained of productive works to be taken in hand, but many many millions of acres and many thousands of miles of water navigation to aid in saving the people alive and in the development of the country.

A friend, who saw a great deal of Sir Arthur in his retirement, declares that he was incessantly engaged with the great subject of irrigation and navigation in India, holding conference with men high in office, delivering lectures and writing pamphlets and letters to the newspapers. His great ideas were :—

First. To establish canals for irrigation wherever they were practicable, and to supersede rain and well-water by river-water, which carried with it fertilizing matter greatly augmenting its value as compared with all other water.

Next. To render irrigation canals navigable, and to establish thousands of miles fit for steamboats to carry the immense amount of produce which could not be moved for internal use or exportation save by the cheapest mode of transit; this could be provided by water alone.

The difficulties he had to encounter, from official sources particularly, seem, to an outsider, almost incomprehensible. At least he had no selfish aim to satisfy. In common parlance he had no axe-edge of his own to sharpen. He was able, proudly, to state to the House of Commons Select Committee on East India Public Works, in 1878: "I have never made this a personal matter, and I trust I am not going to begin in my old age. I never asked for an appointment, or for anything else, except to be allowed to irrigate India. I never possessed property, nor ever took a share in any speculation, that I might have nothing to occupy my thoughts or warp my judgment, but might give myself up to my duty of helping to raise India in this particular point. It has pleased God so to prosper the works I have been engaged in, that the dispute among my adversaries is whether returns are seventeen, twenty-eight, or forty per cent., and, in another, whether the return is not less than eighty-seven per cent." A magnificent, yet modest, boast! Had the percentage been all the other way, had there been loss instead of gain, had no material advantages followed, severe criticism might not have been unexpected. As it was, one noble lord, while Secretary for India, remarked to Manchester men at a public meeting, that water could not be made to run up hill, while a then recently resigned Member of Council invented a range of mountains in order to make it impossible for a canal to be carried across the lower part of Central India. Men learned in the law, like Sir James Fitzjames Stephen, considered themselves capable of teaching the laurel-crowned, successful, old Engineer that they knew more of hydrostatics and water-engineering than did the creator of the Coleroon anicut and the designer of the Dowlaisweram dam.

BEFORE A PARLIAMENTARY COMMITTEE IN 1872.

Twice Sir Arthur appeared before Select Committees of the House of Commons on Indian affairs, in 1872 and in 1878. As the first Committee dealt generally with finance, particularly in connection with military expenses, while the latter had to do solely with public works, it is but natural that his second appearance should be more important than the first. This is why so much space and consideration are given in this chapter to the enquiry of 1878. While more than nine hundred questions were asked of him, in that year, less than three hundred were asked in 1872. And, after enquiries about irrigation on points, all of which were exhaustively dealt with in 1878, and will be found a few pages later, most attention was given to navigation; yet was not irrigation forgotten.[1] Consequently, in the brief reference, which is all that this incident calls for, atten-

[1] "Now," asked the Chairman, the Rt. Hon. A. S. Ayrton, "this system of irrigation has been productive of very great benefit in certain districts; but do you think it is equally applicable to other portions of India as it is to the deltas of great rivers?"

The witness replied: "TO EVERY DISTRICT IN INDIA; *but not with equal benefit, because some districts would be more expensive to irrigate than others*; BUT IT IS EQUALLY APPLICABLE."—Q. 8371, Report, 1872.

tion will be concentrated wholly on the navigation aspect of Sir Arthur Cotton's evidence. In elaborating one of the early questions put to him concerning the population on the banks of the Godavari, the witness mentioned "a very noteworthy fact" concerning that part of the country: "The most palpable and striking result of our government," he said, "has been a steady emigration of a section of the population, constituting forty per cent. of the whole, and the gradual depopulation of the district under our rule." [1]

One feature strongly insisted upon by the witness was the need for plentiful storage if navigation was to be provided the year through: such storage is also pressingly required for irrigation, as Mr. Walch points out in his book, as most of the Indian Members of the Viceregal Legislative Council urged in April, 1900, and as some Indian newspapers have indicated. "It would not require a very large sum, say £200,000, to store water for the completion of the navigation of the Godavari for the whole year," was Sir Arthur Cotton's matured judgment.

It was elicited that repeated requests for funds were sent to successive Secretaries of State without success. "They must have given you some reason why they thought it was undesirable to advance this additional sum of money," persisted the Chairman. "They never gave me any reason at all," responded the witness. "I had continual correspondence with former Secretaries of State, and Lord Halifax, and it was always said the money could not be found." But why it could not be found for works which repaid capital over and over again, Sir Arthur could never make out.

The Chairman: "In your opinion would canal navigation meet the whole transit wants of India, of its commerce, and its people?"

"Perfectly and entirely," was the reply; "without any one defect whatever." Thinking this assertion might be thought too sweeping he qualified it with the remark: "I

[1] Q. 8344, Report, 1872.

do not mean to say that every line in India can be traversed by a canal, but every line on which it is of great importance there should be transit. There may be minor tracts, like some part of the line between Bombay and Madras, which might be better for railways."

To the question as to whether he considered that there was water enough in India to feed all the canals of which he spoke, Sir Arthur, with strong conviction, said:—

"*There is water enough in India for every conceivable purpose ten times over;* THERE IS NO WANT OF WATER."

One more question, quoted because of its bearing on the manner in which the Ellore and East Coast Canal has had its boat licences penalised in the interests of the East Coast Railway,[1] and with it the close of my references to this most disappointing enquiry—singular amongst the many Parlia-

[1] See official documents, pp. 282–284 of this work. A curious feature of this enquiry of 1872 was the most serious mistakes which a leading Indian official made in his evidence. Two questions (8498 and 8499) with their answers are worth quarrying from the ponderous volumes in which they appear:

"8498. [*The Chairman.*] Now the river is opened up to the second barrier, and the traffic, I think you stated, was 20,000 tons the first year. General Strachey states that he believes almost the whole of that traffic was food for the people employed on the works; have you any account of what that traffic consisted of; is it possible that there can have been twenty thousand people employed on that work, and that they could consume, each of them, a ton of food in that period?"

"Here is the report of the navigation for the year 1869–70, which is the last that I have got. The total traffic was 20,500 tons, and of that the Government stores were 1,500, leaving 19,000 tons for general merchandise. I cannot understand how General Strachey, who is so very accurate in general, could have made a mistake of that sort."

"8499. One of General Strachey's objections to the opening of the Godavari is, that it would take off the railway a portion of the existing traffic, and also the further traffic that it was likely to receive: what have you to say to that?"

"I have two things to say to that. One is this: because we have made a railway, are we therefore to compel the people to carry by an expensive mode when they could carry by a cheap one? The other is, that we have nothing to do with the railway in considering the question. There is the question of whether we shall make a line of communication through an important tract of five hundred miles, or have none at all in that five hundred miles."

mentary Committees which have enquired long and ended in nothing.

If, asked the Chairman, it be argued that if you open the Godavari it will compete with the Great Indian Peninsula Railway, will not the projected Indus Valley Railway compete with the river Indus in the same way?

"Yes," was the regretful answer; "but it seems that there is no objection to make a railway to compete with the river, though there is great objection to open a river to compete with a railway."

A HOUSE OF COMMONS DEBATE.

A SEVERE ATTACK UPON AN ABSENT MAN.

So dreadful a famine as that which swept over Southern India in 1876-77, could not pass unnoticed in Parliament. Much discussion on many platforms throughout the country and in almost every newspaper in the United Kingdom made Parliamentary action of some kind inevitable. The Queen's Speech on the opening of the session, contained the following passage:—

"I am thankful that the terrible famine which has ravaged Southern India is nearly at an end. Strenuous and successful exertions have been made by my Local Governments to relieve the sufferings of the population, and in that duty they have been powerfully seconded by the liberal aid of my people at home and in my Colonies. I have directed that an inquiry should be made into the measures most proper to diminish the danger of such calamities for the future."

In the debate which followed in both Houses of Parliament, references to irrigation and to Sir Arthur Cotton's part in it were made. One—that which first follows—shows the harm done to his reputation by the refusal of *The Times* to publish his reply to Sir James Stephen: because no reply appeared to the lawyer's dicta on irrigation it was assumed there was no reply! The Earl of Wharncliffe said:—

" . . . Her Majesty also refers in her gracious speech to the terrible famine which has ravaged Southern India. I rejoice that that great calamity is nearly at an end; and I sincerely trust that the Commission that is to be appointed will be able to discover, in the investigation of the causes of the present famine, the means of preventing these deplorable calamities in the future. The subject is a very difficult one, and it is to be regretted that one of the greatest orators in this country[1] should have recently propounded a scheme, so haphazard and incomplete, that it only needed a stroke of the pen from that distinguished Indian official, Sir James Stephen, to accomplish its entire refutation, and to show how unsound were the premisses of those who supported the plan."

The Earl of Loudoun, on the other hand, supported extension of irrigation. He said:—

. . . "With regard to the Indian Famine, it is gratifying to think that such a calamity has been alleviated by open hearts and hands in England, and by able administration in India itself. The question of irrigation in India is most important, and it is to be hoped that it will receive due consideration. There was an important meeting in Birmingham last night, reported in *The Standard* to-day, at which Sir Arthur Cotton, who has been connected with engineering in India for more than half a century, spoke of the great works of irrigation which had been carried out by the Government, who had spent £20,000,000 on it. But he added that much, of course, remained to be done, and that it was often a very good investment."

In the Commons debate, Mr. Wilbraham Egerton's remarks are almost a replica of Lord Wharncliffe's in the Upper House. He remarked:—

" . . . The good feeling which had long existed between this country and India must have been strengthened by the generous response which had been made, not only by the English people, but by the English race in our Colonies, to the cry for assistance of those who were suffering from the consequences of a dire famine, which would, in his opinion, have resulted in a much greater loss of life but for the facilities which had been afforded by the railways in carrying food at a low rate. The question how

[1] John Bright, who, so far as his time permitted, ardently advocated the adoption of Sir Arthur Cotton's proposals.

to prevent famines in India was now engaging public opinion. The right hon. gentleman the member for Birmingham (Mr. Bright) gave at Manchester some advice on this subject, but his statements were disputed, and his arguments refuted by a very able writer in a leading newspaper. He was glad to see that a Commission was to be appointed to go into the whole subject, and he understood that the additional taxation to be imposed on India was to be devoted either to pay off the loans raised for the famine or to carry on new works, if found necessary."

So soon as discussion upon the answer to Her Majesty's gracious message was concluded, the Under Secretary of State introduced a motion for the appointment of a Select Committee to enquire into and to report as to the expediency of constructing Public Works in India with money raised on loan, both as regards financial results and the prevention of famines. This was the form which, after amendment suggested by Mr. Fawcett and a speech by Mr. John Bright, the motion took.[1] It is essential to a right understanding of the deplorable situation, as regards insufficient extension of irrigation, which resulted from the debate on the appointment of the Committee and the report of the Committee itself, that everything which was said in debate should find record here. I, therefore, abstract from pages 324 to 384 of vol. 237 of *Hansard's Parliamentary Debates*, the speeches which follow:—

LORD GEORGE HAMILTON: Lord Dalhousie suggested a plan by which money might be raised through the agency of

---

[1] The mutations which the original motion underwent are interesting:—

Motion for a Select Committee.

"That a Select Committee be appointed to inquire into and report as to the expediency of constructing Public Works in India with money raised on loan." (Lord George Hamilton.)

Amendment. Mr. Fawcett.

"That the following words be added to the motion of the Under-Secretary of State for India:—

"And further to inquire into the best means to be adopted to prevent the recurrence or to mitigate the intensity of famines in India; and whether by greater economy, especially with regard to certain companies, and, in fact, the making of the desired railways was handed over to those companies, who were induced to find the capital by being guaranteed high rates of interest. That was the origin of guaranteeing railways in India. Lord Dalhousie also proposed to hand over irrigation works to similar companies, and on the abolition of the old Military Boards some few years later, various offices for the construction of public works in connection with the Civil Department were consolidated into a new department, to which the name of the Public Works Department was given. It was proposed that this department should annually expend about £2,000,000 on productive irrigation works. . . . Previous to the establishment of the Public Works Department, a considerable sum had annually been expended in the construction of irrigation works in India; but that was entirely from the ordinary revenue of the year. After the Mutiny, great pressure was put upon the Secretary of State. Certain companies, such as the 'Madras' and the 'Orissa,' were formed for the promotion of irrigation, but they were failures. Lord Lawrence drew attention to the great charges those high guarantees were placing year by year on the revenues of India, and he suggested that in future railways and irrigation works should be constructed by loans. Some years after a proposal was made by the Indian Government, and confirmed by the Home Government, that the Government should in future be entirely responsible for the construction of irrigation works. So long as money was found for these works by private companies, the real state of the case was

---

military and other charges, which are under the control of the Home authorities, a fund for the relief of famines may not be provided without subjecting the people of India to such burdensome taxation as will be imposed upon them by the contemplated increase of the salt duty."

Mr. Grant Duff.

All that he would suggest was the addition of a few words at the end of the motion of the noble lord, namely :—

"Especially such works as may be adapted to prevent the recurrence or mitigate the intensity of famines."

Amendment and motion (by leave) withdrawn.

East India Public Works.

"Select Committee *appointed* to inquire into and report as to the expediency of constructing Public Works in India with money raised on loan, both as regards financial results and the prevention of famine." (Lord George Hamilton.)

obscured; but the moment the State undertook their construction, the whole of the capital embarked was charged against the ordinary revenue of the year. . . . Last session, the Government had proposed a form of account to be sent out to India by which the whole of the transactions connected with railways and irrigation works were brought under one head, and all the interest on the money expended on them, as well as the working expenses, were charged against the receipts, so that at a glance they could see what the actual result of the construction of these works actually was. . . . It was proposed to devote £4,500,000 annually to the construction of Public Works Extraordinary, of which £3,000,000 were to be devoted to railroads and £1,500,000 to irrigation. . . . He had pointed out that the allotment annually given to irrigation had been diminished, and in ordinary times he would not have considered it necessary to call attention to this fact; but, owing to the recent agitation out-of-doors with a view to exercise pressure on the Indian Government, to induce them to spend enormous sums on irrigation works, he felt compelled to refer to this subject. An association, he believed, had been formed, and application had been made to members of Parliament asking their asssistance, in order to induce, if possible, the Indian Government to embark upon a gigantic speculation in that direction. That, however, was the continuance of an old agitation. Some twenty years ago a similar agitation had prevailed, there being a strong impression out-of-doors that they had merely to construct an irrigation work in India, and it must immediately pay. A chief supporter of that view, and a very distinguished engineer, was Sir Arthur Cotton, who, in the early part of his career, had been singularly successful in the construction of certain irrigation works in the Madras delta. Those works had proved satisfactory and had paid well, although what their exact actual returns were, it was difficult to say; but making all allowance, there was no doubt that those works were a great credit to their designers and promoters. But the delta of Madras was exceptionally favourable for such works, and could not be held to be a precedent for other parts of India. Had Sir Arthur Cotton and his friends been content with advocating the construction of works under as favourable circumstances as those he constructed in Madras, he would unquestionably have done unmitigated good to India. But, unfortunately, they went a great deal further, and in all their speeches and statements with reference to the advantages of irrigation, by some curious oversight, those gentlemen had wholly ignored the results of recent experience. Shortly after the Mutiny, great pressure was put upon the Secretary of State to construct irrigation works in Madras by means of a private company. Lord Derby was then Secretary of State for India, and all Lancashire urging him, contrary to the opinion of his Council, he assented to the project and the Madras Irrigation Company was formed. In the prospectus it was represented that the undertaking would be very remunerative, and Sir Arthur Cotton said he would select for execution the work which would, in his judgment, give the best commercial return. In writing to the Indian Government on the scheme, his language was peculiar, considering what the actual results of that company had been. It was stated that when they had secured their plunder, it would be an agreeable task to sit down at their leisure and divide the spoil. It was the actual possession which put everybody in good humour, and the eighty per cent. dividend in the case of the Ganges Company was mentioned. It was further stated that the 'work was composed of distinct parts, each of which formed a complete scheme in itself, and would yield, when executed, its own return independently of the remaining parts.' On the recommendations of so distinguished an authority the Company was constituted with a capital of £1,000,000 sterling, which had been spent without any returns. In consequence of an agitation that was set on foot, the Indian Government was authorised to lend £600,000 to the Company at five per cent. This money also was laid out and no return had been made. Not only so, but the Government had not received any interest; and although they had been paid a small portion of the money so advanced, that Company had never once paid its working expenses. That work ran right through one of the famine districts, and, of course, it did some good; but its most enthusiastic supporter would not say that the crops it had saved were worth a moiety of the expenditure on its construction. It was necessary, therefore, to be cautious in regard to agitation set on foot to put pressure on the Indian Government and to induce it to incur an enormous outlay on undertakings of that character. One of the main points urged on the public was the advantage of cheap water-carriage. No doubt India had a number of magnificent rivers; and of all the rivers in the south, the first, perhaps, was the Godavari. The Indian Government, yielding to an appeal made to it as to the benefits that would accrue from the improvement of the navigation of that river, sanctioned an expenditure for that object. The expenditure was put at £80,000 and the works went on. Lord Mayo took the Public Works Department under his own particular charge, and having heard of the expenditure on the Godavari, sent down gentlemen to enquire what the amount was. The result was startling: no less than £700,000 had been spent without any return. This improvement was intended for the benefit of the Central Provinces. Mr. Norris had written strongly to deprecate the further continuance of these works and had stated that the question in his mind was whether the Government could utilize the expenditure of the past, the main result of which had been, in many places, nothing more valuable than a rich deposit of thick, black mud. The Indian Government sent home the papers relating to the affair, and the conclusion of their despatch was to the effect that the project had swallowed up £700,000, that the work could not be utilized till an expenditure of at least £900,000 had been incurred, and that the river could not be made navigable for less than £1,200,000. It was evident from the circumstances that complete designs were necessary for every project. Woeful as their failures had been, there was still a worse one. The Indian Government had commissioned Sir Arthur Cotton to inspect the Bay of Mahanuddy and to suggest some scheme for securing the neighbourhood from famine. He advocated the expenditure of £13,500,000, but the Government could not accede to that proposal, and, after some delay, it was resolved that the works should be constructed by a private company. Consequently the Orissa Company was formed, with a capital of £1,000,000; but that proved a failure and the Government took over their works at a very high valuation. They then sent down engineers to revise the estimates and it was found that a sum of £2,700,000 would give a return of sixteen per cent. The Duke of Argyll was informed of this, and the Indian Government had reason to believe the estimate safe and sufficient; but only last August it was necessary to write with reference to the affair that, while in 1871 the outlay had been calculated at £2,700,000 and the profit at sixteen per cent., in 1873 the revised estimate amounted to £4,400,000, and at the present time to £6,208,000, the estimated receipts being diminished in an even greater proportion. He had mentioned this fact with the idea that it was desirable to know the results of recent experience, and seeing that, except in the delta, these irrigation works had all failed, he thought it was wrong for any one to support a gigantic agitation to force the Government into incurring an enormous expenditure and yet keep back these notorious facts. Especially was he sorry to find that Sir Arthur Cotton had received countenance from such a high quarter as the right hon. gentleman, the member for Birmingham (Mr. John Bright). His eloquence was so great that it seldom failed to influence the public mind. But that made it all the more necessary for public men of such high position to be careful how they too freely endorsed the ideas of speculative engineers. In purely commercial life he felt certain that the right hon. gentleman would not ask the public to embark in any scheme, respecting the success of which he was not absolutely certain. He ought to be equally cautious in lending his help to an agitation for promoting an immense expenditure of money for purposes which it had been proved would be valueless. Caution and prudence were all the more necessary in this case, because the Indian taxpayer was not directly represented in that House; and of all the departments of the State none was so weakly represented, in a financial sense, as the Indian department. Indian questions were, fortunately, outside the area of party politics. The representative of the India Office could not depend upon that support which party organisation afforded to other departments; and whenever any scheme involving increased expenditure was brought forward, all the advocates of increased expenditure of any sort took good care to prime their friends in the House, so that the representative of the Government found many against him and very few in his favour. He was therefore extremely sorry, and it was doubly unfortunate, that at the Manchester meeting the right hon. gentleman should have taken up one of the wildest and rashest of Sir Arthur Cotton's schemes—that, namely, by which it was proposed to construct a number of navigable canals all over India at a cost of £30,000,000. For his own part, he would like to know what might be expected to be the actual and final cost of such a scheme. He (Lord George Hamilton) did not deny that the reputation of Sir Arthur Cotton was deservedly great, but there was another gentleman, Colonel Chesney, well-versed in such matters, in whose book, to which the right hon. gentleman had alluded, was a passage explaining that the cost of making a canal depended upon the supply of water, the slope of the ground and the drainage of the course. In certain favourable conditions, great canals might be made for a comparatively small sum, and might be navigated cheaply for exactly those reasons which made ocean traffic cheap. But when those favourable conditions were absent, the case wholly changed, and the expenditure on canals was practically indefensible. The best possible way to dispose of Sir Arthur Cotton's ideas would be the appointment of a Select Committee, before whom the advocates of rival opinions could be heard. and their value estimated; but before any committee considered any scheme involving an outlay of £30,000,000, they should first require satisfactory explanations of those past failures to which he had alluded. The recent famine in Madras had, no doubt, directed attention to that part of India, and there were some who thought that much might be done by increasing irrigation in that district to protect it against the recurrence of famine. It had been found by experience that it was no use to construct canals or tanks to prevent drought, which were solely dependent on rainfall for their supply of water. In Madras there were only three rivers, whose sources of supply were independent of the rainfall of Madras and Mysore; and, in the opinions of many competent engineers, it would not be possible to utilise the waters of those rivers to any further considerable extent. Moreover Sir Richard Temple had directed attention to the fact that in the wet lands the famine had been the worst, and he had dwelt on that circumstance in a despatch to Lord Salisbury, concluding by depicting the sheets of water and all the apparatus of irrigation lying useless. From that it was clear, that the construction or tanks or canals, which were not connected with permanent sources would not be sufficient to save the people from famine. In Bengal, the conditions were very different from what they were in Madras, because not only was there a great number of rivers, but the country was flat and the canals were easily constructed. But even in Bengal the results were very remarkable. If he took the total expenditure in Bengal, the result was not altogether unsatisfactory. It appeared, from the last account, that there had been expended about £12,500,000 in Bengal, and the results, including direct and indirect receipts, are a return of 3½ per cent. on the capital. But the moment this sum was analysed, it was found that this revenue was almost exclusively derived from two canals—the Jumna and the Ganges. The capital expended on these two works was £3,500,000 and the result was 10½ per cent. On the whole remaining expenditure in Bengal, which amounted to £9,500,000 there was only a return of half per cent., and this proved very clearly, what recent experience strongly confirmed, that it mainly depended on physical conditions as well as the rainfall, whether a canal paid or not.

General Sir George Balfour asked whether the results referred to in connection with the Jumna canal were independent of the old works?

Lord George Hamilton replied that the Jumna canal was an extension of the old work, and he doubted very much if the old work was included in the calculation. He believed that was not worth very much. Another circumstance to be borne in mind was that it took twelve or fifteen years for the revenue of a canal to be fully developed. The consequence was that if they were, during that period, to adopt a strictly commercial system of increasing the capital account by compound interest, they would make such a capital account as would prevent almost any irrigation work from making the least return. Altogether, the works which the Government had constructed might be divided into three classes—firstly, those which paid well during ordinary years; secondly, those which would not pay during ordinary years, but which averted famines; and, thirdly, those which would not pay in ordinary years and which would not avert famine. It had been shown that it would be a delusion to rely altogether on irrigation, but, on the other hand, it would be a mistake to ignore the service which it had rendered in the past. One of the main questions which the proposed committee would have to enquire into was, what had been the result of irrigation works, and to obtain from the various officers of the Public Works Department the cause of their failures; also to see whether the principle on which their receipts were estimated was sound or not. It was not worth while to enter into a comparison between railroads and canals, because there was not at present data sufficient to enable any one to draw a comparison between them as to their financial results. In the estimated returns from canals, the whole of the indirect receipts, the enhanced value of the land, etc., as well as the direct receipts, were included; but in the case of railways that was not done, although there could be no doubt that railways also enhanced the value of the land, and enabled the Indian Government to largely reduce the number of European troops kept in India.

REPLY TO ADVERSE CRITICISM.

The above speech was delivered on January 22, 1878. Sir Arthur saw it in *The Times* the next day. He immediately prepared a reply to the surprising, even astounding, statements made by Lord George Hamilton. This reply was not sent to the newspapers. He knew he could not expect to receive sufficient space in any journal in which to answer the noble lord's strange travesty of facts or indicate the dis-service done to India by the contracted view taken of irrigation projects. Therefore, he addressed his reply to Viscount Cranbrook, Secretary of State for India, and appealed for justice at his hands. The appeal was in vain. Only by the circulation of his own pamphlet, and at his own expense, did he obtain vindication for himself, and for irrigation as the prime need for India. His reply was in these terms:—

With reference to the late debate on India, in which Lord G. Hamilton was pleased to mention my name, as I was not present to reply to him, and the references to me have been published in all the papers, I have the honour to request that the Secretary of State will, in any way that may seem best to him, place before the public the reply which would have been allowed to me if I had been a member of the House, as I conclude, of course, that the Secretary of State would not wish any one to be thus brought before the public without an opportunity of offering his defence as publicly. It is such an acknowledged right in England that every man should be allowed when accused to state his defence, and *that*[1] before the tribunal before which he has been called, that I need not hesitate to

[1] The italics throughout this reply are Sir Arthur Cotton's.

ask for this, which is essential to a just judgment being formed by the tribunal before which I have been called.

Had these charges been made against me merely in an official paper, I should have had no claim beyond a similar official reply, but having been held up before all the world, by a high authority, it will, of course, be allowed that I ought to be permitted a similar mode of reply.

SIR ARTHUR A DISCRIMINATING ADVOCATE OF IRRIGATION EXTENSION.

His lordship says, " Some twenty years ago there was a strong impression out of doors, that it was only necessary to construct an irrigation works in India and it must necessarily pay. The chief supporter of that view was Sir Arthur Cotton." So directly contrary is this to fact, that one of the main points I continually insisted upon was, that the Ganges Canal was a grand warning against ill-projected works, and I insisted upon the lesson that that work gave us, that great mistakes might be made in such projections, insomuch, that where there were the greatest natural advantages, false projection might cause a comparative failure. His lordship then proceeds to speak in the slightest possible way of the success of the Madras works, in a way that would entirely mislead people as to the actual results, viz., that they had raised Tanjore and Godavari from a very low state to a state of the greatest prosperity (Godavari especially from a state so far below the general low state of the districts at that time, that Sir H. Montgomery was sent as a Special Commissioner to try and raise it from its extreme degradation, to by far the most prosperous state of any district of India), raising the revenue from £400,000 and £230,000 respectively, to £750,000 and £570,000, while the average revenue of all India is £250,000 per district. How completely the public have been misled in this is plainly shown by *The Times* saying, " The Godavari, the Orissa, and the Bengal works have all been more or less failures." Surely such an utterly false statement, gathered from his lordship's speech, requires an official contradiction. I have no doubt these works are the most profitable engineering works in the world. An expenditure of £700,000 has irrigated seven hundred thousand acres, paying eight shillings an acre for water rate alone, amounting to £280,000 a year or forty per cent., while the total revenue of the district has risen from £230,000 to £570,000 a year, the exports have increased from £60,000 to £800,000, and the imports from £20,000 to £200,000. And this is represented to the world as "more or less a failure." Of these works his lordship says, "*What their actual returns were, it was difficult to say.*"[1]

WERE "RECENT RESULTS" EVER IGNORED BY IRRIGATION ADVOCATES?

Further on, he says, "In all their speeches and statements with respect to irrigation, Sir A. Cotton and his friends, by some curious oversight, had wholly ignored the results of recent experience."

In reply to this, I beg to state that in every paper of mine, without a single exception, I have stated the results of the whole of the new works, and every one of my conclusions is drawn from those whole results. I have continually quoted Mr. Thornton, the head of the railway department of the India Office, as to those returns, in respect of the works actually in operation, as he gave them at the Society of Arts. And to those I have added full statements of those works which, through the refusal of the water by the ryots, are only yet in very partial operation. Not a single work has ever been omitted. Especially have I been particular in entering fully into the cases of the two works in which the water has been refused, because it is most essential that it should be known whether those works have, as yet, made no returns from the failure of the *works*, or the failure of *their management.* Nothing can be more mischievous than to confound these two things. If the

[1] See Appendix B.

works themselves are failures, the money is irrecoverably lost, and the only use we can make of them is not to make similar mistakes in future projects. But, if the failure is in the management, we have only to put them into more effective hands, and they will immediately become, like all the thousands of others, highly profitable.

WHY THE TUNGABUDRA WORKS WERE ONLY PARTIALLY SUCCESSFUL.

His Lordship then proceeds to speak of the Tungabudra works, and to make me responsible for their results. The answer to this is very simple. Is the man who recommends a work answerable for all that is done in its execution, and its management when executed? If I were answerable for all the management of irrigation works by the revenue authorities, I should indeed have much to answer for. I don't think Watt is answerable for every steam engine that has failed. However, the Tungabudra works were not only a thoroughly good project, as it is clearly proved to any person who will look into the case, but they have been most successfully executed, and are, as works, an unqualified success, that is, they have been executed at a cost that will give most abundant returns, when they are used, and they have been proved thoroughly sound and good in their standing most severe storms without any injury, while the adjoining railway was destroyed for miles, that is, most seriously injured. They have cost £1,500,000, and they distribute four hundred thousand cubic yards per hour for two hundred days per annum, or a total quantity of two thousand million cubic yards. Taking seven per cent. for interest and management, they thus cost £105,000 a year, which gives a cost of £1 for twenty thousand cubic yards. The question is, Is this a high price or a low one? The natives are in the habit of raising water from wells in millions of cases all over India, at a cost of about three thousand cubic yards per £1, or seven times this cost, and this they willingly pay for well water, entirely without the rich manure contained in river water. Again, the

Government charge in this district for tank water, very inferior to river water, is about ten rupees an acre, that is for about six thousand cubic yards, or at the rate of £1 for six thousand cubic yards, three times the cost of this rich river water. This is perfectly conclusive as to the success of the works, as works. Their failure, therefore, consists solely in the management. Those who have had the charge of the sale of the water have not been clever enough to sell at six rupees per acre what was worth certainly seven times as much, for it is most certain that the natives all over India would not go on raising filtered water from wells at three thousand cubic yards per £1, if it were not worth it. The fact is that the revenue officers, into whose hands the authorities have committed the sale of the water, have entirely failed. We have no proof that the Company, it they had been allowed to manage their own affairs, as every Company in England is, would not have had tact enough to persuade the ryots to take water at one-seventh of its value. Why should not this be tried? These are the things that so effectually keep British capital out of India, and are the reason why British capitalists will readily invest hundreds of millions in America, Turkey, Spain, rather than in our own dominions. This is why India is perishing for want of British capital, while Turkey is carrying on war at our expense. I have spoken only of the value of the water in ordinary years, but who can estimate its value in such a year as the past? In the Company's reports, their effects are thus spoken of: "The value of the crop created by the canal cannot be estimated more nearly than at a million sterling." The whole cost of the works was one and a half millions; thus two-thirds of the whole cost was repaid by a single partial crop, for only one hundred thousand acres were irrigated? Again, in January of this year, 1877, the overseer reports: "The white cholum is magnificent. I have never seen finer crops of this grain. The ears were so full and the plants so thick that they were touching each other." Again, "The average yield per acre is two putties, sold recently at £2 16*s*. per putty, and the straw is almost half as valuable as the grain." Thus the value of the crop was £14, or twenty-four times the year's water-rate. All this in the midst of the terrible desert produced by the drought. One would suppose that to decry such inconceivably important works would be impossible to anybody, and that the only anxiety would be to discover what could be the mistake through which they were rendered even for a time partially useless. Is it possible that the whole Civil Service cannot produce one member with the very moderate tact and talent that would enable him to get over difficulties which have certainly never yet been got over, but this is simply because they have never occurred or been dreamt of in the whole Presidency before in the tens of thousands of irrigation works that are now in operation and have been in operation for thousands of years?

And if such talent cannot at present be found in the Civil Service, surely it would be better to let the Directors of the Irrigation Company search the world for such a man, rather than let the Government and the ryots continue without such inestimable benefits. How strange it seems that it should never have occurred to any of the officials that there must surely be some prodigious mistake, that a thing should occur which has never been heard of in the whole Presidency before. If the whole of this water were used, it would irrigate three hundred thousand acres of rice, producing one hundred and fifty thousand tons, worth £900,000, or sixty per cent. on the cost besides the straw and the cheap transit on some three hundred miles of canal. And the returns to the Company would be, at twelve shillings per acre, £200,000, or fourteen per cent. besides canal tolls. And this supposes the whole of the water is used for rice, whereas it would go much farther if used for wheat and other dry grains. Thus, the temporary failure of this one work out of the thousands of Madras works, solely through mis-management of the revenue officers, is charged upon the Engineers, who up to the point beyond which they were not allowed to interfere, have been eminently and perfectly successful, the revenue officers themselves being the judges.

I must dwell upon this point. If this refusal of the water in one single instance out of the thousands of the Madras irrigation works, new and old, a thing never heard of or thought of before, (I have been all my life employed on these works, and, without exception, always found the natives ten times more eager to get the water than we were to give it to them), if this is represented as the general case, and again, if the failure of these works to afford returns is represented as a failure of the works themselves, in any way, instead of solely the failure in the management, so that at any moment under intelligent management they must inevitably become as profitable as all the other irrigation works in this presidency, without exception; if these things are asserted the whole case is essentially falsified and all our conclusions and proceedings must be utterly wrong.

THE DELTA WORKS IN NORTHERN AND SOUTHERN MADRAS.

To return to the delta works so slightly noticed by the Under Secretary of State, and stated to be more or less failures by *The Times*, what is said of them by others? Mr. Monier Williams, in his letter to *The Times*, giving an account of his tour through the famine districts, says: "All the belts of land reached by the grand system of irrigation which stretches between the Godavari, Kistna, and Cauveri rivers (fertilizing the soil wherever it reaches, and forcing even the haters of English rule to admit that no other raj ever conferred on India such benefits), present a marvellous contrast to the arid tracts which meet the traveller by the Peninsula, Madras, and South India railways." Not a word to this purport has been said either in the Under Secretary's speech, or in any other, on the subject of the famine. From all the accounts of the famine given officially, the public are left in total ignorance of the immeasurable benefits conferred on the presidency by these most beneficent works, but for which the Government would have been overwhelmed. For if, instead of these districts supplying hundreds of thousands of tons of food to their neighbouring tracts, they had added five millions of starving people to the dependents on relief, it is most certain that the Government could not possibly have met the difficulty. The omission of this great fact, therefore, from the reports of the famine quite falsifies the accounts. And the following is the description of these works by the ryots, who are living in immediate contact with, and partaking in the benefits of the works. The ryots of Trichinopoly, on the 13th of November last, thus addressed the Governor: "It was here, in Trichinopoly, that the earliest triumph of hydraulic science was achieved by Captain Cotton. Taking the idea probably from the grand anicut, a most remarkable work of remote times, and a monument of untutored native engineering skill, Captain Cotton conceived and carried out the bold design of controlling the Coleroon by a gigantic dam of masonry, so as to arrest the drying up of the Cauveri, which became imminent year by year. The successful result of the upper and lower anicuts of the Coleroon emboldened that engineer to bridle the Godavari, a river five miles wide at the chosen point, in a similar way and with still more magnificent results. Thenceforward this system of deltaic irrigation has been applied to the Kistna and Pennair, and to the rivers of other presidencies—the Mahanudi in Bengal, the Ganges canal in the Doab, and the Sone in Bengal; all which works have converted *the tracts affected into scenes of matchless fertility and wealth, and have for ever protected them and neighbouring provinces from the disaster of recurring drought.*" This is the way in which the parties most intimately concerned speak of them. These ryots then proceed to press upon the Governor the execution of six extensive projects, which they define, in that one district of Trichinopoly. For one of these they state that they had themselves, years before, subscribed money. In the face of these things the public are led to suppose that the general opposition of the ryots to water is an insuperable difficulty, though the Government are anxious to supply it to them. The ryots conclude by saying : " All these projects will in their humble estimation *bring fertility and wealth to tracts now too frequently exposed to droughts, and which suffered but too severely during the present famine.*" I am persuaded that the English public generally have not the least idea of the true state of the case, either as respects the results of these works or the feelings of the natives about them, or rather that their notions of these are directly contrary to the truth, so completely are they misinformed on the subject.

His lordship then reproves Mr. Bright "for endorsing the speculative ideas of enthusiastic engineers"; these speculations consist exclusively of statements taken from the Blue Books of the actual results of all the works of irrigation, not omitting one, constructed by our Government, illustrated by fifty years of the most thorough practical experience in almost all parts of India. In no single instance is anything in the way of a conclusion stated without the support of facts and figures from the India Office.

THE PROPOSED NAVIGATION CANALS THROUGHOUT INDIA.

His lordship then speaks of "the wildest and rashest of all Sir A. Cotton's schemes," viz. :—to construct navigation canals throughout India, at a cost of thirty millions. But not one word is said to show in what respect this proposition is wild and rash.

In proposing this scheme, I give the most complete data by which anybody can judge of the case, but I may begin my reply to this charge by showing in what good company I am in recommending canals for navigation. Lord Mayo had actually begun a canal by the side of the East India railway for one hundred miles to Ranigunj, and when he stopped it, he said, " Should the discovery of coal at Midnapur result in a coalfield equal to Ranigunj, one of the principal objects of the Damuda canal will no longer exist, because the coal would be carried by the Midnapur canal to Calcutta." *But when it was reported to Lord Mayo that on the removal of the contractor who had charge of the boring, no more coal appeared, the Damuda canal was not resumed.* Thus Lord Mayo first discovered that a canal was essential where £25,000 a mile had been spent upon a railway, after twenty years' trial. And, of course, if a canal was wanted for coal, it was wanted also for ninety-nine hundredths of the traffic, all of which, like coal, require cheapness and not speed. Next, we have the late Bengal Government, which says in its last administration report —that for '75–6—speaking of the communication between the Hooghly and the Ganges, " Although some portion of the traffic is taken off by the railways, still the greater portion follows the water highways, notwithstanding they are so tortuous as to be lengthened out to an excessive distance. It is calculated that a boat plying between Eastern Bengal and Calcutta, travels some two hundred or three hundred miles more than it would if there were anything like a straight route by water. *The obvious remedy will be to construct a canal for navigation across the country from Eastern Bengal to Calcutta.*" And, thirdly, I must quote the present head railway engineer of India, Mr. Leslie, who as soon as he had finished the extension of the East India railway to Goalundo, the confluence of the Ganges and Burhamputra, wrote a letter to the Calcutta merchants, in which he said, " The fact that the railway company has been in the field twelve years, and has literally acquired only a tithe of the traffic, is an unanswerable argument in favour of the canal. The present eastern traffic is one million nine hundred thousand tons per annum, and it is rapidly increasing. A toll of half a crown on this traffic alone would yield a return of £240,000, sufficient to pay all expenses of working and maintenance, and yield a return of eleven per cent. on the capital outlay of £2,000,000. The western traffic would *probably double the receipts* ; at the rate of cost of three shillings and sixpence a ton for tolls and carriage, there would be a saving on the eastern traffic alone of £840,000 a year, as respects the present cost by rail, steamer, and boat." Thus, another *rash* and *wild* engineer calculates that on a line on which £4,000,000 have been spent on a railway (which has been tried for twelve years), if £2,000,000 are spent on a canal, there would be a return on the eastern and western traffic together of twenty-two per cent., and a saving to Calcutta of £1,750,000 a year, on a line of only one hundred and thirty miles direct distance. And this on the present traffic alone, which is rapidly increasing, without the enormous stimulus that such a great reduction of time and freight would cause. Boats, which carry by far the greater part of the traffic, take six weeks to accomplish the four hundred and twenty miles by the rivers. Now we cannot certainly imagine either Lord Mayo, the late Bengal Government, or the head railway engineer, very violently biassed in favour of canals against their own children—the railways—and if they were, the simple figures given by Mr. Leslie are quite decisive to anybody. Since I was ordered to project a work on this line in 1858, when I recommended a canal, at least £20,000,000 have been lost, besides £4,000,000 spent on the railway in cost and debt. This will give some idea *why India is still a poor country.* If by the grievous mistakes that have been made, £24,000,000 have been thrown away on a line of one hundred and thirty miles, what must be the loss on all India for want of cheap transit, and this leaves out of the calculation nine-tenths of the results in the immense traffic that would be created by such effective transit. Of course, what is thus declared to be necessary and practicable on these two lines running out of Calcutta, is equally applicable to all the main lines through similar country. It will be thus seen that there is more than one *rash* and *wild* man connected with India.

CANALS RUNNING PARALLEL WITH RAILWAYS.

There is not the smallest room for question as to the canals being as advisable by the side of the railways after the first hundred miles, as they are for those hundred miles where the face of the country is suitable for canals. Now let us consider what these conclusions imply, to which Lord Mayo, Sir Richard Temple, and the other members of the Indian Government, and the head railway engineer have come. If £1,750,000 a year are lost on the present traffic for want of a steamboat canal between the Hooghly and the Ganges, there cannot be less than three millions a year lost on the three lines out of Calcutta, the Northern, the Western, and the South-Western, on the present traffic alone; consequently, during the thirty years that the railways have been on hand, the loss within one hundred and thirty miles of Calcutta could not have been less than £70,000,000 on the actual traffic, besides the loss from want of the traffic that would have been created. So we are quite safe in saying that £100,000,000 have been lost for want of canals within one hundred and thirty miles of Calcutta, while the railways have been in operation almost all that time. What, then, has been the loss during that same time on all the ten thousand miles of main road that India requires? Certainly *several hundred millions.* Most certainly, if this is well considered, one way of increasing the wealth of India is most palpable and certain. Nobody can answer this argument for cheap transit, based upon the statements and conclusions of the committed railway men themselves.

THE GODAVARI NAVIGATION.

His lordship next proceeds to speak of the Godavari navigation. He says that the estimate was put at £80,000. A first rough estimate was £300,000. But this was not in the ordinary sense of the word an estimate. It was a mere rough guess, preparatory to the formation of an estimate in detail. The remarkable thing is that it has turned out perfectly correct, for it is now certain from what has been expended and effected, that if that sum had been granted at the time it was named, twenty-five years ago, it would have been amply sufficient. But the history of the work is perhaps the most perfect specimen of how not to do a thing, that could be found. Instead of providing £100,000 a year for three years, as any private company would have done, uncertain sums were given from year to year, for twenty years, sometimes more, sometimes less, sometimes none, so that the Engineer never knew what he had to expect. Two or three times the works were suddenly stopped without notice, and the workpeople, who had been collected from great distances, most unjustly dispersed without remuneration, till all confidence was lost, and it was only by very high pay that the people could be collected again. On one occasion the Engineer was compelled to send away the workmen to save them from starving on the spot. Thus the work was spun out for more than twenty years, till the value of money had fallen to half what it was when the work was proposed, and the invaluable time of the most talented and devoted Engineer that India ever had, Colonel Haig, was in a great measure thrown away, and the work cost more than double what it need have done. When an Engineer recommends a work, is he to suppose that such imbecility is to be exhibited in the carrying it out? He necessarily supposes that it will be conducted with ordinary judgment and diligence. But, further, as to the actual cost notwithstanding this astonishing management: his Lordship states that it was £700,000, but *not a word was said as to what was accomplished for this sum.* How can we judge whether money is well spent or not, unless we are told what we get for it? Now the fact is that this sum very nearly completed the works at the Second Barrier, which would have given four hundred miles of navigation, or at the rate of £2,000 a mile. *Now was it no part of the question whether £2,000 a mile for river navigation would be dear or cheap?* A railway has cost from £25,000 a mile to £9,000, and the average charge is one penny per ton, while the cost on the river is one halfpenny per ton, in its present condition, but it might, at a very small expense, be further greatly improved by storing water. It must be stated, however, that, without this stored water, it would only be navigable for seven or eight months in the year, but it would still be a communication of immense value. The Erie Canal in the States is only open seven months in the year, and it conveys four million tons. Had his lordship stated that this navigation would have cost one-tenth of what the great railways have cost, and have carried at half their charge, it might have considerably affected the judgment of the public as to whether it was a wise expenditure or not. The fact is, that it was one of the most profitable undertakings in India, if the works had been completed. It would have laid open the whole district of Nagpur, etc., to the world, whereas it is now paralyzed, solely by being cut off, and isolated by the expense of land carriage.[1] Nothing in the world in the way of internal arrangements will avail to raise this vast tract of Central India from its present state, till it is put within reach of the coast districts and of the world's markets. When Australia was in a state of utter insolvency, and sheep were selling for two shillings each, some clever man discovered that, by converting them into tallow, he could get over the difficulties of carriage, and give them value in the London market; instantly they became of the value of eight shillings each, and Australia entered upon a career of prosperity which has never since been checked, *all having hung upon the cost of transport to foreign markets*. And the same will be the case when Central India can send her excellent cotton, oilseeds, wheat, etc., to the coast at practicable rates, and can receive in return the salt and rice of the coast, and the manufactures of England. At this moment a very small sum is wanted to complete these most essential works, and all Central India *is waiting and must wait till it is done*.

THE ORISSA AND TUNGABUDRA WORKS.

His lordship then goes on to speak of the Orissa works, which is a similar case to that of the Tungabudra, except that it is greatly aggravated there by the dreadful zemind-

[1] See Appendix D.

ari system. The success of the works there also is complete, as works. The failure is solely in the refusal of the water, through the inconceivable evils of the revenue management. The works have cost about £3 an acre, including the navigation, the traffic on which is so great already, that it alone, without irrigation, promises to go far towards paying the interest of the cost. But here, too, we are met with the same sort of false economy which has ruined so many schemes. The navigation between Calcutta and Cuttack has a gap of eighty miles unexecuted, which, of course, keeps the traffic at about a fifth of what it ought to be. What can stand against such a system as this? What would have become of the railways if gaps of eighty miles had been left in them? There is no doubt that the zemindari system is a most terrible difficulty in the way of these works, but I am quite certain that energetic and intelligent men will find their way out of all difficulties there also. But, to represent the present failure of these works to yield returns, as if it were the fault of the works, instead of their management, falsifies the case. When the natives there are asked why they do not use the water, they have often said: "What is the use of it, when, if there is any profit, half of it will go to the money lenders, and the other half to the zemindars?" Of course nothing in the world can stand against such a state of things, but we are surely perfectly justified in hoping that some day some Governor of tact and faithfulness will be found, who will set these things to rights. Some notion of the inconceivable state of things there, may be formed from the following extract from the report of the native deputy superintendent of canals in Midnapur for 1877. "But the most patent cause about the gradual decline of the area leased is the indebtedness of the ryots. They are involved over head and ears, and it is a matter of infinite regret, that their debts are increasing as their connection with government irrigation is growing older. Excepting during the year under review, the canal irrigation has always increased the yield by from 240 to 400 lbs.," (worth about eight shillings,) "but the irrigators are not in a condition to benefit by it; all they obtain from the fields goes *punctually to fill the coffers of the Mahajuns.* They have finally to borrow the money to pay the water rate. The increase of *the crop is sure to prove more than enough for the purpose,* if reserved for the liquidation of the government debt; but no notice is taken of it, and when the irrigator is forced to pay for the irrigation of his land, he blames the canal for the increase of his debt."[1] Such is the state of things, and then the engineers are charged with the failure of the returns. If such a state of things had existed in Madras, the works there, which have yielded fifteen, twenty-one, and eighty-seven per cent., would have as completely failed. On the other hand, the chief engineer says, in his last report, "The returns show a considerable increase of irrigation in Orissa, attributable partly to the deficient rainfall, and partly to a growing appreciation on the part of the cultivators of the value of the canal water in all seasons." We may thus fairly conclude that here also these difficulties will be got over. But nothing can justify the representing of the difficulties which have occurred in these two instances of Orissa and the Tumbudra as if they were generally the case, because it is entirely contrary to the truth.

HAVE ALL THE SOURCES OF IRRIGATION BEEN TAPPED.

Again, his lordship says: "It had been found from experience in Madras that tanks and canals could not be constructed so as to be solely dependent on rainfall, and, in the opinion of many competent Engineers, the waters of the three rivers of Madras could not be much further utilized." It really seems inconceivable that such things could be uttered. We take out of the Godavari 8,000,000,000 of cubic yards, and it discharges about 200,000,000,000 or twenty-five times as much, sufficient to irrigate 30,000,000 acres of rice, and four times as much of dry grains. Out of the Kistna we do not take a fiftieth part. What can be

[1] See Appendix C.

the use of making such statements? In Madras five million acres are irrigated. There is water enough in the rivers to irrigate 100,000,000 acres. But, with respect to the tanks. In the first place only a very few of them are in thorough repair. Then, by far the greatest part of them could be enlarged, and thousands of them supplied from the never-failing rivers. A recent *Friend of India* says: "A native Revenue officer of the Madras Presidency of twenty-six years' standing, Mr. Pillaymootoo Pillay, who has been eleven years in charge of three taluks of North Arcot, tells us, though he witnessed the famines of 1846 and 1866, he has seen no famine before like that he has just passed through." In reply to the question,—"What, in your opinion, is the best way of meeting the difficulty of bad seasons?" Mr. Pillay said: "We ought to increase the supply of water to the cultivator to enable him to grow more crops; for this the tanks must be strengthened. *They must be kept always in good condition.* We must also dig wells widely over the country. In ordinary years we shall be able to grow two crops, and the grain stored would be greater. In this district there are two large tanks. The water has been flowing from these for long past periods, and giving water to the neighbouring lands. This year owing to the water famine, they were dry. They were never so at any previous time. They were built under former rulers, and under our rule were improved. Dams are now constructed so that these tanks are now fed from the Pallaur river. However, as there were no floods in the Pallaur in 1875 and 1876, this led to these tanks becoming dry. By strengthening these tanks and making them capable of growing two crops in ordinary seasons, the stocks of one and a half years could be increased to two and a half. Not only the large tanks but the small ones can be made to hold water enough so as to raise two crops." The fact is that the neglect of these noble native works has been one of the most grievous and most astonishing defects in our government. One of the very first things to be done is thoroughly to examine into the state of all these works, and first, to enlarge them, second, to provide them with ample waste weirs in which they are generally defective, and, lastly, to plan works for filling them from the great rivers that never fail, for, at present, very few of them are so supplied, while thousands can be. Nothing has been more astonishing than the neglect of these essential works by the Civil Service generally. In the last report of the Presidency, of eight hundred pages, no account whatever is given of these works, as if they were matters of no sort of importance, while almost everything else in the Presidency, however insignificant, is given in great detail.

SINGULAR STATEMENTS REQUIRING EXPLANATION.

His lordship goes on to say: "Moreover, Sir Richard Temple had directed attention to the fact that in the wet lands the famine had been the worst." What in the world can this mean? As if famine could be aggravated by water!

He adds: "It was clear that the construction ot tanks and canals which were not connected with permanent sources, was not sufficient to preserve the people from famine." Then why were they not so connected wherever it was possible? What has been done about this? Nothing. This is one of the grievous defects in our Government, and then it is made an excuse for doing nothing. What can be a greater contrast than the way in which these tanks are spoken of by the Under Secretary of State and those in which the same works are mentioned by the Trichinopoly ryots and the Arcot tahsildar?

His lordship then makes a number of statements as to the returns of the Irrigation works and the Railways. As to the Irrigation works, Mr. Thornton has given a statement *in figures* of the whole results of the new works in operation. We cannot suppose that an India Office man would be biassed to overstate these results. He states that the lowest return, even adding to the cost what he supposes had been spent on some of the works before we took them in hand, was four and three-quarters, and the highest forty per cent., and the average, seven and a half per cent. This is direct returns. He gives no report of the change in the districts where the works are, and only speaks of the effects in ordinary years; to which he says must be added the enormous increase in prosperity of the people and the incalculable effects in a year of failure of the season. He says also nothing of the prodigious effects of the cheap transit. But if we put together the accounts of two India Office men respecting the direct returns from irrigation and the statements of official men, which I have given before respecting the effects of transit by canals, we shall certainly arrive at conclusions diametrically opposed to those in his lordship's speech; that is, that notwithstanding the temporary failure of two works owing to the refusal of the water, arising solely from the shocking state of the revenue management of the districts, there is a vast surplus in the treasury from the irrigation works and a far greater saving to the people. The Godavari works alone have, since 1846, when they were begun, raised the revenue by £350,000 a year, or an average about £175,000 for thirty years, amounting to £5,250,000 against £700,000 which they cost and three per cent. for repairs, etc., or ninety per cent. on half the cost, equal together to £300,000, leaving a clear gain of £4,000,000 besides the accumulation of interest. And this is without reckoning the prodigious saving of life, revenue, and property in all the famines that have occurred.[1] And the results of the Railways in point of direct returns are £4,500,000 upon an actual outlay on works and lands of £116,000,000, with an accumulated debt of £45,000,000, being four per cent. on the cost and three per cent. on the cost and debt, leaving a loss on the cost and debt together of £3,000,000 a year, for the total charge upon the Treasury is five per cent. on £94,000,000, the share capital, and four per cent. on the remaining £67,000,000, or £7,500,000.

[1] See Appendix B.

THE DELUSION ABOUT THE BEST MEANS OF TRANSIT IN INDIA.

But this loss is nothing to the terrible mischief of the delusion which they have caused about transit, the authorities and the public both dreaming that they provided the country with effective transit, when Lord Mayo, the Lieutenant-Governor of Bengal, and Mr. Leslie, all declare that they have so failed that it is now necessary to cut canals by their side, and the latter showing by plain figures that the loss is of millions, even within one hundred and thirty miles of Calcutta. Further, we have continually such statements as the following in corroboration of these statements, viz. :—from a late Calcutta paper, "In the Resolution on the Burdwan report, there is the statement that the Midnapur canals carried no less than eighty thousand tons of rice during 1876–77. Side by side with this is the statement that the railway failed entirely to take off the supplies brought to its stations, great quantities having to be carted down to Calcutta by road. Here are two of the navigable canals carrying even under unfavourable circumstances all the vast supplies brought to them for transport to the famine-stricken districts. Here is the chief railway of India, close under the eye of the highest authorities, collapsing under the strain put upon its carrying power." This is only one of multitudes of similar statements, made by fervent supporters of railways, as to the utter failure to carry even the insignificant quantities that are brought to them under the present prohibitory charges. In 1850, when the railways were under consideration, not a word of this was allowed to be heard. This really *rash and wild* undertaking, of spending £160,000,000 upon railways was entered upon without the slightest enquiry, though the actual state of things, as represented now by leading railway men, was urged as the certain effects of the railways in 1850. The present Earl of Derby at that time protested against this *wild* scheme. He said in a speech at Manchester that "it seemed to him one of the most practicable things the Association could attend to, was to give information on these points, the two great things, roads and irrigation. As to roads he was afraid we were in danger of being misled by the example of England. It seemed to be thought that because costly lines of railway were suitable for this country (before a line was constructed we had a complete system of canals suited to our heavy traffic), they were equally suitable to India. He believed, and so did more competent judges, that that system was a *complete mistake.* What was wanted, was, not costly lines for rapid travelling, laid down in a few parts, but a comparatively inexpensive though slow means of communication extended over all India." So, also, a former chief engineer of the East India railway, after they had been tried some years, said to a friend of mine: "But railways are a complete mistake. They are not suited to India." And now that they are done and the money is irrecoverable as well as the time, what possible excuse can be found for continuing to deprive India of this priceless advantage of cheap transit, as urged by the railway men themselves?[1]

NAVIGATION CONNECTING LINKS.

But there is, now, another special reason for expending money in this way, which is, that in the different irrigation works, there are, in detached tracts, so many thousand miles of steamboat canal already executed and only wanting short lines to connect them, in order to give effect to ten times the length of those connecting links. Thus on the line between Calcutta and Ludiana, there are already cut, or cutting, the Sirhind, the Ganges, Lower Ganges, and Sone, projects about eight hundred miles, and one hundred miles more are recommended by the Bengal Government, in all nine hundred miles out of a total distance of twelve hundred miles, so that probably a sum of £1,500,000 more would complete this immensely important line, certainly one of the most important that could be found in the world; a very short calculation will show how entirely

[1] See Appendix D.

insignificant such an addition to the expenses incurred in the works now in hand would be, in comparison with the results. The charge for interest and repairs at seven per cent. would be £100,000 a year. It is impossible to say what traffic such a cheap transport, viz. :—one twentieth of a penny a ton a mile,—would create, but we should be quite safe in supposing two million tons on the whole distance, or 2,400,000,000 tons one mile, which would be equal to a charge of one-hundredth of a penny per ton per mile, one shilling for the whole distance, or one-third of a bushel of wheat, for instance. If the cost of carriage were as supposed, one-twentieth of a penny, the charge for bringing a bushel of wheat the whole distance would be three halfpence. Allowing half a crown for the average price there and the same for freight, etc., to London, North-West Provinces wheat could be landed in England for little more than five shillings, while the average price in England is six shillings and sixpence. Thus a vast trade in wheat would be permanently established. This is only a specimen of what could now be attained by a certain outlay on completing the lines of canal already so far in hand. Certainly no money could be laid out in India to greater advantage.

WORKS URGENTLY REQUIRED.

If the various European and Indian testimonies that I have now quoted[1] are carefully considered, I am sure it will be clear that the following are the works that are most urgently required in India to meet its demands both in respect of the famines and its general elevation in material prosperity, viz. :—

1. The repair, enlargement and better supply of the tanks;
2. Construction of the canal from the Hooghly to the Ganges;
3. The completion of all the lines of canal now partially executed;

[1] See Appendices A, B, C, D, E, F.

4. The extension of those lines wherever practicable, especially the completion of the Godavari navigation;
5. The construction of new works of irrigation in every district, where it can be done at a practicable cost.

I must conclude with earnestly requesting a comparison of these works now proposed, especially Mr. Leslie's canal, with those actually in hand at this moment in the way of railways. The sum of half a million is being expended on sixty miles of railway in Nagpur, or nearly £9,000 a mile; the quantity carried on the lines open was twenty thousand tons, the charge fourpence a ton a mile, the actual cost, including loss of interest, sevenpence, and the return last year one per cent., and this on the very line on which a river, the Wurda, could have been made navigable so as to carry at one-tenth of a penny per ton, for £2,000 a mile.

AN APPEAL AND A PATHETIC DEFENCE.

I need hardly repeat my assurance that, after being spoken of in the opprobrious terms that the Under Secretary thought necessary to use, *where he knew that I was not present to give my side of the question*, the Secretary of State will give me the fullest publicity to my defence which the case now admits of.

Whether it was quite becoming, or for the furtherance of the public service, for a young man, who had never been in India, had never seen a tank, an irrigated area, or a mile of steamboat canal, or spoken to a ryot in the irrigated districts, and was consequently, of necessity, very ignorant of the whole subject, to speak before the House and the world in such contemptuous terms of an officer old enough to be his grandfather, who had had more than fifty years of the most thorough practical experience in the matter, who had done good service and shown himself to be a practical man, though he says it himself (for it had pleased God that he should project and execute works that have put millions into the treasury, and scores of millions into the pockets of the ryots, or rather into their cummerbands) and who had urgently pointed out, twenty-five years ago, what is now declared by a Viceroy, an Indian Lieutenant-Governor and his Council, and several railway engineers, viz. :—that "the railways cannot carry either the *quantities*, or at the *price*, that is essential in India," whether it was becoming or useful for a young man so to speak, is a point which I beg, respectfully, to offer for the consideration of the Right Hon. the Secretary of State and his Council. The Under Secretary of State may possibly even accomplish something himself yet for India, and he will then think it but just and honourable that he should be accused where he can have an opportunity of answering for himself, and for the two hundred and fifty millions of India. For nothing can be more certain than that in the present case the future of India's millions depends greatly upon whether money is still expended upon Railways, to cost £9,000 a mile and carry thirty thousand tons at one penny, or upon canals to cost from £2,000 to £8,000 and carry two or three million tons at one-twentieth of a penny, and whether districts are to be put into the state of Tanjore, Kistna, and Godavari, or left in the state of the rest of the Carnatic last year, and of Orissa, Behar, and Central India a few years ago.

APPENDIX A.

In '71, Assistant Surgeon Wright was sent to inquire into the cause of the fever which had been bad in that Northern part of the Madras Presidency, and the following are extracts from the Sanitary Commissioner's remarks on that officer's report. "It has seemed to me to be a point of the very greatest importance to determine whether the periodical outbreaks of fever in this district have increased in severity since the Godavari Irrigation Works have been completed." He then shows that the average loss of life from fever in five years had been eight and a half per cent. in the Irrigated Taluks, and eleven per cent. in the Upper Taluks, and adds, "My conviction is that the accessions of fever are due to the geographical position of the district," and again, "the fever is due to the northerly winds sweeping over the malarious jungles of the hill tracts. The results of five years' registration demonstrate in a very clear manner that the intensity of fever in any taluk, has no relation to the extent of Irrigation of the land."

APPENDIX B.

The following extracts from the excellent official *Descriptive and Historical Account of the Godavari District*, by Mr. Henry Morris, of the Madras Civil Service, will place in a striking light the change which Irrigation has made in the district. "A severe famine desolated the Northern Circars (the name by which the Northern districts of Madras are commonly known there), in 1791. The effect of the famine was terrific, it was computed that one-fourth of the population fell victims to want, or emigrated." Again, "but the most calamitous season perhaps that has ever been experienced in the Northern Circars, was that of 1833. The crushing misery that daily came upon the people was appalling; Madras being the seat of Government, thousands repaired there. The great Northern road soon became one long graveyard, etc." Again in 1844, it is said in the same book, "About this time the district had fallen into a state so far below even the then generally sad state of the Northern districts, that Sir Henry Montgomery was deputed as a special Commissioner to report what could be done to raise it from its lamentable state of depression. That experienced officer having come from Tanjore, where he had seen the great results of attention to Irrigation, strongly urged the examination of the Delta by an experienced engineer, with a view to the execution of such a system of works for the regulation of the water, as would effectually lead to the realisation of the wonderful amount of produce, which the large extent of fertile soil might be expected to yield, if it were supplied with water, relieved from floods, and provided with navigation." And he concludes his account with saying, "through all these changes (up to 1846), they passed comparatively unchanged; but their present condition is incomparably better than anything they had ever before enjoyed."

Again, "At the commencement of our rule it constituted a portion of a neglected province, and at one time it was brought into a state of extreme impoverishment and distress. It was desolated by famine, and misgoverned by the numerous land owners and their advisers. Since the introduction, however, of the admirable system of Irrigation, it has brightened and revived. Famine is unknown. The people are prosperous and contented. It is the garden of the great Northern Province. The revenue, instead of being reduced, as it once was, to the verge of bankruptcy, is more elastic than it has ever been; its population has more than doubled; the material prosperity of its inhabitants is proved by their being better fed, better clothed, and better educated than formerly; its commerce has flourished, and its trade has developed in a marvellous degree; and it may confidently be asserted that it is in as peaceful, happy and prosperous condition as any part of Her Imperial Majesty's dominions." This is said of a district surrounded by districts overwhelmed by the most desolating famine ever known, to which it was formerly as subject as all the others, but not a word of this must be said in any report or speech about the famine. And the Under Secretary of State actually says that, "In the wet lands the famine had been the worst." Is it possible that words could be uttered more completely perverting the facts of the case? Mr. Morris gives the population in 1842 at 560,000, and by the last census, 1,600,000. The mortality on the average preceding 1872, was under two per cent., and this included the upper feverish taluks. This is pretty strong proof of the healthiness of India, where the water is regulated.

I may take this opportunity of saying a few words on the subject of Revenue management in connection with Irrigation and Navigation, as the matter has been forced upon me in the course of my experience. Of course, even water itself cannot suffice without effective governing. All the water poured over Tanjore and Godavari would not have raised those districts to their present pitch of prosperity unless they had had previously and subsequently able and just rulers. Without this we should undoubtedly have seen there, in great measure, what we now see partially on the Tungabudra and, more fully, in Bengal. Tanjore has been as much favoured in its management as it has in its irrigation. It has had such a succession of able, faithful, and laborious Collectors (as they are so absurdly called still), as I believe no other district of India was ever favoured with. Though the name was a most suitable one when they were first constituted, for the idea of collecting Revenue was the only important thing in the minds of the East India Directors, I wish the name could be now altered to one more suitable to their present noble functions. Before Tanjore was watered, it had thus been prepared for it, for it was in a thoroughly healthy state of Revenue management, etc. And at the time the great works there were begun, and for thirteen years, there was ruling over the district, a gentleman, Mr. Kindersley, who, I have no doubt, was the ablest and most faithful Collector that I ever met with or ever heard of in India. And this is saying much indeed, for I am quite satisfied that there never has been in this world a body of officials so faithful, laborious, upright and able as the Indian Civil Service, nor anything to compare with it, even in England, though, of course, with some serious defects and some shocking exceptions. It has often been remarked that every civilian who came out of Mr. Kindersley's school, almost without exception, turned out a trump. Especially Sir Henry Montgomery and Mr. Henry Forbes, who both took such prominent parts in the restoration of Godavari. Godavari had been under the withering influence of the zemindari system some years before, for there, as in Bengal, the Government had coolly taken the land away from its real owners, the ryots, and made a present of it to other men, whom they called zemindars, and the consequence of this robbery was the utter ruin of the district. Happily the ruin was so complete that the system ruined itself, and the zemindaries were almost all forfeited. And the end was that the district was left in such a state, that the Government were compelled to look out for the ablest man they could find, to try if he could remedy matters. Happily they pitched upon Sir Henry Montgomery, late of the India Council, and he found the district fully prepared for him, that is, everything in utter ruin, so that he had only to clear away the rubbish and lay a new foundation entirely, just the very field for such a man. He first laid a solid foundation, in respect of Revenue system, the soundness of which is shown by the state of the district at this moment. All this is admirably described by the editor of the *Description of the District*, just now ready for publication—Mr. Henry Morris. To me this work seems to be the very thing that is wanted just now, to instruct us in connection with the state of things in Orissa and Bengal. When Sir Henry had laid his foundation in Revenue matters, he then said: "But there remains one thing to give full effect to management, and that is water," having seen with his own eyes what it could do, even without navigation. He was followed by another most upright and able Collector, Mr. Prendergast, under whom it was that the Irrigation works were carried out, but another essential element in the effectual execution of the works was the appointment of another from Mr. Kindersley's school, Mr. Henry Forbes, late Member of the Council in India. To him was assigned the office of providing the Engineers with men and materials, which called for all his tact, self-denial, and talent to the utmost, for it was no small matter to carry out such a vast system of works in a district where there were hardly any mechanics, and the whole population were sunk in such a state of despondence, that they were literally like a slave population. It was thus that it pleased God to bring about such a concurrence of circumstances, as was really essential to the wonderful success of the attempt to raise the district from being probably quite the lowest in India, to be the second in revenue, and by far the first in prosperity, in all India; to such a state as is described in the concluding paragraph of Mr. Morris's book. If such men as Sir Henry and Mr. Forbes could be found and sent to Kurnool, or the Tungabudra, I have not the smallest doubt that in one year everything would be in order there, and in a few years the district would be in such a state of prosperity as Godavari is in now. There is nothing in the world to prevent it. It would no doubt take a man indeed to root out the dreadful system in Orissa and Bengal, which has taken far deeper root, yet I am persuaded that even there matters could in the main be set to right, if a man of talent and decision were allowed to work out his own plans without interference. But it would no doubt be a most severe labour, and try any man to the utmost.

APPENDIX C.

Speech of the Lieutenant-Governor of Bengal at Sonepur, on the Sone, in November, 1877.

"*Now the only way of averting famines arising from drought is to make the greatest use, which science and experience can suggest, of the supply of water which fortunately Nature has given us in Behar in the shape of rivers, but which supply we have hitherto allowed to run to waste, while the fields, through which these rivers pass, have been parchea and waste for want of water.* A large and comprehensive system of irrigation is under construction in Behar, the object of which is to utilise the water of the river Sone in parts especially liable to drought. Other similar schemes are being worked out in Orissa. This of course cannot be done without the expenditure of money, and the question is, who, in fairness and justice, should find this money. After very careful consideration I came to the conclusion that, as the whole of the province of Bengal suffered when there were such famines as have occurred of late years in Orissa and Behar, it was fair that a large proportion ot the cost should be borne by a tax laid upon the public at large. But it also seemed to me fair, and I believe you will agree with me if you will give the subject your unprejudiced consideration, that a share of the cost should fall on the people who directly benefit by the introduction of water to the neighbourhood of their fields, and are thus assured of a good crop at all seasons, instead of being exposed to the risk, every few years, of absolute failure. When I proposed this, I was told that the people did not want water, that they would sooner be left alone to bear the risk of famine, and I was even told that the water of the Sone was destructive to fields. Shortly after this discussion took place, the periodical rains were suspended, and then we had practical proof as to whether or not the Sone water was considered injurious or prejudicial. The people clamoured for water, and to meet this demand we were forced to open our unfinished canals, by means of which we have irrigated during the last few months 200,000 acres of land,[1] which would otherwise have remained waste for the year, but which are now covered with luxuriant crops. The produce of this land represents food grain of the value of £550,000, and of this, crops to the value of £400,000, certainly, would have been entirely lost, if it had not been for the supply of canal water, but it also represents the rent of the land, of which the landholder would have been otherwise deprived, and to this must be added the outlay, which would fall on him, if he had again to give relief to his tenantry in consequence of famine.

"I have just returned from visiting the part of the country where this system has been introduced. I saw what every one *admitted to be the finest crops ever seen in Behar,* in the irrigated fields, while the unirrigated fields by their side were parched, and had hardly

[1] In Jannary, 1878—300,000 acres. [In March, 1899—440,796 acres.]

a blade of vegetation on them. I drove for sixty miles through the irrigated tracts, and returned by one of the main canals. Nothing but this ocular demonstration could have convinced me of the enormous benefits which have been conferred upon the people by irrigation, and throughout the *only complaints which I received from the people with whom I conversed, were of the non-extension of the water supply to these villages*, though I, not unnaturally, was told by some of the ryots that they wanted the water without payment."

APPENDIX D.

Extracts trom the Great Indian Peninsula Railway Report of Meeting, December 7, 1877.

The Chairman said,—"We are informed that on the 30th of June last there were some 400,000 tons of linseed, grain, cotton, and other goods, waiting for transport, to the very great loss of the mercantile community, as can easily be understood." Here is a complete acknowledgment that the railway totally fails to carry the quantity required, even at their paralyzing rates. What could they do with the quantity that would have to be moved at the prices that Indian transit required, one-tenth or one-twentieth of that charged on the railway? Again,—"The Great Indian Peninsula carried grain at a little over a half-penny a ton a mile. They would continue to do so as long as they found it profitable to do so, but no longer,"

This is ten times what it could be carried for by steamboat canal. Thus with a charge of ten times that required on a canal, they still had hundreds of thousands of tons lying on the railway.

Again, Mr. Jones, a shareholder, said,—"I should be glad to know how it is we have paid thirty shillings a ton for our coal." He continued,—"The importance of having cheap traffic on this line is very material, not only to the shareholders, but also to the English public. If our grain is drawn from *our* territory instead of from the American, our goods will go in at a small, unimportant duty, instead of being taxed with so heavy a duty as they are there." Again he says,—"You charge £3 a ton on the cotton traffic. This seems a very heavy burthen, seeing the freight from Bombay to England is only thirty shillings, of which ten shillings is paid to the canal, leaving only £1." To these things the Chairman replies,—"The reason why this cheap coal to the East

India Railway Company is dear to us, is that the transport of that cheap coal over six hundred miles, makes it very costly to us, so that while it costs that company six shillings, it costs us thirty-six," that is, thirty shillings for six hundred miles of carriage by the railway, or a little more than a halfpenny a ton a mile. Thus we see, curiously enough, the railway men complaining of the sad effects of the high cost of railway transit. They cannot but feel it themselves.

He then speaks of the coal being brought by the new line opened to the Chanda coalfield, fifty miles from their line. The charge for this is five shillings a ton. This line has cost £9,000 a mile, and the returns last year on the part opened were one per cent. On this very line from the coal pits to the Railway, the river Wurdah could be opened for a cost of £2,000 a mile by the estimate, prepared on good data, and the coal might be carried by it at a tenth of a penny per mile. What could put the infatuation of the present proceedings with respect to transit, on this line, in a stronger light than the complaint of the Chairman, compared with the proceedings of the Government to relieve them from the burden of the cost of transit? The end of this is that the railway men themselves find that the carriage by rail is so expensive, that they bring a large portion of their coal all the way from England.

It is very curious thus to see the railway men themselves stating how they are hampered by the enormous expense of carrying by their own railways. And the Chairman's reply to Mr. Jones on the subject of the heavy charge on cotton was, "Now this is a rather delicate point for the shareholders to urge. All I can say is, that unless we proceed with a great deal of care and forethought in reducing our charge upon cotton, you will not get many surplus dividends. Our actual charge upon cotton all over the line is about 2¼d. a ton per mile, which I do not think is excessive." This charge makes the cost of carriage from Nagpur to Bombay, about £5 10*s*., or more than a half-penny a pound. Now if the Godavari Navigation had been thoroughly completed, the cotton could be conveyed to Cocanada for about 10*s*. or £1, saving a halfpenny a pound, a difference which a Manchester manufacturer would consider very important. For the sums of £700,000 already spent on the Godavari, and £500,000 spent on the sixty miles of railways in that part, the whole line of navigation from the Upper Wurda, might have been abundantly completed for the whole year's navigation, if the works had been carried out with anything like efficiency, when the works were first proposed; and even when the Godavari works were stopped, the £500,000 spent on sixty miles of railway, would have both improved the Upper Wurda, giving the railway cheap coal, and have stored water for the Godavari, and finished the second barrier works, leaving only the third barrier works to be executed. Thus the railway men by urging the minor railways, are effectually injuring their main works. They, like all other interests, need cheap transit, and are terribly troubled that they are obliged to carry their coal six hundred miles by land. And thus, also, we see from this report how utterly incapable the railways are of carrying even the small quantities that their high charges admit of moving at all.

APPENDIX E.

Extracts from Report of Mr. Robertson, Superintendent Government Farms at Madras, in the Coimbatore District, 1876.

Mr. Robertson divides his report into three heads: lands irrigated by rivers and tanks, by wells, and unirrigated. The total area under irrigation of any kind is only about four per cent. of the land under cultivation; but it pays one quarter of the land revenue. The average rent of the irrigated land is about fifteen shillings, whilst the dry land is about two shillings per acre. About 88,622 acres of Government land are watered from rivers and tanks. Mr. Robertson deprecates the present wasteful method of using the water, being convinced that a larger area might be treated with equal results. Rice is the principal crop, and for five months one inch of depth daily is consumed, which makes a depth of 12 feet.

Again,—"But, inasmuch as the water is frequently derived from granite ranges, it contains the manurial qualities, and the silt is doubtless of value; hence the more water applied, the larger proportion of silt. It appears that the crops under irrigation, even where no manure is applied, are as good now as they were twenty or thirty years since. Now, whilst it is evidently the interest of the ryot who does not properly cultivate and manure to use as much water as possible, it is altogether different for the Government who find the water, and have ninety per cent. of their land unwatered. Some regulation as to the quantity of water is desirable. Mr. Robertson calculates that, according to the water generally employed, each acre of land receives about two tons of silt; if half the water only were used, one ton of silt would have to be replaced by an equivalent of manure. Although the position of the ryots, who occupy irrigated lands, is very superior to the dry farmers, it often happens that the cultivation is not one whit better, owing to the pernicious system of sub-letting, which resembles the Irish middlemen.

Again,—"From experiments Mr. Robertson found that the cost of each watering when the water was raised twenty feet from wells, was about four shillings an acre; and, as each crop of cumboo, cholum, or ragi requires ten or twelve waterings, the total cost is £2 to £2 8*s*. 6*d*.

Again,—"Unfortunately for the natives, upwards of two million acres of the occupied land are altogether unaided by irrigation. The rain as registered varies from 17 inches to 36 inches in the different districts; most of this falls in May, October, and November, and often there are months together without any appreciable downfall. The consequence is, that the crops are extremely precarious, and in a time of drought the suffering is widespread and often terrible.

The reviewer concludes,—"But immediate help is needed. Why cannot the Government make loans at reasonable rates of interest, to be paid off in a certain number of years? Works for increasing the irrigated area would be most useful and profitable; and something might be done in the way of well sinking. It is to be hoped that the fearful sufferings, which we may hope are now over, may lead to permanent progress."

APPENDIX F.

"While fever is so prevalent in Calcutta, it seems also to be raging with some severity in many parts of the province, a correspondent draws a sad picture of the state of several villages not far from the metropolis, specifying Mitahari, Sharulia, and Senargati. Fever, he says, has been raging there with the violence of an epidemic for a year and a half. He gives no statement of the mortality but represents the people as quite heartless and hopeless. The native *kobirajes* are baffled by the fever; and quinine, he says, is ineffectual. In their distress the villagers are turning despairing eyes to the Government, wondering why a beneficent *raj* does not send them medical aid.

"Another correspondent informs us that Halishahar has been suffering severely from epidemic fever since the middle of October. Application has been made by the inhabitants to the sub-divisional officer to move the proper authorities to send, temporarily, a medical officer and a supply of medicines to the place."

These fevers are actually owing to the want of irrigation works, to the sea of mud in which the people live in the monsoon, and the filthy water collected in pits, and filled with every pollution, which they drink in the dry season. If the water were regulated, the country properly drained during the monsoon, and streams of fresh river water were flowing through every village throughout the year, the fever would be almost entirely subdued, as it is in Godavari and Tanjore.

Had Lord Cranbrook widely circulated this communication it might—it possibly would—have completely changed public opinion. Its arguments are convincing, its reasoning satisfactory.

PARLIAMENTARY SPEECHES IN SUPPORT OF SIR ARTHUR COTTON.

My father was not wanting in defenders in the House. I give here what was said by other speakers both for and against him and his projects. This is essential. In the steps which must immediately be taken to preserve India from chronic famine, the statements and arguments herein employed are certain to be revived. It is but right the reader should know them from the start.

MR. HENRY FAWCETT.

. . . When it was stated that expendidure on irrigation works would yield a return of seventy per cent. or eighty per cent., why, he asked, did not the capitalists and commercial men of large means, who made these assertions, embark their money in so splendid an enterprise? He strongly deprecated any partisan feeling in discussing the question whether railways or works of irrigation were the better calculated to yield a profitable return, and to prevent the recurrence of famine. He was quite aware that railways had done great things for India; but, on the

17

other hand, all the railways had not paid, and, in the same way, some irrigation works had been disastrous failures, while some, no doubt, had been attended with success.

MR. JOHN BRIGHT.

Why should not this Committee be appointed for the express purpose of ascertaining from such evidence as we can get in England, and, if necessary, such as we can get from India, how it is that after so many years of possession—one hundred years of possession—of this very part of the country, still we have got no further than this, that there is a drought, and then a famine? There is no failure of water except at particular times, and over a particular district. But, take the year through, almost without exception, in India there is far more water than is necessary there for what is required for the cultivation of the soil, yet almost no step has been taken to provide irrigation works. We hear that there has been £9,000,000 or £16,000,000 spent on such works. What is that in India? The town of Manchester alone, with a population of 500,000, has spent £2,000,000 already, and is coming to Parliament now to ask to be allowed to spend £3,500,000 more: that will be £5,500,000 to supply the population of that town and its immediate surroundings with pure water, and a sufficient quantity of it. But in India we have 200,000,000 of population subject to the English Government, and with a vast supply of rainfall, and great rivers running through it with the means—as I believe there are the means—of abundant irrigation, and still the whole sum expended has been only £16,000,000. We have heard some authorities say it is £20,000,000; but be it £16,000,000 or £20,000,000, what is it when we consider the vast extent of the country, and the greatness of the need? I remember, years ago, that Sir James Hogg, Chairman of the East India Company, and the late Mr. Mangles, stood up in this House and insisted that the Indian Government had not failed in its duty with regard to public works in India. I showed then—that was in 1856 or 1857—that the Corporation of Manchester had, during the preceding fourteen years, spent more in public works for the good of its own population, than the East India Company had spent in the same fourteen years throughout the whole of the vast territories which were subjected to their care or to their neglect. Now, I have no doubt whatever, notwithstanding what has been said, and notwithstanding what may be said, of the condition of their finances, it is the duty of the Indian Government in some way, if possible, to find a remedy; but, if not possible, of course famine must come, and the doomed must die. But I believe it is possible, and I will not rely on the authority of Sir Arthur Cotton alone; but if hon. members will take that book which the noble lord quoted from, they will find there the evidence—I was going to say of scores of eminent men—as to what ought to be done, and what may be done in India. There is the evidence of Colonel Chesney, in which he shows how much may be done, and how much has been neglected in regard to the question of irrigation. The noble lord stated that the Secretary of State for India had ordered an enquiry to be made in India as to some matters having regard to further progress of works of irrigation. What I want, and what Sir Arthur Cotton wants is, not that you should believe me—for I am no authority on the matter—or even that you should believe him, but that you should have a full and fair enquiry on the spot. . . . If the terms [in which the Committee is moved] were such as I think necessary, they would simply enquire into the desirability of irrigation works for the prevention of famine. The hon. member for Hackney has asked a question which other persons have asked. Why is it that if some of these schemes will pay seventy per cent. or eighty per cent., the people of Manchester, or the city of London, or elsewhere, with capital to employ, do not go India, and establish these great works, and put in their pocket this great profit? I will tell the hon. gentlemen why they will not do it. There are no people in this country who form public companies and expend money in India without a guarantee from the Government. These are circumstances which make it very doubtful whether it would be wise for any man to do it. He had better do it, he thinks, in almost any other country than India. The Indian Government does not like these independent companies. It acts upon the traditions of the old Company. The Indian Government objects to the expenditure of English money which is not under their control . . . I have no doubt that if it were possible to bring all the facts connected with the Madras scheme before the House, it would be shown that a very large proportion of the fault, whatever it is, of the failure of that scheme, has been the mismanagement of the Government in connection with it.

Everybody must admit the tremendous difficulties which any Government must have in managing the affairs of that vast country and its population of two hundred millions of persons. I admit that; and therefore, perhaps, it is not reasonable or just that one should bring strong charges against men who, I daresay, do the best they can in their position, but who fail in much that they do. The noble lord quoted two or three cases in which irrigation works had failed. There may be works of irrigation that pay nothing to Government, but which will save the lives of their people: and I do not like to hear the Secretary of State or the Under Secretary in discussing this question, always treat it as if it were a shopkeeper in London or a merchant in Manchester who was considering whether he should open another shop or another mercantile house. It is not exactly in that spirit in which the question should be dealt with. I believe there are many cases in India in which, probably, it would not be possible for the Government to say: "We shall get ten per cent. out of the expenditure of £1,000,000"; but a year afterwards they might say that the expenditure of that £1,000,000 had probably saved a million of human lives, and therefore, it might be worth while for the Government, as a clear duty, to expend that £1,000,000 in that work. I do not know that I have anything more than this to say. If the noble lord intends that the Committee shall thoroughly examine this question, and if they can do anything in India it should be done by a Commission in India, I do not ask them to take my opinion or the opinion of Sir Arthur Cotton. But Sir Arthur Cotton has lived forty-five years in India. He has more information in connection with works of irrigation than any other engineer. He has given the attention of a lifetime to them; he is a man of the most undoubted honour, and of the highest character; he believes absolutely what he says as to what is necessary to be done, and what may be done. I confess I think it will be difficult—almost impossible—after discussing this question with him, not to come to the opinion that his authority is one which ought to have great weight with the House. He is willing to say—I have myself heard him say—that there have been many mistakes made: there have been mistakes in the railroads, in the irrigation works; but that if famine comes from want of water, clearly to get rid of famine you must have water. You cannot have water except by works of irrigation. You have the rain from heaven; you have the great rivers; and you have a great Government, which has conquered the country, and which, having conquered it, at least ought to exercise all the powers of its intellect for the purpose of saving its people from this suffering and this ruin, and ought to save this country and this Parliament from the degradation and humiliation of allowing it to be known throughout the world that millions of the subjects of the crown in India, in the course of ten years, perish by famine, which great engineers, and men of character and experience, say positively might altogether have been prevented.

SIR GEORGE CAMPBELL.

He would not enter into the question whether or not irrigation works in general were good, right, or proper in themselves—that would be for the proposed Committee to decide—but having had much personal experience in regard to several of the works to which the noble lord, the Under Secretary for India, had referred, he thought it his duty to support him in several of his statements. He felt bound to point out the utterly unreliable character of the reports of Sir Arthur Cotton. That gentleman was a man deserving of very great respect, but he was, in this matter, wholly unreliable. Though he did not doubt Sir Arthur Cotton's honesty, he thought there was some truth in the saying regarding him, that he had water on the brain. He was hopelessly enthusiastic, and had been carried away beyond all bounds of reason in his views, and was neither to bind nor to hold in his statements of what might be done if his recommendations were carried out. It was because of the reckless manner in which he had set forth his views that he had prevailed with so many; but he (Sir George Campbell), was sorry that he had prevailed with the right hon. member for Birmingham (Mr. John Bright). As Lieutenant-Governor of Bengal he had experience of great public works which Sir Arthur Cotton had designed, and forced upon the Government, and, as Chief Commissioner of the Central Provinces, he had also had experience of some of Sir Arthur's projects. The noble lord had stated the facts with regard to one or two of these when he said they never could return interest on the money expended on them, and that they had never extended over more than a limited area, or done more than a very limited amount of good. One of Sir Arthur's projects was to create an enormous reservoir in the centre of India, to store water there during the rainy season, and to let it down on the country when drought prevailed. That scheme was submitted to him as Chief Commissioner of the Central Provinces. He found that Sir Arthur Cotton had never been in the country where he proposed to place his reservoir, and had never obtained information in regard to it. He had simply taken a map, and having found that there were two or three rivers in the country, he had marked a circle on the map and said: "You can make a large reservoir, a grand lake there." They found that Sir Arthur Cotton had no data on which to found his assertions. They obtained men to examine and work out these projects, but having gone into them, they saw that there were physical conditions which made it impossible to carry them into effect. That was the last he had heard of Sir Arthur Cotton until he was resuscitated by the right hon. gentleman, the member for Birmingham. There was another of his projects equally wild. India and China were, Sir Arthur said, great countries. Water was the panacea for all evils, and it was the easiest thing possible to make a canal between the two countries. He was oblivious of the fact that between them there were mountains 19,000 or 20,000 feet high, and when somebody pointed this out, he said it was the simplest thing in the world to make locks. While pointing out the unreliability of Sir Arthur Cotton in these matters, he would admit that this was a great and important subject. . . . He thought the right hon. gentleman, the member for Birmingham, was not justified in saying that the people of this country could not form companies and send out money to India to work out their projects. They had done so in many cases. They had not done so in the case of irrigation works, because money invested in this way had been lost, or only recouped from the Government by means which the hon. member for Hackney had alluded to, and they were not satisfied that it would now yield eighty per cent. or a hundred per cent., as Sir Arthur Cotton had asserted.

GENERAL SIR GEORGE BALFOUR

said he had heard with regret the remarks which the noble lord, the Under Secretary for India, had made with reference to Sir Arthur Cotton. Having had many years' acquaintance with Sir Arthur Cotton, and having examined the works which he had made in Madras, he could say that, so far from Sir Arthur Cotton being justly chargeable with the mistakes attributed to him, he believed him to be entirely free from blame. Standing up before the House he would say that he did not believe that a single work which Sir Arthur Cotton had executed had ever been a failure. Sir Arthur Cotton was a man of mighty genius; he was a man who had done much for the people; he had been a great benefactor to India, and his name would go down to posterity as one who had done great things for that country. His hon. friend, the member for Kirkcaldy (Sir George Campbell), had attacked Sir Arthur Cotton, but he would say that if the hon. gentleman had known Sir Arthur Cotton and his great services as well as he, and those who had worked with him did, he would never have given utterance to the censure he had passed on him. When the investigation was made by the Committee, which he hoped would be made, it would be found that there was no ground for some of the charges that had been made against Sir Arthur Cotton. The Under Secretary had made remarks about the Madras Irrigation Company, with a view of throwing on Sir Arthur Cotton the blame of the failure. But it was the Government itself which assigned to the Company the particular works to be undertaken, and he believed it could be proved that they had not shown good faith to the Madras Irrigation Company. No doubt great mistakes had been made, but the mistakes and bad management were greatly due, as the right hon. gentleman the member for Birmingham had said, to the Government themselves. He believed that if Sir Richard Temple, a man of great independence and integrity, and quite capable of judging about these matters, were examined before the Select Committee it was proposed to appoint, he would show that there was great mismanagement on the part of the Government officers. In many parts of the country the reservoirs were empty, and a large number of tanks in the Madras Presidency were thoroughly out of repair. There was in the Madras Presidency only one irrigation work which Sir Richard Temple asked the Government to carry out. This project, if carried into effect, would have cost only £270,000, and after all expenses had been paid, the Government would have derived from the work an annual revenue of £25,000. The Government of India and the Secretary of State came to the conclusion that this work was not yet matured, though the papers laid before the House of Commons in 1870 showed that the project was matured in all its details.

THE SELECT COMMITTEE OF 1878:

ITS CONSTITUTION, ITS METHODS, ITS RESULT.

Lack of sympathy with his high aims and the total absence of the smallest approach to statesmanlike appreciation of what irrigation really was in itself, were never more conspicuously displayed than in the long examination to which Sir Arthur Cotton was subjected as a witness before the Committee which was the outcome of the debate.

Upon this Committee sat Lord George Hamilton, the Parliamentary Under Secretary for India, who was appointed Chairman; Mr. Balfour, now Leader of the House of Commons; Mr. Henry Fawcett, a diligent student of Indian affairs; the Right Hon. Hugh Childers, ex-Cabinet Minister; Mr. James Ashbury, a yacht-owner, who represented Brighton, and who, according to Dod, was "a builder of railway rolling stock"; Sir George Campbell, an ex-Indian civilian, with an exceedingly varied experience of India; Mr. Denzil Onslow, member for Guildford, who had been private secretary to Sir C. Trevelyan, the Right Hon. W. N. Massey, and Sir Richard Temple; Mr. John Cross, Lancashire cotton-spinner, afterwards Parliamentary Under Secretary for India; Mr. Hardcastle, merchant in Manchester; Sir Joseph M'Kenna, Bart., an Irish barrister; Mr. Sampson Lloyd, a banker in Birmingham; Mr. (now Sir Mountstuart) Grant Duff, subsequently Under Secretary for India and Governor of Madras; Mr. Mulholland, eldest son of an Ulster linen manufacturer, afterwards created a peer as Lord Dunleath; Mr. Eustace Smith, a merchant and shipowner in the North of England; and Mr. R. Vans Agnew, a landed proprietor in Scotland. Mr. Eustace Smith, at an early stage, retired. Mr. Edward Stanhope, afterwards Secretary of State for War, Mr. (afterwards Sir Joseph) Pease, railway director and owner of coal and ironstone mines, and

Mr. Ernest Noel, son of the Hon. and Rev. Baptist W. Noel, were subsequently added to the Committee.

Here was a body of Englishmen, fairly representative of the composite character of our nation, not one of whom was an engineer; not a single one of them had had the slightest acquaintance with irrigation engineering. Of actual Indian administrative experience there was only Sir George Campbell.

Sir George Campbell ought not to have sat on this Committee. As a witness he might be of service; as a judge he was in the position of one who had already made up his mind so far as irrigation was concerned. This is evident from his questions. But there is direct proof. In *Memoirs of my Indian Career*, by Sir George Campbell, this passage appears:—

"I was directed by the Government of India to examine Sir A. Cotton's proposals for great irrigation schemes in the Central Provinces. He wanted to make the Godavari navigable throughout its course, and a great highway of commerce, by removing the barriers which obstructed it; and the deficiency of water during the greater part of the year he proposed to cure by the construction of enormous resorvoirs, on an unprecedented scale, on the upper basins of its affluents, from whence also a magnificent system of irrigation was to be derived.

"On looking into the matter I found that the so-called barriers of the Godavàri were really long stretches of rocky and utterly unnavigable channel, which could only be surmounted by canalising a great portion of the river on a large scale and at a very great expense, and that, even if this were done, the river would be navigable but a small part of the year. I found also that the bulky traffic of the Central Provinces flowed west, not east—its surplus grain was wanted on the Bombay side, not on the Madras coast, and the cotton and other valuable products had their natural outlet at Bombay. As to the great reservoirs, I discovered, to my surprise, that Sir A. Cotton had never himself worked out his projects, but had merely drawn lines on the map and said, 'Make them there,' without any real examination whatever.[1] I very greatly doubted the safety of prodigious embankments impounding enormous quantities of water such as he proposed, even if it were practicable; and seeing that we had already a very excellent system of irrigation on a less ambitious scale, and that there was no great necessity for another system,[2] I was not anxious to incur the risk. I accordingly reported against the whole scheme; it was afterwards dropped, and has not been revived. The tide turned and Sir Arthur Cotton ceased to be regarded as a prophet, though his name must always be inseparably connected with several very creditable works which he carried out in Madras."

That is to say, Sir George Campbell did not sit on the Committee to ascertain the facts regarding irrigation, but simply to register a foregone conclusion. With what consequences, let the "terrible" (the word is the Viceroy's) condition of the famine-stricken people in these Central Provinces, ruled by Sir George Campbell, testify.

A general survey of the three days on which Sir Arthur Cotton was under examination will give an idea of two things—one, the wide range of the witness's acquaintance with India irrigationally, and the other, the narrow and hostile attitude towards a general extension of irrigation throughout the various Presidencies, Provinces, and Chief Commissionerships, manifested by the Committee

[1] Sir George Campbell, when he wrote this, had heard Sir Arthur Cotton say (of this very reservoir) in 1878: "But I have seen it; I have been up there, as I say, at the very spot," and yet, in his autobiography, written in 1891 and 1892, he repeats the charge.

[2] The value of the condemnation of Sir Arthur Cotton may be judged by the untrustworthiness of this *ex cathedra* deliverance: "Already . . . an excellent system, . . . no great necessity for another system." And, yet, in the very provinces Sir George Campbell was referring to, there have, within four years, been two destructive famines, and forty per cent. of the people in one district are receiving Government relief at the time when this note is penned (June, 1900). ". . . no great necessity for another system!"

throughout. All who know anything of the Committee Rooms of the House of Commons can readily picture the scene. Those who do not know these interiors may imagine a big, square, room, lighted by high gothic windows overlooking the Thames, containing a large horse-shoe shaped table, around which the members of the Committee are assembled, while inside, the witness under examination, the stenographer in near proximity to him.

Probably, at no time did Sir Arthur Cotton so fully set forth his plans for Indian regeneration as when before this Committee; certainly on no single occasion did he cover so wide a range. The hostile questions put to him never once caused him embarrassment; on the contrary, they served to bring out in more striking manner his wonderful mastery of all the details of varied needs in wholly dissimilar localities.

It is desirable that Sir Arthur Cotton's plans for the restoration of prosperity to India should find adequate expression in this Memoir, as an act of justice to his foresight and character and as an equal act of justice to the suffering people of India. A synopsis of his evidence, with excerpts from the Blue Book record, will enable this to be done.

The first day's examination was on Thursday, 20th June. Of the sixteen members constituting the Committee only nine were present, the absentees apparently being Mr. Balfour, Mr. Fawcett, Mr. Childers, Sir Joseph M'Kenna, Mr. Grant Duff, Mr. Edward Stanhope, and Mr. Pease. But, seemingly, there is a mistake in the list of attendances; Mr. Childers asked some questions, and, therefore, must have been present. Considering who the witness of the day was to be (and each Committee-man would know, in advance, who was to be examined), it does not say much for their notion of public duty or their sense of responsibility towards India that so many and such important members of the Committee were absent. For example, had Mr. Fawcett heard Sir Arthur Cotton's most cogent statements, how much of force and practicality might have been given to what he afterwards did for India while a member of the House of Commons.

More than nine hundred questions, in all, were asked of Sir Arthur Cotton. Lord George Hamilton, as Chairman, began by inviting the witness to describe his experience in India, and generally to give his "opinion as regards the remunerativeness or direct returns from public works in India."

The answer embraced these points :—

1. Direct returns from public works nationally undertaken are not a sufficient guide; "the Government are not in the position of a private company but of a statesman." The amount of direct returns is important, but only of relative importance. "For instance, the Tanjore works have been the principal means of raising the condition of two and a quarter millions of people to such a state of wealth and prosperity as we may safely believe no district of India ever attained before." The revenue in that district has increased by £330,000 a year. Such results are good but they are secondary to the other effects upon so large a population. Food can always be obtained and healthiness promoted by proper drainage.

2. "The utterly inadequate feeding of the people (of India) is perfectly astonishing."

3. Transit and cost of transport are hardly less important than irrigation. Nay,—

"I have so far changed my views that I consider this THE PRIMARY QUESTION IN THE MATERIAL IMPROVEMENT OF INDIA, *and before that of irrigation in importance.*"

"We have before us this awful fact, that from ten to twenty-five per cent. have perished in Madras districts while there was food enough in India, and therefore, solely from want of efficient transit."[1]

[1] Striking confirmation of present-day experience to the same end comes before me whilst the proofs of this chapter are being corrected. From *The Times* of August 10, 1900, I quote the following communication from India, written by Sir Arthur Cotton's old comrade

"In Madras, Mysore, Hyderabad, four or five millions (must have) perished,[1] after spending £120,000,000 on railways,[2] besides incurring a debt on them of £50,000,000."

---

in-arms, General Fischer, R.E., whose evidence, quoted in the appendix to this chapter, is of great value :—

TO THE EDITOR OF *The Times.*

SIR,—I send you below a copy of a telegraphic notice which appeared in the *Madras Mail* of July 12, 1900, and which appears also in other Indian papers :—

"*Railway Difficulties in Northern India.*

"LUCKNOW, *July 11th.*—The B.B. and C.I. Railway Company has advised other railways that through bookings of food-stuffs for places on the Rajputana-Malwa Railway cannot be accepted, owing to the impossibility of working the food traffic, in the absence of water supply for the engines."

If you will be good enough to publish the above in London, it will give the good people of England a better idea of the fearful famine now raging in India than anything else is likely to do. People at home have been led to believe that railways in India are all that is needed to protect this country from famine, and that a good and sufficient water supply was a mere craze of the late Sir Arthur Cotton's. As it now appears that railways cannot be worked without a proper and sufficient supply of water, and as it is officially declared that the mortality among the ryots' cattle is perfectly appalling, and the losses incurred thereby beyond computation, and as a blade of grass cannot be grown in India without water, which cannot now be obtained even for the favoured railway works, nor at any time when the rains fail, as they do so frequently nowadays, by the destruction of the forests and jungle to supply the railways with cheap fuel, is it not time for the people of England to inquire why good reservoirs cannot be established in India similar to that now constructing on the Nile, and so preserve this country from the dire effects of famine, without coming on their charity every two or three years?

Yours truly,

BANGALORE, *July* 14. J. F. FISCHER, *General, R.E.*

P.S.—It is now officially known that the destruction of the ryots' live-stock cannot be estimated ; to all this loss we must add the losses of human lives and the labour of years, all caused by the want of a proper water supply, which can be very easily remedied in India, if only the opposition to this in England were once got rid of.—J. F. F.

[1] This was an under-estimate. In the places named, the total famine deaths in 1876–78 cannot have been much less than seven millions of human beings.

[2] In a later chapter it will be shown that the highest average mortality of this period (1877–78) was in railway-traversed districts.

Railways, as compared with canals, are unable to convey all the traffic of prosperous districts, save at a great cost.

Water traffic is conveyed very much cheaper than land traffic.

Enormous sums have been expended on railways as compared with irrigation.

To 1876.

Railways, £170,000,000; £3,000,000 per annum interest loss on money expended.	Irrigation, £16,000,000; net gain, yearly, of £500,000.

[If railways (which produce nothing) had been equal in interest-paying power to irrigation works, instead of there being a deficit of £3,000,000, there would have been a net revenue of £5,000,000.]

4. "So far as our irrigation works extend, they have completely protected the people from death by famine, and we have no reason for supposing they will not always do that."

"In this fundamental particular THE IRRIGATION AND NAVIGATION HAVE BEEN A COMPLETE SUCCESS, AND THE RAILWAYS A COMPLETE FAILURE."

As to increase of productiveness when river water was available for cultivation, "in Godavari we used to reckon that it increased the crop in grain by Rs. 20 an acre at least." In the North-Western Provinces and in Orissa the increase has been put at Rs. 15 per acre.

"This is besides the cheap transit, the drainage, the security from river floods, the abundance of forage, the supply of wholesome drinking water, etc."

"In Godavari the passengers are carried eight miles for a penny, and the canals are crowded with passenger boats.[1] *This perfect liberty of intercourse is the very life of the district.* If all India were supplied with such cheap passenger

[1] This is now (1900) being altered as the boat licences, etc., have been increased in the interests of a competing railway only just constructed. See pp. 282–284.

transport, where the passengers could be taken up and put down anywhere, and every one was free to travel either in his own boat or by any passenger or goods boat, at any hour of the day or night, and at any speed, without having to wait for a train or go to a station, it would be impossible to estimate the benefits it would confer."

"The effects of railways must be stated rather by what they do not do than by what they do do.

"They do *not* provide food for man or beast;

"They do *not* carry the great traffic of the country;

"They do *not* carry cheaply enough to answer their main purpose;

"They do *not* touch the local traffic, either of passengers or goods, perceptibly;

"They do *not* pay the interest of their cost and debt;[1]

"They do *not* drain the country;

"They do *not* provide wholesome drinking-water;

"They do *not* prevent fever;

"They do *not* create traffic; and, what is a most important point, in case of disturbance it will be impossible to protect them, because you cannot patrol them with trains of armed men while the ordinary traffic is running."

"In short, as a chief railway engineer said to a friend of mine, they are not suited at all to the circumstances of the country, and India is, at this moment, in as great want of a complete system of water carriage as if no railways existed."

Objections to irrigation:—

1. Fever. "I have lived all my life in the paddy fields and never had myself, or knew of, an attack of fever in others, from irrigation."
2. Efflorescence called reh.[2] "I never saw an instance of it.

[1] At this time the amount which had had to be found from the general revenue to pay the guaranteed interest was no less than £24,658,649. (See remarks at the close of this chapter.)

[2] Reh is the vernacular name in India for efflorescent salts which accumulate in the soil and subsoil waters of large tracts of India.

It is quite an exceptional thing, and, therefore, is no more a reason for giving up irrigation than a death on a railway in England is an argument for abolishing railways here."

3. Diminished produce. "At least twenty millions of acres from one end of India to the other have been irrigated for hundreds of years, from rivers, tanks, and wells, without any diminution of produce." The Trichinopoly ryots in an address to the Governor of Madras in 1877, said: "All the great irrigation works have converted the tracts into scenes of matchless fertility and wealth, and have for ever protected them from the disaster of recurring droughts."
4. Refusal of Water. "In Madras, out of thousands of works, we have only had one single instance of any difficulty of this kind."

When this takes place to a serious extent, the land is rendered sterile. In the Upper Punjab efflorescence is known as *kallar*, and in Oudh and other parts of India the affected lands are called *usar*. Ball (*Economic Geology*, III., 696) writes: "As affecting the general prosperity and revenues of the country, the subject of how to mitigate or diminish the evil has naturally attracted a good deal of attention, and numerous reports and papers have been published which contain more or less trustworthy information, and more or less of practical suggestion." "Primarily the saline matters are derived from the decomposition of rocks, and, taking the case of Northern India, the rivers descending from the Himalayas carry down in solution proportions of salt which vary with the character of the strata traversed. The salts so carried in solution consist principally of calcium and magnesium carbonates, and sodium sulphate and chloride. In addition, of course, the alluvium or silt which is brought down, consisting of finely comminuted minerals, includes materials which, on decomposition, are capable of supplying bases for the ultimate formation of the same salts under suitable conditions. In a region of intense evaporation, and where there is not a free drainage outlet of water, these salts, by long continued concentration, accumulate in the soil or in the subsoil waters, and over and above this, rain water charged with carbonic acid, falling on a porous soil, has the effect of decomposing its mineral constituents and of carrying down the salts so formed in solution either to the region of subsoil water, or else for only a few inches or

5. Great Expense of Locks in making Canals Navigable. "This is a mistake." After giving instances, "The cost of the locks, therefore, on all the main lines of India is by no means a serious objection." In the Carnatic there would be six hundred miles without a lock.
6. Evaporation of Water. "This is quite an insignificant matter."
7. The Great Cost in Upland Districts. Grant this. "It has nothing to do with the hundreds of millions of acres in the plains of the Ganges, the Indus, the Brahmaputra," still capable of being irrigated.

Answers to objections as to profit of works in Tanjore, extent of land cultivated, and actual returns to revenue—only assertions made, no disproofs being furnished. So with Godavari and the works carried out there.

---

feet below the surface. When the surface of the ground again becomes dry, this saline water rises by capillary attraction and evaporates, and a salt efflorescence remains, which at length so permeates the superficial layer of soil that cultivation becomes impossible. With free underground drainage, which would admit of the rain passing through and washing the soil, this would not occur, especially where the surface was well protected from evaporation by vegetation."

"Irrigation by canal water, when not accompanied by deep drainage has had the effect of increasing the amount of reh deposit, and large tracts have been in consequence thrown out of cultivation. The indirect action which has produced this result has been fully explained by Mr. Medlicott (*Selections from the Records of the Government of India*, No. xlii., p. 32, of 1864). In this case, the direct increase in the amount of saline matter is inconsiderable owing to the comparative purity of canal water; but the so-called table of subsoil saline water has, by the addition of irrigation water, without an increase in the drainage, had its level raised to an extent which has rendered capillary attraction operative, and so these saline waters, which were previously to a great extent innocuous, have been brought into injurious contiguity with the superficial layers of soil. Thus is explained the apparently paradoxical fact that irrigation, by comparatively pure canal water, has been followed by an increase of salts in the superficial soils."—*Dictionary of the Economic Products of India*, pp. 400–401.

Why have the works in Orissa so far failed? "The expensive head works having been executed, the distribution works were stopped in the middle; the canals were begun at both ends, and then the link to unite them and allow them to effect anything was refused."

[A wholly independent authority was quite of a different opinion from Sir George Campbell and the members of the Committee.

"As it happens," he[1] says, "there is another point of view from which this investment can be regarded, and from which the scheme assumes another aspect. Subject to frequent floods, to occasional droughts, and to the interruption of its communications, the district was formerly always on the verge of famine. When any of these catastrophes did occur, the density of the population rendered them terribly disastrous. The floods, in one district, in one season, destroyed crops valued at £1,000,000. The famine of 1865-66 cost the lives of one million people, and the Government £1,500,000 to save the remainder. During a period of thirty-six years the remissions made by the State amounted to nearly a twelfth of all the revenue received. Prior to these works the whole province depended upon one crop in the year; if this failed, from excess or deficiency of moisture, all failed, and there was nothing but starvation before the people. To-day there are two hundred and fifty thousand acres commanded upon which one crop can be saved, or upon which another can be raised in its stead, three hundred and seventy-five thousand acres are protected from floods, and there are one hundred and seventy-seven miles of canal, by means of which produce can be transported to any region of dearth. If the fifth canal were locked like the other four, this would be much increased. Thus, after all, a permanent protection has been afforded at no greater cost than would be spent in two years in the spasmodic effort to save life and mitigate disaster. If the works had been undertaken with this

[1] Hon. A. Deakin, M.L.A., in *Irrigated India*, pp. 286-287.

end alone, they would be pronounced successful. In such an aspect they have fully justified their existence. The failure has been in theory and in prophecy, and the success in fact."]

Foolish evidence had been given to the Committee as to proposed lines of canals. "It has been stated in evidence," said Sir Arthur, "that there is a range of mountains between the east and the west coast on the line of the Godavari—*there is no such thing*." "The watershed between the Poorna and the Warda is without the sign of a hill, and it is just the same as the line between the Sutlej and the Jumna, on which the canal is nearly completed." "There is not a single serious natural obstacle from sea to sea."

"Madras, Cocanada, and Surat ought all to be coaling ports at this moment, and millions of tons of manure ought to be supplied to the land instead of being burnt."

"I will venture to say that hardly any country ever underwent such a change from poverty and inanition as these provinces (Central Provinces) would undergo if they were thrown open to the world."[1]

"There can hardly be any doubt that the increase of salt revenue alone in these tracts would pay the whole interest and expenditure of this line of canals."

"The little State of Travancore, with a revenue of half a million, has spent £100,000 a year on a canal and other public works."

"I do wish we could condescend to learn a lesson from our native friends, or borrow some dark Commissioners from them for our own provinces, and see if we could stir up our Governors to do for our vast provinces what they are doing with a thousandth part of our means."

"The canal to connect Cuttack and the Upper Mahanadi with Calcutta has been left with eighty miles in the middle uncut. The vast headworks of the irrigation, which give command over a vast tract of country, are now charged

[1] The contrast between the might-have-been predicted in 1878 and the distressful condition of these very provinces in 1900 is appalling.

to quite a small tract, and the canal extends to sixty miles from Calcutta and then stops in the middle of the delta, *at nothing*, and then the engineer is charged with the failure of the works! . . . Is it not incomprehensible that such imbecility should be shown?"

"*Suppose the railways had been dealt with in this way, the great station at Calcutta built and the road carried one hundred miles, and another executed out of Benares, and then the works stopped, what would be the result?*"

"The [navigable] works are all but completed, and the canals have cost £2,000 a mile, against £20,000 for railways, and £9,000 for the petty railways in that part of the country. Think of £500,000 being expended on sixty miles of railway, while money could not be found to complete this four hundred miles of main (canal) communication!"

So much for the witness's main statements. Now for some of the questions put to him and his replies thereto:—

Replying to Lord George Hamilton, in an answer of great length and of the highest value, the witness incidentally remarked:—

"The enormous returns of the Godavari works are in spite of every effort to prevent their being completed. It has taken thirty-two years to obtain £700,000 for them; £20,000 a year for works which, from the very first, have been a most prodigious success, and nothing would induce the authorities to carry them on with ordinary vigour.

> "*To this day money cannot be found to complete them, while the only dispute is whether they yield twenty-seven, twenty-eight, or forty per cent.; and now, after thirty-two years, only seven hundred thousand acres out of one million are irrigated.* IF £100,000 PER YEAR HAD BEEN GRANTED FOR FIVE YEARS, THE WHOLE DELTA WOULD HAVE BEEN IRRIGATED TWENTY-SEVEN YEARS AGO, before the great rise in the cost of labour, and the district would have been yielding a revenue of £750,000 a year for the last twenty-seven

years, making an addition of many millions in the treasury beyond what they have returned."

"*During this time* there was not the least question about supplying £500,000 for the sixty miles of railway to Nagpur, which, it was acknowledged, would not pay four per cent."

"The plain fact is that the dread of the officials is cheap transit; the whole power of the Government, with its Treasury, is to force the people to carry dearly a small quantity by the railways, rather than allow an enormous traffic to grow up at an almost nominal cost by the canals. This is what stopped the Damodhur canal from the coal-fields to Calcutta, the completion of the Orissa canals, the Godavari navigation, etc."

"I am quite certain that if these works are carried out by men heartily forwarding them, not by men secretly endeavouring to their utmost to prevent their producing their legitimate effects, they will not only almost completely prevent famines, but add hundreds of millions to the value of Indian produce."

"What India wants, I am fully persuaded, is that at least £30,000 should be spent in every district on an average per annum on irrigation, besides carrying out a complete system of navigation to the same extent of expenditure—together £10,000,000.[1] We should see such a revolution as hardly any country ever underwent."

"A steamboat canal can be made cheaper than a railway; it can carry cheaper; it can carry all that is wanted, and that a railway cannot; and it can carry at ample speed for every purpose. . . . It can, in most cases, be combined with irrigation and drainage; the supply of good, wholesome, drinking water will always accompany it."

"In setting about to judge between myself and my

[1] This must be a misprint. Take one hundred and sixty-four districts, and £30,000 for each district, the amount would be £59,200,000, which sum may be compared with the sum expended on railways, namely, including cost of land and other items, nearly £200,000,000.

opponents, may it not be justly considered whether a man who has certainly been most successful, and has had by far the longest experience [of any irrigation engineer in India], knows what he is talking about; and then cannot wise men judge of the plain facts and figures which he has set before them?"

"Are Tanjore, Kistna, and Godavari at this moment strewn with hundreds of thousands of the skeletons of victims of famine?"

"Are the districts of Bengal and Madras, on which millions have been spent on railways, rolling in wealth and plenty, in freedom from fever and death?"

"Has the revenue of Bengal, have the revenues of the railway districts of Madras, been raised by an addition of one hundred and fifty per cent?"

"Did any railway ever raise a crop of human food worth a million of money in the midst of the famine as the Madras Company's irrigation works did, saving the Government £500,000 in their famine expenditure?"

"Supposing these facts were brought forward by a man who, after fifty-seven years' practical experience, did not know how to cut a canal, or where one could be cut, how would that alter the matter?"

The Chairman (Lord George Hamilton) asked a large number of questions, chiefly upon the statements summarised above. Especially concerning the great works undertaken in the preceding twenty years, which did not then pay, the witness was pressed to admit he was wrong in his statements. At last an admission was obtained, but it did not help the noble questioner much. "Yes," Sir Arthur consented, "sanguine anticipations" had not then been realised. But, he reminded the Committee, neither had they any returns from the Godavari navigation. Why? Here is the kernel to much of the dissatisfaction to that date. "A work estimated twenty-five years ago is put off, stopped, gone on with, stopped again, and gone on with again for twenty-five years . . . and then, just at the last moment, when it is entering the populous country, it is put a stop to altogether, and you say that the engineer is at fault, that his estimates have failed. What can stand against that?" What, indeed? It does not appear that the irrigation engineers have had fair play—certainly not as compared with railway engineers and contractors.

"Although to you the Indian Government may seem to have been very unreasonable, it is possible, is it not, that they may have had good grounds for not going on?"

"No," said the undaunted engineer, "they had no grounds whatever. That is what I insist upon and am prepared to prove."[1]

"Unfortunately, the Warda canal would not have been navigable at the very time that it would have been wanted," said authority.

"We are not obliged to carry coal at any particular time. It is quite a mistake to suppose that a line of transit is of no value that is not open the whole year round. The Erie canal is open only seven months in the year, and it is the great artery of the United States."

[1] "The tone of the Orders of Government on these reports is still less satisfactory; still less encourages any hope of decisive improvement hereafter. The object most conspicuously observable in them is to get rid of the papers. No real interest is exhibited in the question; no anxiety is evinced to call forth the zeal of officers, or to promote improvement of their districts in this respect; no interest is manifested in the pictures which they draw of the want of roads, or any sympathy in the feelings with which they cannot but look on the reality daily before their eyes; and on the other hand, there is no word of disapproval, of admonition, or of instruction, for those who have no eyes for these vital wants of their districts, or who, seeing them, are indifferent, and make no effort or suggestion for their removal. In short, these Orders afford no evidence of any real sense on the part of the Government, of the entire absence of roads, or of the social backwardness and disability, which such a state necessarily implies, or of the intimate connection between the state of the communications and the revenue, or any real anxiety to promote their improvement. On the contrary, there is a manifest unwillingness to recognise the real, wretched state of the communications as detailed by some Collectors—a disposition to make the most of the very small improvements reported, or aid afforded by Government, and an anxiety to throw upon the people themselves the task, to which they are utterly unequal, of improving the roads."

"Did ever any canal cost as little as £1,000 a mile?"

"Yes, the Kistna and Godavari canal, ninety miles, cost £1,000 a mile right across the lay of the country."

"You admit only three navigable canals pay?"

The witness admitted that was so, and proceeded to ask if any railways whatsoever would have paid if they had been stopped in the midst of an unpopulated country, far away from any great centre of traffic, although costly stations had been built in which to accommodate the traffic. "And, besides, had kept the construction work hanging on for twenty years."[1]

[1] In further elucidation of this point the witness said: "The Ganges canal was brought to Cawnpore, and had six essential defects in it, and the locks connecting it with the river were not allowed to be used. The Orissa canal was carried sixty miles from Calcutta, and ended in the middle of the delta. Supposing they had done that with the railways. What in the world had those got to do with the actual returns of the canal? And this canal, carried from Calcutta and ending at nothing, not even in a great town in the heart of the delta, is now actually yielding three and a half per cent., and increasing most rapidly." On this latter point a most valuable minute by Colonel (now General) F. H. Rundall, R.E., then Inspector-General of Irrigation, was placed before the Committee. In it Colonel Rundall said:—

"As an illustration of the manner in which boats ply from one distant place to another, I may mention that, when inspecting the Midnapore canal the other day, I found boats from such opposite places as Benares, Dacca, and Patna, all plying in that canal, though only six months had elapsed since it had been opened for through traffic.

"The activity on the canals during the past year has been very considerable. On the Ganges canal there has been a traffic of ninety-one thousand tons carried probably between two hundred and three hundred miles.

"On the Calcutta canals about one million eight hundred thousand tons have been moved.

"On the Orissa canals there have been two hundred and twenty-one thousand tons lifted on two hundred and ten miles, or, at the rate of one thousand tons per mile.

"On the Godavari canals eight hundred and seventy thousand tons were lifted over a length of three hundred miles, or, at the rate of two thousand nine hundred tons per mile.

"No figures for comparison with the railway for the current year are yet available, but, during the first half-year of 1872, six hundred

"Do you really mean to say that you think that for the last twenty years every Viceroy and every official connected with the Public Works Department and the Council of India generally, and all the Secretaries of State, have been actuated by, as you put it, the dread of cheap transit?"

"Yes, I only say what are facts. I ask, Have you *finished* anything irrigationally? It is not what I say. These are facts."

Mr. Sampson Lloyd was much puzzled at these statements; he could not believe what he had heard. "Why should any man dread cheap transit?"[1]

Readily came the reply: "Because it would stultify the railways; that is the sole point."

"Only think," he scornfully added, "of a canal by the side of the Eastern Bengal railway, which carries some two hundred thousand tons, carrying two million tons, and swarming with passengers, and goods, and boats! What a terrible affront to the railway that must be!"

The Chairman could not accept this view, and pressed

---

and forty-six thousand tons were lifted over a length of one thousand two hundred and eighty miles on the East Indian railway, giving about five hundred tons per mile of railway, or, if an equal amount of traffic obtained in the second half of the same year, the total lifted was about one thousand tons per mile during the year."

[1] Later, Mr. Sampson Lloyd having communicated with Colonel Fischer, R.E., respecting the traffic on the Godavari canals, to support the evidence he gave, received the following statement for 1877-78:—

1. Number of passenger boats licensed	120
2. Number of cargo boats licensed	1,671
3. Register tonnage, cargo boats	36,011
4. Timber rafts	3,639
5. Tonnage in canals	536,672
6. Ton mileage	12,658,265
	£
7. Value of cargoes estimated or declared	3,696,502
8. Navigation receipts	4,496

"The number of passengers is not given, but one hundred and twenty boats took out licenses, and these carry on an average fifty a day."

for further statements—which were given, and all of the same tenour.

Perhaps, to show how little things change in the immemorial East, even under a British Government, evidence may here be submitted showing that navigation canals are still subject to biassed treatment when a railway has to be protected against water cheapness. The incident occurred in 1898, while Lord George Hamilton has been Secretary of State for India, and therefore, cannot fail at least to interest him.

My authority is a work published in 1899 by the Superintendent of the Government Press, Madras. Here is a narrative which I find begins on p. 168, and which, because of its importance, I quote in full in the text. It cannot be relegated either to an appendix or embodied in a foot-note. The official narrative proceeds:—

"The rates sanctioned in 1883 on the Ellore canal remained in force for upwards of fifteen years, but have now (1898) been increased as explained below.

"Early in 1893 that portion of the East Coast (State) Railway which runs along the Ellore canal of the Godavari and Kistna systems was opened between the two rivers, and later in the year completed to Cocanada; it is in order that some idea may be formed of the effect of the railway on the canal traffic that, in the statement on pages 164–165, it has been shown what that traffic was in 1892–93 (*i.e.*, 1st April, 1892, to 31st March, 1893), as well as in 1896–97.

Railway v. Canals.

"The railway between Bezwada and Cocanada had not long been opened, when its officers began to complain that it could not successfully compete with the water carriage, without a considerable enhancement of the charges for use of the canals, or at all events of the line between Bezwada and Cocanada, consisting of the Kistna-Ellore canal and the Godavari, Ellore and Cocanada canals. Many ways were urged of effecting this, the most favoured being an almost prohibitory toll at the Godavari river locks. The matter was in 1896 referred to a committee, who recommended a reversion to the arrangement in force before 1883 (see statement on page 166), by which the Godavari, Kistna, and East Coast, or Buckingham canals were treated as separate and independent systems of navigation, with the fees to be paid for their use very largely enhanced, in some cases quadrupled, from those in force since 1883, and a preliminary notice to this effect was published. This would have been handicapping the canals with a vengeance, and not only the canals with which the railway is in direct rivalry, but also those which serve parts of the country which the railway does not reach, and which are positively 'feeders' to it; the result would have been that the best interests of the public and the Government would have been sacrificed, with the object that a portion of the traffic, which preferred to use the *State* canals, might be *forced* on to the *State* railway, so that the latter might be thus artificially made to show better returns.

"Fortunately, before the Government was finally committed to this course, further consideration was given to the subject and wiser counsels prevailed. After some time the matter was ably dealt with by the Chief Engineer for Irrigation, Mr. W. Hughes, in a note which will be found with P.M.G., No. 319 I., dated April 18th, 1898. In this, he points out that in all the most advanced countries of Europe 'the tendency is to treat canals as roads, freeing them from all charges except remuneration for services actually rendered, and looking for a return in the general increase of the prosperity of the country which the canals serve. They are considered rather as complements than rivals to railways, each kind of transport being specially suitable for certain kinds of traffic. In no progressive country is any direct profit on (canal) navigation sought' by the State; and that it is 'felt to be a national misfortune,' that, 'in England the railway companies were allowed to get control of many of the canals.'

"He deprecates the attempt 'to adopt the same system here,' and he combats the idea 'that the railway cannot get a fair amount of traffic owing to the through traffic on the canals, unless the latter be so taxed as to prevent boats carrying for less than 4½ pies per ton per mile.' As regards this he says:—

"'The railway traffic between Bezwada and Cocanada in 1896 was 72,000 tons, which is nearly the amount by which the canal traffic fell off. The railway was at the time charging 2¾ pies per ton per mile, but was handicapped by the breakage of bulk and delay and exposure of goods at the Godavari crossing. Nevertheless, practically all the salt, cotton, and oil-seeds, which constituted the more valuable part of the canal traffic went to the railway, and there seems no reason to doubt that the railway can largely increase its rates and still keep the valuable traffic when the Godavari bridge is completed, or other arrangements made to take loaded waggons across the river. The experience of other countries all goes to show that since the great improvements of recent times in permanent way and rolling stock, railways running in competition with canals get nearly all the more valuable traffic, leaving the canals to carry goods of much bulk or little value, trade in which is effected by a very slight difference in freight.'

"He then commends the scale of licenses for use of the canals which will be found in the remarks which follow, and which need not be set out in detail here.

"With reference to his proposed enhancements of navigation charges, the Chief Engineer of Irrigation remarks:—'This is a tariff for revenue to satisfy the objection of the Government of India that the navigation is being worked at a loss. The amount of additional revenue required to cover the present deficit and the further falling off, which will occur when the Madras-Bezwada line is opened, is, of course, purely conjectural. The rates entered are such as it is thought traffic will bear without sensible injury. The rates for annual licenses are increased twenty to thirty-three per cent., and for six weeks' licenses, twenty to one hundred and fifty per cent.—the reason for the great variation in the latter case being that, in the 1883 tariff, a uniform rate of eight annas was imposed in lieu of two tolls irrespective of the class of vessels. The six weeks' rates now proposed are roughly one-fifth of the annual rates. The rates for steamers are trebled. The canals are generally not deep enough for steam traffic, and steamers, unless very small, and worked at a low speed, do much injury to the banks. It is decidedly a bad time to increase rates at all, but the increase cannot be avoided if the receipts and charges are to be made to balance.'

"Government accepted the recommendations made, and the new scale of fees came into force in May, 1898."

After this let there be no more official indignation when irrigation engineers, and those who believe in the extension of irrigation, declare that the canals do not receive fair play where railway interests are concerned.

Once, and once only it seems, the Chairman had the better of the witness, and was able to quote his own words against him. But the triumph, again, was not for long.

"Do you remember the report you wrote on the Madras Irrigation Project?"

"Yes, I remember it."

The witness had said it was because of the non-completion of these works that they did not pay. The Chairman proceeded: "Did you not say of the Madras Project, 'One great advantage of this system of works is that it is composed of parts each forming a complete system in itself, and which, as soon as completed, will yield its own returns independently of the remaining parts . . . as soon as one part is executed, it will at once come into effective operation and yield returns.' That prediction has not been realised?"

"No," the witness candidly replied, "it has not. The water has been refused by the people. I could not contemplate that. I had been fifty years in the country, and never heard in my life or dreamt of the water being refused by anybody. No one could have supposed that there could have been such inconceivable mismanagement that the people cannot take the water."

Lord George Hamilton was determined the witness should not go unscathed, even though he had so good a plea to urge.

"Still," said the noble lord, "from some unforeseen circumstances your prediction has not been realised?"

Sir Arthur Cotton was a little stung by the persistence of the questioning on this point, but he maintained his coolness.

"Not from any defects in the works, but from a defect in the management. I am a manufacturer, and I make a locomotive, and I say, 'Here is a splendid locomotive,' and it is taken to the railway, it bursts because the man is drunk who works it. Am I answerable for that?"

Mr. Onslow found a way out for the further and complete vindication of the witness.

"What is the defect in the management to which you allude?"

It was explained that the Company had not been fairly treated. "The Duke of Buckingham, who is Governor of Madras, is my authority for that. In the Government Minute it is stated that the Irrigation Company have real cause of complaint. The Government were declared to be under an obligation to set matters on a proper footing without further delay. The Deputy Collector of Kurnool issued orders practically preventing applications for water being made as heretofore by the ryots to the irrigation officers direct."

The answer was complete. Nevertheless, a number of further questions were asked, and were all answered with ready information and complete courtesy. Three years later the Famine Commission of 1878–80 reported on this incident. First, they quoted from the report of Mr. Forster Webster and Major Scott Moncrieff, R.E. (who afterwards did such good irrigation work in Egypt) who inquired into the matter, and reported that they had read up much correspondence, and had taken evidence from various individuals in the Kurnool and Cuddapah districts. Although, for reasons already given, they did not think that under the best auspices the canal could have been a success, they considered Mr. Lister was warranted in ascribing its failure partially to:—

"1. The absence of good revenue administration in the taluks traversed by the canal;

"2. The unsatisfactory relations which have existed between revenue officers and the Company;

"3. The feeling of antagonism that has arisen between the Company and the ryots;

"4. The whole system of management which exposes the ryots to worries and exaction."

The Commissioners themselves were even more emphatic, for they said:—

"It was too readily assumed at the outset that the water would be taken at once, and that it would suffice to entrust the management of the revenues of the canal, and the supply of water, to the ordinary district officials, in addition to their regular duties. Applications for water were to be made to the village accountant, who was to open a register and send in monthly reports. The tahsildars and revenue inspectors were to attend to the control and distribution of the water; in no case was any additional pay given for these additional duties. These arrangements were soon found to be unsatisfactory. Mutual recriminations between the officers of the Government and those of the Company soon began; and, in 1878, after much discussion, a special inquiry took place, from which it appeared that the practical failure in extending the irrigation was mainly attributable to the absence of good revenue administration, unsatisfactory relations between Government officials and the officers of the Company, and antagonism between the Company and the ryots, arising out of a harassing system of management." [1]

Many more questions were asked regarding the Madras Irrigation Company, especially by Sir George Campbell, who rubbed in the remark, "You remember that this work was one which above all others you recommended?" "Yes," was the reply, "and it is one of the most complete and successful works, if the water was used, that could be constructed in India."

But, there was vindication to come even for the Kurnool canal. The Famine Commissioners of 1878 remark: "The canal was of great value during the late famine, as it irrigated 87,226 acres in the Kurnool and Cuddapah districts." [2]

On railways, again, the witness was strongly pressed. He had referred to the absurdity of constructing railways in Bengal.

"Then, it seems now," urged Sir George Campbell, in his least pleasing way, "from our experience you were wrong in your predictions?"

[1] Page 162 of *Famine Commission Report*, part ii. "Measures of Prevention and Protection, 1880."

[2] *Famine Commission Report*, 1878, p. 347.

"No," sturdily answered the much-pressed engineer; "I was quite right, and I call the chief railway engineer to witness."

"How can you be right [when you say it is an absolute failure] if it paid ten per cent.?"

"I say it does not carry the quantity, and it does not carry so cheaply as the country requires; that I call a failure. When the chief railway engineer says, 'Here is a railway which leaves nine-tenths of the passengers and goods behind,' if that is not a failure, what in the world is?"

Over and over again it was sought to overcome the witness by an array of authorities, whose good intentions and honour no one could doubt.

"Are you really serious in stating that you believe successive Governors-General have given their sanction" to this, that, and the other thing?

"I only mention facts," pleaded the witness, and he never budged one inch.

The defects of the rivers—particularly the Ganges and the Jumna—were fully discussed, or perhaps "wrangled over" would be the more correct term, such twistings and turnings marked the questions which were put.

As to the damage done by efflorescence of reh, Sir Arthur declared it to be of little importance. "There are twenty million acres of irrigated land in India. How much of that is covered with reh? Not a thousandth part."

Considerations of space—and, maybe, but I hope not, the reader's patience—forbid anything like adequate treatment of the many aspects of irrigation and navigation which the varied needs of India call forth.

On the great storage reservoir in the centre of India—a project which, it is trusted, may be undertaken as one of the consequences of the present disastrous famine [1]—Lord George Hamilton was particularly antagonistic.

[1] It is pitiable, but it is the fact, that, only on paying the terrible price of famine, are great irrigation works undertaken. Mr. Deakin was struck by this, and, in his *Irrigated India*, p. 143, he says :—

"You never surveyed that scheme?"

"There is an officer now in England who has surveyed it thoroughly; and I know all the papers about it. I have been up to that part of the country. I know the country; I have seen all the papers and reports about it, and I have talked it over with the officer who has seen every bit of it."

"Do you think that it would add to your undoubted reputation as a successful engineer if you advocated the construction of a great reservoir in a district you have never seen?"

"But I have seen it; I have been up there, as I say, at the very spot."

Such an emphatic statement should have been decisive, but it was not.

"Are you aware that that scheme has been very severely criticised and pronounced utterly impossible?"

"Yes, like everything else. The Suez Canal was denounced as impracticable, and that it would be of no use when it was done."

[In this connection, attention may be directed to Sir Arthur's truly noble scheme of a great central reservoir, by quoting what, on another occasion, he put forth in detail concerning this project. He wrote:—

"It is indeed surprising that it is only quite of late years

"The immediate relation between famine and irrigation is perfectly evident in every presidency. The dearth in Madras in the early part of the present century lead to the construction of the anicuts which supply its deltas; that of 1837–38 in Bengal induced the preparation of the project for the Ganges canal; that of 1859–60 in the North-West Provinces determined the State to undertake all future works, so that in 1867–68 Lord Lawrence definitely inaugurated what is known as the policy of Extraordinary Public Works. Altogether there were seven severe famines in Southern India in the first seventy years of this century, all disastrous within varying limits. The terrible famine of 1876–77–78, for which a large relief fund was generously raised throughout Australia, marked the culmination of these awful visitations, 5,250,000 persons dying in the lingering agonies of starvation, although the Government lavished £11,000,000 in relief. The indirect losses occasioned would render this hideous total more imposing still."

that this grand discovery has been made, that the Presidency possesses a basin for a reservoir of stupendous dimensions at a level commanding the whole Peninsula,[1] so favourable in all respects that it can be constructed at a perfectly nominal price compared with the value of water.

"In the evidence given by Colonel Fischer (who has levelled and estimated for this work), he allows for a bund one hundred feet high, retaining the water, ninety miles in length, with the contents of the basin three thousand millions of cubic yards, and the cost £300,000. The river for seventy miles has a fall of only seven inches a mile, and above that ten feet with a broad and long plain on each side, of very little value for cultivation. This must certainly be one of the finest sites in the world for a tank.

"It must be remembered that the quantity of water provided by a tank is not measured by its contents, because water may be drawn from it all the five months in which there is a large body of water in the river, while it is left full at the end of the monsoon, so that such a tank would supply at least twelve thousand million cubic yards, that is eight thousand million during monsoon, and four thousand million in the dry season.

"With respect to the supply of water, all the sources of the Tungabudra are in the Western Ghauts, where the rainfall is from one hundred to one hundred and fifty inches. The area drained is stated to be twelve thousand square miles; allowing only one yard of rain to flow off this area. it would supply thirty-six thousand million cubic yards, or three times the quantity proposed to be drawn from the tank, and twelve times its contents."

[1] "The whole Peninsula" does not mean the Empire from Kashmi to Cape Comorin. During the last century the term Peninsula was applied to that part of India which is south of the Godavari; the expression was in common use in Sir Arthur Cotton's time. For want of properly understanding the term, critics have charged Sir Arthur Cotton with having stated that a reservoir in the Madras Presidency would be of service in the far North of India as well as in the near South.

There is salvation for beast as well as man in India if this project be carried out. Will not the British people insist upon their Indian fellow subjects being saved from all the suffering and loss which the chronic famines now cause?]

A little later, retorting upon the Chairman, the witness gave himself the satisfaction of saying: "The last time I was examined before a Committee of the House of Commons it was, in the way of a taunt, said to me, 'Yes, you would cut a canal from the Sutlej to the Jumna!' *That very thing is done.*"

Sir George Campbell, too, was treated to as pretty a bit of sarcasm as seldom comes in the way of a House of Commons questioner: "Is it not the case that in those famines the rain so far failed that the rivers were not full at the time when they were wanted for irrigation?"

"The Godavari was not full; it *only contained fifty times as much water as we would use:* IT WAS AS EMPTY AS THAT."

The end of the first day's enquiry came appropriately with that and two other questions put by the Chairman:—

"Then the general purport of your evidence is that you have not altered your opinions in the least?"

"Not the slightest in the world," was the cheery retort; "the whole thing that has been done has confirmed me more completely."

"You are not in the least deterred by that admitted failure to which we have alluded both in the case of Madras irrigation and the Orissa works?"

"*Not the least in the world.*"

An interval of a week elapsed, and on Thursday, June 27, the witness was once more in the chair. Thirteen out of the sixteen members were present. The absentees were Mr. Balfour, Sir Joseph M'Kenna, and Mr. Grant Duff. Mr. Ernest Noel appears among the Committee on this occasion.

Sir Arthur Cotton started early with a definite statement: "No one line of canal navigation has ever been completed." To ask, therefore, for satisfactory navigation returns was to ask for the impossible.

Sir George Campbell began the examination. He was particularly curious as to canals, and asked no fewer than one hundred and one questions, with a short break of two from Mr. Fawcett. Then he started again, and asked one hundred and twenty more! Not only navigating canals in India, but also in England, Scotland, France, the United States, were laid under contribution. Sir Arthur advanced a fair argument when he suggested no tolls should be charged in irrigation-navigation canals. "As the irrigation pays over and over again the interest of all the expenditure, and as there is no wear and tear of the water in navigating the canal, of course the interest of the State is that these canals should be used to the utmost, and should be perfectly free."

Sir George tried a fresh break on the old question as to river navigation being available for only a certain part of the year.

"So," he queried, "it would be a broken and imperfect navigation?"

"Yes," was the cheerful assent, "unless you supply it with water [which could be done with ease in the vast majority of cases]. It is like everything else. If you build nine arches of a bridge and leave the tenth unfinished, you cannot go along it." "When I propose a project," he went on to say, "instead of working according to the project you [meaning the officials] leave out this, and leave out that, and stop it in the middle, and then say, 'Look at your project.'"

The size of a reservoir to hold the water for the maintenance of the necessary height in canals troubled Sir George. "Would it not require an enormous quantity of water?"

"No; all that has been calculated. We know just a well as we know how much water it would take to fill a bucket . . . we have abundant data now for knowing what it would cost to store the water in large reservoirs in the upper part of the district. It is all a matter of calculation—as simple as possible."

One strong point was that an enormous sum of money would have been saved if the Godavari works had been treated as a railway would have been, while the Presidency Treasury would have greatly benefited year by year.

The questioner was not always discreet, and sometimes elicited facts he did not want, as, for example, when it happened (Questions 2561, 2562, and 2563) that it was proved that while the Hyderabad side of the river was "exceedingly fertile, populous, and thriving," the other side (the British Provinces) was "an almost uninhabited and deserted country, little more than a jungle."

Out of Sir George's persistent questioning some good came. Sir Arthur Cotton was afforded an opportunity of setting forth in detail his scheme for canals for affording communication over nearly the whole of India, with many intermediate connections. On the map [*in pocket at end of book*] the whole of these canals will be found. They are commended to the careful consideration of every reader of this book who wishes well to impoverished and suffering India.

"What are these main lines of navigation which you think might be established?"

The answer was:—

1. From Calcutta to Kurrachee—up the valley of the Ganges, across the watershed of the Jumna and the Sutlej, down the valley of the Indus to Kurrachee. The worst part is already cut, the Sirhind canal, across from the Sutlej to the Jumna.
2. By the line of the Godavari and the Tapti from Cocanada to Surat.
3. Up the valley of the Tungabudra and the valley of the Kala Nuddee, crossing the watershed near Da rwar, which is the worst one, two thousand feet, reaching the sea at Karwar.
4. By Palghaut, a breach south of the Neilgherries, up the valley of the Ponang and down the valley of

> Ambravatty, crossing the watershed near Coimbatore, on a level of about one thousand four hundred feet. Two coast lines would meet at Cape Comorin.[1]

In another place the witness thus comments on some details:—"The remarkable fact in connection with the West Coast canal is that a very small State, under a native

[1] In his *Public Works for India*, published in 1881, he elaborates his proposals as hereafter given. These particulars, so far as was possible, have been indicated on the accompanying map:—

1. The completion of the Coast canal from the Godavari to Madras —380 miles.
2. The completion of the Godavari and Kistna Delta works.
3. The completion of the Upper Godavari and Wurda navigation to near Chanda on the Wurda—150 miles.
4. The Junction canal from the Tungabudra canal at Cuddapah to the North Coast canal at Nellore—80 miles.
5. The construction of a great tank on the Tungabudra, west of Bellary, to contain at least 3,000,000,000 cubic yards.
6. The canal from it to the Irrigation Company's canal—200 miles, irrigating 500,000 acres.
7. The complete examination of the whole system of old tanks, perfecting, enlarging, etc.
8. A nearly level canal from the great Tungabudra tank, south to the Cauveri, near Seringapatam, and north across the Kistna and Bheema, passing near Hyderabad to the Godavari—800 miles.
9. Canals leading the water from this main canal to multitudes of old tanks in the Carnatic.
10. A canal from the above main canal in Bellary across the watershed of the Huggry and the Pennair to convey water into the latter river.
11. A bund across the Pennair where it leaves the hills forty miles above Nellore, with canals leading north to the Kistna and south through the Carnatic, to supply old tanks and for irrigation—about 400 miles.
12. The extension of the East Coast canal from the Pallaur, forty miles south of Madras to Cape Comorin—400 miles.
13. The completion of the West Coast canal from Cape Comorin to Karwar—400 miles.
14. The construction of a canal from Madras through the heart of the Carnatic to Ponany on the West Coast through the

Government, has utterly shamed us by making the canal almost through the whole length of Travancore; while we, with our unbounded means and immense interests, have not had the energy to execute the part in our provinces. The only difficult part of the whole line from Cape Comorin to Karwar is in Travancore, but this has thus been done for us. The rest of the line will be very expensive.[1] How sad it is to see this necessity for our being shamed into the execution of works necessary for the well being of the country by a petty Indian State setting us the example.

"There are already small canals on some parts of this

Palghat Pass, of which the canal from the Pennair would form a branch.

15. The continuation of the high level canal from the Kistna anicut south to the Pennair at Nellore—200 miles.
16. The construction of the two great tanks on the Peneh and the Kanhan rivers, north of Nagpur.
17. A canal from them to the Warda, near Chanda, for navigation, irrigating 250,000 acres in Nagpur, and supplying water to keep the Godavari navigable and fill the Delta canals in the dry season.
18. The extension of the East Coast canal from Cocanada to meet the Orissa canals (now being extended to the Chilka lake) at Ganjam, from which there is a canal to the lake—250 miles.
19. A canal for navigation, west of the Tungabudra at the proposed tank to Karwar on the west coast—180 miles.
20. A canal from the Wurda down the valley of the Taptee to Sura —300 miles.
21. The improvement of the navigation of the Kistna and Bheema above the level of the proposed tank, viz. :—Kistna, 150 miles, and Bheema, 200 miles.
22. A breakwater at Ponany, on the west coast.
23. A breakwater at Cape Comorin.
24. A tank on the branch of the Bhowani river in the Neilgherries, fully examined and estimated by the Madras Government many years ago and of great capacity.
25. A tank on the west side of the Ghauts near the source of the Vigny river in Madura, with a tunnel through the Ghauts for the better supply of that river.

[1] That is, because it has been put off until the cost of materials, labour, etc., have greatly risen.

line, but they are much too narrow and too shallow. The whole distance is five hundred and fifty miles. Allowing something for the part executed in Travancore (though it is probable that this also will require enlarging when it forms part of an extensive system), the cost may be, at £2,000 per mile, £1,000,000 in all.

"Now the most remarkable point with reference to this is, that the openings for works are really wonderful. As respects water transit, the whole Presidency is perfectly capable of first-class water transit on all the important lines, and this almost everywhere, in combination with irrigation.

"The Coast canal from Bengal, by Cape Comorin to Karwar on the Western Coast, is all perfectly practicable at quite an insignificant cost. The main lines across the Peninsula from Madras through the heart of the Carnatic to Ponany, and from the same city by Nellore through the Ceded Districts to Karwar, and that up the Godavari and Wurda, and by the line of the Tapti to Surat, are also all perfectly practicable at a small cost compared with their effect.

"From these, thousands of miles of branch canals may be led so as fully to open up this populous country.

"Further, a contour line may be led from the Cauveri near Seringapatam, through Mysore, the Ceded Districts, and Hyderabad, to the Godavari, in the heart of the upper country, thus putting the whole of the interior by means of the east and west canals and rivers and the coast canals, in effective communication with the ports on both coasts, and with Calcutta and the plains of the Ganges and the Punjab. The conveyance of one ton from Lahore to Karwar, three thousand miles, would thus, at one-twentieth of a penny per ton per mile, cost only Rs. 6—about ten per cent. on the value of a ton of grain.

"Take a single item: Coal. What would be the effect of supplying the whole country from the Chanda mines, and making every port on the East and West coasts a coaling port for steamers?

"Take one other item: Salt. The consumption of salt is at present nine pounds per head. Where it is cheapest and the people are in good circumstances the consumption is twenty pounds. An increase of eleven pounds per head for sixty millions would be three hundred thousand tons. What would be the benefit of this to a vegetarian people? And the revenue from this alone would be, at the present rate of tax, three-farthings per pound, equal to two millions a year, which is the interest on sixty millions at three-and-a-half per cent.—more than what the whole of these canals would cost, including a vast system of irrigation from them.

"This alone will help us to judge what a manly, energetic, extension of public works would do for India and its finances, if it were carried out,—

"1. To secure and turn to use for navigation and irrigation many millions of cubic yards of water, which at present carry to the sea an incalculable treasure of fertilizing matter;

"2. To improve and supply from the great rivers many thousands of the old tanks;

"3. To pervade the whole Presidency with a complete system of water transit, carrying any quantity at a nominal price, both of goods and passengers, connecting the whole interior and the valley of the Ganges and Indus with Cape Comorin and the West coast, the best points for the shipping of goods for Africa, Europe, and America; and

"4. The provision of a large extent of irrigation in every district of Madras, and many of Mysore and Hyderabad, from the great rivers, thus securing them against failure of the local rains."

Sir George's penultimate question in that day's enquiry was almost of equal value to that concerning the Central Reservoir. The witness had opportunity, on challenge, to state his matured views as to what parts of India could still be irrigated.

"Will you just point out, generally, what are the parts of

India which you think are now most favourable to the extension of irrigation ?"

It must have been with something of the feeling of an old seer testifying to a heedless generation, that Sir Arthur Cotton replied :—

"There is an enormous proportion of all India ;
"There is all the Punjab ;
"All the remaining portion of the North West ;
"Almost all of Oudh ;
"All Rohilkund ;
"All Bengal ;
"All the delta country ;
"All the plains of the Kistna and the Tungabudra, and
"The vast extent of the Carnatic still unirrigated.

"Many hundred millions of acres are perfectly fit for irrigation."

[Lord Curzon, the present Governor-General of India, has been advised in this year of grace (1900) that only four millions of acres remain which can be "productively" irrigated. An examination of the '98 *Famine Commission Report* shows on what basis the Viceroy's statement was made. It is to be regretted that statement was made without other illustrative particulars. In paras. 574–576 are recommended:—

	Acres.
The Punjab projects	4,000,000
The Sind projects	660,563
The Upper Burma projects	334,000
Total .	4,994,563

Nothing is allowed for all the Presidencies and the other Provinces and Commissionerships throughout the Empire. But, it is admitted, other works "may, no doubt, be sooner or later proposed in these and other provinces." On this point there can be no doubt. There is much land still capable of being irrigated, and it is regrettable Lord Curzon should seem to have minimized the great development which must take place, and take place soon, if India is to be rescued from its present deplorable condition.

On the extensions as a whole, the Commissioners express themselves in this cordial manner:—

"The new works will therefore tend to reduce the pressure of future famines, and to counteract in some degree the effect of the growth of population, while at the same time adding in ordinary years to the general wealth of the country. Their construction may also be recommended as a financial investment, and as strengthening the financial resources of the State. We have already shown that the surplus revenue realized by productive irrigation works, after all interest charges at four per cent. had been paid, amounted in 1896–97 to Rx. 809,173. This was higher than usual on account of drought, but the actual surplus for 1897–98, was even higher, and when the stimulus afforded by famine has passed away the normal surplus will probably not be less than Rx. 700,000, or nearly half the amount of the famine grant. If the new works are as profitable, taken as a whole, as those already constructed, a surplus revenue of £660,000 may be eventually anticipated, or in other words the nett direct financial profit on productive irrigation will be sufficient to meet two-thirds of the whole estimated cost of famine. The value of these works, and in a less degree of protective and minor irrigation works, in strengthening the financial position of the country may, however, be shown in another way. During the years 1896–97 and 1897–98, famine necessitated remissions of land revenues to the amount of Rx. 1,448,000, and there was great loss of revenue under other heads directly or indirectly attributable to famine. The remissions of land revenue and the whole cost of relief would of course have been infinitely greater if these works had not been constructed, but apart from the value of the works in this respect, the revenue earned by irrigation works of all kinds in these two years showed an excess over the normal of Rx. 981,600 which has been directly attributed to famine. It is therefore a special recommendation of these works that while almost all other sources of revenue are certain to be largely reduced in years of famine, irrigation revenue may be expected to increase, while it will be short only in years of abundant and favourable rainfall, where there is an expansion of other sources of revenue consequent on agricultural prosperity." [1]

Mr. Childers took up Sir George Campbell's running, and tried hard to pin Sir Arthur Cotton to an exposition of the financial arrangements required to carry through the big scheme promulgated.

Finance was not the witness's forte. He declined to be fixed to any statement of the kind. It was not his business.

"I must beg to say," he remarked, "that all these are entirely out of my line. I am not a statesman or a man of business. I am an engineer, and, therefore, I have no opinion on these matters. If I am asked I have certain floating ideas about them. I would give much more liberty to the local governments than they have at present. I would have much less interference on the part of the supreme government with the local governments. I see that one misjudging Viceroy can paralyse all India."

On the third occasion of his occupancy of the position of a witness (July 4, 1878), Mr. Onslow asked the early questions, basing them upon a pamphlet which Sir Arthur Cotton, after his preceding examination, had circulated amongst the committee. When dealing, in later pages, with Sir Arthur's views on the opium traffic and the salt tax, reference may be made to some of Mr. Onslow's questions.

It came out that the large scheme previously outlined was intended to join the following rivers and canals :—

The Ravee,	The Orissa,
The Sirhind,	The Godavari,
The Ganges,	The Kistna,
The Lower Ganges,	The Tungabudra, and
The Sone,	others.

Little else of freshness or importance was asked, and the long examination came to an end.

[1] *Famine Commission Report*, 1898, p. 352.

The whole set of works he sketched out was roughly estimated by him, in detail, as follows :—

	£
1. North Coast canal—450 miles, at £1,000 additional . . .	500,000
2. Completion of Godavari and Kistna Delta Works . . .	1,000,000
3. Completion of the Godavari Navigation to Coalfields, exclusive of tanks	1,000,000
4. Cuddapah and Nellore canal .	500,000
5. The Tungabudra tank . . .	250,000
6. The canal thence to Kurnool, with 500,000 acres irrigation .	2,750,000
7. Complete examination, repairs and improvements of the native tanks in Madras, adding 1,000,000 acres irrigation .	3,000,000
8. The Contour canal, north and south from the Toombudra tank—800 miles at £8,000, irrigating 1,000,000 acres . .	7,500,000
9. Canals from this main canal to many tanks	1,000,000
10. Canal from the same main canal across the Huggry to throw water into the Pennair—50 miles at £6,000, say . .	250,000
11. Bund across the Pennair, west of Nellore, with canals north and south—400 miles at £6,000, irrigating 250,000 acres . .	2,750,000
12. Coast canal from the Pallaur to Cape Comorin—400 miles at £3,000	1,250,000
13. Completion of West Coast canal from Cape Comorin to Karwar—400 miles at £3,000	1,250,000

	£
14. Canal from Madras to Ponany on the West Coast—450 miles at £8,000, with 500,000 acres of irrigation at £1 per acre . .	4,000,000
15. Continuation of high level canal from Kistna anicut to Nellore —200 miles at £6,000, to irrigate 250,000 acres . . .	1,250,000
16. Two great tanks on the Peneh and Kanhan rivers in Nagpur .	500,000
17. Canal from them to the Wurda near Chanda—120 miles at £8,000, with 500,000 acres local irrigation	1,500,000
18. Extension of East Coast canal, north from Cocanada to Chilka Lake—250 miles at £6,000 .	1,500,000
19. Canal from Tungabudra tank to Karwar on the West Coast—180 miles, with 2,400 feet of lockage on inclined plains .	2,250,000
20. Canal from Wurda to the West Coast—300 miles at £8,000, with improvement of the Wurda—100 miles at £2,000	2,500,000
21. Canal from Surat to Bombay .	500,000
22. Improvement of Kistna — 150 miles, and Bheema—200 miles, for navigation, at £2,000 . .	750,000
23. Breakwaters at Cape Comorin and Ponany	500,000
24. Periyar tank in Travancore, for the supply of Madura[1] . .	1,000,000
25. Tanks in the Neilgherries with extension of old canals in Coimbatore	2,000,000
	£41,500,000

[1] Done. To end of 1898–99, nearly completed, cost little more than half of estimate.

	£
Brought forward . . .	41,500,000
Add 20 per cent. for interest while under construction, and coming into operation	8,5000,00
Total . .	£50,000,000

Once, in the course of his own examination, Sir George Campbell conceded the whole of Sir Arthur Cotton's case for irrigation as a preventive of famine. "I do not doubt," he remarked, "that if you could have irrigation works extended all over India, all India would be protected from famine." He proceeded, however, to remark: "But, as a matter of fact, if you look at the map and see the parts that are coloured green, you will find that the areas which are irrigable are only of comparatively small extent, and that there still must be a much larger extent of country which is not so protected. In respect to that large country, I think that you must depend as a security against famine and other calamities upon the improved means of communication of which we have heard so much, and that being so, I think you may very well make railways, provided that you have really sure reason to believe that you may obtain from them a moderate return."[1]

This is the crux of the whole situation. This is *the* point of difference :—

EXPERT.

Sir Arthur Cotton declares that there are few parts of India to which water for irrigation and navigation cannot be taken, if adequate storage be provided. Many millions of acres, he asserts, can be brought under cultivation.

NON-EXPERTS.

Sir George Campbell, and some others, including the present Governor-General (himself most favourable to irrigation), declare only a few million more of acres can be irrigated with financial profit.

[1] Q. 1868, Select Committee, 1878, p. 153.

The layman, with all the evidence before him, is inclined to trust the expert as against the non-experts. If it be a matter of doubt, in view of India's need, the decision ought to incline to the adoption of the expert's views. He, at least, spoke from knowledge.

The Select Committee reported in 1879. Probably, Sir Arthur Cotton was never more intensely annoyed and irritated in respect to any public matter than he was with that report. He had good reason for irritation and annoyance. The paragraphs in it which referred to him and to his schemes were needlessly severe, and were not in accordance with the statements he made. The one point which Sir Arthur made perfectly clear and which accounted for failure, namely, the non-connection of the navigation channels with ports or with means of getting to ports, is wholly ignored. Taking all the irrigation works together, there was no loss but considerable profit. It was recorded against Sir Arthur that he had admitted, "None of the great works pay yet," meaning certain new great works. The witness explained, in detail, why, to that point, they had not paid, and had shown that the irrigation engineers were not to blame. All of no use,—four to five per cent. of profit could not be shown on certain works in exceptional circumstances: therefore, irrigation was *anathema*. They did not then pay their way, enterprise by enterprise, though, as a whole, they yielded a large revenue to the State.

But stay: did the railways at that time fulfil the obligation which the official committeemen considered so necessary? Did they? Lump them together as the irrigation works were lumped together: what then? Sir George Campbell and his colleagues did this in their draft report though not, as is done here, for comparison (p. xxviii.). With what result?

	£
Net receipts on all railways to 1877-78 .	44,295,589
Guaranteed interest paid	69,304,366
Loss . . .	£25,008,777

That is, at a time when irrigation works as a whole showed considerable profit, while railways showed a loss of £25,008,777, it was recommended that, *because they did not pay*, therefore no large irrigation projects were to be considered, while railways were to be undertaken in profusion! And so successfully did this Select Committee, led whither he would by Sir George Campbell, impress the Government, that, in spite of the emphatic recommendations of the much more important Famine Commission two years later—to the 31st March, 1898, all that had been spent from capital for irrigation works, was just six millions more than the deficit on railway account twenty years earlier. Thanks, mainly, to the Committee of 1878, this is how the *first* place in provision against famine has been secured for irrigation works:—

	£
Capital Expenditure on *Railways* to 31st March, 1898	130,614,851
Capital Expenditure on *Irrigation* to 31st March, 1898	32,639,803
Difference AGAINST the works of first importance . . .	£97,975,048

The draft report prepared by the Chairman (Lord George Hamilton) was especially uncomplimentary to proposals for the extension of irrigation, but, as it was not accepted, citations need not be made from it.

The report which was accepted called forth from Sir Arthur Cotton a Memorandum, which, though studiously courteous, is bright throughout with an intense fire of indignation. This Memorandum deals so fully with the report that, as an appendix to this chapter, it must be largely quoted from.

I need only here remark that Sir Arthur felt keenly the mode of examination to be unworthy of so important a body and wanting in respect to himself, as indeed it was. After quoting an instance of frivolous enquiry, to which I have not alluded in my summary of his evidence, he says:—"This mode of questioning is worthy of a lawyer trying to put down a witness, totally unworthy of men appointed by the country honestly to ascertain the real opinions of witnesses."

For the rest I most earnestly commend the passages from Sir Arthur's temperate and most excellently reasoned comments upon the Committee's action.

Appendix I

REPORT OF THE SELECT COMMITTEE.

The following are the passages of the Report of the Select Committee, which relates to the works with which Sir Arthur Cotton was associated, and to Madras generally :—

The Madras Works, constructed with borrowed money, and in operation, chiefly consist of works in the deltas of the large rivers; the only works paying [1] being those in the Godavari, Kistna, and Cauveri Delta, to which an excess revenue of 12·94, 9·8, and 81·30 per cent. is respectively credited upon the capital expended. No account is however taken, in the case of the Cauveri works, of the native anicuts; but making all due allowance for this omission, the results of these works reflect great credit upon the officers who designed and carried them out.

The conditions under which they worked were, however, especially favourable, not only to irrigation, but to that combination of irrigation and navigation which is the chief characteristic of this system.[2]

The area to be irrigated consisted of flat, alluvial plains, without roads, through which passed a great and constant supply of river water, independent altogether of the real rainfall, and capable of being easily controlled and directed to any part of the surrounding delta. If, in other parts of India, similar conditions existed, your Committee would have little hesitation in recommending an expenditure for carrying out works, the receipts from which show that they are both useful to the cultivator and remunerative to the State.

The account which your Committee have, however, given of the climate, and conformation of Southern India, show that not only do not these same favourable conditions elsewhere exist, but that they are in many districts reversed. For a very large portion

---

[1] It will be seen, from the extracts (*Madras Administration Reports for* 1897–98), given on pp. 338–342, that, with a very few exceptions, *all* the Madras Works, after providing for interest, are yielding a large surplus revenue. Probably, no Report emanating from a public body has been so completely falsified by results, as has the irrigation section of this deliverance of 1879; and the railway section, too, so far as railways were to be famine preventers.

[2] This is not so as regards the Cauveri: see evidence on preceding pages.

of the country is unsuited to canal irrigation, and the supply of river water, with three exceptions, is precarious.

During the prolonged drought of 1876–77 the vast majority of the rain-fed tanks were either dry or their contents so reduced as to be of little utility. If, then, a drought continues for more than a year, it is clear that tanks, to be a preventive against such a continuance of dry weather, must either contain more than a year's supply of rain, or be connected with streams whose sources are independent of the local rainfall.

The point, therefore, to be solved, and the importance of which has been prominently brought before your Committee by the terrible mortality, notwithstanding the enormous State expenditure during the late Madras famine, is, taking into consideration both the present condition of Indian finance and the natural physical difficulties to be overcome, to prescribe the practical policy to be adopted the most likely to diminish the prospect of a recurrence of such a calamity in Southern India.

Your Committee are aware that a Special Commission has been appointed by the Government of India to locally investigate the causes and magnitude of this disaster, and to report upon the remedies to be adopted. Without in any way attempting those specific or detailed recommendations for the protection of this vast area from famine, such as would necessitate a preliminary inquiry into the wants and capabilities of each separate district, your Committee desire briefly to notice the proposal laid with much confidence before them by Sir Arthur Cotton. This scheme, though applicable to the whole of India, was based upon his personal experience, mainly derived from the working of the irrigation works in the deltas of Madras.

Sir Arthur Cotton proposes the summary and indefinite suspension of nearly all railway schemes and works. He would, however, devote £10,000,000 annually for the next ten or twenty years to irrigation works, mainly canals (Question 2,722), the main canals to be of such dimensions as to permit navigation. By such an expenditure he estimates that ten thousand miles of main line navigation would be constructed at a cost of £30,000,000, dealing with the most populous districts, whilst the remainder of this vast sum was to be spent on feeders or subsidiary works.

Sir Arthur Cotton estimates that such an expenditure would give a large return to Government (Question 2,751), though your Committee were unable to ascertain the data of this conclusion, especially as he does not deem it to be within his province to consider how, or at what rate of interest, the money expended would be raised. Neither has he in any way attempted to estimate or make provision for the immediate rise in the cost of material and labour which so sudden and simultaneous an expenditure throughout India must inevitably produce.

The figures already embodied in this report show how few o

the most carefully examined irrigation schemes have proved remunerative, and these returns are more than confirmed by Sir Arthur Cotton himself, who, in reply to a question asking him to indicate what works constructed by the Government of India during the last twenty years, other than those in the Madras Delta, had proved remunerative, replied, "None of the great works pay yet" (Question 2,214).

It is evident to your Committee that this scheme, though of gigantic dimensions, is of too shadowy and speculative a character to justify their noticing it, except for the purpose of emphatically rejecting it.

That the works in the Madras delta, with which Sir Arthur Cotton's name is so honourably associated, are a success, has been admitted by your Committee. On the other hand, the Orissa works, the Madras irrigation works, and the navigation works of the Upper Godavari, with which his name has more recently been connected, are financially complete failures.

Your Committee cannot, however, pass without comment the statement more than once repeated by him, that the failure of these works was due to the whole power of the Government having been exercised against their completion, on account of their dread of cheap transit (Questions 2,322, 2,264).

The Government were, in the opinion of your Committee, right when, in the exercise of their discretion, they declined to invest further sums in undertakings which, from their commencement, belied the estimates and returns upon which alone they were sanctioned.

Nor do your Committee find that the causes of the financial failure of past schemes was the want of ability or energy on the part of the officers of the Public Works Department. The main cause of that failure[1] appears to have been the placing too great reliance on the hasty generalisations of engineer promoters who, rendered over sanguine by the success of certain other undertakings, have ignored the conditions under which alone their success was achieved, and without which success was impossible.

---

[1] Once more it must be remarked that, taking the whole range of irrigation works, there has been no failure; rather, in the words of Sir James Lyall and his colleagues (*Fam. Com. Report*, p. 339), respecting the extensions since 1880 (and of works earlier completed): "The result has been a great advantage to the State, regarded merely from the direct financial return on the money invested, and apart from their value in increasing the wealth of the country in ordinary years, and in preventing or mitigating famine in years of drought." The Select Committee reported, in the adverse terms quoted above, in 1879; in the following year the Famine Commission said exactly the contrary: "Put irrigation in the FIRST PLACE; go on with it wherever you can," was their recommendation. But this Report was in existence, the men who wrote it in positions of influence, and—India has suffered, is suffering, and will continue to suffer; who knows how long?

Appendix II

EXTRACTS FROM MEMORANDUM BY SIR ARTHUR COTTON ON THE REPORT OF THE SELECT COMMITTEE OF THE HOUSE OF COMMONS ON PUBLIC WORKS IN INDIA, 1879.

This report seems most urgently to call for notice—first, because it does not make the slightest mention of the main point of the whole question, but is wholly occupied with minor and comparatively insignificant ones.

And secondly, because it entirely excludes one side of the question, even in respect to the minor points with which it assumes to deal. Of the constitution of the Committee we may judge from the fact that the only member of the House who was personally acquainted with the public works in India, from having been one of the Commissioners appointed to investigate the subject in Madras in 1852, was not placed on the Committee.

I may premise that, even if such a Committee were *bona fide* intended fairly to investigate a subject, there are essential defects in the system as it is now carried out.

1st. The Committee can call upon what witnesses they may please, and are consequently liable to leave out the most important ones, either from ignorance of a subject with which the members are not conversant, or from bias.

2nd. The witness, when called, may be rendered useless or worse, either from the members not knowing what questions to ask, from their want of real knowledge of the subject, or from their asking only such questions as will in effect set aside the really important information he has to give. The witness is never asked to give his view of the subject, so that he may have an opportunity of speaking upon what he knows or considers to be the really great points of the question.

3rd. But in the present case a new point was introduced which utterly stultifies the whole proceeding; and that was the examining, as a witness, one of the members[1] who, of course, as a member had to *pronounce on the value of his own evidence.* This member, in the course of his examination,[2] made it one main

[1] Sir George Campbell, K.C.S.I., M.P.

[2] His evidence was extremely long.

point to show the extreme of ignorance of one of the other witnesses, and of course it was not to be expected that either he in the report would judge fairly between himself and his adversary, or that his colleagues would so far lay aside their courtesy towards him as to support his adversary, however much they might be convinced by the arguments of the opponent. If one witness is allowed to judge in the cause, certainly another ought to be so too. Two of the witnesses were diametrically at issue, but if one has given his judgment on the matter, surely, in fairness, the other ought to be called upon to report also, otherwise the best possible means are adopted for misleading the public. In a court of law the decision of the case is never left to one of the advocates, but to a third person.

Nothing can be more evident, therefore, than that I have a perfect right to remark upon the evidence given before the Public Works Committee, now that my opposing witness has given his report to the public, and it ought to have the honour of a blue cover, just as much as the one already published. And to this I may add that my own evidence was given on a subject on which my whole attention had been concentrated and practically exercised for nearly sixty years, while my opponent's experience was confined to quite another line; that not only had he never projected a single work of irrigation or navigation, but so entirely unconversant was he with the subject that he objected to certain lines of canal on account of the *ranges of mountains that crossed them, where there is not a vestige of a hill.*[1]

And of the tone of the Committee, and the honesty with which it approached the duty laid upon it by the country, a judgment may be formed from the following questions put to Sir George Campbell by Lord George Hamilton and answered by the former, recorded in the Blue Book (p. 110) :—

No. 1472. "*There are several ranges of mountains between the Godavari and Poinany,. are there not?*" But this was rather too much, and the witness replied, "I should rather say a high tableland." There is not a vestige of either mountain or even high tableland. The height is exactly the same as that between the Sutlej and Jumna, where the Sirhind canal has already been cut.

No. 1474. "Do you think one might just as well say it would take twenty-five millions as two and a half millions" (to cut the canal from the Godavari to the west coast)? The distance is six

[1] The italics in this Memorandum are Sir Arthur Cotton's.

hundred miles, so that twenty-five millions would be £40,000 a mile, the most expensive canal yet cut having cost £6,000 a mile. The witness, of course, courteously replied to this, "Precisely so."

It is impossible to mistake the nature of an investigation carried on in this style. This mode of questioning is worthy of a lawyer trying to put down a witness, totally unworthy of men appointed by the country honestly to ascertain the real opinions of witnesses. As a further proof of the spirit in which this investigation was carried on, one of the members, in my presence, protested to the chairman against the statement I had given in being published in the report of evidence—that is, that the principal part of the evidence of the engineer of incomparably the greatest experience in the matter, and the only one who, according to the Commissioners' own report, had projected and executed highly remunerative public works of any kind in India, should be suppressed. But though not one of the members protested against such a monstrous course of procedure, I suppose it was considered too dangerous an experiment, and the whole of this evidence has been published in the Blue Book.

My first point is that this report entirely omits the main point of the whole question. *It says not a word on the effect of the public works upon India.* In the case of the Suez Canal, which is of most importance, the one or two millions a year it returns to the shareholders, or the connection of Eastern Asia, China, and Australia with Europe? So with the irrigation and navigation in India; which, for instance, is of the most importance, the direct returns to the Treasury, stated in this report to be a quarter of a million for the three irrigated districts of Madras, or the addition of £2 an acre on two million acres, besides other great money returns in ordinary years, and the production of a million tons of food in the late famine, supplying ten millions of people for six months, in the midst of a desperate famine that carried off several millions of people in all the surrounding districts? And, independently of the question of occasional famines, which is of most importance, the payment of a quarter of a million a year into the Treasury, according to the report before us, or the raising five millions of people to a state of plenty and prosperity far beyond those of any other districts in India? and, even merely as a question of finance, the enabling three districts to pay two millions a year in revenue—one million a year more than before the works

—while the average of the other districts is not much more than £250,000, or rather above a third of the former?

And so with respect to transit, which is of most importance —the conveyance of hundreds of millions of passengers and tons of goods cheaply, safely, and quickly, by eight thousand miles of railway, four thousand miles of steamboat canal, ten thousand miles of minor canals, and some fifty thousand miles of good road, or the payment into the Treasury of £300,000 a year, as stated in the report?

Now, I would ask, what are we to think of a report professing to be an investigation of the subject of public works in India, which utterly ignores these incomparably the most important points of the question, and which not only ignores what has been already effected, but also all that would be effected if these comparatively trifling works were extended throughout India? Not one word is said on these the essential points of the matter placed before them. It really seems incredible that such a paper should have been offered to the people of England as the result of an investigation of this subject, in which the well-being not only of the two hundred and sixty millions of the people of India is essentially involved, but that also of the whole British Empire, for all its parts are inseparably united in interest. For instance, as one point, since the improvement of Godavari the trade has increased, not fifty or a hundred per cent., but more than twentyfold. If all India were thus improved, and its trade increased twentyfold, what part of the empire would not partake in the benefit?

Now let us try to form some estimate of the results of the works that have been executed. They are:—

1st. Six million acres irrigated by new great works, besides a vast extension of irrigation under innumerable smaller works improved.

2nd. Four thousand miles of steamboat canal, besides thousands of minor canals, uniting, and so giving effect to a great extent of river navigation besides.

3rd. Eight thousand miles of railway.

4th. Some fifty thousand miles of good common road.

5th. Fifteen thousand [?][1] miles of telegraph.

Besides innumerable minor works all over India.

---

[1] The query is Sir Arthur's; apparently, writing at home, he had not the necessary information.

A very simple calculation will show, beyond all doubt, the vast extent of the benefits received by the immense population of India from these works in money only.

Estimated gain to India by Public Works.

Six million acres, irrigated, at Rs. 15 per acre, increase of produce only—besides enormous other benefits, such as security from river and rain floods, supply of drinking water, sanitary effects, and many others—£9,000,000.

Two million acres, in works not yet opened, but constructed—£3,000,000.

Four thousand miles of steamboat canals (besides smaller canals and river navigations connected with them), carrying about one hundred thousand tons per annum at 1*d*., against 4*d*. on land, or 3*d*. a ton on four hundred million tons—£5,000,000.

Eight thousand miles of railway, carrying, by last report, two thousand million tons at 1*d*., saving 3*d*. per ton—£25,000,000.

Fifty thousand miles of road, saving 2*d*. per ton on probably fifty thousand tons, or two thousand five hundred million tons the mile—£20,000,000. Total £62,000,000.

This £62,000,000 is besides a multitude of savings in money, which cannot be estimated, and besides the transport of thirty-eight million passengers by rail at one third of a penny per mile an average distance of sixty miles, or two thousand four hundred million of passengers the mile; and of many millions by water at one-eighth of a penny per mile. Thus, the mere saving in money cannot be less than £70,000,000 a year, or double the whole taxation of India; for, deducting from the revenue the items of opium, post office, telegraph, etc., which are not *taxes* on India, the remainder is only £35,000,000.

Thus :—

	£
Land	20,750,000
Excise	2,500,000
Customs	2,750,000
Salt	6,000,000
Stamps	2,750,000
Miscellaneous	250,000
	£35,000,000

But, besides direct money returns, who can estimate the effects of this prodigious personal intercourse, and that by letter and telegraph, both in indirect money returns and in the well-being of the people? And these are only the ordinary things. What shall we say of the millions of lives saved in famines, etc., and by the sanitary effects of the regulation and supply of water, etc.? What would have been the additional loss of life in the single famine of the Peninsula had it been without the million tons of food supplied by the irrigated districts, and a large quantity carried by the railways?

And now, after sitting for many months, a Committee of the House of Commons offer to the public of England their deliberate report on the public works of India, and their conclusions as to what should be done in future, without the least attempt to estimate the results of what has been already done! Is it possible that the public can be deluded by such a make-believe document, surely the poorest that has ever been laid upon the table of the House?

And so it has been in the debates in the House. One member brought forward the whole expenditure on public works, also without a word on their effects, and—incredible as it would seem—no other member requested the first to show them the other side of the ledger before they came to a decision on the subject.

Suppose a Committee appointed to report upon the affairs of a bankrupt were to publish a statement of the liabilities without the least notice of the assets, would the creditors and the public be as grave in their reception of such a farce; and, considering it quite satisfactory, proceed to decide what was now to be done, forming their conclusions upon this wise document?

The member who brought before the House the amount of this expenditure spoke exactly as if the money had been thrown into the sea; and, therefore, the conclusion was the simplest thing in the world, viz., that all that *economy* required was to stop the expenditure, on the clear and simple principle that a penny saved is a penny gained. And that is made the climax of statesmanship! As we used to say under our former masters, "Save the rupees; never mind whether they cost a gold mohur apiece," so now the grave conclusion is, Stop the public works; never mind whether they benefit India fifty per cent. in money, or whether scores of millions perish from famine for want of them. The Committee state the whole sum expended on irrigation and navigation to be seventeen millions, *including five millions on works under construction and just on the point of completion, but not then at all in operation ; and three and a quarter millions for works formerly not in operation from refusal of the water, and now irrigated as far as water is supplied ; but the great mass of the land remaining unirrigated solely from want of distributaries.* And the area now actually under irrigation from these works is six million acres, giving £3 per acre as the average cost, and the mere increase of produce due to this has been thoroughly ascertained to be above Rs. 15 per acre, making the return to be about fifty per cent., besides all the other incalculable benefits. And this includes the capital on works not yet in operation. Deducting five millions for these leaves a capital of twelve millions or £2 per acre, and the return seventy-five per cent., this also including three and a quarter millions for works where the water has been till lately refused, and which, of course, under proper management, will be in full operation. Thus we cannot mistake in concluding that, with cheap transit, the saving in famine years, and other money returns, the whole of the works already in a manner finished, and including those of Orissa and the Buramputra, where the difficulty has been about the acceptance of the water, the return to India is one hundred per cent.

In Orissa, where the water was refused, 120,000 acres are now leased for water, and the only thing that limits its use is that the Government have refused to execute the distributaries, and in Midnapur the hindrance is that they have refused to store the additional water required. So also with the Godavari works : though they have been thirty-three years on hand and have from the very first returned twenty or thirty per cent. only £750,000 have been allowed for them, and they are now incomplete—300,000 acres remaining to be supplied with water, while five or six millions of money lie to their credit in the Treasury. *It is in spite of these inconceivable things that these vast results have been obtained.* Had the works been carried out with common vigour to completion, they would certainly now be watering six million more acres and yielding one hundred and fifty per cent.

The whole of the irrigation and navigation works have been thus treated. The Kistna works have been on hand twenty-five years and are not half finished, £500,000 only having been spent on them, though they have been enormously profitable.

The Godavari navigation was carried on at a cost of three-quarters of a million in twenty-five years, and was stopped entirely when it wanted some £20,000 to complete the second barrier works, which would have finished the first part of the project, opening 400 miles of navigation and bringing some ten millions of people within reach of the markets of the world. At this very time the then Secretary of State spent half a million on sixty miles of branch railways in the most out-of-the-way part of Central India, merely to carry coals and cotton, the returns on which were last year £8,500, or 1·7 per cent. So with the Orissa Canal to connect the whole populous delta and the Mahanudi valley with Calcutta. Of this, seventy miles have been cut at one end and sixty at the other, and the connecting eighty miles have been left unexecuted, though upon it depended the whole project; for it is certain that, if the market of Calcutta had been thrown open to the delta, the increased value of all produce would have been so great that the difficulties about the use of the water must have been swept away. This is the case with the whole of these works, and it is an absolute certainty that if they were all at once completed, which could be done for a sum of two or three millions, the returns to the community would be doubled.

In comparing the results of these works with the railways—according to their mode of judging them by the Treasury returns only—not a word of all this is hinted at, though it was all brought before them in evidence, and was not and could not be denied. Think of £114,000,000 being found for railways, besides fifty millions for land and accumulation of debt, the whole now returning five and a quarter millions, or 3 per cent. on cost and debt, while it was impossible to raise one million in thirty-three years for works which the Committee state return 17½ per cent., but which Mr. Thornton, of the India Office, showed returned 40 per cent., and General Strachey, some ten years ago, 28 per cent., and which are actually returning fully 100 per cent. on their cost to the country, viz.: £2 per acre on produce on £1 cost!

And all this concealed by the Committee! Not the slightest hint of it appears in a report placed before the public as the result of a full and faithful investigation of this fundamental point in the management of India. The case actually required that a truthful Committee should have added, "But, it must be clearly understood in making the comparison, that not a single work of irrigation or navigation—even those returning from the first, according to our own statement, 17½ per cent., and even having, sixteen years ago, on an expenditure of one-third of a million, a balance to its credit of one million, without calculating accumulation of interest (App. to report, No. 4)—that not a single work has been carried on vigorously, or even completed to this day, while every railway without exception was carried on, without a moment's delay, to completion, how ever many millions they required, and though all for twenty to twenty-five years did not pay their interest, and have now an accumulated debt of forty millions against them." . . .

Again, one of the witnesses before the Committee quoted the following from a speech of the present Governor of Bengal, speaking of Orissa, one of the two works where the people have refused the water, but which has enjoyed all the other benefits of the irrigation and navigation works. This is the work the Committee bring forward as a proof of the failure of irrigation works. "On visiting Orissa for the first time after eighteen years (in 1878, date of visit), it is a great satisfaction to me to witness the enormous material and moral progress which this interesting province has made. Notwithstanding the fact that it has within that time been desolated by famine, I believe there is no part of India in which the prosperity of the bulk of the people has improved so much. It is four years since my predecessor visited Orissa. The trade, which had then risen to £770,000, is now £1,230,000." (The trade before the works was £30,000: it has increased in a few years forty-fold.) "I see that Orissa exported last year (1877) 115,000 tons of rice and paddy" (worth about a million). "The price represents an enormous increase of wealth to the agricultural classes."

"It is not, therefore, to me a matter of surprise that *improved facilities of intercourse with the outer world* have brought to it such a development of prosperity as has taken place. I have under my consideration to give to Balasur, and even Cuttack, direct inland water communication with Calcutta, etc. If the work be carried out, it will, *I am sure, bring this district into a condition of prosperity which will not be surpassed in any part of India.*"

These astonishing accounts of the effects of the irrigation works are entirely ignored in the report. The last refers to the district where the only failure of the Government irrigation works has occurred, as respects the use of the water, showing, even where it is refused, that the prosperity of the district has been amazingly promoted by the other benefits of the works. Again, in an official paper, dated June 18, 1878, the following account is given of the effects of the irrigated districts in Madras :—"The Godavari and Kistna works, besides supporting the population of their own districts, and a great crowd of hungry immigrants from the surrounding country, and besides exporting over country roads an amount of food grains, which the Collector of Godavari estimates at little less than the amount exported by sea," (viz., 140,000 tons), "supplied very nearly one-fifth of the food exported from places within the Madras Presidency itself for the supply of the famine demand during the same time. Tanjore and Trichinopoly also supported their own and all the immigrant population, besides exporting by road, as well as by sea and rail, etc. It seems to me that schemes for extending and developing the Godavari and Kistna works deserve the heartiest support of the Government of India." Again: "The gross value of the rice raised by the Godavari and Kistna canals during a year of famine, when, to judge from the condition of the neighbouring districts, there would not otherwise have been an acre ripened, *may be taken at £4,950,000, or four times the whole capital outlay to the end of the year.*"

Not a word of this is inserted, or alluded to, in the report, nor in any of the debates on the famine. Think of a report on what is to be done in future in this respect not saying a word about the completion of these works, and of an official statement being made to the House of Commons on the famine, in which not a word about these amazing effects of the Madras irrigation works is mentioned! It is thus that the British public have been utterly misled, and that their ideas about irrigation are utterly contrary to the truth.

With respect to the subject of transit there is no attempt in the report to go into the essential points of the case. The questions, What does India require in this respect? What quantity ought to be carried, and at what prices, in the circumstances of India, in order to give itself and other countries the full benefit of its productions? What means can effect this? Do the railways answer the purpose or do they not—that is, can they carry the quantities, and at the prices that are absolutely necessary for the development of the country? Can canals do this? Are they practicable generally throughout India? etc. None of these, the fundamental points of the question, are touched upon. This is probably owing to not one of the members being conversant with the subject of transit; so that whether 100,000 tons or 5,000,000 require to be carried on a certain line, and whether it will answer the purpose if goods are carried at a penny a ton, or whether they require to be carried at a tenth or a twentieth of a penny, were points which never occurred to them to inquire into. The fact is, the whole subject of transit requires to be inquired into just as if no committee had been appointed. A railway is opened at an enormous expense, and the sole question asked is, Does it pay three or four per cent. *to Government*? as if the Government were a private company, and had nothing to do with the well-being of India. As if, whether it carried the whole quantity required, and at practicable prices, or whether it was little more than a make-believe, and carried a tenth part of what was wanted, and at prohibitory prices, were matters of no moment to the rulers of the country. *The real fact is that after sinking* 170 *millions on railways*[1] *the country is utterly paralysed for want of effective transit at this moment.* For instance, in the famine, tens of thousands of tons of goods were left to rot at numbers of stations because the comparatively small traffic in grain completely choked the roads. Nothing is more urgently required at this moment than a thorough investigation of this subject, *the very first essential for India.* What India wants is to have millions of tons and millions of passengers carried on all the main lines of the country. Take two instances of this. India is deprived of the market of England for her wheat and other grains and pulse, for want of communications that can carry sufficient quantities and sufficiently cheaply; and, with unlimited supplies of coal and wood, it is burning millions of tons of manure solely for want of the means of distributing the proper fuel at practicable rates. It is utterly in vain that God has been pleased to provide the land with unbounded stores of these invaluable productions, if we do not provide the means of distributing them. This He leaves for us to do. . . .

And now with respect to the point on which the Committee

[1] Including cost of land and minus interest charges, etc.

settle the question—that is, the returns to Government. And first of the irrigation. This is given thus:—Capital fifteen and a half millions, net returns £830,000, interest 5·3 per cent., or ·8 above the Government interest. They thus show upon their own statement that *the irrigation works are an actual gain to the Government even in ordinary years*; that they cost the Government nothing. In the first place, must be added to this (even supposing the saving of millions of lives were nothing to great statesmen), the enormous saving in actual money to the Treasury in famines, and in the years following, in consequence of the additional population compared with what would have survived. Thus, in the Madras famine, rice was grown by our irrigation works sufficient to preserve the lives of ten millions of people for six months. What would have been the loss of revenue for many years if these millions had perished? There cannot possibly be any doubt about this, that in one such famine there is a loss of revenue prevented in that and the following years far exceeding the whole cost of the works. Nothing is said about this in the report. Again, in this total expenditure of fifteen and a half millions is included no less than four and a half millions, the cost of the Agra, Lower Ganges, Sone, Mootah Moolla, and Sirhind Canals, and Ekrookh Tank, all of which were under construction and not in operation, being nearly a third of the capital charged. This reduces the capital to ten and a half millions, and raises the return to 7½ per cent. instead of 5¼. Thus there was in 1875-6 a clear profit to the treasury of £350,000, an ordinary year; and, further, this return is for 1875-76. In that year the irrigation was 150,000 acres in Bengal. Last official year the extent was 400,000 acres, so rapidly is it extending. Thus, with all our mistakes, mistakes which, of course, need not be repeated, the revenue has been considerably increased, even in ordinary years, by the Committee's own statement, upon a capital of only ten and a half millions; so that we have certain data for concluding that, when these works are completed, the revenue will be increased by a million a year, besides all the incalculable saving in famines and the years following them. Further, no account whatever is given of the causes of deficient returns in the works that were not remunerative in 1875-76. The cost of these works, viz., the Midnapur and Orissa Canals, was two and a quarter millions. Now, the case of these works was quite an especial one. The failure of returns was not any essential defect in them, but was entirely owing to two removable causes—the first is the non-completion of the works, and the other is the refusal of the water by the ryots. With respect to the latter, it is already removed. It was simply the consequence of a most wretched state of revenue management. In an official report the case is thus stated:—"From his extreme poverty and state of indebtedness, the Midnapur ryot reaps but a questionable benefit even from a bumper crop. Be it a good one or a bad one, it is said that all, beyond a bare subsistence, for a limited time, is absorbed by the landlord's rent, and the claims of his far more exacting creditor, the village money-lender, in whose toils he is hopelessly entangled, and who charges him at the rate of thirty-nine per cent. per annum." What can an engineer do if, when he has executed such invaluable works as these, the country is so utterly neglected by the revenue authorities that the poor people are left in such a state of bondage as this? While the poor people are refusing the Government water, this is the state of demand for it in that very part of the country. General Haig says:—"There is not a single river, drainage watercourse, or channel of any kind, large or small, in the whole district that is not bunded across at frequent intervals from one end to the other for the purpose of storing the water; no pool, puddle, or waterhole that is not most jealously guarded. It is almost incredible the amount of labour and effort that is thus expended by the ryots (the zemindars, as a rule, do nothing) to secure as far as possible every drop of the precious element; and it strikingly illustrates the actual need that is felt for *more* water, for a more continuous supply, in a district where the natural supply might have been supposed to be sufficient." If this does not show some monstrous mismanagement, what could? All this desperate anxiety to procure more water too is expended to get the *poor rain water*, while the water brought to them by the canals is *rich river water*, worth three times as much.

This was allowed to go on for many years, but at length, under a more faithful Government, this difficulty seems to be pretty well got over. A Committee that lately reported on these works (Orissa) say:—"In 1876–77 the area irrigated was 26,000 acres; in 1877–78, 95,000; and this year, 1878–79, it is estimated that 130,000 acres will have taken water." But now, who could imagine that the distributaries are wanting to conduct the water to the remaining area commanded? This is the way in which the whole of these irrigation works have been treated. If a railway were in hand, though it did not pay interest for twenty-five years—it did not signify how many millions it cost—there never was the slightest discussion about the money; but every water-work has been left unfinished. The one thing that has caused all the difficulty about these Orissa works was that the canal connecting them with Calcutta is not completed. The Committee before mentioned say:—"This canal forms an important link in the chain of communication between Cuttack and Calcutta, the completion of which, *first and before all things*, was urged by Colonel Haig in his exhaustive note of May 29, 1873." And the present Governor of Bengal says, as quoted by one of the witnesses to the Committee of last year:—"I trust before long to obtain sanction for the commencement of this work" (the completion of the canal), "and I hope before leaving India to see Cuttack brought within two days' journey of Calcutta. If the work be carried out, it will, I am sure, bring this province into a *condition of prosperity which will not be surpassed in any part of India.*" The value of rice, as given in the Bengal report, is in Orissa Rs. 17 for the produce of an acre, 900 lb.; and in Calcutta Rs. 28. It could be carried by canal for R. 1, giving an increased value of Rs. 10 per acre to the rice alone, or seven times the water-rate. This will give some idea of what the effect of cheap transit is, and of what India is losing for want of it. The moment this canal is opened, it will give an entirely new value to everything in the district, many times the amount of the water-rate. There cannot be a question that, if this canal had been completed, the enormous increase in the value of produce would have in a moment swept away all the difficulties about the use of the water. And as with the navigation, so it is with the irrigation. Under the present weirs no less than 1,500,000 acres are commanded by the water, while only 640,000 are protected by embankments, and only 130,000 are supplied with water. In this way, of course, irrigation may be made to cost anything. If the whole project for the thorough protection, irrigation, and navigation of the whole delta were carried out, it would regulate the water for 2,000,000 acres, and in increased produce and increased value from cheap transit, the return would be fully Rs. 15

per acre, or a total of £3,000,000 a year, and the total cost of the works would certainly not exceed £4,000,000, giving 75 per cent. besides innumerable benefits in the way of sanitation, etc. There is not the smallest room for doubt that the result, as stated by the Lieut.-Governor of Bengal, would be that "the prosperity of the province would not be surpassed by any district in India." Had there been such governors in Bengal as this in previous years, it is certain that this would have been the present state of the region.

But let us now consider once more the expenditure of £500,000 on the coal railways in Nagpur in the upper basin of the Godavari. This, as I have shown, now yields $1\frac{3}{4}$ per cent., or a clear loss to the treasury of £14,000 a year. Had this sum been spent on the lower end of the Godavari in completing the delta works there, and in the Kistna district, it would have been ample for 500,000 acres, the water-rate alone on which would have been Rs. 4 per acre, forty per cent., or £200,000 a year, making the total profit on irrigation £550,000 on £11,000,000, or five per cent. above the Government interest, or half a million in all. Such would have been the return if this one sum had not been thus shamefully perverted. All this was expressly brought to the notice of the then Secretary of State personally at the time, and it was also given in evidence to the Committee. Yet not a word is said in the report about this waste of the public money. What is the object of these inquiries if it is not to point out such misapplication of the public funds, and other causes of the deficiency of the finances, and of the poverty of the people? This half million expended in watering as many acres would have afforded an increase of produce alone of a million a year to the ryots of Godavari, and this is only a small specimen of the enormous misappropriation of the public money. The fact is that the whole tendency of the report is to hush up and conceal the grievous abuses and mistakes that have been made in the public works, instead of exposing them, which was supposed to be the object of the Committee.

But, further, this return from the irrigation and navigation, as reported by the Committee, entirely leaves out of sight all the indirect return from these works. Can the wealth of the people be increased without increasing the general taxes? The Committee credits the works in Godavari with £127,000 a year; then where does the rest of the increase of the revenue of the district come from? The revenue was before the works £220,000. It is now £570,000, an increase of no less than £350,000. Nothing is said about this difference in the report. The fact is that about £300,000 of this is due directly or indirectly to the works, and so with all the great works. On the six millions[1] of acres now watered by them, there is an increase of income to the people of at least £10,000,000 a year, and it is impossible thus to enrich the people without a considerable portion of it coming to the Treasury. Of the total income of the country about ten per cent. is paid as taxes, so that this additional income must add about one million to the finances. And, even merely in respect of the returns to the finances, if this were the sole question, the report is utterly false. The actual returns of the irrigation works alone, direct and indirect, are at this moment probably £2,000,000 a year instead of £130,000 as stated by the report. And with respect to the *prospects* of the works, even as they are, without their being carried out effectively, the gross revenue of those in Bengal, which is stated in the report as £23,000 for 1875-76, was last year £107,000, or five times as great, and there is absolute certainty that they will in a short time return above the Government interest. In that year the area irrigated was 150,000 acres; last official year it was 400,000; the Sone works are now very nearly completed to the extent to which they are now restricted, and they will water 800,000 acres. Not a word of this is stated, but the remarks in the report imply that these works were doing all they could or were ever likely to do. Only think of this sum of £23,000 a year being mentioned as the return of the Bengal works, without adding: "But the four millions of capital here given includes one and a half millions, the cost of the Sone works now approaching completion, but not in operation, which will return £250,000 a year, besides the Orissa and Midnapur works, which will water at least 500,000 acres under the main canals already cut, and yield £100,000 as soon as these difficulties about the acceptance of the water are overcome, and that they are already in fact overcome

[1] The six millions are now (1900) at least fifteen millions. If Sir Arthur's calculations still hold good, the direct contribution to the wealth of the country of the Government works alone is at least £25,000,000 a year. Probably, it is much more.

under the present vigorous government is evident from the fact that 150,000 acres are now irrigated."

Further, in this report nothing is said about this mode of obtaining water from the *rivers*. Was this nothing, and a matter of no question whatever? Might not a laborious investigation have properly included such a fundamental essential point as this? It is continually said, it has been repeated in a late paper on India, "I prefer obtaining water from wells." Now what is right? Who could imagine that the simple answer to this is not alluded to in the report? The case is this. Well water costs, to raise it by bullocks, about R. 1 for 300 cubic yards, while rich river water, full of all the food that plants require, worth three times as much, is brought on the fields at a cost of from 1,000 to 2,000 cubic yards per rupee. The Sone works, for instance, will distribute 3,500 million cubic yards per annum, and cost, at seven per cent. on £2,700,000, £190,000, or 20,000 cubic yards per £1. One would suppose that such a plain calculation as this would set at rest this question. Neither rain nor well water will restore the soil, while the river water does this so effectually that land has been so cultivated for thousands of years without other manure. Even where there is abundance of rain, river water is just as much required. The fields should be emptied of the rain water as soon as possible and refilled from the river. It is, of course, very difficult to get people to believe the violence of the bias of the real old Indian against the use of this invaluable river water. But surely the following fact will prove this unmistakably. A gentleman [1] was lately sent out from England expressly to investigate the terrible famine question as a member of the Committee appointed in India. He went to India and passed throughout the length and breadth of the land, and, one can only suppose, under the influence of the old India atmosphere in which he was immersed, scrupulously avoided seeing what water could do for India. He not only avoided Orissa, where he might have informed himself that, in spite of great difficulties, the district had made considerable progress in rising from its abject state of poverty and despondency, as stated by the Lieut.-Governor of Bengal; but he actually touched at Cocanada, the port of Godavari, where the water works had had their almost full effect and had

[1] The late Sir James Caird, who was a member of the Famine Commission of 1879.

raised a district from below the lowest of the districts to the state of the very highest prosperity in all India, raising the revenue to £570,000 a year, two and a half times that of the districts generally, and he left the port without landing. In the same way he passed by the Kistna district, and in the south went to Trichinopoly, on the confines of Tanjore, the other thoroughly prosperous district paying a revenue of £750,000 a year, and avoided seeing that district also, so that he has returned without seeing what water can do for India. It will seem incredible, of course, that such things could be, but there is the fact. The only districts that have been fully and effectually delivered from famine, and that yield a revenue to Government, which, if it extended throughout India, would make the receipts of the Treasury one hundred millions instead of thirty-five, and that are really a credit to our rule such as no other districts afford, were carefully avoided; and if this gentleman is asked, "But, what conclusion did you come to respecting the difficulties that have been met with in Orissa and the reported complete success of the well-irrigated districts in Madras, both in respect of the famines, and of finance, and the prosperity of the people?" he must say, "I have no personal knowledge of these districts." What are we to think of these things? Were these no questions? What has made these districts the head districts of India? And how far are the means, which have here produced such astonishing effects, applicable to other parts of India?—districts which, in the midst of the most awful famine, which left every surrounding district, even in spite of a million being spent on each in railways, strewed with hundreds of thousands of dead who have perished in this awful manner, both yielded full revenue to the Treasury, sold a full crop at famine prices, kept their own population in plenty—a population of five millions—and fed ten millions of the adjoining districts.

I must advert also to one assertion of the Committee with respect to my evidence. They state that Sir Arthur Cotton's scheme for the irrigation of India was based upon his personal experience, "mainly derived from the working of the irrigation works in the deltas." My objection to this is that it is pure invention. There is not a shadow of ground for it. My words were, "I take the whole cost of irrigation up to this time wherever it has been carried out," and so on. Throughout my examination there is not one word which showed that my calculations were based upon the cost of the works in Godavari. I stated everywhere what was the cost of irrigation in the various parts of India, and the increase of produce due to it. What are we to think of a Committee that can thus recklessly make assertions directly contrary to the fact, when they know that the person of whom they speak will have no opportunity of refuting them?

CHAPTER XI

Railways *v.* Irrigation and Navigation Canals

IRRIGATION "pays the Hindu everywhere, for without it millions could not live at all, and millions more would be decimated by famine every few years. Reckoning its influence upon railways, commerce, and the good government of the country, its value is simply inestimable."—HON. A. DEAKIN, M.L.A., *Victoria.*

THE real point considered in the last chapter, and, indeed, had it done its duty, the real point of the whole enquiry of the Select Committee, was as to the remedy for famine, frequently and certain-recurring famine in India, which is what has now to be faced. Though partly veiled, the actual issue was: "Do railways, or do irrigation and navigation canals, best preserve the country from famine?" Further involved in it was the additional question: "Granting railways are necessary for transport of passengers, goods, and produce, save in respect to certain trunk lines, would not properly-constructed canals serve the full purposes of such a country as India?"

To these questions Sir Arthur had but one answer. To the first he always said, unhesitatingly, and with abundant proof, that railways in India could not possibly compare, or, with fair treatment, compete, with irrigation and navigation canals as a preservative against famine. To the second, he was, all through his life, of the same mind as the late Lord Derby, one of the sanest and most far-seeing of British statesmen, that a multiplicity of railways was not needed in India, while upon irrigation and navigation canals the very existence of India depended.

The official answer ought to have been the same in each

instance as was Sir Arthur Cotton's. What is the record of the authorities in this respect? Their record is, that their own Famine Commission of 1879–80, which made enquiries in India in 1878 and in England in 1879, plainly laid down what was the FIRST DUTY of the Indian Government. At page 150 of part ii. of the Commission's Report, this most significant statement, and this remarkable recommendation (remarkable in view of the balancing and moderate terms in which a Commission usually makes a suggestion) was submitted :—

> "Among the means that may be adopted for giving India *direct protection from famine arising from drought, the* FIRST PLACE *must unquestionably be assigned to works of irrigation.*[1] It has been too much the custom, in discussions as to the policy of constructing such works, to measure their value by their financial success, considered only with reference to the net return to Government on the capital invested in them. The true value of irrigation works is to be judged very differently. First, must be reckoned the direct protection afforded by them in years of drought, by the saving of human life, by the avoidance of loss of revenue remitted, and of the outlay incurred in costly measures of relief. But it is not only in years of drought that they are of value. In seasons of average rainfall they are of great service and a great source of wealth, giving certainty to all agricultural operations, increasing the out-turn per acre of the crops, and enabling more valuable description of crops to be grown. From the Punjab in the north, to Tinnevelly at the southern extremity of the peninsula, wherever irrigation is practised, such results are manifest; and we may see rice, sugar-cane, or wheat taking the place of millet or barley, and broad stretches of indigo growing at a season when unwatered lands must lie absolutely unproductive."

But, on value according to financial success, that is the

[1] The italics are mine in all cases where the contrary is not stated.

payment of a reasonable dividend (and, it ought, but is not, to be the rule to provide a sinking fund also), the same Commission reported emphatically in words which leave the India Office no excuse whatsoever if they refrain even now from taking most energetic steps to carry out Sir Arthur's plans. Their neglect in the past arouses feelings of indignation which I may not express. Two pages after that mentioned above, namely on page 152 of the Commission's Report, it is stated :—

"LOOKING AT THE PRESENT POSITION OF INDIA IN RESPECT TO IRRIGATION, IT WOULD BE HARD TO FIND ANY SYSTEM OF WORKS THAT IS NOT WORTH TO THE COUNTRY THE MONEY THAT HAS BEEN SPENT ON IT; and where the reverse seems to be the case by reason of an unfavourable direct money return on the capital outlay, it will be generally found that it is due to the backwardness of the cultivators in adopting the great change in their customary system of agriculture, which necessarily follows on the introduction of irrigation, or to defects of design, or errors of management which should not have occurred, and which may be remedied more or less completely. *Only where the population is so sparse that use could not be made of irrigation if it were offered, or where the necessary cost of the works would be so exceptionally great, that it would be cheaper to accept the likelihood of expenditure on famine relief than to incur the cost of canals,*

CAN THERE BE ANY DOUBT AS TO THE ADVANTAGE OF IRRIGATION,

or as to the expediency of extending it within the limits which the general financial position of the State imposes on its outlay on such undertakings."

Even this does not exhaust the advice given by the Commissioners. Yet two pages further, and there is this triumphant official vindication—triumphant on the narrow official lines, more than triumphant if all the conditions are taken into account—of all Sir Arthur Cotton's contentions. "But," say the Commissioners, "although we have thus referred to the possible *temporary* ill-success of irrigation works in some cases, *more particularly in the early stages of their development*, we must again repeat THAT THE ACTUAL EXPERIENCE OF INDIA IS ALTOGETHER OPPOSED TO THE VIEW THAT THE EXISTING WORKS OF THIS CLASS, TAKEN AS A WHOLE, ARE OTHERWISE THAN POSITIVELY REMUNERATIVE TO AN EXTENT WHICH COMPLETELY JUSTIFIES THE MEASURES WHICH THE GOVERNMENT OF INDIA HAS CARRIED OUT FOR THEIR EXTENSION DURING THE LAST TWENTY YEARS OR MORE."

". . . The net income of the whole of the works in operation was, in the year 1879–80, £1,165,800, which amounts within a very small fraction to six per cent. on the whole capital outlay, including about £3,250,000 spent on works not yet brought into operation. If this part of the outlay be excluded, the income is found to be more than seven per cent. on the capital actually utilised."

More astounding still, in view of the comparative neglect which afterwards followed, of irrigation extension and the great extension of railways, are the following statements, statements which more than justify Sir Arthur Cotton's unanswerable position. The Commissioners report :—

To show how greatly the wealth and resources of India have been increased by her works of irrigation, the following instances may be quoted from the mass of evidence to the same effect before the Commission.

In the Punjab.

2. The outlay on completed canals in the Punjab up to the close of 1877–78 had been £2,260,000. The total area irrigated by them was 1,324,000 acres. The weight and value of the food grains raised at the high prices which ruled during that year of drought on the two principal canals were calculated as follows :—

	Tons.	Value.
West Jumna Canal	158,000	£1,147,000
Bari Doab Canal	141,400	789,000
	299,400	1,936,000

The value of other crops grown on these two canals (sugar-cane, cotton, dyes, oils, vegetables, etc.) was estimated at £940,000. It may, without exaggeration, be reckoned that one-half of these crops would have perished if unwatered, or would not have been raised at all if the canals had been absent. So that altogether in that one year, the wealth of the Punjab was increased by these two canals by £1,438,000, an amount equal to about two-thirds of the cost of the works; and, but for the protection they afforded, Government would have lost heavily from the necessity of remitting revenue, and providing for famine relief. The net canal revenue for the year in the Punjab was, however, only £119,000, being about five and a half per cent. on the capital outlay on works in operation, a result which obviously supplies a wholly inadequate test of their value to the country.

In the North-west Provinces.

3. Up to the end of 1877–78 the capital outlay on completed canals in the North-west Provinces had been £4,346,000. The area irrigated that year was 1,461,000 acres, the value of the crops raised on which was estimated at £6,020,000. Half the irrigated area was occupied by autumn crops, which, but for irrigation, must have been wholly lost; and it may be safely said that the wealth of these provinces was consequently increased by £3,000,000; so that three-fourths of the entire first cost of the works was thus repaid to the country in that single year. The net revenue to Government from irrigation in these provinces was £315,600, or about seven and a quarter per cent. on the whole capital outlay on five and three-quarter millions of which one and a quarter millions were still unproductive.

In Bengal.

4. The results of irrigation are not so favourable in Bengal and Behar as in the North-west Provinces and Punjab; but here, too, there is abundant evidence of its value, and the receipts have at length exceeded the working expenses. Up to the end of 1878 the outlay on the Sone canals had been £1,908,000, of which probably twenty per cent. is due to

In Behar.

the elaborate provisions made for navigation. In the drought of 1873–74, these canals were very incomplete, and water was rudely poured over the fields through cuts in the banks. The result was that 159,500 acres of rice were saved, worth not less than £600,000. Were a similar season of drought to occur again, 1,000,000 acres might be watered, the value of which would approach £4,000,000 sterling, or about double the cost of the works. It may still be long before a return is obtained equal to the interest at four and a half per cent. on the £3,110,000 spent, or remaining to be spent, in order to complete the canals of Orissa; but should another famine occur after they are completed, their value would be incalculable. In 1865–66, about a million and a half sterling was spent on famine relief in this province; yet about a million persons perished from starvation, and the province was enriched by no single public work to put against the money spent.

In Orissa.

In the Deccan.

5. From the hilly character of the Deccan, the contracted form and broken surface of the valleys, and the absence of large works, irrigation has been more difficult and more costly in Bombay than in other parts of India; but tank irrigation is common, and some of the works by which the waters of the minor streams are utilized, though on a small scale, are extremely productive, and the value of watered crops is, in ordinary years, not less than four times that of others.

Sindh.

6. In Sindh we find a large province in which, without irrigation, agriculture and population would be alike impossible, but the province, which, with this protection has 1,800,000 acres of cultivated land, has reached a fair condition of prosperity, and gives complete evidence of far greater capacities for progress in the future.

In Madras.

7. The three great deltaic systems of irrigation in Madras, the Godavari, the Kistna, and the Cauveri, yield direct returns of 8·7, 6·5, and 31·7 per cent. respectively on the capital spent on them. During 1876–77, a year when every unirrigated district

was importing the food of a large portion of its population, the value of rice produced in the deltas of the Godavari and Kistna is calculated, at the prices then prevailing, to have been not less than £5,000,000 sterling. The quantity exported by sea from Cocanada, the port of the Godavari delta, was valued at £870,000, while an equal quantity is believed to have been exported by land.

Effect of irrigation on crops

8. Over the greater part of India sugar-cane and rice can only be grown with the help of artificial irrigation, and even in Midnapur, in Bengal, with an average rainfall of fifty-five inches, it has been found that the produce of irrigated rice is forty per cent. in excess of that grown on unirrigated lands.

And on rental.

9. The ordinary rental of land in Northern India is doubled by irrigation, while in eleven districts of Madras the average rental rises from Rs. 1.4.0 to Rs. 5.4.0 per acre when supplied with water. In Tinnevelly the increase is nearly tenfold. In the eight years preceding 1875–76, the average selling price of irrigated lands in the Cauveri valley in Mysore was £35 per acre. The best dry land at the same time did not fetch above £2 to £2 10*s*.

The grounds which justify the extension of irrigation.

10. It would indeed be a great error to rest the value of irrigation works on their direct revenue alone. It should be considered rather whether any particular tract is liable to frequent or serious drought, and whether, in the event of famine, the population is such that large outlay would be necessary for its relief, and large loss of revenue would be incurred. If these questions are answered in the affirmative, and if, at the same time, it is possible to introduce irrigation from a source which can be relied on in years of drought, without any excessive cost, Government might usually embark on the enterprise without hesitation. The certain result will be an increase of the prosperity and of the general well-being and productive power of the population, and the development of every

indirect source from which the wealth of the country springs.

When dealing with Mysore, the Commissioners use almost minatory language with regard to the upkeep and extension of irrigation works in the Feudatory States. "With the evidence before us," they say, "of the terrible misery wrought by the recent famine, we would urge, in the strongest manner possible, that some practical system be devised to ensure the efficient maintenance of the works of irrigation, and that, if possible, it should be placed beyond the risk of being subverted, however weak might be the Government or capricious the ruler." Will the British public repeat this advice to the Indian authorities themselves, concerning the British Provinces? *And, having given the advice,* WILL THEY SEE IT IS ACTED UPON?

This, perhaps, is the best place in which to direct attention to a phase of the irrigation question which is seldom considered, and yet it is of vast importance. Under our rule great neglect has marked our action towards the ancient tanks which are to be found in almost every part of the Carnatic. *The Hindu* newspaper[1] of the 10th of May 1900, describes this neglect in the following striking terms: "The tanks and lakes to be found in the country are too few, and for want of occasional digging up and cleansing are often found silted up and too shallow to hold any large quantities of water. Nor is any attention paid to improving the facilities for gathering rain water falling over large areas of land into existing tanks and reservoirs. Owing to this state of things, the occurrence of famine in years when monsoons fail is almost inevitable, and this contingency is in no small measure accelerated by the tendency of avaricious and miscalculating landholders to convert every available piece of land into *nunja*. Small tanks and pools owned by private individuals have been allowed

[1] A daily newspaper, edited, owned, and published in Madras, wholly by Hindus—a strikingly moderate journal.

to be silted up that they might with small labour and outlay be converted into *nunja* lands. Within recent years, the tanks in many of the villages in several districts have become considerably narrowed in their dimensions by the aggression of owners of lands bordering on them, and the quantity of water they hold is too small to leave any surplus available for agricultural purposes after their use for purposes of drinking, bathing, or washing."

There can be no doubt that an immense accession to the present irrigable area in Madras could be obtained were adequate attention given to this matter. After more than a hundred years' administration, the authorities ought to be in a position to deal directly with every acre of water-catchment in the Presidency.

The Hindu, in another part of the same article, declares "the only well-calculated measure against the possibility of the occurrence of famines is the storing up of large quantities of water in spacious and deep reservoirs." How such a pronouncement, coming from an Indian source, would have rejoiced Sir Arthur Cotton!

Those who have studied irrigation and canal navigation under Sir Arthur's guidance, and who have as closely followed the arguments of opponents like Sir George Campbell and others, as they have Sir Arthur's printed works, have taken the line in conversation that, having received from the Commission of their own appointment so distinct and unmistakable a pronouncement as to irrigation being the FIRST, and (so far as any official recommendations have gone) the *only sure preventative of famine*, the authorities were not competent, were greatly failing in their duty, in not following out to the utmost a bold and far-reaching irrigation policy. On that point there was no mistaking the emphasis with which they argued. If the recommendations of a Commission of Enquiry are such as, if carried out, would serve the public good, the authorities may not disregard such recommendation. What was done in this particular instance?

The Famine Commissioners reported in 1880. They said then that, to the date of their enquiry, even on the bare commercial aspect of the undertaking, and leaving everything else out of consideration, irrigation had been fully justified. This was the case, though, as Sir Arthur never tired of pointing out, some most expensive works were never provided with transit outlets, and, for all practical purposes, were left in a desert. Unless navigation were provided as well as irrigation, there was often no temptation to the cultivator to provide capital and additional energy in preparing his land for the richly-nurturing river water. If the cultivator could not easily export the additional produce when he had raised it, where was the return —the hope of gain—to come from which he looked for, and which alone, in such circumstances, will stimulate enterprise?

Have irrigation works continued to deserve so good a word in their financial favour as was pronounced by the Famine Commissioners of 1880? The answer is that twenty years later, they more than justify all that was aforetime said concerning them. The witnesses cited in justification are the administration reports for the various presidencies, provinces, and chief commissionerships for the year 1898–99. They were available in London only in May of this year (1900) and, therefore, are as up-to-date as it is possible for Indian statistical statements to be. Madras, as the oldest presidency and the most important irrigationally, may lead the way in this array of evidence.

STATEMENT CONCERNING ALL IRRIGATION WORKS IN THE MADRAS PRESIDENCY, 1898–99.[1]

SURPLUS REVENUE.

	During 1898–99.	To end of 1898–99.
	Rs.[2]	Rs.[2]
1. GODAVARI DELTA SYSTEM . . "The net revenue from the system during the year, after paying the interest charges, was 15.02 per cent. on the capital outlay 'Direct and Indirect,' against 15.75 per cent. on the previous year. The anticipated ultimate return was 9.4 per cent. per annum on the capital outlay. . . . The receipts from navigation rose from Rs. 76,581 to Rs. 89,663."	19,62,473	3,70,98,763
2. KISTNA DELTA SYSTEM . . "The net return, after paying interest charges, was Rs. 11.32 per cent. on the total capital outlay against 9.49 per cent. in the previous year. The navigation receipts amounted to Rs. 50,857."	15,17,007	2,02,11,515
3. PENNÉRU ANICUT SYSTEM . "The net return, after paying interest charges, was 4.76 per cent. on the capital outlay against 4.12 per cent. in the previous year."	90,492	12,01,401

[1] *Madras Administration Report*, 1898–99, pp. 130–164.

[2] Although it was intended that all money figures should be stated in sterling rather than in rupees, it has been considered wiser, where the statements cover a long series of years, that the figures, exactly as they stand in the official records, should be reproduced here. For rough and ready purposes the reader has only to divide the amounts by 15 to arrive at the present value of the rupee to the £ sterling. In regard to many of the Madras works, and some of those in the North-West Provinces and the Punjab, profits were realized when ten rupees went to the £1.

	During 1898-99.	To end of 1898-99.
	Rs.	Rs.
4. SANGAM ANICUT SYSTEM . . "The net return, after paying interest charges, was Rs. 29,900 against Rs. 16,234 in the previous year. The area irrigated during the year under first crop is the highest on record."	29,900	—5,61,993
5. CAUVERI DELTA SYSTEM . . "The net return, after paying interest charges, was 37.91 per cent. on the capital outlay against 41.26 in the previous year."	8,00,867	2,35,38,320
6. SRIVAIKUNTAM ANICUT SYSTEM "The net return, after paying interest charges, was 1.82 per cent. on the capital outlay against 1.73 in the previous year. "The area irrigated under first crop is only 406 acres less than the highest on record, while that under second crop is the highest limit yet attained. Under this system the area of second crop irrigation bears a much higher proportion to the first crop irrigation than elsewhere."	26,981	77,711
7. GANJAM MINOR RIVERS SYSTEM "The actual return was 8.69 per cent. on the capital outlay."	7,290	4,44,455
8. CUMBUM TANK SYSTEM . . "The actual return was 17.39 per cent. on the capital outlay."	11,204	1,18,838
9. THADAPALLI CHANNEL SYSTEM. "The actual return was 15.94 per cent. on the capital outlay."	20,030	5,20,859
10. ARKENKOTA CHANNEL SYSTEM. "The actual return was 3.78 per cent. on the capital outlay."	3,898	2,566

	During 1898–99.	To end of 1898–99.
	Rs.	Rs.
11. KALINGARAYAN CHANNEL SYSTEM. "The actual return was 12.72 per cent. on the capital outlay."	10,175	—55,673
12. PALAR ANICUT SYSTEM . . "The actual return was 5.92 per cent. on the capital outlay."	1,23,049	16,37,386
13. POINAY ANICUT SYSTEM . . "The actual return was 19.95 per cent. on the capital outlay"	46,204	7,24,044
14. CHEYARU ANICUT SYSTEM . . "The actual return was 7.60 per cent. on the capital outlay."	30,831	3,59,208
15. CHEMBRAMBÁKAM TANK . . "The actual return was 4.16 per cent. on the capital outlay."	31,086	6,63,703
16. MADRAS WATER SUPPLY AND IRRIGATION SYSTEM. "The actual return was 1.21 per cent. on the capital outlay."	21,121	—12,367
17. VALLURU ANICUT SYSTEM . . "The actual return was 5.39 per cent. on the capital outlay."	3,533	39,090
18. TIRUKKOYILUR ANICUT SYSTEM "The actual return was 6.22 per cent. on the capital outlay."	15,826	3,82,514
19. MEHMATTUR ANICUT SYSTEM . "The actual return was 3.50 per cent. on the capital outlay."	2,489	72,183
20. VRIDDHACHALAM ANICUT SYSTEM. "The actual return was 25.46 per cent. on the capital outlay."	12,665	2,08,708

	During 1898-99.	To end of 1898-99.
	Rs.	Rs.
21. SHATIATOPE ANICUT SYSTEM . "The actual return was 40.73 per cent. on the capital outlay."	93,112	21,27,674
22. PELANDORAI ANICUT SYSTEM "The actual return was 3.28 per cent. on the capital outlay."	19,224	—1,73,668
23. LOWER COLEROON ANICUT SYSTEM. "The actual return was 27.26 per cent. on the capital outlay."	2,56,032	94,10,951
24. MARUDUR ANICUT SYSTEM . "The actual return was 114.32 per cent. on the capital outlay."	51,220	13,65,465
25. PROVINCIAL MINOR WORKS AND NAVIGATION. "Minor works for which neither capital nor revenue accounts are kept, but for which continuous records of expenditure and revenue are maintained individually, shew a nett revenue of Rs. 69,85,309."	69,85,309	
Totals . . . Rs.	1,20,72,018	9,94,01,653

Works showing DEFICIT *Revenue.*

	During 1898-99.	To end of 1898-99.
	Rs.	Rs.
1. KURNOOL-CUDDAPAH CANAL .	8,24,352	1,49,49,034
2. BARUR TANK SYSTEM . .	8,577	1,74,321
3. PERIYAR PROJECT . . . "The project is only partly completed and at work."	1,92,396	Figures showing results to end of 1898-99, are not yet available.
4. MAJOR PROTECTIVE WORKS: RUSHIKULYA PROJECT. "The irrigated area both under first and second crops is steadily increasing."	1,27,522	12,18,198
5. NANDYAR CHANNEL . . . "The working expenses exceeded the revenue by Rs. 775."	775	6,139
6. BUCKINGHAM CANAL (NAVIGATION). "The financial result of the year was a deficit of Rs. 8,736. There was a considerable diminution of traffic owing to a fall in the imports of salt, indigo, and coal, and to the Bezwada-Madras Railway having come into working."	8,736	80,949
Totals . . . Rs.	11,62,358	1,64,28,641

Summary.

	No.	Surplus.
		Rs.
Works recording profit in 1898-99 . .	25 .	1,20,72,018
Works recording deficit in 1898-99 . .	6 .	11,62,358
Net surplus profit		Rs. 1,09,09,660

Works under Construction.

1. MUNÉRU PROJECT . . .	[No particulars furnished.]
2. DONDAPAD PROJECT . . .	
3. SAGILERU UPPER PROJECT . "The results of the year show that the financial aspect of the project is fairly promising. . . . There should be a further increase of revenue."	
4. CHOPAUD PROJECT . . .	

The great Australian authority alludes to the Madras works in flattering terms.

The reports of the Madras Irrigation Department, he says, are in some respects the best in India, for though all the provinces publish admirable records of their work, these are exceptionally lucid and well-arranged. A glance at the map prefacing the annual report indicates at once the position and character of the great state undertakings for water supply. At the extreme north, where the east coast curves eastwards to Orissa, is the Ganjam and Gopalpur tidal canal, undertaken as a famine relief work, the estimate for which is £50,000. Southwards, two important rivers—the Godavari and Kistna—pour their streams over two large tracts, which unite to form a great irrigated area. A long, narrow strip in the mountains indicates the one private enterprise, the Madras Company's land, while the Pennar river, to which it leads, has at its mouth its own deltaic scheme. There are three smaller patches near Madras, and one in the interior at the Barur tank. Then come the great delta of Tanjore, watered by the Cauveri; at the extreme south, another delta below Tuticorin, and between the two, inland, the plain of Madura, to be commanded by the great Periyar project, now in course of construction. The five great schemes are deltaic, and similar in character, repeating here, as in Bengal, the likeness and lessons of the country below Cairo. If Egypt is the gift of the Nile, certainly Bengal is the gift of the Ganges; while the Godavari, Kistna, Pennar, Cauveri, and Tambragani have endowed the Coromandel coast with stretches of remarkable fertility, which have enabled its millions to be certain of their harvests year by year.

The water supply expenditure in Madras is dealt with under several heads, distinguishing works which were undertaken as reproductive investments of capital, from those which were executed to protect the country against famine, and from those which were expected to yield some return incidentally, but were not commenced solely with that end. Under the first head, "major productive works," the Presidency has invested £5,300,000 up to the end of 1889–90; upon "protective works," £160,000; and upon "minor works and navigation," £1,200,000. After allowing for interest upon capital, the first class show a profit to the State for the year of £275,000 on five schemes, and a loss of £102,000 on four, or a total net gain of £173,000. The net revenue, after deducting interest charges, is seven per cent., and would be twelve per cent. if the department were responsible only for the works designed and executed by its own officers. Nearly six million acres were watered during the year, of which two million three hundred thousand were under major works. The direct revenue derived from water rates was over £1,750,000, even after deducting remissions to the extent of £100,000. Many of the areas now commanded by State works were irrigated prior to their construction, and in each case the value of the work done in those days appears upon the accounts. Nor is the result in any sense unfavourable to the administration, for by means of the new works, areas in which there were but one million acres irrigated have now nearly two million two hundred and fifty thousand acres, while the revenue they yield has risen from £90,000 to over £500,000. The official estimate of the value of the crops in the one-third of the whole irrigated area, which is supplied by major works, is just short of £5,500,000, and if the remaining two-thirds be only taken at the same sum, this means security for £11,000,000 a year. Such figures should convey to the mind of the Australian the magnitude of the system of irrigation executed in this one presidency—which is, after all, only half the size of New South Wales and not twice the size of Victoria.[1]

None of the other Administration Reports give details in such fulness as does the Madras report. Hence, in those which follow only total results can be given.

THE PUNJAB.[2]

	Rs.
Receipts from all irrigation works	1,27,36,719
Expenditure upon all irrigation works	76,90,644
Profit	Rs. 50,46,075

NORTH-WESTERN PROVINCES AND OUDH,[3]

1898–99.

	Protective Works.	Productive Works.	Minor Works.	Total.
	Rs.	Rs.	Rs.	Rs.
Receipts	1,10,246	85,82,963	3,28,508	90,21,717
Charges	1,09,769	28,54,713	1,82,828	31,47,310
Nett Revenue	477	57,28,250	1,45,680	58,74,407
Interest Charges	1,63,324	30,37,403	——	32,00,727
Profit or Loss	−1,62,847	+26,90,847	+1,45,680	+26,73,680

"The Betwa canal is the only *protective* work in these provinces. The receipts have for a second time just exceeded the direct and indirect charges of the year, but by Rs. 477 only, and were Rs. 1,62,847 short of the interest charges. *Productive* works show a net revenue of Rs. 57,28,250, representing a return of 7.27 per cent. on the capital outlay

[1] *Irrigated India*, pp. 252–254. [2] *Administration Report*, p. 202.
[3] *Administration Report*, p. 118.

to the end of the year on works in operation, and of seven per cent. on the total expenditure on productive works.

"The net revenue, after deducting the interest charges of the year (Rs. 30,37,403, including interest on the expenditure on the Fatehpur division), shows a clear gain of Rs. 26,90,847.

"*Minor* works give a net revenue of Rs. 1,45,680, which is more than forty-five per cent. above the average, and gives a return of 5.17 per cent. on the capital invested in the canals in operation.

"After meeting the total interest charges, the receipts from all the works show a clear profit of Rs. 26,73,680."

	Rs.
Productive works, net revenue . . .	26,90,847
Minor works, net revenue	1,45,680
Profit (less Rs. 1,62,847 Protective) .	Rs. 26,73,680

CENTRAL PROVINCES.[1]

	Acres.
(*a*) Government canals	—
(*b*) Private canals	8,291
(*c*) Tanks	462,598
(*d*) Wells	75,959
(*e*) Other sources	15,780
Total .	562,628

No statistics in rupees available.

BENGAL.[2]

Major Irrigation Works.

	Rs.
Receipts	19,02,205
Expenditure	13,66,707
Profit	Rs. 5,35,498

[1] *Central Provinces: Stat. Tables*, 1897–98.

[2] *Bengal Administration Report*, 1896–97, p. 214.

Minor Irrigation Works.

	Rs.
Receipts	6,60,942
Expenditure	5,76,226
Profit	Rs. 84,716

BOMBAY.

The Bombay Administration Report for 1898–99 gives very meagre figures, and they are not lucid or easily to be understood.

RECEIPTS.

	Rs.
Major Works:	
Protective works	1,63,465
Productive works	4,96,985
Minor Works:	
Imperial	2,52,253
Provincial	31,197
Total . .	Rs. 9,43,500

EXPENDITURE.	Rs.
Works	18,62,085
Repairs	14,11,304
Establishment	8,99,594
Tools and plant	35,040
Total . . .	42,08,023
Less suspense account	11,593
	Rs. 41,96,430

IRRIGATION WORKS THROUGHOUT INDIA.

GOVERNMENT OF INDIA: PUBLIC WORKS DEPARTMENT.

(Compiled from statements showing the financial results of irrigation operations throughout India, for, and to the end of, the year 1898–99

No.		Mileage in Operation: Main Canals.	Distributaries.	Area Irrigated: Old Works.	New Works.
	Baluchistan :—	Miles.	Miles.	Acres.	Acres.
2.	—	4	41½	5,653	—
	Rajputana :—				
3.	—	—	—	—	25,560
	Burma :—				
1.	Major Works . . .	—	—	—	—
6.	Minor Works . . .	—	—	—	—
	Bengal :—				
4.	Major Works (productive).	729	2,644	—	713,443
3.	Minor Works . . .	887,08	—	—	—
	North-West Provinces and Oudh :—				
5.	Major Works (productive).	1,439	9,965	—	2,112,778
1.	Protective and Navigation Works	168	424	—	39,500
5.	Minor Works . . .	—	618	1,653	101,464
	Punjab :—				
7.	Major Works . . .	1,598	7,596	—	3,320,000
1.	Protective and Navigation Works	22	182	—	139,759
6.	Minor Works . . .	1,813	319	—	664,213
	Madras :—				
9.	Major Works . . .	2,024½	5,708¼	1,200,171	2,092,817
1.	Protective Works . .	80	120	47,309	35,566
27.	{Minor Works . . :	1,365¾	1,184⅛	315,487	248,110
	{Navigation Works . .	304½	—	—	—
	Bombay :—				
15.	Major Works . . .	999	165¾	21,910	694,130
6.	Protective Works . .	156¼	166½	—	40,461
34.	Minor and Navigation Works	2,092	228½	295,848	512,374
		13,671¾	29,574	2,085,351	10,650,175

SUMMARY.

Main Canals	13,671¾ miles
Distributaries	29,574 "
Old Works	2,085,351 acres
New Works	10,650,175 "
Total . .	12,725,526 "

CHARACTER OF WORKS.

	Major Works.		Minor Works and Navigation.
	Productive.	Protective.	
Baluchistan	2	—	—
Rajputana	3	—	—
Burma	1	—	6
Bengal	4	—	3
North-West Provinces and Oudh	5	1	5
Punjab	7	1	6
Madras	9	1	27
Bombay	15	6	34
	46	9	81

DETAILS OF WORKING AND AREA IRRIGATED.

Irrigation Works.	Gross Receipts.	Working Expenses.	Surplus Revenue after charging interest.	Area Irrigated.	Percentage of working expenses in Rx.
Major Works, Productive:—	Rx.	Rx.	Rx.	Acres.	
Bengal . . .	176,564	137,744	−200,756	713,442	78·01
N.-W. Provinces and Oudh . . .	858,295	285,470	+269,084	2,112,778	33·26
Punjab . . .	1,195,245	344,358	+525,718	3,320,000	28·81
Madras . . .	777,992	189,042	+340,402	2,692,817	24·30
Bombay . . .	167,942	51,877	+16,045	716,040	30·89
Navigation:—					
Bengal . . .	7,431	5,003	−7,779	—	67·32
Protective:—					
N.-W. Provinces and Oudh . . .	11,025	10,977	−16,284	39,560	99·56
Punjab . . .	45,465	10,793	+19,194	139,759	23·74
Madras . . .	8,782	4,407	−12,753	82,965	50·18
Bombay . . .	16,359	7,732	−23,524	40,461	47·26
Total . . .	3,265,100	1,047,403	+905,003	9,857,823	32·07
Minor Works and Navigation. Irrigation:—					
Baluchistan . .	5,407	2,084	−3,033	5,653	38·55
Rajputana . .	11,908	5,304	−2,901	25,560	44·54
Burma . . .	88,529	23,473	+51,765	—	26·51
Bengal . . .	499	60	−2,278	—	12·02
N.-W. Provinces and Oudh . . .	32,851	18,283	+4,264	103,117	55·65
Punjab . . .	133,122	79,854	+43,221	664,213	59·99
Madras . . .	104,194	27,564	+43,109	563,597	26·45
Bombay . . .	125,754	47,710	+36,740	806,222	37·93
Total . .	502,264	204,332	+170,887	2,168,362	40·68
Navigation Works:—					
Bengal . . .	48,237	36,296	−31,079	—	75·24
Madras . . .	10,550	11,787	−36,318	—	111·72
Total . .	58,757	48,083	−67,397	—	81·79
Total: M. W. and N.	561,051	252,415	+103,490	—	44·99
		COMBINED	TOTALS:—		
Major Works, all Kinds . . .	3,265,100	1,047,403	+905,003	9,857,823	
Minor Works, all Kinds . . .	561,051	252,415	+103,490	2,168,362	
	3,826,151	1,299,818	+1,008,490	12,026,185	

More striking confirmation of the financial success of great public works could not be desired.[1] That being so, it is desirable to observe to what extent the recommendations of the Famine Commissioners of 1880 have been acted upon in regard to occupying the "FIRST PLACE" with irrigation works as against railways, the only other public works of any magnitude carried out in India being buildings and roads, necessary at all times. Each year from 1882–83 to 1897–98 (the latest available) may be taken. I select 1882–83, and not an earlier year, so as to give the authorities two years in which to make the necessary arrangements for carrying out the policy which was described as of "first" importance. The figures are significant. They are more than significant. They suggest the very pointed enquiry as to how far the authorities may be held blameless for their neglect to carry out such plain and obvious reforms. If the responsible officials at the India Office—men of the past who are still living (Lord Salisbury not the least of a large number) as well as of the present—dare consider the preventible suffering now being endured in India, as the consequence of their want of foresight and effort, perhaps they will change their policy.

[1] Reviewing the foregoing works as a whole ten years previously, Mr. Deakin places this judgment on record: "The works as a whole are remunerative. In Madras, the North-West Provinces, the Punjab, and Sind, they yield handsome profits; in Bombay they are likely to pay for themselves, and in Bengal, they are, after all, the cheapest and best means of fighting famine, and saving the public treasury from ruinous drafts in bad seasons. On the merits of the investment, therefore, the stock would be entitled to rank high, apart from the guarantee."—*Irrigated India*, p. 233.

STATEMENT AS TO EXPENDITURE FROM REVENUE IN INDIA AND ENGLAND ON RAILWAYS AND IRRIGATION, 1882–83 TO 1897–98.

(*Abstracted from Nos.* 27 *and* 33 *of the "Statistical Abstract for British India."*)

Year.	Expenditure in India.		Expenditure in England.	Grand Total.	
		Rx.	Rx.	Rx.	Rx. In favour of Rys.
1882–83	Railways . .	6,520,738	6,105,946	12,626,684	
	Irrigation. .	2,480,912	32,386	2,513,298	
		4,039,826	6,073,560		10,113,386
1883–84	Railways . .	6,808,186	5,929,836	12,738,022	
	Irrigation. .	2,440,963	2,039	2,443,002	
		4,367,223	5,927,797		10,295,020
1884–85	Railways . .	8,158,667	6,000,597	14,159,264	
	Irrigation. .	2,501,949	81	2,502,030	
		5,656,718	6,000,516		11,657,234
1885–86	Railways . .	8,975,159	6,661,693	15,636,852	
	Irrigation. .	2,489,964	590	2,490,554	
		6,485,195	6,661,103		13,146,298
1886–87	Railways . .	8,777,884	7,271,620	16,049,504	
	Irrigation. .	2,416,712	1,921	2,418,633	
		6,361,172	7,269,699		13,630,871
1887–88	Railways . .	9,068,422	7,668,269	16,736,691	
	Irrigation. .	2,552,619	33	2,552,652	
		6,515,803	7,668,236		14,184,039
1888–89	Railways . .	9,494,359	8,282,130	17,776,489	
	Irrigation. .	2,692,950	551	2,693,501	
		6,801,409	8,281,579		15,082,988
1889–90	Railways . .	10,336,538	8,126,638	18,463,176	
	Irrigation. .	2,723,146	1,018	2,724,164	
		7,613,392	8,125,620		15,739,012

Year.	Expenditure in India.		Expenditure in England.	Grand Total.	
		Rx.			
1890–91	Railways . .	10,353,049	7,565,408	17,918,457	
	Irrigation. .	2,813,622	2,898	2,816,520	
		8,539,427	7,562,510		15,101,937
1891–92	Railways . .	12,793,700	8,108,138	20,901,938	
	Irrigation. .	3,020,347	2,603	3,022,950	
		9,773,353	8,105,535		17,878,988
1892–93	Railways . .	13,081,225	9,166,886	22,248,111	
	Irrigation. .	2,994,606	6,666	3,001,272	
		10,086,619	9,160,220		19,246,839
1893–94	Railways . .	13,489,992	9,477,341	22,967,333	
	Irrigation. .	2,917,024	1,894	2,918,918	
		10,572,968	9,475,447		20,048,415
1894–95	Railways . .	13,655,371	10,483,754	24,169,125	
	Irrigation. .	2,992,928	2,962	2,995,890	
		10,662,443	10,480,792		21,173,235
1895–96	Railways . .	13,902,214	10,114,771	24,016,985	
	Irrigation. .	3,013,153	1,475	3,014,628	
		10,889,061	10,113,296		21,002,357
1896–97	Railways . .	13,353,383	9,617,168	22,970,551	
	Irrigation. .	3,295,191	2,648	3,297,839	
		10,058,192	9,614,520		19,672,712
1897–98	Railways . .	13,561,896	9,131,606	22,693,502	
	Irrigation. .	3,142,339	1,746	3,144,085	
		10,419,557	9,129,860		19,549,417
					Rx. 257,522,748

EXPENDITURE ON STATE RAILWAYS AND IRRIGATION WORKS IN INDIA.

CHARGEABLE TO CAPITAL.

Year.	Object.		In favour of Irrigation.	In favour of Railways.
		Rx.	Rx.	Rx.
1882	Railways . .	3,931,543		
	Irrigation. .	701,820		3,229,723
1883	Railways . .	2,710,894		
	Irrigation. .	2,994,229[1]	283,335	
1884	Railways . .	4,419,114		
	Irrigation. .	1,010,797[1]		3,408,317
1885	Railways . .	6,050,856		
	Irrigation. .	953,507		5,097,349
1886	Railways . .	7,019,928		
	Irrigation. .	760,810		6,259,118
1887	Railways . .	5,853,479		
	Irrigation. .	664,835		5,188,644
1887–88	Railways . .	2,332,721		
	Irrigation. .	626,849		1,705,872
1888–89	Railways . .	1,236,594		
	Irrigation. .	539,418		697,176

[1] This large expenditure does not represent new works; during these years the authorities purchased the Madras Irrigation Company's works in Kurnool, around which, the reader will remember, so much sharp questioning occurred before the Select Committee of 1878.

Year.	Object.		In favour of Irrigation.	In favour of Railways.
		Rx.	Rx.	Rx
1889–90	Railways . .	2,799,432		
	Irrigation. .	498,802		
				2,300,630
1890–91	Railways . .	2,876,971		
	Irrigation. .	610,484		
				2,266,487
1891–92	Railways . .	3,418,364		
	Irrigation. .	808,108		
				2,610,256
1892–93	Railways . .	4,779,049		
	Irrigation. .	602,394		
				4,176,655
1893–94	Railways . .	4,086,848		
	Irrigation. .	761,389		
				3,325,459
1894–95	Railways . .	4,487,551		
	Irrigation. .	658,918		
				3,828,633
1895–96	Railways . .	3,945,011		
	Irrigation. .	757,918		
				3,187,093
1896–97	Railways . .	4,257,017		
	Irrigation. .	795,818		
				3,461,199
1897–98	Railways . .	3,635,797		
	Irrigation. .	742,663		
				2,893,134

Total expenditure on Irrigation . Rx. 14,488,759

Total expenditure on Railways . Rx. 67,841,169

The tables relating to revenue and capital, have been compiled from the *Statistical Abstract*:—No. 27, pp. 107–109; No. 33, pp. 114–116; No. 21, pp. 118, 119; No. 22, p. 119; No. 27, pp. 128, 129; No. 33, pp. 132, 133.

Summarized, the position, as shown in the foregoing tables, stands thus (Rs. 15 to the £1):—

Expenditure from REVENUE:	£
Railways	201,381,789
Irrigation	29,699,872
Balance *against* IRRIGATION .	£171,681,917

Expenditure from CAPITAL:	£
Railways	45,227,446
Irrigation	9,659,173
Balance *against* IRRIGATION .	£35,568,273

The combined Totals show:—

Expenditure from REVENUE and CAPITAL:

	£
Railways	246,609,235
Irrigation	39,359,045
Balance *against* IRRIGATION .	£207,250,190

Thus was the emphatic recommendation of the Famine Commission, in 1880, to put irrigation "first" carried out by the authorities! Of what use is an enquiry by Royal Commission, when its most important recommendation concerning protection against famine is thus treated?

However, taking the figures given into consideration, what is there to be said for the irrigation that was undertaken? Fortunately, there is official testimony to fall back upon. The "Report of the Famine Commission, 1898," deals exhaustively with the subject, and does so in terms that would have rejoiced the heart of Sir Arthur Cotton could he have seen them. First, this comparison, based on "Productive" irrigation works, is given:

Area protected in 1878–79:	Area protected in 1896–97:
5,171,497 acres.	9,448,692 acres.

Increase: 4,277,195 acres.

"Although the capital outlay on productive irrigation works has been increased by over fifty per cent. since the report of the Famine Commissioners [in 1880], an average return of about six per cent. is still realised; the new projects and extensions undertaken since 1879–80 have been financially as profitable as the works constructed before that date, in spite of the fact that the outlay subsequent to 1879–80 includes the purchase from the Madras Irrigation Company of the Kurnool Cuddapah canal, which, with a capital account of Rx. 2,171,349, barely pays its working expenses."

Sir James Lyall, the President of the Commission of 1898, and his colleagues proceed to remark: "The remunerativeness of these works may be shown in another way. Taking them as a whole, including the works which are never likely to be remunerative and those not yet opened or in full operation, the surplus revenue realised to the end of 1896–97, after paying all interest charges and working expenses, amounted to Rx. 4,829,917, the surplus for the year 1896–97 itself being Rx. 809,173. The interest charges are calculated throughout at four per cent."[1]

This pæan of success is not enough. A few pages farther on in their report, the Commissioners remark that "the result has been

A GREAT ADVANTAGE TO THE STATE,

regarded merely from the direct financial return on the money invested, and apart from their value in increasing the wealth of the country in ordinary years, and in preventing or mitigating famine in years of drought."[2]

What is the position in India which makes a discussion of this nature necessary at the present moment?

It is this: Famine has now become chronic. There are few safe spots outside the irrigation-protected districts.

To what extent has India become chronically subject to famine?

Take the last half of this century, and note the following record of famines compiled from Part III., *Famine Histories*, published in 1881, and the Report of the Indian

[1] *Famine Commission's Report*, p. 334. [2] *Ibid.*, p. 338.

Famine Commission, 1898 ("Narratives of Famines which have occurred since the Famine Commission's Report, 1880").

YEAR.	REGION AFFECTED.
1853	Bombay.
1857–58 . . .	Upper India.
1854	Madras.
1860–61 . . .	North-West Provinces and Punjab.
1865–66 . . .	Orissa.
	Behar and North Bengal.
	Madras.
1868–69 . . .	Rajputana.
	North-West Provinces.
	Punjab.
	Central Provinces.
	Bombay.
1873–74 . . .	Bengal and Behar.
	North-West Provinces and Oudh.
1876–77 . . .	Bombay.
	Hyderabad.
1877–78 . . .	North-West Provinces and Oudh.
1876–78 . . .	Madras.
	Mysore.
1884	Punjab.
1884–85 . . .	Lower Bengal.
	Madras.
1886–87 . . .	Central Provinces.
1888–89 . . .	Behar.
1889	Orissa (Tributary States).
1888–89 . . .	Madras (Ganjam).
1890	Kumaun and Garwhal.
1892	Kumaun and Dehra Doon.
1891–92 . . .	Madras.
	Bombay (Deccan).
	Bengal and Behar.
	Upper Burma.
1890–92 . . .	Ajmere Merwara.
1897–98 . . .	Madras and Bombay.
	Central Provinces.
	North-West Provinces.
	Central India.
1899–1900 . . .	Bombay.
	Punjab.
	Central Provinces.
	Rajputana.
	Central India.
	Hyderabad, Deccan.
	Berar.

Was ever before such a terrible record presented to an over-ruling Power? Forty-six regions affected in forty-seven years!

Yet, to combat the latest famines, and to PREVENT them, as was promised, there have been constructed 12,652 miles of railways, all of which are now working. In 1880, when the Famine Commission reported, the mileage was 9,308; in 1898, it was 21,960. It was indubitably stated that railways were to prevent famines. The advocates never wearied of asserting this. If Sir Arthur Cotton's works, and irrigation works generally, had presented even one-hundredth part of such ignominy and failure, after like confident, almost boastful, prophecy, could words scornful enough have been found for his proposals? "Scornful enough," I ask, because in the draft report of the Select Committee, before which he attended in 1878, there are expressions used concerning his suggestions which were scornful and ill-timed; in the light of the facts of to-day, they stamp their authors as deficient in insight and almost in common sense, altogether lacking in farsightedness and statesmanship.

When, in 1884, a Select Committee of the House of Commons inquired into the desirability of largely extending railways, there was no plea so frequently urged as that the railways would protect the people from famine, and greatly advance the prosperity of the country. For example, on the latter point the late Sir William Hunter, one of the witnesses, had the hardihood to remark [1]:—

"I think that the increase of the prosperity of the country from the railway system which the Government proposes, will be so great that the Government is not only justified, but is bound to face the contingency of a large fall in exchange with reference to the interest payable on these railways. I believe that any probable fall in exchange will be more than counterbalanced by the increase in prosperity which railways produce."

Mr. Dalrymple asked: "I am right in thinking, then,

[1] Q. 7,184, *Minutes of Evidence*, p. 462.

that a greater extension of railways is asked for, especially as a protection against famine?"

"*That*," the same witness answered, "*is the basis of our proposals*; but it is only the basis. The Government fully recognises the commercial aspects of the line, as well as their famine and protective aspects."[1]

In reply to the next question asked of him, the witness added: "The Government of India would have been glad to recommend more railways as a protection at present."

The fundamental error in regard to railways is the assumption by the authorities that if "the problem of *famine relief*" be "nearly solved," that is enough. A confusion of ideas in regard to "relief" and "prevention" vitiates nearly all that even so clever a man as was the late Sir William Hunter wrote or said on this subject. As he, so all the others. But even he more than once got near the truth, as, for example, when it was asked[2]:—

"You made use of a very strong remark when you said that in time of famine the narrow gauge leads to delay and death. Could you give us an instance where the narrow gauge has led to death?"

"No," was the reply; "I am not prepared to give instances, because I do not know of instances in which this has occurred. I was referring to the proposal to make the Jhansi-Manikpur line on the narrow gauge."

Six years before Sir William thus expressed himself, the actual facts in India had proved themselves to be:—

RAILWAY-SERVED DISTRICTS.	IRRIGATED DISTRICTS.
A much higher mortality; money loss and human suffering more than in (not irrigated districts, but) non-railway traversed districts in which there are no irrigation	"During this most awful season of famine, the worst probably ever known in India, when the districts of this Presidency, through which the railways run, lost over eighty-five per cent. of

[1] Q. 7,222, *Minutes of Evidence*, p. 466.
[2] Q. 7,409, *Minutes of Evidence*, p. 477.

works, or, as in Kurnool, where success is denied to them through the system to which they belong being left unfinished, as a railway would never be similarly left.

their revenues, two-thirds of the population, and the whole of their products, for not an acre of land can be made to yield any products by a railway when the rains fail; the Godavari district, by means of its canals, paid double the revenues it had ever yielded in the most prosperous years before these works were constructed, carried on a trade nearly forty-fold in value to what it was when these works were undertaken, and came out of the trial strengthened in all its resources; whilst India has been brought to bankruptcy in spite of all endeavours to bolster up the railway system. If the condition of industry in India had been at all considered and compared with that existing at home, this waste of money, and time, and life would never have been allowed, but now I fear it will be long before India recovers, if she ever does at all, for it is appalling to see the state of these districts."[1]

No argument could be more unsound, more out of accord with facts, than that which contends that railways prevent famines.

[1] Letter to Select Committee, 1878, from Colonel Fischer, R.E.

During the 1876–78 famine in Madras, nine districts were directly affected. Seven of these had a first-class railway, on either the broad or the narrow gauge, running through them; some were served by two such railways. It has been thought well to compare the decrease of the population, through famine, in certain Bombay and Madras districts served by railways and other districts not served by railways. This is how the comparison works out:—

DISTRICTS TRAVERSED BY RAILWAYS.

DISTRICT.	DECREASE. (1881 compared with 1872, and allowing for increase of one per cent. per annum.)[1]	PERCENTAGE OF DECREASE.
Bellary	481,430	26½
Coimbatore	364,275	19
Cuddapah	351,764	24
North Arcot	378,839	17
Sholapore	201,632	27
	Average	22⅘

DISTRICTS NOT TRAVERSED BY RAILWAYS.

DISTRICT.	DECREASE. (1881 compared with 1872, and allowing for increase of one per cent. per annum.)[1]	PERCENTAGE OF DECREASE.
Kurnool	336,800	32
Kaladgi	251,245	29½
Belgaum	166,020	16½
Dharwar	195,835	18
Sattara	95,392	8¼
	Average	20⅘

[1] The Government of India (p. 567, *Report of Select Committee on*

On the ten districts selected the average indicates a difference of two per cent. against railways, *i.e.* the population decreased more rapidly where the districts were served by railways than where there were no railways. This is a protection against famine entirely in the wrong direction. The particular gain from railways is, however, seen by comparing Kurnool with Bellary; but if Kaladgi be put by the side of Sholapore, the gain to the latter, through the railway, is only two and a half per cent. The Bombay districts mentioned are those selected by the Government of Bombay for a test census, while the Madras district (Kurnool) cited in the first-quoted table was by far the worse affected of the districts not served by railways. It will, therefore, be seen that the facts, as the India Office Blue Books furnish them, have been fairly dealt with. North Arcot is a Madras district traversed by *two broad gauge railways*, yet, according to the late Sir William Hunter, in the *Gazetteer of India*, the utmost efforts of Government had to be put forth to prevent the district being depopulated in 1877–78.

The pointed query follows naturally: "Railways having, by official statement, failed to protect the country against famine in the past, what reason is there to suppose that there would be a different result in the future?" The efficacy of railways *during famine* all must admit. As the result of observations in Southern India and Mysore in 1877–79, the present writer is of the opinion that while, with railways, we lost five millions of lives, without them we should have lost ten millions.

At first sight it may appear a hard saying to remark that it is owing to *our* mode of administration in India that famines are now so frequent and so deadly. The Govern-

East India Railway Communication) puts the normal increase at one and a half per cent. per annum. Had the same figures been used, the case against railways, as protectors from famine, would have been of a stronger character than has been stated. The one and a half per cent., as a standard of increase, could not, however, be used; the Indian census returns do not justify it.

ment of India, with Lord Lytton as viceroy, announced this fact, in effect, though it was not put in that way, by introducing a new feature in Indian finance—a Famine Insurance Fund—because, as was stated, famines must henceforth be looked upon as a regular feature in Indian affairs. The effect of our system is to bring sixty millions of people at a time within the scope of death by famine and by our railways to save five or ten. The mischief lies in the circumstance that the sixty millions need not be famine-stricken at all.

Again, consider what all this would have meant had Sir Arthur Cotton's enterprises shown such deplorable results. He, and all who advocated the views he enunciated, would have been hounded out of argumentative existence; their proposals would have been ridiculed; no place would have been found for them even in our varied public life. But, railways being concerned, railway construction being a matter which interested all the steel and iron works, the locomotive builders, and the carriage and truck makers, as well as the very large proportion of the English public who had invested in Indian railways, I verily believe, without conscious knowledge on the part of any one that not good but harm was all the time resulting to the whole interests of India—every official's eyes became blinded, and each one saw not the condition of things as it actually existed, but as he supposed it must necessarily be. All this was good for the trade of England; it has helped to spell ruin to millions of Indian homes, and has done its part in causing more acute physical suffering and mental pain among British subjects than have all the wars waged throughout the world since the nineteenth century dawned.[1] Had half the money thus spent on railways been expended in the construction of navigation and irrigation works, there would have been great prosperity

[1] "The wars of ninety years, down to 1880, involved . . . the loss of 4,470,000 lives."—MULHALL, *Dictionary of Statistics*, p. 586, ed. 1892.

and the avoidance of much, if not of all, of the famine suffering.

What could irrigation engineers do in the face of such determination that their enterprises should not receive fair consideration, as is shown in a statement, gleefully made by Sir George Campbell, as to what he had done to checkmate those too-enthusiastic Water Apostles?

"We calculated in Midnapur,"[1] he says, "that supposing the whole of the water to be taken up which the canal supplies, and a reasonable rate to be paid for it, still the canal would not pay. That calculation was made by Colonel Haig, a man who is honourable and impartial, but who is certainly not prejudiced against canals, and therefore the conclusion we came to was that the Midnapur canal could never pay, although it was so far successful that the people were quite willing to take the water."

Was ever a worse instance known of the civilian blinded by prejudice? The only thing in connection with irrigation which this exceptionally clever civilian could see was the interest on capital expenditure. He did not feel *quite sure* that four or five per cent. would be realised. No calculation was made for navigation returns, no account was taken of the enormous increase in produce, which would give the cultivator more to eat, more clothing to wear, more money (no, not *more* money, but some money perhaps for the first time in his life), to spend on taxable articles which would benefit the Government revenue; above all, a certain insurance against famine. "The people were *quite willing* to take the water." But, Sir George Campbell was not willing they should.

Some day, in the Providence of God, by rebuke and suffering to us here in England, if we will not move of our own motion, adequate attention will be drawn to the famine suffering, and what is, perhaps, worse, the ordinary suffering caused in India by the adoption of the wrong methods of dealing with the condition of things existing

[1] Q. 1721, Select Committee, 1878, p. 123.

there.[1] India is not in its present deplorable condition because of any lack of the essentials to reasonable and fairly happy life. The land is not cursed of God; it is, however, neglected of man, and that man is the representative of a nation favoured above all other nations of the earth.

That nation has sons possessing insight and energy which enable them, the world over, and nowhere more conspicuously than in India, to subdue kingdoms, work righteousness, overcome natural difficulties, wrest from the hard rock-ribs of the world the treasures lying hidden in subterraneous depths, abolish cruel and ghastly ceremonies and punishments, instil into alien or vacant minds a reverence for law and right-dealing, cherish a high ideal for individuals and communities, and laugh at the huge army of obstacles which bar the way to the attainment of desired ends. More than that; by dint of much self-denial the sons and daughters of that nation are to be found in

[1] For example, the increase of deaths from "Fever" (one of the official Indian medical reports speaks of fever as a euphemism for innutrition and insufficient clothing) is terribly alarming :—

Administration.	1888.	1897.	+
Bengal	1,095,300	1,679,132	583,832
N.-W. Provinces and Oudh	1,053,753	1,463,716	409,963
Punjab	379,893	422,826	42,933
Lower Burma	36,391	51,752	15,361
Central Provinces	158,195	389,335	231,140
Assam	71,825	144,307	72,482
Coorg	2,730	7,182	4,452
Madras	204,561	292,292	87,731
Bombay	304,449	452,596	148,147
Berar	29,979	65,611	35,632
Mysore	37,609	47,093	9,484
	3,374,685	5,015,842	+1,641,157

That is to say, from "Fevers" only there were, in 1897, more than one and a half million more deaths than ten years previously. It is within the mark to say 1,500,000 died, practically, from starvation. The ratio per 1,000 population of total Fever deaths is from 9·0 in Madras to 23·62 in Bengal, 31·21 in North-West Provinces, Central Provinces 40·98, Coorg 41·50, 24·59 in Bombay, and 23 in Berar. (Pp. 298–301, *Statistical Abstract oj British India*, 1888–89 to 1897–98.)

all parts of the world devotedly labouring for wholly intangible results, for consequences which cannot be put into any currency, even the spiritual welfare and eternal salvation of the souls of mankind. It is before such a nation the stupendous task lies of obliterating even the footprints of famine in a land where there need no more be famine than there is famine in our own country. Is that nation equal to the performance of its duty?

The means required for the transformation of India are at hand. Amongst the more important of them is a sufficiency of water to furnish liquid and manurial nourishment to the crops which, with the assistance of soil and sun, will always grow; this sufficiency is to be found every year in India. What is needed is the knowledge to use it rightly.

There is no mineral of which we know anything—neither gold nor copper—which, in value, can be compared with water. Twenty-six years have passed since the following comparison was made between the respective values of gold and water; he who made the comparison was the hero of these pages, Sir Arthur Cotton.

"The importance of any subject of investigation," he said, "is measured by the difference between the cost of obtaining it and its value when obtained, that is, in the case of material things. The question is not what is the value of a pound or a ton of anything. If a pound of gold costs more to obtain than its value, we must leave it alone; and if a pound of iron, when obtained, is worth double the cost of mining and smelting it, it is a highly profitable operation. If a thousand cubic yards of water can be made use of at a cost of sixpence, and if its value, so applied, is ten shillings, there is no gold mine in the world that can be compared to an irrigation work. At present it is stated that the average result of gold mining in Victoria is that it merely affords rather high wages to the men actually employed upon it. If so, it is nothing to the results of conducting water to the land in India. If a million a year is spent in gold-mining, and it gives six shillings a day to the miners, who could otherwise be only gaining four shillings, there is a net profit of £330,000 a year; and if a million a year is spent, as the interest at seven per cent. on a capital of £14,000,000, in irrigating ten million acres, yielding in increase of produce and in other things twenty millions a year, it is sixty times as profitable as gold-mining in Victoria."

Allowing for the difference in the cost of labour since 1874, the argument is as good now as then. As are Tanjore, Godavari, and Kistna districts in the Madras Presidency, so, with modifications, might become the greater part of India, and, if such a change be not made, the responsibility rests upon the British people.

Adequate storage of water is the greatest need of India. Immense quantities may be stored at a "cost of £200 per million cubic yards of contents, or £140 per million supplied, and at a cost in interest and repairs at six per cent. of eighty thousand cubic yards per £1, besides the cost of distribution. Some vast sites have been examined and estimated, one to contain two thousand million cubic yards, five hundred times the capacity of the Sheffield reservoir that burst some years ago." [1]

Again, as to the amount of water available in India.

"What quantity of water have we in India," asks Sir Arthur in one of his lectures, "that is at present totally lost, or worse than lost, and, from want of controlling and directing works, is allowed to destroy instead of refresh and fertilize? When the Godavari is full, for instance, it contains about one hundred and eighty millions of cubic yards per hour, or more than four thousand millions a day. This, at two thousand cubic yards per £1, is worth £2,000,000 a day. It is, however, seldom full—perhaps only once in four or five years, and then from one to ten days; but the

[1] "Three Lectures on Irrigation Works in India before the School of Military Engineers," delivered at Chatham in 1875 by Sir Arthur Cotton, p. 22.

total volume flowing into the sea in the year from this one river is enormous. The average fall of rain in its basin is about forty inches, so far as I can judge, and of this, perhaps, one half flows by the river, which would be two hundred thousand million cubic yards, worth, if it could be all used, £100,000,000 sterling a year. This river drains one-tenth of the area of India.

"Leaving out the rainless tract, if an average of one yard of rain falls throughout India it would supply seven thousand five hundred cubic yards, sufficient for one crop of rice and one of other grain on an acre for two-thirds of the whole area, perhaps nearly all that is fit for cultivation. Land so irrigated would produce not much under a ton of food grains per acre, or sufficient for a population of one thousand five hundred per square mile, or six times the present population, and allowing one-third of the area for other things, there would be food for four times the present population. This is sufficient to show the main point, viz., that we have an unlimited supply of this material as far as any present prospects are concerned. We have, therefore, not only a mine of incalculably more value than any gold mine to work upon, but one of unlimited extent. We have in the case of the Godavari added to the income of the people by this means £1 per head or £5 per family, and when the works are completed there will be half as much more, making £7 10*s*. The average income of a family throughout India is, I believe, about £5 a year,[1] at which rate the income in Godavari has been already doubled, and will be eventually increased still more. There are in India fifty million families, so that if the same blessing were extended to the whole of the country it would add £375,000,000 a year to its income, or nine times the amount of the taxes now paid, besides all the incalculable benefits of health, comfort,

[1] This is an under-estimate; the average annual income in India is under £2 per head. When Sir Arthur made his statement the Cromer-Barbour inquiry of 1882 had not been made; this inquiry put the average annual income at Rs. 27, or, at Rs. 15 to the £, 33*s*. 9*d*. per head.

security, freedom from famine, satisfaction of the people under our rule, free intercourse of goods, passengers, etc., and this would be only with the present population, which is rapidly increasing."[1]

Once more the profitableness of water use in India may be mentioned. Iteration and reiteration will be useful in impressing it on the mind. In the third of his Chatham series of lectures, Sir Arthur asked, "If a gold mine could be found in which it would cost £2 to obtain a pound weight of gold, what would be thought of it? Or, a silver mine that would cost three-halfpence to produce an ounce of silver worth four shillings?" How every newspaper would be full of it, but, because these very results are obtained by water, they are not thought worthy of a moment's notice. "That the Godavari works are, at this moment, costing £42,000 a year, producing £1,500,000 from six hundred thousand acres of irrigation, and about five hundred miles of navigation, is as simple and as palpable a fact as could possibly be brought before us. And so with the Sone works this year; before any part of them is finished they have watered one hundred and sixty thousand acres, producing £500,000 worth of grain, in the midst of a famine—about the whole cost of the works up to that time."

The vast storage tanks needed can be economically constructed. Not the least amazing of the great engineer's efforts was the cheapness with which he could make his enormous bunds. That point need not be laboured here, as it has been already dealt with in the description (chap. vii.) of the construction of the Dowlaisweram anicut. But, it must never be lost sight of in the discussion of estimates prepared by hydraulic engineers, who know naught of other than the accepted heavy stone masonry which is in favour generally.

One important feature in regard to irrigation must not

[1] "Three Lectures on Irrigation Works," pp. 29–30.

be overlooked, and that is, even without large rivers, or even any rivers, much may be done to protect crops. "Here in Jaipur State the famine is less severe than it is in Marwar, and in many districts there has been a fair supply of fodder. Moreover, there are appreciable stretches of country where irrigation works have enabled the people to hold out longer than they would otherwise have done. True, the water this year has been scanty, and now, at the end of April, the canals and tanks are giving out ; but there is no doubt that the jealous care with which the scanty rainfall has been husbanded and utilised has done much to add to the staying power of Jaipur. The good work done in this direction is due to the man who, for thirty-three years, has given the whole of his energies to the advancement of Jaipur. Under Colonel Jacob's direction more than a hundred and fifty irrigation works have been carried through, and this in

A COUNTRY WITHOUT RIVERS,

and presenting as hostile a face to schemes of watering as, I suppose, any district in India. The usual plan adopted has been to select the best spots for catching and storing the floods which come with the rains, and then, by means of canals, to lead the water to as many village tanks or reservoirs as possible. Besides replenishing the tanks, the wells for a long way round have the leakage from the tanks to draw upon, so that the water is thoroughly well spread. Irrigation direct from canal to field—the common fashion in India—is also used. The accounts of the Public Works Department show what a splendid investment irrigation has been for Jaipur. On an outlay of five and a quarter millions of rupees there is an annual return of more than three hundred thousand rupees, and although the chief expenditure on capital account took place in the Eighties, the whole outlay since the beginning in 1868, will be recovered in another three years. The benefit to the people themselves may be imagined by those who know what the value of water means in India. I am told that when Colonel Jacob goes about the country, the people of the unirrigated districts surround him as if he were the god of water, and beseech him to give them canals."[1]

RIVER *VERSUS* RAILWAY—TO TAP CENTRAL INDIA.

When the Central Provinces and the Deccan were yet undeveloped by railway communication, Sir Arthur Cotton made most earnest efforts to turn the Godavari to account. Unfortunately, he laboured in India at the most crucial moment, and it is not in India that a decision is taken on such momentous matters. If only he had been in England, and had been able to secure the active (he had the passive) support of the late Earl of Derby (then Lord Stanley, M.P.), it is quite possible he would have succeeded in tapping the cotton country and in opening up the Central Provinces, by way of an Eastern India port. Had only Sir Arthur Cotton's counsel been followed, the Central Provinces would have been saved from four most terrible famines,[2] each succeeding one being more destructive than its predecessor, while the prosperity of the whole of Southern India would have been enhanced.

What Sir Arthur Cotton wrote on this point must be reproduced. Even though the extracts will fill several pages, it is due to his farsightedness, nearly half a century ago, that they should be put upon record, and note taken by all concerned what India would have become by way of credit and legitimate profit to Britain could he have prevailed. There is no sadder "might-have-been" in recent English history than the retrospect of what India, Britain, and humanity have lost because the forces against which Sir Arthur Cotton had to contend were too strong for him.

[1] The *Manchester Guardian* Famine Correspondent, May 25, 1900.

[2] The famines of 1868–69, 1886–87, 1897–98, and 1899–1900.

Here is his own story (written before 1860) of what would have been could he have prevailed :—

What we have now to do is to discover means whereby the cost of transit may be reduced materially, so as to give a real relief to the country, and enable it to compete with other countries. Till this is accomplished nothing is done. All our immense advantages of soil, and climate, and cheapness, and abundance of labour, are lost, or at least the greater part of them. This is well shown in the case of the Berar cotton trade. It is stated by those who have the best means of knowing, that cotton is actually grown and sold at one penny farthing the pound; to this about three farthings is added in bringing it into the great cotton marts of the district where it is cultivated. Fully one penny is added in conveying it to Bombay, and more in taking it to Calcutta; another penny is added to it in bringing it into the English markets, and thus it arrives at Manchester at a cost which only puts it on a par with American cotton grown by slave labour at an enormous expense. At least three-halfpence per lb. could be taken off this cost by improved communications, and by throwing open the country, where so favourable a climate and soil are found for its growth. It is not merely for want of cheap transit a direct charge of one penny or more is added to the cost of the cotton, but for the same reason food, salt, etc., are three or four times the price they need to be. This is only one of many ways that the price of the cotton is indirectly augmented. At present the purchasing of the cotton from the cultivators is entirely in the hands of the ignorant, short-sighted, oppressive, native merchants. The natives begin to be very sensible of the advantage that it would be to deal with the European; but nothing can deliver them from the present system without an open communication with the ports, giving Europeans free access to the districts, and gradually removing the absurd fancies that mercantile men have about living in the interior of the peninsula, as if they could not do it without great risk to their lives.

In the present great question of the cotton supply, there seems to be scarcely any point more worth investigation than this opening of the fine cotton countries of Nagpur to the coast. No doubt the cultivation would extend rapidly along the whole line of the Godavari. It seems now to be generally acknowledged that

Berar is naturally the most suitable climate for cotton for the English market, and that, therefore, we should make it our grand effort to open a cheap line of communication with it, and it is certain that no other line can possibly compare with that of the Godavari for bringing this cotton to the coast. Captain Fenwick tells me that during the three years Palmer's house [1] brought their capital to bear on this tract, the cultivation of cotton and the general welfare of the people increased surprisingly. There is thus a line of five hundred miles of the cheapest communication, leading into the very heart of the country, to be had almost for nothing; even if fifty thousand pounds were spent in improving it, it would still only cost a hundred pounds a mile.

In the paper on the Berar cotton, by Mr. Ashburner, read before the Asiatic Society, in 1837, the importance of the subject is shown on the very best authority. He states that cotton can be cultivated at three pounds for a Bombay candy (less than one penny a pound), and that the only obstacle to its unlimited production is the cost of transport: that it is sent to Bombay on bullocks at two pounds eight shillings a candy (less than three farthings a pound), taking seventy days on the journey; that large quantities cannot reach Bombay before the monsoon, which is consequently liable to be damaged or destroyed; that there was at that time a traffic of twenty thousand tons a year in salt and Berar cotton; that a good carriage road there would be a saving of one hundred and sixty thousand pounds a year. He then goes on to say: "It may be as well, however, to show the productive powers of the country more clearly, to instance the increase which has lately taken place in the amount of cotton exported from Bombay. From 1828 to 1835 the exports averaged one hundred and seventy-eight thousand bales a year, and remained nearly stationary. But the high prices of the latter year lead to more extensive cultivation, and, notwithstanding numerous obstacles to production, the Presidency of Bombay last year produced and exported no less than two hundred and ninety thousand bales of cotton, being an increase of one hundred and twelve thousand

[1] A well-known, and at one time extremely influential, family, the members of which, at Hyderabad, Deccan, transacted the business affairs alike of the Nizam and of the Europeans in the Nizam's Dominions.

bales within the year. Some portion of this increase, no doubt, is attributable to an unusually good season, but by far the largest share arose, as the reports of the revenue collectors show, from extension of cultivation alone." Here, then, is a specimen of what India is capable of doing under favourable circumstances, and there can be no question whatever, that the production of the cotton would, with good roads to the interior, go on increasing as rapidly as it increased during the last twelve months; for the stimulus to cultivation would be as great from decreased expenses as it has lately been from increased prices.

Thus with proper management we might reasonably expect to see the exports of the country in this staple alone swelling at the rate of one hundred thousand bales per annum, and amounting probably, at no distant period, to a million of bales. And what would be the consequences in other respects? Besides benefiting the revenue, and improving the condition of the people of India, such a trade would give employment to a vast amount of British shipping (four hundred thousand tons) at the same time that it created a greater demand for the manufactures of the mother country.

Now if this cotton, instead of being carried, as Mr. Ashburner proposed, by a carriage road, were conveyed down the Godavari at the rate at which goods are carried on the Mississippi, *i.e.* the sixteenth part of a penny per ton per mile, or about five shillings per ton for the whole distance, there would be a saving of £7 a ton, or of £210,000 on the traffic of two hundred thousand tons, besides saving the interest, insurance, waste, etc.

Think of a great portion of this cotton being carried from the banks of the Godavari, five hundred miles from the sea, by a land carriage of five hundred miles to Mirzapur, to be embarked on the Ganges, a point five hundred and fifty miles from Calcutta. But the important point in Mr. Ashburner's paper is his testimony to the astonishing increase of production consequent on an increase of price, showing clearly the grand fact that everything within that tract of country is in a complete state of preparation, and that nothing is wanting, but a relief in the cost of transit to England, to make the cultivation spring up to almost any extent. There are the climate and soil required for a good marketable cotton for England, and there are the people, the cattle, the enterprise, and all other requisites. This line of transit would probably cause a saving of full three half-pence a pound, five times as much as would be sufficient to give a material stimulus to the trade.

There seems, thus, to be no reason why the Godavari may not become the line of a trade for a million tons a year, when once the pent-up treasures of its basin effect a breach in the barriers, which have hitherto shut it up.

India can supply Manchester fully, abundantly, cheaply, with its two essentials, flour and cotton, and nothing whatever prevents its doing so but the public works. If only the country is, by means of irrigation, supplied abundantly and cheaply with food, and, by means of communications, its produce can be cheaply conveyed to the coast, Manchester is safe: its supply with the two things upon which its very existence depends cannot fail. But while three-fourths of the people of India are raising food, and an eighth carrying their produce over the unimproved face ot the country, at a cost that would instantly paralyse England if it were subjected to such an incubus, this magnificent appendage to England must be comparatively thrown away on her, and the prodigious, the incalculable, stimulus that it might give to her manufacturing and general prosperity must be, in a great measure, lost.

* * * * *

I have before reckoned that a stream of a million cubic yards an hour would secure a depth of three or four feet everywhere in the Godavari, and that tanks containing three thousand millions of cubic yards would be ample for this purpose, and would cost about £150,000. If treble this quantity were stored, so as to give a depth of full six feet, and the bed were perfectly clear of rocks so as to allow of the freest passage for steamers, then vessels of any power might be used, and I have little doubt that if kept at this regulated depth, excepting during the freshes, it could be worked at night as well as by day; and if very high speed were required, a mean current of, suppose, two miles an hour would be no obstacle to such vessels as would be worked. A vessel with the speed of twenty miles an hour, for instance, would go up at eighteen, and come down at twenty-two miles. The cost of storing nine thousand millions of cubic yards might be £450,000, and, allowing £50,000 to be spent on the bed of the river, etc., we should have half a million sterling as the cost of at least seven hundred miles of such navigation (besides making the same rivers available for small vessels to a much higher point), which would be at the rate of only £700 a mile, against £2,000 for a steam canal, or £7,000 for a railway. And it would have this vast advantage, that in the very first year the river would be available throughout, and each year the whole navigation would be improved to the full extent of the amount expended. This is precisely what India wants, viz., to have whole lines of transit at once improved to a certain extent. If a high speed railway were laid on this line, it would be many years before the cotton country would be really accessible, and in the meantime, at least ten times the whole cost of the work would be lost for the want of the means of transit. £50,000 laid out in the river would, in the first year, provide a thoroughly good and exceedingly cheap communication from the heart of Berar to the coast, while £50,000 laid out on even a single high-speed railway, would provide for only perhaps seven miles out of the four hundred and fifty; if only a hundred thousand tons were carried per annum there would be a loss of £500,000 for every year that the opening of the communication was delayed.

This shows the real state of the case between the Bombay railway and the Godavari. To reach the centre of the cotton country would require four hundred miles of railway. What has already been done has been at the rate of ten miles a year and £7,000 a mile; and continuing at the same rate they would, if it were not for those plaguey ghâts, reach the Wurda in forty years, after spending about £2,800,000 on the road, and allowing only a traffic of a hundred thousand tons a year for half the time, or twenty years at £6 per ton, there would be an outlay of £12,000,000 on transit alone. And the account would stand thus at the end of forty years, even supposing the trade did not increase in the Godavari, and that goods were carried for nothing by the railroad:

RAILWAY.

400 miles at £7,000 per mile . . .	£2,800,000
100,000 tons per annum for twenty years at £6 a ton	£12,000,000
Total expenditure .	£14,800,000

GODAVARI RIVER.

Improving river to give a constant depth of six feet	£500,000
One hundred thousand tons for forty years at 6*s*. per ton	£1,200,000
Total expenditure .	£1,700,000

But the railways expect to be able to carry goods at twopence-halfpenny per ton, which for four hundred miles would be £4, or two-thirds of what it is now, in which case £8,000,000 more must be placed against the railway, making the expenditure on that line £23,000,000, against £1,700,000 by the river; or thirteen times as much as the latter. Even allowing the railway to be worked for nothing, there would be a difference of £12,000,000.

"Does this admit of an answer?" asks Mr. J. Bruce Norton, in his letter to the Secretary of the Board of Control. He proceeds: "Yet we find that with a natural slope from Berar to the eastern coast, and a river, which has now been proved to be easily navigable, leading down to the smooth-water harbour at Coringa, every argument has been used to drive traffic westward. Indeed, it has been throughout *assumed* that Bombay was the only feasible route by which to convey the cotton of Berar to England; and this, notwithstanding the whole country slopes *up* westward, so that the railway would have to be ascending an inclined plain until it reached a wall of ghâts, up which it must be forced two thousand four hundred feet in order to be dropped three thousand feet on the other side, into the waters of Bombay! Can anything be more conclusive than this?" Yes, says Colonel Cotton, *This*—and sketches on the margin of proof-sheet the following diagram, which I take the liberty of transferring, as it graphically, succinctly, and conclusively, tells the whole story, and embraces the whole question.

Finally, remarked Sir Arthur, if we could have a ship-load of directors, Manchester merchants, Indian reformers, and others interested in this matter landed at Bombay, carried twenty miles by railway, and then on horses and in palanquins three hundred miles to the Wurda, a journey of from eight to twenty days at an expense of £10 each; and, on arriving there, placed on a steamer and floated down to Coringa in thirty or forty hours, for two shillings each, then they would probably return to England with a more correct notion of the real state of the case: parti-

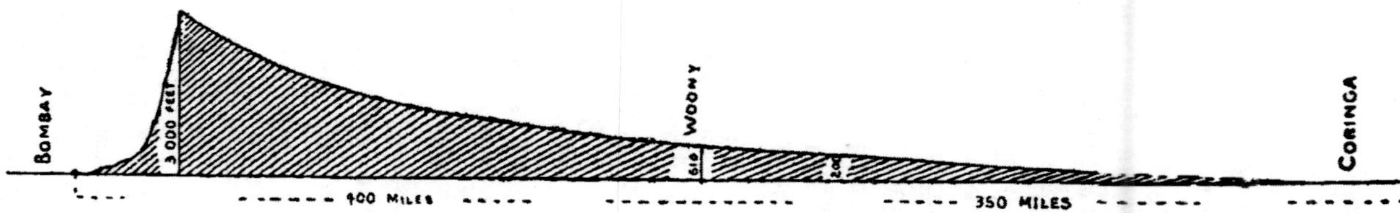

Horizontal Scale, 100 miles = ·715 inch. Vertical Scale, 3,000 feet = ·68 inch.

RAILWAY.

Ascent	2,390 feet.
Descent	3,000 "

Cost: 400 miles × Rs. 70,000 per mile = £2,800,000.

Time for construction: About twenty years.

Charge, per ton, for transit, according to Mr. Chapman's estimate: 400 m. × $2\frac{1}{4}d.$ per m. = 75*s.*

Probable actual charge, at $\frac{3}{4}d.$ per ton: 25*s.*

CANAL.

Ascent	350 feet.
Descent	610 "

River navigable at present for six months in the year.

Cost of improving river for steam navigation throughout the year: 350 m. × Rs. 1,000 = £350,000.

Time required: Two years.

Cost, per ton: 350 m. × $\frac{1}{4}d.$ = 7*s.* $3\frac{1}{2}d.$

cularly as, on the way up, they would have met thousands of worn-out bullocks and drivers carrying cotton at the rate of ten miles a day and at a cost of £6 a ton, whilst on the boats in which they descended the river there would probably be one hundred tons of cotton on freight at 10*s.* a ton. Reaching the end of the railway after a journey of twenty miles, when it had already been two years in progress, and then seeing the frowning ghâts immediately above them, would also be a highly instructive circumstance, which would tend greatly to clear their sight; and there would also be plenty of time for true impressions to be received on their long weary journey of ten or twenty days to the Wurda through a country without roads and across rivers without bridges. What a lively idea they would have of the advantage of inland steam communication long before they reached the Wurda, and with what entire satisfaction would they resign themselves to the sofas in the steamers, and consider themselves as good as at their journey's end.

Surely it cannot be that this record of a life's work and teachings will fail, once the tremendous significance of that work and those teachings is realised, to become instrumental in arousing public attention and lead to the adoption of drastic measures of reform. When we remember the many, many, years during which Sir Arthur laboured, apparently with little result, for a widespread adoption of irrigation, and with no result at all, so far as stopping the extension of railways was concerned, we, not unnaturally, feel intensely anxious as to whether that which will be adequate will be done at once, and before it is too late. At the same time when we call to mind the obstacles with which Sir Arthur had to contend nearly eighty years ago we again begin to be hopeful. For, be it remembered, there is now enough of successful irrigation in India to constitute an object lesson, the teachings of which cannot be mistaken. May we not urge that there is no duty, on its intrinsic merits, which so loudly calls for earnest effort in the United Kingdom as the redemption of Indian daily needs by the adoption of such proposals as Sir Arthur advocated to the last moment of his singularly prolonged life?

Who, in the good Providence of God, will be raised up to carry on this needed work? That which has to be done, it is rightly said, is worthy of the amplest and most elaborate study in every aspect and in all detail. First of all, trustworthy knowledge is required. It would greatly help forward irrigation extension if a succinct history of each scheme, describing and explaining all its failures and all its successes, and depicting its present condition in a clear forcible way, were prepared. "These," says one who himself gave much study to the subject, "should be grouped into systems, their likenesses and differences noted, and the principles which they illustrate set forth, so that even laymen might read and understand, while professional men would acquire fresh evidence and suggestions for new developments of their work. An opportunity remains for the writing, by a competent literary man and engineer, of a book which would be a manual of construction, for many years to come, of the greatest value to the colonies. If complete, it would at the same time offer, to the outer world, the best justification for British supremacy in India, and the best evidence from facts and actions, of the large-minded generosity and courage of its rule." [1]

[1] The author quote from was writing for the Australian colonies, and, consequently, applied his argument to the needs of Australasia. As to the justification the record would afford for British supremacy in India, a hundred times yes—so far as irrigation has been undertaken. But, in view of what needs yet to be done, it is more important we should consider the opportunities we have omitted to turn to account than that we should indulge in self-gratulation. In the presence of ever-increasing starving multitudes in India, it ill-beseemeth us to make boast of our "large-minded generosity and courage"—at the financial risk of India always, be it borne in mind.

Appendices

I.

THE GOVERNOR-GENERAL OF INDIA ON IRRIGATION EXTENSION.

During the Budget Debate, in the Viceregal Council, towards the end of March, 1900, His Excellency Lord Curzon thus expressed himself on this important subject :—

"The second suggestion that is frequently made to me, I admit as a rule from the outside of India, where I am afraid that a good deal of ignorance of the actual position prevails, is that the obvious method to stop famines is to introduce irrigation. Some of these writers seem to plume themselves upon the originality of the idea, and to be unaware that such a thing as irrigation has ever been heard of in India, or has been so much as attempted here. They do not seem to realise that irrigation has been going on in India for quite a considerable number of years, that about nineteen millions [1] of acres in India are already under irrigation, and that upon the works so undertaken has been spent a capital outlay of no less than £25,500,000. Worthy people write me letters, based upon the hypothesis that any Indian river which ultimately discharges its waters into the sea is really so much

[1] It is difficult to understand what His Excellency means in giving this figure. The total area irrigated in India, one harvest, is 30,418,454 acres—for both harvests 33,124,322. At first, I thought Lord Curzon referred to Government Canal Irrigation, but that does not seem to have been the case. The details of the thirty and a half millions are interesting :—

	Acres.
By Canal:	
Government	11,736,755
Private	1,398,432
By Tanks	4,671,195
By Wells	11,328,323
Otherwise	1,283,479
Total	30,418,454
Under second harvest	2,705,868
Acres	33,124,322

(From *Statistical Abstract of British India*, 1898–99, p. 149).

agricultural wealth gone astray, which somehow or other the Government of India ought to have got hold of at an earlier stage, and turned into crops and gardens. Now I have had a very careful estimate made out for me of the extent of fresh ground in the whole of India which we are likely to be able to bring under cultivation, either by new irrigation projects, or by extensions of existing systems. Under the head of Productive works, *i.e.* works which may be expected to yield a net revenue that will more than cover the interest on the capital outlay, the estimated increment is about 3½ million acres, and the estimated outlay between eight and nine millions sterling. Under the head of Protective works, *i.e.* works which will not pay, and which, inasmuch as they constitute a permanent financial burden on the State, can only be undertaken in exceptional cases, and then, as a rule, do very little towards the prevention of famine, we contemplate spending about ten lakhs a year, and shall probably in this way about double the area of 300,000 acres which is covered by that character of work at the present time. It seems, therefore, that the total practicable increase to the irrigable area of India under both heads will not amount to much more than 4,000,000 acres. This increase will, of course, be of value in its addition to the total food-supply of the country, in the employment of labour thereby given, and in its effect upon prices in time of famine. But I am afraid that it cannot be expected to secure immunity from drought to districts now liable to famine, or to help directly their suffering inhabitants. Indeed, when a desert tract is brought under cultivation, a stimulus is given to the growth of population, and more mouths have in time to be fed. The fact remains that the majority of the irrigation works that were most feasible, or most urgently required as protective measures against famine, have now been carried out, and that there is not in irrigation that prospect of quite indefinite expansion with which the popular idea sometimes credits it. At the same time, I am so much in agreement with the general proposition, which has received a good deal of support from many quarters in the course of the present debate, that irrigation should be encouraged, both because of the extension thereby given to the growth of food-supplies in this country, and because, in the case of what are known as Productive works, of the extraordinarily remunerative character of the capital outlay, that I have inaugurated, since I came to India, a definite and, as I hope, a permanent extension (so long as we can find the works to undertake) of our irrigation programme. In my predecessor's time, the annual irrigation grant amounted to 75 lakhs. Last year I persuaded Sir James Westland to increase this; and, in the financial year just expired, we have spent 90 lakhs, some of it being directly applied to the provision of labour in famine districts; while, during the forthcoming year, in spite of the general curtailment of our programme owing to famine, I have prevailed upon Mr. Dawkins to fix the irrigation grant at 100 lakhs, or one crore of rupees. I am hopeful that generosity in this respect will not be a misplaced virtue, either in the direct returns that it will bring in or in its general effect upon the prosperity of the country. For the reasons that I have named, I doubt whether irrigation can continue to do as much in the future as it has done in the past, owing to the gradual exhaustion of the majority of the big schemes. Still, even if our sphere of action is less grandiose and spacious than in bygone days, I believe that for a long time to come, and certainly during my day, we shall find more than enough to occupy our funds with smaller and less ambitious designs."

II.

SIR RICHARD TEMPLE ON IRRIGATION DONE AND TO BE DONE.[1]

Canals have been proposed or projected in general terms or designed more or less in detail, but not yet undertaken, to be derived from the following rivers,—

The Chenab in the Punjab,
The Sarda in Oudh,
The Gandak in Behar,
The lower part of the Pennar on the east coast north of Madras,
The Periyar stream which issues from the Travancore mountains near Madura in the southern peninsula,
The lower part of the Tapti, on the west coast, north of Bombay,

---

[1] Extracts from *India in* 1880, by Sir Richard Temple, pp. 252, 253, and 254.

The lower part of the Nerbudda in the same quarter,
The Wardha, the Wynganga, and lesser streams in the province of Nagpur,
The upper course of the Mahanudi in the eastern extremity of the Central Provinces,
The Chambal in Central India,
The Betwa and the Kene in Bundelkhand, and
The Jumna to carry off surplus water of the rainy season towards the arid tracts east of the Sutlej.

Artificial lakes and several canals, greater or smaller, have been projected in the Deccan districts of the Bombay Presidency, which works have, however, not yet been undertaken. There are, probably, other projects or proposals in different parts of India, for thoughtful officers are constantly busying themselves with plans, whereby the drought so much dreaded in most parts of the empire may be averted.

From this review it will be apparent that the following great rivers have by the British Government been placed under contribution more or less, for the fertilization of provinces or districts in India,—

The Ganges,
The Jumna,
The Sone in Behar,
The Sutlej,
The Ravi in the Punjab,
The Indus,
The lower part of the Mahanudi and some lesser streams in Orissa,
The lower part of the Godavari on the east coast,
The lower part of the Kistna or Krishna,
The Cauveri and Coleroon in the southern peninsula,
The Tunga-badra or Tumbadra in the Deccan,
The upper courses of the Kistna and the Tapti,

and many other lesser rivers and streams, for the formation of artificial lakes, which it would be tedious to enumerate.

The following rivers are known to be capable of affording water for irrigation, but remain yet to be dealt with for this purpose,—

The Gandak in Behar,
The Sarda in Oudh,

The Chenab in the Punjab,
The lesser rivers in Orissa,
The lower part of the Pennar near Madras,
The Periyar river near Madura,
The lower part of the Tapti on the west coast near Bombay,
The lower part of the Nerbudda on the same coast,
The several rivers in the Nagpur province,
The Chambal in Central India,
The Betwa and the Kene in Bundelkhand,

and many other lesser rivers and streams for the formation of reservoirs for irrigation in the Deccan districts of the Bombay Presidency. The only remaining rivers of note are the Jhelum in the Punjab, from which a canal might perhaps be taken; some smaller rivers which flow through Native States, and of which the capabilities are now known; the rivers in the humid regions of lower Bengal, where it is drainage that is wanted rather than irrigation; and the Brahmaputra river and its affluents, the Megna and others, which are not likely ever to supply canals for irrigation.

III.

HOW THE WATER WAS WASTED DURING THE '77 FAMINE.

Even the rain which fell was a source of disquiet, so much of it was wasted. After such a crisis as had been passed through, and with much suffering still to come, arising from the want of water, the least that might have been expected would be that, when the rain did come, it would not be permitted to run to waste. Yet on the day the rains ceased, and for many days after, lamentations were upon almost every lip, as millions of gallons of water were seen to flow away entirely unused, much of which might, and ought, to have been stored against a dry and sunny day—the oriental equivalent for the proverbial "rainy day" of England, which needs to be provided against. As an instance of the frightful waste of water which occurred, the case of the Adyar river may be taken. Nothing was done to conserve the water in its channel. For three days the river flowed full from bank to bank—two hundred and fifty yards wide at the Marmalong bridge. In the middle of the stream, for the width of one hundred yards at the least, the current was moving at the rate of two miles an hour: the depth of water was four feet on an average. It may be that there was not tank accommodation available for the storage of more water. But, even from the tanks, the waste was enormous. The Marmalong Tank at Saidapett (a suburb of Madras) may be taken as an indication of the waste permitted. This tank, when it was seen by the writer, a few days after the rain, was discharging over its waste weir a volume of water six yards wide and one yard deep, flowing at the rate of five miles per hour. The reason given for this outflow was that, if the water were retained, some of the banks of the tank might give way. Yet the level of the water in the tank was below what it frequently had been, and no disaster followed. The truth was this: the budget for petty repairs of tanks was cut down at the beginning of the revenue year, and funds were not available for carrying out such precautionary works as were absolutely needful. The system by which works are done is so unsatisfactory that engineers, though they see the necessity of saving water, are unwilling to take the responsibility of keeping the water in the tanks, in the absence of that protection to the banks which they feel is necessary. They, therefore, choose the lesser of two evils, and, rather than risk a breach of the banks, with consequent flooding of the country around and much damage, they consider it wise to let the water run to waste, and keep the level of the tank very low. Nine months previously, when Lord Lytton issued his Minute on the necessity of economy everywhere, and called upon the local governments to report what savings could be effected upon their budget estimates, the Madras Board of Revenue reported that "a considerable saving could be made on 'estimates' for the annual petty repairs to tanks, channels, etc." The consequences ought to have been obvious. What they were in one instance has been shown, and that was but one instance out of many. Tanks are the prime pre-requisites for cultivation in many parts of India, and, when economy is required, they are the very last things which should be tampered with. When they are neglected, the result is a flow towards the sea of a precious fluid, which represents, in passing away unused, a sacrifice of human lives.[1]

---

[1] Pp. 148–9, 50, vol. i. of *The Famine Campaign in Southern India*, 1876–1878. London, Longmans, Green & Co.

IV.

OBITER DICTA BY SIR GEORGE CAMPBELL, K.C.S.I.

Expressed as a witness before the Public Works Committee of 1878.

"It does seem to me, looking over Sir Arthur Cotton's account of the various irrigation works, that wherever they succeed, the engineers and civilians are both admirable; but, wherever they fail, then the engineers are still admirable, so long as they are not Bengal engineers; but the civilians are detestable, and it is entirely their fault. Where the engineers are Bengal engineers, there both the civilians and the engineers are equally in fault."

[This is a strangely inaccurate remark, and has no relation to Sir Arthur's singularly courteous character. Probably, there never was a man who had less bias or personal feeling: his one thought was the welfare of India.]

A FAMINE ONCE IN ONE HUNDRED YEARS ONLY.

"The general result is to impress me with the idea that, excepting certain special parts of India, which seem to be peculiarly liable to famine, we have no reason to expect a famine to occur oftener than about once in a hundred years in any one tract of country."

[The Central Provinces, at one time ruled by Sir George Campbell, have been visited by famine four times within the past thirty-two years.]

SIR ARTHUR COTTON'S GRAND CANALS FOR BENGAL.

"The only other schemes in Bengal, of which I have any knowledge, were two schemes of Sir Arthur Cotton's. One was to bring a grand canal from the Ganges to Calcutta, and the other was what has been mentioned as the Damuda scheme. I think that the Ganges canal was designed more for navigation than irrigation, but at the same time it was also urged upon the Government, that it would be extremely useful for irrigating Nuddea and other districts. That scheme was a good deal urged upon me during my incumbency in Bengal, but it seemed to me that the project was in so very crude and inchoate a form, and the difficulties were so great, that I declined seriously to entertain it. It involved the making of a great dam to stop the flow of the Ganges, just at the point where it is at its very largest, where it has received all its feeders, and before it has begun to distribute its waters among the channels of the delta. . . .

"I was perhaps a little afraid of once letting in Sir Arthur Cotton and his schemes, for I did not know when we should get them out again."

RAILWAYS IN FAMINE TIMES.

"I will only notice one or two points with regard to the special use of railways in times of famine. I am very much convinced of this, that railways, by increasing the facilities of communication, do very much obviate the future risk of famine; in fact, I think the experience which we have recently had in India almost justifies one in saying that when a complete system of railways is in work throughout India, provided sufficient foresight and care is shown, and sufficient money is forthcoming, no real famine, leading to a very great loss of life, need occur."

THE REMARKABLE FREQUENCY OF FAMINES NOWADAYS.

"That remarkable frequency of famine in recent years, although it may possibly be accidental, is, in my opinion, so serious as to demand very searching inquiry into the questions as to whether modern conditions are not such as to render the country more liable to famine than under the old conditions. It is quite possible that that may be so. To begin with, no doubt, under British peace the population has considerably increased, and, with the population, cultivation has increased. In ordinary times the increase of cultivation counterbalances the increase of population. But, on the other hand, it is my experience that in sparsely populated countries a sparse population has greater resources than a very large population in very fully peopled districts, in time of famine, because where the population is sparse and the uncultivated country is large, there are considerable facilities for resorting to jungle berries and jungle fruits, and one thing and another, so that I think I may state it, as a matter within my own experience, that those jungle districts do not suffer so severely from famine as the more highly populated districts.[1] Then it is certainly the case, although I am inclined to think there has been a good deal of exaggeration in statements which have been made

[1] An exactly opposite experience has been noted during the existing famine (1900) in the Central Provinces and in Eastern Bombay.

regarding the effects of cutting down forests, that considerable effect is produced in the country in the long run by the spread of cultivation, by the cutting down of forests, and by the drainage of the country, which causes the natural water supply to run off more rapidly, and to be less completely stored in the natural reservoirs, which Nature has provided in countries in which the hand of man has not been very active.

"So that on those grounds I think it is quite possible that the country may become more liable to famines. Then there is another very important view, which I think it is necessary to bear in mind. We are very much alive to the fact that improved communications have the effect of enabling us to meet famines in a way in which they never were met before; but we must also remember that there is another view of the question, that those improved communications lead to the export of grain, and a cessation of the old native habit of hoarding grain, which was formerly a very great security against famine. I can speak from my own personal experience. I know parts of the country where, every now and again, when they have had a very good year, the country was perfectly glutted with grain. That was so as regards parts of the Punjab; on the upper part of the Sutlej grain was almost a drug in the market; you could scarcely get anybody to buy it when you had a good season and an enormous produce of grain, and it was the same in the Nerbudda valley, grain was occasionally excessively cheap there. It was the native habit—a habit which no doubt has come down from the time of Joseph—to consider that it was the height of prudence and virtue to store enormous quantities of grain in those cheap years, as a provision against bad years. It was the habit of the native grain dealers, and native zemindars, and cultivators, and others, to make enormous underground pits, in which, in that dry country, they could store grain and keep it for a very large number of years. The consequence was that, under that native system, the difficulty of a market in the plentiful years being so great, there was an immense hoarding of grain, and provision against famine, the great store of which came out in times of famine. Nowadays there has been nothing so conspicuous in recent famines, as the extent to which the country has been denuded of supplies of grain by the facilities of exportation which such means of communication have afforded."

GRAIN STORES IN OLDEN DAYS; NO GRAIN STORES NOW.

"In Orissa it is actually the case that, up to the month of March of the famine year, a very active export of grain was going on, that is, within six weeks of the time when the country was in the throes of the most frightful famine. The traders had miscalculated. In Bengal, during the greater part of the famine, whilst the Government were importing with one hand, the traders were exporting with the other, so that a very great drain took place. I have not the least doubt that on general economical grounds the result of improved communications is a very good result. It is very much better that the cheap grain of cheap years should be brought to market in the quantities in which it is wanted, and that it should be imported in years of dearness and scarcity, but from a financial point of view, it leaves the evil just as great as ever it was, because, although it is perfectly true that the means ot communication enable you to bring into a famine district in a bad year the grain which is there wanted, still that does not give the people the means of buying the grain. What has happened of recent years is that, there being no grain stores in the country where those famines have occurred, the grain being brought in through improved communication, it has been necessary either to supply the grain to the people, or to furnish the means of buying the grain; and, therefore, although you may have succeeded more or less, sometimes more, and sometimes less, in obviating the mortality by famine, you have done so at an enormous expense, and that expense is increasing from famine to famine; therefore it is that there is very great room for question, whether, from a financial point of view at any rate, you are not a good deal more liable to very serious and very expensive famines than you were in former days; I think that is a subject which it will be very necessary to work out fully.

Questions by LORD GEORGE HAMILTON, Chairman:

"You stated that in olden times it was the habit of the natives to store grain, but if a famine occurred the people in the district were still unable to buy that grain, and, unless they had the money, they would not be able to obtain it?—That is so to a very great extent, but the people themselves, the zemindars and the cultivators, sometimes stored a good deal of grain. The grain, too, was very much in the hands of their local bankers and money-lenders, who are in the habit of dealing with people who generally get an advance of grain in time of famine and scarcity to be repaid in time of plenty.

"But unless the people generally are more impoverished now than they were in those times, they would still have the money to buy the grain ?—No; I do not think they either had the money in former days or have it now, but what I believe to be the case is this, that the grain was then in the hands of their own bankers, and traders, and money-lenders, with whom they habitually dealt, and whose very trade and profession it was to advance them what they required in time of need, to be repaid with interest in time of plenty."

THE "GREAT BENGAL FAMINE" OF 1770 EXAGGERATED.

"What I wish to say is that, if we look into the matter historically, I believe no famine ever has occurred, which we could not meet by our present means, that there never has been such a scarcity of grain throughout India that you could not meet the necessities of one part of India from another part of India. Take the great Bengal famine of 1770. In this, as in other matters, I think that distance often leads to a good deal of exaggeration; that famine has been handed down to us as if it were a famine in magnitude quite beyond anything that we have known in modern times. If the Committee will refer to the actual facts as they were extracted by me from the records of the India Office, and which are contained in the paper which I have just put in, it will be found that, in reality, that famine was perhaps scarcely greater than some of our modern famines. It was a very severe famine indeed, and it led to a great loss of population in very considerable parts of Bengal, but by no means in the whole of Bengal. The general result, showing that it was not a famine which threw the country back for hundreds of years, in the way which it has been supposed, will be apparent from some figures which are quoted on page seven of the report which I have put in, for there it will be seen that, the very year following the famine, the revenue rose higher than it had ever been before, and for the next two or three years it continued higher."

WHY HE OPPOSED IRRIGATION EXTENSION.

"And you think, therefore, that the certain danger resulting from an enormous expenditure would more than counterbalance the risk hereafter of some great famine occurring which we could not meet?—That is my view; but at the same time, I think it is very necessary to remember that India contains a very great variety of climatic conditions. I think there are some parts of India in respect of which there is great justification for the irrigation works which have been made, and that there is justification for some additional works. I have wished to go over a rain map with a view of making that clear, but I think I had better postpone that until another day."

HOARDS OF GRAIN IN ANCIENT SCARCITIES.

Questioner: MR. ONSLOW, M.P.

"Was it the fact that the hoards of grain which you mentioned in those different states were compelled to be produced by the different rajahs?—In the native times it is very frequent that a pressure is brought to bear upon the people who have hoarded grain, and who are unwilling to sell it; that is a process which has been well known in Europe, and is well known in Asia, and I believe it was very common in India in native times.

"Under British rule there is no pressure of that kind, I presume?—There has been a good deal of popular pressure; there have been occasions on which riots have taken place; in the famine of 1837–38, there was a good deal of popular disturbance, and a great many grain hoards were plundered."

COLONEL FISCHER, R.E., ON THE GRAND CENTRAL RESERVOIR.

Questioner: SIR GEORGE CAMPBELL.

"We have heard of a grand reservoir scheme, 1,600 feet above the level of the sea, from which all India[1] was to be irrigated; do you know anything about that?—That is the reservoir scheme which I proposed for Bellary; although I did not actually survey the whole of it, I took the levels and proposed it.

"It is the same scheme which Sir Arthur Cotton referred to as

---

[1] "All India!" This was Sir George Campbell's unfair way of begging the question. Not "all India," nor even all Southern India, was to be served by one great reservoir. It will be seen, on reference to Sir Arthur Cotton's map, that a number of storage reservoirs were indicated.

a great reservoir, 1,600 feet high, from which canals are to be carried out to irrigate all India?—Yes, 1,600 feet above the level of the sea; but not to irrigate all India.

"Have you seen Mr. Gordon's surveys?—Yes, he told me himself that he had brought the canal through the hills in exactly the same way as I had proposed, and he went back to finish it; but, in the distribution of the water, the project was so excessively expensive that it was abandoned altogether. I was away from that part of the country, engaged elsewhere, and did not see it at that time; but when I saw the distribution, I saw the mistake which had been made.

"Apart from the distribution, had you the papers regarding the survey which Mr. Gordon had made, which satisfied you that a reservoir on a very large scale was practicable, and upon what scale?—I have no papers here with me, but I think I could point out upon the map of the district something about the extent ot the land which would be submerged by the area of the reservoir.

"Were you satisfied of the practicability of that scheme?—I was then, and I am more so now.

"Do you remember up to what height you proposed to carry the dam?—One hundred feet.

"What was the area of the land to be submerged?—At a level of about one hundred feet you will hold the water back for between eighty and ninety miles up the bed of the river.

"What would be the breadth of the area submerged?—The breadth would vary very much; at the greatest, I suppose, it would be about six or seven miles wide; but then, after you have got up some twenty or thirty miles, the valley narrows very rapidly, and also the bed-face of the river is smaller. . . .

"Is there any existing tank which has an embankment as high as one hundred feet?—I believe the Cumbum tank in the Kurnool district is fully that; it has sixty feet of water over the sluice. I beg to say that I did not intend to make the dam of the reservoir entirely of earth, across such a river as the Tungabudra. If I had to construct it, I should build it with concrete blocks, with a water-tight wall through the centre.

"What would be the length of it?—The length is between eight thousand and nine thousand feet.

"Do you think that it would be safe in time of floods, and that it might not wash away and drown the whole country below?—

At that site I believe it would be perfectly safe; it could not get away there, because the river immediately below goes through a very narrow gorge for forty miles, with hills on either side.

"Could you tell us what was the fate of this scheme?—They abandoned it; after Mr. Gordon made his distribution, they said it would be so expensive that it could not be carried out. I happened to go into the matter again before I left India, and I saw how the distribution had been made, and saw that they were carrying the water in a most unnecessarily expensive manner. I have shown the project to several people, and the way in which the distribution ought to have been made, by which there would not have been that expense. I estimated that you could irrigate one million acres of land in that district for about fifteen rupees an acre.

"You are aware, I think, that Sir Arthur Cotton has alluded to this tank as a grand tank, from which enormous canals might be carried to irrigate, if not all India, at least a very large part ot India; do you concur in the practicability of carrying out a gigantic system of irrigation from this tank to that extent?—In Bellary, I think, it would irrigate somewhere about a million acres, if not much more. Sir Arthur Cotton proposes to utilise a large quantity of the water in the Carnatic plains, but that is a mere suggestion of his, and I think it is well worth looking into and investigating, if you take a large quantity of water and utilise it from the Kistna and Tungabudra rivers."

BELLARY FREQUENTLY FAMINE-STRICKEN.

Questioner: MR. VANS AGNEW.

"You would not consider, then, that those tanks in Bellary, under the Government, were sufficient protection from famine?—Oh, dear no; Bellary has, since 1850, suffered three times from famine."

THE GODAVARI WORKS.

Questioner: SIR G. CAMPBELL.

"Do you consider that those works on the Godavari have been extremely successful?—Certainly.

"Are they without any drawback in respect of unhealthiness or exhaustion of the soil, or anything of that sort?—There is no exhaustion of the soil; the soil is fertilised from the river every year. That is not the thing complained of by the people at all.

"Have you observed any unhealthiness attending the irrigation system?—We had a very unhealthy season indeed in 1869 from fever, but the doctors are of the opinion that it was not due to irrigation. The population has increased very largely, and the people have increased enormously in wealth and comfort.

"On the whole, you are of the opinion that the health of the district has not deteriorated?—I should think that the health of the district has considerably improved.

"Was the district an unhealthy district before?—It was a very feverish one and a very poor one.

"And you think that now there is less fever than there was formerly?—I believe so. The fever was of a very ordinary type. A great deal has been said about it, but during the whole time I was there, and I have treated many cases myself, I never saw a case that could not be easily recovered.

"I believe that the Godavari district is the only part of India in which navigation is largely combined with irrigation; in your opinion has this system of navigation been very successful there?—Most successful.

"Do you see any reason why such a system of navigation should not be applied to other irrigation projects?—It will be carried out in the Kistna delta.

THE CENTRAL RESERVOIR AGAIN.

"Will you tell us some particulars respecting that grand project in Bellary, at a height of 1,600 feet above the sea, to which allusion has already been made?—The proposal is to have a dam across the river in the Bellary district.

"Had you yourself fully surveyed and examined and completed that?—No, I had not completed it; it was never under me for completion.

"Will you have the kindness to tell us how much you had done?—I took the cross sections for the dam.

"Were you the originator of the project?—Yes, for that dam.

"I mean for the whole scheme of the reservoir?—No, Sir Arthur Cotton had proposed a scheme to take a channel out of the river by an ordinary anicut, and to irrigate a large area of Bellary, and to throw a quantity of water into the Pennar for the use of the Nellore district. In going over that project of Sir Arthur Cotton's, and taking the levels up and down the bed of the river, I came upon this site for a reservoir, where the natives had originally intended to build one; an earthwork is there to this day, and when I found this I took it up and proposed it; but as the money had been obtained for carrying on the Kurnool works, and water could be so readily supplied from it for the use of the Koondal valley and the Nellore district, Sir Arthur Cotton abandoned that project at Bellary and went to Kurnool."

Questioner: MR. JOHN CROSS.

"Then you would bank up 250 square miles of water, and with that 250 square miles of water you would propose, I think you said, to irrigate 1,000,000 acres?—One million in Bellary. My estimate for that was fifteen rupees, but more land could be irrigated in Bellary, but it would be very difficult to get at, so that I am afraid that that would raise the average cost of irrigation in Bellary to twenty or twenty-five rupees an acre.

"You say that you would irrigate 1,000,000 acres of land from this great tank; the tank would be 250 square miles; 1,000,000 acres represent, I think, about 1,700 square miles; you would, therefore, have eight miles of irrigated land for one mile of tank? —Yes.

"Is it possible that such a thing would pay at all?—The land pays you nothing now, absolutely nothing. These taluks in the Bellary districts, which would be submerged by this reservoir, have been now for nearly three years almost entirely supported by the Government; they are the most wretched parts of the country and the worst taluks in Bellary. The rains are constantly failing there, and, except a small strip of irrigation along the banks of the Tungabudra river, and one or two other jungle streams about there, they have nothing at all.

"In what period of time do you suppose this 1,000,000 acres would be irrigated from the time that you began the works?—I should think it would take five years to carry out the project to bring the water.

"Have you made any estimate of the cost?—I have made an estimate. This large dam with the head-works I estimate at thirty lakhs of rupees or £300,000; twenty-five miles of canal through the hill, fifty lakhs of rupees or £500,000; forty miles of canal to the Huggary river, including a large aqueduct, £200,000; one hundred and twenty miles of canal towards Kurnool, £150,000; eighty locks for navigation, etc., £200,000; compensation for land, etc., £50,000; minor distributaries, sundries, and supervision, £100,000. That makes a million and a half.

"And that would be in the hope of irrigating 1,000,000 acres?—Yes. I had eight years' constant experience of the Bellary district, being in charge of all the works there, and I never failed to get the water taken for any land which I proposed to irrigate, and which I showed our people could be irrigated. I never failed in one single instance to get the land taken up."

WIDESPREAD BENEFIT OF IRRIGATION.

Questioner: MR. SAMPSON LLOYD.

"So the benefit of these works, in your opinion, is not confined to the amount of direct revenue that it brings to the Government?—Certainly not.

"But it extends to the general comfort, health, and well-being of the people?—Yes, and the preservation of the people of the district.

"And the prevention of future famines?—Yes, and the prevention of famines. That has been a work which has been long under consideration.

"From your own personal knowledge, would you confirm the evidence of that witness,[1] that there is great difficulty in moving barges or boats against the current?—I am entirely against that view. I know that the Italian canals are navigated, although the current is of very much greater velocity than we are using now in the Godavari district. We have never given in our canals a greater slope than five feet a mile, and that is only for half a mile over a large aqueduct. That part is navigable, with difficulty, and I propose, in revising the estimates, to remedy that defect; but the slope that we, generally speaking, give, gives a velocity of under a mile an hour, which is perfectly easy for navigation.

"In fact, I gather from the whole of what you have said, that you consider the uses of irrigation, when properly constructed for navigation, to be most important to the well-being of the people?—I am perfectly certain of it. I can give one or two instances in point if you will allow me. A brother officer and myself had to cut two canals for Sir Arthur Cotton, in 1852, the Nursapur

---

[1] "A witness of great experience," not named, referred to in a previous question.

Canal and the Attaly Canal. The Nursapur Canal was made navigable throughout, and out of 40,000 acres of expected irrigation the people took up over 36,000. The Attaly Canal was simply cut as an irrigation channel, and therefore without any navigation works in it. The area expected to be irrigated by it was about 30,000 acres; but the people never took up more than 12,000 or 13,000 acres. In 1871, when I was carrying out the revised estimates for those works, I put locks into the Attaly Canal to make it navigable, and before we had got the foundations of the first lock in, the people applied for an increase of 10,000 acres of land for irrigation.

"So that as soon as they could get their produce to market by means of a navigable channel they took up more land?—Yes, they took 10,000 acres at once. The whole of the works for the completion of that canal cost £5,600, and £4,000 was returned for water-rate in the first year."

The whole of the preceding passages are taken from the Blue Book: "Report, East India (Public Works), ordered by the House of Commons to be printed, 1 August, 1878." No one, who desires to thoroughly understand the irrigation question, can afford to leave this volume unstudied; notwithstanding the strong bias of leading members of the Committee against irrigation, irrigation comes triumphantly out of the ordeal.

CHAPTER XII

The Cost of a Famine—In Lives and Money

IF, as some allege, and as this work endeavours to prove, famines in India are largely, if not wholly, preventible, it may be pertinent to enquire what is the cost in lives and money of an Indian famine, so as to ascertain whether it would not—to put the matter on the most material basis—be cheaper to provide remedies than to be content with administering relief. An absolutely accurate estimate is not possible, even of money loss. But, so full are the records of some recent famines in India, that a fair approximation of the cost may be made. This is not an idle enquiry. On it depends the material welfare of the people of India. If it be found that, even on a merely money basis, it would have been better to undertake public works which were sufficiently large to mitigate, if not to wholly prevent, famine, we may hope that, even now some steps will be taken towards seeing that this is done in the future.

Unhappily, a feeling prevails, particularly in official circles, that famine in India is to be accepted as an inevitable evil. "Famines," it seems to be argued, "will come, are coming nowadays with a frequency before unknown.[1] It is all very dreadful. But they are the act of God. All we can do, when they come, is to mitigate their consequences as far as may be." Passing by the obvious remark

[1] Sir George Campbell in 1878, and the Famine Commissioners in 1880, used language practically identical with this. The official remarks savour almost of fatalism.

that if famines are the act of God, His creatures, even though they be the rulers of India, ought not to be found fighting against His decrees, it must, in bare justice to the Government of India, be stated that during the past twenty years, they have done wonderfully well in their *treatment* of famine. They have acted in direct contradiction to their argument. They have devised a famine code which, as an attempt to grapple with all phases of relief, has probably never been surpassed in any department of government anywhere. Likewise—but, as I hold, and consider I prove in these pages—not at all wisely, so far as railways are concerned, money has been expended with a lavish hand in the construction of public works, which have always been put forward as means for the prevention of famine. Again, unhappily, the pity and the mischief of it all is, with the best intention in the world, the wrong thing has been done. Successive Governments in India may have desired to *prevent* famine: they must now recognise their efforts have wholly failed, for what they have done is simply to *relieve* the famine-stricken. So long as they can show, with more or less of accuracy, that enough food-grain is reaped year by year in the Empire to give an average of one and a quarter pounds of grain per head of population, per day, with a surplus for emergencies, and, on famine occurring, relieve the people—with their own money, obtained from general taxation—they appear to consider the utmost has been done which can be done. God sends famines; we will relieve all the sufferers we can, and keep everybody alive if that be possible. "We wish we could do more, but we must be content with saving life and preventing extreme suffering."[1]

The most astonishing feature in this distressful state of

[1] So said Lord Lytton and his colleagues, January, 1877. And yet, though it was at the same time laid down ". . . human life *shall* e saved at any cost and at any effort; no man, woman or child *shall* die of starvation," at least five millions in that very famine *did* die of starvation and diseases brought on by innutrition and want generally. The Indian authorities mean well; they go the wrong way to work.

affairs is the fact that the unavoidableness of famine is put forward without disguise. The late Sir James Caird and the Hon. H. E. Sullivan (of the Madras Civil Service) wrote a Minute of Protest against some of the conclusions of their colleagues on the Famine Commission of 1879–80. In paragraph 9, of their protest, they institute a comparison between the free black labourer in the Southern States of America and the Indian labourer. "The common price of grain," where the negro is employed, "is the same as that of the Indian labourer, namely, fifty lbs. to sixty lbs. per rupee." [1] But, the negro's "wages are eight times that of the Indian, two shillings to two and threepence against threepence per day, while the climate is much the same in its demands for clothing and shelter." The protesting Commissioners regard this as a fact of extreme gravity as illustrative of the poverty of the Indian cooly or field labourer. They urge this fact is "not to be met by resting satisfied that 'chronic famine is one of the diseases of the infancy of nations.'" For (they rightly proceed to remark), "India as a nation has long passed its 'infancy,' and the task of the British Government is, by fostering diversity of occupation, to guard it against decline." [2]

Here, a brief interruption of the argument must be accepted by the reader, so that note may be taken whether, now, in 1900, the price of food leaves the Indian labourer in as good a position as he was twenty years ago, when Sir James Caird and Mr. Sullivan made the above comparision. Not the least useful feature in the *Statistical Abstract for British India*, published annually, is the section devoted to Prices Current. Turn to the latest number, that for 1897–98, issued in the autumn of last year. Food prices are given for all parts of the Empire, ranging over the period from 1873 to 1897. The figures given represent number of pounds purchasable for one rupee. I take the first and last years for comparison, exactly as I find them,

[1] Pp. 66–67, *Famine Commission Report, 1880*, Part I.
[2] *Ibid.*, p. 67.

and work them out in English lbs., with a result as follows :—[1]

VARIOUS FOOD GRAINS.	1873.	1897.	
COMMON RICE.	lbs. per rupee.	lbs. per rupee.	FEWER LBS. per rupee in 1897.
Bengal (13 districts), average . .	43·25	19·49	23·76
North-West Provinces and Oudh (11)	28·57	17·40	11·17
Burma (3)	42·17	23·18	18·99
Punjab (6)	23·49	15·53	7·96
Central Provinces (3)	46·80	19·11	27·69
Madras (7)	36·28	20·27	16·01
Bombay and Sind (8)	23·81	15·97	7·84
Assam (4)	47·17	17·78	29·39
WHEAT.			
Bengal (14 districts), average . .	27·31	17·16	10·15
North-West Provinces and Oudh (11)	34·37	20·09	14·28
Punjab (6)	43·75	20·85	22·90
Central Provinces (3)	46·59	18·83[3]	27·76
Bombay (7)	27·91	15·16	12·75
BARLEY.[2]			
Bengal (5 districts), average . .	53·83	22·67	31·16
North-West Provinces and Oudh (10)	59·79	26·30	33·49
Punjab (6)	67·08	28·33	38·74
JOWAR (Great Millet).			
Bengal (2 districts), average . .	41·27	28·88	12·39
North-West Provinces and Oudh (11)	46·10	25·07	21·03
Punjab (6)	57·13	23·63	33·50
Central Provinces (3)	56·79	24·41	32·38
Madras (3)	46·97	28·92	18·05
Bombay and Sind (8)	47·19	22·00	27·19
BAJRA (Bulrush Millet).			
North-West Provinces and Oudh (11) average	40·52	24·83	15·69
Punjab (6)	54·38	20·38	34·00
Madras (4)	57·92	35·78	22·14
Bombay (7)	37·53	19·56	17·97
RAGI.			
Bengal (1 district), average . .	47·24	25·83	21·41
Madras (4)	67·84	32·13	35·71
Bombay (2)	33·09	27·63	5·46

[1] Calculated from particulars on pp. 316–328, *Stat. Abs.*, 1897–98.
[2] The earliest year given for barley is 1886, not 1873 as with others.
[3] There were times and places in the Central Provinces when

Apply Sir James Caird's test to the above figures, and it will be found that in no case is the Indian labourer now on an equal footing, or anything like an equal footing, as regards price of food with the negro labourer. He was twenty years ago. He is not now. On the contrary, in 1897, he got only twenty-one and a half lbs. of common rice for a rupee, instead of from fifty to sixty lbs.—a little more than one-third. Meanwhile there is nothing to show that his wages have increased in Bengal, while, in other Provinces and Presidencies, the increase shown in the accompanying table has in no way been in proportion to the rise in the price of food either for the labourer or for the artisan. And, it must not be overlooked, that, save in large towns, with the advent of high prices and scarcity, work for labourer or artisan almost entirely ceases. The negro artisan, further, certainly earns more than the negro labourer, with whom alone the comparison is made. The increased price, too, affects all classes of the community—not the labourer and artisan simply, whose wages alone are given.

Matters are even worse in regard to wheat. Of this food-stuff—not often consumed by the ordinary labourer—the average in 1897 was 19·69 lbs. per rupee, a big shrinkage by the side of the negro labourer's fifty to sixty lbs. and eight times higher wage.[1]

The commoner grains show a little better, but are woefully short of the fifty-five lbs. per rupee desiderated by Sir James Caird :—

---

nearly sixteen times as much food as is here represented could be obtained. "The price of wheat, rice, and grain (in 1828–29) rose at Bilaspur to 12 seers (25 lbs.) per rupee, and the effect of this rise on the condition of the poorer classes may be judged of from the fact that at that time prices in favourable years were, in Rajpur 400 seers (823 lbs.) to the rupee, while in Bilaspur 120 seers (247 lbs.) of rice and 180 seers (370 lbs.) of kodon had been procurable for a rupee."—Para. 221, p. 156, *Report on the Famine in Central Provinces*, by R. H. Cradock, I.C.S., vol. i. Nagpore, 1898.

[1] The figures for 1898 (available on Sept. 1st, 1900) are better, but only in a few cheap grains, such as barley and jowar, do the figures reach 50 lbs. per rupee. The year after, 1899, famine over a great part of India ran up prices again.

Grain.	Lbs. per rupee in 1897.	LBS. FEWER per rupee.
Barley	25·77	34·45
Jowar	25·49	24·09
Bajra	25·14	22·45
Ragi	28·53	20·86

It will be putting matters in a very moderate form if it be stated that, at the end of twenty-four years, judged by the figures given above, the condition of the negro labourer is not eight times better off than that of his compeer in India but twelve times, with this most important difference: the negro has always work if he cares to do it; the Indian has, in such times of high prices, none at all. Since 1897 there is not likely to have been much, if any, permanent improvement. When a cycle of years of comparative plenty comes again—as it certainly will—it may not be expected prices will drop to the old level. They will not. It is contrary to the nature of things prevailing in India that they should.

The following wages table may be usefully quoted here. (See page 406).

Even in 1879, when the position was much better than it is now, Messrs Caird and Sullivan said, of the Indian labourers: "Already their wages bear a less proportion to the price of food than in any country of which we have knowledge!" The proportion to-day is considerably less than it was then.

The argument interrupted on page 402 may now be resumed. It was broken off at the point where two of the Famine Commissioners protested against India being regarded as a nation in its "infancy," and that famine was a disease incidental to such callowness. With some Indian officials this would seem to be a favourite doctrine. Notwithstanding the manner in which the notion had been shown, by the Famine Commissioners named, to have no relevance, Lieut.-Col. Pitcher,[1] in a letter addressed to his official superiors, dated June 8th, 1888, refers "to the

[1] Officiating Director, Department of Land Records and Agriculture, North-West Provinces and Oudh.

MONTHLY WAGES RATE IN CERTAIN SELECTED STATIONS IN RUPEES, AND NEAREST DECIMALS.[1]

Station.	Able-bodied Agricultural Labourer.			Common Mason, Carpenter, or Blacksmith.		
	1873.	1897.	Increase (+) or Decrease (−) % approx.	1873.	1897.	Increase (+) or Decrease (−) % approx.
Calcutta	—	—	—	7·5 to 10	18 to 20	+140 to 100%
Patna	3 to 4	4 to 5	+33 to 20%	5·6 to 7·5	7 to 8	+25 to 7%
Rangpur	5·5	7.5	+36%	7·5 to 10	15 to 30	+100 to 200%
Backerganj	7·5	10 to 15	+33 to 100%	8 to 15	8 to 15	0
Cawnpore	—	4 to 5	—	7.5	7·5 to 9·4	0 to +25%
Fyzabad	4	1·9 to 4	−52% to 0	8	5·6 to 7·5	−30 to −6%
Meerut	4·5	4·5	0	9	10·5	+17%
Delhi	5·6	7·5	+34%	10	13·1	+31%
Amritsar	6	8	+33%	12·7	15	+18%
Rawalpindi	5·5	6·6	+20%	12	23·1	+92.5%
Karachi	10 to 15	12 to 15	+20% to 0	20 to 25	30 to 45	+50 to 80%
Belgaum	7·5	6	−20%	18·7 to 22·5	14	−33 to −61%
Ahmednagar	4·7	6	+27%	13·1 to 20·6	15 to 30	+14·5 to 46%
Bombay	9	11	+22%	25 to 50	27·5 to 42	+10% to −16%
Ahmadabad	6·1	7	+15%	19·7	22·5	+14%
Jubbulpore	4	3·5	−12·5%	15	10	−33%
Nagpur	5	5	0	12	15	+25%
Raipur	3	4	+33%	11	15	+36%
Bellary	4	6 25	+56%	15	18·75 to 20·6	+25 to 37%
Madras	6	6	0	14·1	13 to 16	−8% to +13%
Salem	2·5	3·8	+52%	13·5	12 to 12·7	−11% to −6%
Rangoon	12	15	+25%	40 to 45	45	+12·5 to 0
Toungoo	15	14	−7%	20	30	+50%

[1] Calculated from particulars on pp. 308–310, *Stat. Abs.*, 1897–98.

state of England in the fifteenth century" as "strangely resembling the state *from which India is gradually emerging.*" He then quotes a "recent writer" without naming him, as having said :—

"There is necessarily a sameness in the records of these pestilences, and this makes it wearisome to dwell upon the sufferings of the people throughout well-nigh the two centuries which lie between the death of Edward I. and the coming of Henry of Richmond. The history of the people of England cannot, however, be understood without dwelling upon the sad monotony of suffering."

"In the pages of the chroniclers we come upon the records of famine and the details of the pestilences which followed closely on the famine. There is hardly any period of five years during that time without these ghastly records." [1]

Colonel Pitcher has only to turn his observation quite round and strengthen it: then, in the light of existing facts, he will be correct. He should have written, "The state into which India is rapidly sinking." It is of common knowledge in India, that, be the reason what it may, the condition of the vast masses of the Indian people, save in the irrigated districts and those districts on the Western coasts and the major part of Bengal, where the rain is always in sufficient quantity, is going from bad to worse. The statistics given above bear mournful witness to this. Although this is not the place in which to argue in detail what, added to the need of further irrigation, is the real cause of the continually increasing distressed condition of India, as the question has been raised by Famine Commissioners and high officials, two brief quotations from Draper's *Intellectual Development of Europe*, relating to our own country at the time referred to by Colonel Pitcher, may be cited. They are as follows :—

[1] Chap. iv., *An Inquiry into the Economic Condition of the Agricultural and Labouring Classes in the North-Western Provinces and Oudh* (Government Printer, Allahabad, 1888), one of the most melancholy records which ever came from the printing press in any country.

"Through the operation of the Crusades all Europe was tributary to the Pope (Innocent III.). . . . There was a steady drain of money from every realm. Fifty years after the time of which we are speaking, Robert Grostête, the Bishop of Lincoln, and friend of Roger Bacon, caused to be ascertained the amount received by foreign ecclesiastics in England. He found it to be thrice the income of the king himself. This was on the occasion of Innocent IV. demanding provision to be made for three hundred additional Italian clergy by the Church of England; and that one of his nephews—a mere boy—should have a stall in Lincoln Cathedral." "In England—for ages a mine of wealth to Rome—the tendency of things was shown by such facts as the Remonstrances of the Commons with the Crown on the appointment of ecclesiastics to all the great offices, and the allegations made by the 'Good Parliament' as to the amount of money drawn by Rome from the kingdom. They asserted that it was five times as much as the taxes levied by the king, and that the Pope's revenue from England was greater than the revenue of any prince in Christendom." "The Parliamentary Bill of 1376 sets forth that the tax paid in England to the Pope for ecclesiastical dignities, is fourfold as much as that coming to the king from the whole realm, that alien clergy, who had never seen, nor cared to see, their flocks, convey away the treasure of the country." [1]

Our enquiry as to the cost of a famine may now be resumed. There appears to be material available for doing this, with any approach to accuracy, only in relation to the calamity which befell Southern India in 1876 to 1878. The famine of that time was regarded as the most widespread and terrible visitation which India had known. It has since been twice eclipsed,—in 1897 to 1898 and in 1899 to 1900.

[1] Draper's *Intellectual Development of Europe*, fifth edition, pp. 365, 397, and 434.

		£
1. Government Expenditure:—		
"The direct outlay on relief reached the sum of nearly"[1]		8,000,000
2. Loss of Land Revenue:—[2]		
1876	£90,000	
1877	1,300,000	
1878	1,130,000	
		2,520,000
3. Loss of Crops:—		
Assume the revenue taken by Government represents, as the Famine Commissioners, on p. 112, of Part II. of their Report say it does, one-sixteenth of the gross produce, the loss to the cultivators is £2,520,000 × 15[3]		37,800,000
4. Loss of Excise Revenue:—[4]		
1877	£76,000	
1878	163,000	
1879	46,000	
		285,000
5. Loss of Customs Revenues:—[5]		
1876	£13,000	
1877	74,000	
1878	118,000	
1879	114,000	
1880	88,000	
1881	72,000	
		479,000

---

[1] *Famine Commission Report*, Part I., 1880, p. 32, para. 96.

[2] P. 27, No. 14, *Statistical Abstract, British India.*

[3] I very much doubt whether this is not greatly overstated, but I take the figures as the Commissioners give them. And yet I find nearly the same proportion of tax to total produce is claimed in the Central Provinces. The land revenue demand "absorbs probably not more than about 6¼ per cent. (or one anna in the rupee) of the value of a normal out-turn." "The poorest parts of the Province . . . where distress has been most severe, pay either no revenue at all (save an insignificant quit rent) to Government . . . or a trifling rate (less than four annas per cultivated acre)." Para. 163, p. 115, *Report on the Famine in Central Provinces*, by R. H. Cradock, I.C.S., vol. i. Nagpore, Secretariat Press, 1898.

[4] No. 14, *Statistical Abstract, British India*, p. 29. [5] *Ibid.*, No. 16, p. 26.

6. Loss of Salt Revenue:—[1] £

		£
1877	£62,000	
1878	211,000	
		273,000

7. Country Silver and Silver Ornaments:—[2]

Bombay Mint returns, for years of the famine, show:—

Year.	Country Silver. Rs.	Silver Ornaments. Rs.	Total. Rs.
1877–78	—	1,24,00,000	1,24,00,000
1878–79	67,00,000	1,16,00,000	1,83,00,000
1879–80	45,00,000	92,00,000	1,37,00,000
	Rs. 1,12,00,000	Rs. 3,32,00,000	Rs. 4,44,00,000

Mr. Barclay said: "The quantity which reached the Mints must have been only a fraction of what was sold by the natives to the dealers." . . . "In the recent famine [1897–98], when the Mints were closed, the silver ornaments would only realise about fifty per cent. in rupees." Sir David Barbour testified: "The return from the Bombay Mint excludes gold; but we know that in the years of the great famine in Madras and Bombay, a large amount of gold was sent from India to England, and, I think, Sir H. Hay said he received a quantity of gold from India which was evidently composed of ornaments melted down."[3]

Take Mr. Barclay's "fraction" as representing only as much more as was actually minted, and Sir David Barbour's exported gold at one million sterling, the reserves drawn upon in Madras and elsewhere (needlessly drawn if only proper means had been adopted to prevent distress) was Rs. 4,44,00,000 × 2 = Rs. 8,88,00,000 @ 2*s.* per rupee = £8,880,000; gold, £1,000,000 . . . 9,880,000

---

[1] No. 16, *Statistical Abstract*, *British India*, p. 27.

[2] "East India Currency Enquiries: Official and other Figures submitted by Mr. Donald Graham, C.I.E., Appendix" [c. 7060–1], 1893, p. 304; also "Evidence of Sir David Barbour, K.C.S.I.," p. 305; and "Evidence of Robert Barclay," Ans. 11,612, Part II., 1899.

[3] "Some lakhs of savings were brought out in the famine of 1876–77; the goldsmith's melting-pots were going day and night for some months

The foregoing is not only of much interest but also of great importance in the light it throws on the "pinch" experienced by the well-to-do classes. The five millions and more who perished in the Madras Presidency, and the millions who were on relief works, or in receipt of charitable relief, would not, I estimate, contribute, Rs. 200,000 towards the Rs. 4,44,00,000 worth of ornaments which disappeared in the melting pot at the Mint. No; all this came from the better-off people, drawn from them by the high price of food. As prices now are always at what used to be considered famine prices, it may be realised how impossible it is for wealth to be accumulated by any class in India.

8. INCREASED PRICE OF FOOD:—

The Famine Commission of 1880 estimated the value of food at £5 per ton. In Madras, during the famine, the Duke of Buckingham and Chandos, the Governor, stated[1] that "two-thirds ot the Presidency were suffering from the high price of food." Two-thirds of the Presidency would be twenty millions of people. Say, they endured these high prices for six months only (an under-estimate), and that the price of food was doubled, £10 per ton, though, as a matter of fact, the price was much more than doubled.[2] The Commissioners considered eight millions of tons per annum were consumed in Madras: take half of that for six months at £5 additional cost,

---

and the Mint Returns alone will show what the accumulation of precious metals in the famine districts must have amounted to."—Hon. J. B. RICHEY, C.S.I., Aug. 15, 1888.

[1] Speech at Famine Relief Meeting held in Madras on August 4th, 1877.

[2] Under normal circumstances at that time one anna would buy i Southern India nearly two lbs. of grain; in August, 1877, it would not purchase more than one-half pound, nor even that quantity. Rice, in ordinary seasons sold at the rate of ten measures per rupee; in the last week of July it was quoted at three or four measures, which was as if the quartern loaf in England, instead of being sixpence, was nearly four times that amount. In merely doubling the price of grain, therefore, the estimate is a moderate one. See *Famine Campaign in Southern India*, 1877–79, vol. i., *passim*.

and the increased price of food represented, 4,000,000 tons × £5 = £20,000,000 : take off one-third, to come into accord with the Duke's (under) statement, and the amount to be brought out is, say . . . . £ 13,000,000

9. Loss of Cattle, Houses, Agricultural Implements, etc. :—

Roughly, in normal years, there are, in the Madras Presidency :—

14,000,000	cattle
8,000,000	sheep
5,000,000	goats
40,000	horses and ponies
100,000	mules and donkeys
Total . . 27,140,000[1]	

Sir Richard Temple, Famine Delegate, in one of his reports, stated "the country was almost entirely bare of all crop or stubble, and there was no sign of fodder or grass." Before the end of December, 1876, in the Bellary district, "one-fourth of the cattle were said to have died, and it was thought more than half would perish before June unless heavy showers fell in January,"[2] but the showers did not fall; "cattle dying for want of fodder" was a frequent item in District Reports. In Bombay careful statements were prepared, such as these :—

Sholapur :—

Cattle before famine	224,599
Cattle in August, 1877	97,167
Loss . .	127,432

"Of these only 44,000 were considered fit for agricultural purposes" :

Madhee and Mohul Taluk :—

Cattle before famine	16,591
Cattle in August, 1877	5,470
Loss . .	11,121

Indee Taluk :—

Cattle before famine	35,747
Cattle in August, 1877	5,644
Loss . .	30,103[3]

[1] *Agricultural Statistics for British India for* 1888–89, p. 229.

[2] P. 56, *Famine Campaign*, vol. i.

[3] *Ibid.*, pp. 364–366.

	£
In view of all this it will not be going too far to assume that one-fourth of the live-stock in the Madras Presidency perished. One-fourth of 27,140,000=6,785,000; taken all round at Rs. 7 each: 6,785,000 × 7 = Rs. 47,495,000, or, at Rs. 10 to the £[1]	4,749,500

10. LOSS OF WAGES:—

Say, 5,000,000 labourers, without work for nine months at Rs. 5·5 per month[2] (the famine extended from the Autumn of 1876 to September, 1877, and much longer in some parts)—5,000,000 × Rs. 5·5 = Rs. 27,500,000: at Rs. 10 to the £ .	2,750,000

11. LOSS OF CAPITAL BY AGRICULTURISTS AND INTEREST BY MONEY-LENDERS AND OTHERS:—

". . . about one-third of the land-holding classes are deeply and inextricably in debt, and at least an equal proportion in debt though not beyond the power of recovering themselves.'[3] The census of 1881[4] gives 6¾ millions of agriculturalists in Madras: say two millions[5] of these indebted at least Rs. 50 each = Rs. 100,000,000; of these assume twenty per cent. lost through the famine Rs. 20,000,000, at Rs. 10 to the £ .	2,000,000

12. LOSS OF PROFIT BY MERCHANTS, TRADERS, ETC., BY DIMINUTION OF BUSINESS:—

This can be no more than a guess, and, unsupported by any authority, my guess must be taken for what it is worth. Considering, however, the great contraction of business throughout the whole Presidency, Rs. 10,000,000 to Rs. 15,000,000 might

[1] It will be seen I have not taken into consideration anything for ruined Houses, loss or sale of Agricultural Implements, etc.; if included, they would make an appreciable difference. Their omission may be covered by any slight excess in what I have estimated.

[2] P. 310, *Statistical Abstract*, 1897–98.

[3] P. 131, *Famine Commission Report*, 1880, Part II.

[4] P. 351, *Census Report*, vol. i.

[5] In all India there were 29,207,150 "Tenant Cultivators"; as a ryotwarry (or peasant-cultivating) province, Madras would have a large proportion of these.

	£
be fairly reckoned, say the smaller sum at Rs. 10 to the £.	1,000,000
Total ascertained and estimated cost of the Madras Famine	**£82,736,500**
Say, *in money*	**£82,000,000**

and THE LIVES OF FIVE MILLIONS OF HUMAN BEINGS.

Who can estimate, in pounds, shillings, and pence, what this terrible loss in lives means!

To the period embraced by the Madras famine the whole expenditure for all India on account of irrigation works was £20,298,000; of this sum £12,769,800 was capital expenditure, and £7,619,000 from current revenue. The accounts for this period, as presented, are somewhat confusing, but it would seem that the capital expenditure in Madras for the twelve years ending 31st March, 1879, was £753,730 only.[1] In 1877 it was £28,589; in 1878, £32,616; in 1879, £19,047. During that same period in the remaining provinces the expenditure was:—

Bengal	£4,741,208
North-West Provinces	2,849,429
Punjab	1,965,752
Bombay	923,446
Rajputana	18,696
Total	£10,498,531

And these were the years in which Sir Arthur Cotton was making his most strenuous endeavours in England to procure adequate irrigation in Madras! It is absolutely safe to say that if, from 1860, when he had to retire from the Service, Sir Arthur Cotton had been retained and had had the £30,000 a year which he desired for expenditure on irrigation works in each of the twenty districts in the Madras Presidency for the succeeding seventeen years,—£10,200,000 in all,—there would have been no famine in Madras in the years 1876 to 1879. More than that: instead

[1] P. 117, *Statistical Abstract*, No. 14.

of a loss to Government and people of seventy millions sterling, so great would have been the gain to both that, probably, a net advantage of two hundred millions would have accrued. There would not have been a broken sluice, a damaged bund, or an empty tank among the sixty thousand in the Presidency; navigation canals would have been constructed in many directions, and storage tanks to keep all channels at a high level would have been provided. The Godavari river would have maintained a large fleet of passenger and cargo steamers, and the Central Provinces, too, would have been saved from three famines. But Sir Arthur Cotton, as John Bright reminds us, was an "enthusiast"[1] in a cause which only enthusiasm *could* lift over all the difficulties in its path.

> Now there was in that country a poor wise man who would have delivered the country from its evils, yet few gave heed unto him, and wisdom was not justified of her son.

---

[1] "They say that Sir Arthur Cotton is an enthusiast. Well, we all have been enthusiasts in our time; it would be a dull world if there were no real and honest enthusiasm in it. But, Sir Arthur Cotton is not surpassed by any man in the Indian service for long experience and for great success in the works with which he has been connected, and which he has undertaken. He has broader and grander views han some of his competitors, or some of his fellow-officers, or those connected with the Government. But he knows that this is a great question, that India is a great country, that two hundred and fifty millions ot people are a great people, and therefore he thinks that a broader and a grander policy is necessary on this occasion."—JOHN BRIGHT, *Speech at Manchester*, December 11, 1877.

Appendix

WHAT THE 1900 FAMINE IS COSTING PEOPLE AND COUNTRY.

Let me turn aside for a moment from the contemplation of the famine in Marwar as it exists to-day, and endeavour to show how deep, how abiding, how slowly effaced are the effects of such an awful drought as that from which Rajputana is now suffering. It was an evil day for India when some secretariat official, whose purview was limited to revenue returns and balance sheets, invented those misleading phrases: "the marvellous recuperative power of the Indian people," "the gratifying elasticity of Indian revenues." The cry has been taken up by every machine politician from Land's End to John O'Groat's, until the impression is general in Great Britain that it needs only a single good year to bring prosperity and contentment to famine-stricken India, and wipe out the influence of widespread crop-failure. A passing acquaintance with any famine area will show how entirely the contrary is the case. Take, for instance, the State of Marwar. It is a comparatively poor country, with a small population scattered over a wide area. The State revenue is derived chiefly from the land tax, and a small toll upon sheep, goats, and buffaloes. This year the whole of the land revenue was remitted, and the mortality amongst the live stock so great, that little was gathered under the second head. A debt of £240,000 was incurred with the Government of India, money was borrowed from other sources where possible, and even the State jewels have been pledged to meet the current expenses of the Maharajah's household. The State will emerge from the crisis saddled with an enormous load of debt, and with the certainty of diminished revenues for at least a decade. Ten years ago the buffaloes, cows, and bullocks in the State were numbered at 1,223,670; of these not five per cent. remain. The camels, sheep, and goats, have stood the strain better. "Unth chodio akro, bakri chodio kakro," ("The camel will eat anything but the ak bush, the goat anything but stones,") runs the Marwari proverb, but even the camels and the goats have been decimated. The principal fount of material wealth has dried up. For years, instead of being a great cattle-exporting territory, Marwar will have to import to repair this terrible wastage. A million sterling might be beneficially expended in relieving the distressed pastoralists in this State alone, and still the havoc would not be made good. The plough bullocks, too, have been swept away. Truly the native says, "My bullock is my life"; with no oxen to yoke to plough and ramp and harrow, much good land will lie fallow at the next sowing, and tens of thousands of acres uncropped at the next harvest. As far as possible camels will be substituted for draught cattle, and light agricultural implements will be introduced suitable for manual labour; but, under the most favourable conditions, not more than one-half the culturable area will be sown this year. I might multiply indefinitely the directions in which famine on a grand scale presses sorely upon this brave people; at least a generation will elapse before its baneful influence is eradicated.—Special Correspondent in India, *Daily Chronicle*, July 2, 1900.

CHAPTER XIII

Is Famine in India due to an Insufficiency of Rain ?

NINETY-FIVE years ago the great Duke of Wellington, then serving in India, urged that there were but two ways of meeting famines. These were:—

(1) By making the more fortunate parts of the community supply the wants of the rest, and the superfluity of one year making good the deficiency of another.

(2) By making as much of the country as is liable to famine by drought safe by an extension of irrigation.

In theory, we have got no farther than the Wellesley of 1805; in practice, the way—a needlessly burdensome, costly, way, for the expense of doing what is necessary will be much greater to-day—is now open to an Administration which will take the trouble to inquire what can be done.

There can be no greater fallacy than that which finds expression in such remarks as that: "God has shut the heavens"—therefore famine prevails: "There has been a rain failure, more or less partial, therefore famine is in our midst." As a fact, not one of the three elements which nature provides in India for the growth of human food ever fails:—

The sun, day by day, never withholds its vivifying power.

The soil remains.

The rain, every year, comes in sufficient quantity to supply the requisite moisture for the necessary crops.

We cannot control the sun or the soil, therefore we do not blame God in connection with either or both, if one should be clouded for a while and the other prove sterile. With the rain it is otherwise. We are too heedless to conserve it when it does fall. Then, when, in accordance with physical laws which, at present, we imperfectly apprehend or do not at all apprehend, the rain falls not exactly to suit agricultural needs, we put the blame upon God, when, instead, we should have built a reservoir. It is the essence of natural law that there should be fluctuations arising out of what science teaches to be the foundation of physical life-motion: with motion and the action and interaction of forces come fluctuations (as we call them), but really movements as regular and as certain as ocean tides, did we but know enough to search them out. Some day we shall. These are owing to the prevalence or absence of sun-spots, variations in temperature, maybe perturbations arising out of the movements of our earth in its orbit. But there is never less moisture or warmth than is needed to ensure seed time and harvest, if only we could learn how to employ all the elements placed at our service to ensure sowing and reaping.

There is nothing the matter with God's world, nothing wrong with that part of it which is called India. There is grievous fault, but it lies at the door of those who, claiming Heaven's light their guide,[1] are content to grope in the darkness and are heedless of the light.[2]

[1] Motto of the Most Illustrious Order of the Star of India.

[2] The late Colonel Chesney, R.E., sometime Conservative M.P. for Oxford, one of the most distinguished of Indian officials, in an article in the *Fortnightly Review*, in 1877, declared that irrigation works which were undertaken by the Indian authorities were extorted from them by famine suffering. He proceeded to say that the Indian Government was very like a father who spends a great deal on the doctor or the nurse if his child is ill and ready to die, but in ordinary times does not take the smallest care of him whatever, or teach him anything with regard to the preservation of his own health. Colonel Chesney, it may be remarked, because of certain detail criticisms, was officially quoted as an authority in opposition to irrigation!

Is it, a reader may, with wonder, ask, really true that always enough rain falls to sufficiently moisten the soil of India, and produce food for man and beast?

"To the law and to the testimony" for the reply to this question.

Twenty-two years ago, the Meteorological Reporter to the Government of India prepared a statement,[1] based on the observations made over a series of years at two hundred and eighty-nine stations scattered throughout the empire. This statement proved that, *on the average*, there is no single month in the year in which some rain does not fall, even though the quantity be as low as 0·02 in Pegu, Upper Burma, in January. The total average annual fall ranges from 251·80 in. at Tsawia, in the Konkan and Ghâts (Bombay), to 4·28 in. in Sind and Cutch—Jacobabad the station. The highest and lowest are, singularly enough, in the same presidency. A summary of the chief table presented by Mr. Blandford, the reporter, cannot fail to interest. It is as shown in the table on the opposite page.

Those are the averages, what are the actuals? Records exist, which may be depended upon, from the following periods:—

Place.	From.
Madras	1813
Bombay	1817
Calcutta	1829
Bangalore	1837
Mysore	1837
Nagpore	1826–32 1855
Jubbulpore	1845

Here are seven fairly representative stations of the whole of India, save the far north, which did not come under our control until nearly half the century had passed, and the North-West Provinces, unaccountably omitted.[2] The table before me takes the figures to 1876, sixty-four years so far as Madras is concerned, sixty in relation to Bombay: in any case a sufficiently long period on which to base trust-

[1] pp. 8–11, *Famine Report*, 1881, Appendix 1. [2] *Ibid.*, p. 10.

TABLE OF AVERAGE RAINFALL IN DIFFERENT PARTS OF INDIA.

DISTRICT OF LOCALITY.	No. of Stations.	Annual Rainfall.
1. Western Himalaya (Punjab and N. W. Provinces)	8	65·07
2. Punjab Plains (Punjab)	29	21·98
3. Upper Gangetic Plains (N.-W. Provinces and Bengal)	50	38·00
4. Eastern Himalaya (Bengal)	4	144·49
5. Lower Gangetic Plains (Bengal)	22	67·20
6. Assam and Eastern Bengal (Assam and Bengal)	16	96·47
7. Western Bengal (Bengal)	10	55·92
8. Central India and Nerbudda (India [1] and Central Provinces)	12	44·30
9. Rajputana and Guzerat (India [1] and Bombay)	16	32·24
10. Sind and Cutch (Bombay)	10	8·79
11. Khandeish and Berar (Bombay and India [1])	7	29·21
12. Central Provinces (South) (Central Provinces)	15	49·09
13. North Deccan Plateaux (Bombay)	13	28·09
14. Hyderabad and South Deccan (India [1] and Madras)	5	25·50
15. Konkan and Ghâts (Bombay)	12	145·20
16. Malabar and Ghâts (Madras)	7	111·77
17. Carnatic (Madras)	28	33·88
18. Northern Circars (Madras)	10	36·16
19. Aralam (British Burma)	3	192·85
20. Pegu	6	76·36
21. Tenasserim	4	173 37
22. Bay Islands	2	108·41

worthy conclusions. From the figures the following facts are garnered :—

MADRAS :—

In sixty-four years the annual fall fluctuated between 88·41 inches in 1827 and 18·45 inches in 1832. The year *preceding* the lowest fall had 44·35 inches ; the year *after* 37·11 inches.

---

[1] In official publications, when allusion is made to Administrations, the word "India" means that the place indicated is under the direct control of the Viceroy and his Executive Council, through the Foreign Office, of which the Viceroy generally takes personal charge.

BOMBAY :—

Sixty years : Highest, 121·98 inches in 1828.
Lowest, 33·87[1] inches in 1824.
Year preceding, 61·70 inches.
Year following, 72·24 inches.

CALCUTTA :—

Forty-eight years : Highest, 91·49 inches in 1868.
Lowest, 43·61 inches in 1837.
Year preceding, 45·66 inches.
Year following, 52·99 inches.

BANGALORE :—

Thirty-nine years : Highest, 63·99 inches in 1867.
Lowest, 16·00 inches in 1838.
Year preceding, 44·30 inches.
Year following, 32·40 inches.

MYSORE :—

Thirty-nine years : Highest, 52·80 inches in 1852.
Lowest, 15·80 inches in 1840.
Year preceding, [no record].
Year following, 33·10 inches.

NAGPORE :—

Twenty-nine years : Highest, 65·31 inches in 1831.
Lowest, 25·49 inches in 1868.
Year preceding, 57·75 inches.
Year following, 33·38 inches.

JUBBULPORE :—

Thirty-two years : Highest, 77·78 inches in 1850.
Lowest, 35·12 inches in 1848.
Year preceding, 44·96 inches.
Year following, 46·92 inches.

It appears almost impossible to over-rate the significance of these figures. They make this, at least, clear, that, given a sufficiency of storage, and this, Sir Arthur Cotton confidently asserted, again and again, is possible almost everywhere in India, there might always have been enough water for the preservation of a certain proportion of crop, enough to maintain the people in their homes and their villages.

[1] In spite of this phenomenally slight fall (it was never again so low, 40·58 inches, no famine, being the nearest), the official records say, "Scarcity, nowhere amounting to famine."

Another feature, in connection with famine as affected by rainfall, which Sir Arthur never tired of mentioning, was that, often-times years of greatest distress were years of considerable rainfall. Frequently the rain came too early. If it were stored that did not matter much; as frequently, perhaps, it came after sowing-time. That, apparently, was fatal for the usual crops, but with the kindly sun ever at hand, in the greater part of India, some crop or other could be obtained. Further, a second crop is nearly always possible. On this point his observations seem to me to be most pertinent. He writes:—

"It will be well, perhaps, to remark on some mistakes which are almost universal on this subject. The first is that, if a tract of land has plenty of rain, there is no necessity for irrigation. . . . No quantity of rain will prevent a famine unless it is tolerably distributed. The fact is, that water from irrigation is required in almost every part of India, even to prevent famine. But, further, there is never a season when, at some time or other, additional water would not improve the crop. Again, when we say 'irrigation,' we always mean the complete regulation of the water, that is, including draining; so there is never a season when there is not, at some moment, excess of rain, which requires to be carried off by a system of drains. It is this REGULATION OF WATER that is needed, and which so abundantly repays the cost of works. God gives us rain, but, as in everything else, He leaves something for us to do, which, if we are too indolent to do, we must suffer for it."

It may be well to show, by a reference to the figures analysed above, what the actual rainfall was, in some instances, in the years when famine prevailed.

Place.	Famine Year.	Rainfall in inches.
Madras	1823-24	26·62 33·72
Bombay	1824-25	33·87 72·24
North-West Provinces	1825	*
Madras	1833-34	37·11 39·00
Bombay	1833	71·39
Upper India	1833	*
Madras	1854	43·20
North-West Provinces and Punjab . .	1860-61	*
Orissa	1865-66	60·00
North Bengal	1865-66	*
Madras	1865-66	41·64 51·39
Northern India	1868-69	*
Central Provinces	1868-69	25·49[1] 33·38
Bombay	1868-69	62·12 91·66
Bengal	1873-74	*
North-West Provinces and Oudh . .	1873-74	*
Bombay	1876-77	50·01[2]
North-West Provinces and Oudh . .	1877-78	*
Madras	1876-78	21·6[3] 66·3 28·7
Mysore	1876-78	22·02[4]

* No record.

[1] For Jubbulpore, another recording station in the Central Provinces, the figures are 28·80 and 62·77 respectively.

[2] 1876 only, 1877 not given.

[3] "Notes of Evidence, Famine Commission, Jan. 30, 1879," by Norman R. Pogson, C.I.E. In those notes Mr. Pogson makes the following most serious statement :—" In my Administration Report to the Madras Government for 1874-75, I made the following remark: 'Five consecutive years of excess having now been experienced, the evident periodicity of tropical rainfall renders it probable that some years of corresponding deficiency may be expected.' This since fully verified prediction, though duly printed in the spare copies of my Report, was suppressed by the compiler of the Annual Volume of Administration Reports for 1874-1875. It is to be regretted that suppressions in and alterations of the Observatory Reports are ever permitted without the Astronomer being allowed a voice in the matter.'

[4] 1876 only, latest year recorded in tables.

The official observations[1] in Madras on the year 1877 were to the effect that the rainfall was remarkable more for its distribution than for actual deficiency. "Taking the mean readings of the two hundred and twenty-eight registering stations under the charge of revenue and other officials, the following were the results :—

Mean of five years ending			1874, 47·87	inches on	62	days.
"	"	"	1875, 37·26	"	·56	"
"	"	"	1876, 27·81	"	42	"
"	"	"	1877, 47·95	"	65	"

In eleven of the revenue districts, namely :—

Bellary	Madura	Tanjore
Coimbatore	Malabar	Tinnevelly
Kistna	Salem	Trichinopoly
Madras	South Arcot	

the total rainfall in 1877 was equal to the average, and, in some cases, very much in excess ; in the other nine districts, namely, in :—

South Canara	Ganjam	Nellore
Chingleput	Godavari	North Arcot and
Cuddapah	Kurnool	Vizagapatam

the aggregate rainfall in 1877 was deficient in comparison with the mean results of the five years ending 1874."

In view of the present famine (1900), and because of its bearing on the storage of rainfall, and the control of river and rain water as a preventive of famine, the following table from Mr. Blandford's Meteorological Report for 1898–99[2] is both interesting and instructive :—

[1] *Madras Administration Report*, 1877–78, p. 40. These figures do not agree with those in the *Famine Commission Report*. Both are official publications, and I quote from each as it stands.

[2] Page 31.

RAINFALL OF SEASON, JUNE TO OCTOBER.

PROVINCE.	Average Actual, 1898.	Average Normal.	Variation from Normal.	Percentage Variation from Normal.
	Inches.	Inches.	Inches.	
Burma	97·60	93·84	+ 3·76	+ 4
Assam	72·75	73·26	− 0·51	− 1
Bengal	68·19	59·84	+ 8·35	+14
Chota Nagpore . .	52·52	47·49	+ 5·03	+11
Bihar	52·49	43·50	+ 8·99	+21
N.-W. Prov. and Oudh	41·75	34·70	+ 7·05	+20
Punjab	12·85	15·15	− 2·30	−15
Central Provinces .	45·61	45·80	− 0·19	0
Central India . .	36·70	40·95	− 4·25	−10
Rajputana	12·16	18·66	− 6·50	−35
Berar	26·31	37·48	−11·17	−30
Bombay	41·59	41·27	+ 0·32	+ 1
Madras	34·84	34·20	+ 0·64	+ 2

The need for water storage is specially shown by the records extant for the district of North Arcot for a period of sixty-eight years. Details which I have examined indicate that during this time there were:—

31 years *below* the average, years in which the rains were deficient or fell at wrong periods.
29 years *above* the average, and fairly prosperous.
8 years which may be denominated medium.

Total 68 years.

The ominous words: "famine," "scarcity," "distress," "lengthened distress," occur many times during this period. With a sufficiency of irrigation channels, and storage to keep the tanks and channels filled, the North Arcot district might have been continuously prosperous.

With such facts on record in official publications, I ask once more, in Sir Arthur's oft-expressed ideas: "Why blame Almighty God for the famines, declaring they occur because He does not send rain, when, as a matter of fact, He does send rain enough for all our needs, but we are too careless to store it against the day of need?"

"Why should the water of any manageable river waste itself in the sea?"[1]

APPENDIX

Through the Famine Districts

IN THE PUNJAB—WHAT IRRIGATION HAS DONE

(*From the Special Correspondent of the "Manchester Guardian,"* May 30, 1900)

HISSAR, PUNJAB.

"Now I have given the darkar [district] of Hissar," so ran a proclamation of Akbar Shah Badshah in 1568, "to the great, the fortunate, the obedient, the pearl of the sea of my kingdom, the star of my Government, the praised of the inhabitants of the sea and land, the apple of my kingdom's eye, my son Sultan Muhamed Salim Bahadur (may God grant him long life and greatness). My wisdom wishes that the hopes, like the fields of those thirsty people, may by the showers of liberality and kindness be made green and flourishing, and that the canal may in my time be renewed, and that other waters may be conducted into it, that thus it may endure for ages. For God has said, From

---

[1] Sir Monier Williams, K.C.I.E., in a letter to *The Times* of Nov. 7, 1877, said: "In other directions we might do more. For example, we might carry on a more systematic defensive warfare against drought and famine by the storage of water in tanks, and its distribution for irrigation. India is blest with abundant rivers. Why are not more aqueducts, canals, and reservoirs made? Why should the water of any manageable river waste itself in the sea?" Sir Monier had shortly before visited India, and, in *The Times*, had placed on record how greatly he had been struck with the advantages of irrigation. "All the belts of land," he remarked, "reached by the grand system of irrigation, which stretches between the Godavari, Kistna, and Cauveri rivers, . . . present a marvellous contrast to the immense tracts of arid waste which meet the eye of the traveller as he travels by the Great Indian Peninsular, the Madras, and the Southern India railways."

water all things were made. Therefore I ordain that this jungle, in which subsistence is obtained with thirst, be converted into a place of comfort, free from all evil." The edict went on to say that the canal was to be "excavated deeper and wider than formerly," and that "on both sides of the canal down to Hissar trees of every description, both for shade and blossom, be planted, so as to make it like the canal under the Tree in Paradise."

The pearl of the sea must have done his work faithfully, for the banks of his canal are shaded with all manner of trees up to and through Hissar, and there is water enough for a good belt of fields on each side, the crops of which were glistening in the sun as I rode along the bank this morning. The oriental fervour of this strange old utterance seems nothing more than natural after a thousand miles of wilderness and the extermination of all agriculture. To see groups of people in the fields again, to see things growing, oxen standing in the shade, squares of land glistening under the film of water from the canal, and, climax of all, a big company of men and women threshing the yellow wheat, is a wonderful thing. But this "place of comfort, free from all evil," is, after all, a narrow strip running through a great waste of wicked desert; and out in the desert, in which their fields have disappeared, the people of Hissar, in numbers that range from a hundred to a hundred and sixty thousand, according to the work to be got elsewhere, are digging tanks and living in famine camps. Numbers of villages are absolutely deserted, and for more than six months past the worst famine within human memory has had its grip on Hissar.

SCARCITY OF FOOD AND FODDER.

The scarcity of food is worst in this southern corner of the Punjab, a corner about as large as Yorkshire; but the fodder famine throughout the whole province has reached a point of such intensity that the Lieutenant-Governor has just declared that, in spite of all the efforts of the local government and the Government of India, it is impossible to secure supplies for keeping life even in the indispensable plough cattle. Thanks to the supplies of fodder from the Chenab and other canals, the calamity has been put off for months, and it is hard, indeed, that this great province should have to look on now while its cattle are dying by hundreds of thousands, as they died last year in Rajputana and Gujerat. It becomes more and more difficult to see how the cultivators of the stricken districts are to get back to work again, in the face of this measureless destruction of their cattle. Even the beasts on the great Government cattle farm, which covers an area of sixty square miles, are in a half-starved state, and it is lamentable to see them roaming about in their vain search for food. The question is forced upon one again whether some system of Government fodder storage or the provision of local ensilage depôts ought not to be energetically taken in hand when once the Government have time to look round. It is rather surprising to find so little attention being paid to this matter. Again and again the peasantry have been stripped bare of their capital, and nothing has been done to provide against future calamities. India has an enormous Forest Department, and it ought surely to be able to take steps for keeping, say, ten per cent. of its live stock from death by famine.

"WHAT ABOUT CANALS?"

"But what about canals?" the reader who has studied irrigation will ask. "Is not the Punjab the classic ground for irrigation?" The answer is that the situation would be far worse—and that hardly puts it strongly enough—but for the magnificent system of artificial watering begun by the old rulers of India and continued, up to a point, by us. Let me deal with the matter more in detail. The total area of crops matured in the Punjab during the year ending September, 1899, was 20,738,687 acres, and of this area 8,967,391 acres, giving a yield of forty-three per cent. of the crops of the year, were cultivated by irrigation. The chief forms of irrigation are—(1) the canal which draws its water all the year round from one of the snow-fed rivers of the Himalayas and spreads them over a great tract of country by a system of minor canals and ducts; (2) the inundation canal, fed by cuts in the river banks through which the waters find an exit in times of flood; and (3) the irrigation wells. The immense importance of the well in Indian agriculture will be seen from these two facts—that during the past ten years more than sixteen thousand new masonry wells have been sunk in the Punjab, to say nothing of the simple pit or cutcha well, and that close on four millions out of the nine millions of irrigated acres were watered by the well. The inundation canals, owing to want of flood-water, did badly, and a decrease of half a million acres of watered lands from the previous year must be set down to their account.

SLOW PROGRESS "NOTHING LESS THAN A TRAGEDY."

Of the great and constant-flowing canals, whose shaded banks are the pleasantest refuges the plains can offer you in the hot weather, it can only be said that they have done so magnificently well that the failure to extend them faster is nothing less than a tragedy. I say nothing at the moment of their financial success, except that they are by far the best investment that the Government of India have ever made. They have largely extended the cultivation of new crops such as rice and sugar, they have given India a permanent granary, and they have opened up huge tracts of desert country to cultivation, relieving the congested districts in the process. This is an old story, no doubt, but the man who comes back from a camel-ride through a once-cultivated desert by way of Sultan Salim's water of Paradise sees more in a canal than the "moral and material progress" Blue-books disclose to him at home.

Take the Chenab canal, the latest big scheme which the Government of India have carried through, and consider its effect, direct and indirect, upon the local famine districts—the rainless corner of Hissar and the half-dozen other districts of the Punjab less severely hit by the food famine than Hissar, but still pretty badly touched. Now the Chenab has opened or is opening up four million acres of pure desert, it has given any quantity of employment to the distressed people during the famine, it looked as if it was going to save the cattle out of its supplies of fodder, and it will certainly give to the Punjab a new productive colony of a quarter of a million or so of workers and their families, all of them carefully selected from the congested districts. That is an achievement of which the proudest Government can afford to be proud, and Colonel Ottley, the master mind of the Chenab, who has gone home to irrigate the minds of the young men at Cooper's Hill, will be glad to know that, in the opinion of a high official of the Government, "the Chenab has largely saved the situation in the Punjab."

THE "EXCESSIVE DELIBERATION" OF GOVERNMENT.

In face of all this, the excessive deliberation with which the Government set about realising the rest of the approved canal schemes is simply mysterious. The Jhelum project was fully authorised in 1888, but nobody seems to quite know when it will be ready to hold water. Then, after the Jhelum, there is the

Sind-Sagar project for spreading Indus waters over another enormous stretch of desert, and there are some enthusiasts who hold the belief that about 1920 there may be a chance for the Montgomery project—a scheme which might have been half put through by this time if the Government had allowed a Company to carry out the work. Some addition is being made this year to the pittance which the Government annually devote to irrigation, but the Punjab presents an irresistible case for large and adequate treatment. A forward policy means, of course, more men and bigger establishments; but then so does a famine. And, for the rest, if the approved schemes are all finished in a dozen years instead of fifty there will still be plenty of work for the engineering staff, even supposing that India is by that time surfeited with canals.

NOT HOPEFUL OF LARGE EXTENSIONS.

To come back to Hissar, I must confess that opinions gathered here and in other parts of the Punjab are not at all hopeful about any extensive scheme of irrigation being possible for this district, and in these matters one is necessarily in the hands of the experts. But, at the worst, a large canal policy would give permanent openings to many people in this famine-haunted region, and abundance of work, at least for a generation, to emigrants during times of famine. The drop of numbers on the relief works from 160,000 to 110,000 is due, so I am told, to the people going off harvesting in the irrigated regions.

MINOR TANKS FOR GROUPS OF VILLAGES.

It is at least satisfactory, too, to know that every stroke of famine labour is making in the direction of more water storage. I visited with Mr. Humphreys, the Deputy Commissioner who is "running the famine," two of the tanks which are being dug out for the future use of groups of villages. A large number of these tanks are being made, and it is work of which the people well know the value. There is no complaint whatever of skulking. The day's work for the gang is marked out, and it is generally done within the day. A leading principle of Major Dunlop-Smith's administration of the last famine was that the people should clearly understand what was expected of them; he found that the trouble taken in explanations was well repaid, and that the results of famine labour compared very fairly with ordinary labour, and evidently the tradition sticks. The people on the works struck me as in good condition, and there was practically no sickness—the best test, I suppose, of good all-round administration. Hissar, however, has not been spared by the cholera, which is raging at the present moment in many of the towns and villages. The famine camps had their worst time some months ago, and there was a terrible outbreak on some canal works, many miles away, to which eleven thousand of the Hissar people had been deported; so bad, indeed, that the whole camp had to be broken up and the people brought back. Mr. Humphreys also took me to the village of Tahvandi Rana, five miles away, a cluster of mud hovels picturesquely heaped together on a mound in the desert, and deserted by all but the aged and infirm, who are receiving a weekly dole. These poor creatures were waiting for us outside the village, formed up in a group under a big sandbank. There were old men leaning on their staffs and women shaking with palsy, the usual collection of village decrepitude, and five blind. On the other side of the road were the fresh applicants for relief, who told their cases. One of them was an old man who had lost two of his sons. He was keeping their wives and their three children and his old mother of ninety. He had no land, and his bullocks, from which he got a living, were dead. He and five more were put upon the list. Altogether in the village, which is a large one, there are thirty-one people on Government and twenty-nine on charitable relief.

CHAPTER XIV

The Money, Moral, and Material Value to India of Sir Arthur Cotton's Work

"With the northern practice the name of Sir Proby Cautley will be handed down to the grateful remembrance of posterity, and with the southern practice, that of Sir Arthur Cotton. Of the many benefactors of India in recent times, there are few who have done more material good than Sir Arthur Cotton during this generation. Both he and Sir Proby Cautley have raised, or contributed to raise, a school of hydraulic engineers, whose deeds have shed lustre on the public service in the Presidencies of Bengal and of Madras. The name of Fife is similarly associated with the irrigation works of the Bombay Presidency."—SIR RICHARD TEMPLE, G.C.S.I., *India in* 1880, p. 257.

IT has been suggested that it might be useful if the value of Sir Arthur Cotton's work to India, reckoned in £ *s. d.*, were computed. If the question be asked, How much is India the better for Lieutenant Cotton's adoption of an Indian career? obviously the answer is difficult. There are certain tangible results which "he may read who runs"; the intangible are harder to indicate. A page or two of this biography, however, may, not unusefully, be devoted to a consideration of this method of estimating Sir Arthur Cotton's work.

I. THE MONEY RETURN.

(a.) *To Government* (*after Interest on Capital Expenditure has been reckoned*).

	Rs.
Godavari Delta System	3,70,98,763
Kistna Delta System	2,02,11,515
Cauveri Delta System	2,35,38,320
Lower Coleroon	94,10,951
Total, Direct	Rs. 9,02,59,549[1]

[1] *Madras Administration Report*, 1898–99, section, "Irrigation."

28

	Rs
Brought forward	9,02,59,549
Of remainder, one-half may be reckoned, as it is certain but for the earlier successes so much irrigation would not have been undertaken .	58,74,758
Total in Madras, Direct and Indirect. .	Rs. 9,61,34,307
Much of this was earned at the old rate of currency (Rs. 10=£1), and might, half of it, be represented at this=£9,508,430. The present rate, however, may be taken, Rs. 15=£1	£6,408,954

Did ever before engineer or civilian in India divert so magnificent a stream of easily-borne revenue into the Government Treasury? And, at the rate of several millions sterling per annum, a contribution to the revenue is going on, and may go on for hundreds of years. Shall he, who provided all this by his courage, ability, and humanity, ever be forgotten? And shall his teaching and example go for nothing?

(b.) *To the Districts Affected, and the People thereof.*

Some difference of opinion exists as to the increase in produce which comes from irrigated land: certain authorities give Rs. 10 per acre in Northern India, Sir Arthur Cotton says Rs. 15,[1] and as he appears to have had good ground for his estimate, it is only fair to him to calculate on his basis. There are 5,875,374 acres under irrigation in Madras. Sir Arthur Cotton, who designed and executed, or (as in Kistna) was the originator and partial designer of the great works, may be credited with this increased produce. The annual increased value thus given to the land, the extra money coming into the hands of the people, is Rs. 8,81,30,610; or, at Rs. 15 to £1 sterling	£5,875,374

[1] I should like to put the Government estimate, but it varies so much that I cannot strike a fair average. Generally, the rate for wet cultivation is four times that for dry cultivation. The Hon. R. A. Dalyell, of the Madras Board of Revenue, gives statistics for 1856 and 1866, which would justify a much higher calculation than is given here, but, all through, I have been desirous to give estimates below the actuals (p. 399, *Administrative Experience Recorded in Former Famines*: 1874).

Sixty years have passed since one of the greatest of Sir Arthur Cotton's works was completed—the Cauveri delta—and nearly fifty since the Godavari began to yield large returns. It would not be unfair to reckon for such an estimate as this, thirty years of the above figures. Such an estimate shows that Sir Arthur Cotton has been the means of adding to the income of the inhabitants of certain districts in Madras only, £5,875,374 × 30 =£176,261,220

Summarised, we have this :—

		£
(a)	Money return to the Government, wholly profit, as interest has been already reckoned, £800,644 per annum, also multiplied by 30	= 24,019,320
(b.)	Money return to the people . . .	176,261,220
	Total	**£200,280,540**

A fairer tribute to Sir Arthur Cotton would have been to add thirty-three per cent. to the above estimate, by giving forty years' amount of the returns, which would reach the sum of **£267,040,720** sterling.

Nothing has been reckoned for the rest of India, though much might, in strict justice, have been reckoned. There can be no doubt that, but for the success in Tanjore and Godavari, very little of the canal irrigation in other parts of India would have been undertaken. Nor is any heed given to the great saving effected through the improvement of the Paumben Channel. Directly and indirectly, Sir Arthur's beneficent work is almost past finding out, certainly it cannot be accurately reckoned up.

2. The Moral and Material Return to Country and to People.

This is incalculable in a double sense. No one can measure the force which prosperity gives in increasing the happiness and comfort of every home affected thereby, or adequately state it, even if it were apprehended. Some idea of the other side of the matter might be obtained if one were to garner and set forth the awful condition which famine causes. Utter destitution falls upon vast multitudes, the money loss from partly-withered crops or from want of crops is great, demoralization affects practically all, and vast numbers become quite destitute and the recipients of Government relief and private charity. As for those others who are able somehow to pull through a time of little or no work and extremely, almost prohibitory, high prices for food, who have to deny themselves everything beyond mere maintenance,—

> "Their skin cleaveth to their bones; it is withered, it is become like a stick."—(*Lam. Jeremiah*, iv. 8.)
>
> "They that are slain with the sword are better than they that be slain with hunger;
>
> "For these pine away, stricken through for want of the fruits of the field."—(*Lam. Jeremiah*, iv. 9.)

All this is impossible where the views of Sir Arthur Cotton have prevailed. In every other part of India it is not only possible, but, in many parts, certain, that hideous suffering recurs at short intervals, as in the case of the Central Provinces, ravaged in 1896–97 and again in 1899–1900, with the consequence that, in one part of that region, forty per cent. of the inhabitants are receiving Government relief!

The Indian people cry, with a loud voice:—

> "How long, O Master, wilt thou permit us thus to suffer? Bring succour that we perish not! How long shall the land mourn, and the herbs of the country wither?"

Alone amongst British subjects do the Indian lieges of the Queen thus suffer. Is it possible, with the teachings of Sir Arthur Cotton in our hands for our guidance, that Englishmen and Englishwomen will permit this state of things to continue?

CHAPTER XV

Work for all India

BEFORE leaving India, Colonel Cotton wrote joyfully of the well-being of his greatest undertaking:—

"I am happy to state that, from whatever cause, the Godavari district is prospering beyond all expectations; we can show that, deducting our large expenditure during the last four years, amounting to £1,110,000, the net revenue has greatly exceeded the average of previous years; the excess in the last year but one is no less than £19,500. That of the last would have been more, but for the destructive flood of last September. The causes to which I attribute this extraordinary improvement, are the large expenditure by the Government and the sugar manufacturers, the extension of irrigation, and the increase of exports under a vigorous revenue management."

He printed for private circulation a pamphlet on Public Works in India. It was afterwards reproduced with an introduction by General Fischer, R.E., and is still of considerable value for the suggestions it contains concerning useful projects. He alludes to some of the former mistakes in the plan and execution of road work, and yet observes, with reference to the improved road from Madras to the westward, that it has saved, in the cost of transit, cent. per cent. on the capital expended upon it. In commenting on this road from Madras he shows that it saves the country £1,850 per mile, on an expenditure of £1,000—nearly 200 per cent.; and that Cochrane's Canal, only ten miles long, yields to the Government annually £3,000, on an outlay of £15,000, or twenty per cent., besides the saving to the community by its cheap transit; and that an expenditure of £25,000 on the Paumben Channel, between the mainland and Ceylon, has reduced the cost of freight between Tanjore and Ceylon by two-thirds, saving in the carriage of grain alone more than £40,000 or 160 per cent.

Most earnestly he was again espousing the cause of navigation on the great rivers, and he argued at length on the commercial advantages of opening up the Upper Godavari, especially for navigation. His project, however, was not accepted by the authorities; it may be hoped that, in the reforms which must come in the early future, its importance may be recognised and the necessary works undertaken.

STORAGE OF SALT WATER.

Another topic, of this time especially, is that of the storage of salt water for the production of salt—"a great necessary of life," and always much prized by the people, though it was an article which they had great difficulty in obtaining. He proved that it would be a great gain "to raise the water to higher levels than the lowest, which alone were occupied in the native manufacture."

In 1862 Sir Arthur left England for India, and investigated the Behar project of irrigation and navigation in the valley of the Sone river, originally examined and estimated by Colonel Dickens, under the orders of Government, and having made a highly favourable report on the project, sent the same to the East India Canal Company, who published it. The Company found they could not raise the requisite capital without a guarantee from the Government, so they were compelled to relinquish all idea of executing the work; it was accordingly taken up by the Government, whose officers have successfully completed it. It proved of most essential service during one of the famines, and irrigated five hundred and fifty-five thousand one hundred and fifty acres, from which otherwise scarcely any crops could have been raised.

His visit to Orissa in 1862 was fruitful of wise comment and judicious observation :—

"All deltas require essentially the same treatment. They are all subject to dreadful evils if unregulated and the rivers left uncontrolled. All are capable of almost incalculable improvements, all cause a far greater expense by their being neglected, than by the execution of the most complete system of works; all require the same means to be used to regulate their waters, and convert the natural constant succession of flood and drought into a constant and invariable supply of that which makes the whole difference between plenty and famine, comfort and misery, wealth and poverty, so far as material things can do it."

"Upon the regulation of the waters of every country depends, incomparably more than on anything else, its material well-being; this is especially the case in all tropical and other countries which have defined periodical rains.

"The cause of all the mischief we are now lamenting [the Orissa famine] is perfectly obvious, and has been clearly pointed out by Captain Short. It is the change that has taken place in the heads of the Kujooree and Mahanudi within the last few years, in consequence of which a much larger portion of the whole water now enters the former river than its lower parts are capable of carrying off. All delta rivers continually change, if left to nature, when, by some change above, the set of the stream is so thrown upon the head of a branch as to widen and deepen it, till the channel is capable of holding the increased body of water down to the sea; but, in the meantime, the mischief that is done by flooding and destroying land is incalculable in a highly-peopled country."

The remedy for this was some trifling works at the point where the evil originates, viz., at the termination of the hill country six miles above Cuttack, by which the excessive evils now experienced could have been stopped at once, and by which they can even now. Indeed, the turning of the water into the Mahanudi had already commenced as the effect of the small works already executed.

In the preceding twenty-three years there had been :—

Three years of famine,
Four years of drought,
Seven years of inundation,
Seven years of moderate seasons.

His practical conclusion, after this inspection, was to this effect, that, "if the works should cost Rs. 5 an acre, the increase of produce would be two hundred or three hundred per cent., abundantly sufficient for our purpose."

In another report, written at the same time, he says :—

"To me it is no more a question whether the waters of the delta ought to be regulated, than whether food ought to be cooked, or a broken leg to be set. It is no more a question whether flood water ought to be let in upon the inhabitants of a delta, than rain water upon those who are living in a barrack; and that before long it will be treated as a matter of course, that £1,300,000 ought to be spent in sheltering two millions of people in a province from the floods and drought, just as much as in sheltering twenty regiments from the weather—that it is as necessary a piece of economy and of mercy."

One party of ryots, in discussing with him the spread of irrigation, finished their statements by saying, "Oh! if you give us such works as you speak of, what with sugar, and all sorts of things that we shall then grow, the land will produce *six times* what it does now!"

In 1864 he wrote to Sir Stafford Northcote as follows:—

"I am not pressing upon your attention a matter which is of comparatively small importance, but one which is certainly at this time one of the great vital questions in the management of India.

"You will see that the views of my opponents and myself are diametrically opposed; one of them must be rejected in the future conduct of the matter. The future progress of India in every respect must most materially depend upon no mistake being made as to which of those views is the true one.

"I have a letter to-day from an Englishman, who has for many years been farming in the delta of the Godavari, who writes as follows:—

"'Last year, in the sub-division of the Godavari district, land yielding £30,000 revenue was thrown up in May, as the ryots saw no chance of obtaining water; in portions of this land the seed had been sown; this was also sacrificed. The navigation in some canals is greatly interfered with by their not being properly cleared of the silt, and many irrigation canals are choked with mud, and are of very little use.

"'The same is the case with the great works in Tanjore.'

"I quote this as a proof of the strange indifference with which this great subject has been treated during the last two viceroyalties of India. I need only refer to the astonishing indifference which has been shown respecting the famine. Not only has there been no effective prosecution of irrigation and navigation for the last five years, but even the successful works yielding such great returns in Madras have not been kept in repair. Nor has anything worth mentioning been done to correct the errors in the Ganges Canal, or to extend its operation; it has been allowed to linger on in an unproductive, and even a dangerous, state, for many years.

"I may add one fact to show the vast importance of this question, if anything were wanted to be added to that of the famine, viz., that the increase of revenue in the Godavari district since the works were begun, has been £270,000 a year, a sum which, if extended to the other one hundred and thirty districts, would amount to £35,000,000, which would be the difference in revenue between India irrigated and India left to the natural state of things, besides the loss of millions of lives by famine."

And to Sir Lewis Pelly (alluding to a pamphlet enclosed):—

"You were good enough to hear what I had to say about the Orissa works. As these are now the works upon which all who are opposed to irrigation and water transit fix their attention, it seems to be of the first importance that their circumstances should be well considered; and I, therefore, try to lay before you in writing what I said at our meeting, with some other things that in the hurry of the meeting I omitted.

"I offer these remarks, not only as having had fifty years' successful experience in these matters, but also as, being out of office, I have time and leisure to examine them in a way that those who are overwhelmed with details, and even that those who are in the thick of the operations, cannot.

"There were four classes of engineers in India—those who aimed at nothing, and succeeded in effecting it; those who aimed at something that was in itself a mistake, and succeeded in doing mischief; those who aimed at something right, but failed through mistakes in carrying it out; and those who aimed at something right and, by God's blessing, succeeded."

In advocacy of the claims of the East India Irrigation Company, and the importance of its promotion, he wrote as follows to the Governor-General:—

"I am informed that the true state of the case is that authority was actually given some time ago to the Governor-General to raise loans to the amount of £20,000,000 in the course of some years, with a full determination that no more projects should be executed by companies (not even in Oudh), though the Government had themselves offered it, and approved of the East India Irrigation Company going to the expense of examining that tract; but that large projects should be executed by Government itself; but since then I hear that these instructions have been countermanded, and that only eight millions should be raised in five years to build barracks, leaving the question of the execution of the great irrigation works where it was before.

"I feel quite certain from all that has passed of late years, that there is not the slightest possibility of any large irrigation works being carried out by the Government; so that if they refuse to let them be done by private companies, it is certain that they won't be done at all. We paid off many millions of debt, while we have withheld £200,000 or £300,000 required for the completion of the Godavari and Kistna works, though that money would yield one hundred per cent. to Government, besides securing the districts from famine and its calamitous consequences.

"The present crisis of the Ganges Canal seems a most favourable opportunity for bringing forward the whole subject, as well as that canal's particular case.

"We have every reason to hope that both the Irrigation Company's great projects, in Madras and in Bengal, will be in extensive operation this year, and they both promise as great returns as those of the Godavari and Kistna."

The vexed question of "mistakes" occupied much of his time and attention, for he was always trying to correct them.

It would often be argued that, if a district were what is called a "rainy" district, the fall in the year being considered good, there was no need there for irrigation. This point Sir Arthur combated strongly on the ground that "the monsoon may be a very heavy one, and yet the land may suffer from famine; as in the case of the Orissa district, where thirty inches fell, and then in the drought that followed the whole of the rice crops were lost. Another thirty inches fell, but it was too late. Famine followed. Had there been a canal system available, this water would have been saved and utilised for the enriching of the country, and all the disasters of a famine averted.

Water must be stored and distributed, or it becomes an enemy—an instrument of destruction and ruin when it does appear, rather than a beneficent friend and life-giving influence; whereas, when it does not come, there is drought and dearth on every side. At all times of the year, too, water is needed." The simplicity of these assertions, one would think, needed no argument or burning eloquence to prove them.

The year 1877 was the worst year of suffering Southern India has ever known. An examination of the rainfall statistics shows 1877 to be a year of heavy rainfall, but twenty-one inches out of the total fell on two or three successive days in May—18 to 20. The quantity which then fell was at least half a year's average normal rainfall.

My attention has been specially drawn to a striking confirmation of Sir Arthur's observations just recorded. He often insisted on the fact that when he used the word irrigation, he meant it as a very comprehensive term. It included storage of water as well as the supplying and drainage of land.

"If," he said, "the careful regulation of the water is attended to, it answers admirably every requirement of the country, bringing prosperity to the population and revenue to the Government. Its necessary outlay in the cost of works is amply repaid over and over again, not only by the wealth, but the health of the territory where the money is spent. Those who are not intimately enough acquainted with the subject have suggested that such a circulation of water must necessarily cause outbreaks of fever. This also is a mistake; it is the undrained swamp, 'combined with insufficient food and clothing,' that creates India's worst scourge—fever. Place the country under a wholesome and continuous system of drainage, and it immediately is free from the dangers of sickness to a very great extent."

THE ENORMOUS VALUE OF RIVER WATER OVER WELL WATER.

By every means in his power he endeavoured to prove that in her rivers, as well as in her rainfall, India possessed a mine of unused, and, as yet, undiscovered, wealth. To quote a favourite sentence of his: "Water is India's greatest treasure." One fact that he would sometimes state was the difference between the "ryot" system of watering the land, and the superior system possible to us by river regulation. The well water raised by the primitive bullock system would provide three hundred cubic yards of water for one rupee, and only just touch the surface of the earth; in river irrigation the rich stream so feeds the crops that no manure is ever required, while the crops follow each other in natural succession year after year. The Government can provide, by means of irrigation works carried out on a right principle, one thousand five hundred cubic yards of water for a rupee, or five times the quantity for the same money of a much more valuable article.

"The difference between well water and river water," he adds, "is this, that well water is not worth one-third of river water, because it contains no food for plants; while river water perfectly renews the soil; and, secondly, because well water costs from five to ten times what river water does. Nobody denies this, yet they always write just as if the one was as good and as cheap as the other. I have shown this in my last paper, as usual. There is no water lost in the canals by percolation. The river water fuddles them perfectly, but the cost of water, delivered on a large scale by river works, is so small that if the canals do lose some by percolation, it is a very small matter, and it must soon stop.

"How strange it seems that people should not ask, What does water cost by such and such a means of bringing it out on the fields? The Tungabudra, the most expensive of all the works, costs £1,600,000, and supplies 2,000 million cubic yards, which, at six per cent., or £100,000 a year, gives 20,000 cubic yards; but this is for bare raising, while the irrigation works include embanking, draining, navigation, etc., besides manure.

"In Godavari, the water costs the Government £1 for 60,000 cubic yards, with all the other effects. Nobody denies this, yet there is not the slightest allusion to it; for instance, in the common report, they write just as if water were water, whether it costs much or little, and whether it manures or not.

"As to the extent of land that could be irrigated at a practicable cost, there is literally no limit to it. At this moment they are watering from one end of India to the other, from millions of wells in every district, at a cost of five or ten times what it would cost to irrigate by works on a large scale.

"Mr. Robertson says that in Coimbatore it costs Rs. 20 an acre per annum. It costs the Government on an average six per cent. on Rs. 25, or Rs. 1½.

"It is passing strange that it should be only in the end of the nineteenth century, that people are beginning to find out that the sufficiency or insufficiency, the abundance or superabundance, the purity or impurity of water, on which depends sickness or health, wealth or want, life or death, ought to be the special subject of the attention of Government; and that when they have completely solved the problem of turning the stormy ocean from the great hindrance into the perfect means of communication between nations, at a nominal price of transport, they should have yet to learn that the same means will answer for the internal transit of countries, and is the only possible effective means; so that while they can bring the corn of India ten thousand miles through the storms of the ocean, they are effectually prevented from making use of it for want of the means of bringing it one thousand miles to the coast from the interior."

NAVIGATION TOPICS AND SCHEMES.

On the question of Indian traffic he writes :—

"The traffic through the Paumben Pass between Ceylon and the mainland is seventeen times what it was before the improvement; the main Godavari canal some twenty-fold probably; that between Orissa and Calcutta forty-fold, although the internal line is not completed.

"I am persuaded that the traffic in the Indus canal, if the North-West and Behar canals are connected, will be beyond any English ideas. Do you see the advertisement about the Panama canal? It gives the traffic in the Suez canal as half a million the first year, and four and a quarter millions now. And this without India being effectually opened. The freight to Kurrachee will soon be £1 10*s*., and with a charge of 10*s*. to Allahabad, together 1*s*. per bushel, the trade in various Indian grains will be immense."

Sir Arthur compares cheapness of water with railway transit in a few terse sentences :—

"I wish we could somehow get Messrs. F. to understand the extraordinary circumstances of Kurrachee, that it must inevitably become one of the principal ports, if not the first; that it is the natural outlet of the whole of North India and of all Central Asia; and this, with its accessibility and nearness to England, gives it advantages which nothing can possibly counteract.

"But that the one thing it wants is *cheap* communication up the valley of the Indus. If a railway could carry at a halfpenny a ton, it would cost £3 10*s*. from the North-West; while a canal, at a tenth of a penny, would charge ten shillings, making a difference of two millions a year on a single million tons of wheat and other grains only, even when the prices in England allow of railway prices at all; but the fact is, it would make the difference between such a trade and none at all.

"In these matters we must always keep in view the conquest of the ocean The cost of transit by sea must greatly fall yet, low as it is. What is now before us in the way of large vessels, 700 or 800 tons, and the use of high pressure, will certainly reduce the cost of sea carriage before long to half of what it is now. The one thing now is to reduce the cost of inland carriage to correspond. If this be done, the increase of trade will be beyond all calculation."

With regard to the Indus navigation schemes, Sir Arthur wrote :—

"I think most probably that the line you suggest will be found the right one, if not the only one. I think there is no water communication between Ferozepur and the Sirhind. A canal of 100 feet by 7 feet would form a good navigation ; but if it is to water half a million acres from the Sutlej in the Punjab, and as many from the Indus in Sind, it must have a section of about 250 square yards, with a current of 3,000 yards.

"It has been of late a great question with me, whether for these large canals it would not be more economical to make them twelve feet deep ; and this is one of the points to be well considered. If twelve feet deep it would require to be sixty yards broad. The cost of the canal is not in proportion to its breadth. The two banks will be the same whether thirty yards apart or sixty. This is one of the things that make the large works so profitable. I think £3,000 a mile would probably be sufficient for the main canal, but to this must be added all the distribution works and river regulation, and drainage works.

"The supply for irrigation must be by leading water from the rivers, because it will be so much cheaper than pumping. The navigation might be supplied by pumping, where no irrigation is, because the quantity is so small.

"Even for navigation purposes the canal must be very large, for we must keep in view a traffic far beyond anything that people usually suppose. We must certainly provide for several million tons. You see how enormously the trade of India is increasing without cheap transit. Really cheap transit will give a stimulus to it that nobody now dreams of. The aqueducts over the Indus and Sutlej would certainly be heavy works, but being only two in a line of nine hundred miles, they would not tell very heavily upon the mileage."

To a leading irrigation official in India he wrote :—

"Thank you for a most encouraging letter. What a wonderful change of affairs! Lord Mayo seems to come into your views astonishingly. Thank you also for the hint about F., which was very important. I have written to Frere,[1] telling him what a hopeful letter you have sent me, and how I hope that his great projects coming under your review will now be heartily forwarded. A year of your reviewing of the great projects now in hand or estimating will, I hope, give such a start to irrigation and navigation as India will never forget, under God's blessing. It seems as if you couldn't have come in at a more critical time, with such a vast extent of work sketched out. The Sind, Ravi, Sutlej, Jumna, main Ganges, Eastern Ganges, Sone, Lower Ganges, Mahanudi, Godavari Delta, Upper Godavari, Kistna, Tungabudra, and Tanjore—fifteen great works all more or less within reach of your revision, involving ultimately more than twenty millions of expenditure and the irrigation of fifteen million acres with ten thousand miles of navigation, besides many minor works, and especially the great storage works. So you have got a field wide enough before you. The completion of the first tank, viz., Ekrookh, is a grand point gained. And at this moment, too, the great point has been conceded and acted upon of borrowing money for such works, only £3,500,000 indeed this year, but I hope you will soon get that increased. That Lord Mayo should at once begin by resuming the Orissa works is beyond all my expectation. Of course, it will be a question at what rate of speed each individual work had best be carried on, but we must always take care rather to err on the side of making hay while the sun shines.

"What a point it is, too, that you can give the Sone

[1] Sir Bartle Frere, G.C.S.I., then a Member of the Secretary of State's Council.

such a start! I think you should do your utmost to get the line undertaken at once throughout its whole length to Allahabad, especially now that the point is established that the communication above is to be continued to that place. I consider this completion of the line up the valley of the Ganges of such extreme importance, that I would press these works on to the utmost. I see in a *Times of India*, to-day, that the railway cannot beat even the Ganges. They are paying, I think, £3,500,000 for goods by railway, on which alone there would be a saving of £3,250,000 if carried by water, and ten times the quantity could be carried. There is a sum of £1,750,000 paid on the Ganges railway alone for goods, on which the saving would be more than £1,500,000 a year, and only about two hundred thousand tons carried instead of two millions for the same money. The canal will certainly force itself on, but I would certainly at once undertake every mile of it that I could. I would also urge the aqueduct at Allahabad to connect the Doab canals with those of the Sone, as an essential work to be commenced at once if possible. Could you not also now put the navigation of the Ganges canal on an efficient footing by putting Government steamers on it?

"Pray consider what I say about your proceeding as soon as you can see your way a little. What is wanted is the connection of the various irrigations, so as to complete steamboat communication from Ludiana, by the Sutlej, Jumna, Sone, Ganges, Mahanudi, Godavari, Kistna boat canals, and one from Nellore through the Carnatic to Ponany, so as to bring produce to a point opposite to Aden at an almost nominal cost. That's the grand object."

To the same correspondent he further wrote:—

"It is impossible to over-estimate the importance of completing the line from Burdwan to Calcutta.

"About crossing the branch rivers, I can't give you my ideas without referring to your note. I would send the water through an aqueduct across the Bhagavati at four thousand or five thousand yards an hour, two or three times the velocity in the canal; it would save so much time as well as money, and I would consider thoroughly how far the work could be hastened by the use of iron, even at an increase of expense. And so with the anicut also, whether you couldn't receive the fall, for instance, on an iron apron instead of stone, as it could be laid in so very short a time. I wish you had sent me profile of the line of canal; I forget the level of Colgong or Rajmahal.

"About the locks for the large steamers, I would not make them for the present river steamers; it would require such an enormous width. When the whole line of canal is completed, of course all the steamers ought to have either stern wheels or twin screws, or, what I think would be best, a large wheel carrying a chain with small plates, say six or twelve inches square, passing over a small wheel in front and rear, so as to give a great resistance by direct action, with very little breadth beyond that of the vessel—the main wheel very large so as to give a high velocity with a slow action of engine.

"You will certainly have a great difficulty in the enormous body of water you will have to dispose of in the river, but your experience in the Muddur branch will come in well there. I think upon your plan of large gabions you would be able to master an immense stream.

"In other respects you certainly have a magnificent site. You do not tell me what you allow for the cost of the anicut; allowing for the difference of length, and three times the cost of labour, it would be £450,000. You estimate the extreme flood at two hundred millions, the same as the Godavari, which is several times independent of the irrigation. You should, of course, have a branch to connect the main canal with the Ganges somewhere about Rampur-Bauleah.

"Have you seen my memo. about high level navigation canals, with a sketch of one to connect the Gorai with Calcutta? I think that would be about the most valuable work that could be executed for the money. The Secretary of State said he had forwarded the papers about it to Calcutta.

"I am putting on paper some loose thoughts about your noble project. I hope to go into it more systematically when I get home. A man who is entirely free from the pressure of the innumerable worries of office has an immense advantage in offering suggestions, though of course most of them may be nothing, because he has not the necessary detailed data; but a wise man may turn some of them to account."

The above letter referred to a large scheme which had been projected for a canal from the Ganges at Sahibgunj to Calcutta, but which was indefinitely shelved.

"I get to-day a letter from [Sir Robert] Montgomery, saying no doubt cheap transit is the great want of India. It is no small matter to have arrived at such a point as that this heresy is held by a Member of Council. And another letter enclosing a pamphlet pointing out the superiority of water to land carriage in the South Mahratta country. There can be no doubt that people are getting upon the right ground now. Fresh water against salt, even with fish in the latter, any day!

THE BENEFICIAL EFFECT OF REDUCING THE LAND TAX.

"The experiments, which have been tried in India with success as respects relief to the finances, are those which have been merciful to the people. One of these is the lowering of the land tax. There are now, happily, many districts which are proof of this. I will give two instances. In South Arcot the average extent of cultivation, for two years before the reductions, was five hundred and ninety thousand acres, and the land tax £230,000. The reductions made amounted to no less than £95,000. The extent cultivated last year was nearly one million acres, and the tax £290,000. So that the same population are now cultivating four hundred thousand acres, or sixty-six per cent., more than they once did, and at the same time the Government are receiving £60,000 more than they did, an increase of twenty-five per cent. And in Trichinopoly in the same way, the increase has been more than fifty per cent. in the area, and £20,000, or sixteen per cent., in the revenue. These are most striking proofs of what the old, ignorant, merciless, suicidal system was, and of the effect of a more merciful one.

"Here is a district cultivating more than two-thirds more land than it did, and, as the whole condition of the people must be greatly improved, there can be no doubt that the whole district is also far better cultivated than formerly; so that probably the land produce of the district is double what it was before the reductions, and the people must be paying £290,000 a year now much more easily than they did £230,000 before. The average land tax has been reduced from Rs. 4 an acre to Rs. 3. Think of a people able to cultivate one million acres, compelled to subsist on the produce of six hundred thousand by the intolerable tax laid upon the land! And, incredible as it may appear, it was chiefly the good land that they were prevented from cultivating by the intolerable tax demanded. It was Lord Harris who made these bold trials of a more merciful system, and the country is most deeply indebted to him, under God, for such a lesson, a lesson applicable to every branch of the management of the country. In these two districts alone is an increase of £80,000 a year, obtained entirely by lowering, not by raising, the taxes."

Still on the question of the work in India, he writes on another occasion:—

"I am so surprised that you have not seen that letter written in November last, but which I only saw the other day. In it S. expressly states that he is quite satisfied that his former views were wrong, and that I was right, and that an officer was to be sent to plan a new head for the canal below the hills. You may suppose what a pretty discussion this has produced in the Council. My friends are urging its publication, which, of course, the rest object to, but they have advised me to get an M.P. to call for it, and I have spoken to one about it, who will probably do so. It is a most remarkable document, and I must confess gives me a new idea of S., for there are very few men who would make such a hearty acknowledgment. It is really a matter of vast importance at this moment.

"I have thought that if I had works to execute again I would look everywhere for a man who had the peculiar talent of choosing modes of execution, and give him that sole department, laying before him the plans and estimates of each kind of work, and requiring of him a report on the kind of apparatus, etc., to be used. I think it would be essential that he should have no charge, but be at liberty to go and get his apparatus to work, for the best-planned apparatus and means require immense work actually to apply them.

"I am very glad to hear such a good account of Fouracres. I thought him a very remarkable man; his management of his industrial school showed that he had some rare talents. Pray remember me to him, and tell him that I am so glad to hear how useful he is.

"You mention the extended Sone project, from which I hope that you are trying to carry out the full project. Pray try and secure the opportunity for completing the line of navigation to Allahabad and Cawnpore. I wish you could take up the high-level canal from Calcutta to the North-East, which I wrote to the India Office about, and which was sent out to Calcutta; it would be a trifling work compared with your others and would be of immense value. I see in a report of D. on what Lawrence did, or rather it should be on what he left undone, that they propose making a connected navigation of all the canals in the Punjab and North-West, eight hundred miles in one line, another proof that they have really learned something about transit."

On another occasion:—

"I am rejoiced to hear that the canal from Cuttack to

tide water is open; that is a grand step. I wish the last link between Calcutta and the Mahanudi were completed; this is of incalculable importance. I hope it is in hand. If you should write again some months hence, pray mention this. I shall be so glad to get an account of your final planning of the Lower Ganges (Rajmahal) project. You could send me a copy of your report on it without any personal labour. It will certainly be the greatest work in the world of that kind, and the most valuable. The traffic on it will be the greatest on any line of transit.

"I am so glad to hear that F. had gone on leave for two months; he certainly greatly required rest. I am in hopes that the Godavari works could now go on under other hands, and that he could be spared for higher work, where he would have less demands upon his physical powers. I wrote to Lord Mayo about him, and I find that Montgomery did the same. It is high time he was relieved from executive duties. I had a letter from him the other day mentioning many items of good news from the Godavari :—

"1st. The merchants have made arrangements for bringing down the cotton from the Warda this year;

"2nd. They have found usable coal at the first barrier;

"3rd. The trade of Cocanada is increasing remarkably. What will it be when the port is the outlet of twenty millions of people? and

"4th. Fischer has found a noble site for a tank with a fall of only four feet per mile, to contain one thousand millions [cubic yards] with a bund only seventy feet high, and four hundred yards long at top. This one would completely keep the Godavari open, and supply the delta in the dry season. The Godavari is lower than ever known, which is all in favour of his present work in the bed.

"The new steamers are a complete success, though still drawing more water than calculated."

A little later, to the same correspondent :—

"I saw Frere in London; he was very anxious to know what you would do about his great Indus project; the last he had heard of it was that the Governor-General was determined to quash it. Of course, I told him you had written to me about it, and you would certainly do all you could to support it. The point he was anxious about was, of course, whether you would be likely to prevent its being quashed.

"I am highly pleased with all I hear respecting H.'s great tanks, and am not sorry one of them has a masonry dam, that they may be fairly compared, though I certainly would not, even on the score of expense, much more on that of safety, have tried a masonry dam, especially in a place where such awful mischief would be done by an instantaneous breach. I am glad to hear it is ten or twelve miles from Poona, but that is too near a great city. If the Sheffield reservoir had been of masonry, and had given way, instead of two hundred and fifty-two deaths, there would have been several thousands.

"Pray look well into the strength given to that bund, and don't spare to add enormous buttresses. If there is not a great superabundance of strength, a terrible accident from one of those great tanks would hinder the storing of water for many years.

"These two tanks give us capital data for the cost of storing; the sites were by no means the best that could be found in India. In many places water could be stored for half or a quarter what they have cost."

"I had to leave off in the middle of my letter yesterday before I had answered your two first letters. I have received no communication from the India Office in reply to my memo. As the Duke of Argyll promised me, so I have written to him to-day to remind him of his promise.

"F. thinks they will at once stop the Godavari works. I have not heard of Chesney's paper; of course they take care that I should not see it. I have not seen Chesney; I was asked to the opening of the Cooper's Hill College, but I didn't go. I have told the Duke that as I am sure he has fulfilled his promise, that he would have my memo.

answered, I trust he will have me furnished with copies of any papers that have been written.

"It is true that there is about an equal quantity of coal carried into London by rail and by sea, but this doesn't affect our question. We are not contending for carriage by sea, but by steamboat canals, and not in England but in India. I am certain that the railways earn less by the carriage of coals, and some of the lines are losing enormously by it; but the price of railway shares rises and falls with the reported amount of traffic.

"There are ten steamers a week each way from the mouth of the Forth and Clyde canal to ports in England, and the railway company there rent the canal at six and a quarter per cent. Their manager on the canal told me, he didn't think a ton of goods was sent from there to London by rail. There are about four thousand steamers a year running along the east coast, carrying, I suppose, much more than a million tons a year, regular ones, besides innumerable ones carrying coal, etc., parallel with the railways, but with a long detour, river charges, etc. The railway running by it, which I suppose is the one that rents it, the North British, I suppose its dividends are not above two per cent. But the peculiar thing about the coal traffic is that accidents are becoming so numerous that some means must soon be adopted to separate the goods and passenger traffic; and it has been actually under consideration to lay a fifth double railway to the north solely for goods traffic. The coal, three and a half million tons, is divided between three double and one treble railway,—four hundred thousand tons per line of rails, or thereabouts.

"I have not the least doubt that locks can be passed in about two minutes when a thousandth part of the thought and money has been expended on steamboat canals that has been applied to the perfecting of railway arrangements. And on many lines in India, such as that from the Punjab to Calcutta, there would be hardly any locks. I consider it now of the very first importance that everything should be done to bring a line of canal to a most effective state for both goods and passenger traffic; one such line would do more than anything else to remove the present ignorant prejudice about water carriage. I was running along the Clyde and its locks in a steamer at from sixteen to eighteen miles an hour, carrying first-class passengers at about one halfpenny per mile, though the boats are laid up half the year or more, and, in an open estuary, are, of course, almost empty in stormy weather. I am sure they could average twenty miles an hour, including locks, in India at one farthing a mile first-class, if the canals were thoroughly suited for high speed. Not that I think speed of any consequence in itself, because I'm sure that for forty-nine-fiftieths of the goods and passenger traffic of India there is no need for speed.

"Brereton has written such an extraordinary account of California and a project for watering the valley of the San Joaquim; the advantage in soil, facilities for storing, and distributing water, etc., are far beyond those of India."

A good prospect opened at one time in the South Mahratta country of a navigation system. Sir Arthur Cotton wrote:—

"A Major D., of the Engineers, has proposed the navigation of the Southern Mahratta rivers, and thinks of trying to form a company for it. A Mr. Andrew Hay, of the Oriental Club, sent me his pamphlet and asked my opinion, and whether I could take a part in the matter. I told him I was no man of business, but I thought he might write to you about it, as it might suit your plans. I entirely approve of the idea, so much so that I got the Irrigation Company to send an engineer to explore the country with that view, and I have his report. But, unfortunately, he preferred his own ideas to mine, and wrote a paper not on navigation but on irrigation, so that it contains very little information that bore upon the question, and he was, like most other people, quite ignorant of the whole subject of transit. It would exactly suit my ideas if this project were to be taken up by a company, so as to afford the instance required of a level tract of country with water carriage. I sent Mr. Hay a letter containing some of my leading ideas on the subject, and have written most of a more digested paper on it.

"It is a perfect field for the exhibition of the system of storing water for the three objects—

"1st. Controlling the floods;

"2nd. Navigating the rivers as they are, that is with partial improvements; and

"3rd. For supplying the irrigation and navigation of the lower works, the Tungabudra, and Kistna delta, in the dry season. One thing Mr. Gordon states is that one hundred and seventy miles of the Kistna have a fall of seven inches a mile, so that a beginning might probably be made by putting steamers on that at once. In the meantime we have data of all kinds to go upon, the steamers on the Godavari, the tanks at Ekrookh and Sholapore, the anicuts and locks on the Godavari, the traffic in the delta, etc. So that a company would start with wonderful advantages.

"They have a magnificent country and a dense population to work upon in the Mahratta country, and nothing wanted, but cheap transit to a capital and port, to put entirely new life into the whole tract."

In another communication, written in 1876, he says:—

"Do you see that the Duke of Buckingham has gone up to see Kistna and Godavari, which looks well? I am glad also to see that they complain of his throwing over his Council. I hope from this that he's going really to govern. I never could see the use of a Governor subordinate to his subordinates." He adds:—

"I am also very glad to see Pelly is to be a member of Council; I hope he will be a great improvement on the old *régime*.

"Pray tell me something about Lord Lytton. I am thinking of writing to him and asking him to let me see him.

"I wrote to Captain Warren to ask him to allow Dr. W. to use his name, which he has readily consented to. He has sent me a most striking pamphlet of his on Palestine, showing how ripe it is for restoration, and wanting nothing but a just government to enable it to start up a young giant."

More details regarding navigation appear in the following letter :—

"I will send you the account of the passage of a regiment of natives through Madras, on their way to Bezwada, by canal. There is only a break of eight miles on that line now, and it will soon be finished. The traffic was three hundred thousand tons on the old canal. What will it be when it is in full operation to Cocanada and the Godavari? The contract rate for the regiment was: sepoys, seven miles for a penny, and the followers fourteen miles for the same amount. I reckon that with steam, even at ten miles an hour, the cost would be almost nominal.

"Fancy the Chamber of Commerce protesting against the Junction Canal being cut! This is a work of immense importance. It is long enough, and on a sufficiently important line, to show very well what water carriage is. Only think what the traffic would now be if the second barrier had been completed, and the third executed, so as to give Madras cheap coal and the whole trade of the Central Provinces! And if the line had been cut to Cuddapah! As it is, there are fourteen miles of connected canal and river open.

"The works in Bengal are getting on very well; everything there is very promising. That's a grand idea of Eden's to open the lower line to Ganjam. There will then be three hundred and fifty miles from Calcutta towards Madras, and four hundred and twenty from Madras towards Calcutta. The Sone works are getting on wonderfully. I had no idea of there being eight hundred thousand acres ready for irrigation. Why, in the estimate for the next year, does Eden suppose that two hundred thousand only will be irrigated? And why should he suppose that the navigation tolls will be the same as this year? I should think it much more likely they would be increased tenfold. We have abundant room for the hope that next year's receipts will be many lakhs more than he estimates. The increase of sugar is a great fact. How immensely important it is that they should store water for that.

"I am so glad to see the way Levinge speaks of shutting the canals; I now hope that this insane proceeding will be stopped. Fouracres's improvement of dredging is a thing of the very first importance. I am greatly pleased with Levinge's letter. It seems to me to show that *he*, at least, takes hold of things by the handle and not by the spout. I think the Sone works must have fully paid their interest this year. Certainly not more than £700,000 can be charged to the works already opened, and £50,000 gives seven per cent. on that. Have they cost two millions up to this time? I wrote to Levinge, and begged him to send me various particulars as to cost, etc., etc.

"I will send you the Madras report. The watershed of the Kala-Nuddee and the Tungabudra is about two thousand feet, that of the Cauveri and Ponany one thousand four hundred feet. I think we should try to concentrate attention on the Carnatic tanks at this time while the iron is hot. C. [Sir James Caird][1] will be examined, and he will not speak out about irrigation. His not seeing the improved districts is conclusive as to his not apprehending the case, or not being willing to face the current. Had he had a right apprehension of the case he would have concluded that the very first thing he had to do was to see the districts which, in point of famine, finance, and social state, were in a perfectly satisfactory condition, and that no others were. Every one of the speakers in the late debate, Bright and all, left out entirely every one of the essential points of the question. Not one word was said of the effect of all the improvements. Have six hundred miles of railway, some five thousand miles of canal, and improved

[1] Sir James Caird, eminent as an English agriculturist, was a member of the Famine Commission of 1879–80; he visited India, but, as Sir Arthur Cotton points out, did *not* visit any of the irrigated districts!

river, and one hundred thousand miles of road, besides innumerable other things, made no difference whatever in the power of the people to pay the taxes?

"In Mr. Hyndman's account of the state of the people, he omits the trifle of the wealthy classes. Fancy a man giving an account of the state of London in respect of property, and utterly ignoring everything west of London Bridge! Of all the enormous wealth of India he says not one word; of all the wealthy landowners, merchants, sowcars, with incomes of £500,000 a year, equal to £1,500,000 in England, downwards, he says nothing. The Rajah of Vizianagram has an income of £120,000 a year over his tribute, equal to £360,000 in England."

Large schemes still occupied Sir Arthur's mind.

"I am writing a paper on Madras," he remarks, "sketching out about twenty-five works, to cost fifty millions.[1] I am myself quite astonished at the result of the investigation. The Presidency may certainly be made into a perfect garden, with the most complete system of cheap transit, and with two ports better situated than any now in existence, Ponany and Cape Comorin.

"With respect to population for the Indus Canal, there are plenty in the Punjab. Fred says a great deal was said about the fear of want in this, in Sind. The land is freely taken up for irrigation in Orissa and Midnapur, to the end of September,—one hundred and thirteen thousand and one hundred thousand acres respectively. There is also a good increase in the Lower Ganges and the Agra; but I am disappointed about the Sone, only seventy-four thousand. What is the cause of this? Ganges Canal, to September, four hundred and twenty-seven thousand; Lower Ganges, twenty-seven thousand; Agra, thirty thousand."

Of the author of two most interesting technical works on the Godavari and Kistna deltas, Sir Arthur remarks:—

[1] See *ante*, pp. 301–303.

"I have had Mr. Walch, of Godavari, with me to-day. He gives a most flourishing account of the state of the Western delta, vast improvements in the works, and a state of prosperity surpassing probably any tract in the world. They will soon irrigate three hundred thousand acres in that delta alone. He says Brownlow and other foreigners expressed their astonishment at the result, and especially at the traffic, in the strongest manner."

To the correspondent who received most of the preceding letters, he wrote in November, 1878:—

"I am astonished to think that I never answered your last most interesting long letter, and now I have another as interesting. I have loads of things to say about both letters. I will begin with the new one. The accounts of Orissa are altogether satisfactory. If I had only had these extracts when I was before the Committee! The water rate levied is a very small matter compared with the water being used. It is, of course, a good stone to throw at a dog to show that the works do not pay the Government. But the great thing is that the country should have the benefit of them.

"Fancy the irrigation under Sir Ashley Eden being already ten times that in Sir George Campbell's time. Is that a result of the change in the works or in the management? I will copy these things for Caird.

"I received the papers about the canal to Calcutta. Mr. Wyllie's report is of the highest importance. What do you now think is the increase of crop due to the irrigation there? F. at first wrote a paper from which I made out that it was about Rs. 15, but since he has made it much less. He said in one paper that the people in Midnapur had begun to empty their fields of rain water in order to fill them with river water. I have no doubt this is the grand thing to get them to do. I reckon that if they carry out the whole scheme the cost will not be more than Rs. 30 an acre, and the water rate alone at Rs. 2½ will be eight per cent., besides tolls, giving a net return of about seven per cent. in all on the cost, and five on cost and interest. But what will the whole return be? At £1 an acre, with saving in carriage, protection of land, etc., certainly fifty per cent. There cannot be a question but that the whole province is now rapidly rising out of its dreadful state of depression. The astonishing increase of trade alone is conclusive of this. What will be the trade when there is direct communication with Calcutta by canal? Pray send me the navigation returns.

"I greatly approve of all that has been done, and the way it has been done. Now suppose that sickness or anything should bring Lord Lytton home, the country would certainly call for Frere, and then what might take place with respect to irrigation and navigation? I am so glad [R. K.] Puckle [of the Madras service] had several interviews with Caird; he knows more about Indian agriculture than anybody, and was just the man to give him solid information. I am glad to hear that [General Sir Richard] Strachey is likely to be at the head of the Commission again. I think he is the best man we could have to be associated with Caird.

"I look upon Cyprus as a most wonderful acquisition, and, in connection with the appointment of Midhat Pasha to Damascus, and the arrangement of a loan for Turkey guaranteed by us on the security of the revenues of Syria, I consider it tantamount to our having the complete control of Palestine."

An important letter, that is to say, one explaining this method for keeping the tanks in the Madras Presidency supplied from the never-failing large rivers in the Peninsula, must be quoted because of the light it throws on the great project Sir Arthur submitted to the Select Committee Inquiry, in 1878. He says:—

"Mrs. Caird read me several extracts from her husband's letters, from the Punjab, North-Western Provinces, Oudh, and Bengal. He was leaving Calcutta for Cocanada. He was greatly interested in Indian agriculture. He said nothing about what he thought of the irrigation works.

He went over the Sone works with Haig. Haig was to leave Calcutta in the middle of last month, and to go to Doomagoodien. Levinge succeeds him. I think he must be the best man for this, and that he will heartily support Eden in his energetic proceedings. I see they are bringing forward a bill for extended irrigation, with compulsory water rates, at Bombay. The amount proposed is £3,500,000. Somehow or other they have made a very poor business of it in Bombay. You see [Sir R.] Strachey is taken off the Commission, and another member has left from ill health. Lord Lytton asked Mr. Caird to select a colleague in place of the last. He wants Scott-Moncrieff.

"I have sent Caird a rough sketch of a project for supplying the Carnatic tanks from the Tungabudra and Kistna, to cost, perhaps, £34,000,000. Its foundation is the great Bellary tank, to contain three thousand million cubic yards, and deliver, during the five months, twelve thousand million cubic yards, leaving it full at the end for dry season watering. From it one large canal on a dead level to the Kistna, where there would be either anicut or a tank, which would support the Tungabudra one. From the reservoir a very large canal to carry the water clear of the hills, and then to divide into four canals. One to carry water to the Eastern ghauts above Chittoor, and discharge its water over the ghauts, into a dead level canal to cross North Arcot on a level of perhaps one thousand feet. A second branch would carry the water to a feeder of the Pennair, and by that river into Nellore, with an anicut at the entrance of the hills to turn the water into a dead level canal from the Kistna to Tinnevelli, and thence to Cape Comorin. Anicuts to be thrown across all the rivers in the Carnatic to turn their waters into the level canal, by which they would be carried both north and south, and distributed to the tanks under it, so as to make the most of the short floods in those rivers. This canal to be one hundred yards broad and four deep. From it two branches would connect it with Madras. From the Kistna I would carry a similar great canal, through the Nizam's country, passing near

Hyderabad to the Godavari and Kistna, having a fall of four or five inches. I would also connect the main canal from the tank with the Irrigation Company's canal, and water a million acres in Bellary. This would give grand lines of communication through Hyderabad, the Ceded Districts and the Carnatic, and secure the irrigation altogether of some twenty million acres of dry cultivation. What do you think of such a project?"

Interesting letters were often received from intelligent inhabitants of Southern India, expressing their gratitude both for personal kindnesses rendered to them, and also for the general prosperity that had come to their districts by the Cottonian irrigation works.

A few of these, herewith given, show both gratitude and appreciation,—yes, gratitude, even though there be those who have resided in India who declare that the quality is unknown to Indian races. One Indian gentleman writes:—

"I always feel thankful, first to God, and then to you, for my prosperity in this world. I have been reading for several years about irrigation works, but, although it is a well-known fact that they are beneficial both to Government and to the public at large, yet it cannot be said when worthy projects will be thoroughly realised.

"It is hard to understand what is meant by the statement that the ryots refuse water, which is contrary to the real fact. The authorities must have accepted the reports of some inexperienced and young officers in India. Some say that the excessive water spoils the land. Allowing it to be so, why not adopt proper measures to make bunds, and so prevent the water submerging the land, and use a proper quantity when required?

"In the month of January last, a member of Parliament came to Madras, and I had the pleasure to meet him at Government House on a certain night, and to hold some conversation with him on irrigation. I explained what was necessary for India, and the benefit derived from the Kistna and Godavari anicuts. I was glad to find that he concurred with me that irrigation works are much needed."

The Godavari District Association wrote of him as "Sir Arthur Cotton, the Father of the Godavari Delta," adding :—

"This Association and the people of this district are immensely pleased to know that he is still strong and active. They ever remember him with feelings of gratitude, and ever pray for his long life and prosperity. The Association has not been able to get his address hitherto, to send him a copy of the Memorials. His views of them will be very valuable indeed, and must necessarily carry great weight.

"The Association proposes to build, rather, is building, a town hall here. It will be a decent building, which will cost between £1,500 and £2,000. It wishes to place in the hall a picture of Sir Arthur Cotton."

The same society, through one of its influential Hindu members, wrote to Sir Arthur, as follows :—

"Allow me, Sir, to assure you, and I hereby convey to you, very feebly, the voice of the people of the Godavari district, that there is not one man in the whole of the district who fails to remember your name on looking at the magnificent anicut that your providential genius has been able to devise and construct for him, and the network of canals that you gave him. He sows the seed in his acres with *your* Godavari water, raises corn with *your* Godavari water, cooks it with *your* Godavari water, eats it with *your* Godavari water, and drinks *your* Godavari water. Your long and arduous labours in connection with these water works have justly placed you on the high and proud pedestal of the Godavari people's grateful memory! And it is a very rare honour, denied to many, that one's name should be gratefully remembered for generation after generation by the people amongst whom he spent the best portion of his life, and for whom he worked with assiduity and at great self-sacrifice.

"The Committee learns with great pleasure and gratitude that, in spite of your retirement and age, you still take a keen and lively interest in Indian engineering, and specially irrigation. It has read, with great interest and respect, your able and recent note on 'Railways *versus* Irrigation.' No one seems to be half as conscious and wide-awake as your worthy self as regards the many vast acres that are lying unused for want of irrigation. The whole of the recent terrible famine, which is still being felt in parts of this presidency, and which must be a recurring thing should irrigation be still neglected, would very probably have been a thing unknown, if one-half of the attention paid to railway extension had been paid to irrigation. The Godavari ryot, with all the canals and huge supply in the river, has still not enough of water, if perchance he has it at all, and not in the right season. Many thousands and hundreds of thousands of acres still lie unploughed. And why is this? The question is simply echoed without any answer. And yet the water tax rose from Rs. 2 to Rs. 3, Rs. 3 to Rs. 4, and now from Rs. 4 to Rs. 5. And heaven knows where it will stop! Drainage system has not been paid any adequate attention to, and yet higher taxation is proposed.

"Your experience of this country entitles your opinion to a great weight. We are a dumb and voiceless people, and we trust in the able advocacy of the people's friends, like you, living in England.

"The Committee will feel greatly obliged if you can kindly favour them with your opinion on the Memorials in question. Their anxiety is to put the ryot's case fairly, and yet accurately, and thus furnish the Government, which has the best of intentions, with an impartial, non-official, view of the question."

In employing water on land, or in conquering it when a part of the ocean, Sir Arthur Cotton was almost equally happy. The chief official of the Godavari District (Mr. E. C. G. Thomas) in the late Seventies, was most anxious that the port of Vizagapatam should be made a protected harbour. Naturally, he turned to Sir Arthur Cotton for counsel, and, as naturally, received what he asked for. The project much interested him. But our space forbids further reference.

THE GANGES CANAL.

CONTROVERSY WITH SIR PROBY CAUTLEY, K.C.B.

The only occasion on which Sir Arthur visited India after his retirement from the service was in 1863, when, at the request of the Directors of the East India Irrigation Company, he investigated the great works then in progress under the management of Sir Proby Cautley, K.C.B. Sir Arthur's Report to the Directors was printed for private circulation, and a copy was placed in the hands of Sir Proby. This led to a most animated discussion.

In his Report Sir Arthur paid a tribute to the usefulness of the canal, even as it had been projected. Had it been carried to completion, instead of, as seems to have happened in *every* irrigation enterprise in India, been dawdled over, it would, before that period, have shown good direct returns. As it was, it had "already saved tens of thousands of lives, and an amount of property probably exceeding its cost, during the late famine." But there were great fundamental mistakes in its projection, and to these the successful engineer from the south directed his attention. Some of these fundamental mistakes, as he terms them, may be summarised thus :—

1. The head of the canal was placed too high, above a tract which had a great and inconvenient fall.

2. The whole canal had been cut so as to carry the water below the level of the surface, entailing a vast unnecessary excavation, and keeping the water below the level at which it was required for irrigation.

3. The whole of the masonry work was of brick, although

suitable stone for hydraulic works was procurable in the sub-Himalayas. (This, Sir Arthur declared, was "a most inexplicable mistake.")

4. The whole of the water was admitted at the head, and some of it, therefore, conveyed three hundred and fifty miles to the land it irrigates.

5. There was no permanent dam across the river at the head of the canal, "so as to secure the supply of water, but temporary works are thrown up after every monsoon, which are liable to be swept away, and have been swept away at the very time when they are most needed."

The mistakes, one to four, had increased the cost threefold, and delayed the completion ten years, with a loss of twenty to thirty per cent. per annum during that period.

A large number of so-called minor mistakes were also pointed out, such as:—

a. The canal was stopped at Cawnpore, instead of being carried on to Allahabad, where the Ganges and the Jumna meet, and river navigation the year through was effective.

b. The slope was continued to Cawnpore, with a consequently large body of water flowing to waste into the river.

c. The bridges were so low as to prevent a fully-loaded boat passing under them.

d. The towing paths were not carried through the arches of the bridges, so that the towing line had to be thrown off at every bridge—that was at every three miles.

And many more of a similar character.[1]

Each of the points raised was fully discussed and answered eagerly by the engineer assailed. It would be

[1] During his examination before the Select Committee on East India Finance in 1872, Sir Arthur Cotton was much pressed concerning the Ganges canal, and why it had not, up to that period, been a profitable enterprise. He told the story as it is described here, only with greater emphasis. "Not one of the bridges," he says, "would allow a fully-loaded boat to go under it; they are at this moment raising fifty bridges to allow the traffic to pass under; that is only one out of six essential mistakes in the construction, and, in spite of that, this traffic of one hundred thousand tons has sprung up. . .

unprofitable, as well as wearisome, to revive this old controversy. But upon one point, around which the differences raged most fiercely, that is, as to the advisability of building a dam across a river on a bed of sand, some few details may be given. Sir Proby Cautley was scornful concerning the possibility of this being done. It must not be forgotten that he and his colleagues, the Bengal irrigation engineers, were at a considerable disadvantage compared with Sir Arthur Cotton and his colleagues: the latter had done the very thing which the former declared impossible—had done it not once, but many times, and under more adverse circumstances than existed in the north. The arguments may be summarised thus :—

Bengal: We have never built weirs across large rivers with sandy beds; therefore they never can be built.

Madras: We have built weirs across rivers of from one thousand yards to four miles broad, with falls per mile of from one foot up to ten, all having beds of nothing but unfathomable loose sand. The weirs so constructed have stood ten, twenty, and thirty, years. Therefore the like can be done again.

Bengal, still unconvinced, again denies the possibility.

Madras: Why, there is in Tanjore such a work, built by the natives in the second century, as is supposed, which is in use to this day. There are nearly two thousand years of experience for you!

Bengal: The slope of the river below the confluence of the Solani is found to be at the lowest estimate one and a quarter feet per mile; it may be two or three feet at that point. So your Madras weirs would not do. Your suggestions are all "visionary."

Madras: Really! The upper anicut on the Cauveri is

They have raised about half of the bridges, and they are raising the others."

"Was that the fault of those who made the canals, or those who made the roads, insisting on low gradients?"

"I think the mistake was in the projection of the canals."

built where there is nothing but sand and a fall of three and a half feet per mile. Again, there is the Pallur anicut, where the bed is also sand, and the fall about ten feet per mile. The work that will stand in Madras in a river with a certain bed and a certain slope would most assuredly stand in the North-West Provinces in a river with the same bed and the same slope. Besides, there is the nearly two thousand years' object lesson!

Bengal: Well, as to another of your criticisms, we did try to establish the head of the canal in the Jumna thirty-six years ago, and abandoned the effort after the first year's work.

Madras: You may have had good reason in 1827 for what you did. But how many works have been completed since? How much has been learned since? Suppose men were to argue now that, because other men did not know how to construct first-class railways in 1827, *therefore* first-class railways cannot be constructed now!

And so it was on all the points of difference. Sir Arthur Cotton had little difficulty in showing, from experience, that his strictures were more than justified.

One more illustration, and this old controversy—of the highest importance to professional men, of minor interest to the general reader—may be passed over.

"I see no remark," says Sir Proby, "in Sir Arthur Cotton's Report tending to show that he looked upon large masses of water as affecting the project. So far from this, he proposes a depth of eighteen feet without the slightest hesitation, and without the most distant idea of having any difficulty in dealing with it."

Sir Arthur Cotton: "Sir Proby Cautley is quite right. I have not the slightest hesitation upon the matter, or the most distant idea of any difficulty in dealing with such masses of water as need to be controlled in order to place the Ganges canal in its proper state, or to ensure its full extent of usefulness. And really there is no particular difficulty in dealing with such a depth of water. The only thing is that, to retain the same current, if the depth is greater the slope of the bed must be less. If we allow a current of three thousand yards for a depth of nine feet, the slope must be six inches. That is all the difference.

"In the Godavari we had to deal with a depth of thirty feet, and eighteen feet passes over the anicut. In the Kistna we have a depth of about thirty-seven feet, and more than twenty feet over the anicut."

Finally, Sir Arthur must close this reference to the controversy in his own words of scornful amazement. "There is to me," he says, "something very curious in hearing now, after thirty years of successful and most abundantly profitable operation of these very works, the self-same language with which I was met when I first urged the construction of the Cauveri or Coleroon anicut. 'An anicut across the Cauveri! What a "visionary" idea!' I thought at that time, 'If I can only get one of these anicuts built, there will be an end to all this; people will see that what was done by the natives hundreds of years ago, in the case of the "Grand Anicut" as it is called, on the Cauveri, with their little science and poor means, can also be done by us, and there will be an end of such exclamations.'

"But, since then, eight such works have been constructed in the very worst situations, as respects foundations, etc., without one failure (not without many accidents), and with unprecedented profits; and now precisely the same cry is heard with respect to a river of one-eighth the volume of water of one of those which has already been mastered, and that not by a non-professional man, by one of our greatest engineers. It seems to me now, that it is as useless waiting till this sort of thing ceases, as it is to wait by the side of the Ganges at Allahabad till all the water runs off. We must be content to go on constructing these visionary works, which produce such uncommonly substantial results as we witness in Madras, and to live and die visionaries for our pains."

It is but fair to Sir Arthur's memory to say that, before entering into controversy on the Ganges canal, he put on record his dislike for contention, and only defended his report on the ground "that the matter dealt with is not a mere personal question, but one of vital importance to India and to the whole British Empire."

On the question as to whether Sir Arthur Cotton's criticisms were relevant, and of service to the enterprise, I prefer myself not to speak; there is no need that I should. Another, an absolutely independent witness, whom I know only through his writings on irrigated India, the Hon. Alfred Deakin, ex-Minister of Lands for Victoria, Australia, has expressed his opinion on the controversy. Referring to the Ganges canal, Mr. Deakin says: "Sir Arthur Cotton, called in to criticise the original plan in 1863, had condemned it almost wholly, and recommended in its stead the construction of a new headwork for a new main canal much lower down the river. Ultimately this proposal of his was adopted in addition to, but not in substitution for, the existing plan." At the same time, Mr. Deakin, "considering that Sir Proby Cautley was the first to undertake the design and execution of a great river canal," and that "the errors in construction have proved to be less serious than was supposed in 1863–64," feels it to be his duty to state that "the general soundness of Sir Proby Cautley's judgment and the wisdom of his project must be conceded." I am glad to be able to close my references to the controversy between my father and the great Bengal engineer with the foregoing commendation of the latter's general design.

CHAPTER XVI

Work in England for India

THE late Sir James Stephen (sometime Law Member of the Viceroy's Council, and afterwards one of Her Majesty's Judges of the High Court, London) wrote a long letter to *The Times,* criticising Sir Arthur Cotton's views. He probably considered that his great forensic reputation, coupled with his five years' tenure of office in India, was sufficient to enable him to controvert statements deduced from accomplished facts and from experience gained during a lifetime's labours. As *The Times* did not print the reply sent to it by Sir Arthur, it is incumbent on his biographer to insert at least the main part in this narrative, so that the independent reader can form his own judgment as to which of the two men was likely to be right. The march of events, and the rapidly increasing prosperity of India in all the irrigated districts, have proved that the judge failed to apprehend the question which he undertook to criticise. The following portion of Sir Arthur's reply sufficiently exposes the weakness of his critic's attack:—

"He (Sir James) speaks as if irrigation were never used except when there was no rain. It is possible that he did not even know that there are some ten millions of acres in India that are watered every year, rain or no rain. He has heard of a single case where the ryots, ignorant of the difference between rain and river water, and acting upon the principle that a penny saved is a penny gained, have refused the water, excepting where they were actually compelled to use it from a total want of moisture. But what has this to do with irrigation in general? Under the old tanks in Madras, four million acres; under the Godavari, seven hundred thousand acres; in Tanjore a million acres; under the Ganges Canal, near a million acres, are irrigated every year, and there are many million more acres in the same condition, whatever rain falls.

"But, further, there is not a single acre in India that would not be the better for rich river water at some period of the crop, even when rain is most abundant, and that not only for rice but for dry grain also.

"He speaks of well or rain water and river water, as if it were all the same,—as if there were no difference either in cost or quantity. A ryot raises well water by bullocks at an average cost of about three hundred yards for a rupee, and it will only moisten the land, whereas river water manures it also, entirely renews it, so that whole districts go on for hundreds of years bearing grain crops without manure.

"The Government deliver the river water on to the land at Rs. 4 for an acre of rice, which is at the rate of fifteen hundred cubic yards per rupee, or a quarter the cost of filtered well water, which is not half its value; and for wheat or ragi, it supplies at about Rs. 2½ an acre, or six hundred cubic yards per rupee.

"So about fever. I believe there are instances of fever accompanying irrigation, but I have lived all my life in the midst of irrigation, and never had a day's fever from it, nor ever knew an instance of it in any of the districts I have been in, though I have had fevers without number in unirrigated districts. In the Godavari district, while the delta has very little fever, the moment you go into the upper tracts you encounter it continually.

"The question in these cases is not what men, entirely without means of knowing, think, but what men thoroughly experienced in such matters, and who have proved themselves to be practical men, think of them.

"If anybody asked me a question of law, I don't know what I would say, but I know what I ought to say. 'I really know nothing about the matter. You should consult Sir James Stephen or some other approved lawyer.'

"I sometimes think we engineers are placed in extraordinary circumstances. No engineer ever thinks of writing a letter of three columns to *The Times* to tell all the world how a hospital ought to be managed, or what is the solution of some intricate and important question of law. The plain fact is, that the rulers of India have most grievously neglected this fundamental duty of rescuing India from famine, and the result we have before our eyes in this terrible disgrace to our rule, and this call upon England for half a million to supplement the millions paid out of the Treasury, and which, if it had only been paid for irrigation and navigation works, would certainly have prevented nine-tenths of the horrors of the famine.

"And what is more, but for the one million that has been spent on the Madras irrigation works, the famine would have been aggravated so fearfully that the Government would have been entirely overwhelmed. With these things staring them in the face, I have a good hope that the people of England will no longer be misled by the old India school, but will insist upon all these imaginary difficulties being forgotten, and the work of relieving India taken up earnestly. I must notice one or two other things in this curious letter. He says, that 'Lord Salisbury said that water will not run up-hill.' There is certainly one thing more extraordinary than this remark of his lordship, that another man can be found to repeat it. I always thought that rain fell on the tops of the hills as well as on the coast; and, consequently, that water could be obtained at any level that was wanted. One of the great tanks is seven thousand feet above the level of the sea, and water is obtainable at every level from that to the coast."

In February, 1875, Sir Arthur Cotton addressed to the Manchester Indian Association a reply to a speech at Manchester, made by the Marquis of Salisbury on the subject of irrigation in India :—

"A single million [of expenditure] has secured two districts and all the surrounding country permanently from famine in the case of Godavari and Kistna, and six and a half millions of expenditure, and perhaps as much more of losses, would have thus permanently secured a tract of some twenty millions of people, or the whole area of the late famine for ever, if the same means had been used. We have shown wisdom in effectually counteracting a famine when it occurred; surely we might go a step further and be wise enough to prevent famines. Most assuredly no other way of doing this has been discovered but by irrigation.

"Millions of acres irrigated, drained, and secured from river floods, the crops in them secured and tripled, hundreds of steamboat canals carrying at a nominal cost, swarming with innumerable boats, conveying a traffic almost wholly created by the canals, tens of millions of people secured from famine, raised from poverty and actual want to abundance and comfort, delivered from living in a sea of mud in the monsoon, and from drinking filthy or mineralised water in the dry season; exports of raw produce for England's manufactories increased ten-fold, and imports of her goods increased twenty-fold, the character of the Government in the eyes of the natives and of foreigners raised highly, millions poured into the Treasury, the greatest returns ever obtained from engineering works in the world—all these were nothing in forming a judgment on the great question whether water is to be given to India or not; the only points worth noticing are a patch or two of the land not yet effectively drained, a patch or two injured by 'reh,' two cases out of thousands in which, through the grossest mismanagement, the use of the water is delayed for a time; these are the things which are to settle the question. Suppose a commission of inquiry on railways in England were to report that, after a thorough investigation, they had concluded from the facts that one passenger in ten millions was killed, that some of the trains arrived after their due time, that one occasionally caught fire, etc., that the whole system ought to be given up.

"One of the things that I complain of in these Indian reports, when they are given, is that they speak only of the Government profit. It may be very necessary for finance purposes to have works which will pay the interest of the money, but the great question is what effect they have upon the country altogether. That is the question for statesmen. I give you the general results of these irrigation works. We have spent £20,000,000 upon them, and we are spending £10,000,000 more upon them now. And the general result is this—that the average cost of irrigation, draining, embanking, and supplying the land with navigation from great rivers has been £2 an acre, and the average increase of produce alone, due to irrigation, has been £1 10*s*. per acre—sixty-six per cent., besides securing the land from the river floods, carrying off the heavy local rains, and supplying them with carriage at a normal price, so that the works are certainly, on an average, at this moment yielding to the country one hundred per cent."

Special reference was made to the Tungabudra reservoir, which the Government refused; he added that from this, if it were made, there might be laid three or four lines of magnificent irrigating canals to convey the water to vast tracts of country and to a very large portion of the Madras Presidency. "Probably at least ten thousand tanks could be supplied from that one reservoir alone. Such works will cost more than the works already executed, for two reasons. One is, that the upper country is more undulating and rocky, and another is that the value of money has considerably altered. But there is something on the other side, which is this:—You must remember that all we have accomplished is the result of our apprenticeship. Yet even these works return seven and a half per cent. to the Government, and that includes all our mistakes and all our failures. Therefore, we may certainly expect that works executed in the future with all this vast experience must be in some respects cheaper than the old ones."

"With respect to the storing of water, you may imagine what is the quantity to be stored when I tell you that from the Godavari alone five thousand millions of cubic yards flow into the sea in a day of a full river. Many suppose there is a lack of water in India, but there is only a lack of brains, not water. With respect to the storage of water, I have been fighting all my life to get such works executed. It is just fifty years since I pressed upon the Government the necessity for the construction of large reservoirs on the Neilgherries.

"In some of the speeches the subject of the opium revenue was mentioned. I should have wished to add a remark on that point.

"My position is this, that there is not the slightest excuse for our having recourse to such abominable means of balancing our finances.

"There is plenty of money to be made honestly and honourably in India. The revenue of the district of Godavari, in its former neglected state, was £220,000 a year, paid with the greatest difficulty and with positive impoverishment of the people, that is, a considerable proportion was paid out of capital. With the new works, still not completed, the revenue is £570,000 a year, an increase of £350,000, with a great and rapid increase of the wealth of the people. There are yet 300,000 acres to be irrigated; when this is done there will be an increase of water rate alone of £120,000 a year, and a total increase of at least £150,000, or in all, £500,000 a year. Now the net proceeds from opium are about £6,000,000, which, for the one hundred and sixty districts of India, would be about £40,000 per district, so that if all the other districts were improved by wise management only to the extent of one-ninth of the actual present increase in Godavari, and one-twelfth of that when the works are completed, it would fully replace the opium revenue. Now, who can estimate the difference between these two modes of balancing our finances? Which would be safest, as before God? Which would most promote our credit before other nations? Which most strengthen our hold upon the affections of the people of India? Which most tend to promote peace with

China, and legitimate trade with her? And, which would be most in accordance with our own national conscience—of these two modes of making money?

"But while we are keeping the famine mainly in view, let us not for a moment lose sight of the general well-being of India and England; for one of my main fundamental points is that the well-being of the two parts of the British Empire is so bound up together that it is impossible to separate their interests. The one is exactly what the other wants. The one wants hundreds of millions of labourers and millions of tons of food and rough materials, with unlimited purchasers of her manufactures; and the other wants an unlimited market for her produce, and an unlimited supply of manufactured goods, for the one implies the other. An orderly, industrious, population of two hundred and fifty millions cannot be sellers without being purchasers. If they sell us, for instance, £20,000,000 worth of wheat they must have in return some £20,000,000 worth of some kind of goods; and so, also, while we have tens of thousands of young fellows fit for anything and willing for anything and hundreds of millions of unemployed capital (for both which we only require a field), they have an unbounded field for the employment of both. It is impossible that two countries could be connected which more exactly meet each other's wants."

It was evidently felt by the Manchester men who heard him that Sir Arthur Cotton had satisfactorily answered Lord Salisbury. "Can we not," asked Mr. Leese, "undertake an enquiry into the exact state of things for themselves? It was very desirable that either the Chamber of Commerce or the Indian Association should undertake such an enquiry. They had on one occasion sent out an agent, and there was no question of greater importance than irrigation. Lord Salisbury had startled them with his extraordinary statements that the matter ought to be enquired into."

The enquiry, however, does not appear to have been made.

In December, 1877, Sir Arthur Cotton gave an address at a meeting of the Manchester Indian Association, and, two days later, a paper by him was read before the East India Association. In it he again describes the results of recently constructed schemes and the urgent need of further similar works, especially in the shape of those for navigation. These are only referred to here as exemplifying the earnestness with which he emphasized the prosecution of such works, which he was convinced were needful to secure the prevention of famine and to promote the prosperity of India. The point on which he most particularly insists is the advantage of cheap water carriage, as follows: "I must say a few words on the necessary connection of steamboat canals with irrigation. To irrigate a million acres of rice requires a canal two hundred yards broad by three feet deep, with a current of one and a half miles an hour, so that when we come to irrigate on this scale, we actually make the finest highways that could possibly be constructed. Thus the Godavari district has three main canals, each sixty yards broad; the Tungabudra main canal is sixty yards broad; the Sirhind canal is one hundred yards broad; so that nothing is wanted but locks, where the slope of the country is greater than can be allowed in the canal, in order to make the navigation. The locks now constructed are one hundred and fifty feet by twenty, and capable of being filled and emptied in one or two minutes, so that they form very small obstructions. With six feet of water they will admit boats of two hundred and fifty tons, and they may, of course, be worked at any speed that may be required for the traffic to be carried."

On several occasions Sir Arthur found the East India Association a convenient and useful medium for the expression of his views. Always there was discussion which, with much regret, must be passed over so far as these pages are concerned. Of one of these meetings he writes: "There are certainly indications of some change here. We had an adjourned discussion at the East India

Association on railways. There were two indications for good ; one was that Danvers and another India Office man, and Andrews, the Sind Railway man, were present ; they have felt so much pressure that they thought it necessary to abandon their old part of dignified silence and come out and meet me. This gave me a grand opportunity, if I had but had wit enough to take advantage of it. The other was that three or four spoke openly on my side, also quite a new feature. The secretary of the Association (Dadabhai Naoroji, now, in fact, the Association ; how curious that an Indian should have the whole affair in his hands!) has written to me twice for additional copies of my paper, besides three hundred he had distributed. . . . I showed M. one of your letters, and talked to him several times. He is not equal to making a decided stand against the Secretary of State and the whole Council, though he made a good fight about irrigation and gained his point. But this land and water communication touches the very apple of their eye, and they would be frantic if one stood up honestly and boldly on the right side. I don't know exactly what part F. plays in this respect, though I believe he does enough to make himself obnoxious. I sent you some copies of my paper, if you can kindly find means of distributing them. I am sorry to say I have got into a sad scrape. In one of your letters which I cannot now find, though how it can be missing I can't think, I understood you to say that the traffic in the Nuddea river was one million nine hundred thousand tons, and I laid great stress upon this ; but, by the papers you now send, I find the average is only five hundred thousand tons. I shall have to acknowledge this. Of course I have not made any allusion to you. It still shows the greater part of the traffic going by the rivers, but there is a great difference between half a million and two millions. I can't think how the mistake has arisen ; whether I read your letter wrongly or not, though I read it several times. I have the accounts of the cost of working the Brahmaputra steamers and they give under three-eighths of a penny per ton per mile, and the Director told me that they used to send their cargoes from Kushtea by rail at twenty per cent. under their regular charges, but they found it so much cheaper to carry them themselves four hundred miles by the Sunderbunds than to send them one hundred and ten by rail, that they gave up their contract with the railway.

"M. says he approves of my last paper on the Godavari Navigation, if I had only left out one or two paragraphs; no doubt the very ones upon which the whole depends. What I want to make them understand is that I am convinced they are essentially wrong, and this is the advantage of having a man out of office, that he can speak out in a way that perhaps a man in office ought not to do. The Oriyas must certainly be the most degraded race in India. I couldn't have believed that they would not even use the canals.[1] I have hope, however, now that the traffic, with the assistance of McKinnon's steamers, is fairly established."

In 1878, Sir Arthur Cotton gave an address at the Edinburgh Literary Institute in reply to one from Lord Napier of Ettrick, who had been Governor of Madras. The Governor and the engineer did certainly not see eye to eye. The engineer pointed out wherein the difference chiefly lay. He said:—

"I beg now to bring the matter before you in a strong light by contrasting my conclusions with those of your late lecturer, Lord Napier, who certainly had the right to offer his opinions, from his having been the Governor of Madras for several years so lately. I may premise that the first point of all, which constitutes the essential difference between us, is his entire indifference to cheap and effective transit. He makes no mention of this whatever; whereas,

[1] Since the above was written, the canals are being largely used for irrigation and navigation. Concerning them, Mr. Deakin says, in his book (p. 288): "Taking into account the circumstances of India and the character of its people, the Orissa canals cannot be denominated failures, though constructed with a view to the profit of private persons, and now being finished at the public expense as a means of preserving life."

in my opinion, it is most distinctly the very first point in the material improvement of India, and in dealing with those famines, even to be attended to in preference to irrigation itself, if considered as distinct, though it is quite true that the two things are so intimately connected, that in general you find you cannot work separately for the two ends."

It is somewhat amusing to note that he who was now an antagonist of the ex-Governor, hailed the latter's going to Madras with joy. Writing to a friend, he gave the information that Lord Napier of Ettrick, "who has hitherto been in the diplomatic line," was appointed to Madras. "Nassau Jocelyn, Lord Roden's son, says he's a very able and a very practical man. I must say I am heartily glad to hear of a Scotch nobleman going there, and not an old Indian. 'Blessed art thou, O land! when thy king is a son of nobles.'"

Perhaps not the least practical of all the addresses given by Sir Arthur Cotton, during his retirement, were the three which he delivered in Chatham. They constitute, for the space they occupy, the most lucid and informing description of irrigation works in India which is to be found anywhere. Apparently, he bestowed special pains on the preparation of these addresses. In previous chapters, it will be remembered, considerable use has been made of them.

During the latter years of his life he wrote memoranda on—

The Salt Tax: The Poor Man's Income Tax,
The Tungabudra Works,
English Internal Transit,
Communication with the Soudan by the Congo,
Public Works in Madras,
The Opium Revenue (chiefly addressed to the Anti-Opium Society, which he supported very warmly),
Study of Living Languages,
Indian Finance,

Prevention of Famines,
Points for the Consideration of the International Congress at Manchester,
Replies to Sir Walter Trevelyan's Minutes, Lord Napier of Ettrick, Sir Proby Cautley (Ganges Canal),
The Navigation of the Kareen River (Teheran),
and many others.

TAXATION ON SALT.

The heavy taxation on salt, and, consequently, the small quantity consumed by human beings and cattle, was always a source of anxiety to him. He wrote a pamphlet on the subject, entitled *The Poor Man's Income Tax.* Only a few passages can be quoted from a brochure of more than ordinary interest and value.

At the time when the late Mr. Laing was sent out, as Finance Minister to India, there was considerable anxiety as to the deficiency in the revenue, and consequent discussion as to the direction in which additional revenue could be raised, and it was finally unfortunately determined to impose an increased duty on salt. "Now salt is an indispensable condiment for a population whose principal diet is that of cereals or vegetables, especially to Hindus, by whom meat is rarely consumed as food. The manufacture of salt was a Government monopoly, and to so great an extent was the price of it raised, that salt from Cheshire could actually be landed at Calcutta and sold more cheaply than it could be purchased from the Government salt pans. To still further raise the price was to inflict a hardship on the population in the interior. On those on the coast it did not fall so severely, but, of course, when the cost of carriage to the interior came to be added to the Government price, it became a serious burden. The measure was a good deal discussed in the public prints at the time. . .

"In England there was formerly a duty of fifteen shillings per hundredweight on salt, or about three halfpence per pound, but, after the fullest inquiry into the subject, the nation came to the conclusion, chiefly on the opinions of the medical body, that salt was so essential to health, even among a population who used animal food extensively, that nothing could justify a tax on that article; though it yielded between one and two millions sterling, and was one of the most easily collected of taxes, it was, by general consent, given up. Whatever new taxes have since been imposed, this has never been again resorted to. It is well known that animal food is, in a measure, a compensation for salt, but the demand of the human system for this condiment, where vegetable food only is used, is more urgent than for anything except for food itself.

"Now, that a portion of the population is deprived of salt is fully proved by two things. First, by the fact mentioned by Mr. Laing, that the consumption is increasing. Men don't use salt as they do liquors,—that is, sometimes in excess; and, therefore, if the consumption increases, it is conclusive that the population had not enough before. And, secondly, the data as to the consumption afforded by Mr. Laing's paper. The total duty levied last year was £3,500,000 sterling. The average cannot be far from Rs. 2½ per maund, or £6 6*s*. per ton, and, consequently, a total duty of £3,500,000 gives a total consumption of 560,000 tons, which, for a population of one hundred and eighty millions, is seven lb. per head.

"Now, it has been well ascertained that, where the price is low, the consumption is not less than eighteen lb. a head, and it is said that in some parts it is proved to be as high as twenty-two lb.; whatsoever the actual consumption is at present, in any one place, for the reason before given, it ought to be at least that all over India; it might very probably be more; it could not be less. Indeed, there is strong ground to believe that it has never yet reached its proper height in any part of India.

"Now, supposing the labouring man in India to earn two annas a day, and his family one anna, his income is about seventy rupees a year,[1] and the salt duty is a poor man's income tax of

6 per cent. in Bengal,
2½ per cent. in Madras,
5¼ per cent. in Bombay,

so that the average of the poor man's income tax is much above that of the rich man.

"Yet the financier lays this on without discovering that he is actually doing the very thing he professes to abhor; he cannot discern the difference between words and things. What does it signify that one is called an income tax and the other a salt tax, and that, in the one case, the payer receives a receipt, and in the other salt, for which he at the same time pays the cost of manufacture, of carriage, and of dealer's profit besides? It is thus that superficial men are misled by their own words. . . . Now, in England, a man pays for a hundred lb. of salt tenpence, and earns, at two shillings a day and one shilling for his family, fifty pounds a year, so that his salt costs him one twelve-hundredth part of his income, and the poor Indian, with his vegetable diet, would have to pay from one to two hundred times as much, in proportion to his income, of course; the result is, as shown by the small amount of revenue raised, that one hundred millions of the people are almost or quite without this necessary of life. Even before the duty of fifteen per cent. in England was taken off, the English labourer only paid fourteen and sixpence a year, or one-seventieth of his income, and this was, by the voice of the whole country, declared to be so intolerable that a tax between one and two millions was given up to relieve him, while in India, it does not appear that one voice was raised against the atrocious proposal of a large increase of this tax.

[1] Unhappily, the average income of an Indian is nothing like Rs. 70 per year, save in the Cottonian districts. Lord Cromer's investigation in 1882 made it only just two-fifths per head of Rs. 70; the reader will note the effect of this reduction on Sir Arthur's contentions.

"Yet in this same paper the writer dares to quote the Holy Scriptures and say, 'Every enlightened Hindu and Mahommedan, as well as every enlightened Englishman, may cordially unite with us and join us in praying, in the words of the Psalmist, that "our works may be so done in truth and equity as to stand fast for ever and ever."' We do most heartily pray that Mr. Laing's works may not stand for this one year."

Throughout these years, India's needs, and the remedies for those needs, were my father's constant thought. Growing deafness kept him more and more to that privacy which, though a great hindrance to his intercourse with friends, was never allowed to be a hindrance to his literary activity. Much of his conversation was carried on by slips of paper, on which the converser stated his point and Sir Arthur replied *viva voce*. Quite a number of these "conversation" slips are in existence, many of them in the handwriting of Mr. Robert Scott, of *The Christian*, who spent several hours every week with Sir Arthur during the last two years of his life. One of these one-sided records—reminding one of a telephonic conversation heard by a bystander—the answers to which can often readily be imagined, though they cannot be heard, may be given. The "writer" was Bishop Thoburn, a most experienced Indian missionary; the speaker, "whose words are silence," was Sir Arthur.

NOTES OF A CONVERSATION BETWEEN BISHOP THOBURN AND SIR ARTHUR COTTON.

Bishop: We have a mission at Sironcha and one at Ingdalpur in Bastar. Both are new. We wish to open mission work at other points.

I am in my thirty-ninth year of service in India.

It is given out that Lord Cromer cannot leave Egypt this year.

And a strong man is needed as Governor-General.

The whole Godavari country is looking up. We have planned for a mission with stations at Raipur, Ingdalpur, Sironcha, and possibly two other stations in Bastar. We have three thousand famine orphans, and intend to settle many of them there.

I have not been nearer than Jellandu coal-field—two years ago.

General Haig used to worship with us in Calcutta, and held meetings constantly among the seamen. For several years he and I were constantly associated together. He often told me of his work on the Godavari. Some of his mission work is now in our hands.

I superintend our missions all over India. The work has spread down to the Straits, where there are now many Chinese colonists. We are now preaching in twenty-four different languages and districts. We have one hundred and ten thousand Christians of all ages, and two thousand native preachers of all grades. The work extends very rapidly among the lower castes. We are greatly straitened for means, owing to reductions in the grants from home, and the rapid extension of the work. But for this we might succeed to almost any extent.

A Commissioner in North India said some years ago, in his official report, that if our work among the Chumars went on, it would lead to a revolution. He feared for the result. In every direction the lower castes are waking up.

Many of the Hyderabad officials are friendly to our work. They aid us in many ways.

They will take up irrigation again before many years. The Nurbadda could have saved the valley in the recent famine. In all sub-mountain regions irrigation could be introduced by forming reservoirs among the hills. Sir Henry Ramsay did this with perfect success in Kumaon.

Ours is an American mission. I came out in 1859, when twenty-three years of age. Most of our missionaries are Americans, but we have some representing England, Scotland, Ireland, Wales, Germany, and Scandinavia. Our foreign force is not increasing. We aim to give increased responsibility to Indians, and this gradually puts responsibility upon them.

Men love to do as they did in ancient times—follow "the traditions of man."

I am much pleased to find that you have read a brief account of my work, and it greatly encourages me to know you approve my method in baptism. I was *led* into it, and after finding this path I discovered that it is the very way the New Testament deals with the question.

They were left to the development of Providence.

Only the simplest elements of a system of government are found in the church of Pentecost. The situation was new. We are on the threshold of a *new era.*

How many years did you spend in India ?—Forty-five years. I shall quote that freely when I go back to India.

You quite believe in a system of great reservoirs, do you not ?

There has been a revolution in medical treatment even since I came out. They told me I *must* drink brandy-pāni. For thirty-six years I have abstained, and now I feel that I am still a young man. We have now three thousand orphans under our care in India. Most of them are survivors of the late famine. It is a great delight to me to have this interview with you. It will interest people in India intensely to hear of your welfare. You are truly "a wonder unto many."

CHAPTER XVII

Life in England—Letters from Florence Nightingale, Sir Bartle Frere, Sir Colin Scott-Moncrieff, R.E., and others

WHEN my father went to India, after his retirement, and on special irrigation business, we removed from Devonshire to Tunbridge Wells, where we awaited his return. When he rejoined us there, later on, it was his last home-coming; though sundry schemes were on foot in after years, and he had thoughts and opportunities of returning, he did not again leave England. Instead, he endeavoured to serve India in this country, by trying to gain the support of those who had power to carry out his great schemes.

He longed for quiet and freedom from too much social intercourse, and often sighed during the few weeks after his return for a real country life. His resources were endless, and he had never known, perhaps for one moment, the meaning of the word *ennui*; he did not like his time broken up by constant visiting.

While at Tunbridge Wells he thus wrote to a friend: "I find they have been making a great mistake all this time in examining the wrong branch of the Tungabudra for sites for tanks; they have reached the Eastern, which is the one with the great fall. I could not understand what they told me about the site having so great a fall; it never occurred to me as possible that they could be wasting their time on the wrong branch. I forget whether I sent you Fife's letter; if not, I will send it. He was hoping to begin soon upon a tank of three hundred million cubic yards. This is the grand thing; if once the storing of water upon a large scale is begun the battle is won. It is curious how both Calveley and Haig have been baffled on this point for so many years. Rundall has a most noble site, on the Tel, which drains the western slopes of the Eastern Ghauts, when the rains are so excessive, two hundred inches at Jeypore. They plan a tank of two thousand millions with a bund of one hundred feet. I have nothing yet from Calcutta. The India Office Engineers are going to make another desperate effort; they think, I suppose, that C. had not made the most of it."

It was at this juncture that he was summoned, with a party of other engineers, to examine into the cause of the disaster that took place at Sheffield, when the embankment of a reservoir suddenly burst in the middle of the night, and a great portion of the city was flooded. He received a telegram early one morning while we were at breakfast, requesting him to proceed to the spot to aid in investigating the cause. His portmanteau was at once packed, and we went by the next train; I say "we," for he would have me go with him to see the wonderful sight. He suggested our going on to Ireland, that we might pay a visit to Lord Roden, who had married a connection of ours, and had most cordially invited us to stay at his place in County Down.

No sooner said than done. Two hours had not elapsed before we were on our way to Sheffield, and, during our long train journey, I had to listen to the discussions of the five engineers, who were travelling together to inspect this important work.

When we arrived at our hotel the scene was an unparalleled one. Confusion reigned in every street, and the sight that met our eyes was indeed strange. The water was pouring in a vast volume down the river bed and far beyond it on either side, carrying with it houses, haystacks, boats, farming implements, and every other imaginable species of wreckage in conglomerated heaps.

Amongst these strange piles were many bodies of unfortunate people, who had been swept away from their houses by the rising water and drowned, whilst men lined the sides of the river, dragging out the bodies, and laying them on the higher ground. It was altogether a terrible sight, but fortunately lasted only a short time as the torrent naturally soon subsided.

Our two days at Sheffield interested my father greatly, as it lay so entirely in his own line of work. We also visited some of the great steel and iron works, and saw the huge plates for the sides of iron-clad vessels prepared, as well as the delicate manipulation of a dainty pair of scissors.

On our journey from Sheffield, the engine broke down, and for two hours the passengers were delayed. My father devoted the period to a study of the engine and the cause of our misfortune. He soon was master of the whole subject, and when some one commiserated us at the end of the journey on our loss of time through this accident, his reply was, "Loss of time, do you call it? I thought it the most interesting and useful two hours of the whole journey."

We soon arrived in Ireland, and after a long drive of about eighteen miles from the station, we were rewarded by the interest of driving up to the great gates of Tollymore Park: he was perfectly entranced with the view; mountains rising over mountains, all tipped with snow, and also the hills richly wooded, ending abruptly in a delicious ravine, through which a bubbling, rushing stream-torrent flowed, sometimes tumbling over the rocks in waterfalls and cascades. The house stood amongst the woods, surrounded by shrubs, and fronted on the west side by an immense bed of rhododendrons just in flower. But it was the mountain view that so enchanted him. From the house we could see the sea, only two miles off,—a glorious view it was! Mountain, sea, and woods combined! He felt in a moment that this was the air, and this was the scene, that would be the greatest refreshment to him now, wearied as he was in mind and body. And when, in the course of the day, Lord Roden drove him down to see a charming house that he had recently put in order, with a gate that opened into the park, and offered it to him for a few months, he could not resist the temptation of making this his home for a time at least. The climate and scenery were everything to him, and he felt that he could use the one power left now—his pen—in this quiet retreat, better than he could in any more frequented place.

In a very short time we all moved to Bryansford, the pretty village into which the gates of Tollymore opened. And there we remained for three years. He wrote incessantly, morning and evening, and drove in the afternoon through the beautiful scenery of the neighbourhood, or made expeditions to the mountains on foot. He was singularly active and fond of walking, and, however weary he might feel, it always seemed to refresh and invigorate him. He would visit the lonely farms scattered through the mountains, his pockets filled with books, with which he would endeavour to cheer the solitude of these lonely people, who were always grateful and pleased to see, as well as cordial in their welcome of, a visitor. They loved him truly, and many a one would offer their rooms for a little reading or prayer, when he would open his Bible and tell them of the Water of Life, which flows so freely from the Throne of Grace, and can satisfy the most needy heart.

Lord Roden's daughter, the Countess of Gainsborough, one of the Queen's ladies-in-waiting, used often to come to Tollymore to stay with her father;—a most charming woman, with handsome features and queenly presence; none that ever knew her could forget her exquisite manners and delightful conversation. Lord and Lady Dufferin, Lord and Lady Lurgan, Sir Arthur Blackwood, and many other friends used to be the guests of that hospitable home. Miss Marsh, the authoress of *Hedley Vicars*, was one of his favourite visitors; and Mr. Richard Nugent, with his wife and daughters, often came to Tollymore.

We often visited Lord Annesley's beautiful place, Castle Wellan, with its remarkable pinetum and far-reaching lake. The house stood in an exquisite position, looking down on the undulating park, with the water shining between the trees.

Lady Annesley's house at Newcastle, Donard Lodge, was another delightful place in the neighbourhood. It was a real enjoyment to my father to walk on the terraces overlooking the sea, and then to wander in the woods, and watch the splendid waterfalls, which, in winter and after rain, were a sight which people would drive miles to see.

One day when my father was driving with Lord Roden, beside the river that ran through the park, he was pointing to the bridges which crossed it, each of which had its history and its own special character, and greatly added to the charm of the grounds. He pointed to one particular turn of the stream, and said, "We have always wanted a bridge there, but have never put one up." My father immediately said, "You can easily have a wooden chain bridge, swinging across from bank to bank; it would be very ornamental, and exceedingly useful for foot passengers, though it would be too light for carriage traffic." They drove together to the carpenter's shop—always a great scene of interest—attached to the saw mills, where busy work was constantly going on. After a little conversation with the man in charge, it was decided that my father should draw out a plan for the construction of this bridge. This was soon done, and to this day the bridge may be seen, a specimen of light, strong, work, useful for its purpose and picturesque as well.

On the recovery of my father's health, he desired opportunities to extend the irrigation interests of India. For this reason he determined to leave Ireland, and take up his residence within easy reach of London; he finally settled at Dorking in Surrey.

He was on the Committees of the Church Missionary Society, the Bible Society, and the Irish Church Mission. He continued his connection with these Societies for

WOODCOT, DORKING.

p. 497.

many years, his attendance only being prevented afterwards by increasing deafness. He was devoted to active exercise, and used to take very long walks, enjoying the sight of fresh views or new country. His activity was wonderful. After the severe illnesses that he had passed through, and the zeal and labour of his life in India, with its many privations, exposures, and difficulties of a thousand kinds, at the age of sixty-seven years he thought nothing of walking thirteen or fourteen miles in a day.

One day we were crossing some fields, and were obliged to pass a large herd of cattle. Some of them looked rather fierce, and one made a dead set at us with its horns down. I immediately ran to a stile that was near, and got out of the way. When my father joined me he was smiling.

"You are just like a woman," he said; "all women are the same."

"What have I done now," I asked, "to merit such a rebuke?"

His reply was: "A woman runs away when there is no danger; but, when there is danger, she is as brave as a lion and knows no fear!"

When he was walking, or driving, he was often so absorbed in calculations on a gigantic scale, millions of rupees, or miles, or measurements of some kind, that he did not utter a word; and, if he was addressed, he did not appear to be conscious that any one had spoken to him. He could often preserve this abstraction in a crowded room, with people talking all around him; he would busily write out his notes or jot down his figures, carrying out his own line of thought at the time.

We did not reside very long in the cottage that we had rented at first at Dorking; my mother's brothers were anxious to build her a house, and they asked my father to choose the kind of house they both would like. A charming spot was selected—a sunny slope, crowned with a wood, and having a pleasant view. My father had said several times that he would have liked very much to have a house built on the plan of one he had seen on the island of Guernsey, belonging to Colonel de Haviland—an old friend of Indian days who had died a few years previously. The coincidence, which now occurred, is interesting. A new curate had come to the parish; my father met him. In the course of conversation it came out that this clergyman's family belonged to Guernsey.

"Oh," said my father, "that is a very curious thing; I should like to ask if you ever knew General de Haviland, who lived there a few years ago. When I was a young man I stayed at his house, and shall never forget its picturesque inner hall with a gallery round it. I have often said I should like, if ever I had a house built for myself, to have it arranged on that plan."

The curate answered, "Strangely enough an uncle of mine has taken rooms for a few days in this town. He lives in that very house in Guernsey, having rented it since the General's death"; adding, "If you will call upon him, he will be delighted to see you, and perhaps can give you some information about it."

My father walked over to pay this visit and found the gentleman at home. When the inquiries were made, the reply was: "I have here in my desk the actual plans of the house."

Sir Arthur begged the loan of the plans, showed them to an architect, and a house was built which was in accordance with his earliest wish.

My brother was at this time in Northern India, having left Sandhurst with flying colours. He arrived at Woodcot one Saturday afternoon as usual, for he always spent Sunday with us; and, as he came into the room, he greeted my father with the words: "What would you say if I were to tell you that I have won the first prize for fencing?" So saying, he exhibited a very handsome pair of fencing-sticks to our joy and pride. Then he added: "Look at this!" and put into his father's hands a sword; "it is the Good Conduct Sword!" Out of eight hundred young men his son had received this honour! My father's delight and surprise were indeed very great. Soon, however, my brother had to leave to join his regiment; there were sad hearts at Woodcot, for he had always been a devoted son.

From his own correspondence a few excerpts are made to indicate the character of the letters he wrote, and the unceasing interest which he took in everything appertaining to the advantage of India, or the greatness of England.

(1) "*The Daily Telegraph* editor wrote to me that Sir Bartle Frere had told him to apply to me for a series of letters on the famine, which I am now writing; two have appeared, and I have sent a third, and should like to write one or two more. It is a great opportunity, as the *Telegraph* has an enormous circulation.

"Frere seems quite to support me. Sir Lewis Mallet also wrote to me, protesting against spending money on works not suited to India, railways, but seems to think it useless to attempt to oppose the system, only resisting individual works.

"I wrote to call his attention to your translation of the French Commission paper, which he thanks me for and says he has got it. Mr. Waterfield, of the India Office, writes to me, saying that you and I say that goods can be carried by water at one-tenth of a penny, and asks for our authority for it. I told him we both give our authority in the papers, and I repeated it in my answer. This shows that the India Office cannot any longer resist the pressure, but is compelled at last to look into the matter. The fact is they must hear of it now. I said to him what a pity they had not asked the difference between the cost of land and water carriage before they spent one hundred and thirty millions on the former.

"I highly approve of your memo., and have no doubt it will have effect. But all the pressure that can possibly be brought to bear upon the matter in England will be required. There is to be a discussion on it to-night at the Society of Arts, under Sir B. Frere, but I cannot go as I have a cough. Another is to be held by the East India Association next week—a paper by W. Tayler, who asked me to give him a memo. on the subject. I have written two letters to Sir George Campbell, urging the execution of the Navigation canal to Jessore, and the pushing on of the different parts of the main line of canal up the Ganges. I have also written two letters to *The Times*, especially insisting upon this—that one crop in a famine would pay the whole cost of the most expensive irrigation works twice over. It would pay the whole cost of the Orissa works, with accumulations of interest, if not an acre was watered nor a boat passed along the canal for ten years. I am very glad the canal is open to Midnapur. It's also a grand point that you are able to water so much land from the Sone, putting in the strongest light the effect of such works in a famine.

"I think the high level canal I proposed to Jessore and the main Ganges of the greatest importance, as opening the communications for the whole year, at the least possible expense of time and money. F. says he wrote a memo. on it and that he would send it to me, but I have not got it yet. I wish you could get it put in hand now."

(2) "I am anxious to hear, first, what effect upon the whole you think the famine will have upon your project as a speculation—whether you think the depopulation and impoverishment of the district will materially delay the use of the water. That it must seriously affect the traffic there seems no room for doubt. Surely it will fully account for what you say of the small traffic in your last letter.

"Next, what effect will this advance of funds by the Government have upon your works?

"I see they offer £20,000 a month, and that B. has accepted it. Will you be able to make use of it, and find labour enough, and what will it do for you this season?

"I should be very much obliged to you for your opinion of the prospects of the project now. They seem to be now doing everything that they ought to have done fourteen months ago. I should suppose that in your present position, with some of the heavy works finished, the money ought to go far in the distribution.

"I should be glad to see any Indian papers that comment on the Ganges canal controversy. The report was an extraordinary failure. I am so glad they didn't call you in, or anybody on my side. I have the Godavari report, too, quite as complete a failure, though free from bias.

"I wrote to Frere and asked him to help in seeing that the matter received a fair hearing in the India Office.

"I wrote also to Sir Stafford, and begged him to read the papers himself, which he promised to do. They have lately printed for the House of Commons papers about irrigation—a most melancholy affair—papers by almost everybody, but not one single thing *done*, even by Lord Cranbourne. Buckle says most truly that this is the characteristic of the age—everybody writes and says, but nobody *does*.

"And nothing will be done while the Council is the executive in public works; they are an incompetent body, and there is no hope till we have a separate Board of Works, who have time to make themselves acquainted with their business, and to acquire an interest in it, and to have nothing else to attend to.

"They are going on just the same with the Upper Godavari works. Sir Charles Wood told J. B. Smith that the last thing he did before he left the India Office was to order the vigorous prosecution of the Godavari works at all the Barriers; but to this time the Indian Government have not issued the orders, and another season is lost.

"I have some idea of trying to make a move by seeing Frere, Sir Stafford, and others, this month. Frere is a man whose deeds do not belie his words, and perhaps he may effect something. I am writing an answer to the Upper Godavari report. But they now talk of millions as they used to talk of thousands. There never was such an opening in respect of capital; the rogueries of last year have left the public afraid of all private enterprise and the accumulation is prodigious. I suppose any amount could be obtained by Government.

"I am in hopes I may hear from you soon. The majority which the Government have just obtained will probably set Sir Stafford at liberty to attend to his own business; but I see no signs whatever, yet, of anything effective being done about public works, though I am in hopes it may still creep on as it has done of late.

"They have sent another officer, Forbes, down to the Godavari, showing that while they affect to ignore these works, they find them too hard a nut to crack; they will find all sorts of faults with them, quite forgetting that all they say against them will only strengthen my arguments, for if, with all the mistakes, the works have produced such results, it only confirms the more all I say about the profits of irrigation.

"God has favoured us with a termination to the Abyssinian Expedition beyond all our hopes, though I must say it's a terrible disappointment to me, too, for I could not help hoping that we should be inextricably entangled in the country, and be compelled to inaugurate a state of peace and order there and in the surrounding countries.

"I have had some conversation with a Mr. Vesey Fitzgerald, a man of property in Ireland, who takes a great interest in India, and made a tour in it some years ago. He is a literary man and, I believe, a man of some influence; he is a Liberal, but a member of the National Club. He sent for me, and is trying if he cannot do something to force on works in India. In this way there is now a very considerable undercurrent working, but it may yet take long before anything is done.

"If you see the Rajah of Benares, tell him I have just been to see his well, within a few inches of where I was born, in Oxfordshire. It is three hundred and fifty-eight feet deep. It was in beautiful order, and the water was delicious, an invaluable gift to that neighbourhood."

(3) "How astonishing it seems that navigation must

never be mentioned at the India Office or in the House of Commons. I am happy to say the Lower Ganges works, begun at the very spot where C. wrote a book to prove it was the greatest nonsense to talk of an anicut being built, are completely successful; and the Sirhind seems to be going on very well, but the Sone hangs fire still—why I have no idea, for not a word is said on this one fundamental point in the reports; the same with the Tungabudra.

"I had a talk with Mr. Bourke [M.P. for King's Lynn, then appointed Governor of Madras and created Lord Connemara], who seems a very efficient man, and I am in great hopes will do something to restore Madras. I pressed upon him the putting of an able man at the head of the Public Works Department, and taking up earnestly the works on which about three millions sterling have been spent without any result as yet, entirely from want of competent men. I alluded to the harbour, the Coast canal, the Tungabudra works, and the Godavari navigation.

"You see they are taking up in good earnest the North-Western Frontier, so far as advanced posts are concerned; but nothing is being done to prepare the ground base, the Indus, as you advise. This is quite beyond present men, though it is *the* point above all. But we have not a single master mind at present, unless G. expands now that he is brought to the front. I am rejoiced that F. has at last got into work worthy of his talents and of his deep Godliness. We last heard from him at Aden, he having visited all the ports of the Red Sea, and he is to go to Muscat and Bagdad and Damascus, and up the Nile. A more able man to lay the foundation of a great mission around Arabia could not be found. He is sent by the Church Missionary Society. What a grievous thing it is to think how such a man has been thrown away hitherto!

"I must acknowledge that it's a great satisfaction to me that this most able paper was prepared by you, and circulated, for I cannot but hope that it may yet help to resuscitate this most vital subject of irrigation, against which the whole Indian official body, almost, have so entirely set themselves.

"Indeed, a friend of mine, an ex-C.E., has lately written to me that he finds the India Office rather inclined to return to the subject. And I have lately found out that the Punjab Government are really heartily in earnest in the matter, in spite of the superior authorities. They have irrigated three million acres, have another great project in hand, and a further one almost ready for execution.

"But, curiously enough, I have now before me a vast railway project about which I should like greatly to have your advice. It includes such a number of first-class objects that it would quite affect all India, though the line itself is only three hundred miles long. It is from Vizagapatam to Raipur, and has been long talked of, and I rather think is actually begun, but without their the least perceiving the main point, that it is the natural and proper outlet of the whole Upper Gangetic country. I am preparing a memo., which I will submit for your remarks. What I wonder at is that I never perceived the state of the case."

One of his favourite correspondents was Miss Florence Nightingale. On the subject of Indian irrigation she was keenly interested. With a view of drawing the attention of a newly-appointed Governor to this subject and the importance of pushing forward certain works, she wrote :—

"If you could write me one of your most interesting and impressive letters, I might be able to do something with it. Will you give me the latest figures and information of the state of things in this year?"

With regard to the irrigation map that was then being prepared, and which, brought up to date, is published with this memoir, Miss Nightingale writes: "I have had but few copies made, because I hope that every year we shall have to make additions to this map; and that every year it will require correction!"

She alludes to Sir Richard Temple's minute on the famine of 1877–78 :—

"He bore testimony to the tanks, as famine relief

works (in the Bombay Presidency), and to their permanent value for the people. I always think of *you*—their father —when I read any of these passages. The more one hears of this famine, the more one feels that such a hideous record of human suffering and destruction the world has never seen before.

"I am very sorry to hear so poor an account of yourself, but there is a good time coming yet. India is forcing her way to the front. You must live for that."

Sir Arthur Cotton writes to another friend with reference to the making of railways instead of canals :—

"What an inconceivable mistake they have made in forcing on the railways in India. After trying land carriage in England for sixty years, they have decided that it is necessary to spend seven millions in water transit by the side of the rails for thirty-five miles (referring to the Manchester Canal). What a decisive judgment this is as to land carriage in India, where there are lines of one thousand miles in length! The ludicrous part of the matter is that they are working the rails generally at from eight and a half to twelve miles an hour, with only the exception of one or two lines at twenty to twenty-five miles, while canals would certainly have been worked generally at fifteen or twenty miles for whatever required it."

No wonder he adds :—

"The works suggested would secure such a supply of cheap building materials, fuel, salt, etc., as would alter the whole domestic state of the people. The works also provide for about five million acres of irrigation scattered through the whole peninsula, yielding an increased produce of ten millions per annum. This, in addition to the present five million acres in Madras (besides all in Mysore, Hyderabad, and Bombay), would secure food for twenty-five millions of people, and would effectually provide against famine in connection with the abundant means of transport of food throughout the whole peninsula, at a charge which would add very little to its cost. But what would be the prodigious stimulus that this means of intercourse would give to the people, certainly putting new life into the community beyond all we can imagine! Besides the new irrigation, these works, by a more certain supply to the tanks in ordinary years (and that the superior river water), would greatly improve the produce and value of the present irrigation.

"But, further, the improved condition of the people would lead to a vast extension of the ordinary dry cultivation, and by the abundance of fodder, the difficulty for providing for the cattle, in consequence of the diminished area of jungle, would be completely met. The model farms have proved fully that, with a very small supply of water, fodder may be grown for cattle at a very small cost. This is one of the many things that it is necessary to put the people in the way of providing, by European instructors.

"Who, for instance, can estimate the effects of such a state of the people in respect of all necessary things, in enabling them to educate themselves? The change in Godavari in this respect, as certified in one of the Indian papers, will give some idea of this.

"Those only who have seen a famine district can judge of the change in the district of Godavari. In a country where, within living memory, men have died of famine by tens of thousands, and population has been checked by contingent consequences of famine, we now see a teeming population of stout, cheerful, well-proportioned men, women and children that will compare with any in the world for intelligence.

"In the Godavari there is scarcely a symptom of solid prosperity and rational enjoyment that is not displayed.

"Lower down the river and in the delta, the rush for education is incredible, though there are a few instances of apparent reaction."

Once more:—

"According to Whittaker, the present return on irrigation works executed by Government is 4·3 per cent., while money is borrowed at 3 per cent., 'apart from the advantages to cultivators and protection against famine'; and, he should have added, the additional revenue paid in a district, besides the water rate. Thus in Godavari, the water rate is Rs. 5 per acre—on 700,000 acres, Rs. 35,00,000—but the increase of revenue has been Rs. 75,00,000, or double the rates, almost the whole of which is due to the irrigation.

"Thus from water rates alone there is now a clear gain to Government of one and a third per cent. on irrigation expenditure.

"And this is without reckoning the actual saving at this moment to Government in respect of famine relief.

"With respect to water carriage, Mr. L.'s evidence is of inestimable importance, as of a man whose prejudices would necessarily be entirely against canals.

"Surely such a principle could not be allowed in the common business of life,—a contractor having completed his contract, presents his written agreement, and demands a hundred thousand pounds, and he is met by the statement that he is foolish to suppose that it is to be taken literally, that the hundred thousand is a mistake, and that he will receive only a thousand."

He complains that estimates are asked for, and then rejected. And that no notice is taken, when considering the famine, of the results obtained from providing a water supply:—

"A crop was raised that year (1878) worth five millions, where not an acre would have been raised without irrigation (the works having cost £1,500,000), and not only over the population of Godavari, Kistna, and Tanjore, about five millions saved, but enough was exported to save four or five millions in other districts. Not a word has been said about the effect of these works on the famine."

Alluding to the Kurnool Canal, he says:—

"It has proved itself a perfect God-send in this year of drought, and in the direct and indirect benefits it has secured to man and beast within its influence, it has fully justified its existence.

"There can be no doubt whatever that, as years go on, the area irrigated will increase, and eventually be very extensive; provided that the canal is maintained in good order, and every effort made to encourage irrigation, and to give the ryots confidence in the canal's ability to meet all their demands."

From amongst the correspondence which he received during these years are a few letters which may profitably be reproduced.

From Sir Bartle E. Frere, G.C.S.I., *Governor of Cape Colony and High Commissioner for South Africa.*

GOVERNMENT HOUSE, CAPE TOWN,
March 27, 1880.

MY DEAR SIR ARTHUR,—

I have been getting from the India Office and other sources, all the papers that I can regarding irrigation, for which there is an enormous and almost unlimited field in every part of South Africa, and for every description of water storage and irrigational work. I have got a mass of works and reports of various kinds, but nothing that satisfies me as a really complete and comprehensive description of the cost and results of your great Madras works, and I find it impossible to make time to go through Blue Books and draw up, from scattered materials, such a precis as would show my friends here, how vast were the prospects, how economically executed, and how great the financial results of your more important irrigational works.

If you could get for me a summary of a kind which would make a good review article, or, as it were, a kind of index to larger and more detailed reports, it would greatly help us. I hope we are now, in South Africa, at the beginning of a period of active irrigational works. They will not go so fast here as they did with you in Madras, for we have to depend much more upon private enterprise and private money. But the Orange and the Vaal rivers are both sources of water supply on which engineers of your school would very soon persuade the people of South Africa to spend at least as many millions as they are spending on railways with the certainty of larger results ; for the soil is everywhere good and everywhere very sparsely inhabited and almost uncultivated.

I wish a few of the disciples of your school would take South Africa in the course of their search for health, or for a home after they have been used up in India. It is a country where old Indians find they have ten or twelve more years' work in them than when they retire exhausted from India ; and where men, who cannot live at all in India or in a cold climate, thrive amazingly. I know you will not mind trouble in such a cause, and with kindest regards, in which Lady Frere and my daughters join,

I am, my dear Sir Arthur,

Very faithfully yours,

H. B. E. FRERE.

General Sir Arthur Cotton, K.C.B.,
Dorking.

From Sir Colin (then Colonel) Scott-Moncrieff, R.E.

I.

CAIRO, *Nov.* 14, 1885.

MY DEAR SIR ARTHUR,—

I thank you very sincerely for your most kind letter of the 31st. The approval and sympathy of such a veteran as yourself is very gratifying. I am sending you the report on which *The Times* formed their article. Do not for a moment think we have made the Barrage a sound job for twenty-five thousand pounds. Far from it. But we succeeded in holding up three metres head of water at the time of lowest Nile, when the demand for cotton and rice irrigation was at its highest. I cannot say we were quite easy about it. I insisted on a good young English engineer being always there in case of accidents, and there was a sigh of relief when the river began to rise and we could open the gates. I daresay in the old days, when you were curbing the Cauveri with that wonderful light anicut, and were battling for every rupee with an inappreciative Government, you had your anxious moments too.

Now I have got a million of money to spend, which, although not much, will help a great deal, and I have some right good officers from India to help me to spend it. We are quite a little English corps here now. Ten of us from India, and three capital young Englishmen I picked up here. And, though I say it who shouldn't, I think with God's blessing we shall leave some mark for good in Egypt. I never before thought so highly of the Indian school of training. The pashas here stand aghast at the unsparing way in which my officers knock about and work in the hot weather; and, after all, it is no more than dozens are doing daily in India, and without whom India would never have been what it is. We have almost decided to make a second weir over the Damietta branch of the Nile, a few miles north of Benha, where the railway crosses the river. This will cost, I fear, two hundred and fifty thousand pounds, and we shall spend, I fear, quite two hundred thousand pounds on making the existing Barrage quite sound. One work I have near my heart is the abolition of the corvée. When I came here I found an army of one hundred and twenty thousand men, employed annually for six months, without pay or food—a horrid, disorganised, rabble—and a system that gave the fullest play to all the corruption and rascality that flourish here.

No pasha ever sent a man to the corvée. The whole burden fell on the poor. By only a little common sense and arrangement we have shown them that for about two-thirds of the former silt clearances the same quantity of water can be obtained. And now we are battling the system altogether, I have got dredgers in to do a lot of the work. Nubar Pasha is helping us with all his influence, and though, perhaps, I am too sanguine, I am in hopes to leave Egypt two years hence without a forced or unpaid workman. But there are endless little worries and hinderances. French jealousy, palace intrigues, the lowest sense of honour on the part of the employees. In India the path was much clearer. Here we are for ever hoping to arrive at daylight through the political haze, but it seems as thick as ever. Mr. Gladstone seems determined, if he gets the chance, to clear us all out. I disbelieve utterly in a Mohammedan country reforming itself. I know if we were to go they would fall back to their old corrupt, unrighteous, ways, and really did I not believe that somehow, in spite of Mr Gladstone and all the Radicals, we are not going to leave Egypt, I should have little heart to work here.

I have to thank you for kind words of sympathy in my domestic desolation. This is a subject on which I cannot write. Submission to the great Captain's orders is surely the good soldier's duty. Hard work is a great solace, and no one ever had more kind friends than I. Forgive this long letter, and

Believe me,
Yours very sincerely,
C. C. SCOTT-MONCRIEFF.

II.

CAIRO, *Sept.* 7, 1890.

It is true, as you say, that patching and reforming is often harder than originating. On the other hand we in Egypt have had an enormous advantage over what you had in the delta days, in nearness to Europe, and consequent facilities in procuring materials, machinery, and skilled labour. A dozen more steam pumps could be got in a few weeks. Our electric light gave no trouble, and made night work far pleasanter than day during the heat. The best of stone could be got from Trieste; Portland cement as much as we required from England; a light railway carried our materials about cheaply and easily; and then we had the benefit of your old experience to help us. You hadn't that! I think Egypt is really doing well under English guidance. I only regret that the Government at home does not speak out honestly, and say once for all we are *not* going to leave the country. Till we do that and face the opposition it must call forth, I think we are sure to have trouble with the French. It would be more honest on our part, I think. The French thwart us very seriously. A conversion of debt has just been concluded in which they have so effectually put a spoke in the wheels, that Egypt won't get over it for fifteen years. They have sympathised in nothing we have done here. They did their best to oppose a reform, which gives me more satisfaction even than the Barrage. I mean the abolition of the corvée.

We spend annually now four hundred thousand pounds on clearing and repairing canals, embankments, etc., all unskilled labour (except some dredging), and all of which labour was performed by unpaid corvée up to 1884. This has been a great boon to the fellah, as you may suppose.

I am sending you two more notes you may care to see, one on a big flood we had in 1887, the other on the means for remedying defective floods such as we had in 1888, when the long valley of Upper Egypt is apt to be left *shardki*, that is, uncovered by the flood, and therefore incapable of tillage. My excellent second in command, Col. Ross (one of my old Indian assistants) has made this his special study, and I trust in two or three years the Egyptian will no longer be haunted by the nightmare that the Nile flood may fail him, bringing distress, if not actual famine. Our next great step must be the storage of Nile water to increase the summer supply, and this, I think, is not far off. But it is a big job. Yes, I fully recognise with you that the Almighty has blessed our work in Egypt, for which we can only humbly thank Him. He knows how poorly and lamely and selfishly much of it has been done. Yet He has blessed us. Thank you again very heartily for your most kind encouragement.

Believe me,

Yours very sincerely,

COLIN SCOTT-MONCRIEFF.

SIR ARTHUR COTTON (AGED 94)

Standing in front of 6 feet high English wheat.

p. 513.

CHAPTER XVIII

Many Interests at Home and Abroad

MY father did many things. I think I am saying only what is strictly accurate, when I assert that he did them all well. He certainly did them with great thoroughness. Before, however, mentioning these, I may refer to his personal friendships.

One of the friends, who came from time to time to have important conversations with him, was the late Sir William McKinnon, Chairman of that marvellous fleet, the British India Steam Navigation Company. My father had the greatest admiration for Sir William's clear intellect and genius. His Indus steamers, and his great ideas with regard to the opening up of Africa and the improvement of the Congo Territories were a constant source of mutual interest.

Sir William's invitation to us to spend a few weeks with him on the trial trip of one of his new steamers to Norway and Sweden was readily accepted. My father enjoyed intensely the cruise round the west coast of Scotland, where the mountain views seemed to unfold like a wonderful series of pictures. We then cruised northwards, and entered the Norwegian Fjords, where some weeks were spent among scenery which defies description. Great mountains rising sheer out of the water, their sides streaked with loveliest silver streams, growing sometimes into waterfalls of wondrous beauty. My father was in his element. Scenery was always a rare and special delight to him, and he loved the sea. He was an excellent sailor, and had no dislike even to rough weather which would compel many of Sir William's guests to desert the deck.

On our return we stayed at Ballinakill, Sir William's beautiful place on the Argyllshire coast, where we had before often enjoyed his hospitality and rambles amongst the heather.

My father, in spite of stormy weather, used to take long walks on the mountain sides. I well remember how he used to say: "I am off for a ramble, who will come?" Some demurred that it was raining. To which he would reply: "The rain is nothing. Don't let us lose a moment of this delicious day." Away he would go, guiding his party to one of the summits near, whence a beautiful view could be obtained of land and sea, even across to the distant coast of Ireland.

Sir William was in constant correspondence with my father regarding a variety of subjects, such as steamers for river navigation, Stanley's expeditions, the employment of Tippoo Tib (a notorious slave-dealer), the further opening up of the Congo States, and the progress of missions connected with the Free Church of Scotland. Sir William's letters were terse and strong, and his opinions on every subject fully and clearly expressed, as though he had abundant leisure at his command, whereas he was the busiest of men.

DEVELOPING NORTH-WEST AFRICA.

A very interesting correspondence was also carried on with Mr. Donald Mackenzie, on the possibilities of taking to North-West Africa the benefits of commerce and civilization. One of the letters relating to this subject, written for more general reading, may be given here, as, from its lucidity of expression, as well as its highly ambitious suggestions, it forms a unique document, and illustrates the workings of my father's mind, with a practical issue always in view, even during his period of retirement, and at an advanced age;—

NORTH-WEST AFRICAN EXPEDITION.

To the Editor.[1]

SIR,—I am very glad to see an able article in your paper advocating the North-West African Expedition. Surely the time for the emancipation of that terribly oppressed land is now come. There are, at this moment, no less than nine Expeditions that I know of (probably there are others) either now actually in operation or in preparation for the opening up of the two portions of Central Africa,—the north and south. North Central Africa may again be properly divided into east and west—viz., that from Lake Chad to the Nile, and the basin of the Niger, etc.

The following are the Expeditions I refer to, viz.: 1st, that under Col. Gordon, for the purpose of establishing the authority of the Khedive of Egypt about the great lakes at the source of the White Nile, and of destroying the slave trade in that direction,—one of the three great streams of African slavery; 2nd and 3rd, two private Expeditions, I believe Italian, for exploring in that part; 4th, the Church of England Mission near Mombaze, on the east coast, where the liberated slaves are chiefly to be received; 5th, the Free Church of Scotland Mission to Lake Nyassa, near the east coast, now starting; 6th, the Geographical Society's Mission of Lieut. Cameron, of which we heard last that he had left Lake Tanganyika to pass down the Congo to the west coast, but, unhappily, we have known nothing of this Expedition now for twelve months; 7th, Mr. Stanley's Mission to Lake Tanganyika and the westward, of whom we last heard half way from the east coast to the lake; 8th, a German Mission which has lately gone to the mouth of the Congo, on the west coast, with the purpose of exploring *up* the basin of that river; and 9th, the Expedition you have given an account of.

It seems as if in almost all human undertakings every other plan was to be tried before the plain, obvious, simple one. Thus, while the long route of 2,000 miles through various barbarous States and wild desert from Tripoli to Timbuctoo, and that from the Gold Coast through most unhealthy and savage States, and over mountains, and that by a long circuitous and sickly route up the Niger,

[1] This letter was addressed to a Bedfordshire newspaper, and comes nto my hands as a cutting only, without the name of the paper being given.

which it seems is not navigable within some hundred miles of the great bend, and that from the mouth of the Gambia, through savage tribes and over a lofty range of mountains; while these routes, all involving also a long sea voyage, have been talked of and tried or used for centuries, the direct line from England, though urged fifty years ago by an intelligent merchant who had settled in the south of Morocco, has never been attempted. This is certainly the shortest, and all the information we have concurs in showing that it is incomparably the most free from difficulties, even in its present state, besides its offering a possibility of a perfect communication ultimately, if (as seems certainly to be shown by the information we have) there is a long hollow of several hundred miles into which the sea can be brought.

The point of the coast at the mouth of the delta is the nearest to England. The country there is perfectly healthy; the races on the borders of the desert there are represented as by far the most practicable people in West Africa. That part of the coast is neutral ground; it is south of the kingdom of Morocco, north of the French settlements; and the space between Capes Juba and Bogador is represented as merely a sandbank thrown up by the sea, and uninhabited, so that there is a prospect of a footing being obtained somewhere there for an English mercantile and mission settlement without any serious difficulty. It seems quite certain that there is a plain direct from that point of the coast all the way to Timbuctoo, that a portion of this is below the level of the sea, and that there is no high water-shed between the Niger and this desert, but the river actually overflows at times past the city and into the desert. The intermediate distance may be passed perhaps at first by camels, and afterwards either by a very light rail or a canal, or by letting in the sea. At present the only difficulty in the line appears to be about water, but I have myself travelled that distance in Arabia, carrying water with us, excepting a little obtained at one or two places on the road for ourselves, but none for the camels—the small quantity of herbs they picked up by the way serving them both for meat and drink. I should mention also that shelter for vessels is reported to be found on the coast near the point I am speaking of. The extraordinary amount of European manufactures that finds its way to Timbuctoo, in spite of the enormous expense of conveying it such great distances, and through so many dangers and difficulties, though no measure of the traffic there would be if all obstacles were overcome, is yet a sure indication that if the line now proposed were opened and secured, the traffic would increase twenty- or one hundred-fold.

If we thus bring Timbuctoo within a very practicable distance of England, and establish commercial and mission premises there, we seem to strike at the very source of the northern slave trade, and to open the way for every wholesome influence to be brought to bear on the whole of the basin of the Niger and the adjoining provinces and fertile countries; and certainly there seems no comparison between this plan of accomplishing these objects and that by any of the other routes hitherto tried. What is now wanted is to find some new means for the full exploration of this line.

I may mention with respect to the letting of the sea into the depression, there is nothing to prevent a cut through, the bar being kept open, as has been shown in the case of the north end of the Suez Canal.

I must say that I know of no more noble and hopeful project, nor one of greater importance in this day of activity, and I cannot but hope that it is God's gracious purpose thus to help forward peace and truth in these oppressed countries.

The account of the four years of captivity of the missionaries in Coomassie gives us a realising idea of the state of the people, such as we have never obtained before, and cannot but make us anxious to try any hopeful plan, under God's blessing, to bring Christian light into these dark places. I trust that your readers will lend their aid to Mr. Donald Mackenzie in this grand enterprise in any way they can. The interest I take in Africa is my only excuse for asking you to have the kindness to find space for this attempt to supply your readers with an abstract of what is now being done for Africa, and of the information I have obtained respecting this route, which if fully opened would bring Timbuctoo within 2,300 miles and a fortnight of England, and effectually open a new field for British enterprise, occupied by twenty millions of people.

I remain, yours obediently,

ARTHUR COTTON.

June 7.

TEMPERANCE WORK.

The blue ribbon shown in the portrait of my father, which appears as frontispiece, renders it scarcely necessary to say that he was much interested in temperance. This interest dated from a day when, sitting at luncheon, he heard a tragic story of the results of drink which had occurred in his immediate neighbourhood. Turning to the servant, he said: "Take the decanter away. I will not have it before me again. Remember this. Do not put it on the table any more."

From that hour to the day of his death he never tasted alcohol in any shape or form, except when, once or twice, he was compelled by those around him to take a mouthful or two during an attack of faintness. On his death-bed he refused to touch brandy or any other stimulant. During the last thirty years of his life he warmly supported the temperance cause, often taking the chair, and speaking, at meetings in the town; and always, by his persistent wearing of the "Blue Ribbon" indicated where he stood.

Many a young man, starting on his way to India, would be warned by him in a fatherly manner to preserve his health, his activity, and his good name, by strictly repudiating all alcoholic drinks. "If I, an old man, can live without it, and work hard too," he would say, "why should a boy like you require such a crutch? Take my advice, and never let the thing pass your lips. You will be glad of your abstinence by-and-by."

He would collect most carefully the statistics respecting the consumption and consequences of drink, adding his own notes and comments. He thoroughly mastered each question that aroused his interest, and, as his memory was very clear and trustworthy, even to the last week of his life, it was amazing, in conversation with him, to notice the amount of information he possessed. It would have been difficult to find topics of general interest with which his mind was not thoroughly conversant; for with the greatest rapidity he could make himself master of any book worth reading.

OFFER OF A COMMISSION PRESIDENCY.

Although he was not a supporter of the Liberal Party, he was the recipient, whilst the Liberals were in office, of a great compliment from a Cabinet Minister. He relates the incident thus: "Mr. Milner Gibson applied to my friends in London to know whether they could accept for me the appointment of President of the Sewage Commission, saying he required an immediate answer. General Balfour, M.P., said he thought I could not, which was right. Danby Seymour gave Mr. Gibson my address in case he wished to write to me, but, as I did not hear from him, I suppose somebody else was appointed. It would have been out of my line. Had they offered me the Thames Navigation Commission I should have been much inclined to accept it, as it would doubtless have opened the way for me to publish my heterodox views in England. Either would, perhaps, have had a great effect upon the Indian question. It makes such a prodigious difference whether a matter comes from an obscure individual or from a man recognised by the Government." Indeed it does, but the creator of the Tanjore, Godavari, and Kistna Irrigation Works was no obscure individual.

BOAT DESIGNING.

His intense zeal with regard to canal navigation led him to devote much attention to the designing of a boat specially suited for canals. His object was to lessen the resistance or friction which a vessel meets in passing through water. He produced a brass-covered double canoe, which he used to sail on the lake of a friend who lived near us. His experiments were very interesting to himself, but rather hazardous we used to think; as everything had to be tried afresh, the new shape, the new surface, and the new power of speed.

"The resistance to boats on canals," he wrote, "is made up of three items, viz., the simple resistance of displacing the water, as in open waters, that due to the piling as before mentioned, and the friction on the surface of the boat. The first is calculated by dividing thirteen by the square of the ratio of breadth to length of entrance, multiplying the quotient by the area of the midship section in square feet for the resistance in pounds at two and a half miles per hour, the resistance to a square foot at two and a half miles, moving on a line perpendicular to its plane, being thirteen pounds per square foot. The surface friction has been ascertained by experiment to be about one-fifteenth of a pound per square foot of surface of painted wood or iron, moving at two and a half miles, and about half that on an ordinary coppered surface as usually done; but this would probably be considerably reduced by applying thick plates of hard phospho bronze accurately joined, with countersunk screw heads. This is when the surface moves on a line parallel to its plane. But on the bow, with an entrance of one to six, it is found to be double this, and on the experimental run the trials showed that there is no friction. For the resistance from piling, I have not found any investigation or experiments; and I can only make rough calculations from the imperfect data that I have. As I have stated above, if the entrance be greater than one to six, no doubt the friction would be lessened on the bow, and if the ratio be less the friction would be increased. An important point has also been settled by experiment in this respect, viz., that the resistance both from friction and displacement is the same on the same surface and angle of entrance, whether the entrance is vertical or horizontal. The large steamers on the Godavari, one hundred and twenty-four feet by twenty-four, and drawing fifteen inches, are rectangular in transverse section and deck surface, perfectly flat in the bottom, and with a vertical entrance of six to one, and the same length of run.

"These boats have been a complete success in reducing the cost of carriage on a shallow river; and I think there is special reason for giving the same form to canal boats, inasmuch as it would probably reduce the wave on the sides of the canal, there being no lateral pressure from the bow, as in the ordinary boats with horizontal entrances. The boat, therefore, that I would propose would be in plan a rectangle of one hundred and fifty feet by eleven and a half, with a draught of six feet. The entrance, a curved slope of one to ten, and the run of seven to one. This would give a tonnage of about one hundred and sixty-five tons, and, allowing fifteen tons for the engine, a cargo of one hundred and fifty tons."

A PATENT TRICYCLE.

He was also much occupied in trying to patent a tricycle on improved lines of his own. In those days cycles were very clumsy and awkward machines; but he was bent on producing one that would be capable of a much greater speed than those generally used. He used to say to us sometimes, "Perhaps you will live to see the day when there are no cab stands in London, when the horse for transit purposes is a thing of the past; every cab will have its own cycle action and artificial power." He was trying to perfect a brake on his own machine—a brake of his own invention—and also to produce a pointed shield, which would divide the force of the wind, and remove that hindrance to rapid cycling. So intent was he on these discoveries, that when he went out to practice on the roads, he used to ask any one that was passing to come and help him, and to give their opinion on what he was doing. "Now you just watch me, and tell me how many turns this wheel makes in a minute," he would say. The astonished passer-by used invariably to yield to these entreaties, and must have wondered at the ardour of the cyclist of seventy years of age!

One day as I was driving along the high road near Dorking, I was dismayed to see my father coming down the hill near our house on his tricycle at a tremendous pace. He had lost control over his machine and speedily found himself in the hedge. I ran to his rescue, asking anxiously, "What can I do to help you?" His reply was, "Look after the machine. I can take care of myself." He was in a wretched plight, his face full ot scratches, and his arms bruised by the fall. The only remark that he made was, "I hope my cycle is not spoilt"; and then, "I am afraid your mother will be anxious if she knows of this accident."

It was quite true; my mother was very anxious, not to say alarmed, when she heard what had happened, and, as he already had had one or two bad falls, she implored him to discontinue these perilous rides, for they were all experimental ones. His reply was: "Rome was not built in a day; it will take me a long time to complete my patent brake!" Her patience was, however, exhausted, and finding she could not persuade him to give up the cycle for his own sake, she told him a pitiful story of an excellent missionary, who needed better means of getting about his district than his donkey-cart afforded. She prevailed upon my father to send him the tricycle, but what she intended for a kindness proved to be a misfortune, for the missionary met with such a serious accident, when riding the machine one day, that he was compelled to go to the hospital with a broken arm. So the tricycle came back to my father and was eventually given away to a friend who knew how to use it.

My father's genius for invention was extraordinary. He was always working out the "ifs" of life. "If so and so could be done, how wonderful it would be!" was his continual remark.

AN ARABIC PRIMER AND "LIVING LANGUAGES."

Another study that occupied and interested my father greatly at this time was the composition of an Arabic Primer. When he was about seventy, he invited an Arabic student, who could speak some English, to stay with him for several weeks; during this time he spent hours every day in going through sentences of the languages, word by word, with him, thus working out the new Primer, which was to meet the needs of missionaries in Persia and Armenia, and other countries where Arabic is spoken.

This Arabic Primer was printed at his own expense, and the whole theme occupied much of his leisure just then.

He had very strong theories on the subject of learning "Living Languages," his opinion being that, as every child who comes into the world learns its mother tongue orally, and at first without grammar, picking it up sentence by sentence and word by word, from those with whom it is associated, either children or adults as the case may be—the study of grammar being a matter of much later consideration,—so the learning of all modern languages would be very much facilitated by a similar process; that is, that the learner should hear each sentence repeated four or five times by a native of the country, and say it after him. This constant repetition, he considered, would give the sound and knowledge of the word so thoroughly that the mind of the pupil would be almost "possessed" by it, to the exclusion, for the time being, of other subjects. Thus, in perhaps one hundred sentences, sound and pronunciation and spelling would be thoroughly mastered in every detail, the spelling taking a secondary place in the acquisition of the knowledge imparted. The third requirement he looked upon as the grammar, which need not be touched until the language had, to a certain extent, been acquired.

Of one of the before-mentioned pamphlets he remarks: "I have been so delighted with the sale of seventy of the 'Pamphlets on Languages' without a single advertisement. It gives me great hopes that the subject will begin to be discussed. I have been trying the word system in Arabic, in order to obtain some definite idea of the rate of progress a man could make, and have been well satisfied, judging that if a stupid old man, with a stiff tongue and deaf ear, can make certain progress, a young man could make far greater. The matter of time is a small one compared with a perfectly good pronunciation and expression, which, I feel quite sure, would naturally follow the adoption of this method. I am now full of hopes that some hundreds of the pamphlets will be sold and that real investigation will begin; and of this I am satisfied, that the great obstacle of confusion of tongues can be in a large measure removed, as those of time and space have been by steam and telegraphy. Several missionaries have said that it gave them useful hints, but nothing more has come of it. *The Times* made an excellent remark upon the subject; it said the English cannot learn languages, and the consequence is that instead of an Englishman learning Tamil, a million Tamils are obliged to learn English, and this is what is going on all over the world. It will soon become the general language. What a wonderful work God is accomplishing in and by England! She is filling the face of the world with fruit temporal and spiritual. Three hundred and forty millions are now directly under our Empress, and every nation on earth is, in a measure, touched by her influence."

To a friend in Ireland he wrote at the time of the Soudanese War:—

"I am so glad to see your Beidawi Grammar, which contains some curious peculiarities. I had no idea you had found time to go so fully into the subject. It is of great value. By how many is this language spoken? If I were younger, and not deaf, how I should like to try learning it by ear. Is it really true that they have our sound of short 'o'?

"Could they really say Cotton? I never saw a man in India who could utter this sound. They can only pronounce our 'o' as in 'political.' Pray answer this. I wanted much to know whether they have, in Africa, our common short 'o' as in 'not.'

"I am delighted with your book and think it is just what is wanted. We have had two cases of influenza, neither of them severe, but requiring the same advice as the Japanese: 'Don't despise a beaten enemy!' To one who has seen what a demoralized regiment is, the stand made by the Chinese is wonderful, and would be an honour to a British army."

"The escape of the *Gascoyne* is a wonderful proof of the conquest God has given us over the ocean.

"A society, the Land Colonization, has taken up the question of farming, I think, in a practical way at last; and the members seem likely to carry out the essential point of the *improvement* of culture effectively. They have, of course, very few helpers at present, and scarcely any money, but they are persevering, and seem, for their extremely small means, to have accomplished a good deal already. I have considerable hope from them. They are, as yet, the only men that have dared to acknowledge the possibility of improvement.

"I am glad you have brought in the magic lantern to help in Ireland. It seems to me a very important adjunct and calculated to counteract Irish difficulties greatly. If our Lord said, 'He who has not a sword, let him sell his coat and buy one,' surely He would have us keep a sharp look out for any help that may offer."

NILE NAVIGATION WHICH WOULD HAVE SAVED GORDON.

At the time of General Gordon's journey into the Soudan, and, on receiving the news of his death, Sir Arthur Cotton's mind was much exercised with regard to the slowness of communications which were occasioning such dire disasters.

He wrote to a newspaper as follows:—

"The one thing, that has been the complete hindrance in all this strange matter of the Soudan Expedition, is that England could not furnish an engineer conversant with such river navigation. The case was exactly similar to that of the delta irrigation. Millions had been spent on that, in the Barrage and other works, and nothing whatever had been effected, solely because there was no experienced irrigation engineer there.

"When Lord Dufferin went there, he saw at once that the one thing that was wanted to restore Egypt's prosperity was such an engineer, and he sent to India for one, and I believe they sent the ablest man they had. The moment such a man arrived, he, at a trifling expense, turned the Barrage to account, in raising the water in the canals, and a complete revolution has already been effected in a great part of the delta, and Colonel Scott-Moncrieff has been publicly thanked by the community for the prodigious results he has obtained, even before a promised million had been granted him. Thousands of water-wheels and steam engines have already been thrown out of work. What has caused this? Nothing but that an engineer conversant with such work has been called in.

"And nothing else is wanted at once to bring the Nile into effective navigation, nothing but an engineer who is really conversant with such work. Take the following facts to show the consequence of placing the river under the charge of officers who had no experience in such work.

"1st. Millions spent on two hundred miles of railway, by the side of the navigable river, which would convey at one-tenth the cost by rail, without anything spent on the river.

"2nd. The boat that Gordon had conveyed to Khartoum drew six feet of water, I believe, had side paddles, and a speed of seven or eight miles, in every way utterly unfitted for the river.

"3rd. When a small steamer was sent out, it was carried in pieces on the railway, as if a steamer was made to be carried, instead of to carry, just as happened when we introduced wheel-barrows into India,—the Indians carried them on their heads.

"4th. No money was laid out on improving the river by removing rocks, etc.

"5th. To convey a force up the river rowing boats were sent out, and worked up the river by ten thousand men at eight or ten miles a day, while a single steamer could have carried a force of fifteen hundred men.

"How can we bear to think that the lives of Gordon and thousands of others, and millions of money were thrown away, solely because there was nobody who was conversant with such river navigation! Had there been one steamer with stern wheel, drawing one foot, and having a speed of twenty miles only, we should have been in constant communication with Khartoum, and had there been a flotilla of twenty such steamers, the whole force would have been carried up without the least difficulty.

"This year I begged a friend, a member of Parliament, to try and bring this matter forward again, and on his communicating with an official, he was informed that a flotilla had now been ordered. In two months from the time that twelve steamers (of one hundred and twenty feet long) were ordered, they were at Alexandria. Who can imagine why this was not done last year? I hear that at last twenty-five steamers have been ordered, but, I am afraid, all with the essential defect of want of speed. If, however, Gordon could hold Khartoum for many months solely by the help of the clumsy steamers that he had, what may not be done with stern-wheel steamers, drawing one or two feet, even though with too low a speed, if measures are also taken, by removing rocks and concentrating the stream, to improve the river at the same time?

"I have not seen the rapids, but I have read numerous accounts of them, and I can confidently assert, from my experience on the Godavari, that a thoroughly effective navigation can be established:—

"1st. At a cost far below that of hundreds of miles of railway.

"2nd. To carry at one-tenth the cost of railway transit.

"3rd. To carry the enormous quantities that the vast Soudan, extending two thousand miles to the line, will require in import and export, when England takes up the matter effectively and gives peace and just and intelligent rule to that distracted country. Had Gordon had effective steamers on the river in his first government, he could have established effective rule over the whole region.

"The Suakim Railway was a complete mistake. It would, first, be utterly impossible to protect it. Nothing in the world is so helpless as a railway, especially in a desert, as we see in the case of the few miles already laid. It could not carry at a cost that would answer the purpose or the quantities that the case requires.

"It is proposed to charge £2 a ton for this three hundred miles, the cost of carrying from Calcutta to London, eight thousand geographical miles. Not one-twentieth of the goods that ought to be conveyed down the valley of the Nile could bear this cost. And this is besides two transfers.

"I have no doubt that goods could be brought from Khartoum to Cairo or Alexandria for ten shillings a ton, probably for much less, when the river is improved, that is for a great part of the year, and certainly, if regulating weirs are built at the mouths of the great lakes, for the whole year.

"The cost of greatly improving the river would be quite small compared with that of railways, and I feel sure that the worst obstacles can be removed at a cost quite insignificant."

The following letter, probably written to General Gordon, bears reference to the opening up of the Nile communications:—

"I have long wished to get a complete account of the actual state of those rapids, and should be so much obliged to you if you could send me any engineering report on them. I have no distinct idea what the rapids really are. I cannot make out that they have ever been seen by an engineer who has had experience in that way. Could steamers of small draught and high speed run by them all the year, or for any considerable part of it? The Godavari steamers draw eighteen inches and have a speed of ten miles; they have power for about twelve or more, but cannot use it on account of great vibration, not being quite strong enough in their frames. With a little alteration they would carry them up very severe rapids, but they must tow cargoes. On the Godavari our steamers are quite oblong on their plan, quite flat at bottom with perpendicular sides, and fine vertical entrances, five to one, but I think they should be finer, one in ten. I would have for the Nile such a boat two hundred feet long, sixty feet broad, and drawing eighteen or twenty-four inches, displacement six hundred tons, drawing empty ten inches, and carrying engines weighing two hundred tons, working to 4,000 H.P. indicated, and with one hundred and fifty tons of fuel on board, drawing two feet, which I reckon would allow a speed of twenty-five miles at least, and more for a spurt; this is the kind of boat that has been such a complete success on the Godavari. I don't know whether the rapids would allow of steamers so large as this. If the stretches of rapids are straight enough, such a vessel might run up alone, anchor above, and then draw up her barge.

"I wish that they had spent the money that the railway has cost in improving the rapids. Even if the river could only be used for heavy traffic for six months in the year it would be an incalculable benefit. They only use the Erie Canal for seven months, and carry four million tons by it. One thing is to me certain, that if water carriage cannot be established to the lakes, there can be no great traffic; for nothing of any consequence will bear the cost of three thousand miles of land carriage. The present head railway engineer in India, as soon as he had finished the Eastern Bengal Railway, wrote a report, showing that it was absolutely necessary to cut a steamboat canal by the side of it, and that it would return twenty-two per cent. and save one and three-quarter millions a year besides on the present traffic, thus reducing the cost of transit from sixteen shillings a ton to three shillings and sixpence.

"Pray excuse my troubling you with all this. The absolute necessity of water carriage has been so forced upon me in India, that I cannot bear to think of those magnificent highways, ready provided to the centre of Africa, remaining unused, while I remember what is hanging upon their use, nothing less than the rapid opening up of that vast population to all the wholesome influences of the Word of God. It was the most unfortunate thing for Egypt that they employed a railway engineer. Like India, the grand treasure of Egypt is water, and there the railway engineers have been compelled to see that railways are a complete mistake. I beg to offer for your reading some of my late papers, in which you will find many things that bear equally upon Egypt.

"The question of internal improvement there, is now at length, I hope, coming to an issue, but it is a hard fight; the old India party cannot bear to give up their idol—railways—after having spent one hundred and sixty millions on them, but they are terribly puzzled when their own oracle comes forward and insists upon a canal by the side of a railway that has cost £20,000 a mile, and has been tried for twelve years. How wonderfully hopeful all the prospects for Central Africa are now. Every month we hear of some new proof that God is working for its emancipation. May He abundantly prosper your work."

In another letter he continues his suggestions:—

"The works required are:—

"1st. The blasting of dangerous rocks, which can be done at the cost of a few pounds of dynamite.

"2nd. The closing smaller channels by large blocks of stone, so as to concentrate the stream, which also would be a very inexpensive work, if powerful apparatus is used, for it is cheaper to work large blocks than small, the cost of breaking up being saved in the former.

"3rd. Probably in some places throwing rough stone dams of large blocks across the stream, and building locks to pass the boats round them.

"By such means as these an engineer of some experience and talent for such work would very soon effect a perfectly good navigation to Khartoum for most, if not all, of the year. . . .

"But excellent use can certainly be made of the river,

even in its present unimproved state, if only effective steamers are used, carrying all the power they can on one foot draught, 1,000 or 1,500 H.P. in a steamer one hundred and twenty feet long, with stern wheel and a speed of twenty or twenty-five miles.

"One engineer writes that he went up in the clumsy country boats with nothing but sails, probably not more than 20 or 30 T.H.P. of wind, and with this ran up all the rapids, when the river was low. What difficulty could there be with steamers with fifty times as much power on board?

"Having had so long experience in this matter on the Godavari, I cannot but hope you may think it worth while to offer this with other papers on the subject for the consideration of the gentlemen who are preparing to bring the subject of Nile navigation before the public in Manchester and London."

Sir Arthur Cotton's great object in pushing these practical theories was the double one of promoting the welfare, spiritual and temporal, of the people throughout the vast continent of Africa.

In allusion to one of his pamphlets on the subject, Sir Henry Johnstone wrote to him :—

"I sat up late last night, and got up early this morning to read through the pamphlet which you kindly gave me yesterday to look at; and now I have great pleasure in returning it to you before I leave for London.

"I must express my gratitude to you for calling my attention to the observations made by Mr. Picot on his recent visit to the Ashanti capital. His letter is painfully interesting, especially in some parts. Deeds of cruelty and bloodshed are still being perpetrated in that dark land. To all outward appearances it is, as it were, hermetically sealed to the heralds of salvation. I pray God that, in spite of all the efforts made by king and chiefs to prevent it, a way may soon be opened by Him for the introduction of that everlasting Gospel, which alone is capable of changing the hearts and lives of the people.

"I thank you sincerely for all your labours on behalf of my country. May the Lord bless you abundantly, and crown your efforts with success!"

At this time he was also intensely interested in the opening up of Palestine by inter-communications. To the Society of Arts he addressed himself with regard to the Arabian railway to Busrah:—

"It is indeed a question of fundamental importance to the empire. The line from Acre to Damascus will soon be completed, overcoming the only serious difficulty in the connection of the Mediterranean and the Gulf, viz., the deep depression of the Jordan valley, which it crosses at the south end of the lake of Tiberias, leaving only the seven hundred miles of level country between Damascus and Busrah, surely the easiest seven hundred miles in the world for a railway.

"I accompanied a caravan by this line, and, for almost the whole way, the country was one absolute tract of dry alluvium without sand, stones, or waterways, so that, for hundreds of miles, the rails might literally be laid on the ground as it is. There was, for weeks on the journey, a clear, level horizon, like that at sea.

"I may add that all this vast tract of country requires nothing but canals from the Euphrates to make it capable of bearing a population of scores of millions, and these canals might be cut at an expense of one-fourth of that of the great delta irrigation of Madras, owing to the works requiring no provision for heavy local rains such as occur in the Carnatic, and to the small size of the Euphrates, about three hundred yards broad, compared with the Godavari, for instance, four miles broad, the weir for which required just one million tons of masonry, besides one and three-quarter miles of vast earthen embankments.

"This second line of communication with India, as it would be in a certain important manner, will be of incalculable value.

"I ought also to refer to the great point brought forward

in Col. F.'s paper, that these plains are the site of an immeasurable deposit of fuel, in the state of bitumen, and probably also, of course, of coal; so that, independent of the fact that a line of railway across them would help to strengthen the connection of the two halves of the British Empire, it would certainly bring effectively into use a material worth hundreds of millions.

"These three things combined, namely—

"1st. A subsidiary connecting link for England with India, and all the East.

"2nd. The giving access and value to the vast field of fuel.

"3rd. The opening of the way for the population of, perhaps, one hundred thousand square miles of rich alluvial country, combined with assuredly laying the foundations for peace and justice throughout Arabia by English influence, as in Egypt; these things give a weight to the subject of an Arabian railway that no words can express, and render it, perhaps, as great and suitable a subject for the Society's consideration as could possibly be found.

"May I hope that my own experience in respect to the passage of the desert of Arabia, and to irrigation in India, will be allowed to excuse my presuming to offer my thoughts in this matter?

"I might add that the port of Acre, the termination of the railway, is naturally the port of Palestine, as it requires only a breakwater extended from Mount Carmel, which can be constructed at a comparatively small cost, to make a perfect harbour of any size that may be required."

The following letters from one of my father's correspondents interested him very much, and he often quoted sentences from them:—

I.

"I went to Hit to see the bitumen spring in connection with my idea that nearly all our coal is a volcanic product ejected and rained down upon the vegetation to which geologists, I think erroneously, solely ascribe the origin. What I saw there is all in confirmation. But I suspect that under the Euphrates there are vast coal fields, and that this was one of the reasons, no doubt, among others, why, from the Tower of Babel onwards, a great city was never permitted to be built on the Babylon site.

"These coal fields will keep the new route going.

"Both the state of the Turkish Empire and the Egyptian question must force on this acquisition of Arabia, but it will be accomplished, I think, when the Turks have to quit Europe by a Moslem rally at some centre—probably Damascus—this rally being followed by a series of very critical events."

II.

"General N. has the wants of Mesopotamia in view, whereas, I contend, they are secondary to the direct Indian interests in the Egypt and Persian Gulf line, with the virtual annexation of Arabia, nearly all the coast districts of which, from Bahrein to Yeddah, are in a state of Bedouin insurrection, not remotely due, I suspect, to the brisk trade in Martini rifles which, I hear, has been going on through the Persian port of Mohumra.

"I look upon the Arabian line as now essential to the safety and progress of India, and certain to be made before long. One of the points for discussion is whether Alexandria should be the terminus of the route, or an entirely new British port opened somewhere on the Egyptian coast between Port Said and Philistia, quite clear of the Suez Canal and European politics. This question I have not attempted to raise.

"There is no doubt that under comparatively slight British direction of affairs, both Turks and Arabs would make progress at a much more rapid pace than the feebler natives of India. There is no want of either intelligence or enterprise at places like Bagdad. But, as long as Christians and Mohammedans are not equal before the law, and a few hundred oriental fanatics have the control of the revenue, and the real power is in their hands at Constantinople, so long they must be depressed, and nothing can be grown or done in the districts, except by a man with a bludgeon in his hand or a gun at his back.

"I have found the word 'swift beasts' to which you refer: Isaiah lxvi. 20. KURKRUT in Hebrew, or 'running things of the nature of machines,' which the dictionary translates 'dromedaries,' and they do the running now. Exactly the same word I find in Arabic—KARKARA, 'running like a machine,' from the root—Kar, to turn round and round, the origin of the Latin 'curro,' and our 'current,' and other words. My two munshis could not attach any distinct meaning to Karkara, it not being in common use as a noun. It certainly was not their word for dromedary.

"The usual Hebrew word which, I am inclined to consider, means a railway, in prophecy, is MÁSULAH, and 'embankment' from the 'SULAL,' to heap up, which is very suggestive. The translators make it 'highway,' as you are aware.

"Steamers again seem meant by the Hebrew 'KLI GAMA.' The latter is possibly the Arabic—GHAYM, 'cloud,' signifying vapour vessels, in French, 'Vapeurs.'

"There are a number of aged and worthless cattle killed round the large markets from the quality of the steaks one gets, but not nearly enough to produce an improvement of agriculture. With European officials tending to become fewer and fewer, it will be some time before the natives see how they are being eaten out of a subsistence by these vampires. But the Arabian route and its daily mails would bring in a fresh stock of European ideas."

As regards British relations with Egypt, my father puts this distinctly on record as his opinion: "The establishment of British Sole Authority in Egypt is incomparably the greatest political event that has happened in my long life."

On the Opium question, a subject which was always one of keen interest to him, he made proposals of his own for the increase of revenue in the place of the direful growth of that which must, in the end, impoverish rather than enrich the country. He writes:—

"I cannot trust the report. I wish very much to see the real evidence of the anti-opium men. How we are reminded of that word: 'Send help from the Sanctuary, for vain is the help of man.' If God were not dealing with us, as He has not dealt with any nation, what would be the weight of His wrath on a nation guilty of the immeasurable crime of the opium trade?

"But He, Who in infinite patience delivered us from the transgression of slavery, without demanding one drop of blood, can bear with us in this also. And we are to-night to pray hopefully: 'Deliver us from all our transgressions.'"

It will be noticed how, in all these anxious questions, his mind reverted continually to the Divine promise of succour and help to those who trust in the King of Kings and believe His word.

And now for some remarks, which I am fully aware will be wholly inadequate to the importance of the subject, respecting that devotion of his to the soil and its productiveness. It was a great enjoyment to him to lay out the gardens of our new house at Dorking, trenching them after his own fashion, three feet deep, and at the same time manuring highly; afterwards he considered it a mistake to do this on too rich a scale. He took immense pains with the production of both flowers and vegetables; his efforts were rewarded with remarkable success. A plant of American blackberries, for instance, placed in this prepared soil, would produce blackberries of an extraordinary size and flavour. He did the same with everything: currants, gooseberries, and raspberries. Then his potatoes, turnips, and other vegetables were indeed a sight to be remembered. It was a great pride to him to desire the gardener to show us a single potato root, with an enormous crop, both the quality and quantity surpassing anything that one had ordinarily noticed. Then he would have

SIR ARTHUR COTTON (AËTAT 94)
In front of the plot of maize grass grown by him in 1896.

p. 537

it weighed, so that he might know exactly what the produce would amount to per acre. By degrees he interested himself intensely in agriculture, experimenting on wheat, oats, and Indian corn. He found that he could produce seven times the ordinary result from one grain of wheat. In the "Appendix" to this chapter will be found a description of his working out of this problem. He would aerate the ground two or three feet deep, pulverising the soil, his theory being that plants needed air as much as water.

One summer there was a great lack of grass in the neighbourhood, while, of course, the supply of hay was small. But when, that same summer, we visited the experimental plots in his garden, we saw grass growing there quite five feet high, thick and strong, abundantly luxuriant; yet he had never given it one drop of water. It had fared like the rest of the fields as regarded the rain supply. The only difference was in the mode of cultivation. The depth of the soil had been sufficient to feed it, and provide it with this vigour of growth. But, as I said before, his resources were endless. His active brain was always working out some new theory, and, with his natural energy and practical common sense, putting it into everyday use.

On this subject he wrote to the *Manchester Guardian*:—

"Your paper of yesterday contained some remarks on my experiments on cultivation, which do not require any direct answer, as they do not amount to any real description of the great national question of improving cultivation, but I should like to take occasion from them to give some information on this vital subject.

"My first is to repeat the fundamental question: 'What can possibly be the reason why everything else in the kingdom should be under improvement, and that with a success altogether beyond anything thought of beforehand by the improvers, and yet that the whole body of agriculturists, without exception, should utterly refuse to attempt anything in the way of improvement, or even to write or utter a word?' Nobody can possibly answer this question.

"And, still more, these very men are, with the utmost intelligence and perseverance, doing just like all other classes in improving their animals, and with the same results.

"In passing along the roads we meet, continually, such horses, cattle, and sheep as were not thought of seventy or eighty years ago; but, if we look over the hedges, we see precisely the same cultivation, four or five inches deep, the same enormous clods, and the same miserable crops as we did in our boyhood.

"And, again, reports of hundreds of agricultural meetings where thousands of prizes are granted for improved animals, but not one for improved crops in respect of *quantity*, *quality*, or *cost*.

"And, if we read the leading agricultural papers, one thing is certain, that the word improvement as to crops is never admitted. To meet this state of things, I do what I can in my circumstances to try what a certain soil *can* be made to produce, though without the advantages of an ordinary farmer with experience, considerable extent of land, and effective implements, etc. And here the result is, not from any enrichment of the soil, which is a pure imagination of your writer, for the soil is exactly the same as before, a very poor one, much below the average. The only change is by cultivation. The result is such crops, in spite of seasons, as nobody could have thought of, for instance, a plant of wheat from a single grain, six feet high, with one hundred and ninety ears on it.

"And as respects seasons: in a year when not a green blade was seen in June on farm meadows owing to drought, a crop of rye grass five feet high, at the rate of three tons to the acre—this without any watering.

"Upon the whole trial, of ten or twelve years, the produce has been about four times that of the farms in potatoes, wheat, grass, and roots. If any farmer wants to have some idea what it would cost to aerate his soil to the depth of two or three feet, he has only to take an hour to calculate it. He has plenty of materials for this.

"I will only add here what I hear is going on at this time in this way. One man writes, to show how little I know about the matter, that he tried my system, and it was a failure, but that by a system of his own he made a clear profit of £8 an acre the first year, counting all the cost of his permanent improvement as if they were current expenses. This was a curious way of showing I was mistaken in saying that cultivation could be improved! If every acre in England were so cultivated as to yield a profit the first year of £8 per acre, the whole body would at once be set upon its legs, and agriculture would be the most profitable industry in the country.

"Further, I have now full evidence that many farmers are already setting themselves to this grand work.

"Two great landowners that I know of are setting about it in earnest. One writes to me that, the year before last he cultivated twenty-five acres to the depth of eighteen inches, and that he had an astonishing crop of rye grass of three tons per acre, with a promise of as much more by further cuttings. Another man wrote that he saw wheat, on the land of the other landowner, two feet higher than on the adjoining farms.

"I have seen also several letters from tenants saying that they have had splendid crops the first year from improved cultivation. One said sixty-seven bushels of wheat, more than double the average of farm lands, and so on.

"I have no doubt, therefore, that there are now many more improvers, both owners and tenants, scattered over the country, and that none of the present false leaders can possibly stop the change, especially when they write only in the way of your writer, without a word of real argument on the subject.

"I am fully assured, after carefully looking into the whole matter, that, with present prices, agriculture would be the most profitable industry in England, if only the multitude of intelligent men, rich and poor, now engaged on the land, would go to their work every day with one thought in their minds: Improvement.

"The reports of harvest this year give an average of thirty-five bushels of wheat, six above the usual average. Of course, the great question in this case is: 'How much of this is due to the season, and how much to the results of improvement?' I have great reasons to believe that a considerable portion of it is due to the latter; but, of course, no agricultural paper would dare to hint at this.

"This is a great vital question in every way, and I most earnestly beg you to allow your readers to see this side of the question."

To a friend he remarks:—

"We have had glorious weather, exactly what we wanted, both for the hay and the corn; but to-day I am sorry to see the temperature has greatly fallen. The hay is safe, but the wheat is not, and a few cold days now would do terrible mischief to the latter. My wheat promises a crop beyond any former, but it is not safe yet, though much forwarder than that on the farms.

"The progress of the enquiry about the new cultivation is far beyond that hitherto with new discoveries. Two Scotch lairds came to see the wheat. They took great interest in all they saw, and said they would both make experiments in the system."

In allusion to a gift of pamphlets and papers on the all-absorbing question of improving the soil, he writes:—

"We have now intimation from so many quarters that men and women are really setting themselves to answer this question, though, as yet, not a single leader in agriculture has condescended to pay the least attention to the subject. But I am sure that very soon we shall see the same conquest over the land in respect of produce as we already see in the ocean, which has now been made the safe, cheap, and speedy highway, moving all nations, by Him Who declared that such was His purpose, three thousand years ago."

Of his agricultural experiments he never tired. A friend writes :—

"Sir Arthur's wheat, sown last autumn, seed by seed, each on a square foot of land, is now about three feet in height (while the ordinary farmer's sowing is three or four inches), and one hundred to one hundred and twenty straws from each seed, and the ground is so fully occupied as to almost entirely cover the soil.

"I find that some friends in America, to whom I had spoken of the three feet digging, imagined that the seed had to be sown unusually deep,—but this is quite a mistake,—Sir Arthur's seeds were put in at the depth of one inch!"

"The facts I have brought forward," said my father, "are quite conclusive as to the wonderful capacity of the worth of produce, and every one acquainted with cultivation can easily notify himself, by an hour's calculation, that farming can be conducted profitably if anything approaching real cultivation is used. There is, however, now an extensive enquiry going on, and some, even, of the old landowners are honestly setting themselves to investigate the subject. The Government, also, have ordered trials to be made."

Appendix

A MODERN SEER AND A NEW HOPE FOR BRITISH AGRICULTURE

(*By a Student of the System.*)

There is almost a dramatic completeness in Sir Arthur Cotton's life. The great subject of his prime was land and water; and now, in his extreme age, it is land and air. Then he saw, in the waste of India's treasure of flood-waters, the chief cause of her poverty and famine: with equal clearness he now sees a parallel waste in our own home lands—the unthought-of waste of air, that great agent of soil-action and plant-growth. He sees, too, this waste, like that of India's monsoon floods, to be inconceivably vast—vast enough to fully account for our agricultural depression, and all that it involves. He considers this land and air question to be almost as vital to Great Britain as the land and water problem is to India.

The parallel is even closer. He himself solved the Indian question practically—so far as he was allowed—by superbly successful undertakings, the turning of two semi-deserts, the deltas of the Cauveri and Godavari rivers, into gardens; and now, during these last twelve years—from his eighty-fourth to his ninety-sixth year—he has given a remarkable practical answer to the home problem. It matters little that in the latter case the experiments are on a very tiny scale, his garden giving him scarcely a square yard for every square mile he dealt with in India. Each plot bears its exact relation to the acre, and all weights and measurements are made, and all observations taken, with extreme scientific exactness, so that the results are as instructive and reliable as they would have been had the experiments been far larger. The advantage is really on the other side. These experiments have been made by a very old man, without agricultural training, and on so small a scale that labour reaches its highest proportion of expense. As he puts it: "Without horses, or steam, or any agricultural experience, and in old age, I can do nothing here as it might be done on a large scale." Add to this that the land is poor, fully sixteen per cent. below the average for the country, and one feels the growing significance of the wonderful success he has made. How much more may be done under better conditions! Also, he has purposely avoided all other special aids, *e.g.* high fertilizers, in order to establish his one point—the importance of the fuller aeration of the soil. Let these be used in addition and far greater results still may be expected.

HOW THESE EXPERIMENTS BEGAN.

They began with the eighth Marquis of Tweeddale and the Yester Deep Cultivation. The Marquis, as Governor of Madras, had been a great strength to Sir Arthur in his Godavari battle. Their friendship continued, and when Sir Arthur visited him some forty-five years ago, he shewed him twelve hundred acres he was then tilling on the Deep Culture principle. "Four years ago," said he, "I got this farm into my hands, and there is now *four times* the value of produce there was when I came into possession."

Sir Arthur was told of a field on the same estate, which had been so poor, and sour, and cold, that oats would not ripen on it in bad seasons, but which, as a result of the new treatment, had just yielded forty bushels to the acre of the heaviest wheat in Great Britain—sixty-seven lbs. to the bushel. All this, too, in Midlothian, four hundred feet above sea-level, and with mean temperature of 5° below that of the South of England. Here were crops of all kinds surpassing anything he had seen in the South.

And the secret? Aeration—simply a fuller and deeper aeration of the soil. Instead of ploughing six inches only, and with the old style, clod-making plough, Lord Tweeddale had ploughed (with four horses) to a depth of sixteen inches with a plough that *made no clods.*

This set Sir Arthur thinking, and so when some thirty years ago he retired, after forty-five years' service, "old and greatly worn out," as he puts it, "by Indian hard work and sicknesses," he began such "trifling experiments" as opportunity allowed in different gardens belonging to houses occupied for short periods. "It was clear enough," he writes, "that there was something quite wrong about the whole state of farming. . . . What the Marquis had accomplished was sufficient to prove that a radical change was required in the whole farming ideas of the nation; but it was only by slow degrees that I realised the unbounded prospect that lies before us." . . . It was not until 1886, when in his eighty-fourth year, that he was able to begin that series of continuous experiments, which he is still conducting in his garden at Dorking.

THE GREAT PRINCIPLE.

That air is the great agent of soil-action and plant-growth is the great principle, and exposure of the soil to air by pulverization to the greatest possible depth, is the one simple method.

He related to me how the Marquis of Tweeddale, having often spoken to him of a clod-breaking machine he had invented, at his request showed it to him. "I have learnt better than that now," answered the Marquis. "Such a machine only proves bad farming. *There is no such thing as a clod on land that's well farmed.*"

Sir Arthur Cotton's plan is to *trench his land to a depth of three feet,* with a very strong cast-steel fork of his own design,[1] and with

[1] To be got at "One and All" depôts.

the one aim of pulverizing and aerating every particle of the soil. In most cases, and at first, this must be done gradually, going a few inches lower each season; for unaired soil is too unwholesome to be mixed at once, and in large quantities, with the top-spit. The particular methods, however, must be left to individual needs, experiences, and ingenuity. The great thing is to keep well in view the wonderful treasure locked up in common soil, and to remember that air is the key to it. One leading agriculturalist has declared that, of the whole weight taken from the land in the way of produce, *ninety-five per cent. comes from the air.* It is now known that air plays a great part in the nitrification of the soil. There is often plenty of nitrate present—in tropical soils sometimes as much as one per cent. is nitrate; but little of this is in a form available to plant life. Air helps by making much of this available.

Again, want of air often makes soil sour, cold, and even poisonous, and the only cure is air—with plenty of air, sour land grows sweet.

Then air is a poor conductor of heat; and so a well-tilled garden bed, being full of air, is a *blanket* to keep out summer drought and winter frost. This is why frost penetrates hard soil so much more quickly than soft.

Further, well and deeply tilled soil acts as a *sponge* as well as a blanket—*a sponge below and a blanket above*—for friable soil gives some play to the law of capillary attraction, so that deep-tilled soil is always damp six inches below the surface, even in the worst droughts known to this country. Such soil is *far* warmer and drier in winter, and *far* cooler and more moist in summer.

Again, deep tillage gives better play to root action—a most important subject which we are only beginning to explore. I was telling Sir Arthur how a friend of mine, a horticultural expert, had traced the roots of strawberries two feet, carrots three feet, onions four feet, and wheat six feet. In reply, he told me that, at a certain agricultural meeting, Lord Tweeddale was called to question for his deep ploughing—what was the good of it? wheat never required such depth. He reserved his reply till a subsequent gathering, when he gave it in the shape of a glass case in which wheat was growing, and where they could *see its roots eight feet long!* And yet nearly all farmers still plough only four, five or six inches deep, and that with a plough which, while it makes clods above, irons out the earth beneath into an almost impervious pan! No wonder we hear of bad times, and farming that never pays!

DEEP CULTURE VASTLY REDUCES RISK IN BAD SEASONS.

When I asked Sir Arthur Cotton about this, he answered with a quiet smile: "The year 1893 was one of the worst hay years in the century to us in these parts. By the first of June there was not a blade of green grass in any of the fields about Dorking. Yet, on that very day, I cut a plot of rye grass, sown the previous autumn, that stood five feet high, green and luxuriant, yielding at the rate of four and a half tons to the acre of splendid hay—while two subsequent cuttings gave me three tons more! It had received nothing but an ordinary dressing of liquid manure, and the land was poor!

RESULTS.

Potatoes.—1. Planted in deep, rich, sandy soil, in Tunbridge Wells, cultivated once to the depth of three feet. One plant to the square yard, yield fourteen lbs. to each plant (average), or thirty tons to the acre, worth, at 70*s.* per ton, £105.

2. Planted in Dorking in 1895. Yield twenty tons per acre, with cabbages planted between the rows of potatoes, yielding another crop of thirty-five tons to the acre. Potatoes, at 70*s.*= £70, and cabbages (for fodder) at 20*s.*=£35. Total value (at the rate of) £105 per acre.

Maize.—This has fully ripened for some years in succession—a remarkable thing in this country. The corn raised one year is used as the seed of the next in the hope of acclimatizing it as a fodder plant. It has already withstood frost that cut neighbouring potatoes down to the ground, and grows luxuriantly to a height of eight and nine feet, yielding, at the flowering time, thirty-five to forty-five tons to the acre of excellent fodder.

Peas.—This year's crop, despite long drought and poor soil, grew splendidly to a height of eight feet, yielding the finest peas I ever ate. The sweet peas stood six feet high.

Wheat.—Hand-sown, each grain twelve to fifteen inches apart, and bearing often an average of about fifty ears per plant. Once, a single grain produced one hundred and twenty ears, and once one hundred and ninety![1]

The 1896 crop was a marvel, yielding at the rate of some one

[1] This year two plants have produced 120 ears each.—A. C.

hundred and thirty bushels per acre, instead of twenty-nine, the usual average for the country generally. It also yielded straw of remarkable quality, six feet high (average), and weighing at the rate of ten tons to the acre. The grain, too, shows a striking improvement in quality as well as amount.

Rye Grass.—Under ordinary methods this plant has a profitable life of only two years; but Sir Arthur's is now in its *seventh* year. This is the first year it has shewn any decline; but even this diminished crop has weighed at the rate of five tons of splendid hay per acre! During the six previous years, there has been an almost steady yield, in three cuttings, of seven to seven and a half tons of hay to the acre, though some of these seasons have been extremely bad. The *cost* of cultivation has been very small, when spread over these seven years. Besides the cost of seed and harvesting, and four or five ordinary dressings of liquid manure, there was merely the first and only cultivation of the land to a depth of three feet, costing about £25 by hand labour. This crop, therefore, has been enormously profitable.

It is true that these cases enumerated are among the best; still, the average for twelve years, over a great variety of crops and seasons, is fully four times the farm average of the country for similar land, and there is little doubt that better land and better conditions would have yielded still more startling results.

A REMARKABLE DISCOVERY.

"I made a remarkable discovery this year," Sir Arthur said to me, as we were turning away from the wheat plot: "The wheat was sown on the 1st of September, but the birds got at some of it, so there were gaps left which we filled up with fresh sowings about the end of October. Thus we had two crops—the early sown, and the late sown—and the difference in the behaviour of these was very striking. The late sown scarcely grew at all in the winter, and never came to a fair crop at last; but the early sown grew and tillered the whole winter through, without a stop even in frost, and reached an average of forty-five ears per seed sown, against twenty ears only in the case of the late sown. And no wonder! for in the coldest spells of the winter, when the surface was frozen, the thermometer registered 47° at a depth of three feet! Only think what that means—*Deep culture adds three months to the growing season.*"

Talk of Klondike and its gold mines! Here in this discovery

are possibilities enough to stagger the imagination. It tells us of vast wealth hidden, not in the cruel, frozen North, but here close at hand in our own familiar fields.

The power of deep tillage is gradually becoming known. The famous Tintara Vineyards of Australia are cultivated on this principle, and Mr. Cecil Rhodes plants 3,000 fruit trees every year in deep-tilled soil, and says he means to do so as long as he lives. The advantage of deep culture is specially felt in tropical lands. Sir Arthur shewed me a letter from a coffee planter in the West Indies, to whom he had sent two of the garden-forks to be used in place of the hoe. This letter reported that the result of deep culture, by means of these forks, had been to raise the coffee yield per acre from 200–400 lbs. to 2,500 lbs.!

The best of this deep tillage, as Sir Arthur is never tired of pointing out, is its availability to every one who has any land whatever. He who tills but one square yard can turn it into a cubic yard or more and watch the effect; while he who ploughs his hundred acres can plough four times instead of once, to a depth of twelve, fourteen, or eighteen inches, with ploughs that cut and aerate the soil while they make no clods.

The one thing needed in this matter is *faith*. When men discover the presence of enormous wealth one thousand yards beneath the surface, they allow no expense to hinder them. They think and plan and invent till they are able to reach their treasure at a reasonable cost. Once we as a people come to believe in the boundless treasure bound up in soil and air, we, too, shall invent machinery to carry out profitably these new ideas. Indeed, this process has begun already. Several machines have been invented. Amongst others, one used last year by the Duke of Bedford, which rips up the land to a depth of thirty inches at a cost of only 30*s.* per acre, and which pulverizes the top eighteen inches for another 20*s.*, *i.e.* only 50*s.* in all. Early in July this year, some experts visited the Duke's estate to see the wheat on the land so tilled, and one of them reported to me that it stood about two feet higher than other wheat near by on similar land tilled in the old style.

Sir Arthur Cotton believes that land is one of the best of investments, if not the best, and that it may well be made to yield a forty to fifty per cent. return at present prices. Anyway, the question is a national one, and one of incalculable importance.

CHAPTER XIX

The Mainspring and Secret of Arthur Cotton's Life: Character and Characteristics

MY father was never really happy unless he was in some manner promoting what he believed to be the furtherance of the kingdom of God in the world. He lived as one who served his Divine Master; and thus ordered his life and conversation; while a sense of the importance of religion to every one and the great issues of eternity made him ever zealous for the salvation of the souls of men. His ever-abiding sense of God's presence was the secret and the mainstay of his life of manifold activities.

So long ago as one of his visits to Tasmania, he took great interest in evangelistic work amongst the convicts, the southernmost island of the Australian dominion being then a penal colony.

Wherever he was stationed in India, Christian mission work found in him a ready supporter. More particularly was this the case while the great anicut at Dowlâisweram was being constructed. Many instances occurred in which this was evidenced. Young officers, sent to assist him in the carrying out of his great enterprise, were particularly influenced by him for good, and not a few were themselves made the occasion of great good to others.

My father's interest in the extension of Christianity throughout the world was evident from a glance at the little pile of missionary reports, quite up to date, which always lay on a small table by his side, ready to be studied at any leisure moment. To the very last month of his life, he seemed to be cognisant of each fresh effort that was being made to aid the march of Christianity in every part of the world.

A conversation with him would embrace so many different themes and cover such a vast area, that we often used to tell him that we had "heard as much as we could take in for the time being." But his own brain never tired in his search after knowledge, especially in anything that related to the advantage of the British Empire, either spiritually or temporally. Truly, he was a Christian patriot.

When the transcript of the Moabite stone came to light, he used constantly to refer to it. "It seems as if it had been sent to us," he said, "just at a critical moment, when infidelity is trying one of its worst attacks on the inspired Word. This is merely to remind God's believing ones that His Word is true; and that nothing can ever shake the Divine testimony."

In prophecy his interest was unbounded. I can give but a slight sketch of some of his prophetic thoughts:—

"The strange confusion which exists on prophetic subjects surely arises from mixing up things literal, things figurative, and things allegorical. When we read, 'They shall cast lots upon my garment,' we know that this is literal. When, again, we read, 'The man of sin shall be revealed, and he who now lets will let,' we know that it is figurative, because the smallest consideration will satisfy us that it has reference to future events; so that 'he who lets' cannot be a man, and consequently we may say the same of 'the man of sin.' To speak of one person in a certain passage as an individual man and in another a figure of something else is contrary to common sense.

"If we begin by satisfying ourselves whether a passage is literal, figurative, or symbolical, which is easily done, the matter will soon be cleared up to us conclusively. We do this, as a matter of course, when we read *John Bunyan's*, or any other, book. Nobody has any doubt whether his

'Interpreter' is a man who translates one language into another, or whether he is an interpreter of the Word of God.

"But I should like to add one or two remarks on particular points.

"One is about Tarshish. It is asked, Where is it? It is perfectly clear that in the Bible the word 'Tarshish' is used just as we have used the word 'India,'—that is, as a general expression for the distant parts of the earth. We had East India, and the West Indies; we call coloured men, Indians, whether negroes or red Indians. We used to call all large ocean vessels, Indiamen, whereas that was not correct; just as they are called in the Bible, ships of Tarshish. Thus ships went to Tarshish from Ezion-geber, and returned after three years' voyage, with ivory, gold, apes and peacocks, the present four marked products of the highlands of Mysore, in India, and those who went from Tyre to Tarshish brought back silver, tin, and lead, the three products of England still. But also Tarshish is mentioned as a particular locality, just as now we designate our Asiatic Empire, India, as if there were no other. Thus, we read in that most remarkable verse, 'Tarshish, and all the young lions thereof,'—the lion being the official symbol of England, the only State that has young ones. There are no young 'eagles.' Canada, Australia, and South Africa are England's real glorious whelps, as superior to all the rest of the world as their mother is. I would like just to add here, that, in the passage in the 38th chap. of Ezekiel, Tarshish is merely represented as looking on, and saying, sarcastically, 'Art thou come to take a prey?' That is spoken by a person taking an intelligent view of the case; and assuredly anticipating what the end of the contest would be."

He held for many years, latterly very strongly, the Anglo-Israelite theory, and certainly many of his statements, which were the result of close investigation, were very convincing.

The relative to whom the following letters are addressed

was in Ireland for a time, directing the operations of the Irish Church Missions :—

(1) "There are two marked signs of the times in Ireland, one is the hearty union of different portions of Christian men, one a Plymouth Brother, a sectarian of sectarians, uniting himself with Churchmen, as well as others. The other is the spirit of dissension, that God has sent among the enemies of truth and of His kingdom.

"We cannot mistake these signs that the time has come for the deliverance of Ireland from her papal bondage. I don't understand what you say about the supply of scriptures running short. Will not the Bible Society supply any number of copies? How far this state of things is beyond what was thought of two or three years ago! What encouragement for the prayer meeting! We must not be surprised at the troubles in North Africa. Hudson Taylor has met the difficulty in China by appropriating separate ranges of country for the different churches.

"A large number of the converts from heathenism in Orissa owe very much of their awakening to the printed Word. In various branches of the Indian service Christian officers, who may not be able to preach in the vernacular, gladly engage in tract and scripture distribution. The late lamented General Brown, of the Madras Army, did this, saying, 'If I cannot preach the Word on the line of march, I can give away the printed Word.' Another officer in the Madras service purchased a sufficient number of gospels to send to every town and village, and to every native prince and Government official in the district where he was appointed. Our Lord said, 'So is the kingdom of God, as if a man should cast seed into the ground; and should sleep and rise night and day, and the seed should spring and grow up he knoweth not how.'

"David strengthened himself for his contest with Goliath, by remembering what God had done for him on a former occasion, and this record is exactly calculated to strengthen the hands of every one, whether missionary or otherwise who shall help in any way to scatter this living seed. We have every day new proofs that it has in good measure already undermined the great fabrics of Hinduism and Mohammedanism; and the working of this leaven is now appearing on the surface; in the little native churches which have sprung up in many places, before any missionary had reached them.

"In one tract of country, on the confines of the native State of Hyderabad, there are now more than twenty-five villages in which there are well-established native churches, the commencement of this movement was entirely from tracts and scriptures, the native catechist who first visited the neighbourhood finding there a number of Indians who regularly met for Christian worship, and were so far instructed as to be in a great measure prepared for baptism. And we may now confidently expect that such cases will rapidly multiply. There is, as it were, the seed of truth under every sod almost throughout India, and all for many years well-watered by the prayers and tears of faithful men. Let this fact encourage every one to help in a work of such unspeakable importance.

"How terrible it is that God's people should be spending their energies upon each other, instead of upon the enemy! I am persuaded that as yet the only thing is for each body of Christians to carry on its own work in its own way."

(2) "I am so glad to hear you are so grappling with Popery. It must be a most difficult subject, but the end of the fight is certain. Rome will never revive. And all this childish religion in our own churches is a sign that men's consciences are not so fast asleep as in my boyhood.

"I remember many years ago your quoting that verse in John, that the Word should try us at the last day, and have a thousand times referred to it. It speaks authoritatively to the conscience, and the whole system of training of the Papacy is to overpower and stupefy the conscience, in order to get rid of this authority of the Word, acting most wisely in their own interests.

"And that which carries conviction to the understanding is the argument of justification by faith.

"The whole Bible rests upon this; and who could have invented it? It bears its own proof with it. That there should be some intimation of it in another book proves nothing. Every human system contains some scriptural things, both doctrinal and perceptive. How could God's teaching be utterly obliterated? Some things approve themselves to the natural conscience which the heart and life are still entirely opposed to; and these are found in all false religions. But the clear and full declaration of 'faith being counted for righteousness' is the proof that the Bible, which is pervaded by it, and absolutely dependent upon it, is from God. If the records of the Bible are false, of course our faith is vain.

"Every possible thing that could confirm the miracles of our Lord took place, and friends and enemies are equally witnesses to them. The miracle of Peter's at the Temple was a remarkable one of this type. The man afflicted was forty years old, had been long placed in the porch of the Temple, where certainly almost every man in the land must have seen him, and known him as well as the pillars! so that, in every town and village of the land, there must have been witnesses of the leaping and praising God of this well-known object of apostolic commiseration. I often think of his long, weary suffering as a reminder of that word, 'What I do thou knowest not now.' How little people thought of God's purposes in regard to this sufferer!"

One of my father's strongest characteristics was his admiration and support of women's work! He expressed in very ardent terms his feeling that women were called into the world's great arena of need in order that they might, with a gentle hand and skilful instinct, which, he said, were talents granted to them as a special gift, take their own place in undoing the work of evil.

Many an argument I have heard between him and others

who would rather hold back, than encourage, feminine efforts of the kind that he loved and supported.

He would sometimes say to me: "Do something, my girl; do something. Never be idle for a single moment. Remember, Time is short, Eternity is near!"

Though a firm adherent of the Church of England, and loyally devoted to it to the last day of his life, he felt very strongly that it was a mistake for those who had been learning heavenly truths all their lives to sit in their pews twice every Sunday, whilst thousands around them might be classed amongst the non-church-going masses, and were untouched by spiritual work of any kind. He employed a home missionary, who visited from house to house, and held small cottage meetings for the poor. He would often go and take these meetings himself.

There was at this time a young French lady residing in a village in the neigbourhood. She had an extraordinary gift for reaching and benefiting the working classes. Their love for her was unbounded; many a story reached us of her quiet, gentle, power over the roughest of the navvies who were employed in making the London and Brighton railway line. Many of her richer neighbours objected, however, to her efforts. She was winning and raising, refining and softening, these men by the hundred; the wives and children blessed her very name. Yet she was hindered and opposed in every way by those living around her, and it was in discussion of this strange opposition that she said to my father one day, "If our Father in heaven did not wish that women should carry the message of His Gospel to the poor and needy, why did He tell us, in the 11th chapter of 1st Corinthians, exactly what costume we are to wear when we are doing it?" Her quaint way of expressing her argument as she drew attention to this well-known passage, struck him very much. A Bible was called for and the words looked up. "You are quite right," he said, "You are quite right"; and in the most enthusiastic way he expressed his approval of what she was doing.

This brings me to the commencement of my own work

in that neighbourhood, which, from the beginning, he warmly encouraged and supported, and which he really initiated. But, as I have already told that story in my book, *Our Coffee Room*, and as this is the memoir of my father's life, I only allude to the work I have been able to do to show that it had his most eager and interested support.

A rumour spread throughout the neighbourhood one day that a very large number of troops and militia were to be mobilised on one of our commons. A sense of our responsibility moved us to consider what was to be done. "We cannot do anything for so many," was my father's first remark. The next question, however, was: "What are we to do?" Finally, we decided to put up a large wooden room that might be occupied by the troops and militia during their leisure hours. It had to be erected without delay, as the regiments were expected within a couple of days. A carpenter whom we knew in the neighbourhood promised that it should be up and ready for use when the men arrived. We had just met on the common to arrange for the site, when an officer rode up to make his inspection of the ground. Not knowing who he was, we stopped him. He proved to be General Kirby. We told him our plan, namely, the erection of a recreation room for the troops. He said: "You could not have applied to a better person, for I am the officer in command, and I assure you that such a provision for the men exactly meets my views. I will do all I can to help you. Where would you like to place it?"

"As near the tents, as possible and near to the pump, too," was our reply.

He smiled, dismounted, and walked with us through the furze bushes to a clearing that almost adjoined the central road on the common. "I think you could not have a better place than this," he said, and at once gave permission for the erection. Within half-an-hour the workmen were on the spot and the work had begun. We had scarcely put the finishing touch to our hall of delights when the bugle sounded, and a great crowd of men filled it from end to end. Every day my father was there helping me. So great were the numbers who used to come that an application was made to the War Office, which the kind General endorsed on our behalf, with the result that first three tents, and then five, were lent to us to increase the space for the men's requirements, recreation, and shelter.

The men listened eagerly when night by night we read to them; they were thankful for these opportunities, and many of them expressed themselves in the very warmest terms of gratitude for all we had done.

The principle of meeting our fellow-creatures at the point of their threefold need is one that cannot fail of success. My father and I used often to discuss this matter, and we agreed that if we really want to reach the masses, and to satisfy them and help them for time and for eternity, we must follow closely in our Saviour's steps who Himself laid down for us the highest maxims, and left us the plainest, and at the same time the brightest and the most practical, Example. He met the needs of the human race in considering and supplying:—

1st. Their spiritual
2nd. Their mental } wants.
3rd. Their bodily

Sometimes, indeed very generally, He reversed this order, meeting first the bodily wants of the people, and proceeding upward in His dealing with them.

At last a day came when both soldiers and militia were to be moved in a body to Aldershot. We thought our work finished, and were about to take our leave of them, when telegrams came, offering us tents in the camps there, and requesting that we would accompany the men to Aldershot, and continue to carry on the friendly work that had been commenced at Dorking. Of course my father rose to this demand. He said that there should be no difficulty in the way of our carrying out this fresh undertaking. An officer kindly lent us his hut at Aldershot, and our tents for the men were large and commodious. They came to us in such numbers that, to the very end, our only difficulty was the one of accommodation.

Our last meeting, on the Sunday night before they dispersed, was a memorable one, and numbers of men stood up to express their thankfulness, and to say what a blessing their visit to England had been to them. My father spoke to them as one of themselves, telling them that there was no profession like that of the army, alluding to his early experiences in the Burmese war, and exhorting them to become good soldiers of Jesus Christ.

The rapid spread of ritualism and its insidious approaches occasioned my father the deepest anxiety and most constant thought. With that certainty of victory, which buoyed him up through every phase of difficulty, he wrote as follows :—

"I am not one of those who fear for the fall of the Church of England; I feel fully assured that He who planted the truth so firmly in every parish by the thirty-nine Articles and the Liturgy will not suffer the gates of hell to prevail against it. I am satisfied that this is the grand bulwark of the truth in the world, and that the ordinances of the Church are in God's hands exactly what the temple-worship was at Jerusalem, only in a different form suited to the present new dispensation. And, therefore, it is that all the Pharisees, Sadducees, and Herodians of the present day, who thrust themselves into the ministry, are still compelled to use in the ordinances the language of pure scriptural, gospel truth.

"But if we are to contend earnestly for the faith once delivered to the saints, the times most urgently require us to watch and do our utmost to save whatever parish we are connected with from returning to 'the weak and beggarly elements whereunto so many are desiring again to be in bondage.'

"The beginning always is by substituting music for worship, introducing some mummery such as intoning, pretty dresses, or ornament. Here, therefore, never was a time when it was more imperative to keep to the utmost simplicity in our worship, and we cannot possibly be too much on our guard against every movement in the direction of ritualism, which is Popery in a slight disguise. The fact is, multitudes do not consider, and are not sensible that the spirit that dwelleth in us lusteth not only to envy, but in the same way and degree to idolatry, and therefore it is that so many godly men are carried away by the torrent of evil that is now pervading the Church of England.

"They do not keep in mind that great warning: 'Searching diligently lest any bitter root springing up trouble you, and thereby many be defiled'; and therefore they enter upon a course which they do not perceive contains the rudiments of this fatal heresy of ritualism.

"If they did, how could they possibly endorse, for instance, such an abomination as whining before God, or what is called intoning, and other such things with which a beginning is usually made in the downward course, of which there is not a trait in the Articles and Liturgy, and which are entirely contrary to the spirit of them, which is the spirit of the Bible.

"'God made man upright, but he has sought out many *inventions*,' and we cannot, therefore, possibly be sufficiently on our watch against *inventions*."

His own views on the advance of Romanism were distinctly free from the depression that at this time was colouring so much of the writing that emanated from Protestant pens. In a letter to one of the Church journals he said :—

"In a recent periodical I see a statement showing the progress of Popery, which seems to me to call earnestly for some consideration.

"The facts given are stated to be startling, but nothing misleads like facts if they are not thoroughly considered. Bare facts may appear to show what is exactly contrary to the truth.

"In this case it is stated that in 1780 there were 70,000 Roman Catholics in England, in 1845 328,000, n 1871 2,200,000, and in 1885, according to Romanists, 2,500,000.

"If this is truly stated, it leaves the impression that Popery has increased thirty-five-fold in one hundred years in England. But Popery and Papists are two essentially different things.

"First, these figures tell us nothing unless we are informed what number of Irish and Continental Papists are now resident in England. The fact is that the English Roman Catholics form a very small proportion of this two and a half millions—perhaps a tenth, but I don't know exactly. While England is, by God's mercy, such a harbour of refuge as it is, of course multitudes will come from other countries to partake of its blessings. But the increase of Papists does not show the increase of Popery.

"Secondly, the population of England is increasing amazingly. I forget what the increase has been in one hundred years, perhaps two and a half fold; so that, if all these two and a half millions were English, it would be two and a half millions out of fifteen millions. Probably not a thirtieth part of the increase is in English Roman Catholics.

"Again, the Papists state that there are two thousand converts from Protestantism every year. First, of course, this is an exaggeration, for no trust can be placed in Roman Catholic statements of this sort. Secondly, the increase of population is about three hundred thousand a year, so that two thousand would be the one hundred and fiftieth part of it. At this rate how long would it take for Popery to predominate in England? Thirdly, how many Roman Catholics become Protestants every year?

"We need not stop here to think that these two thousand converts, if there were so many, surely represent men turned from one form of ignorance to another; whereas the great majority of Roman Catholics who become Protestants are men who have turned from darkness to light from the power of Satan unto God. . . .

"The Papacy is, indeed, making desperate efforts to recover its lost ground, but they are utterly vain. We cannot be too watchful against those efforts, and they call for incessant fighting; but there is a wide difference between fighting a losing battle and a winning one! Men don't carry on the war with less spirit in the latter case than in the former."

CHAPTER XX

The Eventide of Light and Peace

THE days at Woodcot were spent, as has been already stated, in the study of various subjects and correspondence upon them with a number of friends. In the evening, after his frugal dinner, he would sit in the drawing-room with us, his eyes fixed on the pages of a Bible, in very small print, which he delighted in reading. Owing to his deafness, the conversation around him was no interruption to his thoughts; he would sit perfectly absorbed in the subject before him, sometimes a smile lighting up his face, sometimes with an expression of intense thought as he searched deeply into the Word.

One of us said to him one evening: "You seem very fond of your Bible; I do not think you ever get tired of it." His reply, raising his hand with one of his impressive gestures, was: "I feel like a little child playing on the margin of a lake; all my life I have been studying this book, and I seem hardly to have touched it yet. There are such depths and heights beyond all that I have ever seen or known."

Then would come an interval, after nine o'clock, when he would play his favourite game of Patience. He not only played it regularly, but kept a note-book, in which all his winnings and losings were jotted down, and he would say with mock sadness: "I have lost two games to-night." It seemed to be a relief to his busy, active brain to concentrate it on the numerical problems which this simple recreation afforded him.

It was during one of these peaceful years at Woodcot

that my father heard the tidings of his brother Richard's death. The Provost was a man whose activity and strength were so great that, at the age of eighty-seven, he was doing the same work that he had done thirty years before, attending five services on Sunday and carrying out all the duties of his Provostship.

His life was brought to a close very suddenly. Whilst sitting at dinner one evening, he raised his hands in adoration, and in a low voice began to utter sentences of praise and gratitude to God for all His goodness to him during a long life. He then bowed his head, and, as he did so, seemed to fall forward. One of the members of his family went to him, and asked if he felt ill. He made no reply; his spirit had in that moment passed away. My father felt intensely the loss of his brother, and, as was always the case with him whenever any bereavement or grief crossed his path, he could not utter one word on the subject.

Not very long after this loss, his brother, Sir Sydney Cotton, Governor of the Chelsea Hospital, was taken ill and died, his last hours being as remarkable as the rest of his life. He always used to come into that immense drawing-room about five o'clock to tea, after which we all gathered round him for music, conversation, or merry games. But there came a day when at the usual hour Sir Sydney entered the room, but instead of taking his seat by the tea-table, he said: "I am going upstairs to rest; I am tired." He went to bed, and in a short time it was found that his heart was beginning to fail. Many times in that last illness he spoke of the "glory" into which he was about to enter. He was a good man, respected and honoured by all who knew him, but he was not one who had ever been heard to speak much on religious subjects. I remember, however, his saying to me the last time that I saw him, a fortnight before his death: "I want you to come and pay me a long visit here, and then you can read to my sick men in the infirmary. You shall be my chaplain, and I will give you a pass, that you may read the

Bible to them." During the short time during which his illness lasted—I think only about thirty-six hours—his conversation was most interesting. He appeared to have thought he was entering the gates of glory with a victorious army, and expressed himself somewhat in these words:—"I hear it; yes, I hear it! Music! such music as I never heard before,—and songs! Yes! they are songs of victory and triumph! I am going, going now; I am ready. The Captain waits to meet me—the great Captain." Then, again, he would exclaim,—"Oh, such flowers! I have never seen such flowers!" With a clear, distinct voice he said,—"I know whom I have believed! I am persuaded that He is able to keep that which I have committed to Him. . . . I have finished my course; I have fought a good fight!" It was an unspeakable loss to us all when Sir Sydney passed away. No one could ever fill his place amongst the large circle of friends and relatives, who loved him so much and enjoyed his genial kindness and hospitality.

My brother Alfred, who had been appointed to serve on the Boundary Commission between Afghanistan and Central Asia, under Sir West Ridgeway, now Governor of Ceylon, wrote at this time to his father:—

"My party of sixty-seven men is to form Ridgeway's escort. The calvary escort he had from Zulficar to Marchak does not seem to have been a success.

"I don't think my men will give much trouble. They are great, strong fellows—very cheerful, and it is a point of honour never to admit that they feel tired, or to make an excuse to get off anything. On the other hand, they require to be kept under strict discipline. Of course, my very small command does not occupy me much, and, in addition to my military duties, I have been a member of the political staff since November. Among the people reduced was the commissariat officer, and that part of the work falls to me at present. Ridgeway, however, says he will give some one else a turn of it, after a bit. My first job was to collect the winter supplies for the mission, with very short notice, and I had to get over a good many difficulties. This place belongs to the Wali of Mamiena, who is only a tributary of the Amir. The people are Nabaks and hate the Afghans, and the present chief's government is weak. Thus, between the local authorities fearing that the Afghans would think too much was being done for us, and their inability to force their subjects to do enough, it was hard work to obey a sudden call. However, the work was done all right, and Ridgeway expressed his satisfaction."

Again, Alfred writes from Chilik:—

"Our camp will be five thousand feet high, and we are going there to escape the heat, while we are waiting to hear what Government is going to do with us. While on the move, there is not much time for anything except unavoidable work. We march at 1 a.m., to get as much of our stage as possible done before the sun gets up, so one wants a good sleep in the day, while the march takes about a third of the day, when one does twenty-one miles, as we did this morning, so, as the result, mother's correspondence suffers.

"The present plan, if we can get off, is for Ridgeway, with the cavalry and bulk of the mission, to go by Kabul to Peshawur, while I escort Durand through Chitral, Gilgit, and Kashmir. If we do not do that pretty soon, the high passes will be snowed up, and a new programme will be necessary. It is dreary work waiting about like this, and we had a bad month of it at Karkin.

"It was very hot, and when one stays long in a camp the flies increase in a terrible way. They became so bad that I could do nothing all day except knock them off, until I put my table and chair into a mosquito curtain, which was given me by our geologist, who had a second set. We managed to cool ourselves by making a hedge of green camel-thorn, on the north side of the tent, and engaging a Turk to keep throwing water on it. If the wind blew, and if the Turk did his duty, this arrangement made me quite cold. I have known it to bring the temperature down 30°, but on still days we have no remedy. At Kelig, where we halted yesterday, is the position of the principal ferry, where the main road from Afghanistan to Bokhara crosses the river. The boats are large ones, capable of carrying camels, donkeys, merchandise, and people. The means of propelling is probably unique. Two ponies pull the boat by swimming! They have a single broad surcingle, and to this a rope is fastened, and the other end tied to the boat. A man in the stern does what steering he can by rowing with a long pole, and during the whole passage two assistant mariners in the bows belabour the wretched ponies unmercifully. The current is strong, and takes the boat a long way down in the crossing.

"Talbot, one of the surveyors, is next door, and I have just been to look at his thermometer, which I find stands at 107° now, at 3 p.m. I need not say that I rejected his base suggestion that I should 'put on 10°' for your benefit!

"When describing the boring of an Alpine tunnel the other day, they say 'they reached the limit of human endurance at 96°.' But we are kept going by a wind, though a hot one. In a tunnel there would be no breeze.

"I could not write without the assistance of a small vessel of wet shot, to damp my pen in, every word or two. In the night we crossed the belt of sandy desert that borders the river. At least ten miles of loose sand out of a twenty-one-mile march is no joke, and carrying a rifle and accoutrements, but every one of my men came in smiling! They are a most cheerful lot, but they are very anxious to get away from here now. It is quite unusual to keep native troops so long as this away from their homes."

It may well be imagined that my brother's letters were a constant interest and pleasure to us all. His father looked for them eagerly, and welcomed with a special joy his return on leave at the close of his wanderings. When he returned to England he married May, the eldest daughter of Admiral Sir Leopold Heath, and they returned to India together. It was only a few years after that my brother, on his way home from India, became very ill, and, all remedies failing to bring alleviation to his sufferings, he died on the voyage, leaving his widow to arrive alone, while his parents, who were expecting him to spend Christmas with them, were overcome with grief at the loss of their dearly-loved son. Sir West Ridgeway wrote: "It is with great sorrow that I have read in *The Times* of the sad loss which has fallen on you. I had learned to respect and admire your son's character and worth, and therefore you will pardon my intruding on you at this moment. The Government has lost a most promising officer, who could be always relied upon to do loyally, thoroughly, and well, any work confided to him."

My father at first seemed almost stunned with this succession of bereavements, but he rallied to continue his work of correspondence on the many great topics of universal interest that always absorbed him.

The life of this gallant soldier, ever brave in fighting for the cause of right, whether on the battle-field of war or on the often more severe battle-field of the world, was now drawing to a close, and it is truly wonderful that to the end, and during all the latter years of his greatly prolonged life, he was able to keep pace with the times, interesting himself in all the questions of the day, and ever maintaining touch with the joy and sorrow that fell to the lot of both friends and relatives.

In some of my mother's letters there are interesting passages, which give a little home picture of his thoughts and feelings, and work, too, during these latter years.

"Your father is well and the wheat is gathered in; a finer crop of straw than of grain, he says. However, the tall stalks and good-sized ears look very fine. He has still his maize and sugar beets to watch. A farmer is coming from Rugby to-day to visit him."

After a short absence from home:—

"Your father went straight from the carriage to his dear

wheat and Indian corn and sugar beet, which were all much the same as when he left them. . . .

"Your father and I were much interested in your engineering letter, and he hopes to answer it very soon, to-day if he has time, but this is the long-thought-of day of harvest. The precious wheat is to come down to-day, and every separate plant and the produce of each grain sown has to be calculated, registered, and ticketed—such a business for the dear father, who sits watching the process."

It is interesting to note that my father's last communications to the Press were in the form of letters to *The Times* concerning famines in India. The final words which, for public purposes, came from his pen, were in condemnation of "giving India iron instead of water." "This," he declared, "was the sole cause of all this awful loss of millions of lives and hundreds of millions of money in the value of crops and cattle."

Then, an appeal to *The Times*: "I am sure this terrible question is worthy of the paper that is really at the head of the earthly powers."

Within a few months of his death my father's mind was as much concerned with the good of the Indian people as at any former period, while his grasp of the various schemes he advocated was not less firm. This will be seen by a perusal of a short series of letters which were all addressed to my husband. The letters range from Feb. 26, 1897, to April 20, 1898, and are as follows:—

WOODCOT, DORKING, *Feb.* 26, 1897.

MY DEAR ANTHONY,—

. . . About India and its famine, I cannot tell you my feelings, almost the whole loss of life being due solely to the Government's obstinate rejection of irrigation. There is no want of water or land in the worst of years; the famine is caused by the water being allowed to run to waste in the sea.

About 3 per cent. of the rich monsoon river water is led out upon the land, and 97 per cent. still is lost. The infatuation about this in official circles is wonderful. The few districts in which they have cut canals of irrigation and navigation are at this moment selling a large surplus of rice at famine prices, instead of dying by tens of thousands in each, and have done so three and four times in the last thirty or forty years, and nothing will induce the Calcutta Government or the India Office to hear or utter a word about the remedy that is in their hands.

You will observe that these two words, irrigation and navigation, do not appear in any official paper lately published on the famine.

They have spent £250,000,000 in railways to carry grain, and they are now to spend £45,000,000 more on further railways, while the whole question is about grain to carry, not one bushel of which will railways produce.

—— has made you a copy of my letter to *The Times* about the Government history of the Godavari works, which are about the most successful engineering works in the world, but no mention of them must be made in anything said or written on the famine!

If £50,000,000 had been spent in distributing river water throughout India, the whole country would be now sprinkled over with immense tracts of rice, producing food for 30,000,000 of people for a whole year, and including some 10,000 miles of perfect steam-boat canal, carrying at one-tenth of the cost of railways.

Mr. Bright, Mr. Lowe, and Lord Shaftesbury all separately sent for me two or three times to discuss this subject, but all three ended by concluding that they could not take up the matter without giving up home questions, which involved all their time. It's an extraordinary thing that no member of parliament has seen his way to fight this battle as yet. Mr. Dixon, M.P. for Birmingham, came here a few days ago and took an interest in the subject, but whether he will be able to enter upon it in the House, I don't know.

I am in hopes that amongst your acquaintances you may find some one who could apprehend the immense importance of the subject, with these millions dying before our eyes, and compel the Government to look it in the face. I must tell you that it is now, I believe, a personal question with the great majority of the Civil Service.

A lady said to my wife, "I should think so, indeed, when the whole of our property is invested in railways."

The Government works now in operation provide water for 11,000,000 acres of rice and wheat, and, in the Punjab, through the determined stand made by the local officials, some considerable works are being carried out at present.

What is wanted is that irrigation and navigation should be made one of the very first matters at the India Office. But nobody who has not, like me, fought this battle for forty years, can conceive the difficulty of the task.

Even in the Godavari district itself, where there are 700,000 irrigated acres and 500 miles of steam-boat canal, there are still about 500,000 acres unirrigated, including, in their range, 200 or 300 miles of navigation. Lord Wenlock, late Governor of Madras, has been lecturing on his province, but not a word does he say about the incalculable effect the five extensively watered districts of his presidency have upon the present famine.

This Godavari work was begun entirely by the individual effort of Lord Tweeddale, when Governor of Madras, in spite of the whole body of officials at Calcutta and Madras.

. . . What a grievous thing it is that we have not one great man connected with India at this terrible time! But "the Lord reigneth," and He can both send a gracious rain and say to the pestilence—"Be still," and of one thing I am sure, He will deliver us out of all this confusion.

With respect to railways, I may mention that I consider that 600 or 800 miles of main line to connect the capitals with the ports, and with each other, were an absolute necessity; but to spend hundreds of millions on small branch lines, while the irrigation and navigation were neglected, was a great wrong, as is shown by actual results at this time.

Ever yours affectionately,
ARTHUR.

DORKING, *Mar.* 29, 1898.

MY DEAR ANTHONY,—

I have to thank you much for your letter of the 8th, and have not yet answered it, not being sure it would find you.

Thank you also so much for getting the letter to *The Times* reprinted, and for the copies you sent me. Mr. Price, M.P. for East Norfolk, came to talk to me about irrigation.

He is giving time to the matter, and has been to the India Office about it. I hope he may be able to take up the question in the House, but it would require much time and trouble to force the matter upon public attention.

The religious paper in which my letter was, was *The Friend of China.* It was the same letter as that to *The Times.*

With respect to Sir W. Muir's paper, after his speaking of tracts, where irrigation cannot be applied,—Is the question about such tracts, or about such as can be watered? What should we think of a paper on railways which began by saying that rails could not be laid across the Channel? There are many millions of acres that can be watered from unfailing rivers. So, Lord Harris says the irrigation works near Bombay only pay one per cent. Do famines pay one per cent. profit?

The pamphlet I send you now contains much information both on irrigation and navigation. I should be so glad if you could find time to run your eye over it. It will give you some idea of the strange fear of the railway men; but the subject should be really investigated.

I am trying to write a short memo. of what I think is now wanted in this matter, and hope to send you a copy.

The most terrible news I have yet heard is that China

has completely surrendered to Russia. She has agreed to its making three lines of railway in China, with any number of soldiers resident on them that she may deem necessary to defend them. This will bring Russia into direct contact with us, in a way in which we must choose between defending our missionaries or leaving them to the same treatment as Englishmen are receiving in Madagascar, for the Greek Church will no more permit Protestant missions than Papists do.

I hope you will be able to give some time to the Indian water question, to see Mr. Price and Mr. Dixon now; the future of India immensely depends upon it.

Nothing else can deliver it from its famines and satisfy the people that we are equal to the task God has set us, and above all deliver us from the insane idea that nothing can provide for the expenses of Government but that which is the cause of all our failures, the cursed Opium Trade, the one grand disgrace of our present national position, and the real source of all these judgments of God. "Yet will I not leave you wholly unpunished," is what He says in the midst of all the endless blessings which He promises us.

I find no end of papers of mine going fully into every point of the subject of water for India.

With great affection, yours,

ARTHUR.

DORKING, *April* 9, 1898.

MY DEAR ANTHONY,—

In compliance with B.'s telegram, I have sent some papers on irrigation. I find no end of papers that I have written, containing in every form all I have to say on these subjects upon which I am fully persuaded that the temporal well-being of India entirely depends, that water is as completely the great treasure of India as it is of Egypt, and that what is now wanted in the former is exactly the sort of a man who was sent to Egypt, Lord Dufferin, who had the statesmanship to say, Before we proceed to other matters we must lay our foundation by the water, as that on which all depends, as being the only thing which can give us standing ground by setting the finances to rights. Nay, it is still more than that in India, because it is that alone on which the lives of its hundreds of millions depend.

They have spent hundreds of millions on railways, and are there not now tens of thousands of lives being lost notwithstanding?

There are millions of cubic yards of water, all loaded with vegetable food, flowing into the sea, and millions of square miles of land, scattered over all India, in which it ought to have been distributed, and might have been at practicable cost. Nothing but the removal of this opposition from the Indian Council and the Civil Service can save India, either as to life or finance. I am trying to write for Mr. Price a short memo. of what I am sure ought to be done now, without a moment's delay, in the way of navigation and irrigation; but I cannot write such a paper effectively immediately.

I hope, however, to send you a copy of it soon.

Think of its having actually cost only Rs. 18 an acre to water 700,000 acres in Godavari, including 500 miles of the finest internal navigation in the world, while the increase in value of crop due to it is 40 rupees per acre, and there are about 500,000 acres more in that small district, capable of irrigation by means of works which would, at the same time, provide about 350 miles of canal and 150 of river navigation.

I think the irrigation in the upper non-delta districts would cost, perhaps, double what it has done in the delta; but if it cost five times as much, it would be nothing in comparison to its benefits, even in money only, while for life it is essential.

It is true that three of the great Government works are not now paying to the Treasury interest for the cost, but this is solely because they were not in the hands of those who were determined that they should pay. Nothing ever succeeds in the hands of men who have previously made up their minds that they shan't succeed. In every work mistakes are made and difficulties are met with, which can only be overcome by enthusiasts who are determined that they shall succeed.

In Godavari we made plenty of mistakes and have had abundance to learn, and our success is entirely due to the determination and indomitable patience of the long succession of engineers that have had charge of the works.

All the non-paying works are really paying enormously in fact, though so small a proportion reaches the Treasury directly. The Government are not mere investors but rulers, and the question is not, What returns reach the Treasury? but, What are the profits to the people, without speaking of life? It is not even a question of what reaches the Treasury in water-rates only, but what in revenue generally.

The water-rates in Godavari are 5 rupees per acre, 35 lacs a year, but the increase of revenue is 80 lacs, all due to the works. I am fully persuaded that all the non-paying works would abundantly pay interest to the Treasury, if they were fully carried out.

For instance, the vast head-works in the Mahanudi command some 2,000,000 acres of delta, while the water is distributed only over some 200,000 acres. Of course nothing can ever pay if carried on in this way. And not one of the great works, even of those which are acknowledged successes, are yet provided with a most important aid in large tanks in the upper country, which could provide a store of water for the dry season; this could be done at a very trifling comparative cost. Immense reservoir sites have been reported on to supply these great works, but none have yet been executed. India has abundance of openings in this way, if the India Office would but look into the matter. But the whole subject is ignored, and everybody who dares to mention the subject must expect to meet with the treatment I have experienced; and the Government allow things to continue in this state! Pray bear with me.

Ever yours affectionately,
ARTHUR.

DORKING, *April* 20, 1898.

MY DEAR ANTHONY,—

I am sending you copies of a memo. I have written for Mr. Price, as to what I consider is wanted to *prevent* famines in India.

There is a long article in *The Times* to-day about the Agricultural Commission in India, in which everything is spoken of, except the one on which all depends, Water. Nothing can be more certain and obvious than that the whole of the famines depend upon one thing, the want of water; and the ablest men were sent out, at any expense, to consider eighteen years ago on the subject, and the one point on which they, and those who appoint them, are all agreed is, that they shall not mention the word *water*. Who can measure the perverseness of this? A moment's investigation shows certainly that there is no want of water in India in the worst year, and there is no want of land over which it can be taken at a practicable cost, and we have now eight or ten immense works in actual operation, not only supplying millions with food in the midst of this present famine, but even yielding enormous profits on the capital, taking only the direct water-rates and leaving out the principal returns to Government in the general increase of revenue, the result solely of those works. And this, without taking note of by far the largest part of the result in the profits gained by the people.

The cost in interest and management per acre in Godavari is one rupee, and the increase of value of produce about forty rupees.

And all this leaves out the incalculable benefits of cheap carriage by water, the one thing that India wants after securing peace and food.

Among the printed papers sent you is the account of my contest at Manchester with Lord Salisbury, which I had quite forgotten, but which really contains all the great points of the question, all the unaccountable misstatements made by my opponents, and the simple facts stated by me. I shall be glad, indeed, if you can see your way to give some time and attention to this subject, which is indeed a great one, in view of the millions of lives dependent upon it and the hundreds of millions of money that we are losing by neglecting irrigation and navigation, while we are incurring God's judgment in raising a few millions by the Opium Traffic, the greatest disgrace ever brought upon itself by any Government, and bringing reproach upon the name of Christianity throughout China.

Ever yours,
ARTHUR.

Even after he had attained the age of ninety-six he suffered from no illness whatever. "His eye was not dim nor was his natural force abated."

One Saturday in June, 1899, he was very much delighted at receiving a visit from his brother Fred and one or two other friends, and conversed with them freely on every topic brought forward. So well he seemed that we were greatly surprised when, on the next Monday, he said he felt very weak and could not get up. It was evident that his strength had suddenly left him, and though, during the next three weeks, he rallied more than once and was even able to come downstairs, we all saw that a great change had come over him.

My mother writes of those days :—

"On Sunday, July 9, he lay on his sofa downstairs, very cheerful and bright, reading his Bible a good deal, but not inclining much to any other book. The exertion of sitting up through the whole service in church had become too great for him, and latterly he had gone only for the Communion service.

"That Sunday we were at home together, and, in the evening, he said he would try to walk in the garden. With the help of a stick and my shoulder, he reached a seat under the trees, and sat long there enjoying the lovely summer air, the beauty of the scene, and the sweet quiet.

"His heart was full of praise for God's great goodness, especially dwelling at that time on the comfort we had had in this house and garden. 'Exactly suited to us,' he said, and then he spoke of the beauty of the flowers, and the various interests so graciously given, as well as the kindness of dear friends. He did not appear at all conscious that his end was so near.

"Walking up and down stairs had become too great a fatigue, and he was carried for a few days longer from his bed to the sitting-room; but during that week his strength gave way so much that he could no longer leave his room. He was still pleased to see visitors for a few moments.

"Early one morning," my mother wrote, "he looked up at me with a strangely earnest expression on his face, as he used these words: 'I have had such a wonderful night,—a wonderful night,—a revelation, a manifestation of God to my soul. He showed me, in a way that I could never describe, the finished work of Christ upon the Cross, the completeness of salvation,—all is done. I could never tell you what it was; no words can paint it.'"

On the following day, he, the second time, referred to some such experience, fresh and real, and differing slightly from the previous one, but of a similar character.

The cheery smiles and loving hand-clasp with which he greeted those whom he loved were always ready up to the last hours of his life. The welcome we received was ever a warm one. But he would fall asleep again, dozing continually. Gradually the power of speech seemed to forsake him. Even in those hours of intense weakness he would rouse himself to ask about the probabilities of war in the Transvaal, the height of his wheat, the last Protestant or missionary news, and any scraps of information that we could convey to him in large writing in his note-book.

My mother again writes:—

"On the night of the 14th July he was feverish and restless, and it may have been that he became aware then how ill he was. He poured out a remarkable prayer—pleading God's promises, and committing himself and those he loved to the gracious Promiser in a way never to be forgotten; the remembrance is full of comfort to those who remain. After that his strength rapidly declined and his speech became unintelligible, but, up to the very last, there were loving, recognising looks, and the end was 'perfect peace.'"

On the day of the funeral the warmest sympathy and love were shown by our neighbours, both rich and poor, who came in large numbers to the picturesque cemetery, near Dorking, in which he was laid to rest. The touching pathos of the hymns sung, and the words spoken, were all in keeping with the memories of the past, as well as the Union Jack that covered the coffin and the volley fired at the open grave by the Volunteers, symbolising his life-long devotion to his country and his loyalty to the army in which he had served, and of which he ever spoke with the utmost enthusiasm. A beautiful wreath of white hot-house flowers was sent by the Corps of Royal Engineers with a few much-valued sentences.

A friend, Mr. Francis W. Fox, who knew him well, and who had been engaged with him in different phases of work, a few months afterwards, wrote as follows :—

"As I had the privilege, between the years 1874 and '99, of occasionally meeting Sir Arthur Cotton, I had some opportunity of appreciating his fine Christian and lovable character, how rare an order were his mental endowments, and with what power and clear perception he grasped the details and general surroundings of any new problem or complicated question that was laid before him!

"The remarkable success of his great irrigation works in the Madras Presidency, with which his name will be for ever associated, naturally formed a prominent subject of conversation in connection with the development and extension of similar works in India. As his life was so prolonged, he was permitted, in an exceptional manner, to witness the beneficent and altogether brilliant results which flowed from his great works, and he was always most earnestly desirous that the Government of India should introduce the blessings and realise those splendid financial results that he had seen developed in his own works, in other parts of India.

"When the severe famine visited India during the years 1877 to '79, he felt it his duty to deliver addresses in several English towns on irrigation, showing, by statistical facts, how India could be effectually protected against famine by the judicious construction of irrigation canals.

"He addressed at this time a large and influential meeting at the Victoria Rooms, Clifton, and from Clifton he proceeded to Rochdale, where he was guest at the house of the late Right Hon. John Bright, M.P. Subsequently a meeting was held at Manchester, presided over by his distinguished host, who cordially sympathised with him in his views on irrigation, and supported them, in and out of Parliament.

"He had the deepest sympathy for all objects and lines of policy which were calculated to spread in the world the blessings of the Gospel.

"I recollect how especially interested he was in the opening up of the Dark Continent of Africa during the years '74 to '79, for it was during these years that the later discoveries of Livingstone, as well as those of Stanley and Cameron, were made known to the world.

"His friend, the late General Gordon, was also then Governor-General of the Soudan, and I remember the intense pleasure it was to him to hear occasionally from Gordon about the great possibilities of the Nile Basin, and the immense responsibilities which had been placed upon him in those vast regions.

"Sir Arthur Cotton, in connection with his own engineering labours and investigations, ever seemed to be earnestly anxious that these should be the means of ameliorating in some way the moral and material condition of his fellow-men.

"On another occasion, when Sir Arthur Cotton was staying at Grove House, Stoke Bishop, in order to carry out some experiments in connection with a steam turbine engine he had designed, the late Admiral Sir James Hope joined him there on his way from Torquay, where, as Chairman of a Royal Commission of Inquiry into the stability of the "Invincible Class" of battleships, he had been the guest of the late Mr. Froude (brother of the historian), to investigate the result of some naval experiments that Froude had been making with models on the artificial lake at his Torquay house.

"Sir James Hope accompanied Sir Arthur Cotton on this occasion to witness, at some works near Bristol, his steam turbine working at several hundred revolutions per minute, a speed so great that the arms of the turbine itself became quite invisible.

"During one of Sir Arthur Cotton's sojourns at Grove House, a visit was paid to the late George Müller, the founder of the great orphanages on Ashley Down. Sir Arthur Cotton, when a young man, had stopped at Bagdad on an overland journey to India, where he became acquainted with the well-known missionary family of the late Anthony Groves, one of whose sisters became the first wife of George Müller. Both Sir Arthur Cotton and George Müller were pleased to form each other's acquaintance for the first time, and, by a curious coincidence, he met, a few hours after this visit, at the Bristol railway station, Francis W. Newman (the brother of Cardinal Newman), whom he had not seen since those early days at Bagdad, where F. W. Newman was then assisting Anthony Groves in missionary work.

"In concluding these few brief and imperfect reminiscences of your much esteemed father, may I be allowed to say that Sir Arthur Cotton's gentleness and sympathy, combined with an intense force of character, an invincible determination to follow what he believed to be his duty, and a hatred of evil in all its manifestations, that all these characteristics united in giving him the influence which he acquired over the hearts and minds of those who knew him best and who gladly recognised that he, like the original 'King Arthur of the Round Table,' was a true knight that all loved and revered."

Sir Richard Sankey, R.E., K.C.B., in his letter of sympathy to my mother, remarked :—

"Though from your husband's extraordinary health and vitality, the result of a really temperate life, we might have all expected him to survive the century; still, at his very great age, the sorrowful event could not have been very long deferred; but I need hardly say how much, now that it has happened, I, and all who knew your husband, sympathise with you in your affliction. His was a life which, judged by any test, was one of true greatness, such as is only given to very few to attain in this world. He has left behind him a fame and a name which must endure to all time; whether as a scientific officer, or as a practical philanthropist,—the creator of those splendid works along the East coast of India which have already saved thousands of lives, and will continue to do so as long as the world lasts."

These must be the final words of this Memoir. They are the noblest words which can be spoken of any man, and constitute the grandest testimony which can be desired; for only things such as these endure :—

> "His works . . . have already saved thousands of lives, and will continue to do so as long as the world lasts."

Index

A

Abyssinia : Expedition, 502.
Acre : 532 ; 533.
Adam's Bridge : 15.
Aden : 453 ; 503.
Administrative Experience Recorded in Former Famines, 1874 : 434.
Administration Reports :
  Bengal, 346.
  Bombay, 347.
  Central Provinces, 346.
  Madras, 338 ; 345 ; 424 ; 425 ; 433.
  North-West Provinces and Oudh, 345.
  Punjab, 345.
Adyar : 386.
Aeration of Soil : wonderful results by Sir A. Cotton, 536–547.
Afghanistan : 563 ; 564.
Africa : 297 ; 513 ; 517 ; 524 ; 529 ; 577.
— Central : 530.
— North : 551.
— North-West : 514.
— South : 508 ; 550.
— West : 516.
Agnew, R. Vans : 264 ; 395.
Agra : 320 ; 462.
Agriculture : Indian, 464 ; 573.
— Implements, 412 ; 413.
— New hope for British : 541–547.
Agricultural Statistics for British India, 1888–89 : 412.
Agriculturalists : 413.
Ahmadabad : 406.
Ahmednagar : 406.
Ajmere-Merwara : 358.
Akbar Shah Badshah, 1568 : "God has said, 'From water all things are made' " : 209 ; 427.
Aldershot : 556.
Alexandria : 27 ; 28 ; 29 ; 527 ; 528 ; 534.
Allahabad : 75 ; 407 ; 447 ; 450 ; 454 ; 470 ; 473.
Amalapur : canal, 89.
Ambravatty : 294.
America : 228 ; 297 ; 402 ; 490 ; 541.
Amritsar : 406.
Andaman Islands : 71.
Andrews, Mr. : Sind Railway, 483.
Anglo-Israelite Theory : 550.
Anicuts :
  Cauvery, 63 ; 473.
  Cheyaru, 340.
  Coleroon, Lower, 341 ; 473.
  Dowlaisweram, 370 ; 548.
  Godavari, 102 ; 140.
  " Grand Anicut," 102 ; 139 ; 473.
  Marudur, 341.
  Mehmattur, 340.
  Palar, 340.
  Pelandorai, 341.
  Pennéru, 338.
  Poinay, 340.
  Sangam, 339.
  Shatiatope, 341.
  Srivaikuntam, 339.
  Tirukkoyilur, 340.
  Valluru, 340.
  Vriddhachalam, 340.
Annesley, Lord and Lady : 496.
Aqueduct over Godavari : 143 (picture).
Arabia : 503 ; 517 ; 533 ; 534.
Arabian Railway : to Busrah, 532–3 ; 534.
—, Sea : 78.
Arabic Primer by Sir A. Cotton : 169 ; 522.
Arabs : 33 ; 34.
Aralam : 421.

Arbuthnot, Sir Alexander: *re* Mr. W. N. Kindersley, 52.
Cauveri Works, 56.
Arcot:
Nawab of, speech by Edmund Burke, 61.
North, 240; 241; 362; 363; 425; 426; 465.
South, 62; 196; 425; 452.
Argyll, Duke of: 220.
Promised consideration of Sir A. Cotton's proposals, 456.
— shire: 514.
Arkenkota: 339.
Arkwright, R., 80.
"Arthur, King, of the Round Table": 579.
Arts, Society of: 226; 499; 532.
Ashantee: 531.
Ashburner, Mr., paper on Berar Cotton, 374; 375.
Ashbury, Mr. James: 264.
Ashley Down: 578.
Asia: 311; 393; 447.
Asiatic Society, the Royal: paper by Mr. Ashburner, 374.
Assad Shidiak: 30; 31.
Assam: 366; 402; 421; 426.
Athenæum: Madras newspaper, 150.
Attaly: 399.
Australia:
Discovery of gold, 44. Manna, 43. Visits of Captain Cotton, 38; 40; 41; 42; 70; 117. Water storage, project of Capt. Cotton, 46–49.
Gen. refs.: 142; 237; 289; 311; 548; 550.
Avignon: 27.
Ayrton, Rt. Hon. A. S.: Chn. Parl. Com., 1872, 211.

B

Babel: Tower of, 534.
Babylon: 534.
Bacon, Roger: 408.
Bakerganj: 406.
Bagdad: 26; 29; 31; 32; 34; 35; 36; 37; 503; 534; 578.
Bahrein: 534.
Bajra (Bulrush millet): average price of, 1873 and 1897, 403; 405.
Balasur: 317.
Balfour, Rt. Hon. A. J.: 264; 267; 291.
Balfour, Gen. Sir George: 223; speech supporting Sir A. Cotton, 262–264; 519.
Ball, Mr.: author of *Economic Geology*, 272.
Ballarat: 190.
Balmoral: 179.
Baluchistan: 348; 349; 350.
Bangalore: 156; 166; 269; 420; 422.
Bank Canal: 89.
Barbour, Sir David: 369; 410.
Barclay, Robert: 410.
Bari-Doab Canal: 331.
Barley: average price of, 1873 and 1897, 403; 405.
Barnet: 172; 173.
Barnstaple: 182.
Barrage, Egypt: 137; 509; 510; 512; 525; 526.
Barur: 342; 343.
Bastar: 489.
Bay Islands: 421.
Beckenham: 169.
Bedford, Duke of: 547.
Behar: 247; 251; 252; 332; 358; 384; 385; 426; 438; 447.
Belgaum: 362; 406.
Bellary: 294; 362; 363; 393; 395; 396; 397; 398; 406; 412; 425; 465; 466.
Benares: 280.
— Maharajah of, 502.
Bengal: 176; 222; 225; 231; 233; 234; 235; 249; 250; 251; 252; 278; 287; 289; 296; 298; 320; 322; 324; 332; 334; 343; 344; 348; 349; 350; 351; 358; 366; 386; 388; 391; 392; 403; 404; 407; 414; 421; 424; 426; 433; 443; 460; 464; 471; 472; 688.
Bengal:
Bay of, 78; 130; 167.
Berar: 75; 358; 363; 373; 378; 421; 426.
Betwa: 345; 385; 386.
Bevan, Mr. and Mrs. R. C. L.: 175.
Beyrout: 29.
Bezwada: 127; 282; 283; 284; 460.
Bhagavati, river: 176; 451.
Bheema: 294; 302.
Bhowany: 295.
Bhurtpore: 8.
Bible: Reading, Sir A. Cotton's delight in, 19; 20; 168.
— Society: 496; 551.
Bilaspur: 404.
Bimlipatam: 95.
Bingen: 78.

Birmingham : 215 ; 216 ; 221 ; 264.
Blackwood's Magazine : 11 ; 139.
Blackwood, Sir Arthur : 495.
Blandford, Mr. : 420.
Boat designing, by Sir A. Cotton : 519–521.
Bokhara : 564.
Bombay : 35 ; 37 ; 38 ; 78 ; 213 ; 253 ; 254 ; 265 ; 302 ; 333 ; 347 ; 348 ; 349 ; 350 ; 351 ; 358 ; 363 ; 366 ; 374 ; 377 ; 378 ; 384 ; 385 ; 386 ; 389 ; 403 ; 406 ; 412 ; 414 ; 420 ; 421 ; 422 ; 426 ; 465 ; 488 ; 505.
Books : Capt. Cotton's advice on, 24.
Bosworth-Smith, R., M.A. : *Life of Lord Lawrence*, 9.
Bowden, Mr. : 153.
Brahmaputra : 75 ; 233 ; 273 ; 315 ; 386 ; 483.
Brereton, Mr. : 458.
Bridgewater Treatises : 50.
Bright, Rt. Hon. John : 215 ; 216 ; 221 ; 232 ; 258-261 ; 415 ; 461 ; 567 ; 577.
Brighton : 264 ; 554.
Brindisi : 26.
Bristol : 578.
B.I.S.N. Co. : 513.
British Rule in India : 393.
British Supremacy in India : 381.
Brown, Gen. : 551.
Brownlow, Mr. : 463.
Bruges : 26.
Brussels : 27.
Bryansford : 495.
Buckingham and Chandos, Duke of, Governor of Madras : 286 ; 411 ; 412 ; 459.
Buckingham Canal : 134 ; 282 ; 342.
Buckle, Henry T. : 501.
Bundelkhand : 385 ; 386.
Bunyan, John : 549.
Burdwan : 243 ; 450.
Burke, Edmund : 61 ; 65.
Burma : 298 ; 348 ; 349 ; 350 ; 358 ; 366 ; 403 ; 420 ; 426. First War : 16 ; 17 ; 18 ; 557.
Bushire : 37 ; 38.
Bussorah : 35 ; 532.

C

Caird, Sir James : 325 ; 402 ; 404 ; 405 ; 461 ; 463 ; 464 ; 465.
Caird, Mrs. : 464.
Cairo : 28 ; 78 ; 343 ; 509 ; 528.
Calcutta : 102 ; 130 ; 233 ; 234 ; 235 ; 238 ; 243 ; 244 ; 276 ; 277 ; 280 ; 293 ; 296 ; 316 ; 317 ; 322 ; 373 ; 375 ; 388 ; 406 ; 420 ; 422 ; 447 ; 450 ; 451 ; 452 ; 454 ; 455 ; 457 ; 460 ; 463 ; 464 ; 465 ; 486 ; 490 ; 493 ; 528 ; 568.
Caldwell, Colonel : 51.
California : 458.
Camels : 33 ; 417.
Cameron, Lieut. : 515 ; 577.
Campbell, Sir George : 203 ; 393 ; 395 ; 400 ; 463 ; 500 ; *Memoirs of My Indian Career*, 265 ; *Obiter Dicta*, 388 – 393 (see *Obiter Dicta*) ; opposition to irrigation extension : speech in Parliament, 261 ; 262 ; Select Committee, 264 ; reasons, 265 ; 266.
Canada : 550.
Canals : 212 ; 277 ; 282 ; 284 ; 291 ; 292 ; 384–386 ; 388 ; 415 ; 427 ; 428 ; 429 ; 457 ; 458 ; 461.
  Compared with railways : 67–69 ; 234 ; diagram, 379.
  Cost of deep, 448.
  Attaly, 399.
  Bari-Doab, 331.
  Chenab, 384 ; 386 ; 428 ; 430.
  Coast : East, 213 ; 282 ; 295 ; 302 ; 502.
    North, 294 ; 301.
    West, 294 ; 301.
  Cochrane, 437.
  Contour, 301.
  Erie, 237 ; 279 ; 529.
  Forth and Clyde, 450.
  Ganges (*see* Ganges).
  Indus, 447.
  Inundation, 429.
  Irrigation, 294.
  Italian, 398.
  Junction, 460.
  Manchester, 505.
  North-Western and Behar, 447.
  Panama, 447.
  Suez, 289, 447.
Canara, South : 425.
Canning, Lord : 10.
Cape Town : 508.
Capital : and interest, loss of, during famine, 1877–1878, 413 ; 429.
Carmel, Mt. : 29 ; 532.
Carnatic : 27 ; 61 ; 247 ; 273 ; 294 ; 296 ; 298 ; 335 ; 395 ; 421 ; 450 ; 461 ; 465 ; 466 ; 532.
Cattle : loss of, during 1877–78 famine, 412 ; 428 ; 429 ; 430.

Cautley, Sir Proby: engineer, 178; 433; Ganges Canal Controversy with Sir A. Cotton, 469–474.
Cauveri: Capt. Cotton appointed to charge of works, 20; Col. Caldwell's opinion, 1804, 51; nature of river, 52, 58; Col. Baird-Smith's, Mr. Kindersley's, Col. Sim's, opinion, 52, 53; state of district, 52; scheme of work, 57; expected results, 59; opinion of Board of Revenue, after ten years, 63; official figures after fourteen years of Upper and Lower Coleroon anicuts, 63; opinion of Hon. John Sullivan, 64; of Principal Collector of Tanjore, 64.
Gen. refs.: 93; 139; 230; 231; 294; 296; 306; 333; 334; 339; 343; 344; 385; 427; 433; 435; 461; 471; 473; 509; 542.
Cawnpore: 280; 406; 454; 470.
Ceded Districts: 94; 296; 466.
Census Report: 413.
Central Provinces: 75; 220; 346; 358; 366; 385; 388; 389; 403; 415; 421; 424; 426; 436; 460.
— Attempt to open up, by river and canal navigation, before 1860, 372–380.
— Stoppage of irrigation in, by Sir George Campbell, 265.
— *Report on Famine in*, 404; 409; 410.
Ceylon: 15; 16; 438; 447.
Ceylon, by Sir E. Tennent, 198.
Chad, lake: 515.
Chalmers, Rev. F.: in Burmese War, 169; rector of Beckenham, 169.
Chambal: 385.
Chanda: 254; 294; 295; 296; 302.
Changras: 55.
Chapman, Mr.: 370.
Chatham: 14; lectures, 57; 370; 485.
Chembrambakam Tank: 340.
Chenab: 384; 386; 428; 430.
Chesney, Col., R.E.: 221; 259; 456; "Irrigation extension extorted by famine suffering," 419.
Cheshire: 18; 486.
Cheyaru: 340.
Childers, Rt. Hon. H.: 264; 267; 300.
Chumars: 490.
Chilik: 563.
Chilka lake: 295, 302.
China: 262; 311; 481; 551; 570.
Chinese: 490; 524.
Chingleput: 425.
Chinnoor: 150.
Chittoor: 465.
Chitral: 563.
Cholera: 432.
Chota-Nagpur: 426.
Chronicle, Daily, The: 416.
Church Missionary Society: 496; 503.
Circars, Northern: 248; 421.
Civil Service, Indian: 229; 250.
Clyde: 457; 458.
Coal: 232; 233; 253; 277; 296; 316; 323; 455; 457; 460; 534.
Coanud: 59.
Coblentz: 78.
Cocanada: 82; 89; 91; 134; 135; 254; 275; 282; 283; 293; 295; 302; 325; 334; 455; 460; 464.
Cochrane's Canal; 437.
"*Coffee Room, Our*": 555.
Coimbatore: 16; 27; 255; 294; 302; 362; 425.
Colair Lake: 131; 145.
Coleroon: 22; 44; 52; 57; 58; 59; 63; 93; 124; 139; 146; 211; 231; 341; 385; 433; 473.
Colgong: 451.
Combermere:
Abbey, 7. Baron: 8.
Commons, House of: 501; 503; 577.
Select Committee, 1872, 211–214.
Queen's Speech, 1878: 214; Speech on Address, Wilbraham Egerton, 215.
Debate on motion for Select Committee: Lord George Hamilton, 216–224; Henry Fawcett, 257; John Bright, 258–261; Sir George Campbell, 261, 262; Sir G. Balfour, 262–264.
Select Committee, 1878: terms of motion, 216–217; Sir A. Cotton's defence of his integrity, 210. Members of, 264; Sir G. Campbell as judge and witness, 265, 266; *First day's examination*, 267–291; *Second day*, 291–300; *Third day*, 300. Report of Committee, 304; 306–308; Memorandum in reply by Sir A. Cotton, 309–327; extracts from evidence of Sir G. Campbell, Col. Fischer, 388–399; general refs., 328, 354; 464.
Select Committee on extension of railways, 1884: 359; 360; 361; 363.
Commons, Remonstrances of the: 408.

Comorin, Cape: 290; 294; 295; 296; 297; 301; 302; 462; 465.
Congleton, Lord: 31; 37.
Congo States: 513; 514; 515.
Congress, International: 486.
Connemara, Lord: 135; 503.
Constantinople: 36; 535.
Control, Board of: 199; 205; 378.
Coomassie: 517.
Cooper's Hill: 430; 456.
Coorg: 366.
Coringa: 82; 89; 135; 142; 145; 150; 163; 378.
Cornwallis, Lord: 191.
Coromandel coast: 79; 344.
Cotswold Hills: 170.
COTTON, GENERAL SIR ARTHUR T.:
Summary of character in Prologue, 3, 4, 5; birth, parentage, descent, 7; early characteristics, canal-making as amusement, 12; fearlessness, 12; cadetship for India, 13; Addiscombe Military College, 13; appt. to Royal Engineers, 14; Chatham, 14; Ordnance Survey in Wales, 15; Madras, 1821, 15; appointment to Tank Dept., 15; survey of Paumben Pass, 15; supervision of Tank repairs in Southern District, 16; work on military buildings, St. Thomas' Mount, 16; First Burmese War, 16–18; dislike to card-playing, 18; beginnings of religious life, 19; appointed superintendent engineer central division Tank Department, 20; breakdown in health, 20; Paumben Pass improvement, 20; promoted to Captain, 20; appointed to charge of Cauveri irrigation, 20; plans for work evolved and sanctioned, 21; assistance of Lieut. Fred Cotton, 21; repeated attacks of jungle fever, sick-leave to Europe, 21; absent two and a half years, 21; serious tastes in life, 21; return to India overland through Belgium, Switzerland, France, Egypt, Syria, Palestine, Damascus, Bagdad, 26–31; stay at Mission House, 31; letter from Bagdad, 32–37; left for Bombay, May 21, 1833, 37; serious illness at Bushire, "grave dug," 37; arrival in India, resumption of work on Cauveri, 38; steady work for six years, controlled and utilised river by means of anicuts, 51–61; Madras Harbour Scheme, 65; report to Board of Revenue on duties of Irrigation Department and value of Tanks, 65; superintendence of construction of railway, Madras to Red Hills, 38, 66; completion hindered, 67; breakdown in health, visit to Tasmania, 38; Hobart Town, experiments—centrifugal steam engine, serious accident, 39; engagement to Miss Learmonth, 23; met Sir John and Lady Franklin, great favourite, 40; arrival in Tasmania of South Pole Expedition, 40; return to Madras, 23; doctors ordered extension of leave, 23; return to Tasmania, 23; marriage, 23; return to India, 24; health not robust, 70; appointed to Vizagapatam, 70; cyclone on voyage, 71; erection of church, 72; construction of groynes, 72; deep religious convictions, 73; influence over Hindus, 74; saved vessel from wreckers, 74; project to make Vizagapatam a principal port of India, 74–76; appointed to Rajahmundry, 77; Godavari—Before and After, 77–92; report on control of river and irrigation of delta, 94–98; letter to Fred Cotton, 98; details of proposed work, estimates, 107–111; approval of Court of Directors, 112; work begun on Godavari, 1847, 115; hindered for want of artizans, 115; huge establishment, 115; fears from freshes, 116; satisfactory progress, 117; breakdown in health, sick leave to Australia, 117; letter to Fred Cotton, 117–120; visit to Mauritius, Melbourne, 40–44; further progress on Godavari works, 120; difficulties overcome, 121; splendid completion, 122; report to Board of Revenue, 123–126; congratulations from Madras Government, 126; also from Court of Directors, 146; a Hindu overseer, Veenem Veranah, 128, 129; appointed chief engineer of Presidency, 129; extended works, 131; development of navigable channels, 131–134; founder of

COTTON, GENERAL SIR ARTHUR T., *continued* :—
cheapest school of engineering in the world, 137; opposition of Government, 138; recognition of success of works, 134; 135; 139; constant activity, 142; family life during progress of Godavari works, 151–163; sick leave to the hills, 164; disappearance of Ootacamund lake, 165; home at Palaveram, 165; help to missionary and philanthropic work, 158; 159; 167; health affected, furlough to England, 167; account of voyage, 168; visit to Penge, 169; to Rev. F. Chalmers, 169; to Tunbridge Wells, 170; to Weston-super-Mare, 170; to Cotswold Hills, 170; assistance given to clergy, 170; notes of missionary address, 170–172; return to London, 172; home at Barnet, 172; return to India, 172; chief engineership not kept for him, 176; Commandant of Engineers, 176; letter from Madras Government respecting Colonel Cotton, 177; visit to Major Colin Mackenzie, 175; scheme for control of Bhagavati, opposed, 176; attendance on Gen. Sir P. Grant during Mutiny, 176; guest of Governor of Madras, 177; praise from Sir C. Trevelyan, 1858, 177; report to supreme Government on Orissa Irrigation, 178; visit to Calcutta, 178; lecture on work at Rajmahal, 178; report on Ganges Canal, 178; retired, 1860, 178; banquet in London, 178; knighthood, 179; work for India in England, 181, 184–203; stay at Barnstaple, 182; humour, 204–208; witness before Parliamentary Committee, 1872, 211–214; House of Commons debate, severe attack on an absent man, 214–224; reply to adverse criticism, 224–247; discriminating advocate of irrigation, 225; recent results not ignored, 226; why the Tungabudra works were only partially successful, 227; delta works in Northern and Southern Madras, 230; navigation canals throughout India, 232; Godavari navigation, 235; Orissa and Tungabudra works,

COTTON, GENERAL SIR ARTHUR T., *continued* :—
237; irrigation sources to be tapped, 239; singular statements, 241; delusion as to transit in India, 243; navigation connecting links, 244; works urgently required, 245; an appeal and a pathetic defence, 246; Select Committee of 1878: hostile attitude of committee, 265; complete answers to all questions, nine hundred questions asked, summary of views, irrigation, navigation, what railways do *not* do, objections to irrigation, range of mountains invented, Godavari works unfinished in 1878, official dread of cheap transit, £30,000 for irrigation in every district per annum, steamboat canals in every way cheaper than railways, vacillating policy, authorities not justified in stopping supplies, Kurnool canal mismanagement, neglect by authorities reaffirmed, great storage reservoir, defence of same, support by Gen. Fischer, the Godavari "as empty as that," 267–291; *Second day's examination*: no navigation canal ever completed, detailed statement of main lines of navigation all over India, twenty-five schemes for Madras, "many hundred millions of acres fit for irrigation," declines discussion of financial provision, 291–300; *Third day's examination*: rivers proposed to be utilised, sketch of works, estimate of cost, £50,000,000, Sir George Campbell's concession, expert *v.* non-expert, 300–303; 567; report of Committee, 304; 306–308; unfairness to Sir A. Cotton, 304; railway receipts and losses to 1878, 304; capital expenditure on railways and irrigation, 305; frivolous mode of questioning, 305; Memorandum by Sir A. Cotton on Report of Select Committee: estimated gain to India by public works, 309–327; no precious metal to be compared for value with water, 367; more precious than gold in Australia, 367; sixty times as valuable, 368; detailed statements regarding the opening of the Central Provinces by river

COTTON, GENERAL SIR ARTHUR T., *continued* :—
and canal, 372–381 ; enthusiasm, 415 ; money, moral, material value to India of Sir A. Cotton's work, 433–436 ; storage of salt water, 438 ; the Orissa visit, 1862, 439 ; project to supply the Carnatic Tanks, 465 ; Indian tributes, 466–468 ; "Father of the Godavari delta," 467 ; controversy with Sir Proby Cautley, regarding Ganges Canal, 469–474 ; reply to Sir James Stephen, 475–477 ; addresses Manchester Indian Association, 477–482 ; do. Edinburgh Literary Institute, 484 ; visit to Sheffield reservoir, 494 ; stay in Ireland, Bryansford, Tollymore Park, 494–496 ; settling at Dorking, 496 ; committee work, 496–7 ; curious coincidence concerning plans of Woodcot, 498 ; letters to Miss Florence Nightingale and others, 499–508 ; letters to Sir Bartle Frere, Sir Colin Scott-Moncrieff, 508–512 ; Nile navigation which would have saved Gordon, 525–529 ; trip to Norway and Sweden, 513 ; visit to Ballinakill, Scotland, 514 ; temperance work, 518 ; suggested Presidency of Sewage Commission, 519 ; experiments with boats, 519–521 ; improved tricycle, 521 ; various writings (see pp. 525–566) ; death and funeral, 574–76 ; tributes from Mr. F. W. Fox and Gen. Sir R. Sankey, 576–579.

Extracts from writings and letters : Poverty of India, its cause, 186 ; value of water, 189 ; neglect of ancient irrigation works, comparison of British with irrigation policy of ancient rulers, 193 ; comparison of irrigated district (Tanjore) with unirrigated (Guntoor), 199 ; Tanjore—results of liberal treatment, 202 ; great putty case, 204 ; road-making, 206 ; pamphlet on public works in India, 294, 437 ; river *v.* railway, to tap Central India, 372–378 ; on Orissa, 439 ; irrigation and navigation, 441 ; East India Irrigation Co., 442 ; enormous value of river water over well water, 445 ; navigation topics and schemes, 447–452 ;

COTTON, GENERAL SIR ARTHUR T., *continued* :—
beneficial effect of reducing land-tax, 452 ; on various works in India, 453–460 ; salt tax, the poor man's income-tax, 486–489 ; Tungabudra works, English internal transit, communication with Soudan by the Congo, opium revenue, study of living languages, Indian finance, 485 ; prevention of famines, International Congress at Manchester, navigation of Kareen river, 486 ; N. W. African expedition, 514–517 ; Arabic Primer, 169, 522 ; Nile navigation that would have saved Gordon, 525–531 ; cultivation and aeration of soil, 536–547 ; letter to *Manchester Guardian*, 537–540 ; letter to *The Times*, 566.

Cotton, Arthur, steamer, 135.

Cotton family, the : chief members of, since 1535, 7 ; 8 ; 9 ; 10 ; 11.
- Mrs. Calveley Cotton : mother of Sir Arthur Cotton, 12.
- Charles Conyers Cotton : brother of Sir Arthur Cotton, Indian civilian, 10.
- Francis Vere Cotton : brother of Sir Arthur Cotton, Admiral, 10.
- Frederick Calveley Cotton : brother of Sir Arthur Cotton, retired Major-General, C.S.I., 10 ; article in *Blackwood's Magazine*, May, 1900, 11 ; Cauveri works, 21 ; letter on Sir Arthur's opinions regarding railways and irrigation, 67–69 ; letter to, from Capt. Arthur Cotton, 117–120 ; appointed to charge of Godavari works, 129 ; dams in sandy beds, 139 ; population in Sind, 462 ; 574.
- Henry Calveley Cotton : father of Sir Arthur Cotton, 7.
- Hugh Calveley Cotton : brother of Sir Arthur Cotton, Indian irrigation works, Kurnool anicut, 10 ; 493.
- Richard Lynch Cotton : brother of Sir Arthur Cotton, Provost of Oriel, 10 ; 35 ; died at 87, 561.
- Sydney Cotton, Sir : brother of Sir Arthur Cotton, services during Mutiny, 8 ; letter from Lord Lawrence, 9, 10 ; Governor of Chelsea Hospital, 561 ; his last hours, 561–2.

Lady Cotton: wife of Sir Arthur Cotton, 117; reminiscences, 151–156; Bangalore, 156; recollections of Sir Arthur's last illness, 574–576.
Alfred Cotton: son of Sir Arthur Cotton, "left Sandhurst with flying colours," 498; served on Boundary Commission, Afghanistan, 562–4; married Miss May Heath, 564; letters from, 562–4; died on voyage to England, 565; Sir West Ridgeway's testimony, 565.
Combermere, Baron: 8.
Cotton plant: profitable growth, transit of, 373–376.
Cradock, R. H.: 404; 409.
Cranbourne, Lord, 501. (*See* Salisbury).
Cranbrook, Lord: Sir A. Cotton's appeal to, 224; 257.
Crawford, Capt. R. D.: 168.
Cromer, Lord: 369; 488; 489.
Cronin, Mr.: 31.
Crops: 422; 429; 430.
Loss of, during 1877–78 famine, 409. Enormous returns from deep cultivation in England, 542–7.
Cross, Mr. John: 264; 397.
Crozier, Capt.: 40.
Crusades: 408.
Cuddapah: 286; 287; 294; 301; 342; 357; 362; 425; 460.
Cultivation: Deep, 542–547.
Cumbum Tank: 339; 394.
Cure Pipe, Mauritius: 41.
Curzon, Lord, of Kedleston: area for profitable irrigation, 209, 210; speech on Indian Budget, March, 1900, 382; incomplete figures, *re* irrigation, 382; increased expenditure on irrigation, 384.
Customs Revenue: 313; loss of, during 1877–78 famine, 409.
Cutch: 420; 421.
Cuttack: 238; 275; 317; 322; 439; 454.
Cyprus: 464.

D

Dacca: 280.
Dalhousie, Lord: 216.
Dalrymple, Mr., M.P.: 359.
Dalyell, Hon. A. R.: 434.
Damascus: 30; 32; 34; 464; 503; 532.
Dams: 104; 139.
Damuda: 233; 277; 388.
Danvers, Sir Juland: 483.
Darling, river: 47; 48; 49.
Darwar: 293.
Dawkins, Hon. Clinton: 384.
Dead Sea: 29.
Dharwar: 362.
Deakin, Hon. A., M.L.A.: 50; 55; 58; 66; 84; 87; 88; 93; 180; 274; 288; 328; 343; 345; 351; 381; 474; 484.
Deccan: 128; 333; 358; 385; 386; 421.
Dehra Doon: 358.
Delhi: 406.
Delki: 62.
Deltas: treatment of, 439, 440.
Denny, T. Anthony: four letters from Sir Arthur Cotton, 566–574.
Derby, Lord: 68; 219; 243; 328; 372.
Derwent river: Tasmania, 39, 40.
Devonshire: 182; 493.
Dhaupat Rai: 128.
Dickens, Col.: 438.
Dictionary, Econ. Prod.: 273.
Dictionary of Statistics, Mulhall: 364.
Dixon, Mr., M.P.: 567; 570.
Doab; 231; 331; 450.
Dod's Parl. Comp.: 264.
Dolphin's Nose: 72; 73; 75; 76.
Dondapad: 343.
Doomagoodien: 465.
Dorking: 496; 497; 536; 556.
Dowlaisweram: 53; 79; 103; 120; 123; 124; 129; 136; 137; 148; 211; 370.
Draper's *Intellectual Development of Europe*: 407; 408.
Duff, Sir M. Grant: 127; 217; 264; 267; 291.
Dufferin, The Marquis of: 495; 525; 570.
Dunleath, Lord: 264.
Durand, Sir Mortimer, K.C.S.I.: 563.
Dutt, R. C., C.I.E.; 85.
Dykes, Mr.: 194.

E

East Coast Canal: 213; 282; 295.
East India Association: 54, 482, 483, 499.

East India Canal and Irrigation Company: 438; 442; 443; 469.
East India Company: 36; 80; 150; 205; 208; 250.
East India Currency Enquiries: Donald Graham, C.I.E., 410.
Economic Condition in N.W.P. and Oudh: 407.
Economic Geology: Ball, 272.
Eden, Sir Ashley: 317; 322; 323; 325; 460; 463; 465.
Edinburgh: 137.
Literary Institute, 484.
Edward I.: 407.
Edwardes, Sir Herbert: 9; 73; 74; 173.
Egerton, Wilbraham: 215.
Egypt: 28; 137; 343; 510; 511; 512; 525; 530; 535; 570; 577.
—, Khedive of: 515.
Ekrookh: 320; 449; 459.
Ellore Canal: 89; 91; 142; 213; 282.
Elphinstone, Sir James, Bart., M.P.: 16.
E. L. K.: 82.
England: 36; 78; 167; 187; 253; 292; 319; 378; 407; 447; 457; 462; 481; 486; 488; 490; 493; 499; 505; 510; 519; 524; 525; 550; 557; 559.
—, Church of: 515.
English Hearts and English Hands: Dr. Marsh, 169.
Engineers in India: 442.
Erebus: 40.
Erie Canal: 237; 279; 529.
Esdraelon: 36.
Euphrates: 33; 34; 36; 532; 534.
Europe: 297; 311; 393; 408; 534.
Excise Revenue, 313.
Loss of, in 1877–78 famine, 409.
Expenditure: Government on, in 1877–78 famine, 409.
Ezekiel: 550.
Ezion-geber: 550.

F

Famines:
Record since 1853, 357–8.
Forty famines or scarcities in nearly fifty years, 359.
Railways not preservative, 362–3.
Insurance fund, 364.
"Once in a hundred years," 388.
Famines, *continued:*—
Remarkable frequency now, 389.
Bengal, of 1770, 392.
Determination to save life, 401.
In England, 407.
Alleged insufficiency of rain, 418–27.
Camps, 428; 431; 432.
Prevention of, 486.
— *Campaign in Southern India*, 387; 411; 412.
— Commission 1880: 357; 359; 420; 424.
Alleged irrigation failure, 286–7.
Irrigation to have "FIRST PLACE," 329; 336; 351.
All irrigation works justified, 330; 331; 334; 337.
Irrigation in Punjab, N.W. Prov., Bengal, Behar, 332; Orissa, Deccan, Sind, Madras, 333.
Better crops, higher rentals, 334.
Mysore blameable, 335.
Recommendations neglected, 351; 356.
"Great advantage to State," 357.
— Commission, 1898: 5,000,000 acres irrigable, 298; food prices, 404.
— Cost of, 1877–8:
Govt. Expend., 409.
Loss land revenue, 409.
,, crops, 409.
,, excise revenue, 409.
,, customs ,, 409.
,, salt ,, 410.
Country silver and silver ornaments sold, 410.
Increased price of food, 411.
Loss cattle, houses, agricultural implements, 412.
Loss wages, 413.
,, capital, interest, 413.
,, profits, 413.
Total cost, money and lives, 414.
Water wasted, 386–7.
— Cost of, 1900: partial, 416–7.
Famine Histories, 357.
Gen. refs., 60; 80; 214; 289; 357; 431; 432; 477; 478; 504.
Fawcett, Henry, M.P.: 216; 257; 264; 267; 292.
Fenwick, Capt.: 374.
Ferozepur: 448.
Feudatory States: 335.
Fever: 247; 256; 257; 366; 396; 444; 476.
Fife, Mr.: 433; 493.
Finances, Indian: 485.

Fischer, Gen.: 269; 281; 290; 361; 393–99; 437; 455.
Fitzgerald, Vesey: 502.
Fodder: 412; 428; 429; 430.
Food: 403–405; 411; 428.
Forbes, H.: 129; 130; 147; 148; 250; 251.
—, Mr.: 502.
Forest Dept.: 429.
Fort St. George: 150; 179.
Fort St. George Gazette: 179.
Forth Canal: 457.
Fortnightly Review: 419.
Fouracres, Mr.: 454; 461.
Fox, F. W.: 576–579.
— Rev. H.: C.M.S., 153.
France: 26; 46; 292; 511.
Franklin, Sir John: 40.
Frere, Sir Bartle: 449; 455; 464; 499; 501; 508.
Friend of China: 569.
— — *India*: 440.
Froude, Mr.: 578.
Fullerton, Capt.: 15.
Fyzabad: 406.

G

Gainsborough, Countess of: 495.
Gambia: 516.
Gandak: 384; 385.
Ganges: canal, plains, river: 75; 78; 79; 178; 190; 219; 223; 225; 231; 233; 235; 244; 245; 273; 280; 288; 289; 293; 296; 297; 300; 320; 421; 441; 443; 449; 450; 455; 462; 469–474; 476; 500; 501; 503; 504.
Ganjam: 90; 295; 339; 343; 358; 425; 460.
Garwhal: 358.
Gascoyne: S.S., 525.
Gautami: 79; 135.
Gazetteer of India: 363.
Geelong: 42.
Geneva: 27.
Geographical Society, Royal: 515.
Germany: 490.
Ghauts: Eastern, 78; 295; 421; 465; 493.
—: Western, 290; 420; 421.
Ghent: 27.
Gibson, Milner: 519.
Gilgit: 563.
G. I. P. Railway: 253; 427.
Gladstone, Rt. Hon. W. E.: 511.
Gloucestershire: 170; 172.
Goalunda: 233.
Godavari: description river, 77–9; factories, 80; "Great Famine," 1833, 80–2; cyclone, 1839, 82; Sir H. Montgomery, 83; increase population, revenue, 84; do. revenue, 480; imports, exports, wealth, 85; improved condition of people, 86–7; succour to distressed regions, 88; testimony native Indian official, 89–92; works: 40; 44; 53; 75; 76; sugar cultivation, irrigation, 94; general state of irrigation, 96; details of proposed work, 103–111; economy in dam construction, 104; estimate of cost, probable profits, 107–9; approval, 112; damage to anicut, 120–2; "veritable triumph of engineering skill," 122; report, April, 1852, 123–6; congratulation, Government, Directors, 126; enthusiastic praise from beneficiaries, 127; "liquid gold," 128; steamers necessary, 130; development navigation, 131–134; "cheapest school of engineering in world," 137; Government indifference, 138; recognition of success, 1882, 139; 1883, 134; 1890, 135; extensions, 142; summary history project, 150; singularly accurate prediction, 192; works unfinished even in 1878, 315; railway to Bombay *v.* river to Cocanada, 379; Gen. Fischer on Godavari works, 398; success of works, 437; District Association, address to "the Father of the Godavari Delta," 467.
— General refs.: 40; 44; 53; 75; 76; 151; 157; 160; 163; 165; 190; 203; 213; 220; 225; 230; 231; 235; 239; 242; 246; 247; 249; 250; 251; 254; 255; 257; 265; 270; 273; 275; 276; 277; 278; 280; 281; 282; 283; 284; 291; 293; 294; 295; 296; 300; 301; 306; 308; 310; 312; 315; 316; 318; 323; 325; 327; 333; 334; 338; 343; 344; 361; 368; 369; 370; 373; 374; 375; 376; 377; 385; 395; 396; 398; 415; 425; 427; 433; 435; 437; 438; 441; 443; 446; 447; 449; 450; 451; 455; 456; 459; 460; 462; 466; 467; 468; 469; 473; 476; 478; 480; 482; 484; 489; 480; 501; 502; 503; 506; 507; 519; 520; 527; 528; 529; 531; 532; 542; 567; 568; 571; 572.

Godavari, History of, J. H. Morris: 144–149.
Gold: water "liquid gold," 128; 149.
— coast: 515.
Gopalpur: 343.
Gorai: 451.
Gordon, "Chinese": 525; 526; 527; 528; 577.
Gordon, Mr.: 394; 395; 459.
Government: orders of, 2; 126; 279; 438.
Graham, Donald, C.I.E., 410.
Grain: stores, 391; 393; prices of in 1873–97, 403; trade in, 447.
Grant, Gen. Sir P., 176.
Grostête, Bishop: 408.
Groves, A. N.: 31; 37; 578.
,, Henry: 37.
Groynes: 72; 176.
Guernsey: 498.
Guildford: 264.
Gulf Stream: 182.
Gunnaram, Aqueduct, The, over Godavari river: facing 143.
Guntoor: 80; 81; 127; 199–201.
Guyon, Madame: 157.
Guzerat: 421; 428.

H

Haig, Gen., R.E.: 119; 236; 321; 322; 365; 456; 465; 490; 493.
often referred to in letters as *H.*
Halifax, Lord: 179; 212; 501.
Halishahar: 257.
Hamilton, Lord George: speech in debate, 1878, official review of irrigation, 216–224; questions during '78 enquiry, *passim*, 264–303, 391; 305; 310.
Hansard: Parl. Debates, 216.
Hanuman, the Monkey God: 15.
Hardcastle, Mr.: 264.
Harris, Lord: 569.
Hastings, Mr., Rev.: 43.
de Haviland, Col.: 65; 498.
Hay, Andrew: 458; 459.
Hay, Sir H.: 410.
Heath, Sir Leopold: 564.
— Miss May: 564.
Helena, St.: 45.
Henry of Richmond: 407.
Henry VIII.: 7.
Himalayas: 272; 421; 429; 470.
Hindu, The, Madras: neglected tanks, spacious reservoirs, 335–6.
Hissar: 209; 427; 428; 430; 431; 432.
Hit: bitumen spring, 533.
Hobart Town: 23; 38; 39; 70.
Hogg, Sir J. W.: 112–115; 258.
Hope, Admiral Sir J.: 578.
Horace: 150.
Hour, The: newspaper, 202.
Huggry: 294; 301; 397.
Hughes, W.: 283–4.
Hughli: 233; 235; 245.
Humphreys, Mr.: 431–2.
Hunter, Sir W. W.: railways alleged preservatives from famine, 359–60; 363.
Hutchinson, Capt.: 123.
Hyderabad: 94; 208; 269; 293; 294; 296; 297; 358; 374; 421; 466; 490; 505; 552.
Hyndman, H. M.: 462.

I

Ibrahim, Pasha: 30; 31; 34.
Income: average Indian, 369.
Indee: 412.
India: its influence on English thought, 73; creates special type of Christians, 73; "mine of wealth," 142; 462; poverty of, 186–191; special responsibility of Sec. of State to limit expenditure (Lord G. Hamilton), 221; "India perishing for want of British capital," 228.
Gen. refs.: 228; 358; 366; 421; 424; 426; 434; 447; 457; 474; 481; 487; 488; 490; 491; 496; 497; 502; 504; 505; 509; 510; 525; 526; 529; 530; 534; 542; 548; 550; 564; 565; 570; 571; 576; 579.
India in 1880, by Sir R. Temple: 384–6; 433.
India Irrigated: *see* Deakin.
— Office: 232; 241; 316; 330; 351; 363; 392; 454; 456; 493; 499; 501; 503; 504; 508; 567; 568.
Indian trustworthiness, 128–9.
Indies: West, 547; 550.
Indus: canal, river, valley, railway, 78; 214; 273; 293; 297; 385; 447; 448; 455; 462; 513.
Ingaram: 82.

Ingdalpur, 489.
Innocent III. ; IV. : 408.
Intellectual Development in Europe: 408.
Inundation Canals : 429.
Ireland : visit to Lord Roden, 493 ; 495 ; 496.
Gen. refs : 490 ; 502 ; 524 ; 525 ; 551.
Irish Church Mission : 496 ; 551.
Irrigation : Egyptian inferior to Indian, 29 ; needed in Australia, 43 ; ancient works, 58 ; 61 ; 193 ; 198 ; 471 ; 473 ; gain all round from, 60 ; 196 ; 299 ; letter from F. Cotton, 67–69 ; ancient and modern systems contrasted, 194–5 ; responsibility of government, 198 ; comparison —irrigated and unirrigated districts, 199–201 ; objections to, answered, 271–3 ; "many hundred millions of acres perfectly fit for irrigation," 298 ; Sir A. Cotton's £50,000,000 scheme for Madras Presidency, 301–3 ; capital expenditure on, to 1898, 305 ; report Select Committee, 306–8 ; memorandum in reply to report, 309–327 ; Famine Commission, 1880 : strong commendation irrigation everywhere possible, 329 ; "FIRST PLACE," 329, 336, 351 ; results in Punjab, 331 ; N.W. Prov., Bengal, Behar, 332 ; Orissa, Deccan, Sind, Madras, 333 ; mileage, area, financial results works under P.W.D., 348–9 ; expenditure all sources, all objects, 1882–3 to 1897–8, 352–355 ; summary, 356 ; area protected, '78–9–96–7, 356 ; Sir J. Lyall on success of works, 357 ; railway served and irrigated districts contrasted, 360–3 ; lectures at Chatham, 370 ; Lord Curzon's speech, 382 ; increased expenditure promised, 384 ; Sir R. Temple on, 384–6 ; extracts in appendix IV., 388–399 ; expenditure on, 414 ; "irrigation works extorted by famine," 419 ; irrigation involves regulation, 423, 426, 444 ; Hissar, 427–32 ; money and material value Sir A. Cotton's work, 433–436 ; neglect, 441–3 ; results of, 479 ; "10,000 tanks could be supplied from one reservoir," 479.
Gen. refs. : 210 ; 242 ; 249 ; 289 ; 298 ; 433 ; 437 ; 438 ; 449 ; 458 ; 460 ; 464 ; 465 ; 466 ; 468 ; 475 ; 476 ; 478 ; 481.

J

Jacob, Col. : 128 ; irrigated a country without rivers, 371 ; 372.
Jacobabad : 420.
Jaffa : 29.
Jaipur : 128 ; a country without rivers, but with one hundred and fifty irrigation works, 371.
Japanese : 524.
Jellandu : 490.
Jerusalem : 29 ; 557.
Jessore : 500.
Jeypore : 493.
Jhansi-Manikpur railway : 360.
Jhelum : 386 ; 430.
Jocelyn, Nassau : 485.
John o' Groats : 416.
Johnstone, Sir Henry : 531.
Jones, Mr. : 253.
Jordan, river : 532.
Joseph : famine minister of Egypt, 390.
Jowar : average price, '73 and '97, 403 ; 405.
Jubbulpore : 406 ; 420 ; 422 ; 424.
Jumna : canal, river : 223 ; 275 ; 288 ; 291 ; 293 ; 310 ; 331 ; 449 ; 450 ; 470 ; 472.
Junction Canal : 460.

K

Kabul : 563.
Kakien : 16.
Kaladgi : 362 ; 363.
Kala-Nuddee : 293 ; 461.
Kalingarayan : 340.
Kanhan : 295 ; 302.
Karachee : 293 ; 406 ; 447.
Kareen, navigation of : 486.
Karkin : 563.
Karwar : 293 ; 295 ; 296 ; 301 ; 302.
Kashmir : 290 ; 563.
Kelig : 564.
Kene : 385 ; 386.
Keppel, Admiral : 42.
Khandeish : 421.
Khartoum : 526 ; 527 ; 528 ; 530.
Kindersley, W. N. : 52 ; 64 ; 250.

Kinnaird, Lord : 175.
Kirby, Gen. : 555.
Kircaldy : 263.
Kistna : 21 ; 75 ; 112 ; 124 ; 127 ; 134 ; 145 ; 150 ; 190 ; 230 ; 231 ; 239 ; 247 ; 278 ; 280 ; 282 ; 294 ; 295 ; 298 ; 300 ; 301 ; 302 ; 306 ; 315 ; 318 ; 323 ; 326 ; 333 ; 334 ; 338 ; 343 ; 344 ; 368 ; 385 ; 395 ; 396 ; 425 ; 427 ; 433 ; 449 ; 450 ; 459 ; 462 ; 465 ; 466 ; 467 ; 473 ; 478 ; 507 ; 519.
Klondike : 546.
Kodon : 404.
Konkan : 420 ; 421.
Koondal : 397.
Kotaphali : 80.
Kujoree : 439.
Kumaon : 358 ; 490.
Kurnool : 251 ; 286 ; 287 ; 301 ; 342 ; 354 ; 357 ; 361 ; 362 ; 363 ; 394 ; 397 ; 425 ; 507.
Kushtea : 484.

L

Labourer, English : 488.
— Indian : 402 ; 404 ; 405.
— Negro : 402 ; 404 ; 405.
Lachlan, river : 48.
Lahore : 296.
Laing, S. : 486 ; 487 ; 489.
Lancashire : 219.
Land Colonisation Society : 525.
— Revenue : 188 ; 313.
Loss of, in 1877–8 famine, 409.
Effect of reduction of, 452–3.
Land's End : 417.
Languages, Study of Living : 485 ; 523.
Laulgoody : 59.
Launceston, Tasmania : 40.
Lawe, Lieut.-Col. : 115.
Lawrence, Lord : 73 ; 217 ; 289 ; 454.
Lawrence, Lord, Life of, by R. Bosworth Smith, M.A. : 9.
Learmonth, T. : 23.
—, Miss E. : 23.
Lebanon : 30.
Leese, Mr. : 481.
Lennon, Lieut. : 150.
Leslie, Mr. : 233 ; 234 ; 243 ; 246.
Letchee : 159.
Levinge, Mr. : 461.
Lister, Mr. : 286.
Livingstone, Dr. : 173 ; 577.
Lloyd, Sampson : 264 ; 281 ; 398.
London : 137 ; 169 ; 172 ; 178 ; 245 ; 269 ; 457 ; 462 ; 496 ; 528 ; 531 ; 554.
Lords, House of : Queen's Speech, 214 ; address in reply, Earl of Wharncliffe, 214 ; Earl of Loudoun, 215.
Loudoun, Earl of : 215.
Lowe, Robert : 201 ; 567.
Lucknow : 269.
Ludiana : 450.
Lurgan, Lord and Lady : 495.
Lushington, Gen. : 9.
Lyall, Sir James : President Famine Com., 1898 : remunerativeness of irrigation works, 308 ; 357.
Lyons : 27.
Lytton, Lord : 387 ; 459 ; 464 ; 465.
Famine Insurance Fund, 364.
"Human life to be saved at any cost and at any effort," 401.

M

Mackenzie, Gen. Colin : 175 ; 176.
— Mr. : 94.
— Donald : 514 ; 517.
Mackinnon, Sir W. : 164 ; 484 ; 513 ; 514.
M'Kenna, Sir Joseph : 264 ; 267 ; 291.
Madagascar : 570.
Madhee : 412.
Madras : 38 ; 65 ; 66 ; 75 ; 78 ; 102 ; 134 ; 140 ; 163 ; 164 ; 165 ; 167 ; 176 ; 179 ; 184 ; 205 ; 206 ; 208 ; 218 ; 219 ; 222 ; 225 ; 229 ; 230 ; 239 ; 240 ; 248 ; 255 ; 259 ; 263 ; 264 ; 265 ; 266 ; 268 ; 269 ; 272 ; 275 ; 278 ; 284 ; 285 ; 286 ; 287 ; 289 ; 290 ; 294 ; 296 ; 297 ; 301 ; 302 ; 306 ; 307 ; 308 ; 311 ; 318 ; 320 ; 326 ; 333 ; 334 ; 335 ; 336 ; 337 ; 338–345 ; 348 ; 349 ; 350 ; 351 ; 357 ; 358 ; 363 ; 366 ; 384 ; 386 ; 387 ; 403 ; 406 ; 411 ; 412 ; 413 ; 414 ; 420 ; 421 ; 424 ; 425 ; 426 ; 427 ; 433 ; 434 ; 435 ; 437 ; 441 ; 443 ; 460 ; 461 ; 462 ; 464 ; 465 ; 466 ; 471 ; 472 ; 473 ; 476 ; 477 ; 479 ; 488 ; 503 ; 505 ; 508 ; 532 ; 568 ; 576.
— Army : 551.
— Government of : 134 ; 146 ; 295.
— Irrigation and Canal Co : 178 ; 217 ; 219 ; 227–230 ; 278 ; 285 ; 286 ; 287 ; 308 ; 343 ; 354 ; 357.

Madras Mail: 269.
Madras Water Supply and Irrigation System : 340.
Madura : 16 ; 302 ; 343 ; 384 ; 386 ; 425.
Mahanudi : 220 ; 231 ; 275 ; 316 ; 385 ; 439 ; 440 ; 449 ; 450 ; 455.
Mahratta, South : 452 ; 458 ; 459.
Mahrattas, The : 94.
Maine, Sir H. S. : 73.
Malabar : 425.
Mallet, Sir Louis : 499.
Mamiena, Wali of : 563.
Manchester : 216 ; 221 ; 243 ; 254 ; 258 ; 259 ; 260 ; 373 ; 376 ; 378 ; 415 ; 477 ; 481 ; 482 ; 531 ; 573 ; 577.
Manchester Guardian, The : 128 ; 372 ; 427 ; 537–540.
Mandapeta Canal : 89.
Mangles, Mr. : 258.
Manikpur : 360.
Manna in Australia : 43.
Marmalong : 386 ; 387.
Maronite Monastery : 30.
Marseilles : 27.
Marsh, Rev. W., D.D. : 169.
— Miss : 169 ; 495.
Marudur : 341.
Marwar : 371 ; 416 ; 617.
Massey, Right Hon. W. N. : 264.
Masulipatam : 135 ; 142 ; 147 ; 148 ; 208.
Mauritius : 38 ; 41 ; 42.
Mayo, Lord : 220 ; 232 ; 233 ; 234 ; 235 ; 243 ; 449 ; 455.
Mediterranean : 532.
Medlicott, Mrs. : 273.
Meerut : 406.
Megasthenes : 58.
Megna : 386.
Mehmattur : 340.
Melbourne : 40.
Memoirs : Sir G. Campbell ; 265.
Mergui : 16.
Mesopotamia : 534.
Meteorological Reports : 420 ; 421 ; 422 ; 426.
Midat Pasha : 464.
Midlothian : 543.
Midnapore Canal : 232 ; 233 ; 238 ; 243 ; 280 ; 315 ; 320 ; 321 ; 324 ; 334 ; 365 ; 462 ; 463 ; 500.
Military, Board : 205 ; 217.
Mirzapur : 375.
Missionary Address : 170–172.
Mississippi : 99 ; 375.
Mitahari : 256.
Moabite Stone : 549.
Mohal : 412.
Mohumra : 534.
Mombazi : 515.
Moncrieff, Gen. Sir Scott : 286 ; 465 ; 509 ; 511 ; 526 ; 577.
Money lenders : 391 ; 392 ; 413.
— moral, material value : 433–436.
Montgomery, Sir H., Bart. : 83 ; 93 ; 96 ; 99 ; 225 ; 248 ; 250 ; 251.
— Sir R. : 452 ; 455.
— Project : 431.
Mootah Moolla : 320.
Morocco : 516.
Morris, Henry : *Descriptive and Historical Account of the Godavari District* : 70 ; 80 ; 83 ; 93 ; 144–149 ; 150 ; 250.
Muddoor ; 116 ; 125 ; 141 ; 451.
Muir, Sir Wm., K.C.S.I. : 569.
Mulhall, *Dictionary of Statistics* : 364.
Müller, Geo. : 578.
Mullins, Gen., R.E. : 134.
Muneru : 343.
Muhamed Salim Sultan : 427 ; 430.
Murray river, Australia : 48.
Murshedabad : 176.
Murrumbuggee river, Australia : 48.
Muscat : 503.
Mutiny, Indian : 173 ; 176 ; 217 ; 219.
Mylapur : 66.
Mysore : 27 ; 166 ; 222 ; 269 ; 296 ; 297 ; 335 ; 358 ; 363 ; 366 ; 420 ; 422 ; 424 ; 505 ; 550.

N

Nagpur : 75 ; 237 ; 246 ; 254 ; 277 ; 295 ; 302 ; 323 ; 373 ; 385 ; 386 ; 404 ; 406 ; 420 ; 422.
Namur : 26.
Nandyar ; 342.
Naoroji, Dadabhai : 483.
Napier and Ettrick, Lord : 484.
Napoleon, tomb : 45.
Narsapur : 89 ; 91 ; 398.
Nash, Vaughan : 3 ; 128 ; 372 ; 427–432.
Nathamuni S. Mudaliyar : 89.
Navigation : importance of navigable channels all over India : 132 ; 135 ; 143–4 ; Mr. Walch on, 212 ; main lines of, 293 ; 295 ; 328–337.
Gen. refs. : 243 ; 244 ; 245 ; 350 ; 398 ; 415 ; 438 ; 441 ; 447 ; 454 ; 457 ; 458 ; 460 ; 479.
Negro : wages of, 402 ; 404 ; 405.
Neilgherries : 20 ; 62 ; 77 ; 165 ; 293 ; 295 ; 302 ; 480.

Nellore : 294 ; 295 ; 296 ; 301 ; 302 ; 396 ; 397 ; 425 ; 450 ; 465.
Nerbudda : 290 ; 385 ; 386 ; 390 ; 421 ; 490.
Newman, Cardinal : 578.
— F. W. : 35 ; 578.
New South Wales : 345.
New York : 137.
Nicholson, Brigadier : 9 ; 10.
Nicolayson, Mr. : 30.
Niger : 515.
Nightingale, Miss Florence : 504.
Nile : 28 ; 29 ; 78 ; 269 ; 344 ; 503 ; 509 ; 510 ; 528 ; 529 ; 531 ; 577.
— Navigation that would have saved Gordon : 525–531.
—, White : 515.
Noel, Ernest, M.P. ; 265 ; 291.
— Hon. and Rev. Baptist W. : 265.
Norfolk plains, Tasmania : 40.
Norris, Mr. : 220.
Northcote, Sir Stafford : 440 ; 501 ; 502.
North Coast Canal : 294 ; 301.
North Pole : 40.
North-West Provinces : 270 ; 289 ; 298 ; 332 ; 338 ; 345 ; 348 ; 349 ; 350 ; 351 ; 358 ; 366 ; 403 ; 414 ; 420 ; 421 ; 424 ; 426 ; 454 ; 464 ; 472.
Norton, J. Bruce : 150 ; 196 ; 199 ; 201 ; 378.
Norway : 513.
Nubar Pasha : 510.
Nuddea : 388 ; 483.
Nugent, Mr. and Mrs. Richd. : 495.
Nungumbaukum ; 66.
Nunja lands : 336.
Nyassa : 515.

O

Obiter Dicta by Sir Geo. Campbell : Sir A. Cotton and Bengal civilians and engineers, Famine once in one hundred years, Grand canals for Bengal, Railways in famine times, Remarkable frequency of famines, Grain stores, ancient and modern, Famine of 1770 exaggerated, Why he opposed irrigation extension, Hoards of grain in ancient scarcity, 388–393.
Olives, Mount of : 29.
Onslow, Denzil, M.P. : 264 ; 285 ; 300 ; 393.
Ootacamund : 165.
Opium Question : 300 ; 480 ; 485 ; 535.
Orange River : 508.
Ornaments, Silver : melted down, 1877–78, 410.
Orissa : 178 ; 217 ; 220 ; 225 ; 237 ; 239 ; 247 ; 250 ; 251 ; 252 ; 270 ; 274 ; 277 ; 280 ; 291 ; 295 ; 300 ; 308 ; 315 ; 316 ; 317 ; 320 ; 321 ; 322 ; 324 ; 325 ; 326 ; 333 ; 343 ; 358 ; 385 ; 386 ; 391 ; 424 ; 439 ; 440 ; 442 ; 443 ; 447 ; 449 ; 462 ; 463 ; 484 ; 500 ; 551.
Orr, Capt., R.E. : 120 ; 122 ; 123 ; 125 ; 129.
Ostend : 26.
Ottley, Col. : 430.
Oudh : 272 ; 298 ; 345 ; 348 ; 349 ; 350 ; 366 ; 384 ; 403 ; 426 ; 442 ; 464.

P

Pactolus : "Every river in India a," 136.
Paddy : cultivation of, 89.
Palar : 62 ; 240 ; 294 ; 301 ; 340 ; 472.
Palaveram : 165.
Palestine : 460 ; 464 ; 532 ; 533.
Palghaut : 293 ; 295.
Palmer, Messrs. : 150 ; 374.
Panama Canal : 447.
Paradise : 428 ; 430.
Parliamentary Bill of 1376 : 408.
Patna : 280 ; 406.
Paumben Pass : 15 ; 20 ; 65 ; 435 ; 438 ; 447.
Pease, Sir J. : 264 ; 267.
Pegu : 420 ; 421.
Peishcush : 92 ; 110.
Pelandori : 341.
Pelly, Sir Lewis : 442 ; 459.
Peneh : 295 ; 302.
Penge : 169.
Peninsula : 290.
Pennair : 231 ; 294 ; 295 ; 301 343 ; 344 ; 384 ; 386 ; 465.
Pennefather, Rev. W. ; 172.
Penneru : 338.
People of India, improved condition : 434 ; 435 ; 436 ; 444.
Pentecost : 491.
Periyar : 302 ; 342 ; 343 ; 384 ; 386.
Persian Gulf : 532.
Peshawur : 8 ; 9 ; 10.

Piccottah : 110.
Picot, Mr. : 531.
Pillay, P. M. : 240.
Pioneers : 206 : 207 ; 208.
Pitcher, Col. : 405 ; 407.
Plymouth Brother : 551.
Pogson, N. R., C.I.E. : 424.
Poinay : 310 ; 340.
Polaveram : 79.
Ponang : 293.
Ponany : 294 ; 295 ; 296 ; 302 ; 450 ; 461 ; 462.
Ponies as tow-boats : 564.
Poona : 456.
Poonamallee : 208.
Poorneah : 275.
Port Louis, Mauritius : 41.
— Philip, Australia : 189 ; 190 ; 191.
— Said : 534.
Poverty in India : 44 ; 186–191 ; 389.
Power, Mr. : 135.
Prendergast, Mr. : 251.
Price, R. J., M.P. : 569 ; 570 ; 571 ; 573.
Prices current : 402–5.
Prince Consort : 10.
Profit, loss of, during 1877 – 8 famine : 413.
Progress in Madras Presidency during past Forty Years. S. Srinavasa Raghava, Iyengar, C.I.E., Dewan Baroda : 89.
Prologue : 3–5.
Property : increased value of, 334.
Provincial Minor Works : 341 ; 348 ; 350.
Public Works : Sir A. Cotton's suggestions, 294 ; 297 ; 313 ; 437 ; 485.
— — : Commissioners' valuable report on irrigation published about 1852, 193 ; 195–9.
— — Department : 176 ; 177 ; 217 ; 218 ; 220 ; 223 ; 308 ; 310 ; 348 ; 503.
Puckle, R. K. : 464.
Punjab : 75 ; 209 ; 272 ; 296 ; 298 ; 329 ; 338 ; 345 ; 348 ; 349 ; 351 ; 358 ; 366 ; 384 ; 385 ; 386 ; 390 ; 403 ; 414 ; 421 ; 424 ; 426 ; 427 – 432 ; 428 ; 448 ; 454 ; 457 ; 462 ; 464 ; 504 ; 568.
Pushkaram : 79.
Putty case, The great : 204–6.
Pyramids : 28.

Q

Queen's Speech, 1878 : 214.

R

Raghava, S. S., Iyengar, C.I.E., Dewan of Baroda : 89.
Ragi : average price of, 1873 and 1897, 403 ; 405 ; 476.
Railways, Why Sir A. Cotton opposed, in India (Fred. Cotton) : 67–69 ; loss on, to 1876, 270 ; do. to 1878, 304 ; what railways do not do, 271 ; capital expenditure, to 1898, 305 ; *v.* irrigation and navigation canals, 185 ; 243 ; 244 ; 277 ; 282 ; 284 ; 328 ; 372 – 380 ; 399 ; 447 ; 450 468 ; 505 ; 529.
Expenditure all sources, all objects, 1882–3 to 1897–8, 352–356 ; mistake of Indian Government that railways protect country against famine, 360 ; railway-served and irrigated districts compared, 360–364.
Gen. refs. : 214 ; 230 ; 232 ; 253 ; 254 ; 255 ; 269 ; 281 ; 282 ; 388 ; 427 ; 457 ; 461 ; 478.
Rainfall : 80 ; 83 ; 419 ; 420-26 ; 443 ; 444.
— Famine in India not due to insufficiency of : 418–426.
Raipur : 404 ; 406 ; 489 ; 504.
Rajahmundry : 77 ; 80 ; 82 : 91 ; 93 ; 109 ; 113 ; 132 ; 135 ; 146 ; 147 ; 148 ; 151 ; 175 ; 190 ; 192 ; 203.
Rajmahal : 451 ; 455.
Rajputana : 269 ; 348 ; 349 ; 350 ; 358 ; 414 ; 416 ; 421 ; 426 ; 428.
Rallee : 116 ; 148.
Rampur-Bauleah : 451.
Ramsay, Sir Henry : 490.
Rangoon : 16 ; 406.
Rangpur : 406.
Ranigunj : 232.
Ratcliffe, R. : 173.
Ravee : 300 ; 385 ; 449.
Rawalpindi : 406.
Red Hills : 38 ; 66 ; 67 ; 69.
— Sea : 503.
Rees, Hon. J. D., C.I.E. : 135.
Reh : 271 ; 288 ; 478.
Reservoirs : 46 ; 47 ; 61 ; 62 ; 292 ; 297 ; 336 ; 393–399 ; 419 ; 427 ; 479.

Revenue: 193; 249; 344; 356.
—, Board of: 94; 96; 101; 115; 123; 130; 140.
Rhodes, Cecil: 547.
Rice, average price of, in 1873 and 1897; 403; 404; 411; 430.
Richey, Hon. J. B., C.S.I.: 411.
Ridgeway, Sir West, K.C.B., Governor of Ceylon: 562; 563; 565.
Rivers of India, value of: 325; 427; 445.
Roads: 206–8; 437.
Robertson, W. R.: 255; 256; 446.
Roden, Lord: 493; 496.
Rohilkund: 298.
Romance: an Indian, 139.
Rome: 408; 522; 552.
Ross, Sir James: 40.
—, Col.: 512.
Rugby: 565.
Rundall, Gen. F. A.: 73; 88; 195; 280; 493.
Ruripur: 75.
Rushikulya: 342.
Russia: 570.
Ryots, 144; 145; eagerness for canal water, 440; 466; 468.

S

Sagileru: 343.
Sahibgunj: 452.
Saidapett: 387.
St. Helena: 45.
St. Thomas' Mount: 16; 66.
Salem: 194; 195; 406; 425.
Salisbury, Lord: 222; 351; 477; 481; 573. (*See* Cranbourne.)
Salt, loss of revenue in famine, 1877–78, 410; gen. refs., 297; 300; 313; 438; the Poor Man's Income-tax, 485; 486–9.
Samaria: 29.
Samulcotta: 82; 147; 197.
Sandhurst: 498.
San Francisco: 137.
Sangam: 339.
Sankey, Sir R.; 579.
Sanyassee: 74.
Sarda: 384; 385.
Sattara: 362.
Scandinavia: 490.
Scotland: 78; 292; 490; 513; 514.
—, Church of: 515.
Scott, R.: 489.
Scott-Moncrieff, Sir Colin: (*see* Moncrieff).
Seer, a Modern: 541–547.
Selenkos Nikator: 58.
Senargati: 256.
Seringapatam: 294; 296.
Seringam: 62.
Sewage Commission, offer of Presidency to Sir A. Cotton: 519.
Seymour, Danby: 519.
Shaftesbury, Lord: 567.
Shatiatope: 341.
Sheffield: 368; 456; 493–4.
Shevaroys: 77; 150.
Sholapur: 362; 363; 412.
Short, Capt.: 439.
Silver: country, and ornaments minted in 1877–80, 410.
Sim, Col. Duncan: 53; 194.
Sind: 298; 333; 351; 403; 420; 448; 449; 462.
— Sagar project, Punjab: 431.
Sirhind Canal: 55; 244; 293; 300; 310; 320; 448; 482.
Sironcha: 489.
Skinner, Major: 30; 35.
Smith, Col. Baird: 52.
—, Eustace: 264.
—, Major Dunlop: 431.
—, J. B., M.P.: 501.
Snakes: 161; 174.
Solani: 471.
Sone: 231; 244; 251; 252; 300; 320; 324; 325; 332; 370; 385; 438; 449; 450; 454; 460; 461; 462; 465; 500.
Sonepur: 251.
Soudan: 485; 525; 527; 577.
South Pole: 40.
Spain:
Srivaikuntam: 339.
Stamps: 313.
Standard, The: 215.
Stanhope, Rt. Hon. E.: 264; 267.
Stanley, Lord: (*see* Derby).
—, Sir H. M.: 514; 515; 577.
Statistical Abstract: 352–55; 366; 382; 402; 403; 406; 409; 410; 413; 414.
Steamboats: 36; 130; 270; 450; 451; 455; 459; 483.
Stephen, Sir James: 211: 215; 475; 477.
Storage of water: 289; 290; 368; 370; 393–399; 415; 425; 426; 431; 438; 443; 459; 461; 479; 480.
Strachey, Gen. Sir R.: 213; 316; 464; 465.
Suakim: 527.

Suez Canal: 289; 311; 447; 517.
Sugar cultivation: 89; 94; 202; 430; 437; 440; 461.
Sullivan, Hon. H. E.: 402; 405.
— Hon. John: (1840), 64.
— Mr. John: (1779), 150.
Sunderbunds: 484.
Surat: 275; 293; 296; 302.
Sutlej: 275; 291; 293; 310; 385; 390; 448; 449; 450.
Sweden: 513.
Switzerland: 26.
Syria: 30; 464.

T

Tahvandi Rana: 432.
Talbot, Mr.: 564.
Tambragani: 344
Tamil: 524.
Tanjore: 16; 21; 38; 51; 57; 59; 61; 62; 64; 85; 102; 104; 105; 114; 119; 146; 195; 199; 202; 206; 225; 247; 248; 249; 250; 257; 268; 273; 278; 326; 343; 368; 425; 435; 438; 441; 449; 471; 476; 507; 519.
Tanks: 61; 65; 66; 240; 245; 297; 301; 333; 335; 339; 340; 342; 346; 370; 387; 397; 415; 427; 428; 431; 456; 476; 477; 479; 504.
Tanganyika, Lake: 515.
Tanuku: 113.
Tapti: 293; 296; 384; 385; 386.
Tarshish: 550.
Tasmania: 22; 23; 38; 548.
Tavoy: 16; 17; 18.
Tayler, W. (of Patna): 499.
Taylor, Col.: 36.
—, Hudson: 551.
—, Mr. and Mrs.: 175.
Tel: 493.
Telegraph, *Daily*, The: 499.
Telugu: 153.
Temperance: why Sir A. Cotton wore the blue ribbon; greatest possible interest in all temperance work, 518.
Temple, Sir Richard, G.C.S.I.: 222; 235; 241; 263; 264; 384; 386; 412; 433; 504.
Tennasserim: 17; 421.
Tennent, Sir Emerson: 198.
Terror: 40.
Testament, New: 491.
Thadapalli: 339.
Thames: 78; 136; 267.
— Navigation Commission, 519.
Thoburn, Bishop: 489.
Thomas, C. E. G.: 469.
Thomson, James: 184.
Thornton, Mr.: 226; 241; 316.
Tiberias: 532.
Tigris: 34; 35.
Timbuctoo: 515; 516; 517.
Times, The: 82; 186; 214; 224; 225; 230; 268; 269; 427; 475; 477; 524; 566; 567; 569; 573.
— *of India*, The: "railway cannot beat even Ganges," 450.
Tinnevelly: 16; 195; 329; 334; 425; 465.
Tintara: 547.
Tippo Tib: 514.
Tirukkoyilur: 340.
Todd, Mr.: 31.
Tollymore Park: 494; 495.
Torquay: 578.
Toungoo: 406.
Trad, Michael: 29.
Transit, Water, in India: 143; 243; 244; 277; 297; 308; 318; 322; 372–378; 446; 447; 448; 450; 454; 459; 462; 505.
— English Internal: 485.
Travancore: 275; 295; 296; 302; 384.
Trevelyan, Sir Charles, Bart.: 2; 78; 177; 264.
Trichinopoly: 16; 50; 59; 62; 146; 195; 231; 241; 272; 326; 425; 453.
Tricycle: patent, invented by Sir A. Cotton: 521–2.
Trieste: 511.
Trimbak: 79.
Tripoli: 515.
Trotter, Capt. and Mrs.: 175.
Tsawia: 420.
Tunbridge Wells: 170; 492.
Tungabudra: 227; 237; 239; 249; 251; 290; 293; 294; 298; 300; 301; 302; 385; 394; 395; 397; 445; 449; 459; 461; 465; 479; 482; 485; 492; 503.
Turkey: 228; 464.
Tuticorin: 343.
Tyre: 550.
Tyrrell, Lieut.: 194; 195.
Tweeddale, Marquis of: Governor of Madras: 97; 542; 543; 544; 568.

U

United States : 279 ; 292.

V

Vaal River : 508.
Valluru : 340.
Veneem Veranah : 129.
Victoria, Australia : 345 ; 367 ; 368 ; 474.
Vigny, River : 295.
Vijaiswaram : 116 ; 121 ; 123 ; 125 ; 148.
Vizagapatam : 70 ; 72 ; 74–76 ; 90 ; 99 ; 425 ; 469 ; 504.
Vriddachalam : 340.

W

Wages : average, 406 ; loss of, in 1877–8 famine, 413.
Walch, G. T., M.I.C.E. : 78 ; 85 ; 134 ; 212 ; 463.
Wales : 490.
Waltair : 72.
Water : storage in Australia, 43 ; 46–49 ; "National Bank of India," 61 ; "liquid gold," 128 ; 149 ; "more precious than gold in Australia," 189 ; 190 ; 368 ; 370 ; no want of, in India, 213 ; 297 ; 420–6 ; 427 ; 480 ; "rain water poor, river water rich," 321 ; 325 ; 445–6 ; regulation of, 423 ; 439 ; 440 ; 444 ; "India's greatest treasure," 445 ; "rich monsoon river water," 567.
Gen. refs : 292 ; 337 ; 368–370 ; 386–7 ; 431 ; 438 ; 468 ; 476 ; 478 ; 507.
Waterfield, Mr. : 499.
Waterloo, field of : 27.
Watt, James : 227.
Warren, Capt. : 459.
Webster, Forster : 286.
Wellington, Duke of : 10 ; 418.
—, Mount : 39.
Wells : 429 ; 445.
Wenlock, Lord : 568.
West Coast Canal : 294.
Westland, Sir J. : 384.
Weston-super-Mare : 170.
Wharncliffe, Earl of, 214, 215.
Wheat : average price of, in 1873 and 1897, 403 ; 404.
Whitaker's Almanack : 506.
Williams, Sir Monier, K.C.I.E. : 230 ; 427.
Women's work greatly helped by Sir A. Cotton : 553–557.
Wood, Sir Charles : (*see* Lord Halifax).
Woodcot, Dorking : 497 ; 498 ; 499 ; 560.
Wright, Surgeon : 247.
Wundy : 197.
Wurda : 246 ; 254 ; 255 ; 275 ; 279 ; 294 ; 295 ; 296 ; 302 ; 377 ; 378 ; 380 ; 385 ; 455.
Wyllie, Mr. : 463.
Wynganga : 385.

Y

Yeddah : 534.
Yorkshire : 428.

Z

Zemindars : 84 ; 146 ; 238 ; 250.

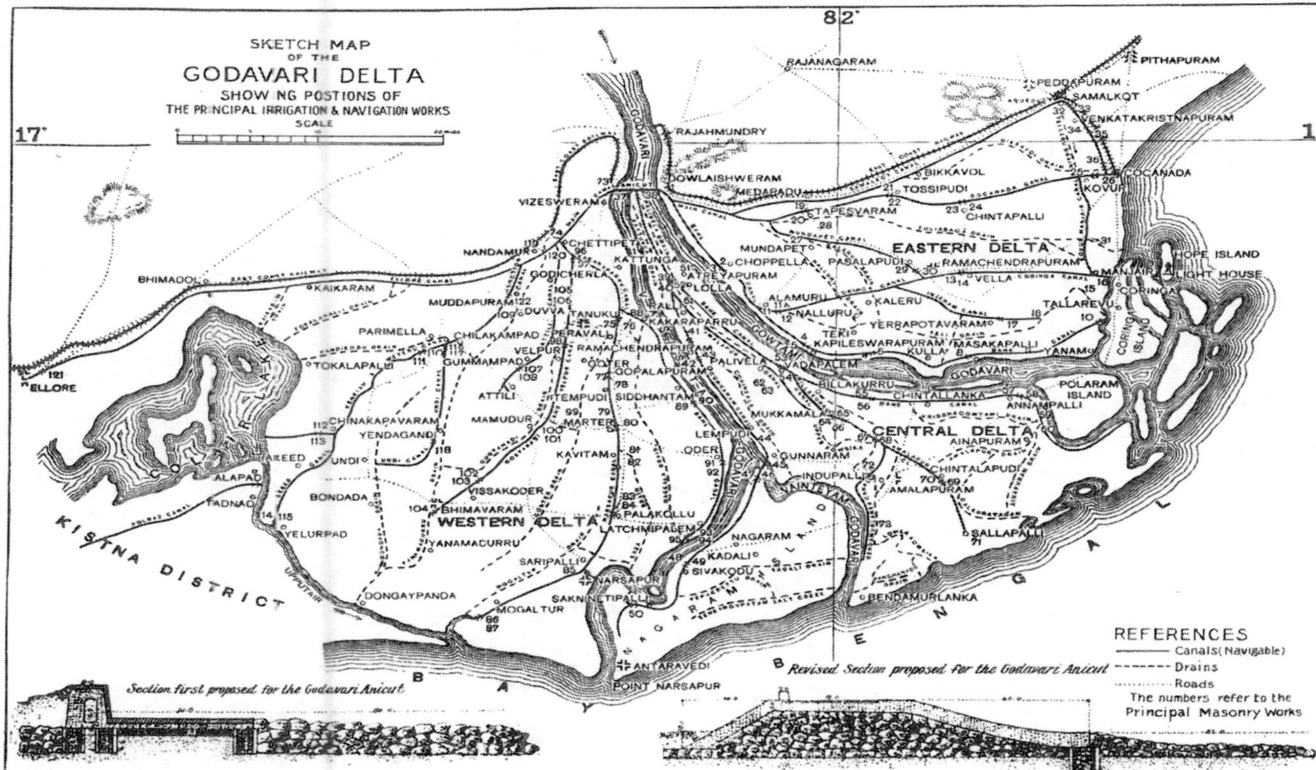
SKETCH MAP OF THE GODAVARI DELTA
SHOWING POSITIONS OF
THE PRINCIPAL IRRIGATION & NAVIGATION WORKS
SCALE
17°
82°
17°
EASTERN DELTA
CENTRAL DELTA
WESTERN DELTA
KISTNA DISTRICT
BAY OF BENGAL
GODAVARI
GOWTAMI
VAINTEYAM
COLAIR LAKE
RAJAHMUNDRY
DOWLAISHWERAM
RAJANAGARAM
PITHAPURAM
PEDDAPURAM
SAMALKOT
VENKATAKRISTNAPURAM
COCANADA
HOPE ISLAND
LIGHT HOUSE
CORINGA ISLAND
POLARAM ISLAND
ELLORE
NARSAPUR
POINT NARSAPUR
ANTARAVEDI
Section first proposed for the Godavari Anicut
Revised Section proposed for the Godavari Anicut
REFERENCES
Canals (Navigable)
Drains
Roads
The numbers refer to the Principal Masonry Works